1987

FOUNDATIONS OF LOGIC AND LINGUISTICS

Problems and Their Solutions

FOUNDATIONS OF LOGIC AND LINGUISTICS

Problems and Their Solutions

Edited by
Georg Dorn
and
P. Weingartner
University of Salzburg
Salzburg, Austria

PLENUM PRESS • NEW YORK AND LONDON

Library of Congress Cataloging in Publication Data

Main entry under title:

International Congress of Logic, Methodology, and Philosophy of Science (7th: 1983: Salzburg, Austria)
Foundations of logic and linguistics.

"A selection of contributed papers from the Seventh International Congress of Logic, Methodology, and Philosophy of Science, held July 11–16, 1983, in Salzburg, Austria"—T.p. verso.
Bibliography: p.
Includes index.
1. Logic—Congresses. 2. Logic, Symbolic and mathematical—Congresses. 3. Language and logic—Congresses. 4. Languages—Philosophy—Congresses. I. Dorn, Georg. II. Weingartner, Paul. III. Title.
BC5.156 1985 160 84-26518
ISBN 0-306-41916-5

A selection of contributed papers from the Seventh International Congress of Logic, Methodology, and Philosophy of Science, held July 11–16, 1983, in Salzburg, Austria

A Division of Plenum Publishing Corporation
233 Spring Street, New York, N.Y. 10013

Printed in the United States of America

PREFACE

This volume comprises a selection of papers that were contributed to the 7th International Congress of Logic, Methodology and Philosophy of Science, which was held in Salzburg from the 11th - 16th July, 1983. There were 14 sections in this congress:

1. *proof theory and foundations of mathematics*
2. *model theory and its application*
3. *recursion theory and theory of computation*
4. *axiomatic set theory*
5. *philosophical logic*
6. *general methodology of science*
7. *foundations of probability and induction*
8. *foundations and philosophy of the physical sciences*
9. *foundations and philosophy of biology*
10. *foundations and philosophy of psychology*
11. *foundations and philosophy of the social sciences*
12. *foundations and philosophy of linguistics*
13. *history of logic, methodology and philosophy of science*
14. *fundamental principles of the ethics of science*

In each section, three or four invited addresses were given, which will be published in the Congress Proceedings (Ruth Barcan Marcus, Georg J. W. Dorn and Paul Weingartner, eds.: Logic, Methodology and Philosophy of Science VII. Proceedings of the Seventh International Congress of Logic, Methodology and Philosophy of

Science, Salzburg, 1983. - Amsterdam, New York, Oxford: North-Holland Publishing Company, 1985.) Every section with the exception of section 14 also contained contributed papers. It has been our aim to make the best of these known beyond the congress audience, and to this end three volumes of selected contributed papers will be published. (The two others are: Otto Neumaier, ed.: Mind, Language and Society. - Wien: Verband der wissenschaftlichen Gesellschaften Österreichs, 1984. This volume comprises selected papers of sections 10 (psychology) and 11 (social sciences). -- Paul Weingartner and Christine Pühringer, eds.: Philosophy of Science - History of Science. A Selection of Contributed Papers of the 7th International Congress of Logic, Methodology and Philosophy of Science, Salzburg, 1983. Special issues 2 and 3 of volume 21 of *Philosophia Naturalis*, 1984. These issues comprise selected papers of sections 6 (general methodology) and 13 (history of methodology).) The present volume contains selected papers of the logic sections 1, 2, 3, 4, 5 and 7 as well as of the linguistics section 12.*

We have organized the material in the following way:

Foundations of Logic
- Mathematical Logic
- Philosophical Logic

Foundations of Linguistics
- Logic and Language
- Philosophy of Language

The central themes of the Mathematical Logic Part are completeness, decidability and reduction. The Philosophical Logic Part mainly

---

* However, not everyone who was invited to contribute his congress paper to this volume was able to do so.

deals with probabilistic semantics, but also treats the old problems of induction and of theory-change in a logical fashion and acquaints the reader with Leśniewski's Ontology as well as with the history of mathematical logic in Continental Europe. The Logic and Language Part starts with two very technical studies in categorial grammars and sense logic, but deals with quantification and relevant entailment as its main topics. Further themes are vagueness of concepts and information in context. The Philosophy of Language Part, finally, is rather historically minded. It centers on Dummett's view of Frege's and Wittgenstein's philosophies of language, treats Quine's thesis of meaning indeterminacy and ends with an empirically oriented study in reference: the naming of colors. --

We thank Miss Eva Stieringer, Secretary of the Philosophy Department of Salzburg University, for having typed this volume in her usual competent and efficient manner.

Salzburg, Austria
September, 1984

Georg J. W. Dorn
Paul Weingartner

CONTENTS

FOUNDATIONS OF LOGIC: MATHEMATICAL LOGIC

FOUNDATIONS OF LOGIC: PHILOSOPHICAL LOGIC

FOUNDATIONS OF LINGUISTICS: LOGIC AND LANGUAGE

FOUNDATIONS OF LOGIC: MATHEMATICAL LOGIC

CONSEQUENCE RELATIONS OF 2-ELEMENT ALGEBRAS

Wolfgang Rautenberg

Institut für Mathematik II
Freie Universität Berlin
D-1000 Berlin 33

Abstract. We show that the consequence determined by a 2-element algebra has at most 7 proper non-trivial extensions and that it is finitely axiomatizable with sequential rules. This implies among other things the finite axiomatizability of each 2-valued consequence in a finite language.

Notation. P, Q, ... denote formulas, X, Y, ... formula sets of a fixed propositional language F. p, q, r, ... denote distinct variables. A *rule* is to mean a finitary sequential rule, given by a skeleton $\rho = (X, Q)$, X finite. If $X = \{P_1, \ldots, P_n\}$ then ρ is denoted by $P_1; \ldots; P_n/Q$. ρ is *proper*, if $X \neq \emptyset$, otherwise *axiomatic*. The symbol $\vdash$ denotes structural consequences (more precisely, consequence relations invariant with respect to substitutions). $\vdash$ is *non-trivial* if $p \nvdash q$. $\vdash$ is *maximal* if $\vdash$ is non-trivial and $\vdash$ has no proper non-trivial extensions (in the same language). $\rho = P_1; \ldots; P_n/Q$ *holds* in $\vdash$ iff $\rho \in \vdash$, i.e., $\{P_1, \ldots, P_n\} \vdash Q$. There are two trivial consequences, the inconsistent, and the one without tautologies, denoted by $\vdash_\emptyset$. $\vdash_M$ denotes the consequence given by a (logical) matrix M = AD, whose underlying algebra is A and whose set of designated elements is D. M is *non-trivial*, if $\emptyset \neq D \neq |A|$, where |A| denotes the domain of A. Note that $\vdash_{A\emptyset} = \vdash_\emptyset$.

1. INTRODUCTION

There are countably many 2-element algebras up to polynomial equivalence, each of a finite type. Fig. 1 shows their expansion diagram. For the sake of convenience, the 2-element algebra with base functions f, g, ... is denoted by (f, g, ...). The diagram slightly differs from the well-known diagram in Post (1941), since iterative systems as defined by Post do not completely coincide with the sets of polynomials of 2-element algebras. In Rautenberg (1981) (henceforth quoted as [R]) it was shown that a structural consequence $\vdash$ in any language F can be viewed as a 2-valued consequence (i.e., $\vdash$ has a 2-element non-trivial adequate matrix) if and only if $\vdash$ is maximal, has a maximal consistent set, and is *congruential*, i.e., the relation $\equiv_X$ defined by $P \equiv_X Q \Leftrightarrow X;P \vdash Q \ \&\ X;Q \vdash P$, is a congruence in F, for each X. Another result from [R] is that each 2-valued $\vdash$ in a finite language is f.a. (*finitely axiomatizable* by means of finitely many sequential rules in the language of $\vdash$). It should be observed that maximality and finite axiomatizability of a 2-valued $\vdash$ cannot be obtained from the well-known special case when the language is functionally complete or contains at least $\rightarrow$. In general, a reduct of a maximal f.a. consequence is neither maximal nor f.a. Examples are easily produced in 3-valued logic (Wroński (1979)).

This paper generalizes some of the results of [R]. The Theorems 1, 2 below immediately imply that each 2-valued $\vdash$ is maximal and f.a., because for lattice theoretic reasons each extension of a f.a. $\vdash$ is f.a., provided $\vdash$ has but finitely many extensions. Both theorems fail for m-element algebras ($m \geq 3$), in general.

We write $A \leq B$ if the algebra A is a reduct of the algebra B, i.e., each polynomial of A is a polynomial of B. Let A be any non-trivial algebra (i.e., card $|A| \geq 2$). We define the *algebraic* consequence $\vdash_A$ as $\cap \{\vdash_{A\{d\}} \mid d \in |A|\}$, so that $\vdash_A = \vdash_{A\{1\}} \cap \vdash_{A\{0\}}$, if

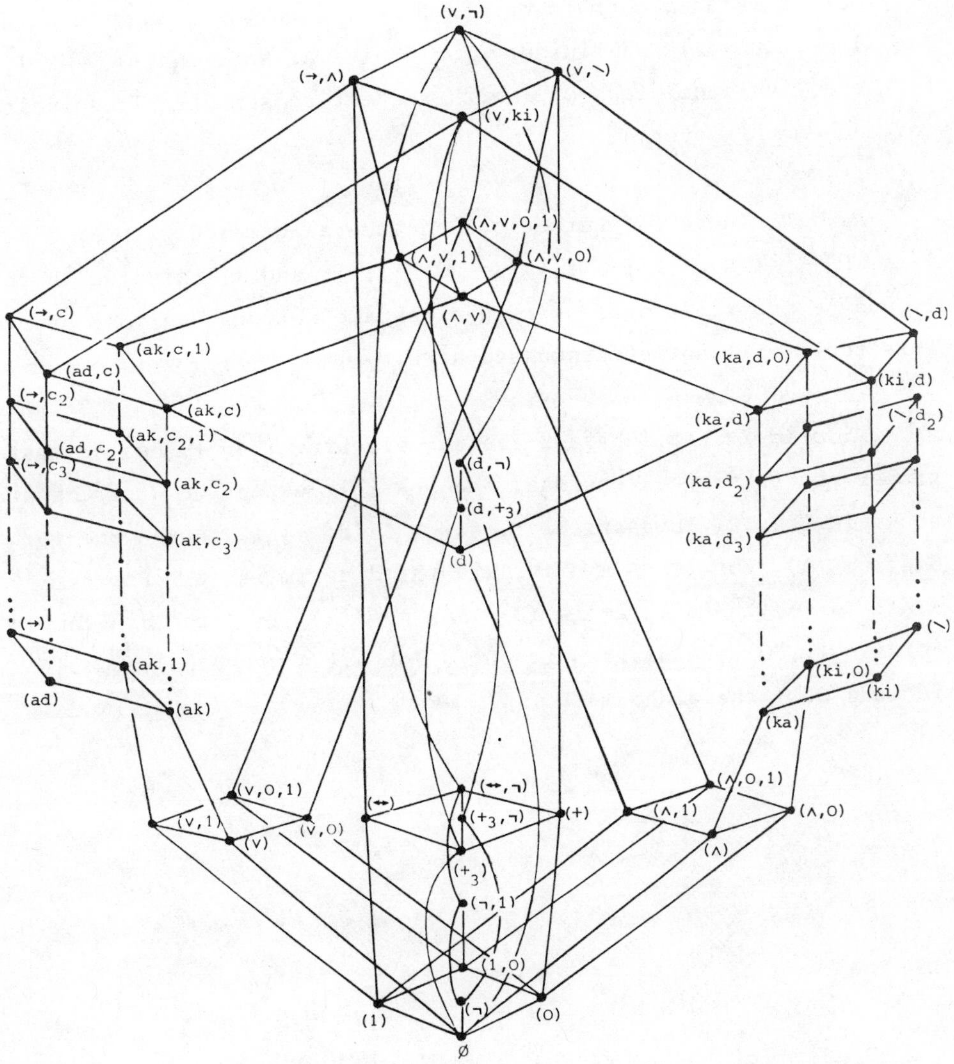

Fig. 1. The expansion diagram of all 2-element algebras. $x \setminus y = x \wedge \neg y$. $+$ (addition mod 2) is the dual of $\leftrightarrow$. $+_3(x, y, z) = x + y + z$. $c_m(x_0, \ldots, x_{m+1}) = \bigwedge_{i=0}^{m+1}(x_0 \vee \ldots \vee x_{i-1} \vee x_{i+1} \vee \ldots \vee x_{m+1})$. $c = c_1$. d_m is the dual of c_m, $d = d_1$. $ak(x, y, z) = x \vee (y \wedge z)$, $ad(x, y, z) = x \vee (y \setminus z)$. ka, ki are the duals of ak, ad respectively.

$|A| = \{0, 1\}$. $\vdash_A$ has no tautologies and hence is the infimum of all $\vdash_M$, where M is an *algebraic* matrix over A (i.e., M = AD with card $D \leq 1$). Clearly, $\vdash_A$ is finitary for finite A. Note that $\{Q \vdash P \vdash_A Q\}$ is the equivalence class of P with respect to semantical equivalence for each matrix over A.

Remark. There is another consequence associated with A, namely $\mid\!\sim_A = \cap\{\vdash_{AD} \mid D \subseteq |A|\}$. If $|A| = \{0, 1\}$, $\vdash_A$ and $\mid\!\sim_A$ coincide. Both $\vdash_A$ and $\mid\!\sim_A$ are related to certain algebraic notions and word problems. This topic will not be discussed here.

Theorem 1. Let A be a 2-element algebra. Then $\vdash_A$ has at most 7 proper non-trivial extensions. The possible extension diagrams are shown in Fig. 2. In particular, for $A \leq (d, \neg)$ it is the one-point diagram (A). For $(\vee) \leq A \leq (\vee, ki)$ the diagram is (B). For $(\vee, 1) \leq$ $\leq A \leq (\rightarrow, \wedge)$ the diagram is (D). For A = (1), $(\leftrightarrow)$ the diagram is (C). For A = $(\vee, 0)$ the diagram is (D*). For all A whose polynomials include 0, 1 the diagram is (E).

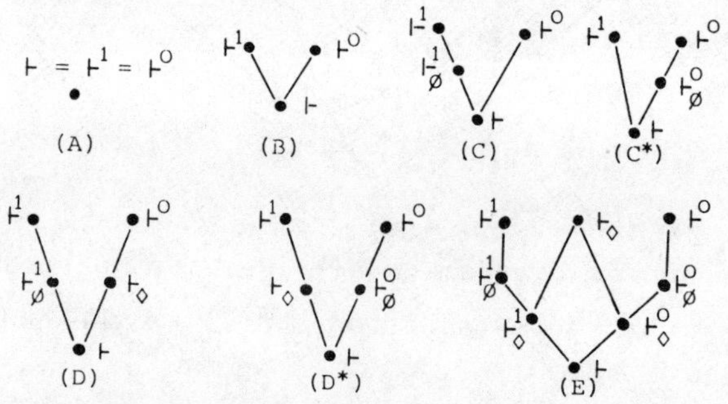

Fig. 2. Classification of extension diagrams for $\vdash := \vdash_A$, $|A| = \{0, 1\}$. $\vdash^i := \vdash_{A\{i\}}$, $\vdash_\Diamond := \vdash_{A\{1\}\times A\{0\}}$, $\vdash^i_\emptyset := \vdash^i \cap \vdash_\emptyset$, $\vdash^i_\Diamond := \vdash^i \cap \vdash_\Diamond$ $(i = 0, 1)$.

Note that Theorem 1 covers all algebras from the left-hand side of Fig. 1., including the diagonal. The diagram for A from the right-hand side is the dual of the diagram for its dual isomorphic copy on the left-hand side. E.g., for ($\leftrightarrow$) the diagram is (C), hence for (+) it is (C*). The diagrams (A), (B) and (E) are self-dual. Note that $\vdash^{i}_{\emptyset}$ derives from $\vdash^{i}$ simply by omitting the tautologies of $\vdash^{i}$.

Theorem 2. For each 2-element algebra A, $\vdash_A$ is finitely axiomatizable.

In order to explain the use of these theorems for logic and linguistics, we start with a simple observation. Consider $\vdash^{\wedge} = \vdash_{(\wedge)\{1\}}$ (the reduct of the classical propositional consequence to formulas in $\wedge$) and $\vdash^{\vee} = \vdash_{(\vee)\{1\}}$. Clearly, the common properties of $\wedge$ and $\vee$ are reflected by the rules of $\vdash^{*} = \vdash^{\wedge} \cap \vdash^{\vee}$, formalized in a language F(*) with one binary connective *. Examples are p*p/p, p/p*p, p*q/q*p etc., expressing the semi-lattice character of $\wedge$ and $\vee$. Some natural questions arise:

(1) To which extent is $\vdash^{*}$ ambiguous, more precisely, how many and which extensions has $\vdash^{*}$?

(2) Is $\vdash^{*}$ f.a., in particular, are the rules expressing the semi-lattice character of $\wedge$, $\vee$ sufficient?

Theorem 1 contains a complete answer to question 1. Note that $\vdash^{\wedge}$ is the same as $\vdash_{(\vee)\{0\}}$, apart from the notation of the connective. Hence, $\vdash^{*} = \vdash_A$ for A = ($\vee$). According to Theorem 1, $\vdash^{*}$ has no proper non-trivial extensions other than $\vdash^{\wedge}$ and $\vdash^{\vee}$ (diagram (B)). Thus, $\vdash^{*}$ is ambiguous to a minimal extent; in other words, the addition of *any* rule distinguishing $\wedge$ and $\vee$ identifies * to be either $\wedge$ or $\vee$. This is perhaps less surprising as in the case of the dual connectives $\leftrightarrow$ (iff) and + (either or). The addition of any rule which holds for + but not for $\leftrightarrow$ to $\vdash^{*} = \vdash^{\leftrightarrow} \cap \vdash^{+}$ (formalized in F(*)), e.g.,

$p*p/p$, forces $*$ to b +. Clearly, $\vdash^{\leftrightarrow}$ cannot be obtained from $\vdash^*$ by adding proper rules, because $\vdash^{\leftrightarrow}$ has tautologies while $\vdash^*$ has not; but if we add any axiomatic rule true for $\leftrightarrow$ (e.g., $p*p$) we already obtain $\vdash^{\leftrightarrow}$ and hence all rules of $\vdash^{\leftrightarrow}$ including its tautologies.

The situation slightly changes if we compare $p \to q$ and its dual $p/q = q\backslash p$. Let $\vdash^*$ formalize the common properties of $\vdash^{\to}$ and $\vdash^{/}$ in $F(*)$, such as $p*p/q*q$ etc. According to Theorem 1, $\vdash^*$ has the extension diagram (D). Thus, if any $\to$-tautology is added to $\vdash^*$ (e.g., $p*p$), we obtain $\vdash^{\to}$. However, if $p*p/q$ is added, which holds for / but not for $\to$, we obtain a system $\vdash_{\Diamond}$ which is somewhat weaker than $\vdash^{/}$, although in $\vdash_{\Diamond}$ each $\to$-tautology is a contradiction. Put $p \circ q = (p*q)*q$, so that $\circ = \vee$ if $* = \to$. Then $\vdash_{\Diamond}$ and $\vdash^*$ have still the same $\circ$-reduct. $\vdash^{/}$ is obtained from $\vdash^*$ by adding any rule $P/Q \in \vdash^{/}\backslash\vdash^{\to}$ such that P is not a $\to$-tautology, for instance $p*q/q$.

We may also ask to which extent the system of those rules containing both $\wedge$ and $\vee$ is ambiguous, which remain true if $\wedge$ and $\vee$ are interchanged. Theorem 1 tells us (for $A = (\vee, \wedge)$) that ambiguity is again as small as it could be. The only complete (i.e., maximal) interpretations are the two standard ones. Things become somewhat more delicate if we consider the corresponding question for a system Φ of Boolean functions by means of which both 0 and 1 are definable. In this case, the consequence $\vdash_{(\Phi)\{1\}} \cap \vdash_{(\Phi)\{0\}}$ has a third complete interpretation, $\vdash_{\Diamond}$, on a 4-valued matrix. $\vdash_{\Diamond}$ has no tautologies and 0, 1 both are contradictions in $\vdash_{\Diamond}$. Note that this includes the special case $(\Phi) = (\to, \wedge, \vee, \neg)$, for which the statement of Theorem 1 was first shown by Malinowski (1981) by quite different methods.

Theorem 2 entails a positive answer to the first part of question 2 above. The axiomatization of $\vdash$ which will explicitly be presented in Section 2 also answers the second part of the question. The unary rules expressing the semilattice character of the connective are insufficient. At least one binary rule is needed. A rule strong enough is p;q*r/p*q which holds for both, $\wedge$ and $\vee$. We will discuss this claim in Section 3.

Notice that the axiomatization of $\vdash_A$ yields at the same time finite axiomatizations of both $\vdash^1$ and $\vdash^0$. In particular, if $\vdash^1$ has tautologies, it suffices to add an arbitrary example.

Theorems 1, 2 also imply the answer to some questions interesting for general matrix theory. What is $\vdash_M$, if M is any (non-trivial) algebraic matrix over a distributive lattice? Here we do not assume that the designated element is the largest element of M. The answer is contained in the following

Corollary. Let M be a non-trivial algebraic semilattice, distributive lattice, Boolean ring or Boolean algebra matrix, respectively. Then $\vdash_M$ is either $\vdash_\nabla$ or $\vdash_\Delta$ or $\vdash_\Diamond$ with $\Diamond = \nabla \times \Delta$, $\nabla = A\{1\}$, $\Delta = A\{0\}$, where A is the corresponding 2-element algebra. $\vdash_M$ is f.a. in each case.

Proof. Well-known facts from general matrix theory and representation theorems imply $\vdash_M \supseteq \vdash_A$ (see, e.g., Sec. 2). In the distributive lattice or semilattice case, $\vdash_M$ is $\vdash_\nabla$ or $\vdash_\Delta$ or $\vdash_{\{\nabla,\Delta\}} = \vdash_A$ according to diagram (B). Since ∇, Δ both are embeddable in $\Diamond$, we have $\vdash_{\{\nabla,\Delta\}} = \vdash_\Diamond$. In the Boolean ring case, we represent A as $A = (1, \leftrightarrow, \vee)$ $(= (\rightarrow, \wedge, \vee))$ with zero 1, addition $\leftrightarrow$, multiplication $\vee$. Then $\vdash_M$ is $\vdash_\nabla$ or $\vdash_\Delta$ or $\vdash^1_\emptyset$ or $\vdash_A$, by diagram (D). Now, $\vdash_M = \vdash^1_\emptyset$ or $\vdash_M = \vdash_A$ is impossible, since $\vdash^1_\emptyset$ and $\vdash_A$ are not uniform in the sense of Łoś and Suszko (1958) (e.g., $p \vdash^1_\emptyset 1$ but not $\vdash^1_\emptyset 1$), hence cannot be represented as single matrix consequences. The Boolean algebra case is treated similarly.

Presently, the proof of Theorem 1 is much easier than that of Theorem 2, where Post's classification is used essentially. It seems worthwhile to look for algebraic reasons for its validity, comparable to well-known algebraic reasons for Lyndon's theorem that the equational theory of each 2-element algebra is finitely based. Although we refer to the latter in our proof, we believe that Theorem 2 cannot be reduced to Lyndon's theorem:

Problem 1 Construct a finite algebra A whose equational and quasi-equational theories are finitely based, but $\vdash_A$ is not.

On the other hand, Theorem 1 and 2 can possibly be generalized as follows: Let τ be any finite type (in particular, that of a single binary operation). Let $\vdash_\tau^2$ denote the intersection of all consequences $\vdash_A$, where A is a 2-element algebra of type τ.

Problem 2 Has $\vdash_\tau^2$ finitely many extensions?

Problem 3 Is $\vdash_\tau^2$ f.a.?

We mention that both problems have a positive answer if τ contains at most unary function symbols.

2. PROOF OF THEOREM 1

Let M, N be matrices. $M \subseteq N$, $M \underset{\sim}{\subset} N$ are to mean that M is a submatrix of N, M is embeddable in N, respectively. TO is the trivial matrix $T\emptyset$, where T is the trivial algebra (in any type). $SP\mathbb{M}$ is the class of submatrices of direct products of members of a class $\mathbb{M}$ of matrices. We will use the following facts: (1) $M \underset{\sim}{\subset} N^I \Rightarrow \vdash_N \subseteq \vdash_M$, (2) $\vdash \supseteq \vdash_{\mathbb{M}} \Rightarrow \vdash = \vdash_{\mathbb{K}}$ for some $\mathbb{K} \subseteq SP\mathbb{M}$ (Woytylak (1979)), (3) if $h: M \xrightarrow{\text{onto}} N$ is a homomorphism such that x is designated in M iff hx is designated in N, then h is (consequence-) *invariant*, i.e., $\vdash_M = \vdash_N$, (4) if M is a non-trivial 2-element matrix and $N \subseteq M^I$ is non-trivial, then $M \underset{\sim}{\subseteq} N$ ([R]).

Let A be any fixed 2-element algebra. We put $\nabla = A\{1\}$, $\Delta = A\{0\}$, $o = A\emptyset$, $\Diamond = \nabla \times \Delta$. Note that $\vdash_o = \vdash_{TO} = \vdash_\emptyset$. Now let $\vdash$ be any non-trivial extension of $\vdash_A = \vdash_{\{\nabla,\Delta\}}$. By (2), $\vdash = \vdash_{\mathbb{K}}$ for some $\mathbb{K} \subseteq SP\{\nabla, \Delta\}$, containing at least one non-trivial member. Without loss of generality, $\mathbb{K}$ has at most one trivial member which may assumed to be o. Let $M \in \mathbb{K}$ be non-trivial, $M \subseteq \nabla^I \times \Delta^J$, say. Clearly, M has a single designated element, denoted by d. We will show that $\vdash_M$ is $\vdash_\nabla$ or $\vdash_\Delta$ or $\vdash_\Diamond$ or $\vdash_{\{\nabla,\Delta\}} = \vdash_A$. Therefore, $\mathbb{K}$ has a consequence-invariant reduction to at most one of the following sets:

$$\{\nabla\},\ \{\Delta\}\ \{\Diamond\},\ \{\nabla, o\},\ \{\Delta, o\},\ \{\nabla, \Diamond\},\ \{\Delta, \Diamond\},\ \{\nabla, \Delta\}.$$

Note that $\{\Diamond, o\}$, ... need not to be included, since $o \underset{\sim}{\subseteq} \Diamond$ and therefore $\vdash_{\{\Diamond,o\}} = \vdash_\Diamond$.

Clearly, it suffices to discuss the case splitting in Theorem 1. Let $A \leq (d, \neg)$. Then $\nabla \simeq \Delta$, so that M is embeddable in a power of ∇. Thus, $\vdash_\nabla \subseteq \vdash_M$. On the other hand, $\nabla \underset{\sim}{\subseteq} M$, by (4), so that $\vdash_M \subseteq \vdash_\nabla$, and consequently $\vdash_M = \vdash_\nabla$. Therefore, $\mathbb{K}$ reduces to $\{\nabla\}$ or to $\{\nabla, o\}$. But $\vdash_\nabla = \vdash_{\{\nabla, o\}}$ since $\vdash_\nabla$ has no tautologies, so that K reduces to $\{\nabla\}$. This yields the one-point diagram (A).

Next consider $(\vee) \leq A \leq (\vee, ki)$ and choose M as above.

Case (a): d (the designated element of M) is maximal and hence the greatest element in the semilattice order of M induced by $\vee$. Then $M \underset{\sim}{\subseteq} \nabla^I$, because $h: M \to \nabla^I$ with $h(x) = (\pi_i(x))_{i\in I}$ is easily seen to be an embedding, ($\pi_i(x)$) is the ith projection of $x \in M$). By (4), $\nabla \underset{\sim}{\subseteq} M$ so that $\vdash_M = \vdash_\nabla$. *Case (b)*: d is a minimal element in the order of M. Then h: $M \to M$ with $h(x) = x \vee d$ is an invariant homomorphism since $h(x \vee y) = hx \vee hy$, $h\, ki(x, y, z) = ki(hx, hy, hz)$, $hx = d \Leftrightarrow$ $\Leftrightarrow x = d$. By (3), $\vdash_M = \vdash_{hM}$. Moreover, d is then smallest element in the order of hM, so that we may assume from the very beginning that d is the smallest element of M. But then h: $x \mapsto (\pi_j(x))_{j\in J}$ is an embedding of M into Δ^J. By (4), $\Delta \subseteq M$, so that $\vdash_M = \vdash_\Delta$ in this case. *Case (c)*: There are, a, b $\in$ M with $a < d < b$. Then {a, d} and {b, d} are submatrices of M isomorphic to ∇, Δ, respectively ($x < y$ implies $ki(u, v, w) \in \{x, y\}$ for $u, v, w \in \{x, y\}$). Thus, $\vdash_M = \vdash_{\{\nabla,\Delta\}}$ in this case. Now, TO is embeddable in both ∇ and Δ, so that $\mathbb{K}$ reduces to $\{\nabla\}$ or $\{\Delta\}$ or $\{\nabla, \Delta\}$. Since $\vdash_\nabla$ and $\vdash_\Delta$ are incomparable ($p/p \vee q \in$ $\in \vdash_\nabla \setminus \vdash_\Delta$, $p \vee q/p \in \vdash_\Delta \setminus \vdash_\nabla$) we obtain diagram (B).

Next suppose $(\vee, 1) \leq A \leq (\to, \wedge)$, $M \in \nabla^I \times \Delta^J$ as before. Note that $1 = 1_M$ is the diagonal of 1's in $\nabla^I \times \Delta^J$.

Case (a): d = 1. Then clearly $J = \emptyset$, so that $M \subseteq \nabla^I$, hence $\vdash_M = \vdash_\nabla$. *Case (b)*: d is minimal in the semi-lattice order of M. As in the previous situation, we may assume that d is the smallest element of M (since $A \leq (\vee, ki, 1)$ and h: $x \mapsto x \vee d$ is an invariant homomorphism from M into M) from which it easily follows that $\vdash_M = \vdash_\Delta$. *Case (c)*: $a < d < 1$ for some $a \in M$. Since $I, J \neq \emptyset$ in the present case, it may be assumed without loss of generality, that $I = J$ and $M \subseteq \Diamond^I$ hence $\vdash_\Diamond \subseteq \vdash_M$. Let N denote the submatrix of N generated by {1, d, a}. Fig. 1 shows $A \geq (\to)$ or else $A \leq (\vee, \wedge, 1)$. In the first case, N contains a further element $b = d \to a$ and $N \simeq \Diamond$. Thus, $\vdash_M \subseteq \vdash_\Diamond$, i.e., $\vdash_M = \vdash_\Diamond$. In the case $A \leq (\vee, \wedge, 1)$, N has the elements 1, d, b only. It is then easily checked that $N \times N$ contains a submatrix which can be mapped onto $\Diamond$ by means of an invariant homomorphism. Therefore, $\vdash_M \subseteq \vdash_\Diamond$ and again $\vdash_N = \vdash_\Diamond$. Since $TO \precsim \Delta \precsim \Diamond$, $\mathbb{K}$ reduces to $\{\nabla\}$ or $\{\Delta\}$ or $\{\Diamond\}$ or $\{\nabla, O\}$ or $\{\nabla, \Delta\}$. This yields diagram (D), provided it has been shown that $\vdash^1, \vdash^1_\emptyset, \vdash_\Diamond, \vdash^0$ are pairwise distinct and $\vdash_\Diamond$ and $\vdash^1$ are incomparable. This is indeed the case, because $\emptyset/1 \in \vdash^1 \backslash \vdash^1_\emptyset$, $p/1 \in \vdash^1_\emptyset \backslash \vdash_\Diamond$, $1/p \in \vdash_\Diamond \backslash \vdash^1_\emptyset$ and $p \vee q/q \in \vdash^0 \backslash \vdash_\Diamond$.

Now consider A = (↔). Clearly, it suffices to show that the extension diagram for its dual isomorphic copy (+) = (+, 0) is (C*). Let M given as above. If d = 0 then obviously $M \subseteq \Delta^I$ and therefore $\vdash_M = \vdash_\Delta$. Let d ≠ 0. M is a subgroup of the Boolean group $G = \nabla^I \times \Delta^J$ which may be considered as a vector space (over the 2-element field). Clearly, there is a linear automorphism f: G → G with $f(d) = 1_G$ (the diagonal of 1's in G). Thus, we may assume without loss of generality, $d = 1_G \in M$. This shows that M is embeddable into a power of ∇. Since $\nabla \underset{\sim}{\subseteq} M$ as well, we obtain $\vdash_M = \vdash_\nabla$. So, 𝕂 reduces to {∇}, or {Δ} or {∇, Δ} or {Δ, O}, because $TO \underset{\sim}{\subseteq} \nabla$. This yields diagram (C*), since $\vdash \subsetneqq \vdash^1_\emptyset \subsetneqq \vdash^1$. The treatment of A = (1) is similar. The case A = (v, 0) is dual to that of A = (v, 1).

Now suppose 0, 1 belong to the polynomials of A. Choose M as above. If $d = 1_M$ or $d = 0_M$, we immediately infer $\vdash_M = \vdash_\nabla$, $\vdash_M = \vdash_\Delta$, respectively. Suppose d ≠ 0, 1. If the subalgebra N generated by d has 4 elements then N is freely generated by d and ¬ belongs to the polynomials of A. Hence, N ≃ ◊ and we infer $\vdash_M = \vdash_\Diamond$ as above. If N = {0, d, 1} (which happens only for A = (0, 1) or for the lattice or semi-lattice expansion of (0, 1)), ◊ is an invariant homomorphic image of N × N, and again $\vdash_N = \vdash_\Diamond$). We thus obtain diagram (E), provided it has been confirmed that its points are pairwise distinct and corresponding incomparability relations hold. This can easily be done by means of a list of rules containing only 0, 1 and a single variable p. This finishes the proof.

3. OUTLINE OF A PROOF OF THEOREM 2

We first describe a certain strategy for constructing a finite axiomatization for $\vdash_A$, where A is any fixed 2-element algebra with at most one non-constant base function (if A = (0, 1), $\vdash_A$ is axiomatized by 0;1/p and for A = (1) no rule is needed at all). Since $\vdash_A$ has no tautologies, we have to work with proper rules only. $\vdash_A$ is the intersection of congruential consequences and hence is itself congruential. According to Lyndon (1951), there is a finite set of equations P = Q which axiomatize the variety V(A) generated by A. Let Γ_A be a suitable set of such equations. Our strategy consists in looking for a calculus $\vdash$, based on a finite set $\mathbb{R}$ of rules, such that

(a) $\vdash$ is correct (i.e., each $\rho \in \mathbb{R}$ holds in $\vdash_A$),
(b) If $P = Q \in \Gamma_A$ then P/Q and Q/P are provable in $\vdash$,
(c) $\vdash$ is congruential.

Suppose such $\vdash$ has been found. We then obtain a complete calculus according to Lemma 1 or 2 below. Thus, the only thing which has to be done is to construct a correct congruential calculus such that (b) is satisfied. As a matter of fact, this is not as easy as it might seem at the first glance. (b) can trivially be satisfied just by choosing the calculus of rules P/Q, Q/P whenever P = Q is in Γ_A. However, this calculus is far from being complete for $\vdash_A$. We therefore have to look for suitable additional rules in order to make the calculus congruential. It is not difficult to prove that a complete calculus for $\vdash_A$ has to include at least one m-ary rule for some $m \geq 2$.

As a rule, condition (c) can only be confirmed by the inductive derivation of one or several Gentzen-style rules which are deduction theorems from the point of view of a sequential rule calculus. This explains why the axiomatization of $\vdash_A$ is more difficult than the axiomatization of the equational or quasi-equational theory of A, where equivalent replacement is present from the very beginning. The inductive proof of suitable Gentzen-style rules necessitates keeping the number of rules as small as possible. Nevertheless, in the more complex cases we had to deal with several dozens of rules.

We will exhibit explicit axiomatizations of $\vdash_A$, following the strategy described above, only for A = ($\vee$), ($\vee$, $\wedge$), ($+_3$) and its expansions by constants (note that ($+_3$, 1) = ($\leftrightarrow$)) and for the exceptions covered by Lemma 2. For the remaining (infinitely many) cases we used uniform axiomatization procedures similar to those of [R].

Lemma 1. Let A $\neq$ ($\neg$), ($\neg$, 1), ($\neg$, $+_3$), ($\neg$, $+_3$, 1) (= ($\neg$, $\leftrightarrow$)), and $\vdash$ be a calculus satisfying (a), (b), (c). Then $\vdash$ is complete for $\vdash_A$.

Proof. $\vdash$ is congruential and therefore (see [R], Sec. 5) permits algebraic semantics, i.e., there is a class $\mathbb{E}$ of matrices for $\vdash$, closed with respect to S, P, such that

(d) each M $\in$ $\mathbb{E}$ is an algebraic matrix,

(e) if P $\vdash$ Q $\vdash$ P and M $\in$ $\mathbb{E}$, then M satisfies the equation P = Q,

(f) $\vdash \; = \; \vdash_{\mathbb{E}}$.

By (b) and (e), the M $\in$ $\mathbb{E}$ satisfy the equations from Γ_A, hence their algebraic reducts belong to V(A). According to Theorem 2 in [R], V(A) = ISP{A} with the 4 exceptions mentioned in the text of the lemma. This, by (d), implies $\mathbb{E} \subseteq$ ISP{∇, Δ, o}, where ∇, Δ, o denote the 3 algebraic matrices belonging to A (Sec. 2). Since o $\subsetsim \nabla \times \Delta$ we obtain

(g) $\mathbb{E} \subseteq$ ISP{∇, Δ}.

Now, (g) and (f) immediately imply $\vdash_A \; = \; \vdash_{\{\nabla,\Delta\}} \subseteq \vdash_{\mathbb{E}} \; = \; \vdash$ and hence the completeness of $\vdash$ for $\vdash_A$.

Lemma 2. Let A be ($\neg$), ($\neg$, 1), ($\neg$, $+_3$), ($\neg$, $\leftrightarrow$) and $\vdash$ a calculus satisfying (a), (b), (c). Then $\vdash_A$ is axiomatized by the calculus $\vdash$, provided p;$\neg$p $\vdash$ q.

Proof. Clearly, $\vdash \subseteq \vdash_A$. In our cases, V(A) = ISP{A} ∪ ISP{A'}, where A' derives from A by putting $\neg_{A'} = id_A$ ([R], p. 341). Choose $\mathbb{E}$ as in the previous lemma, so that each M ∈ $\mathbb{E}$ satisfies the equations from Γ_A. This, by (d), implies $\mathbb{E} \subseteq$ ISP{∇, Δ} ∪ ISP{∇', Δ'}, where ∇' = A'{1}, Δ' = A'{0}. By (3), Section 2, $\vdash = \vdash_{\mathbb{K}}$ for some $\mathbb{K} \subseteq \mathbb{E}$, since $\mathbb{E}$ is closed under S, P. A non-trivial M ∈ $\mathbb{K}$ cannot belong to ISP{∇', Δ'}, because p;$\neg$p/q holds in M, hence must belong to ISP{∇, Δ}. Without loss of generality, o is the only trivial member of $\mathbb{K}$, so that $\mathbb{K} \subseteq$ ISP{∇, Δ}. This yields $\vdash \supseteq \vdash_A$ as in the previous lemma.

First let A = (v). Here are the rules of a complete calculus $\vdash$ for $\vdash_A$ (we omit the writing of the connective and write P.QR for P(QR), etc.):

(0) p;qr/pq, (1) pq/qp, (2) p.qr/pq.r, (3) p/pp, (4) pp/p,
($\check{1}$) u.pq/u.qp, ($\check{2}$) u(p.qr)/u(pq.r), ($\check{3}$) up/u.pp, ($\check{4}$) u.pp/up.

Note that (2') pq.r/p.qr is derivable:

$$pq.r \vdash_{(1)} r.pq \vdash_{(2)} rp.q \vdash_{(1)(2)} qr.p \vdash_{(1)} p.qr.$$

V(A) is the variety of semi-lattices and we take Γ_A to consist of the equations pq = qp, p.qr = pq.r, pp = p. In view of the presence of (1), (2), (2'), (3), (4), condition (b) is satisfied. Since $\vdash$ is correct, the only thing which remains to be done in view of Lemma 1 is to show that $\vdash$ is congruential. This is an obvious consequence of the following

Deduction theorem. $X;R \vdash S \Rightarrow X;TR \vdash TS$.

Proof by induction on the derivability of S from X;R (= X ∪ {R}). Let S ∈ X;R. If S = R, clearly X;TR ⊢ TS. If S ∈ X, the claim follows from $S;TR \vdash_{(0)} ST \vdash_{(1)} TS$. Before starting with the induction step, notice that $\check{\rho}$ holds in ⊢ for each of the 9 rules ρ of ⊢; here $\check{\rho}$ is $uP_1; \dots uP_n/uQ$ if ρ is $P_1; \dots P_n/Q$ (u a variable not occurring in $P_1, \dots, P_n$, Q). This is clear for ρ = (1) - (4). For ρ = $(\check{1})$, rule $\check{\rho}$ follows from $u(v.pq) \vdash_{(2)(\check{1})(2')} u(v.qp)$. Similarly, $\check{\rho}$ is derived for ρ = $(\check{2})$ - $(\check{4})$. For $(\check{0})$ observe $u.qr \vdash_{(2)} uq.r$ and $up;uq.r \vdash_{(0)} up.uq \vdash_{(\check{1})(2')(2)(1)(2')} pq.uu \vdash_{(4)} pq.u \vdash_{(1)} u.pq$, so that up;u.qr ⊢ u.pq. This proves $(\check{0})$. Now suppose X;R ⊢ PQ and PQ is obtained by an application of (0), so that X;R ⊢ P,QQ' for some Q'. By induction hypothesis, X;TR ⊢ TP,T.QQ', and, by $(\check{0})$, TP;T.QQ' ⊢ T.PQ. Thus, X;TR ⊢ T.PQ. Now suppose X;R ⊢ QP by an application of (1), so that X;R ⊢ PQ. By induction hypothesis, $X;TR \vdash T.PQ \vdash_{(\check{1})} T.QP$. Similarly, the induction step is carried out for the other rules ρ with the aide of the provable rule $\check{\rho}$.

Thus, ⊢ is complete for $\vdash_A$. Note that by Theorem 1, from ⊢ we at once obtain axiomatizations of $\vdash^{\vee}$ and $\vdash^{\wedge}$: $\vdash^{\vee}$ = ⊢ + an arbitrary rule which holds for $\vdash^{\vee}$ but not for $\vdash^{\wedge}$, and similarily for ∨, ∧ interchanged. E.g., ⊢ + p/pq = $\vdash^{\vee}$, ⊢ + pq/p = $\vdash^{\wedge}$.

Remark. (0) is the only binary rule of ⊢. In view of the fact that (b) is expressible by unary rules only and that $\vdash^{\vee}$ is indeed f.a. by unary rules (namely (1) - (4) plus p/pq, see [R]), let us ask whether there is a complete calculus for $\vdash_A$ based solely on unary rules. The answer is *no* for the following reason: If ⊢ is any calculus based on unary rules, it is easily shown by induction that $X \vdash P \Rightarrow (\exists Q \in X)(Q \vdash P)$. However, this property does not hold for $\vdash_A$: $p;q \vdash_A pq$, but neither $p \vdash_A pq$ nor $q \vdash_A pq$.

For A = (v, 1), $\vdash_A$ is axiomatized by adding p1/1, 1/p1 to the above calculus. The deduction theorem is preserved; therefore, the extended calculus is congruential and hence complete. Similarly, $\vdash_{(\vee,0)}$ is axiomatized by adding p0/p, p/p0. For A = (v, 0, 1), we add ρ = 0;1/p, in addition. Again, the deduction theorem is maintained. What is needed in order to carry out the induction step for ρ is that $\check{\rho}$ is provable. Here is the proof: u0;u1 ⊢ u, 1 ⊢ u, p1 $\vdash_{(0)}$ up.

It now becomes rather obvious how to axiomatize $\vdash_A$ for A = (v, ∧) and its expansions by constants. We use the language with v, ∧, but we have to keep in mind that a rule in v, ∧ is correct for $\vdash_A$ only if it is correct in the usual sense and remains correct if v, ∧ are interchanged. To each rule ρ, define $\hat{\rho}$ in correspondance to $\check{\rho}$. Then the following 24 rules present a calculus complete for $\vdash_A$ (we include rules for both distributive equations, although in the equational theory one equation is sufficient):

$(0_\vee)$ p;q ∨ r/p ∨ q $(1_\vee)$ p ∨ q/q ∨ p $(2_\vee)$ p $\dot{\vee}$ q ∨ r/p ∨ q $\dot{\vee}$ r
$(3_\vee)$ p $\dot{\vee}$ p ∧ q/p $(4_\vee)$ p/p $\dot{\vee}$ p ∧ q $(\check{1}_\vee)$, $(\check{2}_\vee)$, $(\hat{2}_\vee)$,
$(5_\vee)$ p $\dot{\vee}$ q ∧ r/p ∨ q $\dot{\wedge}$ p ∨ r $(6_\vee)$ p ∨ q $\dot{\wedge}$ p ∨ r/p $\dot{\vee}$ q ∧ r,
$(\hat{5}_\vee)$, $(\check{6}_\vee)$, plus all these rules with ∧, ∨ interchanged.

In view of $(1_\vee)$ - $(6_\vee)$, $(1_\wedge)$ - $(6_\wedge)$, condition (b) is satisfied with respect to the well-known equations P = Q axiomatizing distributive lattices. For each rule ρ, $\check{\rho}$ and $\hat{\rho}$ are provable. Thus, the deduction for ∨ is preserved; moreover it is easily copied for ∧. Thus, ⊢ is congruential and hence complete for $\vdash_A$.

Now we are going to axiomatize $\vdash_A$ for A = $(+_3)$ = $(\leftrightarrow_3)$ and A = $(+_3$, 1) = (↔). The rules are the same; the difference is in the language only. Write PQR for $+_3$(P, Q, R), PQ.RST for PQ(RST), etc. Here are the rules of a complete calculus ⊢ for $\vdash_A$:

(0) p;q;r/pqr (2) pqr/prq (2) pqr/qpr

(3) p/pqq (4) pqq/p (5) pq.rst/pqr.st (the inverse of (5), (5') pqr.st/pq.rst, is provable in this calculus).

The variety $V(+_3)$ of Boolean 3-groups is axiomatized by the equations pqr = prq, pqr = qpr and pq.rst = pqr.st. Thus, in view of (1) - (5), (5'), condition (b) is satisfied. What remains to be shown is that ⊢ is congruential. This needs some preparations.

For $\rho = P_1; \ldots; P_n/Q$ put $\tilde{\rho} = uvp_1; \ldots; uvP_n/uvQ$, where u, v do not occur in $P_1, \ldots, P_n$, Q. Then $\tilde{\rho}$ is provable in ⊢ for ρ = (0) - (5) ([R], p. 331). This, by induction, yields the following deduction theorem. We write P ~ Q if R is derivable from P by means of (1) - (5) and conversely.

Deduction theorem. X;P;Q ⊢ R implies X;P ⊢ PQR or else X;P ⊢ R.

Proof. This is obvious by (0), (3), provided R ∈ X;P;Q.

For the induction step suppose first X;P;Q ⊢ RST by an application of (0), so that X;P;Q ⊢ R,S,T. It has to be shown

(∗) X;P ⊢ PQ.RST or else X;P ⊢ RST.

By induction hypothesis,

X;P ⊢ PQR or X;P ⊢ R, X;P ⊢ PQS or X;P ⊢ S,
X;P ⊢ PQT or X;P ⊢ T.

In the case X;P ⊢ PQR,PQS,PQT, we obtain, by an application of $(\tilde{0})$, X;P ⊢ PQ.RST and consequently (∗). In the case X;P ⊢ R,S,T we get X;P $\vdash_{(0)}$ RST, hence (∗). In the case X;P ⊢ PQR,S,T we obtain X;P ⊢ PQR.ST ~ PQ.RST and the same is obtained in the case

X;P $\vdash$ PQR,PQS,T. This covers all cases up to permutations. Now suppose X;P;Q $\vdash$ RTS was obtained by (1), so that X;P;Q $\vdash$ RST. By induction hypothesis, X;P $\vdash$ PQ.RST $\vdash_{(\tilde{1})}$ PQ.RTS, or else X;P $\vdash$ RST $\vdash_{(1)}$ RTS as we wanted. The induction step for (2) - (5) is similar.

Now we are able to prove that $\vdash$ is congruential. Suppose (1) X;P $\vdash$ P' and (2) X;P' $\vdash$ P. It suffices to show (3) X;PQR $\vdash$ P'QR. By (1), X;PQR;P $\vdash$ P', so that either X;PQR $\vdash$ PQR.PP' or else X;PQR $\vdash$ P' according to the deduction theorem. Now, PQR.PP' $\sim$ P'QR, so that (3) holds in the first case. In the second case we have X;PQR $\vdash$ P (observe (2)). Thus, X;PQR $\vdash_{(0)}$ PP'.PQR $\sim$ P'QR, so that (3) holds in the second case as well. This proves that $\vdash$ is congruential and hence its completeness.

Remark. Clearly, for A = $(+_3, 1)$ = ($\leftrightarrow$), we can rewrite the above rules in terms of $\leftrightarrow$, putting PQR = P $\leftrightarrow$ (Q $\leftrightarrow$ R), 1 = $p_o \leftrightarrow p_o$, say. The ternary rule (0) can then be replaced by the binary rule p;q/p $\leftrightarrow$ q or by p;p $\leftrightarrow$ q/q.

Let us mention next that $\vdash_{(\neg)}$ is axiomatized by means of p/$\neg\neg$p, $\neg\neg$p/p and p;$\neg$p/q. By Lemma 2, it has to be shown that the calculus of these rules is congruential. This is easily seen by proving first Lemma 4 below.

We are now going to axiomatize $\vdash_{(+_3,\ \neg)}$. Write $\neg$PQR for $\neg$(PQR). If ρ = P/Q, let $\overline{\rho}$ denote $\neg$P/$\neg$Q. We add to the calculus for $(+_3)$ the rules

(6) $\neg$pqr/pq$\neg$r, (7) pq$\neg$r/$\neg$pqr, (8) p/$\neg\neg$p, (9) $\neg\neg$p/p,
$(\overline{1})$, $(\overline{5})$, $(\overline{5'})$, $(\overline{6})$, $(\overline{7})$ and (10) p;$\neg$p/q.

For the calculus $\vdash$, obtained in this way, condition (b) is satisfied, because $V(+_3, \neg)$ is axiomatized by adding the equations $\neg pqr = pq\neg r$ and $p = \neg\neg p$ to $\Gamma_{(+3)}$. What remains to be shown according to Lemma 2 is that $\vdash$ is congruential. Let $\vdash^{o}$ denote the calculus obtained from $\vdash$ by ommitting rule (10).

Lemma 3. $X;P;Q \vdash^{o} R$ implies $X;P \vdash^{o} PQR$ or else $X;P \vdash^{o} R$.

Proof. Induction over the rules of $\vdash^{o}$.

Lemma 4. $X;P \vdash Q,\neg Q$ implies $X \vdash \neg P$.

Proof. Without loss of generality, $X;P \vdash^{o} Q,\neg Q$. Clearly, $X \neq \emptyset$, $R \in X$ say. By Lemma 3, $X \vdash^{o} RPQ$ or $X \vdash^{o} Q$ *and* $X \vdash^{o} RP\neg Q$ or $X \vdash^{o} \neg Q$. In case $X \vdash^{o} Q,\neg Q$ clearly $X \vdash \neg P$. In the case $X \vdash^{o} RPQ,\neg Q$, we obtain $X \vdash_{(0)} RPQ.R\neg Q \vdash \neg P$, and similarly in the other cases.

It now easily follows that $\vdash$ is congruential; Lemma 4 yields the congruence property for $\neg$. The corresponding for $+_3$ is shown as in the previous example provided $X;PQR;P$ is consistent. Otherwise $X;PQR \vdash \neg P$ by Lemma 4, and since $X;\neg P \vdash \neg P'$, we obtain $X;PQR \vdash_{(0)} PQR.\neg P\neg P' \vdash P'QR$.

As regards $A = (+_3, \neg, 1) = (\leftrightarrow, 1)$, nothing has to be added to the above rules, simply because $\Gamma_{(+3, \neg, 1)} = \Gamma_{(+3, \neg)}$.

The above examples indicate that the calculi for $\vdash_A$ are rather complex, in general. We axiomatized $\vdash_A$ for the Boolean algebra $B = (\wedge, \vee, \neg) = (\text{ki}, 0, 1)$ in the polynomial base ki, 0, 1. This axiomatization is rather lengthy and artificial. So let us ask the following

Problem 4. Find a nice axiomatization of $\vdash_B$ in $\wedge$, $\vee$, $\neg$.

Note that $\vdash_B$ has neither tautologies nor contradictions. Such a calculus $\vdash$ is highly interesting for methodological reasons: $\vdash$ plus an arbitrary tautology axiomatizes the classical propositional consequence. $\vdash$ plus an arbitrary contradiction does the same, only that $\vee$ has to be read as "and" and $\wedge$ as "or". $\vdash$ axiomatizes, so to speak, the DeMorgan type rules and exhibits the symmetric character of $\wedge$, $\vee$, which usually is recognized in Gentzen-style axiomatizations only.

REFERENCES

Łoś, J. and Suszko, R., 1958, Remarks on Sentential Logics, Ind. Math., 20:177-183.

Lyndon, R. C., 1951, Identities in 2-valued Calculi, Transactions, Am. Math. Soc., 7:457-465.

Malinowski, G., 1981, A Characterization of Strenghtenings of a 2-valued Non-uniform Sentential Calculus, Rep. Math. Logic, 12:17-33.

Post, E., 1941, "Two-valued Iterative Systems of Mathematical Logic," Princeton, Reprint New York 1965.

Rautenberg, W., 1981, 2-element Matrices, Studia Logica, 40:315-353.

Woytylak, P., 1979, Matrix Representation for Structural Strenghtenings of a Propositional Logic, Studia Logica, 38:263-266.

Wroński, A., 1979, A 3-valued Matrix whose Consequence Is Not Finitely Based, Bull. Sec. Logic, 8:68-71.

ON A FORM OF EQUATIONAL INTERPOLATION PROPERTY

Andrzej Wroński

Department of Logic
Jagiellonian University
PL-31-044 Cracow

In this paper we characterize varieties with the amalgamation property and the congruence extension property by means of a condition of proof-theoretic nature resembling a version of Craig's interpolation property due to Maehara (1961).

Preliminaries. To facilitate the presentation we have almost entirely adopted the notation and nomenclature of Burris and Sankappanavar (1981) and the reader will find there all details he might need. However, in opposition to Burris and Sankappanavar (1981), we make no distinction between an identity $p \approx q$ and the pair $\langle p, q \rangle$ and we follow the custom of writing $\mathcal{A}, \mathcal{B}, \ldots$ for algebras and $A, B, \ldots$ for their respective universes. For the reader's convenience some key notation and concepts we use are explained below in detail. The symbol $T(X)$ denotes the set of all terms of a similarity type τ (which will always be clear from the context) over a set of variables X. An identity of type τ over X is a pair $\langle p, q \rangle$ (sometimes written $p \approx q$) where $p, q \in T(X)$. If $T(X) \neq \emptyset$ then we write $\mathcal{T}(X)$ for the term algebra of type τ over X. Given a class V of algebras of type τ, we write $Id_V(X)$ for the set of identities of type τ over X that hold in all algebras from V. If Σ is a set of identities then $\mathrm{Var}(\Sigma)$ stands for the set of all variables occurring in identities from Σ. We use the symbols $\rightarrow$ and & for the familiar logical connectives (implication and conjunction) and occasionally we write $\&(\Sigma)$ for the conjunction of all members of Σ which we allow to be empty or infinite ($\&(\emptyset)$ is to be understood as a logical tautology not involving any variables). A class V of algebras of type τ is a variety iff it consists of all models of $\mathrm{Id}_V(X)$ for a denumerably infinite set of variables X. The class V has the amalgamation property AP iff for every embeddings $\alpha: \mathcal{A} \rightarrow \mathcal{B}$, $\beta: \mathcal{A} \rightarrow \mathcal{C}$ where $\mathcal{A}, \mathcal{B}, \mathcal{C} \in V$ there exists $\mathcal{D} \in V$ and embeddings $\gamma: \mathcal{B} \rightarrow \mathcal{D}$, $\delta: \mathcal{C} \rightarrow \mathcal{D}$ such that $\gamma \cdot \alpha = \delta \cdot \beta$. An algebra $\mathcal{A}$ has the congruence extension property (CEP) iff for every congruence Φ on a subalgebra $\mathcal{B}$ of $\mathcal{A}$ there exists a congruence Θ on $\mathcal{A}$ such that $\Theta\restriction_B = \Phi$. A class of algebras has CEP iff all its members do so. A useful diagrammatic characterization of varieties with CEP is stated in the following lemma whose easy proof is left to the reader.

LEMMA 1. A variety V has CEP iff for every embedding $\alpha: \mathcal{A} \rightarrow \mathcal{B}$ and epimorphism $\beta: \mathcal{A} \rightarrow \mathcal{C}$ where $\mathcal{A}, \mathcal{B}, \mathcal{C} \in V$ there exists $\mathcal{D} \in V$, an epimorphism $\gamma: \mathcal{B} \rightarrow \mathcal{D}$ and an embedding $\delta: \mathcal{C} \rightarrow \mathcal{D}$ such that $\gamma \cdot \alpha = \delta \cdot \beta$.

Also varieties with CEP and AP have an elegant diagrammatic characterization due to Bacsich (1975). Following Bacsich (1975) we say that a variety V has transferable injections (TI) iff for every embedding $\alpha: \mathcal{A} \rightarrow \mathcal{B}$ and homomorphism $\beta: \mathcal{A} \rightarrow \mathcal{C}$ where $\mathcal{A}, \mathcal{B}, \mathcal{C} \in V$ there exists $\mathcal{D} \in V$, a homomorphism $\gamma: \mathcal{B} \rightarrow \mathcal{D}$ and an embedding $\delta: \mathcal{C} \rightarrow \mathcal{D}$ such that $\gamma \cdot \alpha = \delta \cdot \beta$. Then we have:

LEMMA 2 (Bacsich, 1975). A variety has TI iff it has both AP and CEP.

Equational Interpolation Property. The following definition is motivated by Maehara's version of the well-known interpolation theorem of Craig (see Craig (1957); Takeuti (1975)):

DEFINITION. Let V be a variety of some type τ. We say that V has the equation interpolation property (EIP) iff for all finite sets Σ and $\Gamma \cup \{e\}$ of identities of type τ, if $V \models \&(\Sigma \cup \Gamma) \rightarrow e$ and the set of terms of type τ over $Var(\Sigma) \cap Var(\Gamma \cup \{e\})$ is not empty then there exists a finite set Δ of identities of type τ over $Var(\Sigma) \cap (Var(\Gamma \cup \{e\})$ such that $V \models \&(\Sigma) \rightarrow \&(\Delta)$ and $V \models \&(\Delta \cup \Gamma) \rightarrow e$.

Certain forms of equational interpolation property similar to EIP have already been investigated by Jónsson (1965), Pigozzi (1971) and Bacsich (1975). The following remark being an immediate consequence of the compactness theorem for elementary logic gives EIP some model-theoretic flavor and allows for considerable simplifications in various arguments involving EIP.

REMARK. If the sets of identities Σ, Γ and Δ in the above definition were not required to be finite then the resulting property of varieties would remain equivalent to EIP.

The fact just stated will be frequently used without mention in the proof of our main result which is the following:

THEOREM 1. A variety has EIP iff it has both AP and CEP.

PROOF. By virtue of LEMMA 2 it suffices to prove that EIP in varieties is equivalent to TI. To show that EIP implies TI suppose that we are given a variety V, an embedding $\alpha: \mathcal{A} \rightarrow \mathcal{B}$ and a homomorphism $\beta: \mathcal{A} \rightarrow \mathcal{C}$. Choose a set of variables Y big enough to secure the existence of an epimorphism $\varphi_B: \mathcal{T}(Y) \rightarrow \mathcal{B}$ such that $\varphi_B(Y)$ contains a generating set for $\alpha(A)$. Now put $X = Y \cap \varphi_B^{-1}(\alpha(A))$ and define an epimorphism $\varphi_A\colon T(X) \to A$ by $\varphi_A(p) = \alpha^{-1}(\varphi_B(p))$ for every $p \in T(X)$. Next choose a set $Z \supseteq X$ satisfying $Z \cap Y = X$ and as big as is needed to secure the existence of an epimorphism $\varphi_C\colon T(Z) \to C$ which agrees with $\beta \cdot \varphi_A$ on X. Let D be the algebra determined in V by the presentation $\langle Y \cup Z, \ker\varphi_B \cup \ker\varphi_C\rangle$. Then $D = T(Y \cup Z)/\Theta$ where $\langle p, q\rangle \in \Theta$ iff $V \models (\ker\varphi_B \cup \ker\varphi_C) \to p \approx q$ for every $p, q \in T(X \cup Z)$. We define two mappings $\gamma\colon B \to D$ and $\delta\colon C \to D$ putting for every $b \in B$ and $c \in C$, $\gamma(b) = [p]\Theta$ and $\delta(c) = [q]\Theta$ where $p \in \varphi_B^{-1}(b)$ and $q \in \varphi_C^{-1}(c)$. It is clear by construction that the above definition does not depend on the choice of p and q and that both γ and δ are homomorphisms. We shall now prove that $\gamma \cdot \alpha = \delta \cdot \beta$. Take any $a \in A$, $p \in \varphi_B^{-1}(\alpha(a))$ and $q \in \varphi_C^{-1}(\beta(a))$; we claim that $\langle p, q\rangle \in \Theta$. Indeed, since $\varphi_B(p) = \alpha(a)$ then there exists $p' \in T(X)$ such that $\varphi_B(p') = \varphi_B(p)$. Now it follows that $\varphi_A(p') = \alpha^{-1}(\varphi_B(p')) = \alpha^{-1}(\varphi_B(p)) = \alpha^{-1}(\alpha(a)) = a$ and consequently $\varphi_C(q) = \beta(a) = \beta(\varphi_A(p')) = \varphi_C(p')$ which means that $\langle p', q\rangle \in \ker\varphi_C$. Hence $\langle p, p'\rangle, \langle p', q\rangle \in \ker\varphi_B \cup \ker\varphi_C \subseteq \Theta$ and therefore $\langle p, q\rangle \in \Theta$ as claimed. Now we need to show that δ is an embedding and that is the moment when EIP comes in. Suppose that $c, c' \in C$, $q, q' \in T(Z)$, $q \in \varphi_C^{-1}(c)$, $q' \in \varphi_C^{-1}(c')$ and $\langle q, q'\rangle \in \Theta$. Then $V \models \&(\ker\varphi_B \cup \ker\varphi_C) \to q \approx q'$ and applying EIP one obtains a set of identities Δ over X such that $V \models \&(\ker\varphi_B) \to \&(\Delta)$ and $V \models \&(\Delta \cup \ker\varphi_C) \to q \approx q'$. Next one gets easily that $\Delta \subseteq \ker\varphi_B$ and consequently $\Delta \subseteq \ker\varphi_C$ because $\ker\varphi_B\restriction_{T(X)} \subseteq \ker\varphi_A \subseteq \ker\varphi_C$ by construction. Now it follows that $V \models \&(\ker\varphi_C) \to q \approx q'$ and therefore $\langle q, q'\rangle \in \ker\varphi_C$ which implies that $c = \varphi_C(q) = \varphi_C(q') = c'$ ending the proof of the implication from EIP to TI.

To prove the converse implication suppose that $V \models \&(\Sigma \cup \Gamma) \to e$, $Y = Var(\Sigma)$, $Z = Var(\Gamma \cup \{e\})$, $X = Y \cap Z$ and some terms of the considered type over the set of variables X exist. Let Θ_Σ be the smallest congruence of $T(Y)$ containing $\Sigma \cup Id_V(Y)$ and let $\Delta = \Theta_\Sigma\restriction_{T(X)}$.

Then it is obvious that $V \models \&(\Sigma) \to \&(\Delta)$ and it remains to show that $V \models \&(\Delta \cup \Gamma) \to e$ or equivalently that $e \in \Theta_\Gamma$ where Θ_Γ is the smallest congruence of $T(Z)$ containing $\Delta \cup \Gamma \cup Id_V(Z)$. Observe first that the mapping β which sends $[p]\Delta$ into $[p]\Theta_\Gamma$ is a homomorphism of $T(X)/\Delta$ into $T(Z)/\Theta_\Gamma$ whereas the mapping α which sends $[p]\Delta$ into $[p]\Theta_\Sigma$ is an embedding of $T(X)/\Delta$ into $T(Y)/\Theta_\Sigma$. Now by applying TI we pick an algebra $\mathcal{D} \in V$, a homomorphism $\gamma\colon T(Y)/\Theta_\Sigma \to \mathcal{D}$ and an embedding $\delta\colon T(Z)/\Theta_\Gamma \to \mathcal{D}$ such that $\gamma \bullet \alpha = \delta \bullet \beta$. Define a homomorphism $\varphi\colon T(Y \cup Z) \to \mathcal{D}$ putting $\varphi(x) = \gamma([x]\Theta_\Sigma)$ if $x \in Y$ and $\varphi(x) = \delta([x]\Theta_\Gamma)$ if $x \in Z$. The above definition is correct because for every $x \in Y \cap \cap Z = X$ we have $\gamma([x]\Theta_\Sigma) = \gamma(\alpha([x]\Delta)) = \delta(\beta([x]\Delta)) = \delta([x]\Theta_\Gamma)$. Next by induction we get that $\varphi(p) = \gamma([p]\Theta_\Sigma)$ if $p \in T(Y)$ and $\varphi(p) = = \delta([p]\Theta_\Gamma)$ if $p \in T(Z)$. This easily implies that $\Sigma \cup \Gamma \subseteq \ker\varphi$ which leads to the conclusion that $e \in \ker\varphi$ because $V \models \&(\Sigma \cup \Gamma) \to e$ by virtue of the assumption. Thus supposing that $e = p \approx q$ one gets that $\delta([p]\Theta_\Gamma) = \varphi(p) = \varphi(q) = \delta([q]\Theta_\Gamma)$ which yields that $[p]\Theta_\Gamma = [q]\Theta_\Gamma$ because δ is one-to-one. Hence $e \in \Theta_\Gamma$. Q.E.D.

Since interpolation properties of the kind investigated here have their origin in logic it would be particularly interesting to settle the question of EIP for the class of all algebras of a given similarity type. Henceforward it will be convenient to use the notation making similarity type explicit and to denote the class of all algebras of type τ by V_τ. Note first the following simple observation:

LEMMA 3. The class V_τ has CEP iff all operations of type τ are at most unary.

PROOF. Suppose that every operation of type τ is at most unary, $\mathcal{A}, \mathcal{B} \in V_\tau$, $\mathcal{A}$ is a subalgebra of $\mathcal{B}$ and Φ is a congruence of $\mathcal{A}$. Put $\Theta = \Phi \cup \{\langle x, x\rangle\colon x \in B-A\}$ and taking advantage of the restriction on arities of operations in τ verify that Θ is a congruence of $\mathcal{B}$.

To prove the converse implication define a commutative groupoid $A = \langle\{0, 1, 2\}, *\rangle$ by $1 * 2 = 2 * 1 = 2$, $x * x = 0$ and $0 * x = x * 0 = x$. It is easy to see that A^2 does not have CEP. Indeed, $B = \langle\{0, 1\}^2, *\rangle$ is a subalgebra of A^2 and the partition $\{\{\langle 0, 0\rangle, \langle 1, 1\rangle\}, \{\langle 0, 1\rangle, \langle 1, 0\rangle\}\}$ gives rise to a congruence Φ of B that can not be extended to all of A^2. Now suppose that an operation f of type τ is n-ary with $n \geq 2$. We shall define an algebra C of type τ on the universe $\{0, 1, 2\}^2$ by imitating the structure of A^2. For every $x_1, \ldots, x_n \in \{0, 1, 2\}^2$ we put $f^C(x_1, \ldots, x_n) = x_1 * x_2$ and we define all remaining operations of type τ as constant functions of appropriate arity taking only the value $\langle 0, 0\rangle$. Then the same argument as in the case of A^2 shows that CEP fails to hold in C. Q.E.D.

Combining the above lemma with a rather trivial observation that every class of the form V_τ has AP we now obtain:

THEOREM 2. The class V_τ has EIP iff all operations of type τ are at most unary.

The significance of EIP in algebra stems mainly from the fact that it may be used to establish AP for a given variety which in most cases is rather difficult. We hope that deep applications of EIP in this direction may be found by developing calculating procedures for identities modelled after Gentzen techniques of logic.

REFERENCES

Bacsich, P. D., 1972, Injectivity in Model Theory, Colloqu. Math., 25:165.

Bacsich, P. D., 1975, Amalgamation Properties and Interpolation Theorems for Equational Theories, Alg. Universalis, 5:45.

Burris, S., and Sankappanavar, H. P., 1981, "A Course in Universal Algebra," Springer, Berlin.

Craig, W., 1957, Three Uses of the Herbrand-Gentzen Theorem in Relating Model Theory and Proof Theory, J. Symb. Log., 22:269.

Jónsson, B., 1965, Extensions of Relational Structures, *in*: "The Theory of Models, Proceedings of the 1963 Symposium at Berkeley," J. W. Addison, L. Henkin, A. Tarski, eds., North-Holland, Amsterdam.

Maehara, S., 1961, Craig's Interpolation Theorem (in Japanese), Sŭgaku, 235.

Pigozzi, D., 1971, Amalgamation, Congruence-extension, and Interpolation Properties in Algebras, Alg. Universalis, 1:269.

Takeuti, G., 1975, "Proof Theory," North-Holland, Amsterdam.

STRUCTURAL COMPLETENESS OF PURELY IMPLICATIONAL INTERMEDIATE LOGICS

Tadeusz Prucnal

Instytut Matematyki WSP
ul. Konopnickiej 21
PL-25-406 Kielce

0.

The notion of structural completeness was introduced in Pogorzelski (1971). It is known that structural completeness can be characterized in different ways; cf. Mackinson (1976), Pogorzelski and Wojtylak (1982), Pogorzelski (1971), Prucnal and Wroński (1974), Prucnal (1972), and Tsitkin (1978). For example, it can be characterized as follows. Let Cn be any consequence operation in a given language F. Then Cn is structurally complete in the infinitary (finitary) sense if and only if for every (finite) set $Y \subseteq F$ and $x \in F$ the following condition is satisfied:

$$(*) \text{ if } x \notin Cn(Y) \text{ then } \exists_{e \in End(F)} [e(Y) \subseteq Cn(\phi) \wedge e(x) \notin Cn(\phi)],$$

where End(F) denotes the set of all endomorphisms of the algebra F.

The aim of this paper is to give a complete characterization of consequence operations determined by implicational intermediate logics and the modus ponens rule, which are structurally complete in the infinitary sense.

1.

Let F be the set of formulas built from an infinite set $V = \{p_0, p_1, p_2, \ldots\}$ of propositional variables and the binary connective $\rightarrow$. Thus the algebra $\underline{F} = \langle F, \rightarrow\rangle$ is free in the class of all similar algebras. Let INT_c be the set of all purely implicational theses of the intuitionistic propositional calculus. Then by implicational intermediate logic we mean any set $H \subsetneq F$ containing INT_c and closed under the modus ponens rule and the substitution rule. For every implicational intermediate logic H we define the consequence operation C_H in F as follows: $C_H(X)$ is the smallest set containing the set $X \cup H$ and closed with respect to the modus ponens rule. Every set $X \subseteq F$ such that $C_H(X) = X$ will be called an H-system. It is known that for every implicational intermediate logic H, the union of any arbitrary chain of H-systems is an H-system and thus by Kuratowski-Zorn's Lemma the condition $z \notin C_H(X)$ implies the existence of an H-system Y such that $z \notin Y$, $X \subseteq Y$, and Y is a maximal H-system having that property. Every such Y will be called a relatively maximal H-supersystem of X with respect to z. By RMS(H) we denote the family of all relatively maximal H-supersystems; i.e., $Y \in$ RMS(H) if and only if for some $X \subseteq F$ and $z \in F$, Y is a relatively maximal H-supersystem of X with respect to z.

A logical matrix for $\underline{F} = \langle F, \rightarrow\rangle$ is a pair $\mathbb{M} = \langle \underline{M}, \overset{*}{M}\rangle$ where $\underline{M} = \langle M, \Rightarrow\rangle$ is an algebra similar to $\underline{F}$ and $\overset{*}{M} \subseteq M$. A binary relation $\doteq$ on M is called a congruence of the matrix $\mathbb{M} = \langle \underline{M}, \overset{*}{M}\rangle$ if and only if $\doteq$ is a congruence on the algebra $\underline{M}$ satisfying the condition: if $a \in \overset{*}{M}$ then $[a]_{\doteq} \subseteq \overset{*}{M}$, where $[a]_{\doteq} = \{b \in M\colon a \doteq b\}$. Every congruence of $\mathbb{M}$ determines the quotient matrix $\mathbb{M}/_{\doteq} = \langle \underline{M}/_{\doteq}, \overset{*}{M}/_{\doteq}\rangle$ where $\underline{M}/_{\doteq}$ is a quotient algebra and $\overset{*}{M}/_{\doteq} = \{[a]_{\doteq}\colon a \in \overset{*}{M}\}$; cf. Wójcicki (1973).

Let $\mathbb{M}_1 = \langle \underline{M}_1, \overset{*}{M}_1\rangle$ and $\mathbb{M}_2 = \langle \underline{M}_2, \overset{*}{M}_2\rangle$ be two matrices.

We say that a mapping h: $M_1 \to M_2$ is a homomorphism (isomorphism, epimorphism) of the matrix $\mathbb{M}_1$ into (onto) $\mathbb{M}_2$ if and only if the following conditions are satisfied:

(i) h is a homomorphism (isomorphism, epimorphism) of the algebra $\underline{M}_1$ into (onto) algebra $\underline{M}_2$,

(ii) $h(M_1 - \overset{*}{M}_1) \subseteq M_2 - \overset{*}{M}_2$,

(iii) $h(\overset{*}{M}_1) \subseteq \overset{*}{M}_2$.

The matrices $\mathbb{M}_1$, $\mathbb{M}_2$ are said to be isomorphic ($\mathbb{M}_1 \simeq \mathbb{M}_2$) if and only if there is an isomorphism h of the matrix $\mathbb{M}_1$ onto $\mathbb{M}_2$.

Let $\{\mathbb{M}_t : t \in T\}$, $T \neq \emptyset$, be an indexed family of matrices $\mathbb{M}_t = \langle \underline{M}_t, \overset{*}{M}_t \rangle$. The matrix $P_{t \in T} \mathbb{M}_t = \langle P_{t \in T} \underline{M}_t, P_{t \in T} \overset{*}{M}_t \rangle$ is called the product of the family $\{\mathbb{M}_t : t \in T\}$, where $P_{t \in T} \underline{M}_t$ is a product of the algebras $\{\underline{M}_t : t \in T\}$ and $P_{t \in T} \overset{*}{M}_t$ is the Cartesian product of the sets $\{\overset{*}{M}_t : t \in T\}$.

The following definition of the matrix consequence $\overline{\mathbb{M}} : 2^F \to 2^F$ is due to Łoś and Suszko (1959). For every $X \subseteq F$ and $y \in F$:

$$y \in \overline{\mathbb{M}}(X) \text{ iff } \forall_{h \in Hom(\underline{F}, \underline{M})} [h(X) \subseteq \overset{*}{M} \Rightarrow h(y) \in \overset{*}{M}],$$

where Hom($\underline{F}$, $\underline{M}$) is the set of all homomorphisms of the algebra $\underline{F}$ into $\underline{M}$.

The next theorem can be found in Wójcicki (1973).

(1.1) If a matrix $\mathbb{M}_2$ is an epimorphic image of a matrix $\mathbb{M}_1$ then $\overline{\mathbb{M}}_1 = \overline{\mathbb{M}}_2$.

Let H be any implicational intermediate logic. Then any H-supersystem Y determines a binary relation $\doteq_Y$ on F by

$$x \doteq_Y z \text{ iff } x \to z,\ z \to x \in Y.$$

If $Y \in RMS(H)$ then the relation $\doteq_Y$ is a congruence of the matrix $\mathbb{M}_Y = \langle \underline{F}, Y\rangle$. We will write $\doteq$ instead of $\doteq_Y$ if there is no danger of confusion.

The following property follows directly from (1.1).

(1.2) For every implicational intermediate logic H and for any $Y \in RMS(H)$: $\overline{\mathbb{M}}_Y = \overline{\mathbb{M}_Y/\doteq}$.

We also state without proof the following theorem:

(1.3) For every implicational intermediate logic H and any $X \subseteq F$: $C_H(X) = \bigcap\{\overline{\mathbb{M}}_Y(X) : Y \in RMS(H)\}$.

2.

An abstract algebra $\underline{A} = \langle A, \Rightarrow\rangle$ with a two-argument operation $\Rightarrow$ is called a positive implication algebra (cf. Rasiowa (1974)), provided for all a, b, c $\in$ A the following conditions are satisfied:

$$a \Rightarrow (b \Rightarrow c) = (a \Rightarrow b) \Rightarrow (a \Rightarrow c)$$
$$(a \Rightarrow a) \Rightarrow b = b$$
$$(a \Rightarrow b) \Rightarrow ((b \Rightarrow a) \Rightarrow b) = (b \Rightarrow a) \Rightarrow ((a \Rightarrow b) \Rightarrow a).$$

If $\underline{A}$ is a positive implication algebra then for every a, b $\in$ A: $a \Rightarrow a = b \Rightarrow b$. We assume $1_A = a \Rightarrow a$, for $a \in A$. Then the relation $\leq$ defined on A as: $a \leq b$ iff $a \Rightarrow b = 1_A$, is an ordering on A. The element 1_A is the greatest element in the ordered set $\langle A, \leq\rangle$. We say that an algebra $\underline{A} = \langle A, \Rightarrow\rangle$ is strongly compact (SCA) if and only if there exists the greatest element in $A - \{1_A\}$.

A. Wroński states (unpublished) that any positive implication algebra $\underline{A}$ is strongly compact if and only if $\underline{A}$ is subdirectly irreducible.

Let PIA be the variety of all positive implication algebras. From the result of Diego (1966) it is known that

(2.1) Every free algebra of the variety PIA free-generated by a finite set is finite.

Let $\{\underline{A}_t: t \in T\}$, $T \neq \emptyset$, be an indexed family of positive implication algebras and let $\{\mathbb{A}_t: t \in T\}$ be an indexed family of matrices $\mathbb{A}_t = \langle \underline{A}_t, \{1_t\}\rangle$, where $1_t = 1_{A_t}$. Then we prove the following theorem (cf. Zygmunt (1974)):

(2.2) For every $Y \subseteq F$: $\overline{P_{t\in T}\mathbb{A}_t}(Y) = \bigcap\{\overline{\mathbb{A}}_t(Y): t \in T\}$.

Proof. Assume that $x \notin \overline{\mathbb{A}}_s(Y)$ for some $s \in T$. Then there exists a homomorphism $h \in \mathrm{Hom}(\underline{F}, \underline{A}_s)$ such that:

(1) $h(Y) \subseteq \{1_s\}$,
(2) $h(x) \neq 1_s$.

For $i = 0, 1, 2, \ldots$ we define the function $f_i \in P_{t\in T}\underline{A}_t$ as follows:

$$(3)\quad f_i(t) = \begin{cases} h(p_i), & \text{if } t = s \\ 1_t, & \text{if } t \neq s. \end{cases}$$

Let now v be a function such that

(4) $v(p_i) = f_i$, for every $i = 0, 1, 2, \ldots$.

The function $v: V \to P_{t\in T}\underline{A}_t$ can be extended to a homomorphism h^v from the algebra $\underline{F}$ into $P_{t\in T}\underline{A}_t$. Let $\mathbb{1}_T(t) = 1_t$ for every $t \in T$. Then by (1), (2), (3) and (4) we get: $h^v(Y) \subseteq \{\mathbb{1}_T\}$ and $h^v(x) \neq \mathbb{1}_T$. Hence $\overline{P_{t\in T}\mathbb{A}_t}(Y) \subseteq \bigcap\{\overline{\mathbb{A}}_t(Y): t \in T\}$.

The converse inclusion $\supseteq$ follows immediately from the definition of $\overline{P_{t\in T}\mathbb{A}_t}$.

Hint: in this paper we assume that every positive implication algebra $\underline{A}$ is not void.

We shall prove that

(2.3) For every implicational intermediate logic H there exists a family $\{\underline{A}_t: t \in T_H\} \subseteq SCA$ such that:

(i) $C_H = \overline{P_{t\in T_H}\mathbb{A}_t}$

(ii) $\mathbb{A}_{t_1} \not\simeq \mathbb{A}_{t_2}$ if $t_1 \neq t_2$, for every $t_1, t_2 \in T_H$.

Proof. Let H be an implicational intermediate logic. Then by (1.3) we get

(1) $C_H(X) = \bigcap\{\overline{\mathbb{M}}_Y(X): Y \in RMS(H)\}$, where $\mathbb{M}_Y = \langle\underline{F}, Y\rangle$.

Observe that for $Y \in RMS(H)$ we have

(2) $\underline{F}/\dot{=}_Y \in SCA$.

Define now the relation $\approx$ on RMS(H) as follows

(3) $Y' \approx Y''$ iff $\underline{F}/_{\dot{=}Y'} \simeq \underline{F}/_{\dot{=}Y''}$.

This relation is an equivalence relation on RMS(H). Hence, by the axiom of choice, there exists a function S: $RMS(H)/_{\approx} \to RMS(H)$ such that

(4) $S(U) \in U$, for every $U \in RMS(H)/_{\approx}$.

Let now $T_H = S(RMS(H)/_{\approx})$ and $\mathbb{A}_t = \langle \underline{F}/_{\dot{=}t}, \{t\}\rangle$ for $t \in T_H$. Thus the matrix $\mathbb{A}_t$ is an epimorphic image of a matrix $\mathbb{M}_t = \langle \underline{F}, t\rangle$, for every $t \in T_H$. Hence, by (1.1), (1) and (3), we get

(5) $C_H(X) = \bigcap\{\overline{\mathbb{A}}_t(X): t \in T_H\}$ and $\mathbb{A}_{t_1} \not\simeq \mathbb{A}_{t_2}$ for $t_1 \neq t_2$.

Applying now (2.2) we obtain: $C_H(X) = \overline{P_{t\in T_H} \mathbb{A}_t}(X)$, for every $X \subseteq F$.

3.

Define now the formulas: x^i_j, i, j = 0, 1, 2, ... and z^n, n = 3, 4, ... as follows:

$$x^i_j = (p_i \to p_j) \to ((p_j \to p_i) \to p_0), \text{ where } j > i > 0,$$
$$z^n = x^1_2 \to (x^1_3 \to \ldots \to (x^1_n \to (x^2_3 \to (x^2_4 \to \ldots \to (x^{n-1}_n \to p_0)\ldots).$$

It is easy to verify that

(3.1) For every strongly compact algebra $\underline{A} \in$ PIA and for every $n \geq 3$: if $z^n \in \overline{\mathbb{A}}(\emptyset)$ then $card(A) < n$, where card(A) is the cardinal number of the set A.

We say that an implicational intermediate logic H is tabular if and only if $H = \overline{\mathbb{A}}(\emptyset)$ for some finite non-degenerate algebra $\underline{A} \in$ PIA.

We shall show that

(3.2) For every implicational intermediate logic H the following conditions are equivalent:

(c1) H is tabular,

(c2) $z^n \in H$, for some $n \geq 3$.

Proof. The implication (c1) $\Rightarrow$ (c2) follows immediately from the definition of z^n. To prove (c2) $\Rightarrow$ (c1) assume that

(1) $z^n \in H$ for some $n \geq 3$.

Applying (2.3), we obtain:

(2) $H = C_H(\emptyset) = \overline{P_{t \in T_H} \mathbb{A}_t}(\emptyset)$,

(3) $\mathbb{A}_{t_1} \not\equiv \mathbb{A}_{t_2}$ if $t_1 \neq t_2$,

(4) $\underline{A}_t \in SCA$ for all $t \in T_H$.

By (2.2), (1) and (2) we have

(5) $z^n \in \overline{\mathbb{A}}_t(\emptyset)$, for every $t \in T_H$.

Applying now (3.1) and (4), we get

(6) $card(A_t) < n$, for every $t \in T_H$.

Consequently, by (3), the set T_H is finite. Therefore H is tabular.

Let now $Y_o = \{x_j^i : j > i > 0\}$. We shall prove that

(3.3) For every implicational intermediate logic H and for every $e \in End(\underline{F})$: if $e(Y_o) \subseteq H$ then $e(p_0) \in H$.

Proof. Let us assume that

(1) $e(Y_o) \subseteq H$.

We shall define a new function $v_e: V \to V$ as follows

$$(2)\ v_e(p_i) = \begin{cases} p_i, & \text{if } p_i \in V(e(p_0)) \\ p_0, & \text{if } p_i \notin V(e(p_0)), \end{cases}$$

where V(x) is a set of all propositional variables occurring in a formula x. Note that $V(e(p_0))$ is finite.

Let h^{v_e} be the extension of the function v_e to the endomorphism of the algebra $\underline{F}$. Hence, by (1) and (2) we get

(3) $h^{v_e}(e(Y_o)) \subseteq h^{v_e}(H) \subseteq H$, and
(4) $h^{v_e}(e(p_0)) = e(p_0)$.

Applying now (2.1) we obtain:

(5) $h^{v_e}(e(p_i \to p_j)),\ h^{v_e}(e(p_j \to p_i)) \in H$, for some $i < j$.

Thus, by (4), we get $e(p_0) \in H$.

The next theorem can be found in Prucnal (1972).

(3.4) For every implicational intermediate logic H the operation consequence C_H is structurally complete in the finitary sense.

It is easy to verify that

(3.5) For every finite positive implication algebra $\underline{A}$ the following conditions are equivalent:

(c1) the matrix consequence $\overline{\mathbb{A}}$ is structurally complete in the finitary sense,

(c2) $\overline{\mathbb{A}}$ is structurally complete in the infinitary sense.

The following theorem follows directly from: (3.3), (3.2) and (3.2), (2.3), (3.1), (3.5), (3.4).

Theorem. For every implicational intermediate logic H the following conditions are equivalent:

(c1) C_H is structurally complete in the infinitary sense,
(c2) H is tabular.

REFERENCES

Diego, A., 1966, "Sur les algèbres de Hilbert," Paris.

Łoś, J. and Suszko, R., 1959, Remarks on Sentential Logic, Indagationes Mathematicae, 20:177.

Makinson, D., 1976, A Characterization of Structural Completeness of a Structural Consequence Operation, Reports on Mathematical Logic, 6:99.

Pogorzelski, W. A., 1971, Structural Completeness of the Propositional Calculus, Bull. Acad. Polon. Sci., Série Math., Astr., Phys., 19:349.

Pogorzelski, W. A. and Wojtylak, P., 1982, "Elements of the Theory of Completeness in Propositional Logic," Silesian University, Katowice.

Prucnal, T., 1972, On the Structural Completeness of some Pure Implicational Calculi, Studia Logica, 30:45.

Prucnal, T. and Wroński, A., 1974, An Algebraic Characterization of the Notion of Structural Completeness, Bull. of the Section of Logic, 3:30.

Rasiowa, H., 1974, "An Algebraic Approach to Non-classical Logics," PWN, Warsaw.

Tsitkin, A. I., 1978, On Structurally Complete Superintiotionistic Logics, Dokl. Akad. Nauk SSSR, 241:40.

Wójcicki, R., 1973, Matrix Approach in Methodology of Sentential Calculi, Studia Logica, 32:7.

Zygmunt, J., 1974, A Note on Direct Products and Ultraproducts of Logical Matrices, Studia Logica, 33:349.

PROOF-THEORETIC VALIDITY AND THE COMPLETENESS OF INTUITIONISTIC LOGIC

Peter Schroeder-Heister

Fachgruppe Philosophie
Universität Konstanz
D-7750 Konstanz

1. INTRODUCTION

As has often been claimed, the introduction (I) and elimination (E) rules of intuitionistic natural deduction systems stand in a certain harmony with each other. This can be understood in such a way that once the I rules are given the E rules are uniquely determined and vice versa. The following is an attempt to elaborate this claim. More precisely, we define two notions of validity, one based on I rules (valid+) and one based on E rules (valid-), and show: the E rules generate a maximal valid+ extension of the I rules, and the I rules generate a maximal valid- extension of the E rules. That is to say, the calculus consisting of I and E rules (i.e., intuitionistic logic) is sound and complete with respect to both validity+ and validity-. This does not mean that the syntactical form of E rules is determined by the I rules and vice versa, but that the deductive power which E rules bring about in addition to I rules is exactly what can be justified from I rules and vice versa. Concerning the approach based on I rules this was already claimed by Gentzen who considered I rules to give meanings to the logical signs and the E rules to be consequences thereof (Gentzen, 1935, p. 189).

Unfortunately (and contrary to the author's expectation) the approach based on I rules does not work for the full system of intuitionistic logic, but only for the fragment without $\vee$ (and $\exists$ in the quantifier case). The reason for this asymmetry between the two approaches is the indirect character of the E rules for $\vee$ (and $\exists$), as will be shown at the end (see section 4.2 below). Thus from the standpoint of the present investigation preference must be given to the approach based on E rules. This, however, is only a technical argument. Whether one should use I or E rules as the basis of proof-theoretic validity must finally rest on genuine semantical or epistemological arguments which go beyond the scope of this paper.

It is a central feature of the systematics of I and E rules of intuitionistic logic, that an I step followed by an E step whose major premiss is just the conclusion of the I step represents a 'detour' and can be omitted: the premisses of the I step already 'contain' the conclusion of the E step in a certain sense. In Prawitz (1965) this fact is called the 'inversion principle' and used as the basis of the normalization procedures developed there. For example, the sequence of inference steps

$$\begin{array}{ll} & \begin{array}{cc} \cdot & + \\ \cdot & + \\ \cdot & + \end{array} \\ \&I & \dfrac{\alpha \quad \beta}{\alpha \,\&\, \beta} \\ \&E & \dfrac{}{\alpha} \end{array}$$

can be reduced to

$$\begin{array}{c} \cdot \\ \cdot \\ \cdot \\ \alpha, \end{array}$$

the sequence

$$
\begin{array}{llll}
 & \vdots & \overline{\alpha}^{(1)} & \overline{\beta}^{(1)} \\
 & & | & + \\
 & \alpha & | & + \\
\vee I & \overline{\alpha \vee \beta} & | & + \\
 & & \gamma & \gamma \\
\vee E & \multicolumn{3}{l}{\overline{\hphantom{\alpha \vee \beta \quad \gamma \quad \gamma}}\ (1),} \\
 & \gamma & &
\end{array}
$$

where "(1)" marks the discharging of assumptions by the application of $\vee$E, can be reduced to

$$
\begin{array}{c}
\vdots \\
\alpha \\
| \\
| \\
| \\
\gamma
\end{array}
$$

(here the derivations of the minor premisses of $\vee$E must be at one's disposal). Using the concept of the eliminability of a rule from a derivation, which means that the derivation which possibly applies that rule can be transformed into a derivation of the same formula from the same or from fewer assumptions without any application of that rule, these reduction steps can be characterized in two ways:

(i) They show that applications of E rules are eliminable from all derivations in which major premisses of such applications are always conclusions of applications of I rules.

(ii) They show that applications of I rules are eliminable from all derivations in which the conclusions of such applications are always major premisses of applications of E rules.

If one considers eliminability in this sense to be a justification of inference rules, in the first case one takes the elimination procedure to be a justification of the E rules with respect to given I rules (which are considered 'canonical', i.e., justified by definition as meaning-determining rules), and in the second case the same procedure to be a justification of the I rules with respect to given 'canonical' E rules.

This idea can easily be generalized to definitions of validity for arbitrary inference rules ρ of the form

$$\frac{\begin{array}{ccc}\Gamma_1 & & \Gamma_n \\ \alpha_1 & \dots & \alpha_n\end{array}}{\alpha} \quad (n \geq 0),$$

where the Γ_i are (possibly empty) lists of assumptions which may be discharged by the application of ρ in the derivation of α_i from Γ_i. Calling all α_i for which Γ_i is empty the principal premisses of ρ (and correspondingly for applications of ρ) one only has to use what is said in (i) and (ii) about E and I rules, respectively, as the definiens. That is to say, we consider arbitrary inference rules ρ as if they were E rules for their principal premises, or as if they were I rules for their conclusion.

(i') ρ is valid+ if applications of ρ are eliminable from all derivations in which the non-atomic principal premisses of such applications are always conclusions of applications of I rules.

(ii') ρ is valid- if applications of ρ are eliminable from all derivations in which the non-atomic conclusions of applications of ρ are always major premisses of applications of E rules.

These definitions have the disadvantage that validity is not transitive in the sense that rules derived by application of valid rules are valid. E.g., both

$$\frac{(\alpha \mathbin{\&} \beta) \mathbin{\&} \gamma}{\alpha \mathbin{\&} \beta} \quad \text{and} \quad \frac{\alpha \mathbin{\&} \beta}{\alpha}$$

are valid+, but not

$$\frac{(\alpha \mathbin{\&} \beta) \mathbin{\&} \gamma}{\alpha},$$

since there is no elimination procedure for the application ⊠ of the latter rule in the derivation

$$(1) \qquad \boxtimes\,\frac{\dfrac{\overline{\alpha \mathbin{\&} \beta} \qquad \overline{\gamma}}{(\alpha \mathbin{\&} \beta) \mathbin{\&} \gamma}}{\alpha}$$

where $\alpha \mathbin{\&} \beta$ and γ are used as assumptions. Similarly, both

$$\frac{\alpha \quad \beta}{\alpha \mathbin{\&} \beta} \quad \text{and} \quad \frac{\alpha \mathbin{\&} \beta \qquad \gamma}{(\alpha \mathbin{\&} \beta) \mathbin{\&} \gamma}$$

are valid-, but not

$$\frac{\alpha \quad \beta \quad \gamma}{(\alpha \mathbin{\&} \beta) \mathbin{\&} \gamma},$$

since there is no elimination procedure for the application ⊠ of the latter rule in the derivation

$$(2)\qquad \boxtimes\qquad \cfrac{\cfrac{\overline{\alpha}\qquad \overline{\beta}\qquad \overline{\gamma}}{(\alpha \,\&\, \beta) \,\&\, \gamma}}{\alpha \,\&\, \beta}$$

where α, β, γ are assumptions. Another example is the inference rule

$$\frac{\alpha \qquad \begin{matrix}\alpha \vee \beta \\ \alpha \,\&\, \beta\end{matrix}}{\alpha \,\&\, \beta}$$

(where occurrences of $\alpha \vee \beta$ can be discharged by the application of this rule): it is not valid- in the sense of (ii') because it cannot for example be eliminated from the derivation

$$(3)\qquad \boxtimes\qquad \cfrac{\cfrac{\overline{\alpha}\qquad \cfrac{\overline{(\alpha \vee \beta) \supset (\alpha \,\&\, \beta)}\qquad \overline{\alpha \vee \beta}\;{}^{(1)}}{\alpha \,\&\, \beta}}{\alpha \,\&\, \beta}\;{}^{(1)}}{\beta}\;.$$

It can nevertheless be derived by use of the valid- rule

$$\frac{\alpha}{\alpha \vee \beta}\;:$$

$$\text{from}\quad \begin{matrix}+\\+\\+\\ \alpha\end{matrix}\quad \text{and}\quad \begin{matrix}\alpha \vee \beta\\ \vdots \\ \alpha \,\&\, \beta\end{matrix}\quad \text{one obtains}\quad \begin{matrix}+\\+\\+\\ \dfrac{\alpha}{\alpha \vee \beta}\\ \vdots \\ \alpha \,\&\, \beta\end{matrix}\;.$$

Thus the soundness and completeness results which can be proved for intuitionistic logic with respect to the notions of validity defined by (i') and (i'') (cf. Schroeder-Heister, 1983a, 1983b) only lead to an equivalence between derivability in intuitionistic logic and the 'transitive closures' of valid rules; this gives much less information than one would like to have (that is reflected in the fact that the proofs of these results are fairly simple).

This difficulty can be overcome by defining the validity of an inference rule ρ by induction on the complexity of ρ (which will be explicated by the rank $|\rho|$ of ρ). We allow that in eliminating an application of ρ from a derivation, rules which are of lower complexity than ρ may be used. This leads to the following preliminary definitions (for precise definitions see section 2.4 below):

(i'') An atomic rule is valid+ if it is derivable without use of basic rules for operators. A non-atomic rule ρ is valid+ if applications of ρ are eliminable from all derivations in which the non-atomic principal premisses of applications of ρ are always conclusions of applications of I rules, and where, besides I rules, valid+ rules of lower complexity than ρ are at one's disposal.

(ii'') An atomic rule is valid- if it is derivable without use of basic rules for operators. A non-atomic rule ρ is valid- if applications of ρ are eliminable from all derivations in which the non-atomic conclusions of applications of ρ are always major premisses of applications of E rules, and where, besides E rules, valid- rules of lower complexity than ρ are at one's disposal.

Using these definitions the applications ⊠ of the rules considered in the examples above can be eliminated from (1), (2) and (3): We may transform (1) to

$$\dfrac{\dfrac{}{\alpha \,\&\, \beta}}{\alpha}$$

because $\dfrac{\alpha \,\&\, \beta}{\alpha}$ is a valid+ rule of lower complexity than the rule $\dfrac{(\alpha \,\&\, \beta) \,\&\, \gamma}{\alpha}$. (2) can be transformed to

$$\dfrac{\dfrac{}{\alpha} \quad \dfrac{}{\beta}}{\alpha \,\&\, \beta}$$

because $\dfrac{\alpha \quad \beta}{\alpha \,\&\, \beta}$ is a valid- rule of lower complexity than the rule $\dfrac{\alpha \quad \beta \quad \gamma}{(\alpha \,\&\, \beta) \,\&\, \gamma}$. Similarly, we may transform (3) to

$$\dfrac{\dfrac{\dfrac{}{(\alpha \vee \beta) \supset (\alpha \,\&\, \beta)} \quad \dfrac{\dfrac{}{\alpha}}{\alpha \vee \beta}}{\alpha \,\&\, \beta}}{\beta}$$

because $\dfrac{\alpha}{\alpha \vee \beta}$ is a valid- rule of lower complexity than

$$\dfrac{\alpha \quad \begin{matrix} \alpha \vee \beta \\ \alpha \,\&\, \beta \end{matrix}}{\alpha \,\&\, \beta}.$$

It can however be shown that the rule

$$\dfrac{(\alpha \vee \beta) \,\&\, \gamma}{(\alpha \,\&\, \gamma) \vee (\beta \,\&\, \gamma)},$$

for example, is not valid+ in the sense of (i''), because to eliminate it from certain derivations one would have to use an ∨E rule

$$\frac{\alpha \vee \beta \qquad \begin{matrix}\alpha \\ (\alpha \,\&\, \gamma) \vee (\beta \,\&\, \gamma)\end{matrix} \qquad \begin{matrix}\beta \\ (\alpha \,\&\, \gamma) \vee (\beta \,\&\, \gamma)\end{matrix}}{(\alpha \,\&\, \gamma) \vee (\beta \,\&\, \gamma)}$$

which is valid+, but not of lower complexity than the rule above (see section 5.2 below). (i'') will turn out to be adequate only for rules which are built up from formulas without ∨ (and ∃ in the quantifier case). Thus when speaking about validity+ this should always be understood as restricted in this way.

The fact that the so-defined notions of validity are in general transitive, follows immediately from the soundness and completeness results we are going to prove with respect to these notions, i.e., from the fact that a rule ρ is derivable in intuitionistic logic iff it is valid+ and iff it is valid-. Due to lack of space we confine ourselves to sentential logic; the quantifier case is an exercise which gives no new fundamental insight. We shall, however, take atomic bases into account, i.e., consider calculi for atomic formulas which are extended with rules for logically compound formulas.

In the following we shall understand the term 'eliminability' as employed above in its uniform reading. That is to say, the elimination procedures which transform certain derivations of the premisses of a rule into certain derivations of its conclusion must be uniform in the sense that they do not depend on the way the premisses have been derived. This idea will be formally captured by introducing assumption rules, i.e., rules functioning as assumptions, which are a natural counterpart of assumption formulas for natural deduction systems.

Section 2 below will present our system of sentential logic over atomic calculi including assumption rules in detail, more precise re-definitions of validity, and some basic lemmata. Sections 3 and 4 give the soundness and completeness proofs for validity- and validity+, respectively, and section 5 contains, beside some remarks on the extension of our approach to quantifier logic, a discussion of why the conception which is based on I rules fails for formulas containing ∨ (or ∃).

The approach presented here was stimulated by and is closely related to Prawitz' theory of arguments and his definitions of validity (cf. Prawitz, 1971, 1973, 1974, 1984). Because we are concerned mainly with technical matters of proof theory, we always speak of 'derivations' and do not distinguish them from 'arguments'. A comparison of ours and Prawitz' approach cannot be carried out here; we just mention some aspects which must be taken into consideration for such a comparison:

- Prawitz defines the validity of inference rules in terms of the validity of arguments which is the primary notion. We define validity of an inference rule first; a derivation is considered valid if it results from applications of valid inference rules.

- Prawitz' definitions of validity which are based on I rules capture the whole system of intuitionistic logic whereas our notion of validity+ is adequate only for the restricted system without ∨ (and ∃). Conversely, Prawitz' short discussion of a validity notion based on E rules (1971, p. 289 seq.) is restricted to the system without ∨ (and ∃) whereas our notion of validity- is adequate for the full system.

- Prawitz leaves the notion of a 'procedure' unrestricted, whereas we will consider only uniform procedures. It seems to be exactly this restriction which makes the fairly simple completeness proofs for our system possible (whereas the soundness proofs are more complicated because they have to apply the whole power of the normalization theorem). For Prawitz' approach there is an obvious way of proving soundness but it is not at all clear how a completeness proof may proceed. Furthermore, our restriction to uniform procedures is the reason why, when dealing with atomic systems, we need not consider arbitrary extensions of such systems in the definitions of validity.

2. BASIC NOTIONS

2.1 Calculi With Assumption Rules - Uniform Procedures

As stated above we deal with sentential logic which is built over atomic calculi for atomic formulas. An atomic calculus A is given by a set of atomic formulas and a set of inference rules (perhaps including axioms) governing these formulas. The calculus of intuitionistic logic $I(A)$ over A is defined as follows: Formulas of $I(A)$ are formulas of A, and furthermore $(\alpha \,\&\, \beta)$, $(\alpha \vee \beta)$, $(\alpha \supset \beta)$, $\bot$ for formulas α and β of $I(A)$, where outer brackets can be omitted. Such formulas are also called *formulas over* A. For given A, 'α', 'β', 'γ', 'δ', 'ε' (with and without indices) are syntactical variables for formulas over A. Formulas of $I^{o}(A)$ are formulas over A which do not contain $\vee$. *Basic inference rules* (shortly: basic rules) of $I(A)$ are the atomic inference rules of A and the standard I and E rules of intuitionistic sentential logic, i.e.,

&I $\dfrac{\alpha \quad \beta}{\alpha \,\&\, \beta}$ &E $\dfrac{\alpha \,\&\, \beta}{\alpha} \quad \dfrac{\alpha \,\&\, \beta}{\beta}$

$$\vee\mathrm{I}\quad \frac{\alpha}{\alpha \vee \beta} \qquad \frac{\beta}{\alpha \vee \beta} \qquad\qquad \vee\mathrm{E}\quad \frac{\alpha \vee \beta \quad \begin{matrix}\alpha \\ \gamma\end{matrix} \quad \begin{matrix}\beta \\ \gamma\end{matrix}}{\gamma}$$

$$\supset\mathrm{I}\quad \frac{\begin{matrix}\alpha \\ \beta\end{matrix}}{\alpha \supset \beta} \qquad\qquad \supset\mathrm{E}\quad \frac{\alpha \supset \beta \quad \alpha}{\beta}$$

$$[\text{no } \bot\mathrm{I} \text{ rule}] \qquad\qquad \bot\mathrm{E}\quad \frac{\bot}{\alpha}$$

for all α, β, γ. Basic rules of $I^{o}(A)$ are these rules without the $\vee$ rules, where α, β, γ are formulas of $I^{o}(A)$. Note that rules in our sense are not rule schemata so there are, e.g., many $\supset$I rules and not one $\supset$I rule. The formulas standing above a premiss of a rule are those whose occurrences may be discharged by the application of this rule. In the notation of a derivation this discharging must be indicated (e.g., by small numerals in brackets), but not in the notation of a rule, for in the latter case assumptions which are not discharged are never mentioned. As usual, the leftmost formulas of E rules and of applications of E rules are called major premisses.

$I^{+}(A)$ results from $I^{o}(A)$ by omitting the E rules, $I^{-}(A)$ from $I(A)$ by omitting the I rules as basic rules. By I we denote the calculus $I(F)$ over the atomic calculus F where F has denumerably many sentence letters a_1, a_2, ... as formulas and no inference rules. I.e., I is the ordinary calculus of 'formal' intuitionistic sentential logic without an atomic base in the genuine sense. By I^{o}, I^{+} and I^{-} we denote $I^{o}(F)$, $I^{+}(F)$ and $I^{-}(F)$, respectively.

Following Lorenzen (1955), by a *system* of signs we understand a list of signs whose entries are separated by commas and called its members. Note that α is just the system consisting of α only (which is different from the finite set $\{\alpha\}$). If Φ is a system, then $\{\Phi\}$ is the set having as elements the members of Φ. Empty systems are allowed as limiting cases - they have no graphical representation. Syntactical variables for systems of formulas are 'Γ', 'Δ', with and without indices. 'Γ, Δ' denotes the system which is obtained by concatenating the members of Γ and Δ. It will be always obvious from the context, if the comma is used as dividing entries of a system or if it is metalinguistically used in the context of an enumeration.

The general form of an inference rule (shortly: rule) is

$$(4) \qquad \frac{\begin{matrix}\Gamma_1 & & \Gamma_n \\ \alpha_1 & \ldots & \alpha_n\end{matrix}}{\alpha}$$

where Γ_i's may be empty and n may be 0. Syntactical variables for rules are 'ρ', 'ρ_1', 'ρ_2' , ... Rules over A (or 'of $I(A)$') are built up from formulas over A, rules of $I^o(A)$ from formulas over A without $\vee$. As a linear notation for a rule ρ of the form (4) we use

$$<<\Gamma_1> \Rightarrow \alpha_1, \ldots, <\Gamma_n> \Rightarrow \alpha_n> \Rightarrow \alpha$$

where, if Γ_i is empty, $<\Gamma_i> \Rightarrow \alpha_i$ is replaced by α_i and where, if $n = 0$, we write $\Rightarrow\alpha$. By $(\rho)_1$ we denote the system

$$<\Gamma_1> \Rightarrow \alpha_1, \ldots, <\Gamma_n> \Rightarrow \alpha_n$$

and by $(\rho)_2$ the conclusion α. In this linear notation, we write, e.g., $<\alpha, \beta> \Rightarrow \alpha \,\&\, \beta$ for an &I rule and $<\alpha \vee \beta, <\alpha> \Rightarrow \gamma, <\beta> \Rightarrow \gamma> \Rightarrow \gamma$ for an $\vee$E rule. As syntactical variables for systems containing formulas and/or rules of the form $<\Gamma> \Rightarrow \alpha$ we use 'Φ' and 'Ψ' (with and without indices). (Note that Φ and Ψ cannot contain arbitrary rules of the form (4) but only those where all Γ_i are empty.) So a rule ρ of the general form (4) can be represented as $<\Phi> \Rightarrow \alpha$.

The rank of formulas, rules and systems of formulas and rules is denoted by '$|\ |$' and defined as follows:

$|\alpha| = 0$ if α is atomic

$|\bot| = 1$

$|\alpha \,\&\, \beta| = |\alpha \vee \beta| = |\alpha \supset \beta| = \max(|\alpha|, |\beta|) + 1$

$|\Phi| = \max\{|\Psi| / \Psi \text{ is member of } \Phi\}$

$|<\Phi> \Rightarrow \alpha| = \max(|\Phi|, |\alpha|) + 1.$

For example, according to this definition, $\vee$E rules and $\supset$I rules have rank 2 if α, β, γ are all atomic. Note that the rank of a rule is always greater than 0.

Lemma 2.1.1: (i) An I rule with conclusion α has rank $|\alpha| + 1$. The same holds for E rules with α as major premiss, if α is a conjunction or an implication.

(ii) If $|\beta| < |\alpha|$, then $\max(|<\Phi> \Rightarrow \beta| - 1, |\beta| + 1) \leq$ $\leq |<\Phi> \Rightarrow \alpha| - 1$.

Proof (i) trivial.

(ii) $|<\Phi> \Rightarrow \beta| - 1 = \max(|\Phi|, |\beta|) \leq \max(|\Phi|, |\alpha|) =$ $= |<\Phi> \Rightarrow \alpha| - 1$. $|\beta| + 1 \leq |\alpha| \leq \max(|\Phi|, |\alpha|) = |<\Phi> \Rightarrow \alpha| - 1$.

As usual in natural deduction systems, derivations may start with assumptions (or applications of atomic axioms if there are any) and proceed by the application of inference rules where by the application of certain rules assumptions can be discharged, i.e., the dependence on assumptions can be eliminated in the course of a derivation. Unlike usual treatments of natural deduction, however, we permit the application of rules of the form $<\alpha_1, \ldots, \alpha_n> \Rightarrow \alpha$ as additional assumptions. These are not assumptions from which one can start, but assumptions which are applied according to the schema

$$<\alpha_1, \ldots, \alpha_n> \Rightarrow \alpha \qquad \dfrac{\begin{matrix} \vdots & & \vdots \\ \alpha_1 & \ldots & \alpha_n \end{matrix}}{\alpha}$$

and allow one to pass over from derived formulas to another formula. Assumption rules differ from assumption formulas in that, in the framework presented here, there are no rules which allow one to discharge applications of them. We use the term 'assumption' as including assumption formulas and assumption rules. (For a thorough treatment of assumption rules within a framework where they are dischargeable, including the quantifier case, see Schroeder-Heister 1984a, 1984b).

Assumption rules are a natural extension of assumption formulas for the context of natural deduction systems in so far as they can help to explicate the notion of a *uniform* procedure for transforming derivations from assumption formulas; such a notion is important for the definition of the derivability of a rule which allows us to discharge assumptions. Following Lorenzen (1955), in the case of Hilbert-style calculi one can distinguish between the admissibility and the derivability of a rule $<\alpha_1, \ldots, \alpha_n> \Rightarrow \alpha$ in the following way: $<\alpha_1, \ldots, \alpha_n> \Rightarrow \alpha$ is *admissible* if there is a procedure which transforms assumption-free derivations of $\alpha_1, \ldots, \alpha_n$ into an assumption-free derivation of α; it is *derivable* if there is a uniform procedure of this kind, i.e., a procedure which does not depend on the way the $\alpha_1, \ldots, \alpha_n$ may have been derived. The latter can be expressed by saying that α is derivable *from* the assumptions $\alpha_1, \ldots, \alpha_n$. Occurrences of the assumptions $\alpha_1, \ldots, \alpha_n$ in a derivation of α from $\alpha_1, \ldots, \alpha_n$ can be considered as schematic letters representing assumption-free derivations of $\alpha_1, \ldots, \alpha_n$, respectively: instantiation of them by assumption-free derivations uniformly yields an assumption-free derivation of α.

The same distinction can be drawn on the next level with natural deduction calculi. A rule of the form $<<\Gamma_1> \Rightarrow \alpha_1, \ldots, <\Gamma_n> \Rightarrow \Rightarrow \alpha_n> \Rightarrow \alpha$ may be called admissible, if there is a procedure which transforms derivations of α_i from Γ_i (for all i, $1 \leq i \leq n$) into an assumption-free derivation of α, and called derivable if there is a uniform procedure of this kind, i.e., a procedure which does not depend on the way the α_i may have been derived from the Γ_i. The latter can be expressed by saying that α is derivable *from* the assumptions $<\Gamma_1> \Rightarrow \alpha_1, \ldots, <\Gamma_n> \Rightarrow \alpha_n$. Applications of assumptions $<\Gamma_i> \Rightarrow \alpha_i$ in such a derivation can be considered as schematically representing derivations of α_i from Γ_i: replacement of them by derivations of α_i from Γ_i uniformly yields an assumption-free derivation of α.

Consider for example the rule

$$\frac{\begin{array}{cc} \alpha & \beta \\ \beta \,\&\, \gamma & \delta \end{array}}{\alpha \supset \delta}$$

for arbitrary formulas α, β, γ, δ of I. Its derivability in I can be shown using assumption rules in the following way:

$$
\begin{array}{rc}
 & \overline{}\ ^{(1)} \\
 & \alpha \\
\langle\alpha\rangle \Rightarrow \beta \,\&\, \gamma & \overline{} \\
 & \beta \,\&\, \gamma \\
\&E & \overline{} \\
 & \beta \\
\langle\beta\rangle \Rightarrow \delta & \overline{} \\
 & \delta \\
\supset I & \overline{}\ ^{(1)} \\
 & \alpha \supset \delta
\end{array}.
$$

This derivation expresses a uniform procedure because the replacement of

$$\langle\alpha\rangle \Rightarrow \beta \,\&\, \gamma \ \frac{\alpha}{\beta \,\&\, \gamma} \quad \text{and} \quad \langle\beta\rangle \Rightarrow \delta \ \frac{\beta}{\delta}$$

by derivations $\begin{array}{c}\alpha\\ \equiv \\ \beta \,\&\, \gamma\end{array}$ and $\begin{array}{c}\beta\\ \ddagger \\ \delta\end{array}$

uniformly yields the required derivation, no matter how $\equiv$ and $\ddagger$ look.

The distinction between admissibility and derivability breaks down in favour of derivability, however, if one allows additional assumptions from the beginning: If we call $\langle\alpha_1, \ldots, \alpha_n\rangle \Rightarrow \alpha$ admissible if there is a procedure which transforms derivations of α_i *from* Δ $(1 \leq i \leq n)$ into a derivation of α *from* Δ, then by taking Δ to be the system $\alpha_1, \ldots, \alpha_n$ we obtain the derivability of $\langle\alpha_1, \ldots, \alpha_n\rangle \Rightarrow \alpha$ from its admissibility. And similarly, if we call $\langle\langle\Gamma_1\rangle \Rightarrow \alpha_1, \ldots, \langle\Gamma_n\rangle \Rightarrow \alpha_n\rangle \Rightarrow \alpha$ admissible, if there is a procedure which transforms derivations of α_i from Γ_i *and* Φ $(1 \leq i \leq n)$ into a derivation of α *from* Φ, then by taking Φ to be the system $\langle\Gamma_1\rangle \Rightarrow \alpha_1, \ldots, \langle\Gamma_n\rangle \Rightarrow \alpha_n$ so that there are trivial derivations of α_i from Γ_i and Φ $(1 \leq i \leq n)$, we obtain the derivability of the considered rule from its admissibility.

In the following we shall rely on the notion of uniform procedures and thus on assumption rules not only when dealing with derivability in intuitionistic logic but also when dealing with the validity of rules. That means that we may use assumption rules throughout so that elimination procedures are, according to the last paragraph, eo ipso uniform ones.

2.2. Derivability - Canonical Conditions and Consequences

The explication of the notion of assumption rules leads to the following formal definitions of derivation and derivability which correspond to those one can find in Prawitz (1965). Let *K* be one of the calculi defined above. We consider formulas of *K* and rules which are built up from formulas of *K*. Derivations of formulas depending on finite sets of assumptions are defined as follows:

$\overline{\alpha}$ is a derivation of α in *K* depending on the empty set, if $\Rightarrow \alpha$ is a basic rule of *K* (i.e., an axiom), and depending on $\{\alpha\}$ otherwise.

If for each i $(1 \leq i \leq n)$,

$$\begin{array}{c}\overline{\Delta_i}\\ \vdots \\ \alpha_i\end{array}$$

is a derivation of α_i in *K* depending on M_i, then

$$\dfrac{\begin{array}{c}\overline{\Delta_1}^{(x)}\\ \vdots\\ \alpha_1\end{array} \quad \cdots \quad \begin{array}{c}\overline{\Delta_n}^{(x)}\\ \vdots\\ \alpha_n\end{array}}{\alpha}\,(x)$$

is a derivation of α in K depending on $\bigcup_{i=1}^{n}(M_i \setminus \{\Delta_i\})$, if $<<\Delta_1> \Rightarrow \alpha_1, \ldots, <\Delta_n> \Rightarrow \alpha_n> \Rightarrow \alpha$ is a basic rule of K, $\times$ is a numeral which has not been used in the derivation and $\overline{\Delta_i}^{(\times)}$ means that '$(\times)$' is attached to all $\overline{\beta}$ where β is a topmost occurrence of a formula belonging to Δ_i.

If for each i $(1 \leq i \leq n)$,

$$\begin{array}{c} \vdots \\ \alpha_i \end{array}$$

is a derivation of α_i in K depending on M_i, then

$$\frac{\begin{array}{ccc} \vdots & & \vdots \\ \alpha_1 & \ldots & \alpha_n \end{array}}{\alpha}$$

is a derivation of α in K depending on $(\bigcup_{i=1}^{n} M_i) \cup \{<\alpha_1, \ldots, \alpha_n> \Rightarrow \alpha\}$.

The derivations of α_i are called the *immediate subderivations* of the resulting derivation.

If $M \subseteq \{\Phi\}$, then a derivation of α *depending* on M in K is also called a derivation of α *from* Φ in K. α is derivable from Φ in K ($\Phi \vdash_K \alpha$) if there is a derivation of α from Φ in K. A rule ρ is derivable from Φ in K ($\Phi \vdash_K \rho$) iff $\Phi, (\rho)_1 \vdash_K (\rho)_2$. It is derivable in K ($\vdash_K \rho$) iff $(\rho)_1 \vdash_K (\rho)_2$. A system of formulas or rules Ψ is derivable from Φ in K ($\Phi \vdash_K \Psi$) if all its members are derivable from Φ in K.

The definition of the derivability of rules is justified by the remarks in section 2.1 above, according to which the assumption that a derivation of β from Δ is given can be represented by the assumption rule $\langle\Delta\rangle \Rightarrow \beta$ if this assumption is considered as an argument of *uniform* transformations only.

Following this definition the I rules can be conceived of as permitting the inference of formulas from systems of formulas and/or rules, namely of $\alpha \,\&\, \beta$ from the system α, β; of $\alpha \vee \beta$ from the systems α and β and of $\alpha \supset \beta$ from the system $\langle\alpha\rangle \Rightarrow \beta$. $\bot$ as a limiting case cannot be inferred from any system. The E rules can be conceived of as permitting the inference of formulas or rules from formulas, namely of α and β from $\alpha \,\&\, \beta$, of $\langle\langle\alpha\rangle \Rightarrow \gamma, \langle\beta\rangle \Rightarrow \gamma\rangle \Rightarrow \gamma$ for every γ from $\alpha \vee \beta$, of $\langle\alpha\rangle \Rightarrow \beta$ from $\alpha \supset \beta$ and of α for every α from $\bot$. This relationship between formulas and (systems of) rules leads to the following definition: Let α be a formula over A. Then we define the predicate of being an α^{-}, which is a predicate for systems of formulas or rules, as follows:

α is an α^{-} if α is atomic.
β, γ is an α^{-} if α equals $\beta \,\&\, \gamma$.
β is an α^{-} if α equals $\beta \vee \gamma$.
γ is an α^{-} if α equals $\beta \vee \gamma$.
$\langle\beta\rangle \Rightarrow \gamma$ is an α^{-} if α equals $\beta \supset \gamma$.
There is no $\bot^{-}$ (not even the empty system!).

For a rule ρ, we define ρ itself to be a ρ^{-}, and for systems of formulas and/or rules Φ, Φ^{-} is defined memberwise, i.e., $\Psi_1, \ldots, \Psi_n$ is a Φ^{-}, if each Ψ_i is a Φ_i^{-} $(1 \leq i \leq n)$ and Φ equals $\Phi_1, \ldots, \Phi_n$ where each Φ_i $(1 \leq i \leq n)$ is either a formula or a rule. If Φ is empty, Φ is a Φ^{-}.

For given α, the α^{-} can be considered as the possibilities from which α can be introduced by application of an I rule. They will also be called the *canonical conditions* for α, and similarly for Φ^- and Φ.

Conversely, we define the predicate of being an α^+, which is a predicate for formulas or rules, as follows:

α is an α^+ if α is atomic.
β is an α^+ if α equals $\beta \,\&\, \gamma$.
γ is an α^+ if α equals $\beta \,\&\, \gamma$.
For each δ, $\langle\langle\beta\rangle \Rightarrow \delta, \langle\gamma\rangle \Rightarrow \delta\rangle \Rightarrow \delta$ is an α^+ if α equals $\beta \vee \gamma$.
$\langle\beta\rangle \Rightarrow \gamma$ is an α^+ if α equals $\beta \supset \gamma$.
For each γ, γ is an $\bot^+$.

Each α^+ can be considered as a possible consequence of α, if α is used as the major premiss of an E rule. The α^+ will also be called the *canonical consequences* of α.

In the following we shall use 'α^+', 'β^+', ..., 'α^-', 'β^-', ..., 'ρ^-', 'Φ^-', ..., as schematic letters for formulas, rules or systems of formulas and/or rules, which are α^+, β^+, ..., α^-, β^-, ..., ρ^-, Φ^-, ... That is, we also use these metalinguistic predicate signs as schematic letters for what falls under the predicates.

Lemma 2.2.1: (i) From each Φ^-, Φ can be inferred by use of I rules for formulas which are members of Φ.

(ii) Each α^+ can be inferred from α by use of an E rule for α.

Proof: (i) Let Φ be the system $\Phi_1, \ldots, \Phi_n$ where each Φ_i $(1 \le i \le n)$ is either a formula or a rule. We show that for each i $(1 \le i \le n)$, each Φ_i^- implies Φ_i in the described way. If Φ_i is a rule, then each Φ_i^- is identical with Φ_i. Let Φ_i be α. Then the assertion follows from the fact that for all α^-, α follows from α^- by use of the I rule for α. (If α is $\bot$, there is no α^-, so '*for all* α^- ...' is vacuously fulfilled.)

(ii) Immediately from the definition of α^+ and the E rules for α.

Lemma 2.2.2: (i) For each α^- and each α^+: α^+ can be derived from α^- without use of any basic rule.

(ii) For each α there are α^+ such that α can be derived with the help of these α^+ by use of the I rule for α (if α is non-atomic).

Proof: (i) If α is atomic, nothing remains to be shown. If α is $\beta \,\&\, \gamma$, then α^+ is either β or γ and α^- is the system β, γ. Now both β and γ are derivable from β, γ without a basic rule. If α is $\beta \vee \gamma$, then α^- is either β or γ, and each α^+ is of the form $\langle\langle\beta\rangle \Rightarrow \delta, \langle\gamma\rangle \Rightarrow \delta\rangle \Rightarrow \delta$. Now δ follows both from $\beta, \langle\beta\rangle \Rightarrow \delta, \langle\gamma\rangle \Rightarrow \delta$ and from $\gamma, \langle\beta\rangle \Rightarrow \delta, \langle\gamma\rangle \Rightarrow \delta$ without application of a basic rule. If α is $\beta \supset \gamma$, then both α^+ and α^- equal $\langle\beta\rangle \Rightarrow \gamma$, and γ trivially follows from $\beta, \langle\beta\rangle \Rightarrow \gamma$ without application of a basic rule. If α is $\bot$, the assertion is vacuously fulfilled, because there is no $\bot^-$.

(ii) If α is $\beta \,\&\, \gamma$, then both β and γ are α^+, and $\beta \,\&\, \gamma$ follows from β, γ by the I rule for α. If α is $\beta \vee \gamma$, consider $\langle\langle\beta\rangle \Rightarrow \beta \vee \gamma, \langle\gamma\rangle \Rightarrow \beta \vee \gamma\rangle \Rightarrow \beta \vee \gamma$ which is an α^+. With the help of this rule, $\beta \vee \gamma$ can be obtained, since $\beta \vee \gamma$ follows both from β and from γ by the I rule for α. If α is $\beta \supset \gamma$, then each α^+ equals to $\langle\beta\rangle \Rightarrow \gamma$, and $\beta \supset \gamma$ follows from $\langle\beta\rangle \Rightarrow \gamma$ by use of the I rule for α. If α is $\bot$, then $\bot$ itself is an $\bot^+$.

(i) shows that for all α^- and α^+ the way from α^- to α^+ via α is a detour and can be avoided by directly moving from α^- to α^+. This is closely related to the fact that adding I and E rules for logical operators to a calculus forms a conservative extension of that calculus. (ii) shows that I and E rules uniquely determine logical constants: For if α and β are of such a kind that the sets of all α^- and of all β^- are identical as well as of all α^+ and of all β^+ (i.e., α and β have the same canonical conditions and consequences), then we may pass from β by E rules to all α^+, and from some of these α^+ to α by I rules (according to (ii)), and vice versa. I.e., α is uniquely determined by the sets of canonical conditions and canonical consequences of α. (For a general investigation of conservativeness and uniqueness in relation to conditions and consequences of sentences see Došen and Schroeder-Heister, 1984.)

2.3. Validity and Harmony

The concepts of Φ^- and α^+ can now be used to redefine the notions of validity+ and validity- respectively, of a rule $<\Phi> \Rightarrow \alpha$. The idea is roughly as follows: instead of saying that applications of $<\Phi> \Rightarrow \alpha$ can be eliminated from derivations in which the principal premises of applications of this rule are always conclusions of applications of I rules, we could simply formulate that α is derivable from all Φ^- without that rule. For if $<\Phi> \Rightarrow \alpha$ can be eliminated from the described derivations, it can be eliminated from the derivation of α from all Φ^- which infers Φ from Φ^- and then applies $<\Phi> \Rightarrow \alpha$; and if α is derivable from all Φ^-, the eliminability of $<\Phi> \Rightarrow \alpha$ follows because, according to the restrictions on the considered derivations, applications of $<\Phi> \Rightarrow \alpha$ presuppose a derivation of a Φ^- and can be evaded by immediately deriving α from this Φ^-. Similarly, instead of saying that applications of $<\Phi> \Rightarrow \alpha$ can be eliminated from derivations in which the conclusion α of such applications is always a major premiss of an E rule, we could simply formulate that all α^+ are derivable from Φ without that rule. For if

$<\Phi> \Rightarrow \alpha$ can be eliminated from the described derivations it can be eliminated from all derivations of α^+ from Φ which apply $<\Phi> \Rightarrow \alpha$ and then infer α^+ from α; and if all α^+ are derivable from Φ the eliminability of $<\Phi> \Rightarrow \alpha$ follows because, according to the restrictions on the considered derivations, applications of $<\Phi> \Rightarrow \alpha$ are followed by inferring an α^+ in the next step and can be evaded by immediately deriving this α^+ from Φ.

The resulting definitions of validity - according to which, roughly speaking, $<\Phi> \Rightarrow \alpha$ is valid+ if α is derivable from all Φ^- by means of I rules and valid+ rules of lower complexity, and valid- if all α^+ are derivable from Φ by means of E rules and valid- rules of lower complexity (for exact definitions see the next section) - can be programmatically stated as follows, using the terms 'canonical condition' and 'canonical consequence' and neglecting the inductive character of the definitions of validity: A rule is valid+ if its conclusion follows from all canonical conditions of its premisses, and is valid- if from its premisses all canonical consequences of its conclusion follow. In other words, the definitions of validity guarantee that everything that follows from all canonical conditions of a system of formulas and/or rules follows from that system itself, and everything that implies all canonical consequences of a formula implies that formula itself.

This can be put in still another way: Let us call α stronger+ than β if β is derivable from α by means of I rules and valid+ rules, and weaker- than β if α is derivable from β by means of E rules and valid- rules. α is called a strongest+ formula fulfilling a given condition if α is stronger+ than all other formulas β fulfilling this condition. α is called a weakest- formula fulfilling a given condition if α is weaker- than all other formulas β fulfilling this condition. Then each α is a strongest formula which can be inferred from all α^- by I rules and valid+ rules: For if β can be derived from all α^- by such rules, then $<\alpha> \Rightarrow \beta$ is valid+; thus β is derivable from α by means of I rules and valid+ rules. The inductive definition of validity+ can be viewed as a stepwise addition of valid+ rules in order to guarantee this maximal strength of conclusions of I rules. Similarly, each α is a weakest- formula from which each α^+ can be inferred by E rules and valid- rules: For if each α^+ can be derived from β by such rules, then $<\beta> \Rightarrow \alpha$ is valid-; thus α is derivable from β by means of E rules and valid- rules. Again, the inductive definition of validity- adds on each level valid- rules in order to guarantee this minimal strength of major premisses of E rules.

This formulation is very close to what Tennant (1978) calls the Principle of Harmony: "Introduction and elimination rules for a logical operator λ must be formulated so that a sentence with λ dominant expresses the *strongest* proposition which can be inferred from the stated premisses when the conditions for λ-introduction are satisfied; while it expresses the *weakest* proposition which can feature in the way required for λ-elimination." (p. 74)

It should be noted, however, that though the principle of harmony follows from our definitions of validity, the fact that the principle of harmony holds does not guarantee validity. As can easily be checked, the principle of harmony is not affected if one adds unvalid+ E rules as, e.g.,

$$\frac{\alpha \ \& \ \beta}{\gamma} \ .$$

Concerning these nice symmetries between the two approaches to validity one should, however, be aware that only the notion of validity- is adequate for the full system of intuitionistic logic.

2.4. The Definitions of Validity - Basic Lemmata

Let an atomic calculus A be given. We assume that the considered formulas and rules are formulas and rules over A. Without always mentioning it, we assume in all contexts of validity+, $I^{o}(A)$ and $I^{+}(A)$, that the formulas, rules and systems of formulas or rules do not contain $\vee$. Since the definitions of the two validity concepts run completely parallel we give them at the same time, presenting the different formulations for the second notion in square brackets.

A *derivation* is called *k-valid+* [*k-valid-*] in A if it is a derivation in the calculus which results from $I^{+}(A)$ [$I^{-}(A)$] by adding all rules of rank $\leq$ k which are valid+ [valid-] in A. If there is a derivation of α from Φ which is k-valid+ [k-valid-] in A, we write $\Phi \vdash^{A,+}_{k} \alpha$ [$\Phi \vdash^{A,-}_{k} \alpha$]. A *rule* $<\Phi> \Rightarrow \alpha$ is called valid+ [valid-] in A if for all Φ^{-} [α^{+}], $\Phi^{-} \vdash^{A,+}_{|<\Phi> \Rightarrow \alpha| -1} \alpha$ [$\Phi \vdash^{A,-}_{|<\Phi> \Rightarrow \alpha| - 1} \alpha^{+}$].

Obviously, rules of rank 1 are valid+ [valid-] if they are derivable in $I^{+}(A)$ [$I^{-}(A)$] and therefore in A (because their premises and conclusions must be atomic).

An *interpretation in* A is a function which assigns a formula of A to each sentence letter, i.e., a function from the formulas of F into the formulas of A. If ρ is a rule over F (i.e., a rule of I) and φ an interpretation in A, then ρ^{φ} is the rule over A which results from ρ by replacing sentence letters a by $\varphi(a)$ in ρ. Obviously, $|\rho| = |\rho^{\varphi}|$. A rule of I^{o} [I] is called valid+ [valid-] if for each atomic calculus A and for each interpretation φ in A, ρ^{φ} is valid+ [valid-] in A.

Lemma 2.4.1: A rule ρ of I^{o} [I] is valid+ [valid-] iff it is valid+ [valid-] in F.

Proof: The direction from left to right is trivial because the identity is an interpretation in F. For the direction from right to left we use induction on the rank of ρ. Let φ be an interpretation in A. If ρ is of the form $\langle\Phi\rangle \Rightarrow \alpha$ and valid+ [valid-] in F, then for all Φ^- [α^+], $\Phi^- \vdash^{F,\,+}_{|\rho|-1} \alpha$ [$\Phi \vdash^{F,\,-}_{|\rho|-1} \alpha^+$]. Since all basic rules of I^+ [I^-] become basic rules of $I^+(A)$ [$I^-(A)$] when interpreted in A, and the same holds by induction hypothesis for rules of rank $< |\rho|$ which are valid+ [valid-] in A, we have $(\Phi^\varphi)^- \vdash^{A,\,+}_{|\rho|-1} \alpha^\varphi$ [$\Phi^\varphi \vdash^{A,\,-}_{|\rho|-1} (\alpha^\varphi)^+$], i.e., ρ^φ is valid+ [valid-] in A.

Lemma 2.4.2: If $\Phi \vdash^{A,\,+}_{k} \alpha$ [$\Phi \vdash^{A,\,-}_{k} \alpha$], then $\Phi \vdash^{A,\,+}_{1} \alpha$ [$\Phi \vdash^{A,\,-}_{1} \alpha$] for every $1 > k$.

Proof: trivial.

Lemma 2.4.3: If $\langle\Phi\rangle \Rightarrow \alpha$ is valid+ [valid-] in A, then $\langle\Phi, \Psi\rangle \Rightarrow \alpha$ is valid+ [valid-] in A.

Proof: trivial.

Lemma 2.4.4: If $\langle\Phi\rangle \Rightarrow \alpha$ is valid+ [valid-] in A, then $\Phi \vdash^{A,\,+}_{|\langle\Phi\rangle \Rightarrow \alpha|} \alpha$ [$\Phi \vdash^{A,\,-}_{|\langle\Phi\rangle \Rightarrow \alpha|} \alpha$].

Proof: trivial.

Lemma 2.4.5: (i) All basic rules of $I^o(A)$ are valid+ in A.

(ii) All basic rules of $I(A)$ are valid- in A.

Proof: (i) For the basic rules of A nothing remains to be shown. For the I rules the assertion follows by twofold application of lemma 2.2.1(i). For the E rules the assertion follows from lemma 2.2.2(i) where in the case of $\supset$E lemma 2.2.1(i) is still to be applied to the minor premiss.

(ii) For the basic rules of A nothing remains to be shown. For the E rules the assertion follows by twofold application of lemma 2.2.1(ii). For the I rules the assertion follows from lemma 2.2.2(i).

Lemma 2.4.6: If $\langle\Phi\rangle \Rightarrow \alpha$ is valid+ in A and α is different from $\bot$ then for each Φ^- there is an α^- such that $\Phi^- \vdash^{A,+}_{|\langle\Phi\rangle \Rightarrow \alpha| - 1} \alpha^-$.

Proof: By assumption, we have a derivation D of α from Φ^- which is k-valid+ in A for $k = |\langle\Phi\rangle \Rightarrow \alpha| - 1$. If α is atomic, then all α^- are equal to α and nothing remains to be shown. Let α be non-atomic. If $|\Phi| > |\alpha|$, then by lemma 2.4.5(i) and 2.1.1(i) we obtain a derivation of any α^- by application of an E rule to α which is k-valid+ (note that α is not a disjunction). If $|\Phi| \leq |\alpha|$ then $|\langle\Phi\rangle \Rightarrow \alpha| = |\alpha| + 1$. Thus D is $|\alpha|$-valid+ in A. In the last step D cannot apply an assumption rule $\langle\Psi\rangle \Rightarrow \alpha$ belonging to Φ^-, because $|\Phi^-| \leq |\Phi| \leq |\alpha|$, but $|\langle\Psi\rangle \Rightarrow \alpha| > |\alpha|$. Likewise, D cannot apply a rule of rank $\leq |\alpha|$ which is valid+ in A. α cannot even be an assumption formula of D, for then α would belong to a β^- for a member β of Φ, and because α is a formula, $|\alpha| < |\beta|$ would hold, contradicting $|\beta| \leq |\Phi| \leq |\alpha|$ ($|\beta^-| = |\beta|$ only holds if β is an implication and β^- a rule). So D must apply an I rule in the last step.

Lemma 2.4.7: (i) If for all α^-, $\Phi, \alpha^- \vdash^{A,+}_{k} \beta$, then $\Phi, \alpha \vdash^{A,+}_{l} \beta$, where $l = \max(k, |\alpha| + 1)$.

(ii) If for all Φ^-, $\Phi^- \vdash_{I^o(A)} \alpha$, then $\Phi \vdash_{I^o(A)} \alpha$.

Proof: (i) If α^- is identical with α, nothing remains to be shown. If α is a conjunction or implication, apply the E rule for α and use lemma 2.1.1(i). If α is $\bot$, then by applications of $\bot$E rules with atomic conclusions (which are thus of rank $|\alpha| + 1$) we can obtain all atomic subformulas and subformulas of the form $\bot$ of β.

Therefrom β is derivable by use of I rules.

(ii) Similarly.

For the calculus $I(A)$ (and therefore for $I^{o}(A)$) a normalization theorem in the sense of Prawitz (1965) can be proved. Because of the possible occurrence of assumption rules certain modifications are necessary (cf. Schroeder-Heister, 1981) but the central conclusions like the subformula property can be upheld. Without proof we state what we shall need.

Lemma 2.4.8: Let a derivation D of α from Φ in $I(A)$ or $I^{o}(A)$ be given. It can be transformed into a normal derivation D' of α from Φ in $I(A)$ or $I^{o}(A)$, respectively, for which the following holds: if D' applies an E rule in the last step with β as major premiss, then β is a subformula of a formula occurring in Φ and $|\beta| \leq |\Phi|$. Furthermore all applications of $\bot$E rules have atomic conclusions.

3. SOUNDNESS AND COMPLETENESS OF INTUITIONISTIC LOGIC WITH RESPECT TO VALIDITY-

Let an arbitrary atomic calulus A be given.

Theorem 3.1 (Soundness): If $\Phi \vdash_{I(A)} \alpha$, then $\langle\Phi\rangle \Rightarrow \alpha$ is valid- in A. (I.e., each rule which is derivable in $I(A)$ is valid- in A.)

Proof: By lemma 2.4.8 we can assume that derivations in $I(A)$ are in normal form. We proceed by induction on the length of normal derivations. We have to distinguish five main cases according to the kinds of rules which might have been applied in the last step of the given normal derivation D of α from Φ (cf. the clauses in the definition of a derivation).

(i) If D is of the form $\overline{\alpha}$ where $\Rightarrow \alpha$ is a basic rule of $I(A)$, then $\Rightarrow \alpha$ is a basic rule of A (because there are no premiss-free I or E rules), thus $\vdash^{A,\,-}_{0} \alpha$, therefore $<\Phi> \Rightarrow \alpha$ is valid- in A.

(ii) If D is of the form $\overline{\alpha}$ where α is an assumption (thus belonging to Φ), then for all α^+, $\alpha \vdash^{A,\,-}_{0} \alpha^+$ holds by lemma 2.2.1(ii), therefore $<\Phi> \Rightarrow \alpha$ is valid- in A.

(iii) If D applies an I rule in the last step, we distinguish subcases according to the form of α.

a) If α is α_1 & α_2, then D contains derivations of α_1 and of α_2 from Φ as immediate subderivations. Thus by induction hypothesis $<\Phi> \Rightarrow \alpha_1$ and $<\Phi> \Rightarrow \alpha_2$ are valid- in A, i.e., $\Phi \vdash^{A,\,-}_{|<\Phi> \Rightarrow \alpha_i| - 1} \alpha_i^+$ for all α_i^+ $(i = 1, 2)$.

Thus by lemma 2.2.2(ii) and lemma 2.1.1(i):

$$\Phi \vdash^{A,\,-}_{k_i} \alpha_i \quad (i = 1, 2)$$

where $k_i = \max(|<\Phi> \Rightarrow \alpha_i| - 1,\ |\alpha_i| + 1)$.

Thus by lemma 2.1.1(ii):

$$\Phi \vdash^{A,\,-}_{|<\Phi> \Rightarrow \alpha| - 1} \alpha_i \quad (i = 1, 2).$$

b) If α is $\alpha_1 \vee \alpha_2$, then D contains a derivation of α_1 or of α_2 from Φ as an immediate subderivation. Thus by induction hypothesis $<\Phi> \Rightarrow \alpha_i$ is valid- in A for some i $(i = 1, 2)$. As in a) we obtain

$$\Phi \vdash^{A,\,-}_{|<\Phi> \Rightarrow \alpha| - 1} \alpha_i.$$ Thus

$$\Phi, <\alpha_1> \Rightarrow \beta, <\alpha_2> \Rightarrow \beta \vdash^{A, -}_{|<\Phi> \Rightarrow \alpha| - 1} \beta \text{ for each } \beta.$$

c) If α is $\alpha_1 \supset \alpha_2$, then D contains a derivation of α_2 from Φ, α_1 as an immediate subderivation. Thus by induction hypothesis $<\Phi, \alpha_1> \Rightarrow \alpha_2$ is valid- in A. As before we obtain

$$\Phi, \alpha_1 \vdash^{A, -}_{|<\Phi, \alpha_1> \Rightarrow \alpha| - 1} \alpha_2$$

where $|<\Phi, \alpha_1> \Rightarrow \alpha| = |<\Phi> \Rightarrow \alpha|$.

(iv) If D applies an E rule in the last step, we distinguish subcases according to the form of its major premiss δ.

a) If δ is $\alpha \& \beta$ or $\beta \& \alpha$, then D contains a derivation of $\alpha \& \beta$ or $\beta \& \alpha$, respectively, from Φ as an immediate subderivation. By induction hypothesis $<\Phi> \Rightarrow \alpha \& \beta$ or $<\Phi> \Rightarrow \beta \& \alpha$, respectively, is valid- in A, i.e., in particular

$$\Phi \vdash^{A, -}_{|<\Phi> \Rightarrow \alpha \& \beta| - 1} \alpha.$$

Thus by lemma 2.2.1(ii):

$$\Phi \vdash^{A, -}_{|<\Phi> \Rightarrow \alpha \& \beta| - 1} \alpha^+ \text{ for each } \alpha^+.$$

By lemma 2.4.8: $|\Phi| \geq |\alpha \& \beta|$, thus $|<\Phi> \Rightarrow \alpha \& \beta| = |\Phi| + 1 =$
$= |<\Phi> \Rightarrow \alpha|$.

b) If δ is $\beta \vee \gamma$, then D contains derivations of $\beta \vee \gamma$ from Φ, of α from Φ, β and of α from Φ, γ as immediate subderivations. By induction hypothesis $<\Phi> \Rightarrow \beta \vee \gamma$, $<\Phi, \beta> \Rightarrow \alpha$ and $<\Phi, \gamma> \Rightarrow \alpha$ are valid- in A, i.e.,

$$\Phi,\ \langle\beta\rangle \Rightarrow \varepsilon,\ \langle\gamma\rangle \Rightarrow \varepsilon \mathrel{\mathop{\vdash}\limits^{A,\ -}_{|\langle\Phi\rangle \Rightarrow \beta \vee \gamma| - 1}} \varepsilon \text{ for all } \varepsilon$$

$$\Phi,\ \beta \mathrel{\mathop{\vdash}\limits^{A,\ -}_{|\langle\Phi,\ \beta\rangle \Rightarrow \alpha| - 1}} \alpha^+ \text{ for all } \alpha^+$$

$$\Phi,\ \gamma \mathrel{\mathop{\vdash}\limits^{A,\ -}_{|\langle\Phi,\ \gamma\rangle \Rightarrow \alpha| - 1}} \alpha^+ \text{ for all } \alpha^+.$$

By specializing ε to α^+ if α^+ is a formula and to $(\alpha^+)_2$ if α^+ is a rule, we obtain $\Phi \mathrel{\mathop{\vdash}\limits^{A,\ -}_{k-1}} \alpha^+$ for all α^+, where $k = \max(|\langle\Phi\rangle \Rightarrow \beta \vee \gamma|, |\langle\Phi, \beta\rangle \Rightarrow \alpha|, |\langle\Phi, \gamma\rangle \Rightarrow \alpha|)$. By lemma 2.4.8: $|\Phi| \geq |\beta \vee \gamma|$, thus $|\langle\Phi\rangle \Rightarrow \beta \vee \gamma| = |\Phi| + 1 = |\Phi, \beta| + 1 = |\Phi, \gamma| + 1 \leq |\langle\Phi\rangle \Rightarrow \alpha|$.

c) If δ is $\beta \supset \alpha$ then D contains derivations of $\beta \supset \alpha$ from Φ and of β from Φ as immediate subderivations. By induction hypothesis $\langle\Phi\rangle \Rightarrow \beta \supset \alpha$ and $\langle\Phi\rangle \Rightarrow \beta$ are valid- in A, i.e.,

$$\Phi,\ \beta \mathrel{\mathop{\vdash}\limits^{A,\ -}_{|\langle\Phi\rangle \Rightarrow \beta \supset \alpha| - 1}} \alpha$$

and

$$\Phi \mathrel{\mathop{\vdash}\limits^{A,\ -}_{|\langle\Phi\rangle \Rightarrow \beta| - 1}} \beta^+ \text{ for all } \beta^+.$$

Thus by lemma 2.2.2(ii) and lemma 2.1.1(i):

$$\Phi \mathrel{\mathop{\vdash}\limits^{A,\ -}_{k}} \beta$$

where $k = \max(|\langle\Phi\rangle \Rightarrow \beta| - 1, |\beta| + 1)$, thus by lemma 2.1.1(ii)

$$\Phi \mathrel{\mathop{\vdash}\limits^{A,\ -}_{|\langle\Phi\rangle \Rightarrow \beta \supset \alpha| - 1}} \beta, \text{ thus}$$

$$\Phi \mathrel{\mathop{\vdash}\limits^{A,\ -}_{|\langle\Phi\rangle \Rightarrow \beta \supset \alpha| - 1}} \alpha.$$

By lemma 2.2.1(ii):

$$\Phi \mid\frac{A,\ -}{|\langle\Phi\rangle \Rightarrow \beta \supset \alpha| - 1}\alpha^{+} \text{ for all } \alpha^{+}.$$

By lemma 2.4.8: $|\Phi| \geq |\beta \supset \alpha|$, thus $|\langle\Phi\rangle \Rightarrow \beta \supset \alpha| = |\Phi| + 1 =$
$= |\langle\Phi\rangle \Rightarrow \alpha|$.

d) If δ is $\bot$, then D contains a derivation of $\bot$ from Φ as an immediate subderivation. By induction hypothesis $\langle\Phi\rangle \Rightarrow \bot$ is valid- in A, i.e., in particular

$$\Phi \mid\frac{A,\ -}{|\langle\Phi\rangle \Rightarrow \bot| - 1}\alpha.$$

By lemma 2.4.8: $|\Phi| \geq \bot$, thus $|\langle\Phi\rangle \Rightarrow \bot| = |\Phi| + 1 \leq |\langle\Phi\rangle \Rightarrow \alpha|$.
Furthermore α is atomic, i.e., each α^{+} is identical with α.

(v) D applies an assumption rule $\langle\alpha_1, \ldots, \alpha_n\rangle \Rightarrow \alpha$ belonging to Φ in the last step. Then for each i ($1 \leq i \leq n$) D contains derivations of α_i from Φ as immediate subderivations. By induction hypothesis, for each i ($1 \leq i \leq n$), $\langle\Phi\rangle \Rightarrow \alpha_i$ is valid- in A, i.e.,

$$\Phi \mid\frac{A,\ -}{|\langle\Phi\rangle \Rightarrow \alpha_i| - 1}\alpha_i^{+} \text{ for each } \alpha_i^{+}.$$

Thus by lemma 2.2.2(ii) and lemma 2.1.1(i)

$$\Phi \mid\frac{A,\ -}{k_i}\alpha_i \text{ for all i } (1 \leq i \leq n)$$

where $k_i = \max(|\langle\Phi\rangle \Rightarrow \alpha_i| - 1,\ |\alpha_i| + 1)$. Because $\langle\alpha_1, \ldots, \alpha_n\rangle \Rightarrow \alpha$ belongs to Φ, we have $|\alpha| < |\Phi|$ and $|\alpha_i| < |\Phi|$ for all i ($1 \leq i \leq n$). Thus $k_i = |\Phi| = |\langle\Phi\rangle \Rightarrow \alpha| - 1$ for every i ($1 \leq i \leq n$). Thus

$$\Phi \vdash^{A,\,-}_{|\langle\Phi\rangle \Rightarrow \alpha| - 1} \alpha$$

by application of $\langle\alpha_1, \ldots, \alpha_n\rangle \Rightarrow \alpha$ (which belongs to Φ), thus by lemma 2.2.1(ii):

$$\Phi \vdash^{A,\,-}_{|\langle\Phi\rangle \Rightarrow \alpha| - 1} \alpha^+ \text{ for each } \alpha^+.$$

Theorem 3.2 (Completeness): For any k, if $\Phi \vdash^{A,\,-}_{k} \alpha$ then $\Phi \vdash_{I(A)} \alpha$.

Proof: by induction on the pair consisting of k and the length of derivations D of α from Φ which are k-valid- in A. If D is 0-valid- in A, nothing remains to be shown. Let D be k-valid- in A for k > 0.

(i) If D is of the form $\overline{\alpha}$ where $\Rightarrow \alpha$ is a basic rule of $I^-(A)$, then α is a basic rule of A, so D is already 0-valid- in A. If $\Rightarrow \alpha$ is a rule which is valid- in A and for which $|\Rightarrow \alpha| \leq k$, then $\vdash^{A,\,-}_{k-1} \alpha^+$ for all α^+. So by induction hypothesis $\vdash_{I(A)} \alpha^+$ for all α^+, therefore $\vdash_{I(A)} \alpha$ by lemma 2.2.2(ii).

(ii) If D is of the form $\overline{\alpha}$ where α is an assumption (thus belonging to Φ), then $\Phi \vdash_{I(A)} \alpha$ holds trivially.

(iii) If D applies a rule ρ of the form $\langle\langle\Gamma_1\rangle \Rightarrow \alpha_1, \ldots, \langle\Gamma_n\rangle \Rightarrow \alpha_n\rangle \Rightarrow \alpha$ in the last step, then D contains for all i $(1 \leq i \leq n)$ derivations of α_i from Γ_i, Φ as immediate subderivations which are k-valid- in A. By induction hypothesis, we have

(5) $\Gamma_i, \Phi \vdash_{I(A)} \alpha_i$.

We distinguish three subcases:

a) If ρ is valid- in A and $|\rho| \leq k$, then $(\rho)_1 \vdash^{A,-}_{k-1} \alpha^+$ for all α^+. So by induction hypothesis $(\rho)_1 \vdash_{I(A)} \alpha^+$, therefore $(\rho)_1 \vdash_{I(A)} \alpha$ by lemma 2.2.2(ii). Together with (5) we obtain $\Phi \vdash_{I(A)} \alpha$.

b) If ρ is a basic rule of $I^-(A)$ then ρ is also a basic rule of $I(A)$ and together with (5) we obtain $\Phi \vdash_{I(A)} \alpha$.

c) If ρ is an assumption rule then ρ belongs to Φ and together with (5) we obtain $\Phi \vdash_{I(A)} \alpha$.

Corollary 3.3: If $\langle\Phi\rangle \Rightarrow \alpha$ is valid- in A, then $\Phi \vdash_{I(A)} \alpha$ (i.e., each rule which is valid- in A is derivable in $I(A)$).

Proof: From lemma 2.4.4 and theorem 3.2.

Corollary 3.4: If $\Phi \vdash^{A,-}_{k} \alpha$ for some k, then $\langle\Phi\rangle \Rightarrow \alpha$ is valid- in A.

Proof: Theorems 3.2 and 3.1.

This corollary shows that validity- of rules is transitive in the sense that rules which have been derived by successive application of valid- rules are themselves valid-.

Corollary 3.5: A rule over F is derivable in I iff it is valid-.

Proof: Lemma 2.4.1.

This shows that intuitionistic logic with sentence letters is also 'formally' sound and complete with respect to validity-, i.e., sound and complete under all interpretations in atomic calculi.

4. SOUNDNESS AND COMPLETENESS WITH RESPECT TO VALIDITY+

We consider an atomic calculus A and formulas over A which do not contain $\vee$.

Theorem 4.1 (Soundness): If $\Phi \vdash_{I^o(A)} \alpha$, then $\langle\Phi\rangle \Rightarrow \alpha$ is valid+ in A.

Proof: We proceed as in the proof of theorem 3.1, assuming that the given derivation D of α from Φ in $I^o(A)$ is in normal form. The case (i) is treated analogously.

(ii) If D is of the form $\overline{\alpha}$ where α is an assumption (thus belonging to Φ), then $\alpha^- \vdash^{A,\,+}_{0} \alpha$ holds according to lemma 2.2.1(i), therefore $\langle\Phi\rangle \Rightarrow \alpha$ is valid+ in A.

(iii) If D applies an I rule in the last step we distinguish subcases according to the form of α.

a) If α is $\alpha_1 \,\&\, \alpha_2$, then by induction hypothesis $\langle\Phi\rangle \Rightarrow \alpha_1$ and $\langle\Phi\rangle \Rightarrow \alpha_2$ are valid+ in A, i.e., for all Φ^-:

$$\Phi^- \vdash^{A,\,+}_{|\langle\Phi\rangle \Rightarrow \alpha| - 1} \alpha_i \quad (i = 1,\ 2).$$

Thus by application of an &I rule (which is at our disposal in $I^+(A)$):

$$\Phi^- \vdash^{A,\,+}_{|\langle\Phi\rangle \Rightarrow \alpha_i| - 1} \alpha \text{ for all } \Phi^-.$$

b) If α is $\alpha_1 \supset \alpha_2$, then by induction hypothesis $\langle\Phi,\ \alpha_1\rangle \Rightarrow \alpha_2$ is valid+ in A, i.e., for all Φ^-, α_1^-:

$$\Phi^{-},\ \alpha_1^{-} \vdash^{A,\ +}_{|\langle\Phi,\ \alpha_1\rangle \Rightarrow \alpha_2| - 1} \alpha_2, \text{ thus by lemma 2.4.7(i)}$$

$$\Phi^{-},\ \alpha_1 \vdash^{A,\ +}_{|\langle\Phi\rangle \Rightarrow \alpha| - 1} \alpha_2 \quad (\text{note that } |\alpha_1| + 1 \leq |\alpha| < |\langle\Phi\rangle \Rightarrow \alpha|).$$

Thus by application of an ⊃I rule

$$\Phi^{-} \vdash^{A,\ +}_{|\langle\Phi\rangle \Rightarrow \alpha| - 1} \alpha.$$

(iv) If D applies an E rule in the last step, we distinguish subcases according to the form of its major premiss δ.

a) If δ is $\alpha \,\&\, \beta$, then by induction hypothesis $\langle\Phi\rangle \Rightarrow \alpha \,\&\, \beta$ is valid+ in A. Thus by lemma 2.4.6

$$\Phi^{-} \vdash^{A,\ +}_{|\langle\Phi\rangle \Rightarrow \alpha \,\&\, \beta| - 1} \alpha \text{ for all } \Phi^{-}.$$

By lemma 2.4.8, $|\Phi| \geq |\alpha \,\&\, \beta| > |\alpha|$, thus $|\langle\Phi\rangle \Rightarrow \alpha \,\&\, \beta| = |\langle\Phi\rangle \Rightarrow \alpha|$.

b) If δ is $\beta \supset \alpha$, then by induction hypothesis $\langle\Phi\rangle \Rightarrow \beta \supset \alpha$ and $\langle\Phi\rangle \Rightarrow \beta$ are valid+ in A.

Therefore by lemma 2.4.6:

$$\Phi^{-},\ \beta \vdash^{A,\ +}_{|\langle\Phi\rangle \Rightarrow \alpha \supset \beta| - 1} \alpha \text{ for all } \Phi^{-}.$$

Together with

$$\Phi^{-} \vdash^{A,\ +}_{|\langle\Phi\rangle \Rightarrow \beta| - 1} \beta \text{ for all } \Phi^{-}$$

we obtain

$$\Phi^{-} \vdash^{A, +}_{|<\Phi> \Rightarrow \alpha \supset \beta| - 1} \alpha \text{ for all } \Phi^{-}$$

(because $|<\Phi> \Rightarrow \alpha \supset \beta| \geq |<\Phi> \Rightarrow \beta|$). By lemma 2.4.8, $|\Phi| \geq |\alpha \supset \beta| > |\alpha|$, thus $|<\Phi> \Rightarrow \alpha \supset \beta| = |<\Phi> \Rightarrow \alpha|$.

c) If δ is $\perp$, then by induction hypothesis $<\Phi> \Rightarrow \perp$ is valid+ in A, i.e.,

$$\Phi^{-} \vdash^{A, +}_{|<\Phi> \Rightarrow \perp| - 1} \perp \text{ for all } \Phi^{-}.$$

According to lemma 2.4.8, α is atomic, and $\perp$ is a subformula of a formula occurring in Φ. Thus $|\Phi| \geq 1$. If $|\Phi| > 1$, then $|<\Phi> \Rightarrow \perp| = |<\Phi> \Rightarrow \alpha| > 2$. Therefore application of the $\perp$E rule $<\perp> \Rightarrow \alpha$, which is valid+ in A and for which $|<\perp> \Rightarrow \alpha| = 2$ holds, yields

$$\Phi^{-} \vdash^{A, +}_{|<\Phi> \Rightarrow \alpha| - 1} \alpha \text{ for all } \Phi^{-}.$$

If $|\Phi| = 1$, this is vacuously fulfilled, because $\perp$ then is a member of Φ.

(v) If D applies an assumption rule $<\alpha_1, \ldots, \alpha_n> \Rightarrow \alpha$ in the last step, then $<\alpha_1, \ldots, \alpha_n> \Rightarrow \alpha$ belongs to Φ and we have $|\Phi| > |\alpha_i|$ for all i ($1 \leq i \leq n$) and $|\Phi| > |\alpha|$, thus $|<\Phi> \Rightarrow \alpha_i| = |<\Phi> \Rightarrow \alpha| = |\Phi| + 1$ for all i ($1 \leq i \leq n$). By induction hypothesis for each i ($1 \leq i \leq n$), $<\Phi> \Rightarrow \alpha_i$ is valid+ in A, i.e., for all Φ^{-}:

$$\Phi^{-} \vdash^{A, +}_{|\Phi|} \alpha_i.$$

Therefore

$$\Phi^-, \langle\alpha_1, \ldots, \alpha_n\rangle \Rightarrow \alpha \vdash^{A,+}_{|\Phi|} \alpha$$

which is the same as

$$\Phi^- \vdash^{A,+}_{|\langle\Phi\rangle \Rightarrow \alpha| - 1} \alpha$$

because $\langle\alpha_1, \ldots, \alpha_n\rangle \Rightarrow \alpha$ is contained in all Φ^-.

Theorem 4.2 (Completeness): For any k, if $\Phi \vdash^{A,+}_{k} \alpha$, then $\Phi \vdash_{I^o(A)} \alpha$.

Proof: Analogously to the proof of theorem 3.2. We only mark the points where there are differences in argumentation.

(i) If $\Rightarrow \alpha$ is a rule which is valid+ in A and for which $|\Rightarrow \alpha| \leq k$, then $\vdash^{A,+}_{k-1} \alpha$. So by induction hypothesis $\vdash_{I^o(A)} \alpha$.

(iii) a) If D applies a rule $\langle\Psi\rangle \Rightarrow \alpha$ in the last step which is valid+ in A and whose rank is $\leq k$, then by induction hypothesis (concerning the length of derivations)

(6) $\Phi \vdash_{I^o(A)} \Psi$.

Because of the validity+ of $\langle\Psi\rangle \Rightarrow \alpha$ in A we have

$$\Psi^- \vdash^{A,+}_{k-1} \alpha \text{ for all } \Psi^-,$$

so by induction hypothesis (concerning k)

$$\Psi^- \vdash_{I^o(A)} \alpha \text{ for all } \Psi^-,$$

therefore by lemma 2.4.7(ii)

$\Psi \vdash_{\overline{I^o(A)}} \alpha$.

Together with (6) $\Phi \vdash_{\overline{I^o(A)}} \alpha$ follows.

The corollaries 3.3 to 3.5 can easily be taken over.

5. SOME FURTHER POINTS

5.1 Extension to Quantifier Logic

We have restricted ourselves to sentential logic but an extension to quantifier logic presents no additional problem in principle. One would have to introduce individual terms including individual variables, quantified assumption rules $\Delta \Rightarrow_{x_1,\ldots,x_n} \alpha$, and canonical conditions and consequences of formulas $\forall x\alpha(x)$ and $\exists x\alpha(x)$ by defining

the rule $\Rightarrow_x \alpha(x)$ to be an $(\forall x\alpha(x))^-$,
each $\alpha(t)$ for an arbitrary term t to be an $(\exists x\alpha(x))^-$,
each $\alpha(t)$ for an arbitrary term t to be an $(\forall x\alpha(x))^+$,
each rule $\langle\langle\alpha(y)\rangle \Rightarrow_y \beta\rangle \Rightarrow \beta$ for an arbitrary formula β not containing y free to be an $(\exists x\alpha(x))^+$.

The soundness and completeness of intuitionistic quantifier logic can then be proved in a similar way (without $\vee$ and $\exists$ in the I rule approach).

As Prawitz (1971, p. 290) pointed out, in the E rule approach one is even able to handle universal quantification within contexts where the quantifier is not understood in the schematical sense, as e.g., in Peano arithmetic: If numerals *n* are available for every n, we may define each $\alpha(n)$ for arbitrary n to be an $(\forall x\alpha(x))^+$. According to that definition, the induction rules $<\alpha(O)$, $<\alpha(x)> \underset{x}{\Rightarrow} \alpha(x')> \Rightarrow$ $\Rightarrow \forall x\alpha(x)$ turn out to be valid- in the atomic calculus characterizing Peano arithmetic because for each n there is a derivation of $\alpha(n)$ from $\alpha(O)$, $<\alpha(x)> \underset{x}{\Rightarrow} \alpha(x')$ which applies no basic rule. However, unlike Prawitz' sketch for an E rule approach (ibid.), our soundness theorem cannot in that case be transferred to Peano arithmetic. This is due to the fact that our restrictions on the complexity of rules used in k-valid- derivations make it necessary to require normal derivations in $I(A)$ for our soundness theorem which cannot be fully obtained in Peano arithmetic. Another reason is that the important lemma 2.2.2(ii) would not hold for ∀-formulas. The fact that the completeness theorem cannot be upheld follows from Gödel's incompleteness theorem. The inadmissibility of the ω-rule in Peano arithmetic blocks step (iii)a) of the proof of theorem 3.2.

5.2. The Failure of the I Rule Approach for Formulas with ∨.

Lemma 2.1.1(i) is crucial for many succeeding lemmata and for the theorems. It states that the rank of an I rule for α is $|\alpha| + 1$, and that the rank of an E rule with α as its major premiss is $|\alpha| + 1$ if α is not a disjunction or the absurdity. That means that the rank of these rules only depends on the rank of α and not on the rank of any other formula. This no longer holds in the case of ∨E rules

$$\frac{\alpha \vee \beta \quad \begin{matrix}\alpha \\ \gamma\end{matrix} \quad \begin{matrix}\beta \\ \gamma\end{matrix}}{\gamma}\ .$$

Their rank not only depends on the major premiss $\alpha \vee \beta$ but can be arbitrarily high if γ is complex enough. (The same holds for ⊥E, but there it causes no problems because conclusions of applications of ⊥E can be assumed to be atomic.) Thus neither lemma 2.4.6 nor lemma

2.4.7(i) which are important tools in the soundness theorem 4.1 can be proved if $\vee$ is admitted. However, lemma 2.4.7(ii) holds for $I(A)$ instead of $I^{\circ}(A)$, because in $I(A)$ we do not have any restriction on ranks of applied rules. So the completeness theorem 4.2 can be upheld if $\vee$ is included. Furthermore, lemma 2.4.6 remains true in the presence of $\vee$ for the case that $|\Phi| \leq |\alpha|$, as can easily be checked.

These results can be used to demonstrate that a soundness proof for full intuitionistic logic over A including $\vee$ with respect to validity+ in A is not possible for all A. Consider the rule ρ:

$$\frac{(\alpha \vee \beta) \,\&\, \gamma}{(\alpha \,\&\, \gamma) \vee (\beta \,\&\, \gamma)}$$

over F where α, β, γ are atomic formulas (i.e., sentence letters), which is of rank 3. If ρ were valid+ in A, by the part of lemma 2.4.6 which remains provable, we would have

$$\text{either } \alpha \vee \beta, \gamma \vdash^{A,\,+}_{2} \alpha \,\&\, \gamma$$

$$\text{or } \quad \alpha \vee \beta, \gamma \vdash^{A,\,+}_{2} \beta \,\&\, \gamma,$$

thus by the completeness theorem

$$\text{either } \alpha \vee \beta, \gamma \vdash_{I} \alpha \,\&\, \gamma$$

$$\text{or } \quad \alpha \vee \beta, \gamma \vdash_{I} \beta \,\&\, \gamma,$$

which does not hold. ρ is, however, derivable in I by means of the (normal) derivation

$$\dfrac{\dfrac{\dfrac{}{(\alpha \vee \beta) \,\&\, \gamma}}{\alpha \vee \beta} \qquad \dfrac{\dfrac{\dfrac{}{\alpha}{\scriptstyle (1)} \quad \dfrac{\dfrac{}{(\alpha \vee \beta) \,\&\, \gamma}}{\gamma}}{\alpha \,\&\, \gamma}}{(\alpha \,\&\, \gamma) \vee (\beta \,\&\, \gamma)} \qquad \dfrac{\dfrac{\dfrac{}{\beta}{\scriptstyle (1)} \quad \dfrac{\dfrac{}{(\alpha \vee \beta) \,\&\, \gamma}}{\gamma}}{\beta \,\&\, \gamma}}{(\alpha \,\&\, \gamma) \vee (\beta \,\&\, \gamma)}}{(\alpha \,\&\, \gamma) \vee (\beta \,\&\, \gamma)}{\scriptstyle (1)} \quad .$$

One immediately sees that one cannot get rid of the application of the vE rule

$$\dfrac{\alpha \vee \beta \qquad \begin{matrix} \alpha \\ (\alpha \,\&\, \gamma) \vee (\beta \,\&\, \gamma) \end{matrix} \qquad \begin{matrix} \beta \\ (\alpha \,\&\, \gamma) \vee (\beta \,\&\, \gamma) \end{matrix}}{(\alpha \,\&\, \gamma) \vee (\beta \,\&\, \gamma)}$$

which is of rank 4, even if the premisses of ρ are inferred by I rules (so that one has $\alpha \vee \beta$ and γ as undischarged assumptions).

Since soundness, unlike completeness, is a necessary condition for the adequacy of a semantics, the approach based on I rules definitely fails for full intuitionistic logic. It might be noted that Prawitz (1984, section 5) refers to difficulties of the kind just described as being reasons for preferring the validity of derivations ('arguments' in his terminology) instead of rules as the primary notion: He mentions the problem that the derivation of a premiss of an application of an ⊃I rule may essentially contain applications of E rules of higher complexity than the conclusion of this application, which is exactly the case if we extend the derivation given above by application of an ⊃I rule to a derivation of $((\alpha \vee \beta) \,\&\, \gamma) \supset ((\alpha \,\&\, \gamma) \vee (\beta \,\&\, \gamma))$.

Perhaps validity of derivations is the better tool when relying on I inferences, and validity of rules the better tool when relying on E inferences. --

Acknowledgement. I should like to thank Stella Lewis for checking the English.

REFERENCES

Došen, K. and Schroeder-Heister, P., 1984, Conservativeness and Uniqueness. Submitted for publication.

Gentzen, G., 1935, Untersuchungen über das logische Schließen, Math. Zeitschr., 39:176-210 and 405-431.

Lorenzen, P., 1955, "Einführung in die operative Logik und Mathematik," Springer, Berlin. (2nd edition 1969)

Prawitz, D., 1965, "Natural Deduction. A Proof-Theoretical Study," Almqvist & Wiksell, Stockholm.

Prawitz, D., 1971, Ideas and Results in Proof Theory, in: "Proceedings of the 2nd Scandinavian Logic Symposium," J. E. Fenstad, ed., North-Holland, Amsterdam.

Prawitz, D., 1973, Towards a Foundation of a General Proof Theory, in: "Logic, Methodology and Philosophy of Science, IV," P. Suppes. L. Henkin, A. Joja and Gr. C. Moisil, eds., North-Holland, Amsterdam.

Prawitz, D., 1974, On the Idea of a General Proof Theory, Synthese, 27:63-77.

Prawitz, D., 1984, Remarks on some Approaches to the Concept of Logical Consequence (forthcoming).

Schroeder-Heister, P., 1981, "Untersuchungen zur regellogischen Deutung von Aussagenverknüpfungen," Ph. Diss., Bonn.

Schroeder-Heister, P., 1983a, The Completeness of Intuitionistic Logic with Respect to a Validity Concept Based on an Inversion Principle, J. Philos. Log., 12:359-377.

Schroeder-Heister, P., 1983b, Inversion Principles and the Completeness of Intuitionistic Natural Deduction Systems, in: "Abstracts of the 7th International Congress of Logic, Methodology and Philosophy of Science, Salzburg 1983, Vol. 5." Salzburg.

Schroeder-Heister, P., 1984a, A Natural Extension of Natural Deduction, J. Symb. Log. (to appear).

Schroeder-Heister, P., 1984b, Generalized Rules for Quantifiers and the Completeness of the Intuitionistic Operators &, $\vee$, $\supset$, $\curlywedge$, $\forall$, $\exists$, in; "Logic Colloquium '83," M. M. Richter, ed., Springer, Berlin (to appear).

Tennant, N., 1978, "Natural Logic," Edinburgh University Press.

GENTZEN-TYPE OR BETH-TYPE SYSTEMS, CONSTRUCTIVE COMPLETENESS PROOFS AND PRACTICAL DECISION PROCEDURES (WITH SPECIAL ATTENTION TO RELEVANCE LOGIC)

H. C. M. de Swart

Tilburg University
The Netherlands

The aim of this paper is to advertise a notion of provability, originally known as Beth-semantic tableaux (Beth, 1959), then later adapted by R. Smullyan (1971) for classical logic and by M. Fitting (1969) for intuitionistic logic and for the modal system S4.

The notion of provability we have in mind has the subformula property, i.e., each formula occurring in a proof of A is a subformula of A.

Consequently, it is possible to describe a systematic procedure of searching for a proof of A such that (*) if this procedure does not provide a formal proof of A, then it yields a countermodel to A of the appropriate kind. An immediate result of this property (*) is the completeness theorem: if A is valid then A is formally provable. And what may be more important, using these proof systems one can give for many logics very perspicuous decidability proofs: in case the systematic search will terminate for all formulas in finitely many steps, the logic in question is clearly decidable.

The present author has elaborated these ideas for intuitionistic, modal, and counterfactual logics (de Swart, 1976, 1980, 1983). As a consequence, rather theoretical decidability results for intuitionistic, modal, and counterfactual propositional calculi could be replaced by very *practical* decision procedures: given a formula A, the systematic procedure of searching for a proof of A constructs in a small, finite, number n(A) of steps (which, given A, can be determined in advance) either a formal proof of A (in which case A is formally provable and hence valid) or a concrete counterexample to A (in which case A is not valid and hence not formally provable).

A. Urquhart (1972) presents an information-pieces semantics for relevant logic and mentions the decision problem for the set of all formulas valid in his information-pieces semantics as still being open (Urquhard, 198.). Again, a Beth-type formal system can be developed such that the formulas provable in this system are precisely the formulas valid in Urquhart's semantics ($\neg A$ is defined as $A \rightarrow f$). However, in this case the systematic search does not always terminate in finitely many steps.

In part I below we shall present the rules for classical or material implication $\supset$, for intuitionistic implication $\Rightarrow$, for necessity $\Box$, and for relevant implication $\rightarrow$, and demonstrate the systematic procedure for some examples. The case of counterfactuals is too complicated to be treated here. (See de Swart, 1983.)

PART I: A SURVEY

By a *signed formula* we mean any expression of the form TA or FA, where A is a formula, except in the case of relevance logic, where we mean by a signed formula any expression of the form TA_a or FA_a, A being a formula and a being a relevance index, i.e. a finite, unordered, sequence of natural numbers. The *intended interpretation* of signed formulas is as follows:

i) for classical logic, TA : A is true, FA : A is false.
ii) for intuitionistic logic, TA : I have proof of A, FA : I do not have a proof of A.
iii) for modal and counterfactual logic, TA : A holds in the given world, FA : A does not hold in the given world.
iv) for relevance logics, TA_a : A is true on the basis of the information a, which is relevant to A; FA_a : not TA_a.

A *sequent* is a finite, unordered, sequence of signed formulas. The *intended interpretation* of the sequent $TB_1, \ldots, TB_n, FC_1, \ldots, FC_m$ is: if B_1 and ... and B_n then C_1 or ... or C_m. We will use S, S', ... for arbitrary sequents. The intended interpretation of a sequent in the case of relevance logic is not (not yet?) clear.

Some of the rules below contain a horizontal line in order to stress that in applying these rules signed formulas may get lost.

T⊃ $\dfrac{S,\ TB \supset C}{S,\ TB \supset C,\ FB \mid S,\ TB \supset C,\ TC}$ F⊃ $\dfrac{S,\ FB \supset C}{S,\ TB,\ FC}$

T⇒ $\dfrac{S,\ TB \Rightarrow C}{S,\ TB \Rightarrow C,\ FB \mid S,\ TB \Rightarrow C,\ TC}$ F⇒ $\dfrac{S,\ FB \Rightarrow C}{S_T,\ TB,\ FC}$

T□ for KM $\dfrac{S,\ T\Box B}{S,\ T\Box B,\ TB}$ F□ for KM $\dfrac{S,\ F\Box B}{S_\Box,\ FB}$

T→ $\dfrac{S,\ TB \rightarrow C_a}{S,\ TB \rightarrow C_a,\ FB_b \mid S,\ TB \rightarrow C_a,\ TC_{a*b}}$ F→ $\dfrac{S,\ FB \rightarrow C_a}{S,\ TB_{(k)},\ FC_{a*(k)}}$

for any relevance index b.

Where i) S_T is the set of all T-signed formulas in S, ii) $S_\Box$ = = {TE | T□E occurs in S}, iii) k is the least number not occurring in a or in any index of S, iv) a*b is the concatenation of a and b not mentioning the same natural number twice; for instance (1, 2)*(2, 3) = (1, 2, 3).

The rules given above can be read in two ways:

i) From the top down, as *Beth semantic tableaux rules*, interpreting the signed formulas rather than the sequents. Rule F□ for KM, for instance, now says: if □B does not hold in the given world w, then there is a world w', accessible from w, in which B does not hold; w' is such that E holds in w' if □E holds in w.

ii) From the bottom up, as *Gentzen-type rules*, interpreting the sequents rather than the signed formulas. Rule F⇒, for instance, then says in case S = TA, FD : if A ∧ B ⇒ C then A ⇒ (B ⇒ C) ∨ D. Unfortunately, this kind of reading is not (not yet?) available for relevant implication.

A Beth- or Gentzen-type *formal proof* of a sequent S is a finite schema of sequents such that

1. S is the highest sequent,
2. each sequent in the schema, except the highest sequent S, results by applying one of the rules to the sequent immediately above it, and
3. each of the lowest sequents contains either Tf ($Tf_{(\ )}$ in the case of relevance logic, f being falsity) or else both TB and FB for some formula B (TB_b and FB_b in the case of relevance logic).

A is *formally provable* ($\vdash^{!}$ A) if there is a formal proof of FA or in the case of relevance logic, of $FA_{(\ )}$, ( ) being the empty relevance index. The underlying idea in the Beth-type reading of the rules is that A is formally provable if the supposition FA (A does not hold) or $FA_{(\ )}$ in the case of relevance logic, turns out to be impossible; and the underlying idea in the Gentzen-type reading of the rules is that if all the sequents in a certain line are provable, then the sequents immediately above it are provable too, the lowest sequents being of the type "if B and ..., then B or ...".

One easily shows that for each sequent $TB_1, \ldots, TB_n, FC_1, \ldots, FC_m$ in a given formal proof of A it holds that $B_1 \wedge \ldots \wedge B_n \overset{\supset}{\Rightarrow} C_1 \vee \ldots \vee C_m$ is provable in the corresponding Hilbert-type formal system.

Consequently: if $\vdash' A$, then $\vdash A$. However, for the case of relevance logic this is still an open problem. By soundness we have: if $\vdash A$ then $\models A$. And by completeness: if $\models A$ then $\vdash' A$. So the three notions $\vdash' A$, $\vdash A$ and $\models A$ are equivalent both in the case of classical, intuitionistic, modal, and counterfactual logics.

In de Swart (1976) we describe a systematic procedure of searching for an intuitionistic proof of a given formula A. Let us sketch this procedure for the formula $\neg\neg P \Rightarrow P$, i.e., $((P \Rightarrow f) \Rightarrow f) \Rightarrow P$.

Start with	$F((P \Rightarrow f) \Rightarrow f) \Rightarrow P$		0		0R0
	———————				0R1
Apply rule F⇒	$T(P \Rightarrow f) \Rightarrow f,\ FP$		1	$\neg\neg P$	1R1
Next rule T⇒	$FP \Rightarrow f,\ FP$	$Tf,\ FP$			1R2
	———————				2R2
Apply rule F⇒	$TP,\ Ff$		2	P	0R2

We do not find an intuitionistic proof of $\neg\neg P \Rightarrow P$, but, what is more, we actually have constructed a Kripke countermodel to $\neg\neg P \Rightarrow P$, as exhibited to the right. Note that each application of rule F⇒ (containing a horizontal line) results in a new node and that

i) if TE occurs at a given node, then E holds in the corresponding
   model at that node,

ii) if FE occurs at a given node, then E does not hold in the corre-
    sponding model at that node.

Similarly, we described in de Swart (1980) a systematic procedure of searching for a modal proof of a given formula A. We give a
sketch of this procedure in KM for the formula $\Box P \supset \Box\Box P$.

Start with	$F\Box P \supset \Box\Box P$			
Apply rule $F\supset$	$T\Box P,\ F\Box\Box P$	0	P	0R0
Next apply $T\Box$	$T\Box P,\ TP,\ F\Box\Box P$		$\Box P$	0R1
	————————————			
Apply rule $F\Box$	$TP,\ F\Box P$	1	P	1R1
	————————————			1R2
Again apply rule $F\Box$	FP	2		2R2
				not 0R2

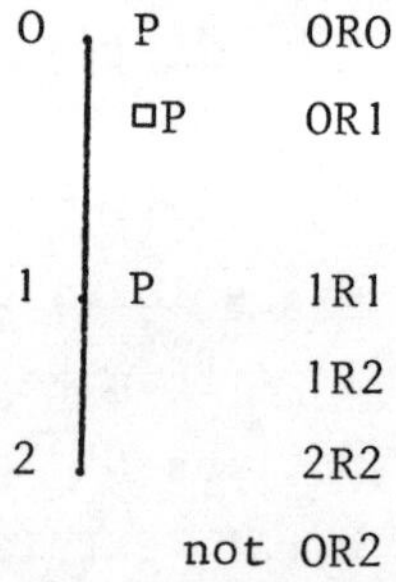

We do not find a formal proof of $\Box P \supset \Box\Box P$ in KM, but we actually
constructed a Kripke counterexample to $\Box P \supset \Box\Box P$ in KM.

In the case of classical, intuitionistic, modal, and counterfactual propositional logics it is clear that the systematic search
for a Beth- or Gentzen-type proof will terminate for all formulas
in finitely many steps and then will result either in a formal proof
or in a countermodel of the appropriate kind. Hence these logics are
decidable in a very practical sense. It should be noted that if we
add quantifiers we loose in general our decidability, since we may
continue to apply the quantifier rules again and again, each time
introducing new variables.

A similar thing is going on in the case of relevance propositional logic where new relevance indices may be introduced all the

time. Consider, for instance, the problem whether $\vdash'$ $((P \to Q) \to \to Q) \to Q$ or not.

Start with $F((P \to Q) \to Q) \to Q)_{(\ )}$

$$T(P \to Q) \to Q_{(1)},\ FQ_{(1)}$$

$$F(P \to Q)_{(\ )},\ T(P \to Q) \to Q_{(1)},\ FQ_{(1)}\ \mid\ TQ_{(1)},\ T(P \to Q) \to Q_{(1)},\ FQ_{(1)}$$

$TP_{(2)},\ FQ_{(2)},$

$,\ F(P \to Q)_{(1)},$

$,\ TP_{(3)},\ FQ_{(1,\ 3)},$

$$FP \to Q_{(2)}$$

and so on, ad infinitum, applying rule T→ again and again.

Now, in this particular case we easily see that we shall never find a formal proof of $((P \to Q) \to Q) \to Q$. In most cases we do find either a formal proof or a counterexample. For instance, consider $P \to (Q \to P)$.

$$FP \to (Q \to P)_{(\ )}$$
$$TP_{(1)},\ FQ \to P_{(1)}$$
$$TP_{(1)},\ TQ_{(2)},\ FP_{(1,\ 2)}.$$

We do not find a formal proof and we actually have constucted a counterexample. Let M be the Urquhart model $\langle I, *, (\ ), \models\rangle$ where (see part II, Definition 1.1) $I = \{(\ ), (1), (2), (1, 2)\}$, $*$ is concatenation not mentioning the same natural number twice (so $(1) * (1) = (1)$) and $M \models_i P$ (P atomic) iff TP_i occurs. Then

i) if TA_i occurs then $M \models_i A$, and
ii) if FA_i occurs then not $M \models_i A$.

It turns out that the formulas valid in Urquhart's information pieces semantics (defining $\neg A$ as $A \to f$) are precisely the formulas provable in our Beth-type formal system and, in addition, are intuitionistically valid.

PART II: INFORMATION PIECES SEMANTICS AND A RELEVANCE FRAGMENT OF INTUITIONISTIC LOGIC

Introduction

A. Urquhart (1972) presents an information-piece semantics for relevant implication ($\rightarrow$) and proves for formulas A containing $\rightarrow$ as the only logical symbol that A is valid with respect to this semantics if and only if A is provable in the system $R_{\rightarrow}$ of Anderson and Belnap (1975, p. 20). Extending this semantics in the "natural" way to cover also conjunction and disjunction makes at least one formula valid, which is not provable in the system R of Anderson and Belnap (1975, p. 340). A. Urquhart calls this formula the formula (D):

$$(A \rightarrow B \vee C) \wedge (C \rightarrow D) \rightarrow (A \rightarrow B \vee D).$$

A. Urquhart (198.) mentions the decision problem for the set of all formulas valid in his information-pieces semantics as still being open.

In this paper we present a Beth-tableaux type formal system such that the formulas provable in this system are precisely the formulas valid in Urquhart's information-pieces semantics. It turns out that these formulas are also intuitionistically valid. The negation $\neg A$ is defined as $A \rightarrow f$. We present a systematic procedure of searching for a proof of a given formula A such that if this procedure doesn't yield a proof of A, then it yields a countermodel to A. It was brought to the author's attention that a similar procedure is described in Urquhart (1971) for formulas having relevant implication as the only connective.

Proving completeness by presenting a systematic procedure of searching for a Beth-tableaux-type formal proof of A such that if this procedure doesn't yield a proof of A, then it yields an appropriate countermodel to A, is very attractive since it provides in a quick and easy way a counterexample to practically all non-valid formulas.

We shall also show that the Hilbert-type (axiomatic) formal system R^iD (where R^i refers to the intuitionistic restriction of the system R and D to Urquhart's formula (D)) has the disjunction property. And in case an appropriate disjunctive normal form "theorem" holds for R^iD (or some appropriate extension), we shall show that provability in R^iD (or some appropriate extension respectively) is equivalent to validity with respect to the information-pieces semantics, too. Unfortunately, the disjunctive normal form "theorem" has still to be shown.

§1 Information Pieces Semantics

We suppose the *alphabet* of our language has the following symbols:

$P_1, P_2, P_3, \ldots$	propositional variables
f	falsity
$\wedge, \vee, \rightarrow$	conjunction, disjunction, relevant implication

We will use P, Q for arbitrary propositional variables, P_i, $i = 1, 2, 3, \ldots$, A and B for arbitrary formulas.

An *atomic formula* is either the symbol f (falsity) or a propositional variable.

Formulas: 1. Every atomic formula is a formula

2. If A and B are formulas, then $(A \wedge B)$, $(A \vee B)$, and $(A \rightarrow B)$ are formulas.

Negation: $\neg A := A \rightarrow f$.

Definition 1.1: $M = \langle I, \cup, 0, \models\rangle$ is a *model* iff

1. I is a non-empty set (regarded as the set of all information pieces).
2. $\cup$ is a binary operation on I, satisfying $i \cup i = i$, $i \cup j = j \cup i$ and $(i \cup j) \cup k = i \cup (j \cup k)$ for all $i, j, k \in I$. ($i \cup j$ is to be regarded as the information of i and j jointly.) We allow the possibility that $\cup$ is only partially defined on I.
3. 0 is an element of I satisfying $i \cup 0 = i$ for all $i \in I$ (0 is to be regarded as the empty piece of information).
4. $\models$ is a relation between the elements of I and atomic formulas ($i \models P$ is to be read as "P is true on the basis of the information in i, all of which is relevant to P), such that not $0 \models f$.

Definition 1.2: For $M = \langle I, \cup, 0, \models\rangle$ a model, $i \in I$ and A a formula, we define $M \models_{i} A$ as follows:

$M \models_{i} P$ iff $i \models P$ (for P a propositional variable)
$M \models_{i} f$ iff $i \models f$
$M \models_{i} B \wedge C$ iff $M \models_{i} B$ and $M \models_{i} C$
$M \models_{i} B \vee C$ iff $M \models_{i} B$ or $M \models_{i} C$
$M \models_{i} B \rightarrow C$ iff for all $j \in I$ if $i \cup j$ is defined either not
$M \models_{j} B$ or $M \models_{i \cup j} C$.

($M \models_{i} A$ is to be read as: A is true on the basis of the information i of the model M, where all the information of i is relevant to A.)

Definition 1.3: $M \models A$ (M is a model for A) iff $M \models_{0} A$.

Definition 1.4: $\models A$ (A is valid) iff $M \models A$ for all models M.

Note that for example $P \to P$ is valid, i.e., $M \models_0 P \to P$ for all M, but that not necessarily $M \models_i P \to P$ for $i \neq 0$, since it may happen that $M \models_j P$ but not $M \models_{i \cup j} P$ (all the information in j may be relevant to P, while not all the information in $i \cup j$ has to be relevant to P).

Remark: Note that we allow the possibility that $M \models_i f$ whence not $\models f \to P$ and that we do not demand that $M \models_i (f \to f)$, whence not $\models P \to t$ where $t := (f \to f)$. Also not $\models P \wedge \neg P \to Q$ and not $\models P \to Q \vee \neg Q$ (see the countermodels further on).

As a consequence, $\to$ satisfies principles of relevance in the following mathematically definite sense: $\models C_1 \wedge \ldots \wedge C_k \to D_1 \vee \ldots \vee D_l$, where each C_i and D_j is an atom (i.e. an atomic formula or the negation of an atomic formula), iff some atom C_i is the same as some atom D_j. The material implication $C_1 \wedge \ldots \wedge C_k \supset D_1 \vee \ldots \vee D_l$, on the contrary, is valid iff

(1) for some variable P, both P and $\neg P$ appear as conjuncts on the left
(2) for some variable P, both P and $\neg P$ appear as disjuncts on the right
(3) some atom occurs as conjunct on the left and as disjunct on the right.

Definition 1.5: Let R^i be the intuitionistic restriction of the system R of Anderson and Belnap, i.e., R^i consists of the following formulas, together with the following rules:

1. $A \to A$
2. $(A \to B) \to ((B \to C) \to (A \to C))$
3. $(A \to (B \to C)) \to (B \to (A \to C))$
4. $(A \to (B \to C)) \to ((A \to B) \to (A \to C))$

$$\frac{A \quad A \to B}{B}\ \text{MP}$$

5. $(A \to B) \wedge (A \to C) \to (A \to B \wedge C)$

$$\frac{B \quad C}{B \wedge C} \wedge$$

6. $A \wedge B \to A$
7. $A \wedge B \to B$
8. $A \to A \vee B$
9. $B \to A \vee B$
10. $(A \to C) \wedge (B \to C) \to (A \vee B \to C)$
11. $A \wedge (B \vee C) \to (A \wedge B) \vee C$

Note that the following formulas are instances of the formulas 2, 3, and 4, respectively, by taking $C = f$.

12. $(A \to B) \to (\neg B \to \neg A)$
13. $(A \to \neg B) \to (B \to \neg A)$
14. $(A \to \neg B) \to ((A \to B) \to \neg A)$

Note that $(A \to B) \to (A \to B)$ together with 3. above and the rule MP yields

15. $A \to ((A \to B) \to B)$ and hence, in particular,
16. $A \to \neg\neg A$.

Note that 1., 3., and 4. above together with MP yield

17. $(A \to (A \to B)) \to (A \to B)$, and hence in particular,
18. $(A \to \neg A) \to \neg A$

The system R^i is equivalent to the system R of Anderson and Belnap, minus A 14, i.e., $\neg\neg A \to A$ (see Anderson and Belnap, 1975, p. 340). So one might call R^i *an intuitionistic version of relevance logic.*

On the other hand, R^i is obtained from the Minimal Kalkül by leaving out the axiom $A \to (B \to A)$, in which the B is not relevant to A and from intuitionistic logic by leaving out also $\neg A \to (A \to B)$, which is equivalent to $f \to B$. So one might say that R^i is *a relevance fragment both of the Minimal Kalkül and of intuitionistic logic.*

I think it is quite unnatural to add $\neg\neg A \to A$, i.e., $((A \to f) \to f) \to A$ to R^i. Only if we take it for granted that $A \vee \neg A$, i.e., $A \vee (A \to f)$ and in addition $f \vdash^r A$, $\neg\neg A \to A$ becomes acceptable. However, $A \vee \neg A$ seems unreasonable since one cannot expect that the empty piece of information always determines A or $\neg A$, and $f \vdash^r A$ seems unreasonable since it would force us to accept $\neg B \wedge B \vdash^r A$.

Remark 1.6:

1) Note that $(B \to A \wedge B) \to (B \to A)$ follows from 2., 3., and 6. together with MP and that $\dfrac{D \to E \quad E \to F}{D \to F}$ is a derived rule of R^i. Hence, *we cannot take* $A \to (B \to A \wedge B)$ *as an axiom* of R^i instead of the $\wedge$-rule, since that would yield $A \to (B \to A)$, in which the B is not relevant to A.
2) *We cannot take* $(A \to B) \to ((A \to C) \to (A \to B \wedge C))$ *as an axiom* instead of 5. For taking B = A we would get $(A \to C) \to (A \to A \wedge C)$, which together with $(A \to A \wedge C) \to (A \to A)$ would yield $(A \to C) \to (A \to A)$, in which $A \to C$ is not relevant to $A \to A$.
3. *We cannot take* $(A \to C) \to ((B \to C) \to (A \vee B \to C))$ *as an axiom* instead of 10. For taking B = C = A we would get $(A \to A) \to ((A \to A) \to (A \to A))$, in which $A \to A$ is not relevant to $(A \to A) \to (A \to A)$.

Lemma 1.7:

(i) All axioms of the system R^i are valid.

(ii) The rules of the system R^i preserve validity, i.e., if $M \models_i B$ and $M \models_i B \to C$, then $M \models_i C$, and if $M \models_i B$ and $M \models_i C$, then $M \models_i B \wedge C$.

(iii) Urquhart's formula (D), $(A \to B \vee C) \wedge (C \to D) \to (A \to B \vee D)$, is valid.

The proof of Lemma 1.7 is straightforward.

In section 2 we shall present a practical method to construct a countermodel for each non-valid formula, in particular for

$P \to (Q \to P)$	$\neg P \,\&\, (P \vee Q) \to Q$
$\neg P \to (P \to Q)$	$(P \to Q) \to ((P \to Q) \to (P \to Q))$
$\neg\neg P \to P$	$((P \to Q) \to P) \to P$
$P \vee \neg P$	$((P \to Q) \to Q) \to Q$
$P \wedge \neg P \to Q$	$(P \to Q \vee R) \to (P \to Q) \vee (P \to R)$
$P \to Q \vee \neg Q$	

Theorem 1.8 (*Replacement*): Let A be a (consecutive) part of C_A and let C_B result from C_A by replacing A by B. If $\models A \sim B$, then $\models C_A \sim C_B$.

The proof is straightforward.

Each Kripke model $M = \langle I, R, \overset{K}{\models}\rangle$ for the intuitionistic propositional calculus (I being a set of finite sequences of natural numbers and $iRj := j$ is an extension of i) can be conceived of as a special kind of Urquhart model $M' = \langle I, U, 0, \overset{u}{\models}\rangle$ with $i \cup j = j$ if iRj, $i \cup j = i$ if jRi and $i \cup j$ undefined otherwise, 0 = the empty sequence and $i \overset{u}{\models} P := i \overset{K}{\models} P$. One easily checks that

i) $M' \overset{u}{\underset{i}{\models}} A$ iff $M \overset{K}{\underset{i}{\models}} A$ and
ii) if $M' \overset{u}{\underset{i}{\models}} A$ then $M' \overset{u}{\underset{i \cup j}{\models}} A$.

Hence we have the following theorem:

Theorem 1.9: If A is valid in Urquhart's information pieces semantics, then A is Kripke valid and hence provable in the intuitionistic propositional calculus.

So, our particular relevance logic, which up till now has been characterized only semantically, is a *subsystem* of intuitionistic propositional calculus.

§2 Beth-Tableaux-Type Formal System

By a (*relevance*) *index* we mean a finite sequence of natural numbers without repetitions, the order of the natural numbers being unimportant. ( ) denotes the empty sequence. We will use a, b, c, ... for arbitrary relevance indices. Our relevance-indices will play the same role as the * and the † in section 3 of Anderson & Belnap (1975).

Let a be the index $(n_1, \ldots, n_k)$ and b the index $(m_1, \ldots, m_l)$, then a * b is by definition the index $(n_1, \ldots, n_k, m_1, \ldots, m_l)$, however not mentioning the same natural number twice.

By a *signed formula* we mean any expression of the form $T(A)_a$ or $F(A)_a$, where A is a formula and a is a relevance index. If it is clear from the context what is meant, we will simply write TA_a instead of $T(A)_a$ and FA_a instead of $F(A)_a$. For example, instead of $T(B \wedge C)_a$ we will mostly write $TB \wedge C_a$.

The intended meanings of TA_a and FA_a are as follows:

TA_a: A is true on the basis of the information a, which is relevant to A,

FA_a: it is not the case that A is true on the basis of a, a being relevant to A.

A *sequent* is a finite (unordered) sequence of signed formulas. We will use S, S', ... for arbitrary sequents.

We will explain the notion of formal provability in terms of finding a counterexample, like Beth did in his semantic tableaux: a formula A is provable if the supposition $FA_{(\,)}$, ( ) being the empty piece of information, turns out to be untenable.

Our rules for →, & and ∨ are the following:

T → $\dfrac{S,\ TB \to C_a}{S,\ TB \to C_a,\ FB_b \mid S,\ TB \to C_a,\ TC_{a * b}}$ for any b

F → $\dfrac{S,\ FB \to C_a}{S,\ TB_{(k)},\ FC_{a * (k)}}$ where k is the least natural number not occurring in a or in any index of S.

T ∧ $\dfrac{S,\ TB \wedge C_a}{S,\ TB_a,\ TC_a}$ F ∧ $\dfrac{S,\ FB \wedge C_a}{S,\ FB_a \mid S,\ FC_a}$

T ∨ $\dfrac{S,\ TB \vee C_a}{S,\ TB_a \mid S,\ TC_a}$ F ∨ $\dfrac{S,\ FB \vee C_a}{S,\ FB_a,\ FC_a}$

Intuitively, the rules T → and F → say the following:

T → : If B → C is true on the basis of the information a, then for any piece of information b it is not the case that B is true on the basis of b or C is true on the basis of a * b.

F → : If it is not the case that B → C is true on the basis of a, then for some piece of information (k) B is true on the basis of (k) and it is not the case that C is true on the basis of a * (k). Since the piece of information (k) need not contain any information already available, we have to demand that k is new.

A sequent S is B(eth)-*provable* iff there is a finite schema of sequents such that

1. the upper sequent is S,
2. each other sequent is the result of an application of one of the rules to a sequent above it,
3. each of the sequents below (in the last line) is *closed*, i.e. either $Tf_{()}$ occurs in it or there is a formula B and an index b such that both TB_b and FB_b occur in it.

$\vdash' A$ (A is B-provable) := $FA_{()}$ is B-provable.

$A^1, \ldots, A^n \vdash' B := TA^1_{(1)}, \ldots, TA^n_{(1)}, FB_{(1)}$ is B-provable.

$A^1, \ldots, A^n \vdash^* B := TA^1_{(1)}, \ldots, TA^n_{(n)}, FB_{(1, \ldots, n)}$ is B-provable.

Clearly: $A_1, \ldots, A_n \vdash' B$ iff $\vdash' A_1 \wedge \ldots \wedge A_n \rightarrow B$,
$A_1, \ldots, A_n \vdash^* B$ iff $\vdash' A_1 \rightarrow (A_2 \rightarrow \ldots (A_n \rightarrow B) \ldots)$.

Examples:

1. $\vdash' ((P \rightarrow P) \rightarrow P) \rightarrow P$. The following schema is a B-proof of $((P \rightarrow P) \rightarrow P) \rightarrow P$:

$$F((P \rightarrow P) \rightarrow P) \rightarrow P_{()}$$
$$T(P \rightarrow P) \rightarrow P_{(1)}, FP_{(1)}$$
$$T(P \rightarrow P) \rightarrow P_{(1)}, FP \rightarrow P_{()}, FP_{(1)} \mid T(P \rightarrow P) \rightarrow P_{(1)}, TP_{(1)}, FP_{(1)}$$
$$T(P \rightarrow P) \rightarrow P_{(1)}, TP_{(2)}, FP_{(2)}, FP_{(1)}$$

2. $\vdash' ((P \vee (P \rightarrow Q)) \rightarrow Q) \rightarrow Q$, in particular $\vdash' \neg\neg(P \vee \neg P)$. The following schema is a B-proof of $((P \vee (P \rightarrow Q)) \rightarrow Q) \rightarrow Q$:

$$F((P \vee (P \to Q)) \to Q) \to Q_{(\ )}$$
$$T(P \vee (P \to Q)) \to Q_{(1)},\ FQ_{(1)}$$
$$T\ ..{}_{(1)},\ FP \vee (P \to Q)_{(1)},\ FQ_{(1)} \mid T\ ..{}_{(1)},\ TQ_{(1)},\ FQ_{(1)}$$
$$T\ ..{}_{(1)},\ FP_{(1)},\ FP \to Q_{(1)},\ FQ_{(1)}$$
$$T\ ..{}_{(1)},\ FP_{(1)},\ TP_{(2)},\ FQ_{(1,2)},\ FQ_{(1)}$$
$$T\ ..{}_{(1)},\ FP \vee (P \to Q)_{(2)},\ FP_{(1)},\ TP_{(2)},\ FQ_{(1,2)},\ FQ_{(1)} \mid \ldots,\ TQ_{(1,2)},\ FQ_{(1,2)}$$
$$FP_{(2)},\ FP \to Q_{(2)},\ FP_{(1)},\ TP_{(2)}$$

Lemma 2.1: The search for a B-proof of A may consist of infinitely many steps, as may become clear from the following infinite schema.

$$T(P \to Q) \to R_{(\ )},\ \ldots$$
$$T(P \to Q) \to R_{(\ )},\ FP \to Q_{(\ )} \mid T(P \to Q) \to R_{(\ )},\ TR_{(\ )}$$
$$,\ TP_{(1)},\ FQ_{(1)}$$
$$T(P \to Q) \to R_{(\ )},\ FP \to Q_{(1)}, TP_{(1)},\ FQ_{(1)} \mid T(P \to Q) \to R_{(\ )},\ TR_{(1)},\ TP_{(1)},\ FQ_{(1)}$$
$$TP_{(2)},\ FQ_{(1,2)}$$
$$T(P \to Q) \to R_{(\ )},\ FP \to Q_{(2)},\ \ldots \mid T(P \to Q) \to R_{(\ )},\ TR_{(2)}$$
$$TP_{(3)},\ FQ_{(2,3)}$$

and so on. □

However, although the search for a B-proof of ((P → Q) → Q) → Q consists of infinitely many steps, it is clear from its structure that not $\vdash^{!}$ ((P → Q) → Q) → Q.

$$F((P \to Q) \to Q) \to Q_{(\ )}$$
$$T(P \to Q) \to Q_{(1)},\ FQ_{(1)}$$
$$FP \to Q_{(\ )},\ T(P \to Q) \to Q_{(1)},\ FQ_{(1)} \mid TQ_{(1)},\ T(P \to Q) \to Q_{(1)},\ FQ_{(1)}$$
$$TP_{(2)},\ FQ_{(2)},$$
$$,\ FP \to Q_{(1)},$$
$$TP_{(3)},\ FQ_{(1,3)},$$
$$,\ FP \to Q_{(2)}$$

and so on, ad infinitum.

Theorem 2.2 (*Soundness*): If $\vdash' A$, then $\models A$.

Proof: Suppose $\vdash' A$, i.e. there is a finite schema of the form

$$FA_{(\ )}$$

$$\cdot \quad \cdot \quad \cdot$$

$$\cdot \quad \cdot \quad \cdot \quad \cdot$$

$$|\ TB_b,\ FB_b,\ \ldots\ |\ TC_c,\ FC_c,\ \ldots\ |\ Tf_{(\ )},\ \ldots\ |\ \ldots$$

In order to prove the soundness it suffices to show the following *claim*: if $TP_{(\ )}, TQ_{(1)}, TR_{(1,2)}, FS_{(2,3)}, FT_{(1,2,3)}$ is a sequent in this schema, then for all models M = <I, U, O, |=> and for all i_1, i_2, i_3 in I, if $M \models_0 P$ and $M \models_{i_1} Q$ and $M \models_{i_1 \cup i_2} R$, then $M \models_{i_2 \cup i_3} S$ or $M \models_{i_1 \cup i_2 \cup i_3} T$.

For the sequents in the last line of the given schema this is immediate. And the proofs of the induction steps are straight forward. □

It is important to note here that we are not able to prove for a Beth-provable sequent of the form TB_b, TD_d, FC_c, FE_e that $\models D \wedge B \to C \vee E$ nor that $\models D \to (B \to C \vee E)$.

Urquhart (1971) describes a procedure for translating Beth-proofs into Hilbert-type proofs for the implicational fragment (see Urquhart, 1971, Lemma 3.2). However, the present author did not succeed in extending this procedure to include also $\vee$.

Theorem 2.3 (*Disjunction Property*): If $\vdash' B \vee C$, then $\vdash' B$ or $\vdash' C$.

Proof: Suppose $\vdash' B \vee C$, i.e. $FB \vee C_{(\ )}$

$$FB_{(\ )},\ FC_{(\ )}$$

yields only closed sequents. However, the only rule which gives a T-signed formula is rule F $\rightarrow$:

$$\frac{S,\ FB \rightarrow C_a}{S,\ TB_{(k)},\ FC_{a*(k)}} \quad \text{where } k \text{ is new.}$$

Since k is new, a closed sequent can never result from an interplay between $FB_{(\ )}$ and $FC_{(\ )}$. Hence $FB_{(\ )}$ alone yields only closed sequents or $FC_{(\ )}$ alone yields only closed sequents. □

$\rightarrow$ satisfies principles of relevance in the following mathematically definite sense:

Theorem 2.4: $\vdash' C_1 \wedge \ldots \wedge C_k \rightarrow D_1 \vee \ldots \vee D_l$, where each C_i and D_j is an atom (i.e. an atomic formula or the negation of an atomic formula), iff some atom C_i is the same as some atom D_j.

The proof is straightforward. The semantic version of this theorem (with $\models$ instead of $\vdash'$) was stated in §1.

Theorem 2.5: There is a systematic procedure of searching for a B-proof of A such that if this procedure doesn't yield a B-proof of A, then it provides a counterexample to A, i.e., a model M = $\langle I, U, 0, \models \rangle$ with $M \not\models_0 A$.

Corollary 2.6 (*Completeness* of B-provability with respect to Urquhart's information pieces semantics): if $\models$ A, then $\vdash'$ A.

Proof of Theorem 2.5: The systematic procedure of searching for a B-proof of A consists of the following possibly infinite number of steps:

Step 0: Start with $FA_{(\,)}$ and apply all F-rules, except F →, as many times as possible.

Step n (n ≥ 1): Apply rule F → (if there is a signed formula of the form $FB \to C_a$) and next apply all other rules, except F →, as many times as possible; in the application of rule T → we can and do restrict ourselves to all indices b, in which no new natural numbers are introduced.

Example 1: We apply our systematic procedure to P ∧ ¬P → Q.

$$FP \wedge (P \to f) \to Q_{(\,)}$$

$$TP \wedge (P \to f)_{(1)},\ FQ_{(1)}$$
$$TP_{(1)},\ TP \to f_{(1)},\ FQ_{(1)}$$
$$TP_{(1)},\ FP_{(\,)},\ TP \to f_{(1)},\ FQ_{(1)} \mid TP_{(1)},\ Tf_{(1)},\ TP \to f_{(1)},\ FQ_{(1)}$$
$$S_1 \quad \mid \quad S_2 \quad \mid \quad S_3 \quad \mid \quad S_4$$

where $S_1 = TP_{(1)},\ FP_{(\,)},\ FP_{(1)},\ TP \to f_{(1)},\ FQ_{(1)}$; closed
$S_2 = TP_{(1)},\ FP_{(\,)},\ Tf_{(1)},\ TP \to f_{(1)},\ FQ_{(1)}$; not closed
$S_3 = TP_{(1)},\ Tf_{(1)},\ FP_{(1)},\ TP \to f_{(1)},\ FP_{(1)}$; closed
$S_4 = TP_{(1)},\ Tf_{(1)},\ Tf_{(1)},\ TP \to f_{(1)},\ FQ_{(1)}$; not closed

Since not all of S_1, S_2, S_3 and S_4 are closed, P ∧ ¬P → Q is not B-provable. We shall soon see that each of the "branches" ending with S_2 or S_4 yields a countermodel to P ∧ ¬P → Q.

Example 2: We apply our systematic procedure to the classically valid formula ((P → Q) → P) → P.

$$F((P \to Q) \to P) \to P_{(\,)}$$

$$T(P \to Q) \to P_{(1)},\ FP_{(1)}$$
$$FP \to Q_{(\,)},\ T(P \to Q) \to P_{(1)},\ FP_{(1)} \mid S_1$$
$$FP \to Q_{(\,)},\ FP \to Q_{(1)},\ T(P \to Q) \to P_{(1)},\ FP_{(1)} \mid S_1 \mid S_1$$

$TP_{(2)}, FQ_{(2)}, FP \to Q_{(1)}, T(P \to Q) \to P_{(1)}, FP_{(1)} \mid S_1 \mid S_1$
$TP_{(2)}, FQ_{(2)}, FP \to Q_{(1)}, FP \to Q_{(2)}, T(P \to Q) \to P_{(1)}, FP_{(1)} \mid S_2 \mid S_1 \mid S_1$

$TP_{(2)}, FQ_{(2)}, TP_{(3)}, FQ_{(1,3)}, FP \to Q_{(2)}, T(P \to Q) \to P_{(1)}, FP_{(1)} \mid S_2 \mid S_1 \mid S_1$
$TP_{(2)}, FQ_{(2)}, TP_{(3)}, FQ_{(1,3)}, FP \to Q_{(2)}, FP \to Q_{(1,3)}, T(P \to Q) \to P_{(1)}, FP_{(1)} \mid \ldots$
and so on

where $S_2 = TP_{(2)}, FQ_{(2)}, FP \to Q_{(1)}, TP_{(1,2)}, T(P \to Q) \to P_{(1)}, FP_{(1)}$
$S_1 = TP_{(1)}, T(P \to Q) \to P_{(1)}, FP_{(1)}$; closed

Since new indices may be introduced all the time, our systematic procedure applied to $((P \to Q) \to P) \to P$ does not end in finitely many steps. (Cf. Lemma 2.1.)

A *branch*, resulting from applying our systematic procedure to a formula A, is a sequence of sequents $S_1, S_2, \ldots$ (possibly finite), where $S_1 = FA_{(\,)}$ and each S_{i+1} is obtained from S_i by application of one of the T- or F-rules.

By definition, if all branches starting with $FA_{(\,)}$ are closed (i.e. contain a closed sequent) then $\vdash'$ A. So if not $\vdash'$ A, then at least one branch starting with $FA_{(\,)}$ is *open*, i.e. not closed. In order to prove theorem 2.5 we still have to show that an open branch starting with $FA_{(\,)}$ yields a countermodel to A.

Lemma 2.7: Let τ be an open branch starting with $FA_{(\,)}$. Let $M_\tau = \langle I_\tau, U_\tau, 0, \models\rangle$ be defined as follows:

i) I_τ is the set of all indices occurring in τ,
ii) $i \cup_\tau j := i * j$ if $i * j \in I_\tau$; $i \cup_\tau j$ undefined, otherwise,
iii) $0 :=$ the empty sequence,
iv) $i \models P :=$ TP_i occurs in τ.

Then for all formulas E and for all $i \in I_\tau$, if TE_i occurs in τ, then $M_\tau \models_i E$, and if FE_i occurs in τ, then not $M_\tau \models_i E$.

The proof of Lemma 2.7 is straightforward, by induction. Note 1) if $TB \to C_i$ occurs in τ then for all $j \in I_\tau$, FB_j or TC_{i*j} occurs in τ and 2) if $FB \to C_i$ occurs in τ then for some k, $TB_{(k)}$ and $FC_{i*(k)}$ both occur in τ. As a consequence, if τ is an open branch starting with $FA_{(\,)}$ then not $M_\tau \models_0 A$. So, if not $\vdash' A$ then not $\models A$.

<u>Example 1</u> (*continued*): The open branch ending with S_2 yields the following countermodel M to $P \wedge \neg P \to Q$:

$M = \langle\{(\,), (1)\}, *, (\,), \models\rangle$ with $(\,) \not\models P$, $(1) \models P$, $(1) \models f$ and $(1) \not\models Q$.

<u>Example 2</u> (*continued*): The left-most branch τ yields the following countermodel M_τ to $((P \to Q) \to P) \to P$.

$M_\tau = \langle I_\tau, U_\tau, 0, \models\rangle$ as defined in Lemma 2.7, i.e. $(\,) \not\models P$, $(1) \not\models P$, for all $n \geq 2$ $(n) \models P$ and for all $i \in I_\tau$, $i \not\models Q$. Then for all $i \in I_\tau$, $M_\tau \not\models_i P \to Q$. Hence $M_\tau \models_{(1)} (P \to Q) \to P$. Therefore $M_\tau \not\models_0 ((P \to Q) \to P) \to P$.

This completes the proof of Theorem 2.5.

Using our systematic procedure one easily finds a counterexample for each non-valid formula, such as

$P \to (Q \to P)$,	$P \wedge \neg P \to Q$,	$(P \to Q) \to ((P \to Q) \to (P \to Q))$
$\neg P \to (P \to Q)$,	$P \to Q \vee \neg Q$,	$(P \to Q \vee R) \to (P \to Q) \vee (P \to R)$
$\neg\neg P \to P$,	$\neg P \,\&\, (P \vee Q) \to Q$,	$(P \to Q) \to ((P \to R) \to (P \to Q \wedge R))$
$P \vee \neg P$,	$((P \to Q) \to Q) \to Q$,	$(P \to R) \to ((Q \to R) \to (P \vee Q \to R))$

Since validity is equivalent to B-provability (Soundness, theorem 2.2, and completeness, corollary 2.6) and since the systematic procedure of searching for a Beth proof of A may consist of infinitely many steps (confer Lemma 2.1 and see the proof of theorem 2.5) the author guesses that Urquhart's notion of validity is undecidable. Motivation: the analogous procedures in the case of classical, intuitionistic, modal, and counterfactual logics terminate after finitely many steps precisely in those cases in which the logic in question is decidable.

Urquhart (198.) mentions the decidability problem for his notion of validity as still being open.

Note that also in the case of purely implicational formulas the systematic procedure may consist of infinitely many steps (see Lemma 2.1), while on the other hand Kripke (1959) claims that the implicational fragment $R_{\rightarrow}$ of R is decidable.

It is also interesting to note that A. Kron (1978) has shown that the positive fragment of R without the axiom schema of contraction, $(A \rightarrow (A \rightarrow B)) \rightarrow (A \rightarrow B)$, is decidable.

Hypothesis 2.8 (*Undecidability*): The set of all formulas valid in Urquhart's information-pieces semantics is undecidable.

§3 Some Properties of the System $R^i D$

In this section we want to develop a notion $A_1, \ldots, A_m \vdash^r B$ (the "r" stands for "relevance") such that

1. if $A_1, \ldots, A_m \vdash^r B$ is the case, then each of the premisses $A_1, \ldots, A_m$ is in some sense (to be specified in definition 3.1) relevant to B, and

2. $A_1, \ldots, A_m \vdash^r B$ iff $A_1, \ldots, A_{m-1} \vdash^r A_m \to B$.

We specify that the notion of relevance is such that not $f \vdash^r B$, and consequently not $\vdash^r \neg A \to (A \to B)$. Also not $\vdash^r A \to (B \to A)$.

Definition 3.1: An *r-deduction of* B *from* $A^1, \ldots, A^m$ is by definition a finite schema of the following form:

$$A^1_{(1)} \ldots A^m_{(m)} \quad \text{axiom}_{(\ )} \quad \text{axiom}_{(\ )}$$

$$\frac{C_c \quad C \to D_d}{D_{c*d}} \qquad \frac{C_c \quad D_c}{C \wedge D_c}$$

$$B_{(1, \ldots, m)}$$

where the axioms still have to be specified in such a way that condition 2 above (the deduction theorem) holds, and c and d are (relevance) indices (see §2).

$A^1, \ldots, A^m \vdash^r B$ (B is *r-reducible from* $A^1, \ldots, A^m$) := there is an r-deduction of B from $A^1, \ldots, A^m$.

In order to be able to prove the deduction theorem we need the following axioma-schemas belong to R^i:

1. $A \to A$
2. $(A \to C) \to ((C \to D) \to (A \to D))$
3. $(A \to (C \to D)) \to (C \to (A \to D))$
4. $(A \to (C \to D)) \to ((A \to C) \to (A \to D))$
5. $(A \to C) \wedge (A \to D) \to (A \to C \wedge D)$

Theorem 3.2 (*Deduction theorem*): $A^1, \ldots, A^m \vdash^r B$ iff $A^1, \ldots, A^{m-1} \vdash^r A^m \to B$.

Proof: From right to left is trivial. From left to right: Suppose $A^1, \ldots, A^m \overset{r}{\vdash} B$. Replace in the given r-deduction of B from $A^1, \ldots, A^m$ each expression E_e with the natural number m occurring in the index e by the expression $A^m \rightarrow E_{e - (m)}$ where the index e - (m) results from e by leaving out m.

The upper line in the resulting schema looks as follows:

$$A^1_{(1)} \ldots A^{m-1}_{(m-1)} \quad A^m \rightarrow A^m_{(\ )} \ \text{axiom}_{(\ )},$$

while the bottom line in the resulting schema just contains

$$A^m \rightarrow B_{(1, \ldots, m-1)}.$$

For Modus Ponens,

$$\frac{C_c \quad C \rightarrow D_d}{D_{c * d}},$$

there are four possibilities:

i) m occurs in c, but not in d. Then we get

$$\frac{A^m \rightarrow C_{c - (m)} \quad C \rightarrow D_d}{A^m \rightarrow D_{c * d - (m)}}$$

and using axiom 2 this is a derived rule of R^i.

ii) m occurs in d, but not in c. Then we get

$$\frac{C_c \quad A^m \rightarrow (C \rightarrow D)_{d - (m)}}{A^m \rightarrow D_{c * d - (m)}}$$

which is a derived rule in R^i by using axiom 3.

iii) m occurs both in c and in d. Then we get

$$\frac{A^m \to C_{c - (m)} \quad A^m \to (C \to D)_{d - (m)}}{A^m \to D_{c * d - (m)}}$$

which is a derived rule of R^i by using axiom 4.

iv) In case m occurs neither in c nor in d, the application of modus ponens remains unchanged.

For the ∧-rule,

$$\frac{C_c \quad D_c}{C \wedge D_c},$$

there are two possibilities:

i) If m does not occur in c, the application of this rule remains unchanged,

ii) if m does occur in c, then we get

$$\frac{A^m \to C_{c - (m)} \quad A^m \to D_{c - (m)}}{A^m \to C \wedge D_{c - (m)}}$$

which is a derived rule of R^i using the ∧-rule and the axiom $(A \to C) \wedge (A \to D) \to (A \to C \wedge D)$. □

<u>Remark 3.3:</u> In remark 1.6, 1) we have seen that $A \to (B \to A \wedge B)$ cannot be taken as an axiom-schema for relevance logic. For that reason the rule $\frac{C \quad D}{C \wedge D}$ was introduced. Now if $\frac{C_c \quad D_d}{C \wedge D_{c * d}}$, with possibly different indices c and d, were a rule, we would need in the proof of the deduction theorem (in case m occurs in c and not in d) $(A \to C) \wedge D \to (A \to C \wedge D)$ as an axiom. But this latter

formula reduces to $D \to (A \to D)$ in case $C = A$ and hence we have to require that in an application of the $\wedge$-rule the indices c and d are equal.

To the axiom-schemas 1, 2, 3, 4, and 5 we can add other axiom-schemas which are valid in Urquhart's information pieces semantics, for instance the schemas of the system R^i, defined in 1.5 and Urquhart's formula (D), defined in Lemma 1.7 (iii). *For the remainder of this section we shall actually do so*, but other axiom-schemas valid in the information pieces semantics might be added.

Lemma 3.4: $A_1, \ldots, A_m \vdash^r B$ iff $\vdash A_1 \to (\ldots \to (A_m \to B) \ldots)$ in R^iD, where R^iD is the system obtained from R^i by adding the schema (D).

Proof: By the deduction theorem $A_1, \ldots, A_m \vdash^r B$ is equivalent to $\vdash^r A_1 \to (\ldots \to (A_m \to B) \ldots)$; and the latter is equivalent to provability in R^iD of the formula in question, given our convention italicized above. □

By Lemma 1.7 we have the following

Corollary 3.5 (*Soundness*): If $A_1, \ldots, A_m \vdash^r B$ then $\models A_1 \to (\ldots \to (A_m \to B) \ldots)$.

The following theorem follows immediately from Corollary 3.5 and Theorem 1.9, but can also be seen directly.

Theorem 3.6: If $A_1, \ldots, A_m \vdash^r B$, then $A_1, \ldots, A_m \vdash B$ intuitionistically; but not conversely.

Proof: An intuitionistic deduction of B from $A_1, \ldots, A_m$ is obtained by leaving out all the relevance indices in a given r-deduction of B from $A_1, \ldots, A_m$.

But A, B $\vdash$ A intuitionistically, while not A, B $\vdash^r$ A by Corollary 3.5. The following schema is an intuitionistic deduction of A from A, B, but not an r-deduction of A from A, B.

$$\dfrac{\dfrac{A \quad B}{A \wedge B} \qquad A \wedge B \rightarrow A}{A}$$

□

<u>Theorem 3.7</u> (*Replacement*): Let A be a (consecutive) part of C_A and let C_B result from C_A by replacing A by B. If A $\vdash^r$ B and B $\vdash^r$ A, then $C_A \vdash^r C_B$ and $C_B \vdash^r C_A$.

The proof is straightforward by induction on the complexity of A. A close inspection of this proof shows that we need all the axioms and rules of R^i in order to be able to prove the replacement theorem. In other words, R^i is the *minimal* system for which both the deduction theorem and the replacement theorem hold.

In order to prove the disjunction property for the system R^iD we introduce a variant of the Kleene slash, introduced in Kleene (1962).

<u>Definition 3.8:</u> $A_1, \ldots, A_m \mid P := A_1, \ldots, A_m \vdash^r P$ for P atomic, $A_1, \ldots, A_m \mid C \wedge D := A_1, \ldots, A_m \mid C$ and $A_1, \ldots, A_m \mid D$, $A_1, \ldots, A_m \mid C \vee D := A_1, \ldots, A_m \Vdash C$ or $A_1, \ldots, A_m \Vdash D$ where $A_1, \ldots, A_m \Vdash C := A_1, \ldots, A_m \mid C$ and $A_1, \ldots, A_m \vdash^r C$, $A_1, \ldots, A_m \mid C \rightarrow D :=$ for each finite (unordered) sequence $B_1, \ldots, B_n$ of formulas, if $B_1, \ldots, B_n \Vdash C$ then $A_1, \ldots, A_m * B_1, \ldots, B_n \mid D$, where $A_1, \ldots, A_m * B_1, \ldots, B_n$ is by definition the finite (unordered) sequence $A_1, \ldots, A_m, B_1, \ldots, B_n$ leaving out double occurrences of the same formula in case $A_i = B_j$ for some i, j. For instance, P, Q * Q, R, S := P, Q, R, S.

<u>Theorem 3.9</u> (*Disjunction Property*): If $A_1, \ldots, A_m \vdash^r E$ and for all i = 1, ..., m $A_i \mid A_i$, then $A_1, \ldots, A_m \mid E$.

Corollary 3.10: If $A_1, \ldots, A_m \vdash^{r} B \vee C$ and $A_i \mid A_i$ for all $i = 1, \ldots, m$ then $A_1, \ldots, A_m \vdash^{r} B$ or $A_1, \ldots, A_m \vdash^{r} C$.

Proof: We show that for any sub-r-deduction of E' from $A_{i_1}, \ldots, A_{i_k}$, occurring in a given r-deduction of E from $A_1, \ldots, A_m$ it holds that $A_{i_1}, \ldots, A_{i_k} \mid E'$.

Case 1: E' is an axiom and k = 0. It is a long but easy exercise to check that for any axiom E' of the system R^iD it holds that $\emptyset \mid E'$.
Case 2: $E' = A_i$ for some i and k = 1. Then $A_i \mid A_i$ by hypothesis.
Case 3: For an application of Modus Ponens we have by the induction hypothesis $A_{i_1}, \ldots, A_{i_k} \Vdash C$ and $A_{j_1}, \ldots, A_{j_1} \mid C \to D$. Hence it follows immediately from the definitions that $A_{i_1}, \ldots, A_{i_k} * A_{j_1}, \ldots, A_{j_1} \mid D$.
Case 4: For an application of the $\wedge$-rule we have by the induction hypothesis $A_{i_1}, \ldots, A_{i_k} \mid C$ and $A_{i_1}, \ldots, A_{i_k} \mid D$. Hence, by definition, $A_{i_1}, \ldots, A_{i_k} \mid C \wedge D$. □

In Theorem 2.2 and Corollary 2.6 we have seen that the notions of $\models A$ and of $\vdash' A$ are equivalent. In Corollary 3.5 we have established that if $\vdash^{r} A$ then $\models A$. The obvious question now is if one can show the converse: if $\models A$ then $\vdash^{r} A$; in other words, whether $\models A$, $\vdash' A$ and $\vdash^{r} A$ are equivalent.

A. Urquhart (1972) has shown that formulas built up from atomic formulas by relevant implication, $\to$, only and valid in the information pieces semantics are r-provable indeed. In order to make this paper self-contained, we repeat here his argument.

Theorem 3.11 (Completeness for implicational formulas): Let A be an implicational formula (i.e. containing no other connectives than $\to$). If $\models A$, then $\vdash^{r} A$.

Proof: Suppose $\models A$. Let $M = \langle I, *, \emptyset, \models\rangle$ be defined as follows. I is the set of all finite, unordered, sequences of implicational formulas; * is defined as in Definition 3.8; $\emptyset$ is the empty sequence; $A_1, \ldots, A_m \models P := A_1, \ldots, A_m \vdash^r P$ for P atomic.

Claim: for all $i \in I$ and for all implicational formulas A, $M \models_i A$ iff $i \vdash^r A$. Since $\models A$ and hence $M \models_\emptyset A$ it follows that $\vdash^r A$.

In order to prove the claim we have to check that $M \models_i B \to C$ iff $i \vdash^r B \to C$, i.e. $\forall j \in I$ [not $M \models_j B$ or $M \models_{i * j} C$] iff $i \vdash^r B \to C$, i.e. (by induction hypothesis) $\forall j \in I$ [not $j \vdash^r B$ or $i * j \vdash^r C$] iff $i \vdash^r B \to C$.

From right to left is trivial. From left to right: Let

$$N^0 D := D$$
$$N^{k+1} D := (N^k D \to N^k D) \to N^k D.$$

Then one shows by induction on k that $N^k D \vdash^r D$ and $D \vdash^r N^k D$; for the latter statement note that $(E \to E) \to (E \to E)$ is an axiom and hence by axiom 3, $E \vdash^r (E \to E) \to E$.

Now take $j = N^k B$ such that $N^k B$ does not occur in i. Then $j \vdash^r B$ and hence $i * j \vdash^r C$, i.e. $i, N^k B \vdash^r C$. It follows that $i \vdash^r B \to C$ (using Theorem 3.7). □

C. Charlwood (1981) proves completeness of an extension of the system R^i with respect to Urquhart's information pieces semantics for formulas A built from a whole hierarchy of languages.

The question remains whether one can show completeness of $R^i D$ or some extension of it for formulas of our simple language.

Below we shall reduce the completeness of R^iD (or some extension of it?) with respect to the information pieces semantics to the problem if the disjunctive normal form theorem holds for R^iD. The latter problem, however, is still *open*.

The idea of proving completeness in this way was given to the author by S. A. Kripke (oral communication), however, for the case of intuitionistic logic.

Open Problem (*Disjunctive normal form "theorem"* for R^iD or some extension of it): Every formula B is r-equivalent to a disjunction $B_1 \vee \ldots \vee B_n$ such that for all i, $1 \leq i \leq n$, $B_i \mid B_i$.

In case this problem has been solved positively, one can generalize Urquhart's completeness proof for implicational formulas to a completeness proof for arbitrary formulas.

Theorem 3.12 (*Completeness* of R^iD with respect to Urquhart's information pieces semantics): If the disjunctive normal form "theorem" for R^iD holds, then for all formulas A, if $\models A$ then $\vdash^r A$.

Proof: Suppose $\models A$. Let $M = \langle I, *, \emptyset, \models\rangle$ be defined as follows. I is the set of all finite, unordered, sequences i of formulas C such that $C \mid C$ for all C in i and $i \models P := i \vdash^r P$, for all $i \in I$ and for P atomic. Again, it suffices to show the *claim*: $M \models_i A$ iff $i \vdash^r A$ for all $i \in I$ and for all formulas A.

Then from $\models A$ it follows that $M \models_\emptyset A$ and hence that $\vdash^r A$.

Proof of claim:

i) $M \models_i P$ iff $i \vdash^r P$ for P atomic, by definition.
Induction hypothesis: $M \models_j B$ iff $j \vdash^r B$ for all $j \in I$,
$M \models_j C$ iff $j \vdash^r C$ for all $j \in I$.

ii) $M \models_i B \wedge C$ iff $M \models_i B$ and $M \models_i C$
iff $i \vdash^r B$ and $i \vdash^r C$
iff $i \vdash^r B \wedge C$.

iii) $M \models_i B \vee C$ iff $M \models_i B$ or $M \models_i C$
iff $i \vdash^r B$ or $i \vdash^r C$
iff $i \vdash^r B \vee C$ (disjunction property).

iv) $M \models_i B \to C$ iff $\forall j \in I$ [not $M \models_j B$ or $M \models_{i*j} C$]
iff $\forall j \in I$ [not $j \vdash^r B$ or $i * j \vdash^r C$] (1)
iff $i \vdash^r B \to C$. (2)

(2) → (1) is straightforward. (1) → (2): Suppose $\forall j \in I$ [not $j \vdash^r B$ or $i * j \vdash^r C$]. By the disjunctive normal form "theorem", B is r-equivalent to some disjunction $B_1 \vee \ldots \vee B_n$ such that $B_j \mid B_j$ for all $j = 1, \ldots, n$. So for all $j = 1, \ldots, n$, $B_j \in I$ and $B_j \vdash^r B$ and therefore $i * B_j \vdash^r C$. (In case B_j occurs in i, B_j should be replaced by $N^k B_j$ for some k.) Hence, $i, B_1 \vee \ldots \vee B_n \vdash^r C$. Therefore, by the deduction theorem, $i \vdash^r B_1 \vee \ldots \vee B_n \to C$. So, by the replacement theorem, $i \vdash^r B \to C$. □

Note that a crucial formula in a proof of the disjunctive normal form "theorem" is the formula $P \to Q \vee R$. Notice also that axiom-schema 11, $A \wedge (B \vee C) \to (A \wedge B) \vee C$ will be needed in a proof of this "theorem".

REFERENCES

Anderson, A. and Belnap, N., 1975, "Entailment: The Logic of Necessity and Relevance," Princeton University Press, Princeton.

Beth, E., 1959, "The Foundations of Mathematics," North-Holland, Amsterdam.

Charlwood, G., 1981, An Axiomatic Version of Positive Semilattice Relevance Logic, The Journal of Symbolic Logic, 46:233-239.

Fitting, M., 1969, "Intuitionistic Logic, Model Theory and Forcing," North-Holland, Amsterdam.

Kleene, S. C., 1962, Disjunction and Existence under Implication in Elementary Intuitionistic Formalisms, The Journal of Symbolic Logic, 27:11-17.

Kripke, S., 1959, The Problem of Entailment, The Journal of Symbolic Logic, 24:324.

Kron, A., 1978, Decision Procedures for two Positive Relevance Logics, Reports on Mathematical Logic, 10:61-78.

Smullyan, R., 1971, "First Order Logic," Springer Verlag, Berlin.

Swart, H. C. M. de, 1976, Another Intuitionistic Completeness Proof, The Journal of Symbolic Logic, 41:644-662.

Swart, H. C. M. de, 1980, Gentzen-type Systems for C, K and Several Extensions of C and K, Logique et Analyse, 90/91:263-284.

Swart, H. C. M. de, 1983, A Gentzen-type or Beth-type System, a Practical Decision Procedure and a Constructive Completeness Proof for the Counterfactual Logics VC and VCS, The Journal of Symbolic Logic, 48:1-20.

Urquhart, A., 1971, Completeness of Weak Implication, Theoria, 37:274-282.

Urquhart, A., 1972, Semantics for Relevant Logics, The Journal of Symbolic Logic, 37:159-169.

Urquhart, A., 198., The Undecidability of Entailment and Relevant Implication. To appear.

SEQUENTIAL CALCULI FOR SYMMETRIC DYNAMIC LOGIC

Regimantas Pliuškevičius

Institute of Mathematics and Cybernetics
Lithuanian SSR Academy of Sciences
SU-232600 Vilnius

The algorithmic logic of Salwicki (1970, 1977) and dynamic logic of Pratt (1976, 1979) represent a rather successful synthesis of modal logic and Hoare's (1969) logic. Algorithmic and dynamic logics are of great importance not only in computer science but also in mathematics: Ershov (1983) has shown that dynamic logic is closely related to admissible sets.

It is known that algorithmic logic consists of infinitary rules of inference. For dynamic logic, which is based on finitary rules of inference for program operators, the following holds: 1) application of the rule for operating with negative occurrences of the iteration operator is far from being mechanical in functional dynamic logic (FDL) and requires to choose "convergents", i.e., total invariants; 2) propositional dynamic logic (PDL), meant for the study of abstract schemes of programs, and FDL have principally different formulations for operating with negative occurrences of the iteration operator; 3) rules of inference for operating with negative and positive occurrences of the iteration operator do not possess any symmetry, which causes various difficulties of a proof theoretical character.

In this paper *symmetric dynamic logic* is proposed in the form of sequential calculi. Symmetric dynamic logic enables us: (1) to obtain uniform calculi definitions for FDL and PDL, possessing better proof-theoretical properties than traditional definitions of FDL and PDL; (2) to prove that the properties of program terminating as well as of total correctness of deterministic programs are decidable in respect to arithmetic with formula variables. (2) agrees with the statement of Meyer and Halpern (1982) that "terminal" assertions are more tractable than those of "partial correctness".

The paper consists of three parts. The first part deals with FDL and symmetric FDL (SFDL); a possibility to confine oneself to highly specialized applications of the cut rule is proved. In the second part the so-called quasimodal SFDL (QSFDL) is analysed, with the aim of proving the traditional properties of programs. It is proved that in the case of QSFDL all applications of the cut rule may be realised in the "logical" part. Hence, as a corollary, the decidability of the total correctness property in respect to arithmetic with formula variables is obtained. The third part considers PDL and symmetric PDL (SPDL). A constructive proof of the elimination theorem for SPDL is presented. The lemmas and theorems are enumerated by a couple of natural numbers i, j, where i indicates the number of the respective part.

PART 1: FDL AND SFDL

For the logical basis of FDL let us take an arithmetical theory T, containing the arithmetical language of the first order with formula variables (see, e.g., Hilbert and Bernays (1934)). Assume that all the axioms, including that of induction, of Peano arithmetic are derivable in T. The formulas of T will be called *program-free* formulas. Let us define the concept of a *program*: 1) if x is a variable and t is a term of T, then $(x \leftarrow t)$ is a program (called *assignment*); if Q is a program-free formula, then the expression $Q?$ is a program (called a *test*); 2) if α, β are programs, then the expressions $(\alpha; \beta)$, $(\alpha \mid \beta)$, α^* are programs (called *composition, nondeterministic choice* and *iteration*, respectively). We shall call programs of the form $(x \leftarrow t)$, $Q?$ elementary. Let us define the concept of a *formula*: 1) every program-free formula is a formula; 2) if B, C are formulas, x is a variable, and α is a program, then the expressions $(B > C)$, $(B \,\&\, C)$, $(B \vee C)$, $\neg B$, $\mathrm{A}xB$, $\mathrm{E}xB$, $\{\alpha\}B$ are formulas.

The expression $B \equiv C$ is an abbreviation of the formula $(B > C) \,\&\, (C > B)$. Notation $\ddot{\mathrm{A}}B$ will denote the closure of the formula B, i.e., the formula of the form $\mathrm{A}x_1, \ldots, x_n B$, where $x_1, \ldots, x_n$ is a list of free variables of the formula B. Let $\Gamma = B_1, \ldots, B_n$ $(n = 0, 1, \ldots)$, then $\{\alpha\}\Gamma$ will denote $\{\alpha\}B_1, \ldots, \{\alpha\}B_n$. By $|\alpha|$ denote the *complexity* of *program* α, defined by the number of occurrences of program operators in program α. By $|B|$ denote the *complexity* of the *formula* B, defined by the number of occurrences of program and logic symbols in the formula B. Though we consider non-deterministic program operators $\mid$ and $*$, we may consider deterministic programs if we use the operators $\mid$ and $*$ only in the following formulas $(Q?; \alpha) \mid (\neg Q?; \beta)$ and $(Q?; \alpha)^*; \neg Q?$. These formulas express deterministic constructions *if* Q *then* α *else* β and *while* Q *do* α, respectively. The formula $\{\alpha\}B$ expresses only partial correctness of program B. The formula $\neg\{\alpha\}\neg B$ expresses the existence of a B-terminating path. In the case of the deterministic program α this formula expresses the total correctness of α relative to B.

A sequent be an expression of the form $\Gamma \rightarrow \Omega$, where Γ, Ω are finite sets of formulas (i.e., in the calculi, here described, structural rules of permutation and contraction of premises appear implicitly). We now give a sequential formulation of FDL. Let K be an arbitrary calculus and the notation $\vdash_K S$ mean that the sequent S is derivable in the calculus K. Let FD be a calculus which includes the Gentzen (1934/35) calculus LK without structural inference rules of permutation and contraction of premises (since we conceive of an antecedent and succedent of a sequent as sets, these structural rules are contained in the calculus FD implicitly) as well as the following postulates:

The axiom scheme: $\vdash_T S$

Rules of inference:

$$\frac{\Gamma \to \Omega,\ Q(t)}{\Gamma \to \Omega,\ \{x \leftarrow t\}Q(x)} \to\leftarrow \qquad \frac{Q(t),\ \Gamma \to \Omega}{\{x \leftarrow t\}Q(x),\ \Gamma \to \Omega} \leftarrow\to$$

where $Q(x)$ is a program-free formula, term t is free for variable x in the formula $Q(x)$.

$$\frac{Q,\ \Gamma \to \Omega,\ B}{\Gamma \to \Omega,\ \{Q?\}B} \to ? \qquad \frac{\Gamma \to \Omega,\ Q\ ;\ B,\ \Gamma \to \Omega}{\{Q?\}B,\ \Gamma \to \Omega} ? \to$$

$$\frac{\Gamma \to \Omega,\ \{\alpha\}\{\beta\}B}{\Gamma \to \Omega,\ \{\alpha\ ;\ \beta\}B} \to ; \qquad \frac{\{\alpha\}\{\beta\}B,\ \Gamma \to \Omega}{\{\alpha\ ;\ \beta\}B,\ \Gamma \to \Omega} ; \to$$

$$\frac{\Gamma \to \Omega,\ \{\alpha\}B;\ \Gamma \to \Omega,\ \{\beta\}B}{\Gamma \to \Omega,\ \{\alpha \mid \beta\}B} \to\mid \qquad \frac{\{\alpha\}B,\ \{\beta\}B,\ \Gamma \to \Omega}{\{\alpha \mid \beta\}B,\ \Gamma \to \Omega} \mid\to$$

$$\frac{\Gamma \to \Omega,\ R;\ R \to \{\alpha\}R;\ R \to B}{\Gamma \to \Omega,\ \{\alpha^*\}B} \to *$$

$$\frac{\to Q'(n+1) > \neg\{\alpha\}\neg Q'(n)}{\to Q'(n) > \neg\{\alpha^*\}\neg Q'(O)} \{\overline{*}\},$$ where Q' is a program-free formula, containing freely natural number n, not occurring in α.

$$\frac{\Gamma \to B}{\{\alpha\}\Gamma \to \{\alpha\}B}\ \{\alpha\},$$

where $\Gamma = B_1, \ldots, B_n$; $n = 0, 1, \ldots$

The calculus *FD* represents a sequential axiomatization of FDL, the calculus *FD* is therefore sound and complete relative to *T* (see, e.g., Harel, Meyer and Pratt (1977) and Harel (1979)).

Lemma 1.1. *Let B be an arbitrary formula of* FDL. *Then there exists a program-free formula Q such that* $\vdash_{FD} \to (B \equiv Q)$.

The proof follows from relative completeness of the calculus *FD* and the theorem on the expressibility of FDL formulas (see, e.g., Theorem 3.2 of Harel (1979)).

Let us introduce a symmetric FDL (SFDL). Program λ, interpreted as a reflexive and transitive binary relation, is also joined to the number of elementary programs of SFDL. Denote by SFD_0 a calculus obtained from *FD* by

1) replacing the rules $\{\overline{*}\}$ and $\{\alpha\}$ with the following ones:

$$\frac{P(\overline{x}),\ \{\lambda\}\ddot{A}(P(\overline{x}) > \{\alpha\}P(\overline{x})),\ \{\lambda\}\ddot{A}(P(\overline{x}) > B),\ \Gamma \to \Omega}{\{\alpha^*\}B,\ \Gamma \to \Omega}\ * \to,$$

where *P* is a predicate symbol (called an *eigen-variable* of the rule $* \to$), not occurring in the conclusion, $\overline{x}$ is the list of free variables occurring in α. Formulas of the type $\{\lambda\}B$ will be called *modalized;*

$$\frac{\nabla,\ \Gamma \to B}{\nabla,\ \{\alpha\}\Gamma \to \{\alpha\}B}\ \{\alpha\}',$$

where ∇ is a set consisting only of modalized formulas.

2) By joining the following rules for operating to the elementary program λ:

$$\frac{\{\lambda\}\Gamma \to B}{\{\lambda\}\Gamma \to \{\lambda\}B} \to \lambda \qquad \frac{B,\ \{\lambda\}B,\ \Gamma \to \Omega}{\{\lambda\}B,\ \Gamma \to \Omega} \lambda \to$$

Remark. Both rules $\to *$ and $* \to$ contain three side formulas bearing definite similarity. Therefore these rules (as well as other rules of the calculus *SFD*), in contrast to those for iteration of the calculus *FD*, show the Gentzen phenomenon, namely, symmetry. The presence of the elementary program λ in the rules $* \to$, $\{\alpha\}'$ enables us to specify the cut rule for SFDL in a more convenient way. At the end of this part an alternative formulation of SFDL will be described, excluding the elementary program λ.

A sequent S which does not contain occurrences of λ will be called λ-*free*.

Let SFD_O' be a calculus obtained from the calculus SFD_O by joining the rules $\{\overline{*}\}$, $\{\alpha\}$ of the calculus *FD* to SFD_O.

Lemma 1.2. *If* $\vdash_{SFD_O'} S$, *then* $\vdash_{FD} S$, *where* S *is a* λ-*free sequent.*

To prove the lemma, let us make use of the induction on the number n of applications of the rule $* \to$ in the given derivation of sequent S in the calculus SFD_O'.

The basis: $n = 0$. Since the sequent S is λ-free it is easily seen that the given derivation is a derivation in the calculus *FD*.

The induction step: $n > 0$. Consider the upper application of the rule $* \rightarrow$ in the given derivation:

$$\frac{D\{P(\overline{x}),\ \{\lambda\}\ddot{A}(P(\overline{x}) > \{\alpha\}P(\overline{x})),\ \{\lambda\}\ddot{A}(P(\overline{x}) > B),\ \Gamma \rightarrow \Omega}{\{\alpha^*\}B,\ \Gamma \rightarrow \Omega} * \rightarrow$$

According to Lemma 1.1 there exists a program-free formula Q such that $\vdash_{FD} \rightarrow \{\alpha^*\}B \equiv Q$ (1). In the derivation D, in the place of all occurrences of the elementary formula $P(\overline{x})$, we shall put the formula Q and eliminate all the ancestors of the singled out occurrence of the symbol $\{\lambda\}$. Instead of the derivation D we shall obtain D_1 in which some applications of the rule $\{\alpha\}'$ are probably destroyed. All the "destroyed" applications of the rule $\{\alpha\}'$ are corrigible by means of the cut rule, making use of (1) and the fact that $\vdash_{FD} \rightarrow \{\alpha^*\}Q > \{\alpha\}\{\alpha^*\}Q$; $\vdash_{FD} \rightarrow \{\alpha^*\}Q > Q$ (2), as well as of the structural rule of thinning. As to the "destroyed" applications of the rule $\lambda \rightarrow$, they will simply vanish since their premise coincides with the conclusion. Since P does not occur in α, B, Γ, Ω, as a result we obtain derivation D_2 of the sequent $S_1 = Q, \ddot{A}(Q > \{\alpha\}Q), \ddot{A}(Q > B), \Gamma \rightarrow \Omega$. With the help of cut and making use of (1) and (2) from the derivation D_2 of the sequent S_1 it is possible to obtain derivation D_3 of the sequent $\{\alpha^*\}B, \Gamma \rightarrow \Omega$ in the calculus SFD'_0 not containing applications of the rule $* \rightarrow$. Replacing the derivation of the sequent $\{\alpha^*\}B, \Gamma \rightarrow \Omega$ in the initial derivation of the sequent S by derivation D_3 we obtain the derivation of the sequent S which contains only $n - 1$ applications of the rule $* \rightarrow$. By applying the inductive assumption to the obtained derivation we get the derivation of the sequent S in the calculus FD. Thus the lemma is proved.

As a corollary from Lemma 1.2 we get the following

Lemma 1.3. *If* $\vdash_{SFD_0} S$, *then* $\vdash_{FD} S$, *where* S *is a* λ*-free sequent.*

Lemma 1.4. *For an arbitrary positive integer k and arbitrary formulas B and C we have:*

$$(1) \vdash_{SFD_o} B,\ \{\lambda\}\ddot{A}(B > \{\alpha\}B) \rightarrow \{\alpha\}^k B;$$
$$(2) \vdash_{SFD_o} \{\alpha\}^k B,\ \{\lambda\}\ddot{A}(B > C) \rightarrow \{\alpha\}^k C,$$

where $\{\alpha\}^k = \{\alpha\} \overset{k\text{-time}}{\cdots\cdots} \{\alpha\}$.

Both parts of the lemma are proved by induction on k.

Let FD_1 be a calculus obtained from the calculus FD by replacing the rule $\rightarrow *$ by the rule in which the formula R is a program-free formula. Let us determine the *degree* of the *considered occurrence* of the *operator* $*$ as the number of occurrences of the operator $*$, present in the area of action of the occurrence of the operator $*$. An *iterative degree* of the *formula* B, denoted by $\|B\|^*$, is defined as max $(j_1, \ldots, j_r)$, where $j_k (1 \leq k \leq r)$ is a degree of the k-th occurrence of the operator $*$ in the formula B. Let S be an arbitrary sequent, an *iterative degree* of the sequent S, denoted by $\|S\|^*$, be defined as max $(\|A_1\|^*, \ldots, \|A_n\|^*)$, where $A_1, \ldots, A_n$ are the terms of the sequent S.

Lemma 1.5. *If* $\vdash_{FD_1} S$, *then* $\vdash_{SFD_o} S$.

To proof this we shall make use of induction on $\|S\|^*\omega+h$, i.e., double induction on $\|S\|^*$ and h, where h is the height of the given derivation. Consider only the case when the rule $\{\overline{*}\}$ was used last in the given derivation (other cases are considered by induction on h):

$$\frac{\rightarrow Q(n+1) > \neg\{\alpha\}\neg Q(n)}{\rightarrow Q(n) > \neg\{\alpha^*\}\neg Q(o)}\ \{\overline{*}\}$$

The formula $Q(n) > \neg\{\alpha^*\}\neg Q(o)$ denotes termination of the program α^* under the assumption $Q(n)$. It means that there exists a somewhat unfixed positive integer k such that $\vdash_{FD_1} \to Q(n) > \neg\{\alpha\}^k\neg Q(o)$. By applying the inductive assumption to the last sequent we obtain $\vdash_{SFD_o} \to Q(n) > \neg\{\alpha\}^k\neg Q(o)$ (1). Since Lemma 1.4 is valid for an arbitrary positive integer k and arbitrary formulas B, C, from (1) and Lemma 1.4(2) follows

$$\vdash_{SFD_o} Q(n),\ \{\alpha\}^k P(\bar{x}),\ \{\lambda\}\ddot{A}(P(\bar{x}) > \neg Q(o)) \to \quad (2),$$

where P is a predicate symbol, not occurring in Q, α. From (2) and Lemma 1.4(1) we get $\vdash_{SFD_o} Q(n),\ P(\bar{x}),\ \{\lambda\}\ddot{A}(P(\bar{x}) > \{\alpha\}P(\bar{x})),$ $\{\lambda\}\ddot{A}(P(\bar{x}) > \neg Q(o)) \to$ (3). By applying the rules $* \to$, $\to \neg$, $\to >$ to (3) we arrive at $\vdash_{SFD_o} \to Q(n) > \neg\{\alpha^*\}\neg Q(o)$. This proves the lemma.

Lemma 1.6. *If* $\vdash_{FD} S$, *then* $\vdash_{SFD_o} S$.

The validity of Lemma 1.6 follows from the Lemmas 1.1, 1.5.

Theorem 1.1. $\vdash_{FD} S$ *iff* $\vdash_{SFD_o} S$, *where* S *is a* λ*-free sequent.*

The validity of the theorem follows from the Lemmas 1.3 and 1.6.

Let SFD_1 be a calculus obtained from the calculus SFD_o by replacing the rule $\{\alpha\}'$ with the following rule:

$$\frac{\nabla,\ \Gamma \to B}{\nabla,\ \{x \leftarrow t\}\Gamma \to \{x \leftarrow t\}B}\ \{x \leftarrow t\},$$

where ∇ is a set consisting of modalized formulas.

Lemma 1.7. *The rule* $\{\alpha\}'$ *is admissible in the calculus* SFD_1.

The lemma is proved by induction on $|\alpha|$.

Let SFD_2 be a calculus, obtained from the calculus SFD_1 by replacing the rule $\rightarrow *$ with $\rightarrow *'$ in which the formula R is program-free.

As a corollary from Theorem 1.1 and Lemmas 1.1, 1.7 follows the validity of

Theorem 1.2. *The calculi* SFD_o, SFD_1, SFD_2 *are equivalent.*

Let SFD_3 be a calculus, obtained from the calculus SFD_2 by replacing the cut rule, i.e., the rule

$$\frac{\Gamma \rightarrow \Omega,\ B\ ;\ B,\ \Pi \rightarrow \Sigma}{\Gamma,\ \Pi \rightarrow \Omega,\ \Sigma},$$

with the following rule

$$\frac{\Gamma \rightarrow \Omega,\ M\ ;\ M,\ \Pi \rightarrow \Sigma}{\Gamma,\ \Pi \rightarrow \Omega,\ \Sigma}\ \text{cut}_a,$$

where M is either a program-free formula or the formula $\{x \leftarrow t\}Q$, and Q is a program-free formula.

The derivation in calculus SFD_2 will be called *pure* if 1) no variable occurs in this proof free and bound at the same time; 2) for each application of the quantifier rules $\rightarrow$ A, E $\rightarrow$ and the rule $* \rightarrow$, the eigen-variable of this application occurs only in the sequents located higher than its conclusion.

Lemma 1.8. *Let S be an arbitrary sequent in which no variable occurs free and bound at the same time. Thus, if* $\vdash_{SFD_0} S$, *then it is possible to construct a pure derivation of the sequent* S *in the calculus* SFD_2.

Proof of the lemma is evident (see, e.g., Lemmas 35, 36, 37, 38 in Kleene (1952)).

Theorem 1.3. *Given a pure derivation of the sequent* S *in the calculus* SFD_2, *it is possible to construct a pure derivation of the sequent* S *in the calculus* SFD_3.

To prove Theorem 1.3, it suffices to prove the following lemma.

Lemma 1.9. *Let a pure derivation of the sequent* S_1 *be given in the calculus* SFD_2, *the last step of which consists in the application of the cut rule, whose premises are the derivations in the calculus* SFD_3. *Then it is possible to construct a pure derivation of the sequent* S_1 *in the calculus* SFD_3.

Proof. The end of the given derivation is of the form

$$\frac{D_1\{\Gamma \to \Omega,\ B\ ;\ D_2\{B,\ \Pi \to \Sigma}{\Gamma,\ \Pi \to \Omega,\ \Sigma}\ cut$$

We shall make use of induction on $\|B|\ \omega + h_1 + h_2$, where h_1, h_2 are heights of the derivations D_1, D_2 and $\|B| = \langle|B|^*,\ |B|\rangle$; $|B|^*$ is an *iterative complexity* of *formula* B, determined by the number of occurrences of the operator $*$ in the formula B ; $|B|$ is the complexity of the formula B. We now must consider all the cases in accordance with what rules of inference i, j are used last in derivations D_1 and D_2 (the case, when one of the premises of the cut rule is an axiom, is analysed trivially). Consider, however, only a few characteristic cases in which both isolated occurrences of formula B are the main formulas of the rules of inference i and j (the case, when one of the isolated occurrences of formula B is not the main formula of the rule of inference i, j, is analysed by induction on height).

1. $i = \{x \leftarrow t\}$; $j = \{x \leftarrow t\}$:

$$\dfrac{\dfrac{\nabla_1,\ \Gamma \to D}{\nabla_1,\ \{x\leftarrow t\}\Gamma \to \{x\leftarrow t\}D}\{x\leftarrow t\} \qquad \dfrac{D,\ \Pi,\ \nabla_2 \to C}{\{x\leftarrow t\}D,\ \{x\leftarrow t\}\Pi,\ \nabla_2 \to \{x\leftarrow t\}C}\{x\leftarrow t\}}{\nabla_1,\ \nabla_2,\ \{x\leftarrow t\}(\Gamma,\ \Pi) \to \{x\leftarrow t\}C}\text{cut}$$

Let us construct the following derivation:

$$\dfrac{\dfrac{\nabla_1,\ \Gamma \to D\ ;\ D,\ \Pi,\ \nabla_2 \to C}{\nabla_1,\ \nabla_2,\ \Gamma,\ \Pi \to C}\text{cut}}{\nabla_1,\ \nabla_2,\ \{x\leftarrow t\}(\Gamma,\ \Pi) \to \{x\leftarrow t\}C}\{x\leftarrow t\}$$

The cut may be eliminated since $|D|^* = |\{x\leftarrow t\}D|^*$ and $|D| < |\{x\leftarrow t\}D|$.

2. $i = \to *$; $j = * \to$

$$\dfrac{\dfrac{\Gamma \to \Omega,\ R\ ;\ R \to \{\alpha\}R\ ;\ R \to D}{\Gamma \to \Omega,\ \{\alpha^*\}D}\to * \qquad \dfrac{D_2'\ \{P(\bar{x}),\ K,\ L,\ \Pi \to \Sigma}{\{\alpha^*\}D,\ \Pi \to \Sigma}* \to}{\Gamma,\ \Pi \to \Omega,\ \Sigma}\text{cut,}$$

where $K = \{\lambda\}\ddot{A}(P(\bar{x}) > \{\alpha\}P(\bar{x}))$; $L = \{\lambda\}\ddot{A}(P(\bar{x}) > D)$. In the derivation D_2' let us substitute a program-free formula R for all the occurrences of the formula $P(\bar{x})$. Since the given derivation is pure, we obtain a derivation D_2'' (instead of the derivation D_2') of the sequent

$$R,\ \{\lambda\}\ddot{A}(R > \{\alpha\}R),\ \{\lambda\}\ddot{A}(R > D),\ \Pi \to \Sigma.$$

It is easily seen that the desired derivation can be obtained from the derivation D_2'' and the derivations of the premises of the rule $\to *$, using induction on $\|B|$. This proves Lemma 1.9 as well as Theorem 1.3.

Let us introduce another alternative formulation of SFDL, which is more adjusted to the transition to the quasimodal SFDL (see part 2 of the given paper). Let us denote by SFD_i' $(i = 0, 1, 2)$ a calculus obtained from the calculus SFD_i (respectively) by the following transformations:

1) The language of the calculus SFD_i' is obtained from that of the calculus SFD_i by removing elementary program λ and adding the list of predicate symbols $\lambda, \lambda_1, \lambda_2, \ldots,$ called *marked predicate symbols;*

2) substituting for the rule $* \to$ the following rule

$$\frac{\lambda(\bar{x}),\ \ddot{A}(\lambda(\bar{x}) > \{\alpha\}\lambda(\bar{x})),\ \ddot{A}(\lambda(\bar{x}) > B),\ \Gamma \to \Omega}{\{\alpha^*\}B,\ \Gamma \to \Omega}\ *' \to,$$

where λ is a marked predicate symbol, not entering the conclusion of the rule $*'\to$; $\bar{x}$ is a list of free variables entering program α.

Formulas of the form $\ddot{A}(\lambda(\bar{x}) > \{\alpha\}\lambda(\bar{x})),\ \ddot{A}(\lambda(\bar{x}) > B)$ will be called *closed marked* formulas. A similar rule was used by Harel, Pnueli and Stavi (1977) in a weaker program logic than FDL.

3) Replacing the rules $\{\alpha\}'$, $\{x \leftarrow t\}$ by those in which set ∇ consists of closed marked formulas;

4) eliminating the rules $\to \lambda$, $\lambda \to$.

A sequent, not containing isolated predicate symbols, will be called λ-pure.

Remark. It is easily seen that Theorems 1.1 and 1.2 will be true if the calculus SFD'_i $(i = 0, 1, 2)$ is substituted for SFD_i.

PART 2: QUASIMODAL SFDL

Let us construct some fragment of SFDL, a quasimodal SFDL (QSFDL), aimed at expressing and proving traditional properties of programs (e.g., equivalence, partial and total correctness, inclusion of programs). In QSFDL there is no rule $\{x \leftarrow t\}$ giving SFDL "a shade" of modal logic, but worsening the proof-theoretical properties of SFDL. A formula $\{\alpha_1\} \ldots \{\alpha_n\}Q$ $(n = 0, 1, \ldots)$, where Q is a program-free formula, will be called *basic*. A formula will be called *quasimodal* if it is composed of basic formulas with the help of propositional connectives. We shall call a sequence $\Gamma \to \Omega$ *quasimodal* if Γ is composed either of quasimodal formulas or of formulas of the form $\ddot{A}(\lambda(\bar{x}) > B)$ (where λ is a marked predicate symbol, B is the basic formula), and Ω is composed either of quasimodal formulas or is an empty set. By *QD* let us denote a calculus, the rules of which are applied to quasimodal sequents and obtained by replacing "program" rules of the calculus SFD with the following ones (below, $\bar{\alpha}$ will mean either an empty word or a word of the form $\{\alpha_1\} \ldots \{\alpha_n\}$). The rules of the first group change the extreme program on the right into basic formulas:

$$\frac{\Gamma \to \Omega,\ \{\bar{\alpha}\}Q(t)}{\Gamma \to \Omega,\ \{\bar{\alpha}\}\{x \leftarrow t\}Q(x)} \to \overline{\leftarrow} \qquad \frac{\{\bar{\alpha}\}Q(t),\ \Gamma \to \Omega}{\{\bar{\alpha}\}\{x \leftarrow t\}Q(x),\ \Gamma \to \Omega} \overline{\leftarrow} \to$$

$$\frac{\Gamma \to \Omega,\ \{\bar{\alpha}\}(Q_1 > Q)}{\Gamma \to \Omega,\ \{\bar{\alpha}\}\{Q_1?\}Q} \to \overline{?} \qquad \frac{\{\bar{\alpha}\}(Q_1 > Q),\ \Gamma \to \Omega}{\{\bar{\alpha}\}\{Q_1?\}Q,\ \Gamma \to \Omega} \overline{?} \to$$

$$\frac{\Gamma \to \Omega,\ \boxed{\alpha}\{\alpha_1\}\{\alpha_2\}Q}{\Gamma \to \Omega,\ \boxed{\alpha}\{\alpha_1\ ;\ \alpha_2\}Q} \to \bar{;} \qquad \frac{\boxed{\alpha}\{\alpha_1\}\{\alpha_2\}Q,\ \Gamma \to \Omega}{\boxed{\alpha}\{\alpha_1\ ;\ \alpha_2\}Q,\ \Gamma \to \Omega} \bar{;} \to$$

$$\frac{\Gamma \to \Omega,\ \boxed{\alpha}\{\alpha_1\}Q;\ \Gamma \to \Omega,\ \boxed{\alpha}\{\alpha_2\}Q}{\Gamma \to \Omega,\ \boxed{\alpha}\{\alpha_1 \mid \alpha_2\}Q} \to \bar{|}$$

$$\frac{\boxed{\alpha}\{\alpha_1\}Q,\ \boxed{\alpha}\{\alpha_2\}Q,\ \Gamma \to \Omega}{\boxed{\alpha}\{\alpha_1 \mid \alpha_2\}Q,\ \Gamma \to \Omega} \bar{|} \to$$

$$\frac{\Gamma \to \Omega,\ \boxed{\alpha}R\ ;\ R \to \{\alpha_1\}R\ ;\ R \to Q}{\Gamma \to \Omega,\ \boxed{\alpha}\{\alpha_1{}^*\}Q} \to \bar{*}$$

$$\frac{\boxed{\alpha}\lambda(\bar{x}),\ \ddot{A}(\lambda(x) > \{\alpha_1\}\lambda(\bar{x})),\ \ddot{A}(\lambda(\bar{x}) > Q),\ \Gamma \to \Omega}{\boxed{\alpha}\{\alpha_1{}^*\}Q,\ \Gamma \to \Omega} \bar{*} \to,$$

where λ is a marked predicate symbol, not entering the conclusion, $\bar{x}$ is the list of free variables entering α_1.

The rules of the second group are quite analogous to the antecedent rules of the first group and transform the extreme program on the right into basic formulas, entering the antecedent ones of the form $\ddot{A}(\lambda > B)$:

$$\frac{\ddot{A}(\lambda(\bar{x}) > \boxed{\alpha}Q(t)),\ \Gamma \to \Omega}{\ddot{A}(\lambda(\bar{x}) > \boxed{\alpha}\{x \leftarrow t\}Q(x)),\ \Gamma \to \Omega}\ \mathrm{A}(x \leftarrow t) \to$$

$$\frac{\ddot{A}(\lambda(\bar{x}) > \boxed{\alpha}(Q_1 > \ Q)),\ \Gamma \to B}{\ddot{A}(\lambda(\bar{x}) > \boxed{\alpha}\{Q_1?\}Q),\ \Gamma \to B}\ \mathrm{A}? \to$$

$$\frac{\ddot{A}(\lambda(\bar{x}) > \boxed{\alpha}\{\alpha_1\}\{\alpha_2\}Q),\ \Gamma \to \Omega}{\ddot{A}(\lambda(\bar{x}) > \boxed{\alpha}\{\alpha_1\ ;\ \alpha_2\}Q),\ \Gamma \to \Omega}\ \mathrm{A}; \to$$

$$\frac{\ddot{A}(\lambda(\bar{x}) > \boxed{\alpha}\{\alpha_1\}Q),\ \ddot{A}(\lambda(\bar{x}) > \boxed{\alpha}\{\alpha_2\}Q),\Gamma \to \Omega}{\ddot{A}(\lambda > \boxed{\alpha}\{\alpha_1 \mid \alpha_2\}Q),\ \Gamma \to \Omega}\ \mathrm{A}| \to$$

$$\frac{\ddot{A}(\lambda(\bar{x}) > \boxed{\alpha}\lambda_1(\bar{x}_1)),\ \ddot{A}(\lambda_1(\bar{x}_1) > \{\alpha_1\}\lambda_1(\bar{x}_1)),\ \ddot{A}(\lambda_1(\bar{x}_1) > Q),\Gamma \to \Omega}{\ddot{A}(\lambda(\bar{x}) > \boxed{\alpha}\{\alpha_1{}^*\}Q),\ \Gamma \to \Omega}\ \mathrm{A}{*}\to,$$

where λ_1 is a marked predicate symbol, not entering the conclusion, $\overline{x}_1$ is the list of variables entering α_1.

Lemma 2.1. *The rules of inference of the calculus QD, besides the rules* $\overline{*}\to$, A$*\to$, *are derivable in the calculus* SFD'_o.

Let us consider only some rules of inference of the calculus *QD*.

1. Rule $\to \overline{;}$

$$\dfrac{\Gamma \to \Omega,\ \boxed{\{\alpha\}}\,\{\alpha_1\}\{\alpha_2\}Q\ ; \qquad \dfrac{\dfrac{\dfrac{\{\alpha_1\}\{\alpha_2\}Q \to \{\alpha_1\}\{\alpha_2\}Q}{\{\alpha_1\}\{\alpha_2\}Q \to \{\alpha_1\ ;\ \alpha_2\}Q}\ \to ;}{\dots}}{\boxed{\{\alpha\}}\,\{\alpha_1\}\{\alpha_2\}Q \to \boxed{\{\alpha\}}\,\{\alpha_1\ ;\ \alpha_2\}Q}\ \{\alpha\}'}{\Gamma \to \Omega,\ \boxed{\{\alpha\}}\,\{\alpha_1\ ;\ \alpha_2\}Q}\ \text{cut}$$

2. Rule $\to \overline{*}$

$$\dfrac{\Gamma \to \Omega,\ \boxed{\{\alpha\}}R \qquad \dfrac{\dfrac{\dfrac{R \to R\ ;\ R \to \{\alpha_1\}R\ ;\ R \to Q}{R \to \{\alpha_1{*}\}Q}\ \to *}{\dots}}{\boxed{\{\alpha\}}R \to \boxed{\{\alpha\}}\,\{\alpha_1{*}\}Q}\ \{\alpha\}'}{\Gamma \to \Omega,\ \boxed{\{\alpha\}}\,\{\alpha_1{*}\}Q}\ \text{cut}$$

Let QD^+ be a calculus obtained from the calculus *QD* by adding the rules of the calculus SFD'_o.

Lemma 2.2. *If* $\vdash_{QD^+} S$, *then* $\vdash_{SFD'_o} S$.

The lemma is proved by induction on the number n of applications of the rules $\overline{*}\rightarrow$, $A{*}\rightarrow$ in the given derivation. In the case of the basis the lemma is true by virtue of Lemma 2.1. The induction step is done analoguously to Lemma 1.2.

As a corollary from Lemma 2.2. we get the following

Lemma 2.3. *If* $\vdash_{QD} S$, *then* $\vdash_{SFD_0'} S$

To prove the inverse implication, we shall introduce an auxiliary calculus *QD'*. The language of the calculus *QD'* is obtained from that of the calculus *QD* by adding the *marked predicate symbols* λ_i' *associated* with the *marked predicate symbols* λ_i $(i = 1, 2, \ldots)$. The postulates of the calculus *QD'* are obtained from those of the calculus *QD* by the following transformations:

1) replacing the rule $\rightarrow\overline{*}$ by the following one:

$$\frac{\Gamma \rightarrow \Omega,\ \{\alpha\}\overline{R}\ ;\ \overline{R} \rightarrow \{\alpha_1\}\overline{R}\ ;\ \overline{R} \rightarrow Q}{\Gamma \rightarrow \Omega,\ \{\alpha\}\,\{\alpha_1^*\}Q} \rightarrow\overline{*}'$$

Here and below $\overline{R} = R(\overline{\lambda}' / \lambda)$; $\overline{\lambda}' = \lambda_1', \ldots, \lambda_n'$; $\overline{\lambda} = \lambda_1, \ldots$ $\ldots, \lambda_n$; $\overline{\lambda}' / \lambda$ denotes a substitution of $\overline{\lambda}'$ by $\overline{\lambda}$; $\overline{\lambda}'$ is called a *connected list* of the rule $\rightarrow\overline{*}'$;

2) adding the following rules:

$$\frac{\Gamma \rightarrow \Omega,\ B(\overline{\lambda})}{\Gamma \rightarrow \Omega,\ B(\overline{\lambda}')} \rightarrow\lambda' \qquad \frac{B(\overline{\lambda}),\ \Gamma \rightarrow \Omega}{B(\overline{\lambda}'),\ \Gamma \rightarrow \Omega} \lambda'\rightarrow$$

Lemma 2.4. *All the rules of inference of the calculus QD', besides the structural rules of thinning and cut, are invertible.*

The lemma is proved by induction on the height of the sequent, having the form of a conclusion of the rule of inference of QD'.

<u>Lemma 2.5.</u> *If* $\vdash_{QD'} \Gamma \to \Omega, \{\!\!\{\alpha\}\!\!\} B$, *then* $\vdash_{QD'} \Gamma \to \Omega, \{\!\!\{\alpha\}\!\!\}(B \vee C)$ *and* $\vdash_{QD'} \Gamma \to \Omega, \{\!\!\{\alpha\}\!\!\}(C \vee B)$.

The lemma is proved by induction on the height of the given derivation.

<u>Lemma 2.6.</u> *In the calculus* QD' *the following rules are admissible:*

$$\frac{\Gamma \to \Omega,\ \{\!\!\{\alpha\}\!\!\}\{\alpha_1\}\{\alpha_2\}\{\beta\}Q}{\Gamma \to \Omega,\ \{\!\!\{\alpha\}\!\!\}\{\alpha_1 ; \alpha_2\}\{\!\!\{\beta\}\!\!\}Q}\ \overline{\to ;'}, \qquad \frac{\{\!\!\{\alpha\}\!\!\}\{\alpha_1\}\{\alpha_2\}\{\!\!\{\beta\}\!\!\}Q,\ \Gamma \to \Omega}{\{\!\!\{\alpha\}\!\!\}\{\alpha_1 ; \alpha_2\}\{\!\!\{\beta\}\!\!\}Q,\ \Gamma \to \Omega}\ \overline{;'\to}$$

$$\frac{\Gamma \to \Omega,\ \{\!\!\{\alpha\}\!\!\}\{\alpha_1\}\{\!\!\{\beta\}\!\!\}Q\ ; \qquad \Gamma \to \Omega,\ \{\!\!\{\alpha\}\!\!\}\{\alpha_2\}\{\!\!\{\beta\}\!\!\}Q}{\Gamma \to \Omega,\ \{\!\!\{\alpha\}\!\!\}\{\alpha_1 \mid \alpha_2\}\{\!\!\{\beta\}\!\!\}Q}\ \overline{\to |'}$$

$$\frac{\{\!\!\{\alpha\}\!\!\}\{\alpha_1\}\{\!\!\{\beta\}\!\!\}Q,\ \{\!\!\{\alpha\}\!\!\}\{\alpha_2\}\{\!\!\{\beta\}\!\!\}Q,\ \Gamma \to \Omega}{\{\!\!\{\alpha\}\!\!\}\{\alpha_1 \mid \alpha_2\}\{\!\!\{\beta\}\!\!\}Q,\ \Gamma \to \Omega}\ \overline{|'\to}$$

$$\frac{\Gamma \to \Omega,\ \{\!\!\{\alpha\}\!\!\}\overline{R}\ ;\ \overline{R} \to \{\alpha_1\}\overline{R}\ ;\ \overline{R} \to \{\!\!\{\beta\}\!\!\}Q}{\Gamma \to \Omega,\ \{\!\!\{\alpha\}\!\!\}\{\alpha_1^*\}\{\!\!\{\beta\}\!\!\}Q}\ \overline{\to *'}$$

$$\frac{\{\!\!\{\alpha\}\!\!\}\lambda(\overline{x}),\ \ddot{A}(\lambda(\overline{x}) > \{\alpha_1\}\lambda(\overline{x})),\ \ddot{A}(\lambda(\overline{x}) > \{\!\!\{\beta\}\!\!\}Q),\ \Gamma \to \Omega}{\{\!\!\{\alpha\}\!\!\}\{\alpha_1^*\}\{\!\!\{\beta\}\!\!\}Q,\ \Gamma \to \Omega}\ \overline{*'\to}$$

The lemma is proved by induction on $|\overline{\beta}|$ using Lemmas 2.4 and 2.5.

<u>Lemma 2.7.</u> *In the calculus* QD' *the following rule is admissible:*

$$\frac{\nabla,\ \{\!\!\{\alpha_1\}\!\!\}Q_1,\ \ldots,\ \{\alpha_n\}Q_n \to \{\!\!\{\alpha_{n+1}\}\!\!\}Q_{n+1}}{\nabla,\ \{x \leftarrow t\}\{\!\!\{\alpha_1\}\!\!\}Q_1,\ \ldots,\ \{x \leftarrow t\}\{\!\!\{\alpha_n\}\!\!\}Q_n \to \{x \leftarrow t\}\{\!\!\{\alpha_{n+1}\}\!\!\}Q_{n+1}}\ \{x \leftarrow t\},$$

where ∇ is a set consisting of the closed marked formulas (see the end of Part 1).

To prove Lemma 2.7 let us make use of induction on $|\overline{\alpha}_1| + \ldots$
$\ldots + |\overline{\alpha}_{n+1}|$.

Basis: $|\overline{\alpha}_1| + \ldots + |\overline{\alpha}_{n+1}| = 0$. In this case the application of the rule $\{x \leftarrow t\}$ is of the form:

$$\frac{D\{\nabla,\ Q_1(x),\ \ldots,\ Q_n(x) \rightarrow Q_{n+1}(x)}{\nabla,\ \{x \leftarrow t\}Q_1(x),\ \ldots,\ \{x \leftarrow t\}Q_n(x) \rightarrow \{x \leftarrow t\}Q_{n+1}(x)}$$

In derivation D substitute a term t for all occurrences of variable x. Instead of derivation D we shall get a derivation D_1 of the sequent $\nabla,\ Q_1(t),\ \ldots,\ Q_n(t) \rightarrow Q_{n+1}(t)$. The derivation of the sequent $\nabla,\ \{x \leftarrow t\}Q_1(x),\ \ldots,\ \{x \leftarrow t\}Q_n(x) \rightarrow \{x \leftarrow t\}Q_{n+1}(x)$ will be obtained from the derivation D_1 by means of application of the rules $\overline{\leftarrow}\rightarrow$, $\rightarrow\overline{\leftarrow}$.

The induction step is done by means of Lemma 2.4. This proves the lemma.

As a corollary from Lemmas 2.6 and 2.7 we get the following

Lemma 2.8. *If* $\vdash_{SFD'_0} S$, *then* $\vdash_{QD'} S$, *where* S *is a quasimodal sequent.*

Let $(j)\ \rightarrow\overline{*}'$ denote an application (in the derivation considered) of the rule $\rightarrow\overline{*}'$, denoted by j ; $(j_1, \ldots, j_n)\ \overline{*}\rightarrow$ denotes n applications of the rule $\overline{*}\rightarrow$ (in the considered derivation, too), denoted by $j_1, \ldots, j_n$. A pair $((j) \rightarrow \overline{*}', (j_1, \ldots, j_n)\overline{*}\rightarrow)$ will be called *associated* if $\overline{\lambda} = \lambda_1, \ldots, \lambda_n$, where $\lambda_1, \ldots, \lambda_n$ are eigen-variables of the applications $j_1, \ldots, j_n$ of the rule $\overline{*}'\rightarrow$, and $\overline{\lambda}'$ is a connected list of the application j of the rule $\rightarrow\overline{*}'$. We shall call an associated pair $((j)\rightarrow\overline{*}', (j_1, \ldots, j_n)\overline{*}\rightarrow)$ *regular* if all the $j_1, \ldots,$

j_n applications of the rule $\overline{*}\rightarrow$ are lower than the j-th application of the rule $\rightarrow\overline{*}'$. The derivation in the calculus QD' will be called *regular* if all the associated pairs of the applications of the rules $\rightarrow\overline{*}'$, $\overline{*}\rightarrow$ are regular.

Lemma 2.9. *An arbitrary derivation in the calculus QD' may be transformed into a regular one with the same last sequent.*

The lemma is proved by induction on the number of irregular associated pairs of applications for the rules $\rightarrow\overline{*}'$, $\overline{*}\rightarrow$. In the case of the basis the lemma is true.

Induction step. Consider the very upper irregular associated pair of applications of the rules $\rightarrow\overline{*}'$, $\overline{*}\rightarrow$. Let D be a derivation of the conclusion of application of the rule $\rightarrow\overline{*}'$ of this pair. To justify the induction step, induction on the height of derivation D is used.

As a corollary from Lemma 2.9 we get the following

Lemma 2.10. *An arbitrary derivation in the calculus QD' may be reconstructed in calculus QD with the same last sequent.*

As a corollary from Lemmas 2.3, 2.8, 2.10 we get

Theorem 2.1. $\vdash_{SFD'_0} S$ *iff* $\vdash_{QD} S$, *where S is a quasimodal sequent.*

Let QD_1 be the calculus obtained from QD by changing the rule $\rightarrow\overline{*}$ into the rule, where R is a program-free formula. As a corollary from theorems 1.1. 1.2 and the remark, concluding Part 1, we obtain

Lemma 2.11. *The calculi QD and QD_1 are equivalent.*

Let QD_2 be a calculus obtained from the calculus QD_1 by changing the cut rule into the rule

$$\frac{\Gamma \to \Omega, Q \; ; \; Q, \Pi \to \Sigma}{\Gamma, \Pi \to \Omega, \Sigma} \text{cut}'$$

where Q is a program-free formula.

Theorem 2.2. *Let a pure derivation of the sequent S in the calculus QD_1 be given. Then we may construct a pure derivation of the sequent S in the calculus QD_2.*

The proof of Theorem 2.2. is analogous to that of Theorem 1.3.

Let QD_3 be a calculus differing from the calculus QD_2 in that the parametric formulas in the cut' rule are program-free.

Lemma 2.12. *If* $\vdash_{QD_2} S$, *then* $\vdash_{QD_3} S$.

The lemma is proved by the number of applications of the cut' rule to the given derivation. To justify the induction step, induction on the derivation height of the conclusion of the very upper application of the cut' rule is used.

As a corollary from Lemma 2.12 as well as from the form of rules of the calculus QD_3 we get

Theorem 2.3. *The sequent* $\to \neg\{\alpha\}\neg B$ *is decidable with respect to theory T.*

PART 3: PDL AND SPDL

The PDL language consists of two types of variables: program variables γ, γ_1, γ_2, ... and propositional variables P, P_1, P_2, ... Let us simultaneously define the concept of a *program* and a *formula* of PDL: 1) every program variable is a program, a propositional variable is a formula; 2) if α, β are programs and B, C are formulas, then the expressions $(\alpha ; \beta)$, $(\alpha \mid \beta)$, α^* are programs and $(B > C)$, $(B \& C)$, $(B \vee C)$, $\neg B$ are formulas. Let us denote by *PD* a calculus obtained from the calculus *FD*: 1) by replacing the predicative calculus *LK* with the propositional calculus *LK*; 2) by eliminating the axiom scheme $\vdash_T S$; 3) by eliminating the rules of inference $\rightarrow\leftarrow$, $\leftarrow\rightarrow$; 4) by replacing the rules of inference $\{*\}$, $\{\alpha\}$ with the following ones, respectively:

$$\frac{B,\ \{\alpha\}\{\alpha^*\}B,\ \Gamma \rightarrow \Omega}{\{\alpha^*\}B,\ \Gamma \rightarrow \Omega}\ *_o\!\rightarrow \qquad \frac{\Gamma \rightarrow B}{\{\gamma\}\Gamma \rightarrow \{\gamma\}B}\ \{\gamma\}$$

The calculus *PD* is a sequential axiomatization of PDL, the completeness of which has been proved by many authors (see, e.g., Parikh (1978), Nishimura (1979)).

Let us introduce the symmetric PDL (SPDL). The language of SPDL is obtained from that of PDL by joining a program variable λ interpreted as a reflexive and transitive binary relation. Let us denote by *SPD* a calculus, obtained from the calculus *PD* 1) by changing the rules $*_o\!\rightarrow$ and $\{\gamma\}$ into the following ones:

$$\frac{P,\ \{\lambda\}(P > \{\alpha\}P),\ \{\lambda\}(P > B),\ \Gamma \rightarrow \Omega}{\{\alpha^*\}B,\ \Gamma \rightarrow \Omega}\ *\!\rightarrow$$

where P is a propositional variable called *eigen-variable* of this rule, not occurring in the conclusion; a formula of the form $\{\lambda\}B$ will be called *modalized;*

$$\frac{\nabla,\ \Gamma \to B}{\nabla,\ \{\gamma\}\Gamma \to \{\gamma\}B}\ \{\gamma\}',$$

where ∇ is a set consisting of modalized formulas; 2) by adding the rules $\to\lambda$, $\lambda\to$ of the calculus SFD_O:

$$\frac{\{\lambda\}\Gamma \to B}{\{\lambda\}\Gamma \to \{\lambda\}B}\ \to\lambda \qquad\qquad \frac{B,\ \{\lambda\}B,\ \Gamma \to \Omega}{\{\lambda\}B,\ \Gamma \to \Omega}\ \lambda\to$$

A sequent not containing the program variable λ will be called *λ-free*.

Remark. The rule for operating with negative occurrences of the operator * in the calculi SFD_O and SPD (contrary to FD and PD) is almost of the same form. The rules of SPD as well as those of SFD_O are symmetric.

Lemma 3.1. *If $\vdash_{SPD} S$, then $\vdash_{PD} S$, where S is a λ-free sequent.*

Lemma 3.1 is proved quite analogously to Lemma 1.3.

Lemma 3.2. *In the calculus SPD the following rule is admissible*

$$\frac{\nabla,\ \Gamma \to B}{\nabla,\ \{\alpha\}\Gamma \to \{\alpha\}B}\ \{\alpha\}'$$

The lemma is proved by induction on $|\alpha|$.

Lemma 3.3. *If $\vdash_{PD} S$, then $\vdash_{SPD} S$.*

To prove the lemma, it suffices to make sure that (a) $\vdash_{SPD} \rightarrow$ $\rightarrow \{\alpha^*\}B > B$; (b) $\vdash_{SPD} \rightarrow \{\alpha^*\}B > \{\alpha\}\{\alpha^*\}B$. For (b) Lemma 3.2. is used.

As a corollary from Lemmas 3.1 and 3.3 we get

Theorem 3.1. $\vdash_{PD} S$ *iff* $\vdash_{SPD} S$, *where* S *is a* λ-*free sequent.*

We shall point out a simple property of the calculus *SPD*, distinguishing it from the calculus *PD*. This property will be important in the constructive proof of the elimination theorem for *SPD*.

We shall call the axiom $B \rightarrow B$ *elementary* if $B = P$ (i.e., B is a propositional variable). The derivation in the calculus *SPD* will be called *reduced* if all the axioms are elementary.

Lemma 3.4. *An arbitrary derivation in the calculus SPD may be transformed into a reduced one with the same last sequent.*

The lemma is proved by induction on $|B|$.

The sequent $\{\alpha^*\}B \rightarrow \{\alpha^*\}B$ is a counterexample to Lemma 3.4 in the case of calculus *PD*.

Let SPD_1 be the calculus, obtained from the calculus *SPD* by changing the axiom $B \rightarrow B$ into the axiom $P \rightarrow P$. As a corollary from Lemma 3.4. we get

Lemma 3.5. $\vdash_{SPD} S$ *iff* $\vdash_{SPD_1} S$.

For the constructive proof of the elimination theorem let us introduce a conservative extension of SPDL, i.e., the so-called SPDL with indices (SPDLI). The SPDLI language is obtained from the SPDL language by adding *propositional variables with the indices* $P_i^{(k)}$, $k = 0, 1, 2, \ldots$, $P_i^{(0)}$ is identified with P_i. To determine the formula, we shall make the restriction that one and the same formula may contain propositional variables only with identical indices. The notation $B^{(i)}$ will mean that formula B contains propositional variables with index i. Denote by SPD_1' the calculus obtained from the calculus SPD_1 by 1) changing the axiom $P \rightarrow P$ into the axiom $P^{(i)} \rightarrow P^{(k)}$; 2) changing the rules $\rightarrow *$, $* \rightarrow$ into the following ones:

$$\frac{\Gamma \rightarrow \Omega,\ R^{(i+1)} \ ;\ R^{(i+1)} \rightarrow \{\alpha\} R^{(i+1)} \ ;\ R^{(i+1)} \rightarrow B^{(i+1)}}{\Gamma \rightarrow \Omega,\ \{\alpha *\} B^{(i)}} \rightarrow *'$$

$$\frac{P^{(i+1)},\ \{\lambda\}(P^{(i+1)} > \{\alpha\} P^{(i+1)})\ \{\lambda\}(P^{(i+1)} > B^{(i+1)}),\ \Gamma \rightarrow \Omega}{\{\alpha *\} B^{(i)},\ \Gamma \rightarrow \Omega} *' \rightarrow,$$

where $P^{(i+1)}$ is a propositional variable not entering the conclusion and called *eigen-variable* of the rule $*' \rightarrow$.

It is obvious that the following lemma is valid.

Lemma 3.6. *Let S be a sequent nor containing propositional variables with indices, then an arbitrary derivation D of the sequent S in the calculus SPD_1' may be reconstructed as a derivation D_1 in the calculus SPD_1, if the derivation D did not have applications of the cut rule, the derivation D_1 does not have applications of the cut rule, either, and conversely, i.e., if $\vdash_{SPD_1} S$ then $\vdash_{SPD_1'} S$.*

Lemma 3.7. *In the calculus SPD_1' the sequent $B^{(i)} \rightarrow B^{(j)}$ is derivable.*

The lemma is proved by induction on $|B|$.

A derivation in the calculus SPD_1' will be called *pure* if for every application of the rule $*' \rightarrow$ the eigen-variable of this application enters only the sequents located higher than this application. It is obvious that the following lemma is valid.

Lemma 3.8. *An arbitrary derivation in the calculus* SPD_1' *may be transformed into a pure one with the same last sequent.*

Theorem 3.2. *Let a derivation of the sequent S in the calculus* SPD_1' *be given. Then it is possible to construct a derivation of the same sequent S, not containing applications of the cut rule.*

To prove Theorem 3.2, it suffices to prove the following

Lemma 3.9. *Let in the calculus* SPD_1' *a pure derivation of the sequent S be given, whose final step consists in the application of the cut rule and which, apart from this, does not contain cuts. Then it is possible to construct a new pure derivation of the sequent* S_1, *not containing cuts.*

The end of the given derivation is of the form:

$$\frac{D_1\{\Gamma \to \Omega, B^{(i)} \quad ; \quad D_2\{B^{(i)}, \Gamma \to \Omega}{\Gamma, \Pi \to \Omega, \Sigma}\text{cut}$$

A pair $<\frac{1}{2i}, |B^{(i)}|>$ will be called the *order* of *formula* $B^{(i)}$. The order of the formula $B^{(i)}$ will be denoted by $\|B^{(i)}\|$. To prove Lemma 3.9, we shall make use of induction on $\|B^{(i)}\|\omega + h_1 + h_2$, where h_i is the height of the derivation D_i $(i = 1, 2)$.

Consider only two typical cases.

1. One of the premises of the cut rule is an axiom. Since axioms are elementary, the cut rule cannot be the main formula for the nonstructural rule j, used in the other premise last. Therefore a

cut may be applied to the premises of the rule j, and after that eliminated, making use of induction on hight. If the rule j is a structural rule of thinning and the cut formula is the main formula for this application, then the desired derivation is obtained from the premise of the considered application of the rule of thinning by means of applying the rule of thinning.

2. The end of the given derivation is of the form:

$$\dfrac{\dfrac{\Gamma \to \Omega,\ R^{(i+1)} \ ;\ R^{(i+1)} \to \{\alpha\}R^{(i+1)} \ ;\ R^{(i+1)} \to B^{(i+1)}}{\Gamma \to \Omega,\ \{\alpha^*\}B^{(i)}} \to *' \qquad \dfrac{D_2'\{\ S_2'}{\{\alpha^*\}B^{(i)},\ \Gamma \to \Omega} *' \to}{\Gamma,\ \Pi \to \Omega,\ \Sigma} cut,$$

where $S_2' = P^{(i+1)},\ \{\lambda\}(P^{(i+1)} > \{\alpha\}P^{(i+1)}),\ \{\lambda\}(P^{(i+1)} > B^{(i+1)}), \Pi \to \Sigma$.

In the derivation D_2' let us substitute formula $R^{(i+1)}$ for all occurrences of the propositional variable $P^{(i+1)}$. Since the given derivation is pure, $R^{(i+1)}$ does not contain eigen-variables of the rule $*' \to$, contained in derivation D_2'. Therefore, using Lemmas 3.7, 3.8 instead of derivation D_2' of the sequent S_2', we can construct a pure derivation D_2'' of the sequent $R^{(i+1)},\ \{\lambda\}(R^{(i+1)} > \{\alpha\}R^{(i+1)}),\ \{\lambda\}(R^{(i+1)} > B^{(i+1)}),\ \Pi \to \Sigma$. The desired derivation may obviously be obtained from the derivations of the premises of rule $\to *'$ and from derivation D_2''. While constructing the derivation, all the occurring applications of the cut rule may be eliminated by induction on the cut rule order.

This proves Lemma 3.9. and Theorem 3.2.

Let SPD_2 be a calculus obtained from the calculus SPD by eliminating the cut rule. As a corollary from Lemmas 3.5, 3.6 and Theorem 3.2 we get

Theorem 3.3. (elimination theorem for SPDL). *The cut rule is admissible in calculus* SPD_2.

Remark 1. The method of indices used for the constructive proof of the elimination theorem for *SPD* can easily be changed to eliminate cut in logics of a higher order implying the properties of symmetry and axiom elementarity.

Remark 2. Analogously, having changed the proof of Theorem 3.1, the elimination theorem for PDL may be obtained.

REFERENCES

Ershov, Y. L., 1983, Dynamic Logic over Admissible Sets, Dokl. Akad. Nauk USSR, 273:1045-1048.

Gentzen, G., 1934/35, Untersuchungen über das logische Schließen, Math. Zeitschr., 39:176-210, 405-431.

Harel, D., 1979, First-order Dynamic Logic, Lect. Notes Comp. Sci., 68.

Harel, D., Meyer, A. R. and Pratt, V. R., 1977, Computability and Completeness in Logic of Programs, in: "Proc. 9th Ann. ACM Symp. on Theory of Computing," Boulder, Col., 261-268.

Harel, D., Pnueli, A. and Stavi, J., 1977, A Complete Axiomatic System for Proving Deductions about Recursive Programs, in: "Proc. 9th Ann. ACM Symp. on Theory of Computing," 249-260.

Hilbert, D. and Bernays, P., 1934, "Grundlagen der Mathematik, I," Springer, Berlin.

Hoare, C. A. R., 1969, An Axiomatic Basis for Computer Programming, Journal of the ACM, 12:576-580.

Kleene, S. K., 1952, "Introduction to Metamathematics," North-Holland, Amsterdam.

Meyer, A. R. and Halpern, J., 1982, Axiomatic Definitions of Programming Languages: A Theoretical Assessment, Journal of the ACM, 29:555-576.

Nishimura, H., 1979, Sequential Method in Propositional Dynamic Logic, Acta Informatica, 12:377-400.

Parikh, R., 1978, A Completeness Result for PDL, Lect. Notes Comp. Sci., 64:403-416.

Pratt, V. R., 1976, Semantical Considerations on Floyd-Hoare Logic, in: "Proc. 17th IEEE Symp. on Found. of Comp. Sci.," 109-121.

Pratt, V. R., 1979, Dynamic Logic, Mathematical Centre Tracts (Amsterdam), 109:53-82.

Salwicki, A., 1970, A Formalized Algorithmic Language, Bull. Acad. Pol. Sci., Ser. Sci. Math. Astr. Phys., 18:227-232.

Salwicki, A., 1977, Algorithmic Logic, a Tool for Investigations of Programs, in: "Proc. of 5th Int. Congress of Logic, Meth. and Ph. of Sci.," I, 281-295, Reidel, Dordrecht.

SEMANTIC GAMES ON FINITE TREES

Jari Talja

Department of Philosophy
University of Turku
SF-20500 Turku 50

1. INTRODUCTION

The early work of Kobrinskii and Trakhtenbrot (1965) and of Büchi (1962) established an "equivalence" between the monadic second-order theory of finite linear orders and the regular sets - in the following sense:

(+) Regular sets are exactly those definable in a second-order monadic predicate language.

McNaughton & Papert (1971) established a similar "equivalence" between the first-order theory of finite linear orders and the star free (non-counting) regular sets.

It was implicit in the work of Büchi that there is a similar "equivalence" between the monadic second-order theory of ω and the ω-regular sets. This result was made explicit by Ladner (1977) by using the very elegant method of model-theoretic games. Ladner also conjectured that there would be a similar "equivalence" between the first-order theory of ω and the ω-star free sets.

The main thrust of this paper is to establish an "equivalence" between the monadic second-order theory of finite trees and the regular forests. The approach will be that of model-theoretic games, and will be rather similar to that of Ladner (1977).

In the case of trees some complications are encountered, however. In proving (+) finite words over a suitable alphabet are regarded as the finite models of the language in question. If L_1 and L_2 are regular languages over the fixed alphabet, it is fairly easy (cf. Ladner (1977) Thm. 4.3) to construct a sentence $A_{L_1L_2}$ such that for every word $x_1 \ldots x_k$ over the fixed alphabet it holds that

$$(1)\ x_1 \ldots x_k \models A_{L_1L_2} \text{ iff } x_1 \ldots x_l \in L_1 \text{ and } x_{l+k} \ldots x_k \in L_2$$
(for some index l)

But, if one considers the counterpart of this for trees, one immediately encounters a difficulty typical for trees. For, consider the z-product of two trees t and u (cf. Section 5 for definitions). In the product tree $t \cdot_z u$ the occurrences of z as labels in u are substituted by the symbol root(t), and hence some nodes in u may be relabelled. For example, consider the trees given in Figure 1.

Their z-product $t \cdot_z u$ is the tree given in Figure 2, where the substitution has taken place in the encircled nodes.

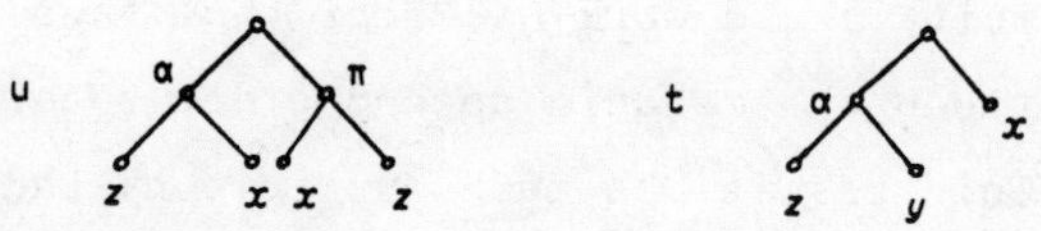

Fig. 1.

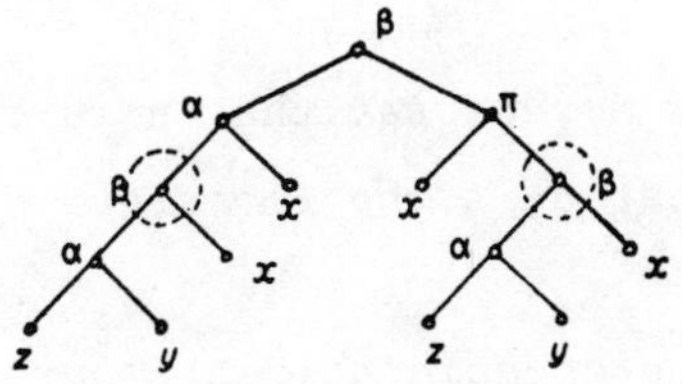

Fig. 2.

If T_1 and T_2 are regular forests and one considers, how to construct a sentence doing the similar job of $A_{L_1L_2}$ in (1), one has to be able to test for a given tree v, whether or not the tree obtained from v by reading it from the root towards the frontier up to some subset X of nodes is in the forest T_1, when the non-leaf nodes of X are relabelled by z. Such a procedure calls for "non-standard" models which allow improper labelling and yet preserve information of the tree. Such non-standard models, below called pseudotrees, are logically handled by a special quantified modal language, containing the usual monadic second-order predicate language.

Section 2 presents the basic definitions concerning trees and pseudotrees. Section 3 presents the object language of our study, and develops the necessary semantical theory for it. Section 4 discusses model-theoretic games on trees and pseudo-trees. Finally, Section 5 presents and proves the main theorem, and considers a simple decision problem.

2. TREE DOMAINS, TREES AND PSEUDOTREES

Let N* = (N, ., 0) be the free monoid generated by the set N of natural numbers (including 0). Define a partial ordering on N* as follows:

$p \leq q$ iff $p \cdot p' = q$ for some $p' \in N^*$

If $p = q \cdot i$ $(i \in N)$, we say that p is the i'th *immediate successor* of q, and that q is the *immediate predecessor* of p.

Definition 2.1. A *tree domain* is a nonempty subset D of N^* satisfying the following three conditions:

(D1) $p \leq q$ and $q \in D$ imply $p \in D$.

(D2) $p \cdot j \in D$ and $i < j$ imply $p \cdot i \in D$ $(i, j \in N)$

(D3) There is a number $n \in N$ such that no element of D has more than n immediate successors in D.

A tree domain may be finite or infinite. In this paper we shall be discussing only finite domains. The elements of a tree domain are called its *nodes*. Nodes maximal with respect to the ordering $\leq$ are called *leaves*. The *rank* of node p, $r_D(p)$, is the number of its immediate successors in D.

Definition 2.2. A tree *subdomain* of a tree domain E is a nonempty subset D of E satisfying the following two conditions.

(SD1) $r \leq p \leq q$, $r \in D$ and $q \in D$ imply $p \in D$.

(SD2) $p \cdot i \in D$ and $p \cdot j \in E$ imply $p \cdot j \in D$.

Definition 2.3. A *ranked alphabet* is a finite nonempty set Σ of symbols with a mapping $r: \Sigma \rightarrow N$ which assigns a non-negative *rank* to each symbol $\delta \in \Sigma$.

Below r is sometimes not mentioned. Instead, Σ is expressed as a union $\Sigma_0 \cup \Sigma_1 \cup \ldots$, where for each $m \geq 0$: $\Sigma_m = \{\delta: r(\delta) = m\}$. Notice that $\Sigma_m \neq \emptyset$ for a finite number of m's only.

Definition 2.4. A Σ-tree over a tree domain D is a mapping $f: D \to \Sigma$ such that for all nodes p in D:

$$r(f(p)) = r_D(p).$$

For each node p in D the element f(p) is called the *label* of p.

Let X be an alphabet (in the ordinary sense) disjoint from the ranked alphabet Σ. Let Σ^X be the ranked alphabet obtained by adding the letters of X to Σ as nullary symbols. Then a Σ*X-tree* is a finite Σ^X-tree as defined above. The set of ΣX-trees is denoted by $F_\Sigma(X)$. Subsets of $F_\Sigma(X)$ are called Σ*X-forests.*

It is often more convenient to define ΣX-trees as Σ-terms in variables X. Then $F_\Sigma(X)$ will be the smallest set such that

(T1) $X \cup \Sigma_0 \subseteq F_\Sigma(X)$

(T2) $\delta(t_1, \ldots, t_m) \in F_\Sigma(X)$ whenever $m \geq 0$, $\delta \in \Sigma_m$ and $t_1, \ldots, t_m \in F_\Sigma(X)$.

There is a simple inductive translation back to the original definition of $F_\Sigma(X)$. Hence, the two definitions can be used in parallel.

Definition 2.5. A Σ*X-pseudotree* defined over a tree domain D is a mapping $f: D \to \Sigma^X$ satisfying

(P1) $f(p) \in \Sigma$ implies $r(f(p)) = r_D(p)$

(P2) $\Sigma_{r_D(p)} \neq \emptyset$ $(\forall p \in D)$.

It follows from the definitions that each ΣX-tree is a ΣX-pseudotree. In a proper ΣX-pseudotree some nodes, which are not leaves, are labeled by symbols from X. However, condition (P2) guarantees that each ΣX-pseudotree can be converted into a ΣX-tree by relabelling some nodes. The set of ΣX-pseudotrees is denoted by $PF_{\Sigma}(X)$.

3. THE OBJECT LANGUAGE

In what follows the ranked alphabet Σ will be kept fixed. In the construction of ΣX-regular forests (cf. Section 5) it may be necessary to use auxiliary terminal alphabets of unlimited (yet finite) cardinality, the symbols of which do not occur in the ΣX-trees themselves. This fact will be of importance in the sequel. Hence, we shall allow the case of X being a denumerably infinite set of symbols such that $\Sigma \cap X = \emptyset$. In every special case we shall consider only finite subsets of X. Hence, it follows that we can stick to those definitions of ΣX-trees and ΣX-pseudotrees which were presented in Section 2.

As the object language of the discussion we shall use a second-order monadic quantified model language $M_{\Sigma X}$, the alphabet of which is given in the next definition.

Definition 3.1. (i) The *logical alphabet* of the language $M_{\Sigma X}$ consists of the following symbols:

(1) $p, q, r, p_1, q_1, \ldots$	individual variables
(2) $P, Q, R, P_1, Q_1, \ldots$	set variables
(3) $\wedge, \vee, \supset, \equiv, \sim$	propositional connectives
(4) $\forall, \exists$	quantifiers
(5) $\circledequal$	identity symbol
(6) $\circledin$	symbol of elementhood
(7) $\Box_x^R$	modal operator for each set variable R and $x \in X$.

(ii) The *non-logical* alphabet of $M_{\Sigma X}$ consists of the following symbols

(8) $\circledless$	binary predicate symbol, first order
(9) U_δ	unary predicate symbol, first order, $\delta \in \Sigma \cup X$
(10) S_i	unary predicate symbol, first order, $i \in N$.

The clause (7) brings a denumerably infinite set of modal operators into the language $M_{\Sigma X}$.

The definition of the well-formed formulas is the standard one, save for the clause for the modal operator:

($\square$) If A is a wff, $x \in X$, and R is a set variable, then $\square_x^R$ A is a wff.

An occurrence of a variable is *bound* if it is in the scope of a corresponding quantifier, otherwise an occurrence is *free*. Hence, in the wff $\square_x^R$ A the occurrence of the variable R attached to the modal operator is always free. A *closed formula* or a *sentence* is a wff with no free variable occurrences.

Next, we shall define the semantics of $M_{\Sigma X}$, and prove some model-theoretic results necessary for our purposes.

Denote by $\Sigma(f)$ the set of those symbols of Σ which occur as labels in the pseudotree f. Let t be a fixed tree. Define the associated set of pseudotrees W_t as follows:

$$W_t = \{f\colon f \in PF_\Sigma(X),\ dom(f) = dom(t),\ \Sigma(f) \subseteq \Sigma(t)\}.$$

In particular then, $t \in W_t$. The set W_t can be thought of as the centered neighbourhood around t. It is the set of those pseudotrees which share the unlabelled tree structure and labels from Σ with t. In modal logical terms, W_t is the set of those points which count in the evaluation of the modal operators.

The semantics of $M_{\Sigma X}$ is a modification of the well-known Scott-Montague semantics for modal logic, cf. Bowen (1979).

Definition 3.2. Let $t \in F_\Sigma(X)$. The *modal t-frame* is the ordered triple $\langle t, D, \emptyset \rangle$ where $D = \mathrm{dom}(t)$ and $\emptyset$ is the mapping

$$\emptyset\colon X \times W_t \times p(D) \rightarrow W_t$$

defined as follows: for each $d \in D$, $f \in W_t$ and $E \in p(D)$:

$$\emptyset(x, f, E)(d) = \begin{cases} f(d), & \text{if } d \notin E \\ x, & \text{if } d \in E \end{cases}$$

Intuitively speaking, $\emptyset$ relabels the nodes in E by x, and leaves others as such. Note that the t-frame is uniquely determined by t.

Definition 3.3. Let $t \in F_\Sigma(X)$ and let $\langle t, D, \emptyset \rangle$ be the modal t-frame. A *t-model* over the frame $\langle t, D, \emptyset \rangle$ is a family of ordered quadruples

$$(A_f)_{f \in W_t} = (\langle f, D_f, \emptyset, V \rangle)_{f \in W_t},$$

where for each f in W_t: $D_f = D$, and V is a valuation function in the ordinary sense of second-order predicate logic, mapping individual variables to elements of D, and set variables to subsets of D.

As symbols for t-models we shall in the sequel use L_t. Each quadruple A_f (f $\in W_t$) is called a *point* or a *possible world* of the t-model L_t.

Each wff is evaluated - as is usual in modal logic - in a point of a t-model L_t. For this, let A_f be an arbitrary point of a t-model L_t. If B is a wff, we shall write $A_f \models B$ to mean "B is satisfied in the possible world A_f". The definition of satisfaction is the usual one for propositional connectives and quantifiers. Satisfaction conditions for other cases are:

(1) $A_f \models p \circledequal r$ iff $V(p) = V(r)$
(2) $A_f \models p \circledless r$ iff $V(p) \leq V(r)$ (ordering in N*)
(3) $A_f \models U_\delta(p)$ iff $f(V(p)) = \delta$
(4) $A_f \models S_i(p)$ iff $V(p) = d \,.\, i$ (for some d $\in$ D)
(5) $A_f \models \Box^R_x B$ iff $A_{\emptyset(x,f,V(R))} \models B$

According to this definition each variable (whether individual or set variable) is regarded as a rigid designator. In other words, a variable designates the same "object" in each point (possible world) of the model. In addition, each object, which "exists" in one of the possible worlds, exists in all of them. On this relies the validity of the generalized Barcan formula (cf. below).

Definition 3.4. (i) A wff A is *valid in the t-model* L_t, if it is satisfied in each point of the model. If A is valid in L_t, we write $L_t \models A$.

(ii) A wff A is *valid* or *universally true*, if A is valid in every model L_t (t $\in F_\Sigma(X)$). If A is valid, we write $\models A$.

Now it is fairly easy to show that each modal operator $\Box^R_x$ distributes over the propositional connectives. In other words, we have

$$\models \Box_x^R \sim A \equiv \sim \Box_x^R A$$
$$\models \Box_x^R (A \wedge B) \equiv (\Box_x^R A \wedge \Box_x^R B)$$
$$\models \Box_x^R (A \vee B) \equiv (\Box_x^R A \vee \Box_x^R B)$$
$$\models \Box_x^R (A \supset B) \equiv (\Box_x^R A \supset \Box_x^R B)$$
$$\models \Box_x^R (A \equiv B) \equiv (\Box_x^R A \equiv \Box_x^R B)$$

By the definition of a universally true wff, we also have:

if $\models A$, then $\models \Box_x^R A$ (for each R and x)

As was already noted, the special feature of the t-models is that the universe of each of the possible worlds is constant, namely the set dom(t). From this it follows that the usual counterexamples to the Barcan formula cannot be constructed, cf. Kripke (1971) and Bowen (1979). In the usual quantified modal logic the Barcan formula is

(B) $\forall x \Box A \supset \Box \forall x A$.

In the language $M_{\Sigma X}$ the Barcan formula has a denumerably infinite number of analogues, since the modal operator brings a free variable occurrence into the formula.

Lemma 3.5. $\models \forall p \Box_x^R A \equiv \Box_x^R \forall p A$.

Proof. Let $t \in F_\Sigma(X)$, $D = \text{dom}(t)$, L_t an arbitrary t-model, and A_f a fixed point of L_t. By the definition of satisfaction we now get the following sequence of equivalences:

$$A_f \models \forall p \Box_x^R A \Leftrightarrow \langle f, D, \emptyset, V(p/d)\rangle \models \Box_x^R A \text{ for every } d \in D$$
$$\Leftrightarrow \langle \emptyset(x, f, V(p/d)(R), \emptyset, V(p/d)\rangle \models A \text{ for every } d \in D$$
$$\Leftrightarrow \emptyset(x, f, V(R)), D, \emptyset, V\rangle \models \forall p A$$

$\Leftrightarrow \langle f, D, \emptyset, V\rangle \models \Box^R_x \forall pA$

$\Leftrightarrow A_f \models \Box^R_x \forall pA$

Hence, it follows that $A_f \models \forall p\, \Box^R_x A \equiv \Box^R_x \forall pA$.

Similarly, it is easy to prove the following:

$\models \exists p\, \Box^R_x A \equiv \Box^R_x \exists p\, A$

$\models \forall P\, \Box^R_x A \equiv \Box^R_x \forall P\, A$, if P and R are different variables

$\models \exists P\, \Box^R_x A \equiv \Box^R_x \exists P\, A$, if P and R are different variables

It is also easy to show that modalities (i.e., sequences of modal operators) of the same type can be reduced:

$\models \Box^R_x \Box^R_x A \equiv \Box^R_x A$.

Hence, it is seen that the operator $\Box^R_x$ is at least an S4-operator, cf. Chellas (1980). Mixed modalities (i.e., sequences of modal operators of different types) cannot in general be reduced.

By using the results above we can now construct a prenex normal form for the wffs of $M_{\Sigma X}$. To that end we must have the Substitution of Equivalents-theorem.

Theorem 3.6. (Substitution of Equivalents). If A, B, C are wffs, B is a subformula of A, and A' has been obtained from the wff A by substituting some (possibly none) occurrences of B by the wff C, then A' is a wff. Moreover, if $\models B \equiv C$, then $\models A \equiv A'$.

The proof is easy and proceeds by induction on the length of the wff A.

The construction of the prenex normal form proceeds by using the standard prenex operations plus the following two.

(U1) Replace $\square_x^R \forall p\ A$ by the wff $\forall p\ \square_x^R\ A$.

(U2) Replace $\square_x^R \forall P\ A$ by the wff $\forall P\ \square_x^R\ A$, if P and R are different variables. If not, replace first $\square_x^R \forall P\ A$ by an alphabetic variant $\square_x^R \forall P' A$, where P' is a variable which does not occur in A at all.

(For details, cf. Shoenfield (1967).) Hence, we get:

Theorem 3.7. (Prenex Normal Form Theorem) For every wff A there is a wff A' such that A' is of the form $Q_1 P_1 \ldots Q_n P_n B$, where each $Q_i \in \{\forall, \exists\}$, and each P_i $(1 \leq i \leq n)$ is a variable, and B is quantifier-free, and such that $\models A \equiv A'$.

Define $M_{X,n}$ to be the set of those sentences of the language $M_{\Sigma X}$ the prenex form of which has prefix-length n. Define

$$SM_{\Sigma X} = \bigcup_{n \in \omega} M_{X,n}.$$

Finally, if $A \in SM_{\Sigma X}$, we have that, if for some t-model L_t it holds that $L_t \models A$, then this holds for all t-models. Hence, we can write in this case: $t \models A$. Define now

$$MOD(A) = \{t \in F_{\Sigma}(X) : t \models A\}.$$

4. SEMANTIC GAMES

Let again Σ be a fixed ranked alphabet and let X be a fixed terminal alphabet. Let D_1 and D_2 be tree domains, and let $f: D_1 \rightarrow \Sigma^X$ and $g: D_2 \rightarrow \Sigma^X$ be fixed pseudotrees. A *semantic game* in the pseudotrees f and g is played by two players, I and II. Player I begins and first chooses the pseudotree in which he plays and then makes in that pseudotree an *individual* move (i.e., chooses a node in the respective tree domain) or a *set* move (i.e., chooses a subset of nodes in the respective tree domain). Player II continues and makes a similar type (individual or set) move in the other pseudotree. After both have made n moves the game ends.

A game can be represented as a sequence of ordered pairs:

$$\begin{array}{ll} (r_i, t_i) \quad (1 \le i \le k) & \\ & (k + 1 = n) \\ (R_j, T_j) \quad (1 \le j \le 1) & \end{array}$$

where the first component expresses a move in the pseudotree f and the second component a move in the pseudotree G, small letters denote individual moves and capital letters denote set moves.

Player II *wins* if all of the following conditions are satisfied by the game:

$$\begin{array}{lll} (S1) & f(r_i) = g(t_i) & 1 \le i \le k \\ (S2) & r_i \le r_j \Leftrightarrow t_i \le t_j & 1 \le i,\ j \le k \\ (S3) & r_i = d \,.\, v \Leftrightarrow t_i = e \,.\, v & d \in D_1,\ e \in D_2,\ v \in N \\ (S4) & r_i \in R_j \Leftrightarrow t_i \in T_j & 1 \le i \le k,\ 1 \le j \le 1 \end{array}$$

Definition 4.1. ΣX-pseudotrees f and g are *ΣX,n-equivalent*, if Player II has a winning strategy in a semantic game played in the pseudotrees f and g, with n moves. If f and g are ΣX,n-equivalent, we write $f \approx^n_{\Sigma X} g$.

It is easy to show that $\approx^n_{\Sigma X}$ is an equivalence relation in the set $PF_\Sigma(X)$.

Lemma 4.2. The relation $\approx^n_{\Sigma X}$ is a congruence relation of the Σ-algebra $(PF_\Sigma(X), \Sigma)$.

Proof. Let $\delta \in \Sigma_m$ and let $f_i \approx^n_{\Sigma X} g_i$ $(1 \leq i \leq m)$. We are to show that

$$\delta(f_1, \ldots, f_m) \approx^n_{\Sigma X} \delta(g_1, \ldots, g_m).$$

The winning strategy of Player II is to play according to his winning strategy in the subpseudotrees f_i and g_i, and to play the identity strategy in the root δ.

The following lemma is of crucial importance for the construction of canonical tree recognizers below.

Lemma 4.3. Let $f, g \in PF_\Sigma(X)$. If $f \approx^n_{\Sigma X} g$, then for any wff A in $M_{X,n}$ it holds that

$$f \in MOD(A) \Leftrightarrow g \in MOD(A).$$

Proof. The proof is a direct modification of the proof of Lemma 3.1 of Ladner (1977). Let dom(f) = D, and dom(g) = E. Suppose now that for some $A \in M_{X,n}$ we have $f \in MOD(A)$ and $g \notin MOD(A)$. We may assume that A is already in prenex normal form. Hence, let $A = Q_1\xi_1 \ldots Q_n\xi_n B$, where B is quantifier-free. Define now

$$\overline{Q} = \begin{cases} \exists, & \text{if } Q = \forall \\ \forall, & \text{if } Q = \exists \end{cases}$$

We have that $\sim A$ is equivalent to $\overline{Q}_1\xi_1 \ldots \overline{Q}_n\xi_n \sim B$.

In what follows the symbol $B[{}^{\xi_1 \ldots \xi_n}_{\alpha_1 \ldots \alpha_n}]$ means that the variable ξ_i (either a set or individual variable) is interpreted as α_i $(1 \leq i \leq n)$, and that all of the variables in B are in the set $\{\xi_1, \ldots, \xi_n\}$. This simplifies the notation.

We now define a winning strategy for Player I in the semantic $\Sigma X,n$-game in f and g such that if the first m moves are $\{(\alpha_i, \beta_i): (1 \le i \le m)\}$ where α_i and β_i are of the appropriate type, then

$$(1)\quad \begin{aligned} f &\models Q_{m+1}\xi_{m+1} \cdots Q_n\xi_n B[{}^{\xi_1 \ldots \xi_m}_{\alpha_1 \ldots \alpha_m}] \\ g &\models \overline{Q}_{m+1}\xi_{m+1} \cdots \overline{Q}_n\xi_n {\sim}B[{}^{\xi_1 \ldots \xi_m}_{\beta_1 \ldots \beta_m}] \end{aligned}$$

This is done by induction on m. Trivially (1) holds if m = 0. Assume now as induction hypotheses that the first m moves satisfy (1). Player I's (m + 1)st play is to play in f if Q_{m+1} is $\exists$ and play in g if Q_{m+1} is $\forall$. The move is an individual move if ξ_{m+1} is an individual variable, and a set move if ξ_{m+1} is a set variable. If, for instance, the move is in f, then choose α_{m+1} so as to force

$$f \models Q_{m+2}\xi_{m+2} \cdots Q_n\xi_n B[{}^{\xi_1 \ldots \xi_{m+1}}_{\alpha_1 \ldots \alpha_{m+1}}]$$

Since $\overline{Q}_{m+1}$ is now $\forall$, then for all β_{m+1} we must have

$$g \models \overline{Q}_{m+2}\xi_{m+2} \cdots \overline{Q}_n\xi_n {\sim}B[{}^{\xi_1 \ldots \xi_{m+1}}_{\beta_1 \ldots \beta_{m+1}}]$$

After n moves we have

$$\begin{aligned} f &\models B[{}^{\xi_1 \ldots \xi_n}_{\alpha_1 \ldots \alpha_n}] \\ g &\models {\sim}B[{}^{\xi_1 \ldots \xi_n}_{\beta_1 \ldots \beta_n}] \end{aligned}$$

By induction on the complexity of the wff B we show now that Player I indeed wins the game.

(1) If B is atomic, Player I wins by definition.

(2) If $B = C \wedge D$, and the assertion holds for C and D, then since $g \models {\sim}(C \wedge D)$, we have that $g \models {\sim}C$ or $g \models {\sim}D$. Because on the other hand $f \models C$ and $f \models D$, Player I wins by the induction hypothesis in both cases.

(3) If $B = \sim C$, and the assertion holds for C, then $f \models \sim C$ and $g \models C$, whence Player I wins by induction hypothesis.

The cases of the other propositional connectives follow from (2) and (3).

(4) $B = \Box_x^R C$, and the assertion holds for C. One of the variables in the list $\xi_1, \ldots, \xi_n$ must be R. Let us assume that $\xi_i = R$. By definition we have that

$$f \models \Box_x^R C[{}^{\xi_1 \ldots \xi_n}_{\alpha_1 \ldots \alpha_n}] \text{ iff } \emptyset(x, f, \alpha_i) \models C[{}^{\xi_1 \ldots \xi_n}_{\alpha_1 \ldots \alpha_n}]$$
$$g \models \sim\Box_x^R C[{}^{\xi_1 \ldots \xi_n}_{\beta_1 \ldots \beta_n}] \text{ iff } \emptyset(x, g, \beta_i) \models \sim C[{}^{\xi_1 \ldots \xi_n}_{\beta_1 \ldots \beta_n}]$$

By the induction hypothesis Player I wins the ΣX,n-game in the pseudotrees $\emptyset(x, f, \alpha_i)$ and $\emptyset(x, g, \beta_i)$. If this is because one of the conditions (S2) - (S4) fails, it follows that Player I also wins the ΣX,n-game in f and g. If, on the other hand, Player I wins the game in $\emptyset(x, f, \alpha_i)$ and $\emptyset(x, g, \beta_i)$ because of the failure of (S1), we have for some move (r_j, t_j):

$$\emptyset(x, f, \alpha_i)(r_j) \neq \emptyset(x, g, \beta_i)(t_j)$$

Then, by definition, one of the following holds:

$r_j \in \alpha_i$ and $t_j \notin \beta_i$
$r_j \notin \alpha_i$ and $t_j \in \beta_i$
$f(r_j) \neq g(t_j)$.

In each case Player I wins the ΣX,n-game in f and g.

Next I will prove that the congruence relation $\approx_{\Sigma X}^n$ is of a finite index. To this purpose, we need a few concepts. Let $\overline{s} = (s_1, \ldots, s_k)$ be a vector of nodes of a tree domain D. Let $m = \max\{r_D(p):$

$p \in D\}$. For any u, $v \geq 1$ let $C(u, v)$ denote the complete u-ary tree of height v. Then define a *packing* of $\bar{s}$ - or an $\bar{s}$-packing - with parameters u and v to be a mapping

$$P(u, v)\colon \{1, \ldots, k\} \to C(u, v)$$

satisfying the condition

$$(P)\ s_i \leq s_j \Leftrightarrow P(u, v)(i) \leq P(u, v)(j).$$

It is easily seen that, if we choose u = m and v = k, there will always be an $\bar{s}$-packing with parameters u and v.

An *optimal* $\bar{s}$*-packing* is an $\bar{s}$-packing with parameters u and v such that for no u' less than u, and for no v' less than v, there is an $\bar{s}$-packing $P(u', v')$. It follows that optimal $\bar{s}$-packings have the same parameters. Denote by $P(\bar{s})$ the set of optimal $\bar{s}$-packings.

Assume now that D and E are tree domains and that $\bar{s} = (s_1, \ldots, s_k) \in D^k$, $\bar{t} = (t_1, \ldots, t_k) \in E^k$. It is easy to show that the following two conditions are equivalent:

(i) $P(\bar{s}) = P(\bar{t})$

(ii) $s_i \leq s_j \Leftrightarrow t_i \leq t_j$ $(1 \leq i, j \leq k)$.

Lemma 4.4. The congruence relation $\approx^n_{\Sigma X}$ is of a finite index.

Proof. Let f be a pseudotree, f; $D \to \Sigma^X$, $m = \max\{r_D(p)\colon p \in D\}$, and let $s_i \in D$ for each $i \in [1, k]$ (integer interval), and $S_j \in p(D)$ for each $j \in [1, 1]$. Define now

$$t_{0,k,1}(f, s_1, \ldots, s_k; S_1, \ldots, S_1) = (\rho, \tau, \nu, P),$$

where

(1) $\rho: \begin{cases} [1, k] \to \Sigma^X \\ i \mapsto f(s_i) \end{cases}$

(2) τ is a mapping $\tau: [1, k] \to 2^{[1,l]}$ such that $s_i \in S_j \Leftrightarrow$ $\Leftrightarrow j \in \tau(i)$.

(3) ν is a mapping $\nu: [1, k] \to [1, m]$ such that $\nu(i) = v$ if and only if $s_i = d \,.\, v$ for some $d \in D$ and some $v \in [1, m]$.

(4) P is the set of optimal $(s_1, \ldots, s_k)$-packings.

Let us further define

$$t_{n+1,k,l}(f;\, s_1, \ldots, s_k;\, S_1, \ldots, S_l) =$$
$$\{t_{n,k+1,l}(f;\, s_1, \ldots, s_{k+1};\, S_1, \ldots, S_l) : s_{k+1} \in D\} \cup$$
$$\cup\ \{t_{n,k,l+1}(f;\, s_1, \ldots, s_k;\, S_1, \ldots, S_{l+1}) : S_{l+1} \in p(D)\}.$$

It is straightforward to prove by induction on n that in a $\Sigma X, n+k+l$-game in pseudotrees f and g, where the moves

$$\{(s_i, t_i) : 1 \le i \le k\}$$
$$\{(S_j, T_j) : 1 \le j \le l\}$$

have already been made, Player II has a winning strategy if and only if

$$t_{n,k,l}(f;\, s_1, \ldots, s_k;\, S_1, \ldots, S_l) = t_{n,k,l}(g;\, t_1, \ldots, t_k;\, T_1, \ldots, T_l)$$

Hence, by definition, we have

$$f \approx^n_{\Sigma X} g \Leftrightarrow t_{n,0,0}(f) = t_{n,0,0}(g).$$

Thus, to prove the lemma, it suffices to show that

$$|\{t_{n,0,0}(f)\colon f \in PF_\Sigma(X)\}| < \infty.$$

To this end, define

$$T_j = \{t_{j,k,l}(f;\, s_1, \ldots, s_k;\, S_1, \ldots, S_l)\colon f \in PF_\Sigma(X),\ s_i \in \mathrm{dom}(f)\ (1 \le i \le k),\ S_j \subseteq \mathrm{dom}(f)\ (1 \le j \le l),\ j + k + l = n\}.$$

It is easy to show that always $T_{j+1} \subseteq T_j$ and that

$$T_n = \{t_{n,0,0}(f)\colon f \in PF_\Sigma(X)\}$$
$$T_0 = \{t_{0,k,l}(f;\, s_1, \ldots, s_k;\, S_1, \ldots, S_l)\colon f \in PF_\Sigma(X),\ s_i \in \mathrm{dom}(f)\ (1 \le i \le k),\ S_j \subseteq \mathrm{dom}(f)\ (1 < j < l),\ k + l = n\}.$$

Since there are only a finite number of mappings satisfying (1) - (3), and only a finite number of optimal packings to be taken into consideration, it follows that $|T_0| < \infty$. Thence,

$$|T_n| \le \underbrace{2^{2^{\cdot^{\cdot^{2^{|T_0|}}}}}}_{n \text{ times}}$$

5. REGULAR FORESTS

We shall first define the *regular operations* on forests. These definitions are taken from Gécseg and Steinby (1982). In what follows we shall use the definition of trees as Σ-terms in variables X, which was given in Section 2 above.

Definition 5.1. Let $(T_x \mid x \in X)$ be an X-indexed family of ΣX-forests. For each ΣX-tree we define a forest $t(x \leftarrow T_x \mid x \in X)$, mostly written simply $t(x \leftarrow T_x)$, as follows:

(1) If $t = z \in X$, then $t(x \leftarrow T_x) = T_z$

(2) If $t = \delta \in \Sigma_0$, then $t(x \leftarrow T_x) = \delta$

(3) If $t = \delta(t_1, \ldots, t_m)$ $(m \geq 1)$, then
$t(x \leftarrow T_x) = \{\delta(s_1, \ldots, s_m) : s_i \in t_i(x \leftarrow T_x),\ 1 \leq i \leq m\}$

The *forest product* of the family $(T_x \mid x \in X)$ with the ΣX-forest T is defined as the ΣX-forest

$$T(x \leftarrow T_x \mid x \in X) = \cup(t(x \leftarrow T_x \mid x \in X) : t \in T).$$

Definition 5.2. Let S and T be ΣX-forests and $z \in X$. The *z-product* of S and T is the forest product

$$S \cdot_z T = T(x \leftarrow T_x \mid x \in X),$$

where $T_z = S$ and $T_x = x$ for all $x \in X$, $x \neq z$.

Intuitively, the trees in $S \cdot_z T$ are obtained by taking a tree t from T and substituting a tree from S for every occurrence of z in t. Different occurrences of z may be replaced by different trees from S.

Definition 5.3. Let T be any ΣX-forest and let $x \in X$. Put

$$T^{0,x} = \{x\}$$
$$T^{j+1,x} = T^{j,x} \cdot_x T \cup T^{j,x}$$

for all $j \geq 0$. Then the *x-iteration* if T is the ΣX-forest

$$T^{*x} = \cup(T^{j,x} \mid j \geq 0).$$

Intuitively, the forest T^{*x} is obtained as follows. First include x. New members of T^{*x} are obtained by substituting in some $t \in T$ for every occurrence of x some tree already known to be in T^{x}. Note that $T^{1,x} = T \cup \{x\}$ and $T^{j,x} \subseteq T^{j+1,x}$ for every $j \geq 0$.

The operations finite union, z-product and z-iteration are called the *regular operations*. A forest is called *regular* if it can be constructed from finite forests by applying a finite number of regular operations. The notion of *regular expression* can easily be generalized to trees; cf. Gécseg and Steinby (1982). It is just because of the ability of the z-product to "destroy" the label z wherever the substitution takes place that in the construction of a regular forest some auxiliary letters may be needed. This is why we have allowed X to be infinite.

The concept of "recognizability" can also be generalized in a natural way to forests; cf. again Gécseg and Steinby (1982). Also, we have the following theorem:

Kleene's Theorem for Forests. A forest is recognizable if and only if it is regular.

A deterministic FR-recognizer (frontier-to-root) is a quadruple $\mathcal{A} = (A, \Sigma, \alpha, A_F)$, where A is the set of states, (A, Σ) is a Σ-algebra, α is the initial assignment, and A_F is the set of accepting states. Each input of the recognizer is a ΣX-tree. Given an input tree t, $\mathcal{A}$ starts reading it from the leaves in states that depend on the labels of the leaves. If a certain leaf is labelled by a frontier letter x, then $\mathcal{A}$ is in state $\alpha(x)$ at that leaf. If the label is a nullary operator δ, then $\mathcal{A}$ starts from that leaf in state δ^A. Now $\mathcal{A}$ moves down all the branches towards the root step by step as follows. If a given node ν is labelled by the m-ary operator δ $(m > 0)$, then $\mathcal{A}$ enters ν in state $\delta^A(a_1, \ldots, a_m)$, where $a_1, \ldots, a_m$ are the states of *A* at the nodes immediately above ν, listed in order from left to right. The tree is accepted if *A* enters the root in an accepting state.

If t is a ΣX-tree, denote by $[t]^n_{\Sigma X}$, or simply by [t], the $^n_{\Sigma X}$-equivalence class determined by t. The *canonical finite tree-automaton* $M_{\Sigma X,n}$ is defined as follows: $M_{\Sigma X,n} = (M, \Sigma, \alpha)$, where

$$M = \{[t]_{\Sigma X,n} : t \in F_\Sigma(X)\}$$

$$\alpha: \begin{cases} X \to [X] \\ x \mapsto [x] \end{cases}$$

The operations δ^M ($\delta \in \Sigma_m$) are defined as follows:

$$(1)\ \delta^M([t_1], \ldots, [t_m]) = [\delta(t_1, \ldots, t_m)].$$

By lemma 4.2. (1) is a good definition, and by lemma 4.4. M is finite.

Lemma 5.1. Let $A \in M_{X,n}$ be a fixed sentence. If T = MOD(A), then T is a regular ΣX-forest.

Proof. Define a finite tree recognizer *M* as follows: $\mathcal{M} = (M, \Sigma, \alpha, M_A)$, where (M, Σ, α) is the canonical tree automaton $M_{\Sigma X,n}$ and

$$M_A = \{[t] : t \in F_\Sigma(X),\ t \models A\}.$$

If *M* enters the root of a tree u in an accepting state, in symbols: $[u]\alpha \in M_A$ (cf. Gécseg and Steinby (1982)), there exists a tree such that $t \approx^n_{\Sigma X} u$ and $t \models A$. By lemma 4.3. it follows that also $u \models A$. Hence, if T(*M*) denotes the forest recognized by *M*, we have $T(\mathcal{M}) \subseteq T$.

If, on the other hand, $t \models A$, then $[t] \in M_A$, whence by construction $[t]\alpha \in M_A$, and it follows that $T \subseteq T(M)$.

Lemma 5.2. If T is a ΣX-regular forest, there is a sentence $A \in M_{\Sigma X}$, such that $T = \mathrm{MOD}(A)$.

Proof. We shall construct for each ΣX-regular forest T a wff $A_T(R)$ such that

$$t \models A_T(R)[{}^R_S] \Leftrightarrow \text{S is a tree subdomain of dom(t) and } t^*|_S \in T, \text{ for some } t^* \in W_t,$$

where t^* is obtained from t by relabelling those maximal nodes in S, which are not leaves of t. Then define

$$A_T(\Omega) \equiv_{df} (\exists R)(\forall r)(r \circledcirc{\in} R \wedge A_T(R)).$$

Now, $A_T(\Omega)$ is the desired sentence A.

The construction of $A_T(R)$ proceeds by regular induction on the construction of T.

(1) If T is a finite forest, $T = \{t_1, \ldots, t_n\}$, it is sufficient to construct the wff $A_{\{t_i\}}(R_i)$ for each t_i and then form their disjunction. For every tree $t \in F_\Sigma(X)$ we construct the wff $A_{\{t\}}(R)$ by induction on the height of t, which is denoted by hg(t).

(1a) hg(t) = 0. In this case $t = \alpha$, where $\alpha \in \Sigma_0 \cup X$. Hence, we may define

$$A_{\{t\}}(R) \equiv_{df} (\exists! p)(p \circledcirc{\in} R \wedge (\forall r)(r \circledcirc{\in} R \supset U_\alpha(r))).$$

(1b) hg(t) = k(k ≥ 1). In this case t = $(t_1, \ldots, t_m)$, $\delta \in \Sigma_m$, and for each i $(1 \leq i \leq m)$ $hg(t_i) < k$. By the induction hypothesis we can find the wffs $A_{\{t_i\}}(R_i)$. Define now

$$\begin{aligned}
A_{\{t\}}(R) \equiv_{df} & (\exists p)(p \textcircled{=} \min(R) \wedge U_\sigma(p) \wedge (\exists R_1) \ldots (\exists R_m)(\exists p_1) \ldots \\
& \ldots (\exists p_m)(\bigwedge_{i=1}^{m}(p_i \textcircled{\in} R)(\bigwedge_{i\neq j}^{m}(R_i \cap R_j \textcircled{=} \emptyset) \wedge \\
& \wedge \bigwedge_{i=1}^{m}(p_i \textcircled{=} \min(R_i) \wedge \bigwedge_{i=1}^{m}(R_i \textcircled{=} Id(p_i, R)) \\
& \bigwedge_{i=1}^{m}(S_i(p_i) \wedge p \prec p_i) \wedge \bigwedge_{i=1}^{m} A_{\{t_i\}}(R_i)),
\end{aligned}$$

where the introduced new symbols are defined as follows:

$$\begin{aligned}
& p \textcircled{=} \min(R) =_{df} (p \textcircled{\in} R \wedge (\forall r)(r \textcircled{\in} R \supset p \textcircled{<} r)) \\
& P \cap Q \textcircled{=} \emptyset =_{df} \sim(\exists p)(p \textcircled{\in} P \wedge p \textcircled{\in} Q) \\
& R_i \textcircled{=} Id(p_i, R) =_{df} (\forall r)(r \in R_i \equiv ((p \textcircled{<} r \vee p \textcircled{=} r) \wedge \\
& \qquad \wedge r \textcircled{\in} R)) \\
& p \prec r =_{df} \sim(\exists q)(\sim p \textcircled{=} q \wedge \sim r \textcircled{=} q \wedge p \textcircled{<} q \wedge q \textcircled{<} r) \wedge \\
& \qquad \wedge p \textcircled{<} r.
\end{aligned}$$

(2) If T is formed as the union of two forests T_1 and T_2, we have simply

$$A_T(R) = A_{T_1}(R) \vee A_{T_2}(R).$$

(3) $T = T_1 \cdot {}_z T_2$ $(z \in X)$

By the induction hypothesis we can construct the wffs $A_{T_1}(R_1)$ and $A_{T_2}(R_2)$. Now we define

$$\begin{aligned}
A_{T_1 \cdot {}_z T_2}(R) \quad {}_{df} \quad & (\exists P)(\exists p)(\exists Q)(P \subseteq R \wedge Q \subseteq R \wedge p \textcircled{=} \min(R) \wedge \\
& \wedge (\forall r)(r \textcircled{\in} Q \equiv (p \textcircled{<} r \wedge \sim(\exists q)(q \textcircled{\in} P \wedge \\
& \wedge \sim q \textcircled{=} r \wedge q \textcircled{<} r \wedge \Box_z^P A_{T_2}(Q) \wedge \\
& \wedge (\forall S)(\forall q)((q \textcircled{\in} P \wedge S \textcircled{=} Id(q, R)) \supset \\
& \supset A_{T_1}(S))),
\end{aligned}$$

where we define: $P \subseteq R =_{df} (\forall r)(r \textcircled{\in} P \supset r \textcircled{\in} Q)$.

Intuitively speaking, P will be the set of those nodes, in which the substitution takes place, and Q will be the set of those nodes, which constitute the tree in T_2. Pictorially the situation is illustrated in Figure 3.

(4) $T = T_1^{*z}$ $(z \in X)$

By the induction hypothesis again, we can construct the wff $A_{T_1}(R)$. We can define, then

$$\begin{aligned} A_T(R) \equiv_{df}\ & (\exists!)p(p \textcircled{\in} R \wedge (\forall r)(r \textcircled{\in} R \supset U_z(r))) \vee A_{T_1}(R) \vee \\ & \vee (\exists p)(\exists P)(P \subseteq R \wedge p \textcircled{=} \min(R) \wedge \sim p \textcircled{\in} P \wedge \\ & \wedge (\forall Q)((Q \subsetneq R \wedge (\exists P')((Q \textcircled{=} CI(P, p) \wedge P' \textcircled{=} P) \vee \\ & \vee (\exists r)(r \textcircled{\in} P \wedge Q \textcircled{=} CI(P, r) \wedge P' \textcircled{=} P - r)) \supset \\ & \supset \Box_z^{P'} A_{T_1}(Q)), \end{aligned}$$

where we define

$$\begin{aligned} Q \textcircled{=} CI(P, p) =_{df}\ & (\forall q)(q \textcircled{\in} Q \equiv (p < q \wedge \sim(\exists s)(s \textcircled{\in} P \wedge \\ & \wedge \sim s \textcircled{=} q \wedge s \textcircled{<} q)) \\ P' \textcircled{=} P - r =_{df}\ & (\forall q)(q \textcircled{\in} P' \equiv (q \textcircled{\in} P \wedge \sim q \textcircled{=} r)). \end{aligned}$$

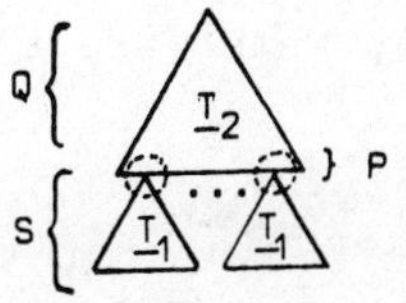

Fig. 3

Notice that the disjuncts of $A_{T}(R)$ correspond directly to the clauses in the definition of z-iteration. Intuitively speaking, P will again be the set of those nodes in which the substitution takes place. The meaning of P' is to make sure that at each stage the root of the tree subdomain Q is not relabelled when it is tested whether or not the tree read from Q after relabelling the nodes in P' by z in the forest T_1 or not.

This concludes the proof.

By lemmas 5.1 and 5.2 we now have the following main theorem, which - in a sense - generalizes Büchli's theorem.

Theorem 5.3. Let T be a ΣX-forest. Then T is ΣX-regular if and only if there is a sentence $A \in M_{\Sigma X}$ such that $T = MOD(A)$.

As a simple byproduct of our approach, we shall obtain a decision procedure for the monadic second-order theory of branch-limited unlabelled trees.

Let k be a fixed natural number, $k \geq 1$. Call an unlabelled tree t *k-ary*, if each node of t has at most k immediate successors. Let $\Sigma = \Sigma_1 \cup \ldots \cup \Sigma_k$, $\Sigma_i = \{\sigma_i\}$ $(1 \leq i \leq k)$, and let $X = \{x\}$. There is, then, a bijective correspondence between the k-ary unlabelled trees and the forest $F_{\Sigma}(X)$.

Now delete from the language $M_{\Sigma X}$ the modal operators and the predicate symbols U_{σ}. Call the obtained language the language L. The *second-order semantic theory of k-ary unlabelled trees* is the set of those sentences of L, which are true in every k-ary unlabelled tree.

Let A be a sentence of *L*. We may assume that A is already in prenex normal form. Assume that the prefix-length of A is n. Notice that now we also have: $A \in M_{X,n}$.

The canonical tree recognizer M_A is connected, and the cardinality of M is the index of the congruence $\approx^n_{\Sigma X}$. Denote this index by $m_{\Sigma X}(n)$.

It is known (cf. Gécseg and Steinby (1982), Section 10) that in a connected tree-automaton with k states each state can be reached from the initial states by a tree of height less than k. Hence, each state [t] of M_A can be reached by a tree u of height less than $m_{\Sigma X}(n)$. In other words, for each t there is a tree u such that

$$t \approx^n_{\Sigma X} u \text{ and } hg(u) < m_{\Sigma X}(n).$$

The sentence A is true in all k-ary trees if and only if $T(M_A) = F_\Sigma(X)$, or equivalently, if $M_A = M$. Now it can effectively be tested, whether or not $t \models A$ for all t of height less than $m_{\Sigma X}(n)$. Finally, notice that the proof of lemma 4.4 gives an effective - although completely impracticable - upper limit for $m_{\Sigma X}(n)$. Hence, it follows that

> the monadic second-order theory of finite k-ary trees is decidable.

REFERENCES

Bowen, K. A., 1979, "Model Theory for Modal Logic. Kripke Models for Modal Logic," Synthese Library Vol. 127, Reidel, Dordrecht.

Büchi, J. R., 1962, On a Decision Method in Restricted Second Order Arithmetic, in: "Proc. 1960 Int. Cong. for Logic, Method. and Philos. of Sci.," Stanford Univ. Press, Stanford, Calif.

Chellas, B. F., 1980, "Modal Logic," Cambridge University Press, Cambridge, England.

Gécseg, F. and Steinby, M., 1982, "Tree Automata," Akadémia Kiadó, Budapest (to appear in 1983).

Kobrinskii, N. E. and Trakhtenbrot, B. A., 1965, "A Theory of Finite Automata," North-Holland, Amsterdam.

Kripke, S. A., 1971, Semantical Considerations on Modal Logic, in: "Reference and Modality," L. Linsky, ed., Oxford University Press, Oxford.

Ladner, R. E., 1977, Application of Model Theoretic Games to Discrete Linear Orders and Finite Automata, Inf. and Contr., 33:281-303.

McNaughton, R. and Papert, S., 1971, "Counter Free Automata," MIT Press, Cambridge, Mass.

Shoenfield, J. R., 1967, "Mathematical Logic," Addison-Wesley, Reading.

Steinby, M., 1982, Systolic Trees and Systolic Language Recognition by Tree Automata, to appear in Theor. Comp. Sci. 1983.

Thomas, W., 1981, A Combinatorial Approach to the Theory of ω-Automata, Inf. and Contr., 48:261-283.

TO THE DECISION PROBLEM FOR BRANCHING TIME LOGIC***

Yuri Gurevich***

Electrical Engineering and Computer Science Department
University of Michigan
Ann Arbor, MI 48109, USA

Saharon Shelah

Mathematics Department
Hebrew University
Jerusalem 91904, Israel

SECTION 1. INTRODUCTION

First we describe a certain branching time logic. We borrow this logic from Prior (1967) and call it BTL. It is a propositional logic whose formulas are built from propositional symbols by means of usual boolean connectives and additional unary connectives PAST, FUTURE, NECESSARY.

---

* The Main Theorem was proven in principle during the Jerusalem Logic Year 1980-81 when both authors were fellows in the Institute for Advanced Studies of Hebrew University.

** Supported in part by the United States - Israel Binational Science Foundation.

*** Supported in part by NSF grant MCS83-01022.

Models for BTL are trees with additional unary predicates. Recall that a tree is a partially ordered set where the predecessors of any element are totally ordered. Think about elements of a given tree as possible states of the world, branches (i.e., maximal totally ordered subsets) as possible courses of history, and the partial order as the relation "later". The restriction to trees reflects the idea of one past but many possible futures.

Trees with additional unary predicates will be called colored trees. In other words, the additional unary predicates will be called colors. We suppose that any colored tree has finitely many colors. A tree with colors $P_1, \ldots, P_m$ interprets BTL formulas with propositional symbols $P_1, \ldots, P_m$. The interpretation of a formula at element t with respect to a branch B through t is defined inductively:

P_i holds at t wrt B if and only if $t \varepsilon P_i$,

NOT (φ) holds at t wrt B if and only if
φ does not hold at t wrt B,

φ_1 & φ_2 holds at t wrt B if and only if
both φ_1 and φ_2 hold at t wrt B,

PAST(φ) holds at t wrt B if and only if
there is $u < t$ such that φ holds at u wrt B,

FUTURE(φ) holds at t wrt B if and only if
there is $u > t$ such that $u \varepsilon B$ and φ holds at u wrt B,

NECESSARY(φ) holds at t wrt B if and only if
for all branches C through t, φ holds at t wrt C.

A BTL formula φ is a *theorem* of BTL if for every tree T with appropriate colors, every element t of T and every branch B through t in T, φ holds at t with respect to B in T. Note that the semantics of BTL is defined in terms of a certain theory of trees.

Definition. Extend the first-order language of colored trees by an infinite list of unary predicate variables henceforth called *branch variables*. Allow quantification of branch variables. A tree T with colors P_1, ... P_m provides a standard interpretation for a portion of the extended language (i.e., for formulas with unary predicate constants among $P_1, \ldots, P_m$) under the stipulation that the branch variables range over all branches of T. The theory of these standard interpretations will be called TREE.

Remark. The first-order language of colored trees contains infinitely many unary predicate constants whereas each colored tree contains only finitely many colors. This does not constitute a contradiction. Theorems of the first-order theory of colored trees hold in those colored trees where they are defined. The same relates to TREE and other formal theories in this paper.

Definition. A formal theory T1 *reduces* to a formal theory T2 if there is an algorithm (the *reduction algorithm*) which associates a sentence $\varphi2$ in the language of T2 with each sentence $\varphi1$ in the language of T1 in such a way that $\varphi1$ is a theorem of T1 if and only if $\varphi2$ is a theorem of T2.

Strictly speaking, a reduction algorithm in the sense of the above definition reduces the decision problem for T1 to the decision problem for T2. All reduction algorithms in this paper will be systematic translations from one language to another.

Obviously, BTL reduces to TREE. Moreover, the extension of BTL by means of binary connectives SINCE and UNTIL, and many other extensions and variations of BTL reduce to TREE. This raises the question whether TREE is a decidable theory.

In our lecture in Salzburg we announced the decidability of the theory of trees with quantification over nodes and branches and sketched our decidability proof. (This theory of trees and the theory TREE readily reduce to each other: colors are easily coded.) In this paper we reduce the theory TREE to the first-order theory of binary colored trees which are bounded and well-founded. We prove the decidability of the latter theory elsewhere (Gurevich and Shelah, 1984). Thus TREE is decidable. Hence, BTL is decidable and all other formalizations of branching time logic reducible to TREE are decidable.

We believe that our interpretation of arbitrary trees in colored well-founded trees is of interest in its own right. --

Acknowledgement. We thank John Burgess for posing to us the question whether TREE is decidable (when he visited Jerusalem during the Logic Year 1980-81). John also explained to us the connection between TREE and branching time logic. We thank Andreas Blass for useful comments.

SECTION 2. MAIN THEOREM

First we define bounded trees and reduce the theory TREE to the first-order theory of bounded colored trees.

Definition. A branch of a tree is *bounded* if it has a maximal element, otherwise the branch is *unbounded*. A tree is *bounded* if all its branches are bounded.

Proposition 1. Every tree is embeddable into a bounded tree. Hence the theory TREE reduces to the first-order theory of bounded colored trees.

Proof is clear.

We imagine our trees growing upward (in contrast to computer science trees which usually grow downward). Elements of a tree are *nodes*. Maximal nodes are *leaves*. If x, y are nodes and $x < y$ we say that x is below y and y is above x.

We use terminology of genealogical trees but we imagine our trees growing toward future (whereas genealogical trees grow toward past). If x, y are nodes and $x \leq y$ we say that x is an *ancestor* of y and y is a *descendant* of x.

If x, y are nodes of a tree, $x < y$ and there is no z with $x < z < y$ then x is the *father* of y and y is a *son* of x. Sons of the same father are *brothers*. (We could use terms "mother", "daughter" and "sister". There is no room however for both sexes. Our choice is not an expression of male chauvinism. We just prefer to make fun of our own sex.)

Definition. A tree is *binary* if no node has more than two sons.

If x_1, x_2, y are nodes of the same tree and $y = \inf\{x_1, x_2\}$ then y will be called the *meet* of x_1, x_2.

Definition. A tree is *well-founded* if the ancestors of any node are well ordered and every pair of nodes has a meet.

Remark. Usually, the first condition in the above definition defines well-founded trees. We will not be interested in trees satisfying the first but not the second condition. In the presence of the first condition the second condition ensures existence of a least element (the *root*) and ensures that every bounded, nonempty, totally ordered subset (i.e., every bounded *chain*) has an extremum.

Main Theorem. The first-order theory of bounded colored trees reduces to the first-order theory of binary, bounded, colored, well-founded trees.

The Main Theorem is proved in the sequel. It follows from Proposition 1 in Section 3, Proposition 1 in Section 4 and Proposition 1 in Section 5.

SECTION 3. COMPLETE TREES

In this section we define complete trees and reduce the first-order theory of bounded colored trees to the first-order theory of any class of bounded colored trees which contains all bounded, colored, complete trees.

A subset of a tree will be called *open* if it contains all descendants of any of its elements. This defines the tree topology.

Recall that a topological space is *connected* if it cannot be split into two disjoint nonempty open subsets. A subset of a topological space is *connected* if it is connected as a subspace. A maximal connected subset of a topological space is called a *component* or a *connected component*.

Lemma 1. Two nodes of a tree T belong to the same component of T if and only if they have a common ancestor in T.

Proof. The relation E = {(x, y): x, y have a common ancestor} is an equivalence relation on T. For it obviously is reflexive and symmetric. To check transitivity suppose $E(x_1, x_2)$ and $E(x_2, x_3)$. Let y be a common ancestor of x_1, x_2 and z be a common ancestor of x_2, x_3. Since y, z have a common descendant x_2, they are comparable. The least between them is a common ancestor of x_1, x_3. Hence, (x_1, x_3) belongs to E.

Every equivalence class of E obviously is open. It suffices to prove that every equivalence class X of E is connected.

By contradiction suppose that the subspace X splits into non-empty, disjoint, open subsets Y, Z. Pick $y \varepsilon Y$ and $z \varepsilon Z$. Let $x \varepsilon X$ be a common ancestor of y, z. Without loss of generality $x \varepsilon Y$. Hence $z \varepsilon Y$ which is impossible.□

Lemma 1 implies that components of any open subset of a tree are open.

Lemma 2. Let X be a connected, nonempty, open set of nodes of a tree. If $x \varepsilon X$, $y \not\varepsilon X$ and $y < x$ then y is a lower bound for X. If Y is another connected open set which properly includes X then Y contains a proper lower bound for X.

Proof. First suppose that $x \varepsilon X$, $y \not\varepsilon X$ and $y < x$. For an arbitrary $x' \varepsilon X$ let x'' be a common ancestor of x and x' in X. The nodes x'' and y have a common descendant x and are comparable. If $x'' \leq y$ then $y \varepsilon X$ which is impossible. Hence $y < x'$.

Next suppose that Y is another connected open set of nodes which properly includes X. Pick $x \varepsilon X$, $z \varepsilon Y-X$ and a common ancestor y of x, z in Y. Use the first statement of the lemma.□

Definition. Let X be an arbitrary set of nodes in a tree. L(X) (respectively PL(X)) is the set of lower (resp. proper lower) bounds for X. In other words, y belongs to L(X) (resp. to PL(X)) if $y \le x$ (resp. $y < x$) for all x in X.

If X is empty then either of L(X), PL(X) is the whole tree. If X is not empty then either of L(X), PL(X) is either the empty set or a bounded chain.

Definition. Let X be an arbitrary bounded set of nodes in a tree. U(X) is the set of upper bounds for X. If $X = \{x\}$ we call U(X) a *cone* and write Cone(x) instead of $U(\{x\})$. It is easy to see that if U(X) has a minimum y then U(X) = Cone(y). If U(X) is not empty but does not have a minimum we call it a *pseudo-cone*.

Lemma 3. If Y = L(X) then Y = L(U(Y)), and if Y = U(X) then Y = U(L(Y)).

Proof. The definitions of L(X) and U(X) make sense for an arbitrary partially ordered set. It suffices to prove either of the two statements of Lemma 3 in the case of a partially ordered set.

Clearly, $Y \subseteq U(L(Y))$ for any Y. If Y = U(X) then $X \subseteq L(Y)$ and we have also $U(L(Y)) \subseteq U(X) = Y$.□

Remark. Let X be a set of nodes in a tree such that U(X) is not empty. Then X is empty or X is a chain. If X has a supremum then U(X) is a cone, otherwise U(X) is a pseudo-cone.

Lemma 4. Let G be a pseudo-cone and X be a connected, nonempty, open subset of G. Then X is a connected component of G if and only if PL(X) = L(G).

Proof. Clearly $L(G) = PL(G) \subseteq PL(X)$ and $L(G)$ is an initial segment of $PL(X)$.

If $L(G)$ is a proper initial segment of $PL(X)$ pick a node y in $PL(X)-L(G)$. By Lemma 3, G equals $U(L(G))$. Hence $y \varepsilon G$. Thus X is a proper part of the component of G which contains y.

If X is a proper part of some component Y of G then, by Lemma 2, Y contains a proper lower bound y for X. Hence $L(G) = PL(G) \neq PL(X)$.□

Definition. A tree is *complete* if every nonempty set of nodes has an infimum.

Lemma 5. A tree is complete if and only if there is a least node (the *root*) and every bounded chain has a supremum.

Proof is clear.

Theorem 1. Every tree T is embeddable into a complete tree S.

Proof. Our S consists of nonempty sets U(X) where X is a subset of T. We order S by reverse inclusion. In particular, T itself is the least member of S. Clearly, S is a partially ordered set. To embed T into S we assign Cone(x) to each x in T. It remains to prove that S is a complete tree.

Claim 1. Suppose that X_1, X_2 are S-ancestors of some Y. Then X_1, X_2 are S-comparable. Hence S is a tree.

Proof of Claim 1. Without loss of generality Y is a cone. Let Y_i be the component of X_i which includes Y. If $Y_j - Y_i$ is not empty pick an element y there. By Lemma 2, y is a proper lower bound for Y_i. If X_i is connected then $X_i = Y_i \subset Y_j \subseteq X_j$. If X_i is disconnected then, by Lemma 4, $y \varepsilon L(X_i)$ and $X_i \subset \text{Cone}(y) \subseteq Y_j \subseteq X_j$.

Suppose that $Y_1 = Y_2$. If some Y_i is connected then $X_i = Y_i = Y_j \subseteq X_j$. Suppose that both X_1 and X_2 are disconnected. By Lemma 4, $L(X_1) = L(X_2)$. By Lemma 3, $X_1 = X_2$. Claim 1 is proved.□

Claim 2. Every nonempty subset K of S has an infimum in S.

Proof of Claim 2. Let G be the union of members of K and $G^* = U(L(G))$. Then G^* is an S-lower bound for K. If X is an S-lower bound for K then $X \supseteq G$, $L(X) \subseteq L(G)$ and $X = U(L(X)) \supseteq U(L(G)) = G^*$ i.e., $X \leq G^*$. Thus G^* is the desired infimum. Claim 2 is proved. Theorem 1 is proved.□

Proposition 1. Let K be an arbitrary class of bounded colored trees which contains every bounded, colored, complete tree. The first-order theory of bounded colored trees reduces to the first-order theory of K.

Proof. Given a sentence φ in the first-order language of colored trees find the first unary predicate constant P which does not appear in φ. Write a sentence φ_1 in the vocabulary $\{<, P\}$ whose meaning on any bounded tree is that P is not empty and every branch of the subtree P has a maximum (for every leaf a there is $b \leq a$ such that P(b) and for every $c \leq a$, if P(c) then $c \leq b$).

Further let φ_2 be the result of restricting the quantifiers of φ by P. The desired reduction algorithm transforms φ into $\varphi_1 \rightarrow \varphi_2$.□

SECTION 4. ORIENTED WELL-FOUNDED TREES

In this section we make the crucial translation to well-founded trees. The simple technique of interpreting by embedding fails here. A non-well-founded tree is not embeddable into a well-founded tree. To overcome this difficulty we introduce oriented trees where in addition to the upward tree ordering (the vertical order) there is also a horizontal order: sons of the same father are partially ordered (from left to right). An important task of the next section will be to get rid of orientations.

The contribution of this section toward the Main Theorem is a reduction of the first-order theory of one class of bounded trees, that contains every bounded, colored, complete tree, to the first-order theory of bounded, colored, oriented, well-founded trees.

Recall that a tree is well-founded if the ancestors of any node are well-ordered and every pair of nodes has an infimum (called the meet). The *height* of a node x in a well-founded tree is the ordinal type of the sequence $\langle y: y < x \rangle$.

Lemma 1. Every well-founded tree is complete.

Proof. Let T be a well-founded tree. The unique element of T of height 0 is the root of T. If C is a bounded chain in T then a node in U(C) of minimal height is a supremum of C. Now use Lemma 5 in Section 3.□

Definition. A strict partial order H on a tree is an *orientation* of the tree if

(i) for every (x, y) in H the nodes x and y are brothers,
(ii) every node belongs to a unique maximal H-chain (in other words, the set of nodes, partially ordered by H, is a disjoint union of H-chains), and
(iii) every maximal H-chain has an H-maximal element.

A tree with an orientation is an *oriented tree*.

Lemma 2. Let H be an orientation of a tree. Then the relation "either $x < y$ or there exists z such that xHz and $z \leq y$" is the transitive closure of the union of the relations H and <.

Proof. The relation in question includes the union of H and <. It is included into the transitive closure of the union. And it is transitive.□

Theorem 1. For every complete tree T there is a well-founded tree T' and an orientation H of T' such that

(i) T and T' have the same nodes, and
(ii) For all nodes x and y, x is a proper T-ancestor of y if and only if either x is a proper T' ancestor of y or there is a node z such that xHz and z is a T'-ancestor of y.

Proof. Work in a complete tree T. For every nonempty, connected, open subset X choose a point p(X) in X such that p(X) = min(X) if X is a cone. Let C(X) be the chain $\{x \varepsilon X: x \leq p(X)\}$.

Construct a decreasing sequence of open subsets as follows:

$$S_o = T,$$
$$S_\alpha = \cap\{S_\beta : \beta < \alpha\} \text{ if } \alpha \text{ is limit, and}$$
$$S_{\alpha+1} = \cup\{X - C(X): X \text{ is a connected component of } S_\alpha\}.$$

The construction halts when the empty set is reached. If $x \varepsilon S_\alpha - S_{\alpha+1}$ we say that α is the *rank* of x. Clearly, every node is ranked and rank(x) $\leq$ rank(y) if $x \leq y$ (because the sets S_α are open).

Claim 1. Suppose that α is limit and S_α is not empty. Then every component X of S_α is a cone.

Proof of Claim 1. It suffices to check that $x = \inf(X)$ belongs to S_α. Let $\beta = \text{rank}(x)$. By contradiction suppose that $\beta < \alpha$. By Lemma 2 in Section 3, the component of Y of $S_{\beta+1}$ which includes X contains a proper lower bound y for X. Then $y \leq x$ which is impossible. Claim 1 is proved.□

If X is a component of some nonempty $S_{\alpha+1}$ then the supremum y of PL(X) will be called the *patriarch* of X and X will be called a *clan* of y.

Claim 2. Suppose that X is a component of some nonempty $S_{\alpha+1}$ and y is the patriarch of X. Then $\text{rank}(y) = \alpha$ and either $y = \inf(X)$ or there is a son x of y such that $X = \text{Cone}(x)$.

Proof of Claim 2. Let Y be the connected component of S_α which includes X. By Lemma 2 in Section 3, Y contains a proper lower bound y' for X. If z is a proper lower bound for X of rank $\geq \alpha$ then $z \varepsilon Y$ (because y' and z are comparable) and z does not belong to any component of $S_{\alpha+1}$. Hence $z \leq p(Y)$. But y is the supremum of such nodes z, hence $y \varepsilon C(Y)$ and $\text{rank}(y) = \alpha$.

Next, let $x = \inf(X)$. If $x \notin X$ then x is the patriarch of X and the claim is proved. Let $x \varepsilon X$. Then $X = \text{Cone}(x)$ and x is a son of y. For, if $y < z < x$ then z is a proper lower bound for X above y which is impossible. Claim 2 is proved.□

Let R be the relation "x is the patriarch of a clan which contains y". Clearly, xRy implies $x < y$, and R is transitive. Hence R defines a new tree T' on the nodes of T. Clearly, every R-chain is well-ordered. The next claim completes the proof that T' is a well-founded tree.

Claim 3. For all nodes x_1 and x_2 there is a T'-meet of x_1, x_2.

Proof of Claim 3. Let x be the T-meet of x_1 and x_2. Every common T'-ancestor of x_1, x_2 is a T-ancestor of x. If x has a T'-father y then y is a common T'-ancestor of x_1, x_2. Hence either x or y is the T'-meet.

Suppose that x does not have a T'-father. Then α = rank(x) is limit. By Claim 1, the component S_α which contains x is a cone. By the definition of sets S_α, this component is Cone(x). By Claim 2, x is the patriarch of any component of $S_{\alpha+1}$ which meets Cone(x) (hence is included into Cone (x)). Hence x is the T'-meet of x_1, x_2. Claim 3 is proved. □

Let H be the relation "there exists α and a component Z of $S_{\alpha+1}$ such that x and y belong to Z and $x < y \leq p(Z)$". It is easy to see that H orients T'. In particular, if xHy and $\alpha+1$ = rank(x) and Z is the component of $S_{\alpha+1}$ which contains x, y, then the patriarch of Z is a T'-father of x, y.

Finally, we prove the statement (ii) of Theorem 1. The "if" implication is obvious.

Claim 4. Suppose that x is a proper T-ancestor of y. Then either xHy holds or x is a proper T'-ancestor of y or there is z such that xHz holds and z is a T'-ancestor of y.

Proof of Claim 4. Let α = rank(x) and X be the component of S_α which contains x. If $x' > x$ is a node of rank α then C(X) is not singleton, X is not a cone, α is successor (by Claim 1), and therefore xHx' holds. In particular, if rank(y) = α then xHy holds.

Suppose that rank(y) > α. Let Y be the component of $S_{\alpha+1}$ which contains y and let z be the patriarch of Y. If x = z then x is a proper T'-ancestor of y. Suppose that $x \neq z$. By Lemma 2 in Section 3, x is a proper lower bound for Y. Hence $x < z$. By Claim 2, rank(z) = α and z is a proper T'-ancestor of y. By the previous paragraph, xHz holds. Claim 4 is proved. Theorem 1 is proved.□

Theorem 2. Let T be a tree, T' be a well-founded tree and H be an orientation of T'. Suppose that T, T' and H satisfy the statements (i) and (ii) of Theorem 1. Then T is bounded if and only if T' is bounded.

Proof. The "only if" implication is clear. We prove the "if" implication. By contradiction suppose that T' is bounded but T has an unbounded branch B. Let A be the set of T'-heights of elements in B.

If A has a maximal element α then B has a final segment which is an H-chain. By the definition of orientations, this H-chain has an H-upper bound x. Clearly, x is a T-upper bound for B, which is impossible.

Hence A does not have a maximal element. For every $\alpha+1$ in A, all nodes in B of T'-height $\alpha+1$ are sons of the same T'-father. These T'-fathers are cofinal in B and form a T'-chain. Any T'-upper bound for this T'-chain is a T-upper bound for B which is impossible.□

Proposition 1. Let K be the class of colored trees T such that there exists a bounded well-founded tree T' and an orientation H of T' which satisfy the statements (i) and (ii) of Theorem 1. Then every colored tree in K is bounded, every bounded, colored, complete tree belongs to K, and the first-order theory of K reduces to the first-order theory of bounded, colored, oriented, well-founded trees.

Proof. The first statement follows from Theorem 2. The second statement follows from Theorems 1 and 2. The third statement is obvious.□

SECTION 5. BINARY TREES

In this section we reduce the first-order theory of bounded, colored, oriented, well-founded trees to the first-order theory of binary, bounded, colored, well-founded trees.

An orientation of H of a binary tree looks especially simple. Every maximal H-chain consists of at most two nodes. If $(x, y) \varepsilon H$ and z is the father of x, y then we say that x is the *left son* of z and y is the *right son* of z. H defines the following *lexicographic order* on the tree: x *lexicographically precedes* y if the meet of x, y has two sons, the sons are H-ordered, x descends from the left son and y descends from the right son.

Lemma 1. Every linear order C is isomorphic to the lexicographic order of leaves (i.e., maximal nodes) of some binary, bounded, oriented, well-founded tree.

Proof. The desired tree T will be a set of non-empty segments of C ordered by reverse inclusion. If A is a segment of C with at least two points we split A into a nonempty initial segment (called the *left part* of A) and the remaining nonempty final segment (the *right part* of A). If A will be a node of T then the left part of A and the right part of A will be the left and the right sons of A in T.

We construct a decreasing sequence of equivalence relations on C whose equivalence classes are segments of C. We start with $E_o = CxC$. If α is limit then E_α is the intersection of all E_α with $\beta < \alpha$. For every α, $E_{\alpha+1}$ is the relation "x and y belong to the same part of the same equivalence class of E_α". The construction is completed when the equality relation is reached. The desired tree T consists of all equivalence classes of all these equivalence relations.□

Theorem 1. For every well-founded tree T with an orientation H there is a binary, bounded, oriented, well-founded tree T' such that

(i) the universe of T' extends the universe of T,

(ii) for all x, y in T, x < y in T iff x < y in T', and

(iii) for every pair (x, y) of T-brothers, (x, y)εH iff x lexicographically precedes y in T'.

Proof. By Lemma 1, for every maximal H-chain C there is a binary, bounded, oriented, well-founded tree Tr(c) such that C is isomorphic to the set of leaves of Tr(C) with the lexicographical order. Let I(C) be an isomorphism from C to the chain of leaves of Tr(C).

For every nonsingleton maximal H-chain C we add some auxiliary nodes to T. Let x be the T-father of nodes in C. Graft a copy of Tr(C) at x in such a way that the root of Tr(C) becomes a son of x, and identify nodes of C with leaves of Tr(C) with respect to I(C). The resulting tree is the desired binary tree. We orient this binary tree with respect to the grafts. In other words, the union of the orientations of the grafts is the orientation of our binary tree.□

Proposition 1. The first-order theory of bounded, colored, oriented, well-founded trees reduces to the first-order theory of binary, bounded, colored, well-founded trees.

Proof. Let φ be a first-order sentence in a vocabulary comprising the binary predicate symbols <, H and a number of unary predicate constants. Find first unary predicate constants L, P, which do not appear in φ.

Write a first-order sentence φ_1 and a first-order formula L*(u, v) in the vocabulary {<, L} such that if T is a binary tree with a color L which satisfies φ_1 then for every pair of brother nodes in T exactly one brother belongs to L, and an arbitrary pair (x, y) of nodes satisfies L*(x, y) in T if and only if there exist nodes x', y', z such that $x' \leq x$, $y' \leq y$, x' and y' are different sons of z and $x' \varepsilon L$.

Write a first-order sentence φ_2 in the vocabulary {<, L, P} such that if T is a bounded well-founded tree with colors L, P which satisfies φ_2, then P forms a bounded well-founded subtree of T and L* is an orientation of the subtree P. Let φ_3 be the result of the following changes in φ: first restrict all quantifiers in φ by P, then replace H by L*. It is easy to see that

$$\varphi \mapsto (\varphi_1 \ \& \ \varphi_2 \rightarrow \varphi_3)$$

is the desired reduction.□

REFERENCES

Gurevich, Y., and Shelah, S., 1984, The Decision Problem for Branching Time Logic, J. Symbolic Logic, to appear.

Prior, A. N., 1967, "Past, Present and Future," Clarendon Press, Oxford.

REDUCTIONS OF THEORIES FOR ANALYSIS

Wilfried Sieg
Department of Philosophy
Columbia University in the City of New York
New York, N.Y. 10027/USA

INTRODUCTION

The formal theories considered here are all subsystems of second order arithmetic with the full comprehension principle, briefly (CA). They are theories for classical analysis: Hilbert used a theory equivalent to (CA) as a formal framework for mathematical analysis in lectures during the early twenties; an extensive portion of analysis had already earlier been developed by Weyl in a weak subsystem of (CA). Weyl's work aimed at *rebuilding parts of analysis on a "sound" basis*, and that meant, above all, avoiding impredicative principles. Hilbert, in contrast, set himself the task of securing the instrumental usefulness of all of classical mathematics. He hoped to achieve that aim by *reducing analysis* and even set theory *to a fixed, absolutely fundamental part of arithmetic*, so-called finitist mathematics. The specific proposal of how to achieve such a reduction is the mathematical centerpiece of Hilbert's program; it was refuted by Gödel's Incompleteness Theorems.

A generalized reductive program has been pursued for analysis, and significant progress has been made. Indeed, progress has been made in two complementary directions. On the one hand, the work of Weyl and of other predicatively or constructively inclined mathematicians has been extended to show that all of classical analysis can be carried out in theories that are reducible to elementary arithmetic. On the other hand, strong impredicative subsystems of (CA) have been reduced to constructively acceptable theories of inductive definitions. These results lead naturally to a distinction between two types of reductions. The two types are distinguished from each other not by the techniques for obtaining them, but rather by programmatic aims. FOUNDATIONAL REDUCTIONS are to provide a constructive basis for strong and (from certain foundational perspectives) problematic parts of (CA); COMPUTATIONAL REDUCTIONS are to yield algorithmic information from proofs in weak and (even from a finitist standpoint) unproblematic parts of (CA).

It is via foundational reductions that the generalized program is pushed forward in an attempt to answer the question "WHAT MORE THAN FINITIST MATHEMATICS DO WE HAVE TO KNOW TO RECOGNIZE THE (PARTIAL) SOUNDNESS OF A STRONG THEORY?". Computational reductions answer in a specific way Kreisel's question "WHAT MORE THAN ITS TRUTH DO WE KNOW, IF WE HAVE PROVED A THEOREM BY RESTRICTED MEANS (HERE: IN A WEAK SUBSYSTEM)?". Answers to the latter question are of mainly mathematical interest, whereas answers to the former question are of more philosophical significance: in any event, they provide detailed material for reflections on the epistemology of mathematics.

A concise formulation of the generalized reductive program is given below, and the aims of proof-theoretic investigations are discussed in greater detail. Some of the results which have been obtained more recently are described, and there is even a new theorem or two. However, the paper is expository and reflective. I hope it will be informative and accesible to non-proof-theorists, as I believe that the broad themes are, or should be, of general interest to philosophers concerned with the foundations of mathematics and the sciences. In part A, I start out with a few historical remarks on the context in which the Hilbert program arose, because it is still widely and deeply misunderstood as an ad-hoc-weapon against the growing influence of Brouwer's intuitionism. (A fuller account of this context is given in Sieg, 1984. See also Giaquinto, 1983.) At the end of part A the crucial features of one proof-theoretic tool, sequent calculi, are presented. Part B gives examples of the two types of reductions. Foundational reductions of impredicative parts of (CA) to intuitionistic theories of constructive, well-founded trees are given in B1. B2 contains computational reductions; in particular, I will show that an interesting, weak subsystem can be reduced to a proper part of primitive recursive arithmetic (PRA).

A. REDUCTIVE AIMS OF PROOF THEORY

The problems that motivated Hilbert's program can be traced back to the central foundational issue in 19th century mathematics, namely securing a basis for analysis. A possible resolution is indicated by the slogan "Arithmetize analysis". That direction was given already by Gauss, and its meaning can be fathomed from Dirichlet's claim (reported by Dedekind), that *any* theorem of analysis can be formulated as a theorem concerning the natural numbers. For some the arithmetization of analysis was accomplished by the work of Cantor, Dedekind, and Weierstrass; for others, e.g., Kronecker, a stricter arithmetization was required which would base the whole content of all mathematical disciplines (with the exception of geometry and mechanics) "on the concept of number taken in its most narrow sense, and thus to strip away the modifications and extensions of this concept, which have been brought about in most cases by applications in geometry and mechanics" (Kronecker, 1887, 253.) (In a footnote, Kronecker makes clear that he has in mind "in particular the addition of the irrational and continuous magnitudes".) Kronecker strongly opposed Cantor's and Dedekind's free use of set-theoretic notions, as it violated methodological restrictions on ("legitimate") mathematical concepts and arguments. Cantor suggested a way to turn such a restrictive position to positive work and formulated "certain advantages".

> If, as it is assumed here [i.e., from such a restrictive position], only the natural numbers are real and all others just relational forms, then it can be required that the proofs of theorems in analysis are checked as to their "number-theoretic content" and that every gap, which is discovered, is filled according to the principles of arithmetic. The feasibility of such a supplementation is viewed as the true touchstone for the genuineness and complete rigor of those proofs. It is not to be denied, that in this way the foundation of many theorems can be perfected and that also other methodological improvements in various branches of analysis can be effected. Adherence to the principles justified from this viewpoint, it is also believed, secures against any kind of absurdities or mistakes. (Cantor, 1883, 173.)

Hilbert may have been influenced by such considerations when he gave up - in his Heidelberg address of 1904 - his first attempt of circumventing the Cantorian problems in set theory as far as they effected analysis. The then recently discovered elementary contradictions of Zermelo and Russell had changed his outlook on these problems. Bernays is quoted in Reid's biography of Hilbert as saying:

> Under the influence of the discovery of the antinomies in set theory, Hilbert temporarily thought that Kronecker had probably been right there. [i.e., right in insisting on restricted methods.] But soon he changed his mind. Now it became his goal,

one might say, to do battle with Kronecker with his own weapons of finiteness by means of a modified conception of mathematics. (Reid, 1970, 173)

The key question was, how might that be done?

A1. Reflection

The radicalization of the axiomatic method, high-lighted in Hilbert's own "Grundlagen der Geometrie", and the fresh developments in logic due to Frege and Peano provided the basic background for Hilbert's way of answering the question. The ultimate goal of his proposal in 1904 was the same as the one he had formulated in "Über den Zahlbegriff" (1900) and his famous Paris lectures, namely to establish by means of a consistency proof the existence of the set of natural and real numbers and of the Cantorian alephs. Hilbert indicated now a possibility of giving such a proof without presupposing basic set-theoretic notions as he had done earlier. He proposed a simultaneous *formal* development of logic and arithmetic, so that proofs could be viewed as *finite* mathematical structures. The new task was to show by elementary mathematical means that such formal proofs cannot lead to a contradiction.*

* From a much later perspective Bernays describes the fundamental conception as follows: "... in taking the deductive structure of a formalized theory as an object, the theory is projected so-to-speak into number theory. The structure obtained in this way is in general essentially different from the structure intended by the theory. However, it [the deductive structure] can serve the purpose of recognizing the consistency of the theory from a standpoint which is more elementary than the assumption of the intended structure." (Bernays, 1970, 186)

This formulation foreshadowed aspects of the proof-theoretic program Hilbert pursued in the twenties together with, e.g., Bernays, Ackermann, von Neumann, Herbrand. There was, however, a crucial and sophisticated shift in what a consistency proof was to establish. (Recall, above it was the existence of infinite mathematical systems.) To bring this out clearly, let P be a formal theory in which mathematical practice can be represented and let F be a theory formulating principles of finitist mathematics. Under weak assumptions on P (satisfied by the usual formal theories) the consistency statement for P is equivalent to the *reflection principle*

$$Pr(a, '\psi') \rightarrow \psi;$$

Pr is the canonical proof-predicate for P, 'ψ' the translation of the F-statement ψ into the language of P. Proving the reflection principle in F amounts to recognizing - from the restricted standpoint of F - the truth of F-statements whose translations have been derived in P. As a matter of fact, the proof would yield a method turning any P-proof of 'ψ' into an F-proof of ψ. In this way a consistency proof would achieve what Hilbert used to call the elimination of ideal elements from proofs of real statements.* Finitist mathematics was viewed as a fixed part of elementary arithmetic, as I mentioned already; its philosophical justification seemed to be unproblematic. Thus Hilbert thought that the consistency proof for P would solve the foundational problems "once and for all" and would achieve this by mathematical considerations. "This is precisely the great advantage of Hilbert's proposal, that the problems and difficulties arising

---

* Compare this with Cantor's remarks quoted above. But note that this goal is quite in accord with the positivist-instrumentalist ZEITGEIST of the early decades of this century. Vide Bernays, 1922, 18-19.

in the foundations of mathematics are transferred from the epistemological-philosophical to the genuinely mathematical domain." (Bernays, 1922, 19.)

A2. Incompleteness

The radical foundational aims of Hilbert's program had to be abandoned on account of Gödel's Incompleteness Theorems. A generalization of the program was developed in response to Gödel's results, and it has been pursued with great vigor and mathematical success - for parts of analysis. Bernays and later Kreisel were highly influential in this development. (For relatively recent and polished formulations, see Bernays, 1970, pp. 186-187 and Kreisel, 1968, pp. 321-323.) The basic task of the generalized reductive program can be seen as follows: find for a significant part of classical mathematical practice, formalized in a theory P*, an appropriate constructive theory F*, such that F* proves the partial reflection principle for P*. I.e., F* proves for any P*-derivation D

$$Pr^*(D, '\psi') \rightarrow \psi.$$

ψ is in a class Λ of F*-statements. It follows immediately that P* is conservative over F* with respect to the statements in Λ; consequently, P* is consistent relative to F*. (I made the assumption, satisfied by the theories discussed below, that F* is easily seen to be contained in P*. If that is not the case, reductions in both directions have to be established.)

The Gödel-Gentzen-reduction of classical elementary arithmetic (Z) to its intuitionistic version (HA) is the early paradigm of a successful contribution to the generalized program. Clearly, (Z) is taken as P*, (HA) as F*, and Λ consists of all negative arithmetic and Π^0_2-sentences.* It was incidentally this result which showed to the Hilbert-school that intuitionistic and finitist reasoning did not coincide, "contrary to the prevailing views at the time" as Bernays puts it. In addition, it gave an important positive impetus to(wards) the generalized program.

> It thus became apparent that the "finite Standpunkt" is not the only alternative to classical ways of reasoning and is not necessarily implied by the idea of proof theory. An enlarging of the methods of proof theory was therefore suggested: instead of a restriction to finitist methods of reasoning, it was required only that the arguments be of a constructive character, allowing us to deal with more general forms of inferences. (Bernays, 1967.)

The question which had sweeping, general answers in the original Hilbert program had to be addressed anew, indeed in a more subtle way. Which parts of classical mathematical practice can be represented in a certain theory P*? What are (the grounds for) the principles of a "corresponding" constructive F*? Briefly put, if a metamathematical conservation result has been obtained, it has to be complemented by additional mathematical and philosophical work establishing its foundational interest by answering these questions. - Classical analysis was viewed as decisive for the generalized program. Its basic notions and results were carefully and in detail presented by Hilbert and Bernays (Supplement IV of their "Grundlagen der Mathematik, II").

---

* The negative arithmetic are those sentences in the language of arithmetic which are either atomic or use in their build-up only the logical connectives $\rightarrow$, &, $\forall$. - Gödel and Gentzen established the result for negative arithmetic sentences, Kreisel (1958) extended it to Π^0_2-sentences, and Friedman (1978) gave a very simple syntactic argument for this extension.

Remark. The language of analysis is chosen here to be that of second order arithmetic with function variables (and quantifiers) and names for all primitive recursive functions. The axioms of the base theory (BT) include (a) the axioms for zero, successor, and the defining equations for all primitive recursive functions, (b) the induction principle for quantifier-free formulas, and (c) quantifier-free comprehension. Full classical analysis (CA) is obtained from (BT) by adding the comprehension principle for all formulas of the language. Subsystems of analysis are principally distinguished by their restricted function (or set) existence principles. They include, for example, the comprehension principle or forms of the axiom of choice only for certain classes of formulas (like Π^0_n, Π^0_∞, Π^1_n). There is a second important distinguishing feature. The induction principle can be formulated either as a schema for all formulas of the language or as a second-order axiom. In the latter case, the principle is available only for functions (sets) which can be proved to exist in the theory. For example, (Π^0_∞-CA) denotes the theory obtained from (BT) by adding the arithmetic comprehension principle and the full induction schema; (Π^0_∞-CA)$\restriction$, "restricted -(Π^0_∞-CA)", is the corresponding theory with the induction axiom. Clearly, (Π^0_∞-CA)$\restriction$ is equivalent to the theory obtained from (BT) by just the arithmetic comprehension principle. This is Weyl's theory. (BT) is conservative over (PRA). (Π^0_∞-CA)$\restriction$ is conservative over elementary arithmetic, whereas (Π^0_∞-CA) proves the consistency of (Z).

In the case of analysis the first question can be more sharply focused: which set or function-existence principles are sufficient (and necessary) to prove central facts? The surprising answer is that arithmetic comprehension suffices. This is the outcome of work by Takeuti (1978), Feferman (e.g., 1977), and Friedman (e.g., 1980). Obviously, their investigations lie in a rather long tradition of persistent efforts to pursue analysis by restricted means. The work of constructivists like Kronecker, Brouwer, and Bishop is part of that tradition. Predicatively inclined mathematicians contributed also significantly; indeed, Weyl's "Das Kontinuum" is an early landmark of that kind of research.

From results of Friedman and Simpson one can infer that weaker theories will not do for all of analysis as some crucial theorems are actually equivalent to the arithmetic comprehension principle. Examples of such theorems are the Bolzano-Weierstrass-Theorem and the fact that every Cauchy-sequence is convergent. Nevertheless, in a theory isolated by Friedman a good deal of analysis can be developed, and that theory is conservative over primitive recursive arithmetic (PRA). It is the first theory I consider to be of interest for computational reductions. Theories like $(\Pi^1_1\text{-CA})\upharpoonright$ and $(\Sigma^1_2\text{-AC})$ for which foundational reductions are available are thus for the actual practice of analysis far too strong. The F*'s to which they can be reduced are, ironically, justified from an intuitionistic standpoint. They are theories for constructive trees, and we have a(n intuitionistically) convincing answer to a sharpening of the second question: what are (the principles for) constructive mathematical objects? - Before turning to the detailed discussion of these reductive results I want to outline one way of establishing conservative extension results by proof-theoretic means.

A3. Sequent Calculi

A variety of technical tools have been employed in proof-theory; for example the ε-calculus, the no-counterexample-interpretation, the Dialectica-interpretation. The tools most directly useful for the reductive aims are in my view finitary and infinitary sequent calculi for which the cut-elimination-theorem can be established. (Clearly, in the case of infinitary calculi, the proof-theoretic treatment has to be kept constructive.) The subformula-property is the crucial feature of cut-free derivations. This feature makes it possible to use truth-definitions for formulas of restricted syntactic complexity and to establish formally the truth of statements. Let me explain this for the usual finitary calculi.

The classical sequent calculi are assumed to be in the style of Tait, 1968; i.e., finite sets of formulas are proved, negation is directly available only for atomic formulas. (For complex formulas it is defined in the obvious way.) Thus, the basic logical symbols are just &, ∨, ∀, ∃. The rules of the calculi are included among the following ones, where Γ is used as a syntactic variable ranging over finite sets of formulas.

<u>LA</u> $\Gamma, \psi, \neg\psi$ (ψ is atomic)

<u>&</u> $$\frac{\Gamma, \psi_1 \qquad \Gamma, \psi_2}{\Gamma, \psi_1 \,\&\, \psi_2}$$

<u>∨</u>$_i$ $$\frac{\Gamma, \psi_i}{\Gamma, \psi_1 \vee \psi_2} \qquad i = 1, 2$$

<u>C</u>(ut) $$\frac{\Gamma, \psi \qquad \Gamma, \neg\psi}{\Gamma}$$

When appropriate, rules for quantification are available. In case of (extensions of) number theory we have the rules

<u>∀</u> $$\frac{\Gamma, \psi a}{\Gamma, (\forall x)\psi x}$$ (a must not occur in Γ) <u>∃</u> $$\frac{\Gamma, \psi t}{\Gamma, (\exists x)\psi x};$$

The rules for function-quantification are analogous. Identity rules can be taken in the form

$$\frac{\Gamma, \psi t}{s \neq t, \Gamma, \psi s} \qquad \frac{\Gamma, \psi t}{t \neq s, \Gamma, \psi s};$$

the axiom for identity is

<u>IA</u> Γ, a = a.

(An intuitionistic version of this calculus can be formulated in a straightforward, though more complicated way.) Derivations are built up in tree-form as usual; let me use D, E, ... as syntactic variables ranging over derivations. A derivation is called cut-free or normal, if it does not contain an occurrence of the cut-rule <u>C</u>. Two facts concerning the invertibility of quantifier-rules will be extremely useful. I formulate them only for number-quantifiers, but analogous results hold for function-quantifiers as well.

$\forall$-*inversion.* If D is a normal derivation of Δ, $(\forall x)\psi x$, then there is a normal derivation E of Δ, ψc; c is a parameter not used in D and E is not longer than D.

The second fact concerns the invertibility of <u>$\exists$</u>; this is possible only in restricted contexts and is a form of Herbrand's Theorem. I refer to it also as an Herbrand-type lemma.

$\exists$-*inversion.* Let Δ contain only purely existential formulas and let ψa be quantifier-free; if D is a normal derivation of Δ, $(\exists x)\ \psi x$, then there is a finite sequence of terms $t_1, \ldots, t_n$ and a normal derivation E of Δ, $\psi t_1, \ldots, \psi t_n$. Again, E is not longer than D.

Due to Gentzen's Hauptsatz, the fundamental fact for these finitary calculi, the restriction to normal derivations in the above lemmata is not restrictive. After all, any derivation can be effectively transformed into a normal one with the same endsequent. By inspection of the rules it can be seen immediately that all formulas occurring in a normal derivation of Δ are subformulas of elements of Δ.

Let me explain through an example how the subformula-property is exploited for proofs of (partial) reflection principles. The underlying idea is simple, pervasive, and quite elegant. Consider a fragment of arithmetic, say (HAN); it has the usual axioms for zero and successor, defining equations for finitely many primitive recursive functions, and the induction schema for just quantifier-free formulas. Consequently, all of the axioms can be taken to be in quantifier-free form. Now assume that (HAN) proves (a Π^0_1-statement and thus by $\forall$-inversion) a quantifier-free statement ψ. A normal derivation of Δ, ψ can then be obtained, where Δ contains only negations of HAN-axioms. These considerations can actually be carried out in (PRA), i.e.,

$$(\text{PRA}) \vdash \text{Pf}_{\text{HAN}}(\ulcorner\psi\urcorner) \rightarrow \text{Pf}^n(\ulcorner\Delta, \psi\urcorner);$$

Pf_{HAN} and Pf^n express that there is a derivation in (HAN), respectively a normal derivation in the sequent calculus. A normal derivation of Δ, ψ contains only subformulas of elements in its endsequent. So one can use an adequate, quantifier-free truth-definition Tr (for quantifier-free formulas) to show that

$$(\text{PRA}) \vdash \text{Pf}^n(\ulcorner\Delta, \psi\urcorner) \rightarrow \text{Tr}(\ulcorner\mathbb{W}\Delta, \psi\urcorner);$$

$\mathbb{W}\Delta, \psi$ is the disjunction of the formulas in Δ, ψ. This is possible, as the language of (HAN) contains only finitely many symbols for primitive recursive functions: we can easily define a primitive recursive valuation function for all terms built up from them. More generally, but for the same reason, (HAN) could contain all functions of a fixed segment of the Grzegorczyk-hierarchy. (For details concerning the standard part of truth-definitions see Schwichtenberg, 1977, 893-894.) As Tr is provably adequate we have

$$(\text{PRA}) \vdash \text{Tr}(\ulcorner\mathbb{W}\Delta, \psi\urcorner) \rightarrow \mathbb{W}\Delta, \psi$$

and thus

$$(PRA) \vdash Pf_{HAN}(\ulcorner\psi\urcorner) \to \psi.$$

This step can be taken, as the axioms of (HAN) are axioms of (PRA). Note that the above is essentially Gentzen's way of establishing the consistency result due to Ackermann, von Neumann, and Herbrand.

For the last step it was obviously crucial that the axioms of (HAN) are available in (PRA). The basic structure of the argument can be modified, however, for theories P* whose principles are not recognizable (i.e., provable) in F*. The strategy is to eliminate those principles from derivations (of certain classes of formulas). Eliminations can be effected by (i) the embedding of finitary into infinitary calculi, and (ii) the extraction of information from a given finitary or infinitary normal derivation via an Herbrand-type lemma. An example of (i) is the embedding of (Z) into a calculus with the ω-rule replacing the induction principle. (See Schwichtenberg (1977) for a lucid presentation.) Lorenzen and Schütte introduced this technique to recast Gentzen's consistency proof for (Z), and extensions have been used widely. For the foundational reductions below one uses infinitary calculi with inferences involving constructive tree classes $\mathcal{O}_\alpha$. These inferences are of the form

$$\frac{\Delta,\ \psi e}{\Delta,\ (\forall x)(\mathcal{O}_\alpha x \to \psi x)} \quad \text{for all } e \text{ in } \mathcal{O}_\alpha;$$

in case $\alpha = 0$, this is just a form of the ω-rule. For the reductive program it is crucial that the infinitary derivations needed for the embedding and subsequent proof-theoretic investigation can be treated constructively, and that means first of all that they are constructive mathematical objects.* Examples of (ii) can be found in Tait (1968), in Feferman and Sieg (1981b) and in Sieg (1983); the extracted information is used to eliminate various forms of the axiom of (dependent) choice in favor of the comprehension principle. One achieves by this technique a constructive understanding of the quantifier combination $\forall \exists$ in a classical, albeit restricted context. - This brings us directly to the eliminative considerations for foundational and computational reductions.

B. REDUCTIVE RESULTS FOR PARTS OF ANALYSIS

Before describing such results, I want to make some brief remarks on one facet of proof theory which is sometimes taken as the most enlightening one. I am alluding to (the use of) systems of ordinal notations. Indeed, from Gentzen's (second) consistency proof for (Z) emerged a program which is more specific than the generalized reductive program described earlier. Gentzen's argument, recall, can be carried out in (PRA) extended by the principles of transfinite recursion and transfinite induction for the first ε-number ε_o. ε_o is the smallest ordinal with this property. Gentzen wanted to characterize the strength of stronger and stronger theories by their uniquely determined "proof-theoretic ordinals". This is a fascinating, relatively precise technical problem, and a great deal of sophisticated work has been devoted to it. The foundational interest of such

* Compare this with the (modified) version of the Hilbert program as described by Bernays (1970, 186) and in A2. Recall also that the restriction to finite derivation figures in Hilbert's metamathematics aroused very early on the criticism of people with completely different foundational views; e.g., Brouwer (1927) and Zermelo (1931 and 1935). See also the last section of Sieg (1984).

investigations rests, however, on the constructive character of the ordinals used. Gentzen saw quite clearly that "one has to carry out investigations [in parallel to establishing consistency via transfinite induction] with the aim of making the validity of transfinite induction for larger and larger limit numbers constructively intelligible". (In a letter to Bernays in 1936.) The point I want to make is quite simply that the determination of the proof-theoretic ordinal of a theory T is not the ultimate aim of investigations in proof-theory and presumably not even the central one (unless further research *shows* that ordinals are conceptually central in constructive mathematics and thus for the general reductive aims). In any event, the foundational reductions for some impredicative parts of (CA) discussed in B1 do not use special systems of ordinal notations. The strongest of the theories treated there is $(\Delta^1_2\text{-CA})$. B2 presents computational reductions of two weak subsystems which are conservative over (a fragment of) (PRA). Details of the argument for the latter result are indicated in B3.

B1. Foundational Reductions

Generalized inductive definitions* play a central role here, both technically and conceptually. Classes given by inductive definitions, i.d. classes for short, have been used in constructive mathematics ever since Brouwer. Two familiar examples of such classes are well-founded trees of finite sequences of natural numbers ("unsecured sequences") and Borel sets. The former were employed in Brouwer's justification of bar-induction; the latter in Bishop's

* In contrast to elementary inductive definitions by means of which exactly the recursively enumerable sets of natural numbers are definable.

original development of measure theory. In spite of the fact that i.d. classes can be avoided in the current practice of constructive analysis, particular ones are of intrinsic mathematical and foundational interest.

The constructive (well-founded) trees form such a distinguished class, called $\mathcal{O}$. It is given by two inductive clauses, namely (i) if e is 0, then e is in $\mathcal{O}$, and (ii) if e is (the Gödel-number of) a recursive function enumerating elements of $\mathcal{O}$, then e is in $\mathcal{O}$.* - The elements of $\mathcal{O}$ are thus generated by joining recursively given sequences of previously generated elements of $\mathcal{O}$ and can be pictured as infinite, well-founded trees. Locally, the structure of such a tree is as follows:

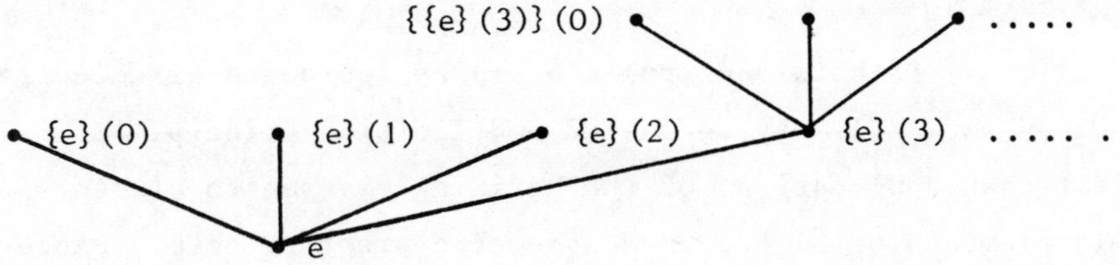

Higher tree classes are obtained by a suitable iteration of this definition along a given recursive well-ordering of the natural numbers. Suitable means here that branchings in trees are not only taken over the natural numbers but also over already given lower tree classes.

---

* The antecedents of these generating clauses can be expressed by a formula which is arithmetic in $\mathcal{O}$. Their disjunction is abbreviated by $A(\mathcal{O}, e)$.

These special i.d. classes have been investigated by Brouwer, Church, Kleene, and others; they have also played a significant role in metamathematical studies of theories for classical and intuitionistic analysis. Their constructive appeal consists partly in this: the trees reflect their build-up according to the generating clauses of their definition directly and locally in an effective way. If one views the clauses as inference rules, the constructive trees are infinitary derivations and show that they fall under their definition. Constructive theories for $\mathcal{O}$ have been formulated as extensions of intuitionistic arithmetic with the following principles for $\mathcal{O}$ (cp. fn. on preceding page):

$\mathcal{O}1.\quad (\forall x)(A(\mathcal{O}, x) \rightarrow \mathcal{O}x)$

$\mathcal{O}2.\quad (\forall x)(A(\psi, x) \rightarrow \psi x) \rightarrow (\forall x)(\mathcal{O}x \rightarrow \psi x).$

$A(\psi, x)$ is obtained from $A(\mathcal{O}, x)$ by replacing all occurrences of $\mathcal{O}z$ by ψz. - $\mathcal{O}1.$ may be called a definition principle making explicit that applications of the defining clauses to elements of $\mathcal{O}$ yield elements of $\mathcal{O}$. $\mathcal{O}2.$ is a schematic proof principle expressing that one can give arguments by induction on $\mathcal{O}$ (employing any formula ψz of the language). Proofs by this principle follow or parallel the construction of the elements in $\mathcal{O}$. The resulting theory is called $ID_1(\mathcal{O})$. For the higher tree classes the definition and proof principles can be formulated in a similar, though more complicated manner. The theory is denoted by $ID_{<\lambda}(\mathcal{O})$, when the iteration proceeds along arbitrary initial segments of the given well-ordering of type λ. (For the detailed formulation the reader is referred to Feferman and Sieg, 1981a.)

These theories (for higher tree classes) are also meaningful from a classical point of view, even when more general defining clauses are considered. Let P be a unary predicate variable and call a formula $A(P, x)$ positive in P if P does not occur in the scope of a negation sign or in the antecedent of a conditional. Each such formula determines an i.d. class P^A which is definable in second-order logic by

$$P^A a \leftrightarrow (\forall P)((\forall x)(A(P, x) \rightarrow Px) \rightarrow Pa);$$

for convenience we make use of a second-order language with predicate variables. P^A exists as a set by an impredicative instance of the comprehension principle, as positive formulas satisfy the following monotonicity condition

$$(\forall x)(Px \rightarrow Qx) \rightarrow (\forall x)(A(P, x) \rightarrow A(Q, x)).$$

The theories obtained from classical number theory by adding the definition and proof principles for all i.d. classes P^A given by positive A is denoted by ID_1^c. As above, one can consider iterations of such definitions and obtain theories $ID_{<\lambda}^c$. Feferman (1970) and Friedman (1970) established that for example $(\Pi_1^1\text{-CA})\restriction$, $(\Delta_2^1\text{-CR})$, and $(\Delta_2^1\text{-CA})$ are equivalent to $ID_{<\omega}^c$, $ID_{<\omega^\omega}^c$, respectively $ID_{<\varepsilon_0}^c$. Thus, it is sufficient - for reducing the above impredicative subsystem - to reduce the theories of iterated inductive definitions. That was achieved among other things by Buchholz, Pohlers, and myself in 1977. Our work is reported in volume 897 of the Springer Lecture Notes in Mathematics. (Buchholz and Pohlers determined in addition the proof theoretic ordinals of the theories.) The reduction I achieved is formulated in the next theorem.

Theorem. For any primitive recursive well-ordering of limit characteristic λ, $ID_{<\lambda}^c$ is conservative over $ID_{<\lambda}(\mathcal{O})$ for all negative arithmetic and Π_2^0-formulas.

The proof, inspired by Tait (1970), employs the strong infinitary calculi described at the end of A3 and exploits the close interrelation between constructive trees, derivations in those calculi, and positive inductive definitions. A detailed informal description of the argument is given in Sieg (1984), a full account in Sieg (1981).

The reductions to theories of tree classes are most satisfactory from an intuitionistic point of view. The question clearly is whether still stronger parts of (CA) can be reduced in the same way. Unfortunately, the answer is "NO". It is a well-known result of Addison and Kleene that the iteration of the hyperjump (and thus of inductive definitions) along recursive ordinals leads only to Δ^1_2-sets. Consequently, theories for i.d. classes cannot be used for reductions of $(\Pi^1_n\text{-CA})$ with $n \geq 2$. Here is a major conceptual problem, it seems to me, namely to find a broad notion of "constructive mathematical objects" and suitable principles for them which can serve as a starting point for foundational reductions of parts of analysis beyond $(\Delta^1_2\text{-CA})$.* There are also some precise and important open questions concerning the theories for i.d. classes (cp. Sieg, 1981, and Feferman, 1982). Problem 1: Is ID^c_α conservative over $ID_\alpha(\mathcal{O})$ for negative arithmetic and Π^o_2-sentences ... for all (primitive) recursive α? Problem 2: Is ID^{mon}_α conservative over $ID_\alpha(\mathcal{O})$ for all arithmetic sentences? (ID^{mon}_α is the intuitionistic theory for i.d. classes given by provably monotone clauses.)

* There are results for $(\Delta^1_2\text{-CA})$+BI): Jäger and Pohlers determined the proof-theoretic ordinal, and Jäger reduced it to Feferman's constructive theory T_0. (This establishes with earlier work of Feferman's the equivalence of these theories.)

B2. Computational Reductions

It was already pointed out in A2 that all of classical analysis can be formally developed in various conservative extensions of elementary arithmetic, and that one cannot do better as some central theorems are over (BT) equivalent to the arithmetic comprehension principle. If one concentrates, however, on proper parts one can get by with weaker systems. Friedman (1975) isolated a particularly interesting system. I present it in an equivalent formulation that is more suitable for the subsequent proof-theoretic treatment. The theory, call it (F), extends (BT) by the axiom of choice for Σ_1^0-formulas, Σ_1^0-AC_0,

$$(\forall x)(\exists y)\psi xy \rightarrow (\exists f)(\forall x)\psi xf(x),$$

the induction principle for Σ_1^0-formulas, Σ_1^0-IA, and König's Lemma for binary trees, WKL,

$$(\forall f)(T(f) \ \& \ (\forall x)(\exists y)(lh(y) = x \ \& \ f(y) = 1) \rightarrow (\exists g)(\forall x)f(\overline{g}(x)) = 1.$$

$T(f)$ expresses that f is (the characteristic function of) a tree of 0-1-sequences, lh is the length-function for sequence numbers. $T(f)$ is the purely universal formula

$$(\forall x)(\forall y)((f(x * y) = 1 \rightarrow f(x) = 1) \ \& \ (f(x * \langle y\rangle) = 1 \rightarrow y \leq 1)).$$

(F) is surprisingly strong for mathematical work and quite weak from a metamathematical point of view, namely conservative over (PRA) for Π_2^0-statements.

Remarks. (i) Let me indicate what kind of facts can be established in (F) and point to the phenomenon of "reverse mathematics". In (F^-), i.e., (F) without WKL, one can establish the equivalence of the following statements: (1) WKL, (2) the Heine-Borel Theorem (every covering of the unit interval by a countable sequence of open intervals has a finite subcovering), (3) every continuous function on the unit interval is uniformly continuous, (4) every continuous function on the unit interval is bounded, (5) every continuous function on the unit interval has a supremum and attains it, (6) the Cauchy-Peano Theorem on the existence of solutions for ordinary differential equations. - The equivalence between (1) and (2) was established by Friedman; the other equivalences are due to Simpson (1982a and 1982b).

(ii) Minc (1976) introduced a subsystem, proved it to be conservative over (PRA) for Π^0_2-sentences, and established Gödel's Completeness Theorem in it. The system, call it (M^-), is essentially (BT) together with the comprehension principle for Π^0_1-formulas WITHOUT function parameters and the induction rule for Π^0_2-formulas WITHOUT function parameters. The crucial step in the argument for the completeness theorem is a proof of WKL for primitive recursive trees. Indeed, the extension of (M^-) by WKL yields a theory (M) which is conservative over (PRA) for Π^0_2-sentences. (Sieg, 1983.)

Friedman established the conservation result mentioned just before the remarks by model-theoretic methods. In Sieg (1983) I gave a purely proof-theoretic argument.* (F) is thus directly justified on finitist grounds. The result has also a computationally informative consequence.

Corollary. There is a primitive recursive function f and a proof in (PRA) of $\psi af(a)$ in case (F) proves $(\forall x)(\exists y)\psi xy$; ψ is quantifier-free.

---

* A proof theoretic argument for this and some other results was given by A. Cantini in a very recent, unpublished paper "On the proof theory of Weak König's Lemma."

The corollary implies that the provably recursive functions of (F) are exactly the primitive recursive ones. It is through a characterization of the provably recursive functions of a theory T that one answer to Kreisel's question can be given. The chances for obtaining an interesting answer are obviously greater when T is extremely restricted, yet mathematically still powerful. It seems to me that the work of Friedman and Simpson has improved our chances dramatically; so much so that further systematic studies are justified, not just ad-hoc constructions.

Remark. Kreisel has urged to explore "the mathematical significance of consistency proofs", in particular in his 1958 paper of that very title. He emphasized two uses of a characterization of T's provably recursive functions: (1) to obtain more explicit solutions for Π^o_2-theorems in the sense of the above corollary;* (2) to give independence arguments concerning Π^o_2-sentences. To see the latter assume that $(\forall x)(\exists y)\psi xy$ is true, but that for no f in the class of provably recursive functions of T $(\forall x)\psi xf(x)$ is true; then $(\forall x)(\exists y)\psi xy$ is independent of T. A beautiful example of that strategy is given in Graham et al. (1982), to establish the independence of the Paris-Harrington-Ramsey statement. (They make use of the fact that the provably recursive functions of (Z) are exactly the $<\varepsilon_o$-recursive ones.)

From a mathematical-computational vantage point one is really looking for refinements of the corollary, i.e., for subsystems whose

---

* In addition, they should be extracted efficiently from given proofs. That is most important, but requires work in a different direction. One has to pay close attention to the computational complexity of (presentations of) elementary syntax and of proof-theoretic operations on (restricted classes of) derivations.

provably recursive functions are in a small subclass of the primitive recursive functions. I have one relevant result whose proof I will describe in the next section. Let (ET) be like (BT), but admit only names for the Kalmar-elementary functions into the language. Naturally, the axioms include just the defining equations for them. (KEA) is (PRA) restricted in the same way.

Theorem. Let (K) be (ET + Σ_1^0-AC_0 + WKL); (K) is conservative over (KEA) for Π_2^0-sentences.

The theorem has as an immediate consequence a refinement of the earlier corollary.

Corollary. There is a Kalmar-elementary function f and a proof in (KEA) of $\psi af(a)$ in case (K) proves $(\forall x)(\exists y)\psi xy$; ψ is quantifier-free.

Thus, the provably recursive functions of (K) are exactly the Kalmar-elementary ones. - A first candidate for testing the usefulness of (K) is Artin and Schreier's Theorem, that every positive definite rational function with rational coefficients is a sum of squares. This is a solution to Hilbert's 17th problem, and Kreisel showed that the number and degrees of the squares are bounded by a (specific) primitive recursive function of the degree and the number of variables of the given positive definite function. That there is such a primitive recursive function follows immediately from the fact that Artin and Schreier's Theorem can be established in (F), according to Friedman et al. (1983). A proof in (K) would yield a Kalmar-elementary bounding function. (That an elementary function can be found was shown recently by Friedman.)

There are some obvious questions to be asked. (1) Can one push the proof-theoretic considerations further and treat theories whose provably recursive functions are computationally feasible? (2) Which parts of mathematics can be developed somewhat systematically in such weak systems? And, finally, leaving aside a systematic development, (3) which interesting Π^o_2-statements can be proved in them? - Further refined computational reductions, if accompanied by informative applications, would be of real mathematical interest.

B3. Proof Theoretic Facts Used for Establishing the Theorem Concerning (K)

If we want to follow the strategy suggested in A3, the work is cut out for us: we have to eliminate Weak König's Lemma and the Σ^o_1-axiom of choice (indeed, only the quantifier-free one, as these two forms are equivalent over (ET)). Let me formulate the two crucial elimination lemmata. In their formulation I assume that Δ consists only of purely existential formulas. $\Delta[\neg QF\text{-}AC_o]$ denotes the sequent obtained from Δ by adding instances of the negation of the quantifier-free axiom of choice; $\Delta[\neg WKL]$ and $\Delta[\neg QF\text{-}CA]$ are defined similarly.

$QF\text{-}AC_o$-Elimination. If D is a normal derivation of $\Delta[\neg QF\text{-}AC_o]$, then there is a normal derivation E of $\Delta[\neg QF\text{-}CA]$.

I.e., the quantifier-free axiom of choice is eliminated in favor of quantifier-free comprehension; the same fact holds for Weak König's Lemma.

WKL-Elimination. If D is a normal derivation of $\Delta[\neg WKL]$, then there is a normal derivation E of $\Delta[\neg QF\text{-}CA]$.

Assuming these two lemmata I sketch the proof of the theorem concerning (K). Notice, first of all, that a normal derivation in (K) of the Π^o_2-statement $(\forall x)(\exists y)\psi xy$ is a normal derivation with an end-sequent of the form

$$\Delta[\neg\text{QF-CA}, \neg\text{QF-AC}_0, \neg\text{WKL}], (\forall x)(\exists y)\psi xy,$$

where Δ contains only negations of other, purely universal axioms of (K). By $\forall$-inversion the endsequent can be assumed to be of the form

$$\Delta[\neg\text{QF-CA}, \neg\text{QF-AC}_0, \neg\text{WKL}], (\exists y)\psi ay.$$

The main argument proceeds now by induction on (the length of) normal derivations D with endsequents of this form and establishes that such D can be transformed into normal derivations E of

$$\Delta[\neg\text{QF-CA}], (\exists y)\psi ay.$$

The induction step is trivial in case the last rule in D effects an element of Δ, an instance of $\neg$QF-CA or $(\exists y)\psi ay$. If the last rule introduces an instance of $\neg\text{QF-AC}_0$ or $\neg$WKL one appeals (first to the induction hypothesis and then) to the appropriate elimination-lemma. For this to be possible, the comprehension principle has to be formulated in purely universal form, e.g., by using λ-terms as $(\forall x)\lambda y.\ t[y, \ldots](x) = t[x, \ldots]$. This establishes the conservativeness of (K) over (ET) for Π^0_2-statements; the latter theory is easily seen to be conservative over (KEA).

Now let me turn to the proofs of the elimination lemmata. The QF-AC_0-elimination is obtained in a way which is completely analogous to establishing the Main-Lemma in Feferman and Sieg (1981, 2.1.3, p. 105). The $\exists$-inversion lemma is used crucially to define a choice-function when, in the course of an inductive argument on the length of D, one has to treat the case that the last rule in D introduces an instance of $\neg\text{QF-AC}_0$. The WKL-elimination lemma is also proved by induction on the length of normal derivations. I concentrate on the central case when the last rule in D introduces an instance of $\neg$WKL, i.e.,

$$T(f) \ \& \ (\forall x)(\exists y)(lh(y) = x \ \& \ f(y) = 1) \ \& \ \neg(\exists g)(\forall x) \ f(\overline{g}(x)) = 1.$$

Then there are derivations D_1, D_2, D_3, all shorter than D, of

$\Delta[\neg WKL]$, $T(f)$,
$\Delta[\neg WKL]$, $(\forall x)(\exists y(lh(y) = x \ \& \ f(y) = 1)$, and
$\Delta[\neg WKL]$, $(\forall g)(\exists x)f(\overline{g}(x)) \neq 1$.

Using $\forall$-inversion and the induction-hypothesis one obtains derivations E_1, E_2, E_3 of

$\Delta[\neg QF\text{-}CA]$, $T(f)$,
$\Delta[\neg QF\text{-}CA]$, $(\exists y)(lh(y) = c \ \& \ f(y) = 1)$, and
$\Delta[\neg QF\text{-}CA]$, $(\exists x)f(\overline{u}(x)) \neq 1$.

$\exists$-inversion and definition by cases (available for elementary functions) provide terms t and s and derivations F_2 and F_3 of

$\Delta[\neg QF\text{-}CA]$, $lh(t[c]) = c \ \& \ f(t[c]) = 1$,
$\Delta[\neg QF\text{-}CA]$, $f(\overline{u}(s)) \neq 1$.

Now observe (i) that t yields sequences of arbitrary length in f which do not necessarily form a branch, and (ii) that the right-most formula in the endsequent of F_3 expresses the well-foundedness of f. In short, we have a binary tree (according to E_1), that is well-founded and contains sequences of arbitrary length. To exploit this situation let me first make the simplifying assumption that s is a closed term with numerical value k. Let t[k] be the 0-1-sequence $t_o, \ldots, t_{k-1}$ and define with QF-CA the function u* by

$$u^*(n) = \begin{cases} t_n & \text{if } n < k \\ o & \text{otherwise.} \end{cases}$$

Obviously, $\overline{u^*}(s) = t[k]$. Replacing u in F_3 by u* yields a derivation of

$$\Delta[\neg QF\text{-}CA],\ f(\overline{u^*}(s)) \neq 1$$

and indeed a G_3 of

$$\Delta[\neg QF\text{-}CA],\ f(t[k]) \neq 1,$$

when taking into account the equation $\overline{u^*}(s) = t[k]$. A derivation G_2 is obtained from F_2 by &-inversion and replacing c by k; G_2 has the endsequent

$$\Delta[\neg QF\text{-}CA],\ f(t[k]) = 1.$$

Cutting G_3 with G_2 and subsequent normalizing yields a normal derivation of

$$\Delta[\neg QF\text{-}CA].$$

The simplifying assumption concerning s can be eliminated. s contains in general occurrences of u and f; both u and f can be assumed to be majorized by the function which is identically 1. Let $2_m(x)$ be defined by $2_o(x) = x$ and $2_{n+1} = 2^{2_n(x)}$. The usual argument showing that for any elementary function g(x) there is a k, such that for all x: $g(x) \leq 2_k(x)$, can be specialized and carried out in (ET) to obtain a closed term s* majorizing s. As f is a tree,

$$\Delta[\neg QF\text{-}Ca],\ f(\overline{u}(s^*)) \neq 1$$

can be proved, and one can complete the argument as above.

TWO RESULTS AND THREE CONJECTURES

Via the Herbrand-Theorem as formulated in Shoenfield (1967) the above argument can be extended to prove that (K) is conservative over (ET) for Π^1_1-sentences. The proof of Sieg (1983) showing that (F) is conservative over (PRA) can similarly be modified to show that (BT + Σ^0_1-AC_0 + WKL) is conservative over (BT) for Π^1_1-sentences. These results imply that (K) is conservative over (KEA^+) and that (BT + Σ^0_1-AC_0 + WKL) is conservative over (PRA^+); the +-sign indicates that (KEA) and (PRA) have been expanded by first order logic. So we have two subsystems of analysis which are fully conservative over fragments of elementary number theory. I conjecture three further and more interesting such results.

Conjecture 1: (F) is conservative over (Σ^0_1-IA), i.e., over (Z) with the induction principle restricted to Σ^0_1-formulas.

This yields in particular Harrington's result that (F) is conservative for Π^1_1-sentences over (BT + Σ^0_1-AC_0 + Σ^0_1-IA). - Define (F_n) as (BT + Σ^0_1-AC_0 + Σ^0_n-IA + WKL).

Conjecture 2: (F_n) is conservative over (Σ^0_n-IA).

From this one can establish Kreisel's old theorem (see Kreisel et al., 1975), that (BT + Σ^1_∞-IA + Σ^0_1-AC_0 + WKL) is conservative over (Z). Finally let (FF_n) be a suitable finite type extension of (F_n).

Conjecture 3: (FF_n) is conservative over (Σ^0_n-IA).

The last conjecture is of special interest, as Feferman has urged to consider, has used and investigated finite type theories instead of just second order theories. The reason is straightforward and convincing: mathematical practice is much more directly and naturally represented in them.

CONCLUDING REMARKS

Many fascinating mathematical and logical problems are left open by the work reported here; I indicated some of them. These problems are partly precise (meta-) mathematical, partly broad conceptual ones. The accomplished work on the open questions are both integrated to the generalized reductive program. That is not seen, in sharp contrast to the original Hilbert program, as an instrument to solve the foundational problem of mathematics once and for all; it is rather viewed as a coherent scheme guiding foundational research. This research has yielded rich (meta-) mathematical results, and it continues to provide us with detailed material for philosophical reflections on the nature of our mathematical experience.

Through this work we have gained a much clearer understanding of the mathematical strength of (weak) classical theories, the relation between classical and constructive theories, and the nature of constructive principles and their relative strength. Here is a body of definite results which should inform the philosophical discussion of foundational issues today. But the reductive results do not only provide information; they present also a deep philosophical challenge. The reductions do secure, after all, classical theories on the basis of theories which can justly be called more elementary. In this sense they are epistemological reductions, whose precise character awaits philosophical analysis. It seems to me that such an analysis would throw considerable light on issues discussed under the heading of platonistic and constructivistic tendencies in mathematics.

REFERENCES

I use some abbreviations which are not standard or self-explanatory, namely,

HB for "Handbook of Mathematical Logic," J. Barwise, ed., North-Holland, Amsterdam, 1977.

IPT for "Intuitionism and Proof Theory. Proceedings of the Summer Conference at Buffalo, N.Y., 1968," A. Kino, J. Myhill and R. E. Vesley, eds., North-Holland, Amsterdam, 1970.

LNM for Lecture Notes in Mathematics, Springer, Berlin.

Bernays, P., 1922, Über Hilberts Gedanken zur Grundlegung der Arithmetik, Jahresbericht DMV, 31:10-19.

Bernays, P., 1967, Hilbert, David, in: "The Encyclopedia of Philosophy," Vol. III, P. Edwards, ed., Macmillan, New York.

Bernays, P., 1970, Die schematische Korrespondenz und die idealisierten Strukturen, Dialectica, 24:53-66. (Reprinted in 1976.)

Bernays, P., 1976, "Abhandlungen zur Philosophie der Mathematik," Wissenschaftliche Buchgesellschaft, Darmstadt.

Brouwer, L. E. J., 1927, Über Definitionsbereiche von Funktionen, Math. Annalen, 97:60-75.

Buchholz, W., 1981a, The $\Omega_{\mu+1}$-rule, LNM, 897:188-233.

Buchholz, W., 1981b, Ordinal Analysis of ID_ν, LNM, 897:234-260.

Cantor, G., 1883, Grundlagen einer allgemeinen Mannigfaltigkeitslehre. Reprinted in: "Gesammelte Abhandlungen," E. Zermelo, ed., Springer, Berlin 1932.

Feferman, S., 1970, Formal Theories for Transfinite Iterations of Generalized Inductive Definitions and Some Subsystems of Analysis, in: IPT.

Feferman, S., 1977, Theories of Finite Type Related to Mathematical Practice, in: HB.

Feferman, S., 1979, Constructive Theories of Functions and Classes, in: "Logic Colloquium '78," North-Holland, Amsterdam.

Feferman, S., 1982, Monotone Inductive Definitions, in: "The L. E. J. Brouwer Centenary Symposium," North-Holland, Amsterdam.

Feferman, S. and Sieg, W., 1981a, Iterated Inductive Definitions and Subsystems of Analysis, LNM, 897:16-77.

Feferman, S. and Sieg, W., 1981b, Proof-theoretic Equivalences between Classical and Constructive Theories for Analysis, LNM, 897:78-142.

Friedman, H., 1970, Iterated Inductive Definitions and Σ^1_2-AC, in: IPT.

Friedman, H., 1975, Some Systems of Second Order Arithmetic and their Use, Proc. Int. Cong. Mathe. Vancouver, 1:235-242.

Friedman, H., 1978, Classically and Intuitionistically Provably Recursive Functions, LNM, 669:21-27.

Friedman, H., 1980, A Strong Conservative Extension of Peano Arithmetic, in: "Kleene Symposium," North-Holland, Amsterdam.

Friedman, H., Simpson, S. and Smith, R., 1983, Countable Algebra and Set Existence Axioms. Annals of Pure and Applied Logic, 25:141-183.

Giaquinto, M., 1983, Hilbert's Philosophy of Mathematics, Brit. J. Phil. Sci., 34:119-132.

Graham, R., Rothschild, B. and Spencer, J., 1980, "Ramsey Theory," Wiley & Sons, New York.

Hilbert, D., 1900, Über den Zahlbegriff, Jahresbericht DMV, 8:180-194.

Hilbert, D., 1904, Über die Grundlagen der Logik und Arithmetik, in: "Verhandlungen des Dritten Int. Math. Kongr. in Heidelberg," Teubner, Leipzig, 1905.

Kreisel, G., 1958, Mathematical Significance of Consistency Proofs, JSL, 23:155-182.

Kreisel, G., 1968, A Survey of Proof Theory, JSL, 33:321-388.

Kreisel, G., Minc, G. and Simpson, S., 1975, The Use of Abstract Languages in Elementary Metamathematics: Some Pedagogic Examples, LNM, 453:38-129.

Kronecker, L., 1887, Über den Zahlbegriff, in: Werke, Vol. III, 251-274.

Minc, G., 1976, What Can Be Done in PRA? Zapiski Nauchuyh Seminarov LOMI, 60:93-102.

Pohlers, W., 1981, Proof-theoretical Analysis of ID_ν by the Method of Local Predicativity, LNM, 897:261-357.

Reid, C., 1970, "Hilbert," Springer, Berlin.

Schwichtenberg, H., 1977, Proof Theory: Some Applications of Cut-elimination, in: HB.

Shoenfield, J., 1967, Mathematical Logic, Addison-Wesley, Reading.

Sieg, W., 1981, Inductive Definitions, Constructive Ordinals, and Normal Derivations, LNM, 897:143-187.

Sieg, W., 1983, Fragments of Arithmetic. To appear in: Annals of Pure and Applied Logic.

Sieg, W., 1984, Foundations for Analysis and Proof Theory, to appear in Synthese.

Simpson, S., 1982a, Reverse Mathematics, to appear in: "Proc. AMS Summer Institute in Recursion Theory, Cornell University."

Simpson, S., 1982b, Which Set Existence Axioms Are Needed to Prove the Cauchy/Peano Theorem for Ordinary Differential Equations? To appear in: JSL.

Tait, W. W., 1968, Normal Derivability in Classical Logic, LNM, 72:204-236.

Tait, W. W., 1970, Applications of the Cut-elimination Theorem to some Subsystems of Classical Analysis, in: IPT.

Takeuti, G., 1978, "Two Applications of Logic to Mathematics," Princeton University Press, Princeton.

Weyl, H., 1918, "Das Kontinuum," Leipzig.

Zermelo, E., 1931, Über Stufen der Quantifikation und die Logik des Unendlichen, Jahresbericht DMV, 31:85-88.

Zermelo, E., 1935, Grundlagen einer allgemeinen Theorie der mathematischen Satzsysteme, Fund. Math., 25:136-146.

THE INCOMPLETENESS THEOREMS AND RELATED RESULTS FOR NONCONSTRUCTIVE THEORIES

Vladimir I. Stepanov

Department of Mathematical Logic, Faculty of Mathematics
and Mechanics, Moscow State University
Moscow, USSR

After the discovery of the arithmetical hierarchy Mostowski realized that there are further general recursion-theoretic facts which lie in the foundation of the incompleteness theorems and related results. In his articles (see Mostowski, 1979) he has made attempts to investigate formal systems from the recursion-theoretic point of view. Particularly, he has shown that the restriction to recursively enumerable systems is irrelevant for the 1st incompleteness theorem.

It is well known that incompleteness and undecidability of formal systems have played an important role in the beginning of the development of the recursion theory. This concerns not only the introduction of recursive and recursively enumerable sets but also a different kind of reducibility. Particularly, the notion of creative set is an abstract form of the incompleteness phenomenon, which was discovered by Gödel (see, for instance, Davis, 1965).

On the other hand an effective numeration of syntax permits us to consider formal systems as special objects of recursion theory. As a confirmation of this point of view let us show how to generalize theorems of Gödel, Rosser, Sheperdson, Boolos and others to nonconstructive theories.

1. INCOMPLETENESS THEOREMS

By a theory we understand a 1st order theory in the language of the Peano arithmetic PA (see Kleene, 1952; Shoenfield, 1967). Ax_T is the set of nonlogical axioms of a theory T. An effective numeration of the language PA is fixed. $\ulcorner\varphi\urcorner$ is a numeral which denotes the number of the formula φ. Identification of a formula with its number allows us to speak about recursive, recursively enumerable, Σ^o_n (Π^o_n, Δ^o_n) - sets of formulas and about Turing reducibility of one set of formulas to another one (see Rogers, 1967; Shoenfield, 1967). $\omega^A_o, \ldots, \omega^A_n \ldots$ is a standard numeration of sets which is recursively enumerable in A (see Rogers, 1967). T(i) is the theory of which the nonlogical axioms are $Ax_T \cup \omega_i^{Ax_T}$ (see Rogers, 1967). It is assumed that there are desirable primitive recursive terms available. For example, terms *neg*, *conj*, *imp*, *Sub*, satisfy the following conditions:

$$T \vdash neg\,(\ulcorner\varphi\urcorner) = \ulcorner\neg\varphi\urcorner;$$

$$T \vdash imp\,(\ulcorner\varphi\urcorner, \ulcorner\psi\urcorner) = \ulcorner\varphi \rightarrow \psi\urcorner;$$

$$T \vdash conj\,(\ulcorner\varphi\urcorner, \ulcorner\psi\urcorner) = \ulcorner\varphi \,\&\, \psi\urcorner;$$

$$T \vdash Sub\,(\ulcorner\varphi(x)\urcorner, \bar{n}) = \ulcorner\varphi(\bar{n})\urcorner.$$

Instead of *Sub* $(\ulcorner\varphi(x)\urcorner, y)$ we write $\ulcorner\varphi(\dot{y})\urcorner$ (see Feferman, 1960; Smorynski, 1980). We get similarly $\ulcorner\varphi(\dot{x}_1, \ldots, \dot{x}_n)\urcorner$.

Now, for every formula $\varphi(x_1, \ldots, x_n)$ which has n free variables one can effectively find a formula $\varphi(x_1, \ldots, x_{n-1})$ such that $T \vdash \varphi(x_1, \ldots, x_{n-1}) \leftrightarrow \psi(x_1, \ldots, x_{n-1}, \ulcorner\varphi(x_1, \ldots, x_{n-1})\urcorner)$. This is Gödel's or the standard diagonalization lemma (see Feferman, 1960, 1962).

A relation $\rho \subset \omega^k$ $(k \geq 1)$ is said to be representable in theory T if there is a formula $\varphi(x_1, \ldots, x_k)$ such that

$$T \vdash \varphi(\bar{n}_1, \ldots, \bar{n}_k) \Leftrightarrow \langle \bar{n}_1, \ldots, \bar{n}_k \rangle \in \rho.$$

A relation $\rho \subset \omega^k$ $(k \geq 1)$ is said to be definable in theory T if there is a formula $\varphi(x_1, \ldots, x_k)$ such that φ represents ρ in T and $\neg\varphi$ represents $\omega^k \setminus \rho$ in T.

Definition: A theory T is said to be self-referential if every relation $\rho \subset \omega^k$ $(k \geq 1)$ which is recursive in Ax_T (Turing reducible to Ax_T), is definable in T.

Let T be a self-referential theory. Then there is a relation R, recursive in Ax_T, such that $T(i) \vdash \varphi \Leftrightarrow \exists sR(s, i, \text{num } \varphi)$.

Relation R is definable in T by the formula $Prf_T(x, z, y)$. $Pr_T(z, y) \rightleftharpoons \exists x Prf_T(x, z, y)$.

It is easy to see that for every $i \in \omega$

(A) $T(i) \vdash \varphi \Rightarrow T(i) \vdash Pr_T(\bar{i}, \ulcorner\varphi\urcorner)$.

Theorem 1 (1st generalisation of Gödel's incompleteness theorem): For every self-referential theory T there is a recursive function f such that for every $i \in \omega$

1) $T(i)$ is consistent $\Rightarrow$ $f(i)$ is an unprovable sentence of $T(i)$,
2) $T(i)$ is ω-consistent $\Rightarrow$ $f(i)$ is an undecidable sentence of $T(i)$.

Proof: By Gödel's lemma, for every $i \in \omega$ we can effectively find a sentence ψ_i for which $T \vdash \psi_i \leftrightarrow Pr_T(\bar{i}, \ulcorner\psi_i\urcorner)$.

It is easy to see that for any consistent theory T(i) we have $T(i) \nvdash \psi_i$ and for ω-consistent $T(i) \nvdash \neg\psi_i$.

Definition: Let T be a self-referential theory. A proof's predicate $Pr_T(\bar{i}, y)$ is said to be standard for $i \in \omega$ if

$$(B)\ T(i) \vdash Pr_T(\bar{i}, y) \,\&\, Pr_T(\bar{i}, imp(y, t)) \rightarrow Pr_T(\bar{i}, t)$$
$$(C)\ T(i) \vdash Pr_T(\bar{i}, y) \rightarrow Pr_T(\bar{i}, \ulcorner Pr_T(\bar{i}, y)\urcorner).$$

A proof's predicate $Pr_T(\bar{i}, y)$ is said to be uniformly standard if it satisfies (B) and (C) for every $i \in \omega$.

Conditions (A), (B), (C) are also called Hilbert-Bernays conditions. Let

$$con_T(z) \rightleftharpoons \neg Pr_T(z, \ulcorner \bar{0} = \bar{1}\urcorner),$$
$${}^{G}con_T(z) \rightleftharpoons \forall y \neg (Pr_T(z, y) \,\&\, Pr_T(z, neg(y))),$$
$${}^{\varphi}con_T(z) \rightleftharpoons \neg (Pr_T(z, \ulcorner\varphi\urcorner) \,\&\, Pr_T(z, \ulcorner\neg\varphi\urcorner)).$$

Similar to the case of constructively defined theories it is proved

Lemma 1: Let T be a self-referential theory and $Pr_T(\bar{i}, y)$ satisfies (B). Then

1) $T(i) \vdash \varphi \rightarrow \psi \Rightarrow T(i) \vdash Pr_T(\bar{i}, \ulcorner\varphi\urcorner) \rightarrow Pr_T(\bar{i}, \ulcorner\psi\urcorner)$,
2) $T(i) \vdash Pr_T(\bar{i}, \ulcorner\varphi \,\&\, \psi\urcorner) \leftrightarrow Pr_T(\bar{i}, \ulcorner\varphi\urcorner) \,\&\, Pr_T(\bar{i}, \ulcorner\psi\urcorner)$,
3) $T(i) \vdash \neg Pr_T(\bar{i}, \ulcorner\varphi\urcorner) \rightarrow con_T(\bar{i})$,
4) $T(i) \vdash con_T(\bar{i}) \leftrightarrow {}^{\varphi}con_T(\bar{i})$,
5) $T(i) \vdash con_T(i) \leftrightarrow {}^{G}con_T(\bar{i})$.

Lemma 2: Let T be a self-referential theory and $Pr_T(\bar{i}, y)$

satisfies (C). Then

$$T(i) \text{ is consistent} \Rightarrow T(i) \nvdash {}^{G}\mathrm{con}_T(i).$$

Using lemmata 1 and 2 one can get

Theorem 2 (2nd generalisation of Gödel's incompleteness theorem): Let T be a self-referential theory and $\mathrm{Pr}_T(z, y)$ a uniformly standard proof's predicate. Then for every $i \in \omega$

1) $T(i)$ is consistent $\Rightarrow T(i) \nvdash \mathrm{con}_T(\bar{i})$,
2) $T(i)$ is ω-consistent $\Rightarrow T(i) \nvdash \neg\mathrm{con}_T(\bar{i})$.

Rosser (see Davis, 1965) strengthened Gödel's 1st theorem by introducing an other proof's predicate. His result will be generalized as above.

Theorem 3 (generalisation of Rosser's theorem): Let T be a self-referential theory and for every $n \in \omega$

$$T \vdash x \le \bar{n} \vee \bar{n} \le x; \; T \vdash x \le \bar{n} \to x = \bar{0} \vee \dots \vee x = \bar{n}.$$

Then there is formula $\psi(y)$ such that if $T(i)$ is consistent then $\psi(\bar{i})$ is an undecidable sentence of $T(i)$.

Proof: Let us define Rosser's proof's predicate for T

$$\mathrm{Prf}_T^R(x, z, y) \rightleftarrows \mathrm{Prf}_T(x, z, y) \;\&\; \forall u(u \le x \to \neg\mathrm{Prf}_T(u, z, \mathrm{neg}(y))),$$
$$\mathrm{Pr}_T^R(z, y) \rightleftarrows \exists x \mathrm{Prf}_T^R(x, z, y).$$

It is easy to verify that $\mathrm{Pr}_T^R(\bar{i}, y)$ satisfies (A). Moreover:

$$(A^*)\; T(i) \vdash \neg\varphi \Rightarrow T(i) \vdash \neg\mathrm{Pr}_T^R(\bar{i}, \ulcorner\varphi\urcorner).$$

Indeed: if $T(i) \vdash \neg\varphi$ then for some $p \in \omega$

$$T(i) \vdash Prf_T(\bar{p}, \bar{i}, \ulcorner\neg\varphi\urcorner)$$

and for every $s \in \omega$

$$T(i) \vdash \neg Prf_T(\bar{s}, \bar{i}, \ulcorner\varphi\urcorner).$$

Then

$$T(i) \vdash \bar{p} \leq x \rightarrow \bar{p} \leq x \ \&\ Prf_T(\bar{p}, \bar{i}, \ulcorner\neg\varphi\urcorner),$$
$$T(i) \vdash x \leq \bar{p} \rightarrow \neg Prf_T(x, \bar{i}, \ulcorner\varphi\urcorner).$$

So we have

$$T(i) \vdash \neg Prf_T(x, i, \ulcorner\varphi\urcorner) \vee \exists u(u \leq x \ \&\ Prf_T(u, \bar{i}, \ulcorner\neg\varphi\urcorner))$$

or

$$T(i) \vdash \neg Pr_T^R(\bar{i}, \ulcorner\varphi\urcorner).$$

Then by (A*) and (A) a sentence ψ_i such that

$$T(i) \vdash \psi_i \leftrightarrow \neg Pr_T^R(\bar{i}, \psi_i)$$

is an undecidable sentence for theory $T(i)$ if $T(i)$ is consistent. So one can take $\psi(y)$ as formula $\neg Pr_T^R(y, f(y))$ where primitive recursive term f is such that $T \vdash f(\bar{i}) = \ulcorner\psi_i\urcorner$ for every $i \in \omega$.

Theorem 4 (generalisation of Löb's theorem): Let T be a self-referential theory and $Pr_T(\bar{i}, y)$ a standard proof's predicate, then for every sentence φ

1) $T(i) \vdash \varphi \Leftrightarrow T(i) \vdash Pr_T(\bar{i}, \ulcorner\varphi\urcorner) \to \varphi$,
2) $T(i) \vdash Pr_T(\bar{i}, \ulcorner Pr_T(\bar{i}, \ulcorner\varphi\urcorner)\urcorner \to Pr_T(\bar{i}, \ulcorner\varphi\urcorner)$.

The proof is omitted because one can verify Theorem 4 by Löb's (1955) own arguments. Note that for Rosser's proof's predicate the following conditions are fulfilled:

$$T(i) \vdash \bar{0} = \bar{0} \leftrightarrow Pr_T^R(\bar{i}, \ulcorner\bar{0} = \bar{0}\urcorner),$$
$$T(i) \vdash \bar{0} = \bar{1} \leftrightarrow Pr_T^R(\bar{i}, \ulcorner\bar{0} = \bar{1}\urcorner).$$

So Löb's theorem does not hold for Pr_T^R.

2. EXAMPLES OF NONCONSTRUCTIVE SELF-REFERENTIAL THEORIES

For every $n > 0$ the set of nonlogical axioms of T_n is defined as

$$Ax_{T_n} = \{\varphi \in \Pi_n \mid \varphi \in St, \langle\omega, +, \cdot, 0, 1\rangle \models \varphi\} \cup Ax_{PA}.$$

First of all let us introduce the proof's predicate for the theory T_n. Remember that proof's predicate Pr_φ for formula φ is defined as follows:

$$Prf_\varphi(x, y) \rightleftharpoons Seg(x) \mathbin{\&} \forall u \le lh(x)((LAx((x)_u) \vee Ax_{PA}((x)_u) \vee$$
$$\vee\ \varphi((x)_u) \vee \exists z, v < u((x)_z = imp((x)_v, (x)_u) \vee (x)_u =$$
$$= Gen((x)_z))) \mathbin{\&} Form(x)_u) \mathbin{\&} y = (x)_{lh(x)};$$
$$Pr_\varphi(y) \rightleftharpoons \exists x Prf_\varphi(x, y),$$

where

$$Ax_{PA}, LAx, imp, Gen, Seg, lh, (\cdot)_u,$$

are appropriate primitive recursive formulas or terms (see Feferman,

1960; Shoenfield, 1967). As φ-formula we take the truth definitional Π_n-formula Tr_n for any Π_n-formulas, i.e.,

$$(*)\ PA \vdash \varphi(x) \leftrightarrow Tr_n(\ulcorner\varphi(\dot{x})\urcorner)\ (\varphi \in \Pi_n).$$

Theorem 5: $Pr_{Tr_n}(y)$ is a standard proof's predicate of the theory T_n.

Proof: The condition $T_n \vdash \varphi \Leftrightarrow T_n \vdash Pr_{Tr_n}(\ulcorner\varphi\urcorner)$ results from the definition of Pr_{Tr_n}. Let us verify that $PA \vdash Pr_{Tr_n}(y) \rightarrow \rightarrow Pr_{Tr_n}(\ulcorner Pr_{Tr_n}(\dot{y})\urcorner)$. Let $\varphi(y)$ be a Π_n-formula. By (*) we have $PA \vdash \varphi(y) \rightarrow Pr_{Tr_n}(\ulcorner\varphi(\dot{y})\urcorner)$. Then $PA \vdash \exists y\varphi(y) \rightarrow Pr_{Tr_n}(\ulcorner\exists y\varphi(y)\urcorner)$. It is easy to see that Pr_{Tr_n} is provably equivalent in PA to a Σ_{n+1}-formula. To complete the proof we note that the condition $PA \vdash Pr_{Tr_n}(y)\ \&\ Pr_{Tr_n}(imp(y, y_1)) \rightarrow Pr_{Tr_n}(y_2)$ results from the theorem 4.6 in Feferman (1960).

Let A, B be disjoint Σ^0_{n+1}-sets and Σ_{n+1}-formulae $\exists z\psi(z, y)$ and $\exists z\varphi(z, y)$ be such that

$$n \in A \Leftrightarrow \langle\omega, +, \cdot, 0, 1\rangle \models \exists z\psi(z, \bar{n}),$$
$$n \in B \Leftrightarrow \langle\omega, +, \cdot, 0, 1\rangle \models \exists z\varphi(z, \bar{n}),$$

where ψ, φ are Π_n-formulas. Let us take Sheperdson's formula

$$Sh_n(y, x) \rightleftharpoons \exists z Prf_{Tr_n}(z, neg(Sub(x, y))) \vee \psi(z, y))\ \&$$
$$\&\ \forall u(u \leq z \rightarrow \neg Prf_{Tr_n}(u, Sub(x,y))\ \&\ \neg\varphi(u, y)).$$

By Gödel's lemma we have

$$PA \vdash \chi(y) \leftrightarrow Sh_n(y, \ulcorner\chi(y)\urcorner).$$

Then like in Smorynski (1980) the following theorem holds.

Theorem 6: Let A, B be disjoint Σ^o_{n+1}-sets. Then Σ_{n+1}-formula $\chi(y)$ represents A in T_n and $\neg\chi(y)$ represents B in T_n.

Corollary:

a) Every Δ^o_{n+1}-set is definable in T_n.
b) T_n is a self-referential theory.

To construct the uniformly standard proof's predicate for the theory T_n let us consider the relation $W^{(n)}$

$$m_2 = [k, i] \ \& \ m_1 \in \omega_i^{Ax}T_n \Leftrightarrow \langle m_1, m_2\rangle \in W^{(n)}$$

to at most k steps in enumeration $\omega_i^{Ax}T_n$. It is easy to see that $W^{(n)}$ is recursive in Ax_{T_n}. Then by the hierarchy theorem $W^{(n)}$ is a Δ^o_{n+1}-set and by corollary (a) definable in T_n. Let $\omega^{(n)}$ be a Σ_{n+1}-formula which defines $W^{(n)}$ in T_n.

Let us denote the formula which is constructed from Pr through substitution of $Tr_n(x)$ by $Tr_n(x) \vee \omega^{(n)}(x, [x_1, v] (y))$ by $Prf_{Tr_n}(x_1, v, y)$.

Put $Pr_{Tr_n}(v, y) \rightleftarrows \exists x_1 Prf_{Tr_n}(x_1, v, y)$. Then we have: for every $i \in \omega$

1) $T_n(i) \vdash \varphi \Rightarrow T_n(i) \vdash Pr_{Tr_n}(\bar{i}, \ulcorner\varphi\urcorner)$,
2) $PA \vdash Pr_{Tr_n}(\bar{i}, y) \ \& \ Pr_{Tr_n}(\bar{i}, imp(y, t)) \rightarrow Pr_{Tr_n}(\bar{i}, t)$,
3) $PA \vdash Pr_{Tr_n}(\bar{i}, y) \rightarrow Pr_{Tr_n}(\bar{i}, \ulcorner Pr_{Tr_n}(\bar{i}, \dot{y})\urcorner)$.

CONCLUSION

In Boolos (1976, 1977) considerations are based on the Hilbert-Bernays conditions and on the provability of the formalized Löb-theorem in PA. The same holds for self-referential theories. So Boolos results for such theories can be generalized.

It is well known that in 2nd order arithmetic A_2 the sentence con_{PA} is provable. If we take

$$con_{T_n} \rightleftharpoons \neg Pr_{Tr_n}(\ulcorner \overline{0} = \overline{1} \urcorner),$$

then we have

$$A_2 \vdash con_{T_n} .$$

On the other hand

$$T_n \nvdash con_{T_n} .$$

Now one can try to generalize other metamathematical results like those in Feferman (1960), Kreisel (1962), Smorynski (1980). As a rule, proofs are similar. The reason for it is evident if we look at metamathematics from the point of view of the recursion theory.--

The author would like to thank Academician A. N. Kolmogorov for his support and Professor G. Kreisel for good advice.

REFERENCES AND RELATED WORKS

Boolos, G., 1976, On Deciding the Truth of Certain Fixed Point Statements Involving the Notion of Consistency, J.S.L., 41:177-178.
Boolos, G., 1977, On Deciding the Provability of Certain Fixed Point Statements, J.S.L., 42:191-193.
Davis, M., 1965, "The Undecidable," Raven Press, New York.
Erchov, Y. L., 1980, "The Undecidability Problems and Constructive Models," Nauka, Moscow (in Russian).

Feferman, S., 1960, Arithmetization of Metamathematics in General Setting, Fund.Math., 49:35-92.

Feferman, S., 1962, Transfinite Recursive Progression of Axiomatic Theories, J.S.L., 27:259-316.

Kleene, S. C., 1952, "Introduction to Metamathematics," North-Holland, Amsterdam.

Kreisel, G., 1962, On Weak Completeness of Intuitionistic Predicate Logic, J.S.L., 27:139-158.

Kreisel, G., and Takeuti, G., 1974, Formally Self-referential Propositions for Cut-free Classical Analysis and Related Systems, Diss.Math., 118:50 pp.

Löb, M., 1955, Solution of a Problem of Leon Henkin, J.S.L., 20:115-118.

Mostowski, A., 1979, "Foundational Studies, I, II," North Holland, Amsterdam.

Rogers, H., 1967, "Theory of Recursive Functions and Effective Computability," McGraw-Hill, New York.

Shoenfield, J. R., 1967, "Mathematical Logic," Addison-Wesley, Reading.

Smorynski, C., 1980, Calculating Self-referential Statements, Fund. Math., 109:189-210.

Stepanov, V. I., 1982, On an Application of the Hierarchy-formulas of the Peaono Arithmetic, in: "6th All-Union Conference on Mathematical Logic," Tiflis (in Russian).

Stepanov, V. I., 1982, The Second Order Arithmetic and Consistency of a First Order Theory, Usp. Math. Nauk, 4:177-178 (in Russian).

A TYPED λ-CALCULUS AND GIRARD'S MODEL OF PTYKES

Peter Päppinghaus

Institut für Mathematik
Universität Hannover
D-3000 Hannover

0. INTRODUCTION

In a fundamental paper inaugurating Π^1_2-logic Girard (1981) introduced the notion of a dilator as a functor from the category of ordinals into itself preserving direct limits and pull-backs. In Chapter 12 of a forthcoming book (Girard (198.)) he generalizes this notion to all finite types. For every finite type σ a category PT^σ is defined whose objects form a (proper) class Pt^σ and are called *ptykes* of type σ. In annex 12.A of his book Girard proves the ptykes of finite types to be a model of a variant T' of Gödel's T. Using this new model he proposes an intrinsic "ordinal assignment" to terms of T'. To (closed) terms of type $o \to o$, in particular, their value at ω is assigned. We are interested in determining these values. From earlier work on theories of functionals of finite type over the countable ordinals - well surveyed in Zucker (1973, 6.8.6., pp. 442-446) - the following answer to this question is to be expected:

$$\{t\omega \mid t \text{ closed T'-term of type } o \to o\} = \eta_o,$$

where $\eta_o := \varphi_{\varepsilon_{\Omega+1}}(0)$ denotes the so-called Bachmann-Howard-ordinal. This has been conjectured by Girard. The aim of this paper is to prove the inclusion "$\subset$" of the equation above. The reverse inclusion will be proved elsewhere.

The types and the categories PT^σ are inductively defined as follows (see Girard (198.)):

- o is a type, and PT^o is the category ON of ordinals. Pt^o is the class On of all ordinals. For x, y $\in Pt^o$ the set of morphisms $I^o(x, y)$ is the set of all order-preserving maps from x to y.
- If σ and τ are types, then $(\sigma \to \tau)$ is a type. $Pt^{\sigma\to\tau}$ is the class of all functors from PT^σ to PT^τ preserving direct limits and pull-backs. For A, B $\in Pt^{\sigma\to\tau}$ the set of morphisms $I^{\sigma\to\tau}(A, B)$ is the set of all natural transformations from A to B.
- If σ and τ are types, then $(\sigma \times \tau)$ is a type. $Pt^{\sigma\times\tau} := Pt^\sigma \times Pt^\tau$ and $I^{\sigma\times\tau}((A, B), (A', B')) := I^\sigma(A, A') \times I^\tau(B, B')$.

If one wants to define (impredicative) primitive recursion for ptykes, one encounters the difficulty that this notion cannot be defined exactly as customary in type structures.

Consider a ptyx A of type o $\to$ o, ordinals $x \leq y$ and the embedding $E_{xy} \in I^o(x,y)$. $A(E_{xy}) \in I^o(Ax, Ay)$ implies that $Ax \leq Ay$, and so only non-decreasing functions can possibly be induced by ptykes of type o $\to$ o. Girard takes this into account by modifying the scheme for primitive recursion at type σ in the following way. For a $\in Pt^\sigma$, b $\in Pt^{\sigma\to(o\to\sigma)}$, x $\in Pt^o$:

$(R_\sigma 0)$ $\quad R_\sigma ab0 = a,$

$(R_\sigma S)$ $\quad R_\sigma ab(x + 1) = R_\sigma abx +_\sigma b(R_\sigma abx)x,$

where $+_\sigma$ is a previously defined ptyx of type $\sigma \to (\sigma \to \sigma)$.

This modification in the recursion equation makes it possible to define for every finite type σ a ptyx R_σ of type $\sigma \to ((\sigma \to o \to \sigma) \to (o \to \sigma))$ satisfying the equations above (see Girard (198.), Annex 12.A).

The set of primitive recursive ptykes can now be described as the least set of ptykes, which contains $0 \in Pt^{o}$, $S \in Pt^{o\to o}$ (successor), every $+_\sigma \in Pt^{\sigma\to\sigma\to\sigma}$ and every $R_\sigma \in Pt^{\sigma\to(\sigma\to o\to\sigma)\to o\to\sigma}$ and is closed under explicit definitions.

The ptykes of finite types are distinguished from the type structure of the classical, set-theoretical functionals over the ordinals by the fact that functors act on *morphisms* as well as on *objects*. It turns out, however, that this enrichment of structure is not relevant for finding a bound for $A\omega$, A a primitive recursive ptyx of type $o \to o$.

For the *definition* of the ptykes R_σ the action on *morphisms* plays the following role. Equations ($R_\sigma 0$) and ($R_\sigma S$) have natural analogues for the action of R_σ on morphisms. A fundamental fact proved in Girard (1981) says that every ordinal is a direct limit of a directed system of natural numbers.

By preservation of direct limits this entails that the ptyx R_σ is uniquely determined by the equations ($R_\sigma 0$) and ($R_\sigma S$) and their analogues for the action on morphisms.

On the other hand the action of this uniquely determined ptyx R_σ on *objects* can also be described in the following way. There is a natural notion of sup at type σ, defined as a direct limit of a suitable directed system in the category PT^{σ} (see Girard (198.), Section 12.2), w.r.t. which R_σ satisfies the following equation.

For $a \in PT^{\sigma}$, $b \in Pt^{\sigma\to o\to\sigma}$, x a limit ordinal:

$$(R_\sigma \sup) \qquad R_\sigma abx = \sup_{y<x} R_\sigma aby.$$

Furthermore $+_{\sigma\to\tau}$ and sup at type $\sigma \to \tau$ satisfy

$$(A +_{\sigma\to\tau} B)a = (Aa) +_\tau (Ba) \text{ and } (\sup_{y<x} Ay)a = \sup_{y<x} (Aya),$$

and $+_{\sigma\times\tau}$ and sup at type $\sigma \times \tau$ satisfy

$$(A, B) +_{\sigma\times\tau} (A', B') = (A +_\sigma A', B +_\tau B') \text{ and}$$
$$\sup_{y<x} (Ay, By) = (\sup_{y<x} Ay, \sup_{y<x} By).$$

This shows that the values down at type o can be completely described solely in terms of the action of higher type ptykes on objects. And so one would expect the same bounds for $A\omega$ to hold for primitive recursive objects A in every type structure over the ordinals, provided only the equations above are satisfied.

In order to prove this, several methods suggest themselves from the literature (see e.g. Feferman (1968), §3 or Zucker (1973)). We have chosen the following approach, which is quite similar to Zucker's method of determining the ordinal of his theory T_2 of trees (see Zucker (1973), Thm. 6.6.8, p. 419f.). We set up a typed λ-calculus of ordinal operator terms, λ-OT, which extends T', and define a notion of reduction reflecting the defining equations of the constants. By routine methods we prove this notion of reduction to be *Church-Rosser* (see Barendregt (1981), Def. 3.1.11, p. 53f.) and *strongly normalizing* (see Barendregt (1981), Def. 3.1.22, p. 57). A closed term of type o in normal form is of one of the following forms: 0, St with t also a closed term of type o in normal form, or $\sup_{x<\alpha} t[x]$, where α is a limit ordinal and t[x] a normal term of type o. So we can use the normal form of a closed term t of type o to determine inductively $|t|$, the intended value of t: $|0| := 0$, $|St| := |t| + 1$, and $|\sup_{x<\alpha} t[x]| := \sup_{\beta<\alpha} |NF(t[\underline{\beta}])|$, where $\underline{\beta}$ is a closed term of type o denoting β.

This definition is by induction on an inductively defined class OC_o of "ordinally computable" closed terms of type o. In the same way as the notion of computability is frequently used in proofs of normalizability, we generalize the notion of ordinal computability to all finite types and prove that every closed term is ordinally computable. This proof is modelled on Zucker's proof of computability of the closed terms of his theory T_2 of trees in Zucker (1973), §4, pp. 404-407.

In order to obtain a bound for $|t|$, we restrict the system λ-OT to terms of the form $\sup_{x<\alpha} t$ with $\alpha < \Lambda$ for some fixed $\Lambda \leq \eta_o$, and observe that for this restricted system the proof of "$t \in OC_o$" can be formalized in the theory ID_1 of one inductive definition. Applying the proof theory of ID_1 it follows that for terms of the restricted system $|t|$ is bounded above by η_o (see Buchholz et al. (1981), Ch. IV, §δ, p. 333).

And so the same bound holds for the value of t in an arbitrary canonical model of λ-OT (i.e.: a model where the domain of type o is an ordinal). For it is easy to see that in such models $|t|$ equals the value of t in the model.

Unfortunately the type structure of the ptykes is not a model of the full language of λ-OT. This is because the sup of a family of ptykes does not always exist. This difficulty is overcome by restricting λ-OT to a suitable syntactically defined subclass of terms. We show that the ptykes are a model of the resulting subsystem $PT < \Lambda$ of λ-OT.

Together these results establish that η_o is closed under primitive recursive ptykes of type $o \to o \to \ldots \to o$.

1. TYPED λ-CALCULUS λ-OT

The types are defined as in §0; as usual $\sigma_1 \to \sigma_2 \to \ldots \to \sigma_n$ is a shorthand for $(\sigma_1 \to (\sigma_2 \to (\ldots \to \sigma_n)))$.

Definition 1.1:

The classes OTm_σ of *ordinal-λ-terms* of type σ are inductively defined by:

Variables: $a^\sigma, b^\sigma, c^\sigma, \ldots \in OTm_\sigma$.

Constants: $0 \in OTm_o$, $S \in OTm_{o\to o}$, $+ \in OTm_{o\to o\to o}$, $R_\sigma \in OTm_{\sigma\to(\sigma\to o\to\sigma)\to o\to\sigma}$.

⊠-terms: $s \in OTm_\sigma$, $t \in OTm_\tau \Rightarrow (s \boxtimes t) \in OTm_{\sigma\times\tau}$.

π-terms: $t \in OTm_{\sigma\times\tau} \Rightarrow (\pi^1 t) \in OTm_\sigma$, $(\pi^2 t) \in OTm_\tau$.

App-terms: $t \in OTm_{\sigma\to\tau}$, $s \in OTm_\sigma \Rightarrow (ts) \in OTm_\tau$.

λ-terms: $t \in OTm_\tau$, a^σ variable $\Rightarrow (\lambda a^\sigma.t) \in OTm_{\sigma\to\tau}$.

Sup-terms: $t \in OTm_o$, α limit ordinal, x^o variable $\Rightarrow (\sup_{x^o<\alpha} t) \in OTm_o$.

As usual we take $t_1t_2t_3\ldots t_n$ to abbreviate $(\ldots((t_1t_2)t_3)\ldots t_n)$, drop type superscripts or subscripts if possible without ambiguity, and adapt the definitions of free and bound variables, closed terms and substitution in the obvious way (see, e.g., Barendregt (1981), pp. 24-27). We reserve the letters x, y, z, ... for variables of type o. Following Barendregt we tacitly identify terms, which can be obtained from each other by correctly renaming bound variables (α-congruent terms), and adopt his *variable convention* that in a given context all bound variables are chosen to be different from the free variables. This effects that operations like substitution can always be carried out freely (see Barendregt (1981), pp. 26f., 575-577). The result of substituting $s \in OTm_\sigma$ for the free occurrences of a^σ in $t \in OTm_\tau$ is denoted by $t[a^\sigma := s]$ or simply by $t[s]$ when t is written as $t[a^\sigma]$.

In order to define a notion of reduction on the terms of the OTm_σ, we introduce the following abbreviations.

Definition 1.2:

(i) $CTm_\sigma := \{t \in OTm_\sigma \mid t \text{ closed}\}$

(ii) $+_0 :\equiv + \in CTm_{0\to 0\to 0}$

$+_{\sigma\to\tau} :\equiv \lambda a.\lambda b.\lambda c\ +_\tau\ (ac)(bc) \in CTm_{(\sigma\to\tau)\to(\sigma\to\tau)\to(\sigma\to\tau)}$

$+_{\sigma\times\tau} :\equiv \lambda a.\lambda b.\ +_\sigma\ (\pi^1 a)(\pi^1 b) \boxtimes +_\tau\ (\pi^2 a)(\pi^2 b) \in$
$\in CTm_{(\sigma\times\tau)\to(\sigma\times\tau)\to(\sigma\times\tau)}$

(iii) for $t \in OTm_{\sigma\to\tau}$: $(\sup_{x<\alpha} t) :\equiv \lambda a.\sup_{x<\alpha}(ta) \in OTm_{\sigma\to\tau}$

for $t \in OTm_{\sigma\times\tau}$: $(\sup_{x<\alpha} t) :\equiv \sup_{x<\alpha} (\pi^1 t) \boxtimes \sup_{x<\alpha} (\pi^2 t) \in OTm_{\sigma\times\tau}$

Definition 1.3:

(i) The *notion of reduction* $\succ$ is defined by the following *contraction rules.*

(λ)	$(\lambda a^\sigma.t[a])s \succ t[s]$ for $t[a] \in OTm_\tau$, $s \in OTm_\sigma$
(π)	$\pi^1(s \boxtimes t) \succ s$, $\pi^2(s \boxtimes t) \succ t$
$(+0)$	$+t0 \succ t$
$(+S)$	$+t(Su) \succ S(+tu)$
$(+\sup)$	$+t(\sup_{x<\alpha} u) \succ \sup_{x<\alpha} (+tu)$
$(R_\sigma 0)$	$R_\sigma tu0 \succ t$
$(R_\sigma S)$	$R_\sigma tu(Sv) \succ +_\sigma (R_\sigma tuv)(u(R_\sigma tuv)v)$
$(R_\sigma \sup)$	$R_\sigma tu(\sup_{x<\alpha} v) \succ \sup_{x<\alpha} (R_\sigma tuv)$

Note that the variable convention implicitly requires x to be chosen different from the free variables of t in (+sup), and different from the free variables of t, u in ($R_\sigma$sup).

(ii) *One step reduction* $\rightarrow$ is defined to be the compatible closure of $\succ\!\!-$, i.e., the closure of $\succ\!\!-$ under the term forming operations (see Barendregt (1981), Def. 3.1.5, p. 51 and Lemma 3.1.9, p. 53).

(iii) *Reduction* $\twoheadrightarrow$ is defined to be the reflexive, transitive closure of one step reduction $\rightarrow$.

(iv) As usual a term on the l.h.s. of "$\succ\!\!-$" is called a *redex*, and the corresponding term on the r.h.s. its *contractum*. A term is called *normal*, if it contains no redex as a subterm.

Like for most λ-calculi our notion of reduction is *Church-Rosser*. The proof of this fact is routine and sketched in Appendix 1.

<u>Proposition 1.4:</u>

(i) $\twoheadrightarrow$ satisfies the *diamond property*, i.e.:
$s \twoheadrightarrow t_1 \wedge s \twoheadrightarrow t_2 \Rightarrow \exists u\colon t_1 \twoheadrightarrow u \wedge t_2 \twoheadrightarrow u.$

(ii) Normal forms are unique, i.e.:
$s \twoheadrightarrow t_1,\ s \twoheadrightarrow t_2,\ t_1, t_2 \text{ normal} \Rightarrow t_1 \equiv t_2.$

<u>Definition 1.5:</u>

(i) $NTm_\sigma := \{t \in OTm_\sigma \mid t \text{ is normal}\}$

(ii) If $t \twoheadrightarrow t'$ and t' is normal, then t' is called the *normal form* of t:
$NF(t) :\equiv t'$.

In order to see that every term has a normal form, we note that by an adaption of standard methods as outlined in Appendix 2, one can prove a strong normalization theorem for our notion of reduction.

Definition 1.6: Strong Normalizability

$t \in SN_\sigma :\Leftrightarrow t \in OTm_\sigma$ and every reduction path starting with t (see Barendregt (1981), Def. 3.1.17, p. 55) is finite.

Proposition 1.7:

$\succ$ is *strongly normalizing*, i.e.: for every type σ: $SN_\sigma = OTm_\sigma$.

The fact that $\succ$ is strongly normalizing is not very strong, in fact for each fixed term $t \in OTm_\sigma$ the proof of "$t \in SN_\sigma$" can be formalized in intuitionistic first order arithmetic (compare Troelstra (1973), 2.3.11, pp. 119-121). This is not surprising, because the contradiction rules do not express in any way the meaning of the ordinals in the subscript of "sup".

2. ORDINAL COMPUTABILITY IN λ-OT

We want to define $|t|$, the intended value of a closed term of type o. To do this, it is helpful to use its normal form NF(t), because closed terms of type o in normal form are of a special syntactical form lending itself readily to such a definition.

Definition 2.1: Principal Constituent of a Term

(i) If t is a variable, constant, λ-term, $\boxtimes$-term or sup-term, then t is the principal constituent of t.

(ii) If $t \equiv t_1 t_2$, then the principal constituent of t is the principal constituent of t_1.

(iii) If $t \equiv \pi^i t'$, then the principal constituent of t is the principal constituent of t'.

Lemma 2.2:

(i) Every term t has a uniquely determined principal constituent s. s is a subterm of t, and the type of t is a subtype of the type of s.

(ii) If t is closed, then the principal constituent of t is closed.

(iii) If s is the principal constituent of t, t normal, $s \not\equiv t$, then s is neither a λ-term nor a $\boxtimes$-term.

(iv) If $t \in NTm_o \cap CTm_o$, then the principal constituent of t is a constant or a sup-term.

Lemma 2.3:

If $t \in NTm_o \cap CTm_o$, then $t \equiv 0$ or $t \equiv St'$ for some $t' \in NTm_o \cap CTm_o$ or $t \equiv \sup_{x<\alpha} t'$ for some $t' \in NTm_o$.

Proof: By induction on the length of t. Let s be the principal constituent of t and apply Lemma 2.2 (iv). If $s \equiv +$, then there are $u, v \in NTm_o \cap CTm_o$ s.t. $t \equiv +uv$. If $s \equiv R_\sigma$, then there are closed, normal terms u_1, u_2, v s.t. $R_\sigma u_1 u_2 v$ is a subterm of t. Applying I. H. to v we obtain a contradiction to t being normal.

It follows that s ≡ 0 or s ≡ S or s is a sup-term, and hence t ≡ 0 or t ≡ St' or t is a sup-term as required.

Definition 2.4:

(i) For every ordinal α we define $\underline{\alpha} \in CTm_o \cap NTm_o$ as follows: $\underline{0} :\equiv 0$, $\underline{\alpha+1} :\equiv S\underline{\alpha}$, and for a limit ordinal α: $\underline{\alpha} :\equiv \sup_{x<\alpha} x$.

(ii) For every type σ and every ordinal α we define $\underline{\alpha}_\sigma \in CTm_\sigma \cap NTm_\sigma$ as follows: $\underline{\alpha}_o :\equiv \underline{\alpha}$, $\underline{\alpha}_{\sigma\to\tau} :\equiv \lambda a^\sigma . \underline{\alpha}_\tau$, $\underline{\alpha}_{\sigma\times\tau} :\equiv \underline{\alpha}_\sigma \boxtimes \underline{\alpha}_\tau$.

Definition 2.5: Ordinally Computable Terms of Type o

OC_o is the least subset of CTm_o satisfying the following closure conditions:

(0) $NF(t) \equiv 0 \Rightarrow t \in OC_o$.

(S) $NF(t) \equiv St' \wedge t' \in OC_o \Rightarrow t \in OC_o$.

(sup) $NF(t) \equiv \sup_{x<\alpha} t'[x] \wedge \forall\beta < \alpha: t'[\underline{\beta}] \in OC_o \Rightarrow t \in OC_o$.

Definition 2.6: $|\ |: OC_o \to On$

By induction on "$t \in OC_o$" we define:

(0) $NF(t) \equiv 0 \Rightarrow |t| := 0$.

(S) $NF(t) \equiv St' \Rightarrow |t| := |t'| + 1$.

(sup) $NF(t) \equiv \sup_{x<\alpha} t'[x] \Rightarrow |t| := \sup_{\beta<\alpha} |t'[\underline{\beta}]|$.

In order to prove that $|t|$ is in fact defined for every closed term of type o, we generalize the notion of ordinal computability to all finite types.

Definition 2.7: Ordinally Computable Terms

(i) $t \in OC_{\sigma\to\tau} :\Leftrightarrow t \in CTm_{\sigma\to\tau} \wedge \forall s \in OC_\sigma: ts \in OC_\tau$.

(ii) $t \in OC_{\sigma\times\tau} :\Leftrightarrow t \in CTm_{\sigma\times\tau} \wedge \pi^1 t \in OC_\sigma \wedge \pi^2 t \in OC_\tau$.

Lemma 2.8:

(i) $t, t' \in CTm_\sigma \wedge NF(t) \equiv NF(t') \Rightarrow (t \in OC_\sigma \Leftrightarrow t' \in OC_\sigma)$.

(ii) $\lambda a.t[a] \in OC_{\sigma\to\tau} \Leftrightarrow \forall s \in OC_\sigma: t[s] \in OC_\tau$.

(iii) $s \boxtimes t \in OC_{\sigma\times\tau} \Leftrightarrow s \in OC_\sigma \wedge t \in OC_\tau$.

(iv) $\sup_{x<\alpha} t[x] \in OC_\sigma \Leftrightarrow \forall\beta < \alpha: t[\underline{\beta}] \in OC_\sigma$.

(v) $\forall\alpha \in On: \underline{\alpha}_\sigma \in OC_\sigma$.

Proof:

(i) By induction on σ.

$\sigma = \rho \to \tau$: Observe that by virtue of Church-Rosser-property $NF(ts) \equiv NF(NF(t)s)$.

$\sigma = \rho \times \tau$: Observe that $NF(\pi^i t) \equiv \pi^i NF(t)$.

(ii), (iii) follows by (i) from the definition of $OC_{\sigma\to\tau}$, $OC_{\sigma\times\tau}$.

(iv) By induction on σ.

$\sigma = o$: Let $t'[x] :\equiv NF(t[x])$. Then $NF(\sup_{x<\alpha} t[x]) \equiv \sup_{x<\alpha} t'[x]$, and so $\sup_{x<\alpha} t[x] \in OC_o$ iff for every $\beta < \alpha$: $t'[\underline{\beta}] \in OC_o$. But $NF(t'[\underline{\beta}]) \equiv NF(t[\underline{\beta}])$, and so the claim follows by (i).

$\sigma = \rho \to \tau$: $\sup_{x<\alpha} t[x] \in OC_{\rho\to\tau} \underset{(ii)}{\Leftrightarrow} \forall s \in OC_\rho$:
$\sup_{x<\alpha} (t[x]s) \in OC_\tau \underset{I.H.}{\Leftrightarrow} \forall\beta < \alpha$:
$\forall s \in OC_\rho: t[\underline{\beta}]s \in OC_\tau \Leftrightarrow \forall\beta < \alpha: t[\underline{\beta}] \in OC_{\sigma\to\tau}$.

$\sigma = \rho \times \tau$: $\sup_{x<\alpha} t[x] \in OC_{\rho\times\tau} \overset{\Leftrightarrow}{(iii)} \sup_{x<\alpha} \pi^1 t[x] \in OC_\rho \wedge \sup_{x<\alpha} \pi^2 t[x] \in OC_\tau$
$\underset{I.H.}{\Leftrightarrow} \forall\beta < \alpha: \pi^1 t[\underline{\beta}] \in OC_\rho \wedge \pi^2 t[\underline{\beta}] \in OC_\tau$
$\Leftrightarrow \forall\beta < \alpha: t[\underline{\beta}] \in OC_{\sigma\times\tau}$.

(v) By induction on σ.

$\sigma = o$: By induction on α.
$\sigma = \rho \to \tau$: By (ii).
$\sigma = \rho \times \tau$: By (iii).

<u>Lemma 2.9:</u>

(i) $S \in OC_{o\to o}$
(ii) $+_\sigma \in OC_{\sigma\to\sigma\to\sigma}$
(iii) $R_\sigma \in OC_{\sigma\to(\sigma\to o\to\sigma)\to o\to\sigma}$

Proof:

(i) $St \in OC_o \Leftrightarrow NF(t) \in OC_o \Leftrightarrow t \in OC_o$.

(ii) By induction on σ.

$\sigma = o$: By induction on "$u \in OC_o$" we prove that
$t \in OC_o \wedge u \in OC_o \Rightarrow NF(+tu) \in OC_o$.
Case 1: $NF(u) \equiv 0 \Rightarrow NF(+tu) \equiv NF(t) \in OC_o$.
Case 2: $NF(u) \equiv Su' \Rightarrow NF(+tu) \equiv S(NF(+tu'))$.
I.H. $\Rightarrow NF(+tu') \in OC_o \underset{(i)}{\Rightarrow}$ q.e.d.
Case 3: $NF(u) \equiv \sup_{x<\alpha} u'[x] \Rightarrow NF(+tu) \equiv \sup_{x<\alpha} NF(+tu'[x])$.
I.H. $\Rightarrow \forall\beta < \alpha: NF(+tu'[\underline{\beta}]) \in OC_o \underset{L.2.8(iv)}{\Rightarrow}$ q.e.d.
$\sigma = \rho \to \tau$: Let $s_1, s_2 \in OC_\sigma$, $r \in OC_\rho$ be given. Then $s_1 r, s_2 r \in OC_\tau$, and so by I.H.: $+_\tau(s_1 r)(s_2 r) \in OC_\tau$. By Lemma 2.8 (ii) this proves the claim.

$\sigma = \rho \times \tau$: Let s, $t \in OC_{\rho\times\tau}$ be given. Then $\pi^1 s$, $\pi^1 t \in OC_\rho$, $\pi^2 s$, $\pi^2 t \in OC_\tau$, and so by I.H.: $+_\rho(\pi^1 s)(\pi^1 t) \in OC_\rho$, $+_\tau(\pi^2 s)(\pi^2 t) \in OC_\tau$, and by Lemma 2.8(iii): $+_\rho(\pi^1 s)(\pi^1 t) \boxtimes +_\tau(\pi^2 s)(\pi^2 t) \in OC_{\rho\times\tau}$. By Lemma 2.8(ii) this proves the claim.

(iii) By induction on "$v \in OC_o$" we show that

$$t \in OC_\sigma \wedge u \in OC_{\sigma\to o\to\sigma} \wedge v \in OC_o \Rightarrow NF(R_\sigma tuv) \in OC_\sigma.$$

Case 1: $NF(v) \equiv 0$, then $NF(R_\sigma tuv) \equiv NF(t) \in OC_\sigma$.

Case 2: $NF(v) \equiv Sv'$, then $NF(R_\sigma tuv) \equiv NF(+_\sigma (R_\sigma tuv')(u(R_\sigma tuv')v'))$ $\equiv NF(+_\sigma (NF(R_\sigma tuv'))(u(NF(R_\sigma tuv'))v'))$.
Apply I.H., (ii), and Lemma 2.8. (i).

Case 3: $NF(v) \equiv \sup_{x<\alpha} v'[x]$, then $NF(R_\sigma tuv) \equiv \sup_{x<\alpha} NF(R_\sigma tuv'[x])$.
I.H. $\Rightarrow \forall\beta < \alpha$: $NF(R_\sigma tuv'[\underline{\beta}]) \in OC_\sigma$.
Now the claim follows from Lemma 2.8 (iv).

Definition 2.10: Ordinal Computability under Substitution of Closed Terms

Let $t[a_1^{\sigma_1}, \ldots, a_n^{\sigma_n}] \in OTm_\tau$ be such that the free variables of t are among $a_1^{\sigma_1}, \ldots, a_n^{\sigma_n}$.

$$t[a_1, \ldots, a_n] \in OC_\tau^* :\Leftrightarrow \forall s_1 \in OC_{\sigma_1} \ldots \forall s_n \in OC_{\sigma_n} : t[s_1, \ldots, s_n] \in OC_\tau.$$

Theorem 2.11:

For every type σ:

(i) $OC_\sigma^* = OTm_\sigma$

(ii) $OC_\sigma = CTm_\sigma$

Proof:

(i) By induction on terms. We confine ourselves to the less easy cases.

Case 1: $t[a_1, \ldots, a_n] \equiv \lambda a.t'[a_1, \ldots, a_n, a]$. Let $s_i \in OC_{\sigma_i}$, $s \in OC_\sigma$. By I.H. we see that $t'[s_1, \ldots, s_n, s] \in OC_\sigma$, and so by Lemma 2.8(ii): $\lambda a.t'[s_1, \ldots, s_n, a] \in OC_{\sigma\to\tau}$, which is to be shown.

Case 2: $t[a_1, \ldots, a_n] \equiv \underset{x<\alpha}{\sup}\, t'[a_1, \ldots, a_n, x]$. Let $s_i \in OC_{\sigma_i}$ and $\beta < \alpha$. By Lemma 2.8 (v) and I.H. we have that $t'[s_1, \ldots, s_n, \underline{\beta}] \in OC_o$, and so by Lemma 2.8 (iv): $\underset{x<\alpha}{\sup}\, t'[s_1, \ldots, s_n, x] \in OC_o$, which is to be shown.

In order to find bounds for $|t|$, we want to apply proof theory. So we have to determine the proof-theoretical strength of the methods used in the preceeding proof of "$t \in OC_o$". We observe that beyond elementary syntactical reasoning we have repeatedly used induction on OC_o and at one place transfinite induction, namely in the proof of "$\underline{\alpha} \in OC_o$" (see Lemma 2.8 (v)). So the strength of the proof of "$t \in OC_o$" depends essentially on the size of the ordinals α, for which "$\underset{x<\alpha}{\sup}$" occurs in t.

To put this more formally, let Λ be a recursive ordinal and let $\prec$ be a primitive recursive well-ordering on $\mathbb{N}$ of order type Λ. We restrict the system λ-OT to terms having only $\alpha < \Lambda$ in the subscript of "sup", and change the rule for formation of sup-terms, so that the terms of the resulting system $\underline{\lambda\text{-OT} < \Lambda}$ are finitary objects. This can be done as follows: If $n \in \mathbb{N}$ is such that $|n|_\prec$ is a limit ordinal, and if $t \in OTm_o$, then $(\underset{x\prec n}{\sup}\, t) \in OTm_o$. Now assume some canonical coding of the syntax of $\lambda\text{-OT} < \Lambda$ to be given. For every specific term $t \in CTm_o$ the proof of Theorem 2.11 can be formalized in the intuitionistic theory of the inductively defined set OC_o

plus transfinite induction on initial segments of $\prec$ (for details of formalization consult Troelstra (1973), Ch. I, §5 and Ch. II, §3).

Moreover for $\Lambda \leq \eta_o$ this transfinite induction is provable in ID_1, so we obtain the following theorem.

Theorem 2.12:

For every $t \in CTm_o$ of λ-OT $< \Lambda$:

(i) For some $n \in \mathbb{N}$: $ID_1(OC_o) + TI_{\prec}(n) \vdash OC_o(\ulcorner t \urcorner)$.

(ii) If $\Lambda \leq \eta_o$, then $ID_1 \vdash OC_o(\ulcorner t \urcorner)$.

(It is to be understood that here OC_o is a predicate constant and $\ulcorner t \urcorner$ denotes the Gödel-number of t.)

Let for every $t \in OC_o$ the earliest ordinal stage at which t is put into OC_o be denoted by $|t|_{OC_o}$ (cf., e.g., Buchholz et al. (1981), Ch. I, §11, p. 20f. or Zucker (1973), 6.2.1, p. 397).

The following boundness result is well-known from the proof theory of ID_1 (see, e.g., Buchholz et al. (1981), Ch. VI, §γ, Theorem 2.7, p. 325):

$$ID_1 \vdash OC_o(\ulcorner t \urcorner) \Rightarrow |t|_{OC_o} < \eta_o.$$

A straightforward induction on OC_o shows moreover that for every $t \in OC_o$:

$$|t| \leq |t|_{OC_o}.$$

Putting together Theorem 2.12 (ii) and this information, we arrive at our main theorem.

Theorem 2.13:

$$t \in CTm_o \text{ of } \lambda\text{-OT} < \Lambda \wedge \Lambda \leqq \eta_o \Rightarrow |t| < \eta_o.$$

3. TYPED λ-CALCULUS PT < Λ AND MODELS

Having estimated $|t|$, it remains to relate this syntactically defined value of t to values in models, in order to obtain the result about ptykes we are interested in.

The definition of the notion of a model is a bit cumbersome because of the presence of λ-terms and sup-terms. A detailed discussion of the trouble with λ-terms can be found in Barendregt (1981), Ch. 5, §§1 and 2, so we treat this matter rather casually.

The sup-terms present another difficulty, because for ptykes the "sup" does not always exist.

We solve the problem by restricting λ-OT to a syntactically defined subclass of OTm_σ, which is big enough for our purpose and for which the ptykes can be shown to form a model.

Definition 3.1:

The notion of a *distinguished variable* (d. var.) is inductively defined as follows:

(i) x is d. var. of $x \in OTm_0$.

(ii) x is d. var. of $u \in OTm_0$, x is not free in $t \in OTm_0 \Rightarrow$
$\Rightarrow x$ is d. var. of $+tu \in OTm_0$.

(iii) x is d. var. of $v \in OTm_0$, x is not free in $t \in OTm_\sigma$,
$u \in OTm_{\sigma\to 0\to\sigma} \Rightarrow x$ is d. var. of $R_\sigma tuv \in OTm_\sigma$.

(iv) x is d. var. of $t \in OTm_{\sigma\to\tau}$, x is not free in $s \in OTm_\sigma \Rightarrow$
$\Rightarrow x$ is d. var. of $ts \in OTm_\sigma$.

(v) x is d. var. of $t \in OTm_{\sigma\times\tau} \Rightarrow x$ is d. var. of $\pi^1 t \in OTm_\sigma$,
$\pi^2 t \in OTm_\tau$.

We note without proof some elementary properties of this notion.

<u>Lemma 3.2:</u>

(i) Every term has at most one distinguished variable.

(ii) x d. var. of $t \Rightarrow x$ has exactly one free occurence in t.

(iii) x d. var. of $+tu$, $+tu \twoheadrightarrow s \Rightarrow \exists t', u': t \twoheadrightarrow t', u \twoheadrightarrow u'$,
$s \equiv +t'u'$, x d. var. of u', s.

(iv) x d. var. of $R_\sigma tuv$, $R_\sigma tuv \twoheadrightarrow s \Rightarrow \exists t', u', v': t \twoheadrightarrow t'$,
$u \twoheadrightarrow u'$, $v \twoheadrightarrow v'$, $s \equiv R_\sigma t'u'v'$, x d. var. of v', s.

(v) x d. var. of ts, $t \in OTm_{\sigma\to\tau}$, $s \in OTm_\sigma$, $ts \twoheadrightarrow u \Rightarrow \exists t', s'$:
$t \twoheadrightarrow t'$, $s \twoheadrightarrow s'$, $u \equiv t's'$, x d. var. of t', u.

(vi) x d. var. of $\pi^i t$, $t \in OTm_{\sigma\times\tau}$, $\pi^i t \twoheadrightarrow s \Rightarrow \exists t': t \twoheadrightarrow t'$,
$s \equiv \pi^i t$

(vii) x d. var. of $t[a^\sigma]$, $a^\sigma \not\equiv x$, x not free in $s \in OTm_\sigma \Rightarrow x$
d. var. of $t[s]$.

In the following let Λ be a fixed ordinal or Λ = On. The typed λ-calculus <u>PT < Λ</u> is given by the same notions of reduction $\succ\!\!-$, $\to$, $\twoheadrightarrow$ as λ-OT, however restricted to the following class PTm < Λ of ptyx-terms.

Definition 3.3:

$PTm_\sigma < \Lambda$, σ type, is the family of the smallest subclasses of OTm_σ containing all variables and constants of λ-OT, and closed under formation of ⊠-terms, π-terms, app-terms and λ-terms, and under the following rule of term formation:

(P-sup) $t \in PTm_0 < \Lambda$, x d. var. of t, $\alpha < \Lambda$, α limit ordinal ⇒ ⇒ $(\sup_{x<\alpha} t) \in PTm_0 < \Lambda$.

By $CPTm_\sigma < \Lambda$ we denote the subclass consisting of the closed terms of $PTm_\sigma < \Lambda$.

Remark: Observe that for $\Lambda = \omega$ there are no sup-terms, and so $PT < \omega$ is Girard's variant T' of Gödel's T (see Girard (198.), Annex 12.A).

In the following lemma we collect some closure properties of $PTm_\sigma < \Lambda$, in particular we see that reduction does not lead out of $PTm_\sigma < \Lambda$.

Lemma 3.4:

(i) $+_\sigma \in CPTm_{\sigma\to\sigma\to\sigma} < \Lambda$

(ii) $\alpha < \Lambda \Rightarrow \underline{\alpha}_\sigma \in CPTm_\sigma < \Lambda$

(iii) $t \in PTm_\sigma < \Lambda$, x d. var. of t, $\alpha < \Lambda$, α limit ordinal ⇒ ⇒ $\sup_{x<\alpha} t \in PTm_\sigma < \Lambda$

(iv) $t[a^\sigma] \in PTm_\tau < \Lambda$, $s \in PTm_\sigma < \Lambda \Rightarrow t[s] \in PTm_\tau < \Lambda$

(v) $t \in PTm_\sigma < \Lambda$, $t \succ t' \Rightarrow t' \in PTm_\sigma < \Lambda$

(vi) $t \in PTm_\sigma < \Lambda$, $t \to t' \Rightarrow t' \in PTm_\sigma < \Lambda$

(vii) $t \in PTm_\sigma < \Lambda$, $t \twoheadrightarrow t' \Rightarrow t' \in PTm_\sigma < \Lambda$

Proof:

(iii) By induction on σ using the definition of sup for terms of higher types.

(iv) By induction on t[a]. We confine ourselves to the case, where $t[a] \equiv \sup_{x<\alpha} t'[x, a] \in PTm_o < \Lambda$. Then we have that x is d. var. of $t'[x, a] \in PTm_o < \Lambda$, $\alpha < \Lambda$. By I.H. $t'[x, s] \in PTm_o < \Lambda$ and by Lemma 3.2 (vii) x is d. var. of t'[x, s], and so by rule (P-sup): $t[s] \equiv \sup_{x<\alpha} t'[x, s] \in PTm_o < \Lambda$.

(v) By inspection of the contraction rules.

(vi) By induction on "$\rightarrow$". Look at the case, where $\sup_{x<\alpha} t \rightarrow \sup_{x<\alpha} t'$ is inferred from $t \rightarrow t'$. By I.H. we see that $t' \in PTm_o < \Lambda$. From Lemma 3.2 (iii) - (vi) it follows that x is d. var. of t' and so by the term formation rule (P-sup): $(\sup_{x<\alpha} t') \in PTm_o < \Lambda$.

<u>Definition 3.5: Type Structure</u>

A type structure is a quadrupel

$M = \langle \{M_\sigma \mid \sigma \text{ type}\}, \{\cdot_{\sigma\tau} \mid \sigma, \tau \text{ types}\}, \{\boxtimes_{\sigma\tau} \mid \sigma, \tau \text{ types}\}, \{\pi^i_{\sigma\tau} \mid \sigma, \tau \text{ types}, i = 1, 2\}\rangle$

such that

(i) $\cdot_{\sigma\tau} : M_{\sigma\rightarrow\tau} \times M_\sigma \rightarrow M_\tau$ (write $a \cdot b$ for $\cdot_{\sigma\tau}(a, b)$),

(ii) $\boxtimes_{\sigma\tau} : M_\sigma \times M_\tau \rightarrow M_{\sigma\times\tau}$ (write $a \boxtimes b$ for $\boxtimes_{\sigma\tau}(a, b)$),

(iii) $\pi^1_{\sigma\tau} : M_{\sigma\times\tau} \rightarrow M_\sigma$, $\pi^2_{\sigma\tau} : M_{\sigma\times\tau} \rightarrow M_\tau$,

(iv) $\forall a \in M_\sigma\ \forall b \in M_\tau : \pi^1_{\sigma\tau}(a \boxtimes b) = a$, $\pi^2_{\sigma\tau}(a \boxtimes b) = b$.

Definition 3.6: Ordinal Operator Structure Over Λ

An ordinal operator structure over Λ (Λ-OOS) is a pair $<\mathcal{M}, *>$ such that $\mathcal{M}$ is a type structure, M_o is a limit ordinal $\geq \Lambda$ or Λ = On, and $*$ is a map associating with every term $t \in PTm_\tau < \Lambda$ and every sequence $a_1^{\sigma_1}, \ldots, a_n^{\sigma_n}$ of distinct variables containing the free variables of t a map $t^*: M_{\sigma_1} \times \ldots \times M_{\sigma_n} \to M_\tau$ satisfying the following:

(i) t^* is "independent of the naming and ordering of the variables", which means precisely: If $a_1^{\sigma_1}, \ldots a_n^{\sigma_n}$ contains exactly the free variables of t, $n \leq k$, $\pi: \{1, \ldots, n\} \to \{1, \ldots, k\}$ is an injective map, $b_1^{\tau_1}, \ldots, b_k^{\tau_k}$ is a sequence of distinct variables s.t. $\tau_{\pi i} = \sigma_i$, and s is obtained from t by renaming bound variables and simultaneously substituting $b_{\pi 1}^{\sigma_1}, \ldots, b_{\pi n}^{\sigma_n}$ for $a_1^{\sigma_1}, \ldots, a_n^{\sigma_n}$, then for all $c_1 \in M_{\tau_1}, \ldots, c_k \in M_{\tau_k}$:

$$s^*(c_1, \ldots, c_k) = t^*(c_{\pi 1}, \ldots, c_{\pi n}).$$

We use this independence to admit a certain notational ambiguity: we do not distinguish between the different maps t^* associated with t. Since their relationship is clear by the above requirement, we can thus avoid awkward notations.

(ii) $(a^\sigma)^*(c) = c \in M_\sigma$

(iii) $(ts)^*(c_1, \ldots, c_n) = t^*(c_1, \ldots, c_n) \cdot_{\sigma\tau} s^*(c_1, \ldots, c_n)$

(iv) $(\pi^i t)^*(c_1, \ldots, c_n) = \pi^i_{\sigma\tau}(t^*(c_1, \ldots, c_n))$

(v) $(s \boxtimes t)^*(c_1, \ldots, c_n) = s^*(c_1, \ldots, c_n) \boxtimes_{\sigma\tau} t^*(c_1, \ldots, c_n)$

(vi) $(\lambda a^\sigma . t)^*(c_1, \ldots, c_n) \cdot_{\sigma\tau} d = t^*(c_1, \ldots, c_n, d)$ for every $d \in M_\sigma$.

(vii) $0^* = 0 \in M_o$

(viii) $S^* . \alpha = \alpha + 1$ for every $\alpha \in M_o$.

(ix) $(\sup_{x<\alpha} t)^*(c_1, \ldots, c_n) = \sup_{\beta<\alpha} t^*(c_1, \ldots, c_n, \beta) \in M_o$

In order to guarantee that the reduction rules generate valid equations in a Λ-OOS, we must impose certain additional requirements, some of which give the right meaning to + and R_σ, and some amount to uniformity conditions for the interpretation of λ-terms. The latter are always trivially satisfied in extensional type structures, but somewhat awkward in the non-extensional case (cf. Barendregt (1981), Ch. 5, §2, pp. 90-95, 99f.).

Definition 3.7: Canonical Pseudo-model of PT < Λ

A canonical pseudo-model of PT < Λ is a Λ-OOS $\langle M, *\rangle$ satisfying the following requirements:

(i) $t[a^\sigma] \in PTm_\tau < \Lambda$, $s \in PTm_\sigma < \Lambda$, a^σ not free in $s \Rightarrow$
$\Rightarrow (t[s])^*(c_1, \ldots, c_n) = t^*(c_1, \ldots, c_n, s^*(c_1, \ldots, c_n))$.

(ii) x distinguished variable of $t \in PTm_\sigma < \Lambda$, $\alpha < \Lambda$ limit ordinal $\Rightarrow (\sup_{x<\alpha} t)^*(c_1, \ldots, c_n) = t^*(c_1, \ldots, c_n, \alpha)$.

(iii) $+^*\cdot\alpha\cdot\beta = \alpha + \beta \in M_o$ for all $\alpha, \beta \in M_o$.

(iv) $R^*_\sigma\cdot c\cdot d\cdot 0 = c$,
$R^*_\sigma\cdot c\cdot d\cdot(\alpha + 1) = +^*_\sigma\cdot(R_\sigma\cdot c\cdot d\cdot\alpha)\cdot(d\cdot(R^*_\sigma\cdot c\cdot d\cdot\alpha)\cdot\alpha)$ for every $\alpha \in M_o$.

Remark 3.8:

If $\langle M, *\rangle$ is a canonical pseudo-model of $PT < \Lambda_1$ and $\Lambda_o < \Lambda_1$, then $\langle M, *\rangle$ is also a canonical pseudo-model of $PT < \Lambda_o$.

Lemma 3.9:

Let $\langle M, *\rangle$ be a canonical pseudo-model of PT < Λ. Then for t, $s \in PTm_\sigma < \Lambda$: $t \succ\!\!- s \Rightarrow t^* = s^*$.

Proof: By inspection of the contraction rules.

Case 1: $(\lambda a.t[a])s \succ t[s]$.

$((\lambda a.t[a])s)^*(c_1, \ldots, c_n) = (\lambda a.t[a])^*(c_1, \ldots, c_n)\cdot s^*(c_1, \ldots, c_n) = t^*(c_1, \ldots, c_n, s^*(c_1, \ldots, c_n)) = (t[s])^*(c_1, \ldots, c_n)$.

Case 2: $+t(\sup_{x<\alpha} u) \succ \sup_{x<\alpha} (+tu)$.

$(+t(\sup_{x<\alpha} u))^*(c_1, \ldots, c_n) = +^*\cdot t^*(c_1, \ldots, c_n)\cdot(\sup_{x<\alpha} u)^*(c_1, \ldots, c_n) = t^*(c_1, \ldots, c_n) + u^*(c_1, \ldots, c_n, \alpha) =$
$= (+tu)^*(c_1, \ldots, c_n, \alpha) = (\sup_{x<\alpha} (+tu))^*(c_1, \ldots, c_n)$.

Case 3: $R_\sigma tu(\sup_{x<\alpha} v)) \succ \sup_{x<\alpha} (R_\sigma tuv)$.

$(R_\sigma tu(\sup_{x<\alpha} v))^*(c_1, \ldots, c_n) = R_\sigma^*\cdot t^*(c_1, \ldots, c_n)\cdot u^*(c_1, \ldots, c_n)\cdot(\sup_{x<\alpha} v)^*(c_1, \ldots, c_n) = R_\sigma^*\cdot t^*(c_1, \ldots, c_n)\cdot u^*(c_1, \ldots, c_n)\cdot v^*(c_1, \ldots, c_n, \alpha) = (R_\sigma tuv)^*(c_1, \ldots, c_n, \alpha) =$
$= (\sup_{x<\alpha} (R_\sigma tuv))^*(c_1, \ldots, c_n)$.

The remaining cases are straightforward.

In the generation of the reduction relation $\twoheadrightarrow$ there occurs the clause "$t \twoheadrightarrow s \Rightarrow \lambda a.t \twoheadrightarrow \lambda a.s$". Validity of this clause imposes another uniformity requirement on the interpretation of λ-terms, which for simplicity we have chosen not to demand. (The term "pseudo" in our notion of model is meant to indicate this lack.) So we introduce a restricted reduction relation $\bar{\twoheadrightarrow}$, where this clause is not used.

<u>Definition 3.10: Weak Reduction $\bar{\twoheadrightarrow}$</u>

The relation $\bar{\twoheadrightarrow}$ of weak reduction is defined by the following inductive clauses.

(i) $t \mathrel{\overline{\twoheadrightarrow}} t$,

(ii) $t \succ s \Rightarrow t \mathrel{\overline{\twoheadrightarrow}} s$,

(iii) $t \mathrel{\overline{\twoheadrightarrow}} t', s \mathrel{\overline{\twoheadrightarrow}} s' \Rightarrow ts \mathrel{\overline{\twoheadrightarrow}} t's'$,

(iv) $t \mathrel{\overline{\twoheadrightarrow}} t', s \mathrel{\overline{\twoheadrightarrow}} s' \Rightarrow t \boxtimes s \mathrel{\overline{\twoheadrightarrow}} t' \boxtimes s'$,

(v) $t \mathrel{\overline{\twoheadrightarrow}} t' \Rightarrow \pi^i t \mathrel{\overline{\twoheadrightarrow}} \pi^i t'$,

(vi) $t \mathrel{\overline{\twoheadrightarrow}} t', \sup_{x<\alpha} t \in PTm_o < \Lambda \Rightarrow \sup_{x<\alpha} t \mathrel{\overline{\twoheadrightarrow}} \sup_{x<\alpha} t'$,

(vii) $t \mathrel{\overline{\twoheadrightarrow}} s, s \mathrel{\overline{\twoheadrightarrow}} u \Rightarrow t \mathrel{\overline{\twoheadrightarrow}} u$.

<u>Proposition 3.11:</u>

Let $\langle \mathcal{M}, * \rangle$ be a canonical pseudo-model of $PT < \Lambda$. Then for $t, s \in PTm_\sigma < \Lambda$:

$$t \mathrel{\overline{\twoheadrightarrow}} s \Rightarrow t^* = s^*.$$

Proof: Straightforward by induction on $\overline{\twoheadrightarrow}$.

Now we can for $t \in CPTm_o < \Lambda$ relate $|t|$ to the value t^* in canonical pseudo-models of $PT < \Lambda$. Weak reduction is sufficient, because for reduction of terms of type o we can avoid contractions inside of λ-terms. Namely by virtue of the strong normalization theorem one can always reduce a maximal (outermost) redex.

<u>Lemma 3.12:</u>

Let $\langle \mathcal{M}, * \rangle$ be a canonical pseudo-model of $PT < \Lambda$.

(i) $t \in CPTm_o < \Lambda \Rightarrow t^* = NF(t)^*$.

(ii) $\alpha < \Lambda \Rightarrow \underline{\alpha}^* = \alpha$.

Proof:

(i) Follows from Proposition 3.11, since by the above remarks $t \twoheadrightarrow NF(t)$.

(ii) By induction on α. $\underline{0}^* = 0^* = 0$. $\underline{\alpha + 1}^* \equiv (S\underline{\alpha})^* \underset{(I.H.)}{=} S^*\cdot\alpha = \alpha + 1$. For α limit: $\underline{\alpha}^* \equiv (\sup_{x<\alpha} x)^* = (x)^*(\alpha) = \alpha$.

Theorem 3.13:

Let $\langle M, *\rangle$ be a canonical pseudo-model of PT $< \Lambda$. Then for every $t \in CPTm_o < \Lambda$: $|t| = t^*$.

Proof: By induction on OC_o.

Case 1: $NF(t) \equiv 0$: $t^* = 0^* = 0 = |t|$.
Case 2: $NF(t) \equiv St_1$: $t^* = (St_1)^* = t_1^* + 1 \underset{(I.H.)}{=} |t_1| + t = |t|$.
Case 3: $NF(t) \equiv \sup_{x<\alpha} t_1[x]$:

$$t^* = (\sup_{x<\alpha} t_1[x])^* \underset{(3.6\ (ix))}{=} \sup_{\beta<\alpha} (t_1[x]^*(\beta)) = \sup_{\beta<\alpha} (t_1[x]^*(\underline{\beta}^*)) \underset{(3.7\ (i))}{=} \sup_{\beta<\alpha} (t_1[\underline{\beta}])^* \underset{(I.H.)}{=} \sup_{\beta<\alpha} |t_1[\underline{\beta}]| = |t|.$$

From the main result of the preceding section we obtain the following consequence.

Corollary 3.14:

Let $\langle M, *\rangle$ be a canonical pseudo-model of PT $< \Lambda$, $\Lambda \leq \eta_o$, $t \in CPTm_o < \Lambda$: then $t^* < \eta_o$.

In the final section we will introduce the ptykes of finite types as a canonical pseudo-model of PT < On, and apply our result to this model.

4. THE MODEL OF PTYKES

Since Girard's (198.) book has not yet appeared, we will not go very deeply into the theory of ptykes. We rather confine ourselves to reviewing and explaining the main properties of ptykes of finite types, which are needed to see that they form indeed a canonical pseudo-model of PT < On as desired.

Beyond what has been said in the introduction, the following facts are important. For every finite type σ there is a partial order $\leqq^{\sigma}$ on Pt^{σ}, which is characterized by:

(1) $A \leqq^{\sigma} B$ iff an "embedding" morphism $E^{\sigma}_{AB} \in I^{\sigma}(A, B)$ is well defined.

(2) $\leqq^{o}$ is the usual order on ordinals, and for higher types we have: $A \leqq^{\sigma\to\tau} B \Rightarrow \forall a \in Pt^{\sigma}: Aa \leqq^{\tau} Ba$ (but the converse does not hold in general), and $(A, A') \leqq^{\sigma\times\tau} (B, B') \Leftrightarrow A \leqq^{\sigma} B \wedge A' \leqq^{\tau} B'$.

Using the embedding morphisms, one can define $\sup_{i\in I} A_i$ in a natural way as the direct limit of the directed system $(A_i, E^{\sigma}_{A_iA_j})_{i,j\in I}$ provided that for all $i, j \in I$: $i \leqq j \Rightarrow A_i \leqq^{\sigma} A_j$. This notion of sup satisfies:

(3) $A = \sup_{i\in I} A_i$ in $PT^{\sigma\to\tau} \Rightarrow \forall a \in Pt^{\sigma}: Aa = \sup_{i\in I} A_i a$, and $(A, B) = \sup_{i\in I} (A_i, B_i)$ in $PT^{\sigma\times\tau} \Leftrightarrow A = \sup_{i\in I} A_i$ in $PT^{\sigma} \wedge B = \sup_{i\in I} B_i$ in PT^{τ}.

A ptyx $A \in Pt^{\sigma\to\tau}$ is said to be a *flower* iff

(4) $\forall a, b \in Pt^{\sigma}: a \leq^{\sigma} b \Rightarrow A(E^{\sigma}_{ab}) = E^{\tau}_{Aa,Ab}$.

Since ptykes preserve direct limits, this entails immediately that flowers commute with sups. So we see that for a flower $A \in Pt^{0\to\sigma}$, $\sup_{y<x} Ay$ is in fact well-defined in the category $PT^{0\to\sigma}$ and satisfies

(5) $Ax = \sup_{y<x} Ay$.

For the ptykes $R_{\sigma} \in Pt^{\sigma\to(\sigma\to 0\to\sigma)\to 0\to\sigma}$ defined in annex 12.A of Girard (198.) we have indeed that for all $a \in Pt^{\sigma}$ and $b \in Pt^{\sigma\to 0\to\sigma}$

(6) $R_{\sigma}ab \in Pt^{0\to\sigma}$ is a flower.

To get an idea of why this is so, we should point out that $\leq^{\sigma}$ can also be characterized by

(7) $a \leq^{\sigma} b \Leftrightarrow \exists c \in Pt^{\sigma}: a +_{\sigma} c = b$.

So by the very choice of the recursion equation for $R_{\sigma}ab(x + 1)$, one sees immediately that $R_{\sigma}abx \leq^{\sigma} R_{\sigma}ab(x + 1)$.

The construction of the canonical pseudo-model PT of the ptykes of finite types can now be outlined as follows.

Pt^{σ} is taken to be the domain of objects of type σ. $\cdot_{\sigma\tau}$, $\boxtimes_{\sigma\tau}$, $\pi^{i}_{\sigma\tau}$ are the application, pairing and unpairing of ptykes of corresponding types. Thus PT is a type structure. To define the map *, we simultaneously define t* as required in Definition 3.6 and in addition for every sequence of morphisms $T_1 \in I^{\sigma_1}(A_1, A'_1), \ldots, T_n \in I^{\sigma_n}(A_n, A'_n)$ a morphism $t^*(T_1, \ldots, T_n) \in I^{\tau}(t^*(A_1, \ldots, A_n), t^*(A'_1, \ldots, A'_n))$. Beyond the requirements of Definition 3.6. we demand that

(8) (i) $t^*(E^{\sigma 1}_{A_1}, \ldots, E^{\sigma n}_{A_n}) = E^{\tau}_{t^*(A_1,\ldots,A_n)}$,

(ii) $t^*(T_1, \ldots, T_n)t^*(T'_1, \ldots, T'_n) = t^*(T_1T'_1, \ldots, T_nT'_n)$,

(iii) $t^*(T_1, \ldots, T_n) \wedge t^*(T'_1, \ldots, T'_n) = t^*(T_1 \wedge T'_n, \ldots, T_n \wedge T'_n)$,

(iv) $(A_1, T_{1i}) = \varinjlim_{i \in I} (A_{1i}, T_{1ij}), \ldots, (A_n, T_{ni}) =$
$= \varinjlim_{i \in I} (A_{ni}, T_{nij}) \Rightarrow (t^*(A_1, \ldots, A_n), t^*(T_{1i}, \ldots, T_{ni}))$
$= \varinjlim_{i \in I} (t^*(A_{1i}, \ldots, A_{ni}), t^*(T_{1ij}, \ldots, T_{nij}))$

It is now easy to define these maps t* by induction on the complexity of the term t. Observe that by the acting of t* on objects *and* morphisms, the solution is indeed uniquely determined even for λ -terms. For details see annex 12.A of Girard's (198.) book.

Simultaneously with the definition the claimed properties are proved inductively, and in addition the following can be proved.

(9) If the free variables of $t \in PTm_\tau < On$ are among $a_1^{\sigma 1}, \ldots, a_n^{\sigma n}$, x^o, and x^o is distinguished variable of t, then for $\alpha \leq \beta \in On$:

$$t^*(E^{\sigma 1}_{A_1}, \ldots, E^{\sigma n}_{A_n}, E^{o}_{\alpha\beta}) = E^{\tau}_{t^*(A_1,\ldots,A_n,\alpha)t^*(A_1,\ldots,A_n,\beta)}.$$

By virtue of this, we can define the interpretation of sup-terms simply as follows:

(10) $(\sup_{x<\alpha} t)^*(A_1, \ldots, A_n) := t^*(A_1, \ldots, A_n, \alpha)$,
$(\sup_{x<\alpha} t)^*(T_1, \ldots, T_n) := t^*(T_1, \ldots, T_n, E^o_\alpha)$.

With these definitions it can be shown that <*PT*, *> is indeed a canonical pseudo-model of PT < On. In particular 3.7 (ii) - (iv) follow immediately by definition, and 3.7 (i) can be proved by induction on $t[a^\sigma] \in PTm_\tau < On$. By an application of Corollary 3.14 to the model <*PT*, *> we finally obtain our main result.

Theorem 4.1:

Let $t \in PTm_o < \omega$ be such that all free variables of t are among $x_1^o, \ldots, x_n^o$. Then for $<PT, *>$: $\alpha_1, \ldots, \alpha_n < \eta_o \Rightarrow t^*(\alpha_1, \ldots, \alpha_n) < \eta_o$.

Proof: Simply observe that for $t \equiv t[x_1, \ldots, x_n]$ as above, $t[\underline{\alpha}_1, \ldots, \underline{\alpha}_n] \in CPTm_o < \eta_o$ and $(t[\underline{\alpha}_1, \ldots, \underline{\alpha}_n])^* = t^*(\alpha_1, \ldots, \alpha_n)$, and apply Corollary 3.14 and Remark 3.8 to $<PT, *>$.

A similar result holds, of course, for every canonical pseudo-model of $PT < \eta_o$, in particular for the classical full (extensional) type structure over some regular ordinal $\Lambda > \omega$.

APPENDIX 1: CHURCH-ROSSER-THEOREM FOR λ-OT

The diamond property for $\twoheadrightarrow$ can be proved by an adaption of a method of W. W. Tait and P. Martin-Löf. We follow the presentation of Barendregt (1981) in Ch. 3, §2 and confine ourselves to a sketch of the main steps.

The main tool is the definition of a relation $\underset{1}{\twoheadrightarrow}$ ("parallel one step reduction") which can be proved to satisfy the diamond property.

Definition A 1.1:

(refl) $t \underset{1}{\twoheadrightarrow} t$

(λ) $t[a^\sigma] \underset{1}{\twoheadrightarrow} t'[a^\sigma],\ s \underset{1}{\twoheadrightarrow} s' \in OTm_\sigma \Rightarrow (\lambda a^\sigma.t[a^\sigma])s \underset{1}{\twoheadrightarrow} t'[s']$

(π) $s \underset{1}{\twoheadrightarrow} s',\ t \underset{1}{\twoheadrightarrow} t' \Rightarrow \pi^1(s \boxtimes t) \underset{1}{\twoheadrightarrow} s',\ \pi^2(s \boxtimes t) \underset{1}{\twoheadrightarrow} t'$

(+0) $t \underset{1}{\twoheadrightarrow} t' \in OTm_o \Rightarrow +t0 \underset{1}{\twoheadrightarrow} t'$

(+S) $t \underset{1}{\twoheadrightarrow} t' \in OTm_o,\ u \underset{1}{\twoheadrightarrow} u' \in OTm_o \Rightarrow +t(Su) \underset{1}{\twoheadrightarrow} S(+t'u')$

(+sup) $t \underset{1}{\twoheadrightarrow} t' \in OTm_o,\ u \underset{1}{\twoheadrightarrow} u' \in OTm_o \Rightarrow +t(\sup_{x<\alpha} u) \underset{1}{\twoheadrightarrow} \sup_{x<\alpha} (+t'u')$

$(R_\sigma 0)$ $\quad t \underset{1}{\twoheadrightarrow} t' \Rightarrow R_\sigma tu0 \underset{1}{\twoheadrightarrow} t'$

$(R_\sigma S)$ $\quad t \underset{1}{\twoheadrightarrow} t', u \underset{1}{\twoheadrightarrow} u', v \underset{1}{\twoheadrightarrow} v' \Rightarrow$

$\Rightarrow R_\sigma tu(Sv) \underset{1}{\twoheadrightarrow} +_\sigma (R_\sigma t'u'v')(u'(R_\sigma t'u'v')v')$

$(R_\sigma \sup)$ $\quad t \underset{1}{\twoheadrightarrow} t', u \underset{1}{\twoheadrightarrow} u', v \underset{1}{\twoheadrightarrow} v' \Rightarrow R_\sigma tu(\sup_{x<\alpha} v) \underset{1}{\twoheadrightarrow} \sup_{x<\alpha} (R_\sigma t'u'v')$

(app-comp) $\quad t \underset{1}{\twoheadrightarrow} t' \in OTm_{\sigma\to\tau}, s \underset{1}{\twoheadrightarrow} s' \in OTm_\sigma \Rightarrow ts \underset{1}{\twoheadrightarrow} t's'$

(λ-comp) $\quad t \underset{1}{\twoheadrightarrow} t' \Rightarrow \lambda a^\sigma.t \underset{1}{\twoheadrightarrow} \lambda a^\sigma.t'$

(π-comp) $\quad t \underset{1}{\twoheadrightarrow} t' \Rightarrow \pi^1 t \underset{1}{\twoheadrightarrow} \pi^1 t', \pi^2 t \underset{1}{\twoheadrightarrow} \pi^2 t'$

($\boxtimes$-comp) $\quad s \underset{1}{\twoheadrightarrow} s', t \underset{1}{\twoheadrightarrow} t' \Rightarrow s \boxtimes t \underset{1}{\twoheadrightarrow} s' \boxtimes t'$

(sup-comp) $\quad t \underset{1}{\twoheadrightarrow} t' \in OTm_o \Rightarrow \sup_{x<\alpha} t \underset{1}{\twoheadrightarrow} \sup_{x<\alpha} t'$

Lemma A 1.2:

$$t[a^\sigma] \underset{1}{\twoheadrightarrow} t'[a^\sigma],\ s \underset{1}{\twoheadrightarrow} s' \in OTm_\sigma \Rightarrow t[s] \underset{1}{\twoheadrightarrow} t'[s'].$$

Proof: Straightforward adaption of Barendregt (1981), Lemma 3.2.4, p. 60f.

Lemma A 1.3:

$\underset{1}{\twoheadrightarrow}$ satisfies the diamond property.

Proof: Adaption of Barendregt (1981), Lemma 3.2.6, p. 61 f. One has to distinguish an awful lot of cases, but everything works straigthforwardly.

Lemma A 1.4:

$\twoheadrightarrow$ is the transitive closure of $\underset{1}{\twoheadrightarrow}$.

Proposition 1.4 (i) now follows by a simple diagram chase from Lemmas A 1.3 and A 1.4, and Proposition 1.4 (ii) from (i) by observing that for a normal term t, $t \twoheadrightarrow t'$ entails that $t \equiv t'$.

APPENDIX 2: STRONG NORMALIZATION THEOREM FOR λ-OT

The strong normalization theorem for λ-OT can be proved using the method of strong computability invented by W. W. Tait. We follow the presentation of Troelstra (1973), 2.2.12 - 2.2.19, 2.2.30 - 2.2.31 and 2.3.7 and confine ourselves to a sketch of the main steps.

Definition A 2.1: Strong Computability

(i) $t \in SC_o :\Leftrightarrow t \in SN_o$ (see Definition 1.6).

(ii) $t \in SC_{\sigma\to\tau} :\Leftrightarrow t \in OTm_{\sigma\to\tau} \wedge \forall s \in SC_\sigma : ts \in SC_\tau$.

(iii) $t \in SC_{\sigma\times\tau} :\Leftrightarrow t \in OTm_{\sigma\times\tau} \wedge \pi^1 t \in SC_\sigma \wedge \pi^2 t \in SC_\tau$.

We associate with every type σ finite sequences of types $\sigma_1, \ldots, \sigma_n$ and characteristic terms $t\langle a^\sigma, a_1^{\sigma_1}, \ldots, a_n^{\sigma_n}\rangle$ corresponding to the possibilities of arriving from type σ-objects by applications and projections at type o-objects.

Definition A 2.2: Characteristic Terms for a Type

(i) $t\langle x^o\rangle$ is a characteristic term for type o $:\Leftrightarrow t\langle x^o\rangle \equiv x^o$.

(ii) $t\langle a^{\sigma\to\tau}, a_o^\sigma, a_1^{\sigma_1}, \ldots, a_n^{\sigma_n}\rangle$ is a characteristic term for type $\sigma \to \tau :\Leftrightarrow t\langle\ldots\rangle \equiv s\langle(a^{\sigma\to\tau} a_o^\sigma), a_1^{\sigma_1}, \ldots, a_n^{\sigma_n}\rangle$ for some characteristic term $s\langle b^\tau, a_1^{\sigma_1}, \ldots, a_n^{\sigma_n}\rangle$ for type τ.

(iii) $t\langle a^{\sigma\times\tau}, a_1^{\sigma_1}, \ldots, a_n^{\sigma_n}\rangle$ is a characteristic term for type $\sigma \times \tau$ $:\Leftrightarrow$ $t\langle\ldots\rangle \equiv s\langle\pi^1 a^{\sigma\times\tau}, a_1^{\sigma_1}, \ldots, a_n^{\sigma_n}\rangle$ for some characteristic term $s\langle b^\sigma, a_1^{\sigma_1}, \ldots, a_n^{\sigma_n}\rangle$ for type σ, or $t\langle\ldots\rangle \equiv s\langle\pi^2 a^{\sigma\times\tau}, a_1^{\sigma_1}, \ldots, a_n^{\sigma_n}\rangle$ for some characteristic term $s\langle b^\tau, a_1^{\sigma_1}, \ldots, a_n^{\sigma_n}\rangle$ for type τ.

It is to be understood here that the free variables are chosen pairwisely distinct and that the result of simultaneously substituting $s_1 \in OTm_{\sigma_1}, \ldots s_n \in OTm_{\sigma_n}$ for the variables in $t\langle a_1^{\sigma_1}, \ldots, a_n^{\sigma_n}\rangle$ is denoted by $t\langle s_1, \ldots, s_n\rangle$.

Lemma A 2.3:

(i) If $t\langle a^\sigma, a_1^{\sigma_1}, \ldots, a_n^{\sigma_n}\rangle$ is a characteristic term for type σ, then every σ_i is a subtype of σ and t itself is of type o.

(ii) $t \in SC_\sigma$ iff $t \in OTm_\sigma$ and for every characteristic term $u\langle a^\sigma, a_1^{\sigma_1}, \ldots, a_n^{\sigma_n}\rangle$ for type σ and all $s_1 \in SC_{\sigma_1}, \ldots, s_n \in SC_{\sigma_n}$: $u\langle t, s_1, \ldots, s_n\rangle \in SN_o$.

Lemma A 2.4:

(i) $s \in SC_\sigma \wedge s \twoheadrightarrow t \Rightarrow t \in SC_\sigma$.

(ii) $\lambda a.t[a] \in SC_{\sigma\to\tau} \Leftrightarrow \forall s \in SC_\sigma : t[s] \in SC_\tau$.

(iii) $s \boxtimes t \in SC_{\sigma\times\tau} \Leftrightarrow s \in SC_\sigma \wedge t \in SC_\tau$.

(iv) $\sup_{x<\alpha} t \in SC_\sigma \Leftrightarrow t \in SC_\sigma$.

Proof of (ii): "$\Rightarrow$" follows from the definition of $SC_{\sigma\to\tau}$ and (i). "$\Leftarrow$": Let $u\langle b^\tau, b_1^{\tau_1}, \ldots, b_n^{\tau_n}\rangle$ be a characteristic term for type τ, $t_1 \in SC_{\tau_1}, \ldots, t_n \in SC_{\tau_n}$, $s \in SC_\sigma$, and consider an arbitrary reduction path starting with $u\langle\lambda a.t[a]s, t_1, \ldots, t_n\rangle$. It must be of the form ..., $u\langle\lambda a.t'[a]s', t_1', \ldots, t_n'\rangle$, $u\langle t'[s'], t_1', \ldots, t_n'\rangle$, ... with $\lambda a.t[a] \twoheadrightarrow \lambda a.t'[a]$, $s \twoheadrightarrow s'$, $t_i \twoheadrightarrow t_i'$. Hence $t[s] \twoheadrightarrow t'[s']$, and so $t'[s'] \in SC_\tau$, $t_i' \in SC_{\tau_i}$. It follows that $u\langle t'[s'], t_1', \ldots, t_n'\rangle \in SN_o$, and so the considered reduction path must be finite. Now Lemma A 2.3 (ii) yields the result.

Lemma A 2.5:

(i) $t \in SC_\sigma \Rightarrow t \in SN_\sigma$.

(ii) $a^\sigma \in SC_\sigma$.

Proof: Simultaneously by induction on σ, for details see Troelstra (1973), Lemma 2.2.15, p. 105f.

Lemma A 2.6:

(i) $S \in SC_{o\to o}$

(ii) $+_\sigma \in SC_{\sigma\to\sigma\to\sigma}$

(iii) $R_\sigma \in SC_{\sigma\to(\sigma\to o\to\sigma)\to o\to\sigma}$

Proof:

(ii) By induction on σ. σ = 0: We have to show that for every $t, u \in SN_o$: $+tu \in SN_o$. NF(u) is of the form ...S(...(sup(...u'... ...))...)... with u' not a sup-term nor of the form u' ≡ Su". Let #(u) be the number of symbols S or sup used in constructing NF(u) from u'. The claim is proved by induction on #(u) through an inspection of an arbitrary reduction path starting with +tu. For details see Troelstra (1973), Thm. 2.2.19 (vi), p. 107f. For the induction step compare the proof of Lemma 2.9 (ii).

(iii) By induction on $\#(v)$ (see (ii)) we show that $t \in SC_\sigma$, $u \in SC_{\sigma\to o\to\sigma}$, $v \in SN_o \Rightarrow R_\sigma tuv \in SC_\sigma$. To prove this, consider for an arbitrary characteristic term $w\langle a^\sigma, a_1^{\sigma_1}, \ldots, a_n^{\sigma_n}\rangle$ for type σ and $s_i \in SC_{\sigma_i}$ a reduction path starting with $w\langle R_\sigma tuv, s_1, \ldots, s_n\rangle$. For details see again Troelstra (1973), Thm. 2.2.19 (vi), p. 107f.

Definition A 2.7: Strong Computability Under Substitution

Let $t[a_1^{\sigma_1}, \ldots, a_n^{\sigma_n}] \in OTm_\tau$ be such that the free variables of t are among $a_1^{\sigma_1}, \ldots, a_n^{\sigma_n}$.

$$t[a_1, \ldots, a_n] \in SC^*_\tau :\Leftrightarrow \forall s_1 \in SC_{\sigma_1} \ldots \forall s_n \in SC_{\sigma_n}: t[s_1, \ldots, s_n] \in SC_\tau.$$

Proposition A 2.8:

$$SC^*_\sigma = SC_\sigma = SN_\sigma = OTm_\sigma.$$

Proof: By induction on t one shows that for every $t \in OTm_\sigma$: $t \in SC^*_\sigma$. The proof is straightforward using the previous lemmas.

REFERENCES

Barendregt, H. P., 1981, "The Lambda Calculus," North-Holland, Amsterdam.

Buchholz, W., Feferman, S., Pohlers, W., and Sieg, W., 1981, "Iterated Inductive Definitions and Subsystems of Analysis: Recent Proof-Theoretical Studies," Springer, Berlin.

Feferman, S., 1968, "Ordinals Associated with Theories for One Inductively Defined Set," unpublished typescript (of a lecture given at the 1968 summer conference at Buffalo, New York).

Girard, J.-Y., 1981, Π^1_2-Logic, Part 1: Dilators, Annals of Math. Logic, 21:75-219.

Girard, J.-Y., 198., "Proof Theory and Logical Complexity," Bibliopolis, Naples (to appear).

Troelstra, A. S., 1973, "Metamathematical Investigation of Intuitionistic Arithmetic and Analysis," Springer, Berlin.

Zucker, J. I., 1973, Iterated Inductive Definitions, Trees and Ordinals, in: Troelstra (1973, pp. 392-453).

WELLORDERING THEOREMS IN TOPOLOGY

Norbert Brunner

Institut für Mathematik und angewandte Statistik
Universität für Bodenkultur
A-1180 Wien

1. INTRODUCTION

In this paper we consider topological variants of Zermelo's wellordering theorem. Given topological notions, P, Q of the form "some class of subsets of a space X is wellorderable", we consider assertions of the form "if a space X satisfies P, also Q holds for X". The properties to be considered here are related to the following cardinal invariants: cardinality of the topology, weight, density, Lindelöf-degree, spread, (hereditary) cellularity. Accordingly we define for a topological space (X, $\mathcal{X}$):

X is o, if $\mathcal{X}$ is wellorderable (the topology)
X is w, if X has a wellorderable base
X is d, if there is a dense, wellorderable subset of X
X is ℓ, if every open cover has a wellorderable subcover
X is s, if every discrete subset is wellorderable
X is c, if every family of pairwise disjoint open sets is wellorderable
X is h, if every subset is c.

If we combine these properties, we get 21 different assertions. Their interdependence is illustrated in figure 1. Using it, one easily verifies that there are indeed no other combinations.

These implications are proved within ZF set theory; i.e. the axiom of choice AC is not used. If AC is assumed, every space is od (= o and d), whence in figure 1 everything is equivalent. We will show in this paper, that no additional arrow can be proved in ZF and that in many cases an arrow which does not appear in figure 1 is equivalent to the axiom of choice. No separation axioms are assumed throughout this paper. Therefore, for example, od is not equivalent to o, as it would be the case for T_1-spaces.

2. MAIN RESULTS

In this section we prove, that figure 1 is complete for ZF set theory.

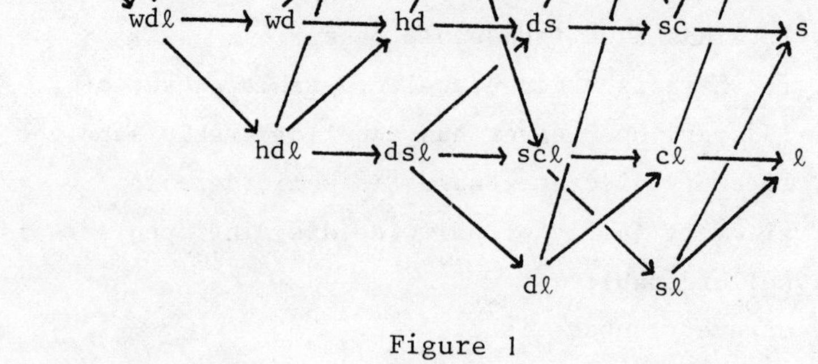

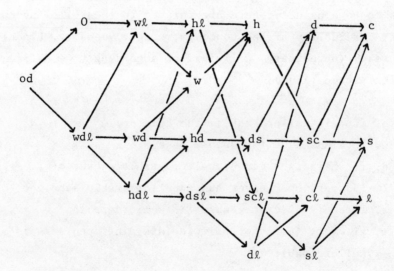

Figure 1

Lemma 1: The following assertions are equivalent to AC:

(1) $\ell \to c$

(2) $wd\ell \to o$.

Proof: Let X be a set and Y = X ∪ {p} be the Alexandroff one-point-compactification of the discrete topology on X; i.e.: open neighborhoods of p are cofinite, while points x ∈ X are isolated. Y is called the Fort-topology in Steen and Seebach (1978). Since Y is compact, Y is ℓ. (1) If Y is c, X is wellorderable. (2) If X is wellorderable, Y is ℓ, d and w. But if Y is o, then $P(X) \subseteq \mathcal{Y}$ is wellorderable, whence Rubin's axiom PW holds: The power set of an ordinal is wellorderable. In ZF, PW implies AC; cf. Rubin and Rubin (1985). q.e.d.

Lemma 2: $d \to \ell$ is equivalent to AC.

Proof: Let X be a set and define the Sierpinski space Y = X ∪ {p} as follows: $O \neq \phi$ is open, if and only if $p \in O$. Since {p} is dense, Y is d. $\mathcal{O} = \{\{x, p\}: x \in X\}$ is an open cover of Y. If Y is ℓ, then there is a wellorderable subcover $\mathcal{P}$ of $\mathcal{O}$. But since $\cup\mathcal{P} \neq Y$, whenever $\mathcal{P} \subseteq \mathcal{O}$ and $\mathcal{P} \neq \mathcal{O}$, we have: $\mathcal{P} = \mathcal{O}$ and X is wellorderable. q.e.d.

Lemma 3: The following arrows are equivalent to AC:

(1) $d\ell \to s$

(2) $h\ell \to d$.

Proof: Let $(X, \mathcal{X})$ be a space and define its open extension $Y = X \cup \{p\}$ as follows: $O \in \mathcal{Y}$, if and only if $O \in \mathcal{X}$ or $O = Y$. Since every open covering of Y contains Y as an element, Y is compact (i.e.: Y is always ℓ). For (1), let $X_1 = X \cup \{p_1\}$ be the Sierpinski space and $X_2 = X_1 \cup \{p_2\}$ be its open extension. $\{p_1\}$ is dense in X_2, and so X_2 is dℓ. Since X is discrete in X_2, s implies that X is wellorderable. In case (2), let *X* be the following topology: $O \neq \phi$ is open, if and only if $X \setminus O$ is wellorderable. Y is the open extension of X. Since X is easily shown to be h, so is Y, whence Y is hℓ. If Y is d, also its open subspace X is d. But if $D \subseteq X$ is dense and wellorderable, then $D = D^{-} = X$. q.e.d.

Lemma 4: hdℓ → w is equivalent to AC.

Proof: Let *X* be the cofinite topology on X (complements of finite sets are open). X_1 is the so-called closed extension of X: $X_1 = X \cup \{p_1\}$ and $\mathcal{X}_1 = \{\phi, O \cup \{p_1\}: O \in \mathcal{X}\}$. X_2 is the open extension of X_1. As above, X_2 is hdℓ. If X_2 is w, X is w, too. Therefore X is a wellorderable union of finite sets (the complements of the base sets). As is shown in Rubin and Rubin (1985), from this axiom (Levy's axiom of multiple choice) we get AC. q.e.d.

The author does not know, whether s → c is equivalent to AC. In this case also s → ℓ is equivalent to AC.

Is h → ℓ equivalent to AC? It can easily be seen that the axiom of choice for wellorderable families of sets AC^{wo} implies w → ℓ and w → d. For the latter arrow we even get an equivalence.

Lemma 5: w → d is equivalent to AC^{wo}.

Proof: Let *F* be a wellorderable family of pairwise disjoint, nonempty sets. $X = \cup F$ and *X* is generated by the base $F \cup \{\phi\}$. If $D \subseteq X$ is dense and wellorderable, $f(F) = \min D \cap F$ is a choice function. q.e.d.

If the axiom of foundation is not assumed, PW implies w → o + ℓ, but PW does not imply AC^{wo}. So w → ℓ does not imply AC^{wo}. We do not know, what happens if the axiom of foundation is assumed. In the following example we prove, that those arrows, that do neither appear in figure 1 nor can be shown to be equivalent to AC by an application of lemmas 1 to 4, do depend on the axiom of choice.

Example: The following assertions depend on AC:

(1) $o \to d$

(2) $wd \to \ell$

(3) $s\ell \to c$

(4) $ds\ell \to h$

Proof: (1) By applying transfer to a permutation model, where AC^{wo} fails, one gets a model of ZF with a family F of disjoint sets, such that the powerset $P(F)$ is wellorderable and F has no choice function. Topologizing $\bigcup F$ as in lemma 5, we get an o + not d space. For a description of the transfer technique consult Jech (1973). (2) is due to Jech (1968): $\mathbb{R}$ is w + d, but if there is an infinite, Dedekind-finite subset of $\mathbb{R}$, $\mathbb{R}$ is not ℓ. One can prove even more under this assumption, namely, that every Lindelöf + T_1 space is compact (Brunner (1984)). For (3) we recall from Brunner (1982a) that there is a model of ZF which contains a Dedekind-finite subset F of disjoint finite sets (F indeed is amorphous), such that no infinite subset of F has a choice function. $X = \bigcup F$ with the same topology as in lemma 5 is obviously not c (or ℓ), but it is s, since every discrete subset D of X is finite, as it is a choice set for F. The open extension X_1 of X is ℓs and not c. (4) The closed extension X_2 of X_1 is ℓsd, but not h. q.e.d.

Combining the above results with figure 1, we obtain figure 2 which gives an almost complete description of the strength of the topological wellordering theorems "every P space is Q", P, Q from

P \ Q	o	w	h	d	s	c	ℓ
od	→	→	→	→	→	→	→
o	→	→	→	∧	→	→	→
wdℓ	AC	→	→	→	→	→	→
wℓ	AC	→	→	∧	→	→	→
wd	AC	→	→	→	→	→	∧
hdℓ	AC	AC	→	→	→	→	→
hℓ	AC	AC	→	AC	→	→	→
w	AC	→	→	∧	→	→	∧
hd	AC	AC	→	→	→	→	Z
dsℓ	AC	AC	∧	→	→	→	→
h	AC	AC	→	AC	→	→	Z
ds	AC	AC	∧	→	→	→	Z
scℓ	AC	AC	∧	AC	→	→	→
dℓ	AC	AC	AC	→	AC	→	→
d	AC	AC	AC	→	AC	→	AC
sc	AC	AC	∧	AC	→	→	Z
cℓ	AC	AC	AC	AC	AC	→	→
sℓ	AC	AC	∧	AC	→	∧	→
c	AC	AC	AC	AC	AC	→	AC
s	AC	AC	∧(')	AC	→	∧	Z
ℓ	AC	AC	AC	AC	AC	AC	→

Figure 2: P → Q in ZF

figure 1. In figure 2 we shall insert an arrow, if P → Q is true in ZF; AC, if P → Q is equivalent to AC in ZF; ∧, if P → Q is not provable in ZF but P → Q does not imply AC in ZF; Z, if P → Q depends on AC but we do not know, if it is equivalent to AC. We conclude:

Corollary: In ZF, in figure 1 no arrow can be added. For P in figure 1, the assertion "every topological space is P" is equivalent to AC.

3. ADDITIONAL REMARKS

In Brunner (1983) similar investigations were done for T_2-spaces. Since in this situation it is even difficult to prove that some arrow depends on AC, it is no surprise that almost nothing is known about combined properties in the T_2-case. As an example we solve a problem, left open in Brunner (1983).

Example: One cannot prove in ZF that a wellorderable T_2 space has a wellorderable local base.

Proof: We work in the Levy-Solovay model (Solovay (1970)), where every set of reals is Lebesgue-measurable. In this model every uncountable set of reals has a perfect subset. It follows that every wellorderable subset of $\mathbb{R}$ is countable. In this model we consider the Appert space $X = \omega \cup \{p\}$, which is defined as follows: points $n \in \omega$ are isolated and neighborhoods U of p have a lower density 1, i.e., $\liminf \frac{1}{n}|U \cap n| = 1$. X is a countable T_2 space. If $(U_n)_n$ were a countable local base at p, the sequence $x_n = \min\{x \in U_n \cap \omega: s > e^n\}$ would define a neighborhood $U = X \setminus \{x_n: n \in \omega\}$ of p (observe, that $\frac{1}{n}|U \cap n| \geq 1 - \frac{\ln(n)}{n}$) which does not contain any U_n; this would constitute a contradiction. If $\mathcal{U}$ is a wellorderable local base at p, $\mathcal{U}$ induces a wellorderable subset of $P(\omega)$, and so $\mathcal{U}$ is countable. It follows that X does not have a wellorderable local base at p. q.e.d.

In a similar way one proves that in the Levy-Solovay model $2^{\mathbb{R}}$ is separable, but no point is an intersection of a wellorderable family of open sets; here one uses the principle of dependent choice.

This remark answers another question of Brunner (1983). As was observed in the above example, in the Lefy-Solovay model [0,1] is a compact, connected, linearly ordered space which has no uncountable wellordered subset. In permutation models such a space has no non-constant, continuous real valued functions (this was proved in Brunner (1982b)), whence we have here an example of a topological result, which is provable in permutation models, but not in ZF.

As a final remark we note that without the axiom of foundation several of the equivalents to AC proved in section 2 are lost. Moreover, in this weaker set theory $s \to c$ does not imply AC, because $s \to c$ holds in the Fraenkel-Halpern model. For the proof one combines the following facts: (1) in this model a set which is not wellorderable contains an infinite subset, coded by an infinite set of urelements (cf. Brunner (1982a)), and (2) every such family has a choice function (cf. Brunner (1983)).* --

The author wants to express his gratitude to Professors Jean and Herman Rubin for several stimulating conversations and to Purdue University for the hospitality extended to the author during 1983/1984 when this paper was written.

REFERENCES

Brunner, N., 1982a, Dedekind-Endlichkeit und Wohlordenbarkeit, Mh. Math., 94:9-31.

---

* It was pointed out to the author by Arthur Rubin that a similar argument is valid in the Cohen-Halpern-Levy model of ZF. Therefore $s \to h$ is in the class $\wedge$.

Brunner, N., 1982b, Geordnete Läuchli Kontinuen, Fund. Math., 116:67-73.

Brunner, N., 1983, The Axiom of Choice in Topology, Notre Dame J. F. L., 24:305-317.

Brunner, N., 1984, Hewitt Spaces, Math. Balkanica (to appear).

Jech, T., 1968, Bemerkungen zum Auswahlaxiom, Casopis pest. mat., 93:30-31.

Jech, T., 1973, "The Axiom of Choice," North-Holland, Amsterdam.

Rubin, H. and Rubin, J. E., 1985, Equivalents of the Axiom of Choice II, in: "Studies in Logic," North Holland, (to appear).

Steen, L. A. and Seebach, J. A., 1978, "Counterexamples in Topology," Springer, New York.

Solovay, R., 1970, A Model of Set Theory in which every Set of Reals is Lebesgue Measurable, Ann. Math., 92:1-56.

FOUNDATIONS OF LOGIC: PHILOSOPHICAL LOGIC

MATHEMATICAL LOGIC AND CONTINENTAL PHILOSOPHERS

Josef M. Bocheński

University of Fribourg
Switzerland

1.

1.1. Mathematical logic (abridged as "ML") was received with little sympathy - indeed with much hostility - by the majority of continental philosophers during the years following the Second World War. By "continental philosophers" the philosophers of European countries are meant, with the exception of Great Britain and Scandinavia, but including the Soviet Union. This hostility was an astonishing fact to most mathematical logicians: ML was so much superior to conventional logic (used by the philosophers), that the question how it was possible to reject it in favour of the latter was and is a serious problem.

The scope of this paper is not to study the history of the opposition between philosophers and mathematical logicians; it is not historical but rather systematic. The problem at hand is: *why* was it so? Why did this hostility and opposition arise?

1.2. To make at least two historical remarks, we may say, first, that continental philosophers did not, in the majority of cases, take any notice of ML before the end of the Second World War. This is not astonishing. The attention of a larger public was first drawn to ML by the *Principia*, which were published immediately before the First World War and became seriously known after it. In fact the first extensive paper on ML published in an important philosophical magazine was that by Canon Robert Feys (1924 / 25). However, most discussions concerning ML did not develop until a quarter of century later - the most relevant among them being probably that which took place in the Soviet Union around 1960. - The second historical remark to be made here is that these discussions seem now to be over: ML has been introduced into most philosophy departments of continental Europe, at least outside France. We are dealing, therefore, with a closed period.

1.3. This is however no reason for the discussions and struggles concerning ML to be forgotten. They offer some historical interest, as the struggle sometimes took rather dramatic forms. One young Polish logician was nearly driven to suicide because of persecution by philosophers. Some Soviet mathematical logicians showed much courage, fighting against adversaries who would gladly have sent them to concentration camps. Some of their Western colleagues were threatened in their existence: to cite just two instances, Fr. Clark was prohibited from teaching and the present writer nearly lost his chair twice because of denunciations by philosophers. Above all, the discussions about ML are not deprived of systematic interest. The study of these discussions may clarify the presuppositions and views of logic accepted by the philosophers concerned.

1.4. Our problem is, as said, why did ML meet with so much opposition from continental philosophers? There seem to have been two kinds of reasons: subjective and objective. Among the first, some were moral, like aggressivity, laziness and conservatism; some intellectual, namely misunderstandings and confusions: ML was confused with the philosophy of the logicians and with general logic. The objective reasons consisted in philosophical or logical assumptions made by philosophers. In the first class we find above all hostility toward mathematics and condemnation of all formal logic. Logical assumptions, which seem to have been the most important were either particular - as the rejection of logic of propositions (after the fashion of the old Peripateticians) - and the opposition against Boolean syllogistics. The general assumptions were, first of all, the condemnation of formalism, of extensionalism and of the logic in terms of laws.

These reasons may be tabulated as follows:

REASONS FOR REJECTING ML	SUBJECTIVE	MORAL		AGGRESSIVITY OF THE LOGICIANS	1
				LAZINESS	2
				CONSERVATISM	3
		INTELLECTUAL = confusions with		PHILOSOPHY	4
				GENERAL LOGIC	5
	OBJECTIVE	PHILOSOPHICAL		CONDEMNATION OF FORMAL LOGIC	6
				HOSTILITY TOWARD MATHEMATICS	7
		LOGICAL	PARICULAR= rejection of	LOGIC OF PROPOSITIONS	8
				BOOLEAN SYLLOGISTICS	9
			GENERAL= rejection of	FORMALISM	10
				EXTENSIONALISM	11
				LOGIC OF PROPOSITIONS	12

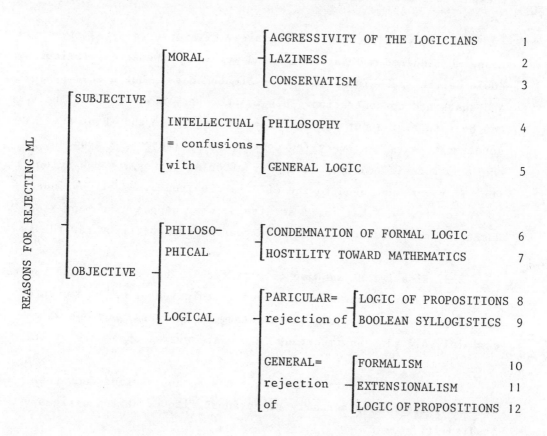

2.

2.1. One obvious reason why so many continental philosophers rejected ML was the attitude of many of the new logicians. They were often aggressive and even impolite. They said sometimes in so many words that conventional logic - the only one known by the philosophers - was rubbish and that it was a disgrace to adhere to it. There were, surely, some attenuating circumstances for that aggressivity: conventional logic *was* often rubbish and many continental philosophers were ignoramusses with regard to their own logical tradition. Yet, the said aggressivity rendered the reception of ML by philosophers more difficult. It strengthened the opposition against it, and caused the philosophers to be the more adverse to ML.

2.2. Many philosophers were guilty of another sin, namely laziness. ML required much attention and work. A mathematical-logical book could not be read "in diagonal" as Frenchmen say, but needed serious and sustained concentration. This was not very new - exactly the same can be said e.g. about the *Analytics* of Aristotle and about the scholastic texts. But very few continental philosophers read the *Analytics*: their tradition was very often a literary, not a scientific one. They were not used to the efforts required by ML. It was easier to reject it. And that is, I am afraid, what happened so many times. Human laziness was one of the main reasons for hostility toward ML.

2.3. Finally, ML was not only difficult, but also new and had to face the conservatism, deeply rooted in thinking of men and even of philosophers. This is just another form of laziness, but one which certainly did play an important role with several opponents of ML.

One result of that attitude was the rather curious fact that so many philosophers actually rejected ML without having seriously studied it.

2.4. However, not all continental philosophers who opposed ML were guilty of such laziness and ignorance. Some - it is true that they were few - did read some ML-al texts. If they rejected ML, this was often due to confusion concerning it. Among such confusions two seem to have been the most frequent: the confusion of ML with the philosophy of certain logicians and with general logic. ML was defended, for a time, principally by neo-positivists, who were known for their radical nominalism and positivism. And already before them one great name in ML was that of Bertrand Russell, who was not only a logician but also a sort of twentieth century Voltaire. His philosophy, like that of the members of the Vienna Circle, was taken to be identical with ML - in spite of the obvious fact that this was not so.

2.5. On the other hand ML was often confused with general logic, whereas it is basically just *formal* logic. Formal logic is actually pure logic, while general logic contains also, along with this, at least two sorts of applied logic (semiotics and general methodology) as well as the philosophy of logic. All these disciplines may be considered as parts of general logic. Now conventional logic did usually contain such general logic, while ML did not. Philosophers who did not understand that rejected ML as being inadequate.

2.6. If we now come to the objective reasons, we meet, first of all, with *philosophical* assumptions. One of them is the doctrine, according to which logic and especially formal logic is not a legitimate tool of thought; this was equivalent with its rejection in favour of some more or less irrational methods. Such rejection has been known, it is true, in the past, but the relative novelty of the modern discussions consists in the fact that logic was rejected now not only by professed irrationalists or sceptics, but also by philosophers who claimed to be partisans of reason, e.g. by thomists and kantians.

2.7. At the same time another assumption, relevant in our context, seems to have often been made: that whatever is mathematical is foreign to philosophy and hardly useful in it. This is probably the result of the trauma caused by the rise of Galilean, mathematical natural science. Some modern philosophers were so scared by it, that they tried hard to find a field free from the dreaded mathematics. But with ML even logic was becoming mathematical. No wonder that these philosophers should consider ML as a deep perversion of the true, qualitative logic.

2.8. Along with these two philosophical assumptions some properly *logical* doctrines played an important role in the hostility toward ML. One of them was the theory according to which the whole of formal logic may be reduced to or based on Aristotelian syllogistics - in other terms the rejection of propositional logic, which is basic in ML as it was for the Stoics and Scholastics. This is again nothing very new, as a similar doctrine was also held by ancient Peripateticians in their discussions with the Stoics. The most astonishing fact in this respect is that most of the Neo-scholastics diligently expurgated from their logic every trace of propositional logic, which was highly developed in mediaeval Scholasticism.

2.9. Another similar logical assumption was the rejection of Boolean (and as a matter of fact, of every non-Aristotelian) syllogistics. It was said to be false, the only true syllogistics being those of Aristotle, or rather of Ockham (for the modern philosophers knew the syllogistics of the Organon only in its Ockhamist rewriting). One must confess that several mathematical logicians committed a similar error, asserting, on the contrary, the primacy of Boolean syllogistics, while we know that everything depends here on the system of axiomatics used.

2.10. If both the above reasons were concerned with parts of formal logic, some other arguments were made in the field of methodology of logic. One consisted in saying that every formal logic has to be intentional (with "t"), i.e., that no use should be made of formalism in its development. Logic has to be "meaningful" and one is, therefore, not allowed to abstract from the meaning of the symbols used in proofs.

2.11. Logic had not only to be intentional (with "t") but also intensional (with "s"), i.e., it should not be an extensional system. The fervent defenders of the supposedly intensional logic of Aristotle did not seem to notice that he had himself formulated - indeed better than Leibniz - the *principium indiscernibilium*, which is the masterpiece of extensionalism. Anyway, they rejected ML as being extensional. What intensional logic would be according to them, they never did say clearly - at least in as far as is known to the present writer.

2.12. Finally the old quarrel of Logic of Laws (Aristotelian) as against Logic of Rules (Stoic) was revived. The philosophers had opted for the latter, while ML was written up to the middle of the thirties exclusively in terms of laws, not of rules. It was therefore rejected as a wrong sort of logic, or, indeed, as not being logic at all.

3.

3.1. The foregoing are some of the reasons which were named by philosophers in order to justify their opposition to ML. Those reasons are many - too many, one would say. So the suspicion arises that they were not the true reasons for the refusal to acknowledge the new logic, but served only to cover one single, deeper and true reason. What can it possibly be?

Two answers are suggested to that question, one by the general history of thought, the other by the history of formal logic.

3.2. There is a striking analogy between our case and that of the philosophers who refused Galilean astronomy - and even refused to look through his telescope. Those philosophers were so much used to the received ways and methods of thinking, that they found it extremely difficult to accept anything as different from them as the new astronomy was. Something similar seems to have happened here. A whole period of the history of philosophy - of pretty bad philosophy, one must say - was coming to an end and new ways of thinking were being inaugurated. Among them, ML was the outstanding source of new and better methods. It was comparable with the mathematics and the telescope of Galileo. But the acquired habits were so strong that many philosophers found it extremely difficult to acknowledge its legitimacy.

Seen in that light, the opposition to ML was simply an expression of the refusal of the new by the old, so common in history.

3.3. Another answer is suggested by the history of formal logic. There exists namely a close analogy between what happened during the middle of the twentieth century and phenomena observed during several other periods of the history of Formal Logic. We notice that, several times, after logic had attained a high level of sophistication, violent opposition arose against it. This happened at least twice in our part of the world. The first time with Cicero the rhetorician, ridiculing the propositional logic of the Stoics, and again with the humanists, men like Lorenzo Valla and Erasmus of Rotterdam, ridiculing the scholastics, mostly for their use of logic.

It looks at if we were passing through a similar period. Logic obtained as ML a very high degree of sophistication. As its predecessor, the Stoic and Scholastic logic, it was rejected by many. The rejection of ML, like that of the older types of formal logic, was a rejection of rational methods in favour of more intuitive ones - of science in favour of poetry.

3.4. If this is true it will appear that out of our twelve reasons for rejecting ML two were decisive: the second and, above all, the sixth.

This means that our enterprise ends with a partial success only: we were not able to find a single cause. But even the reduction to two causes may help to understand the curious phenomenon of the opposition of philosophers against ML.

REFERENCE AND RELATED WORKS

Banks, P., 1950, On the Philosophical Interpretation of Logic, Dominican Studies, 3:138-153.

Feys, R., 1924/25, La Transcription Logique du Raisonnement. Son Intérêt et ses Limites, Revue Néoscolastique de Philosophie, 26:299-324, 417-451, and 27:61-86.

Jacoby, G., 1962, "Die Ansprüche der Logistiker auf die Logik und ihre Geschichtsschreibung," Kohlhammer, Stuttgart.

Lear, J., 1980, "Aristotle and Logical Theory," Cambridge University Press, Cambridge.

Veatch, H., 1950, In Defense of Syllogism. The Modern Schoolman, 27:182-202.

Veatch, H., 1950, Aristotelian and Mathematical Logic, The Thomist, 13:50-96.

Veatch, H., 1951, Basic Confusions in Current Notions of Propositional Calculi, The Thomist, 14:238-258.

THE NON-EXISTENCE OF PROBABILISTIC INDUCTIVE SUPPORT

Karl R. Popper

Fallowfield, Manor Close, Manor Road
Penn, Buckinghamshire
England

1. INTRODUCTION: PROBABILISTIC SUPPORT

Using a minimum of propositional logic and of the elementary calculus of probability (see Appendix), David Miller and I (Popper and Miller, 1983) published a very short paper in which we proved that *probabilistic support* in the sense of the calculus of probability *can never be inductive support*. As some knowledgeable people remained unconvinced, I am here restating our case, adding some further proofs.

Probabilistic support of x by y may be defined by

1.1 $$s(x, y) = p(x, y) - p(x)$$

or the support of x by y in the presence of z by

1.2 $$s(x, y, z) = p(x, yz) - p(x, z),$$

where yz is the conjunction, "y and z", so that xy will be the conjunction "x and y". The first of these formulae defines $s(x, y)$ as the difference between the *relative or conditional* probability of x, given y (or in the presence of y), and the absolute or unconditional probability of x. Each of these probabilities can be defined in terms of the other. The absolute probability $p(x)$ can be defined by

$$1.3 \qquad p(x) = p(x, x \rightarrow x) = p(x, x \leftarrow x),$$

where $x \rightarrow y = y \leftarrow x$ is the conditional "If x then y" or "y if x", so that $x \rightarrow x$ and $x \leftarrow x$ are tautologies.

The relative probability can be defined in terms of absolute probability only under the condition that the second of the defining absolute probabilities is not zero, because division by zero is impermissible:*

1.4 If $p(y) = 0$ then

$$p(x, y) = \frac{p(xy)}{p(y)}$$

where xy is (as before) the conjunction of x and y. Thus formula 1.1 (and 1.2) defines the support of x by y (or, of x given z by y given z) as the *increase* of the probability of x owing to the presence of y.

It is possible that y supports x, in which case $0 < s(x, y)$, so that the support is positive; or that y *countersupports* x, in which case $0 > s(x, y)$, so that the support is negative. In this case the *countersupport*, cs, will be positive: $0 < cs(x, y)$ if and only if $0 > s(x, y)$. So countersupport can be defined:

$$1.5 \qquad cs(x, y) = -s(x, y),$$

* In my axiom systems for relative probability (see the Appendix, and Popper (1959, ^{11}1983)), $p(x, y)$ is meaningful even if $p(y) = 0$, and even if $y = (-x)x$. But this is a special merit of these (demonstrably consistent) systems, and here no use is made of it.

and similarly (cp. 1.2)

1.6 $\quad cs(x, y, z) = -s(x, y, z).$

It is also possible that $0 = s(x, y, z) = cs(x, y, z)$. In this case we say that x and y are, in the presence of z, probabilistically *independent*.

Since for absolute or unconditional probabilities we have*

1.7 $\quad 0 \leq p(x) \leq 1$

and similarly for relative or conditional probabilities

1.8 $\quad 0 \leq p(x, y) \leq 1$

it follows from 1.1 and 1.7 that

1.9 $\quad -1 \leq s(x, y) \leq 1$ (1.1; 1.7)

and similarly from 1.2 and 1.8 that

1.10 $\quad -1 \leq s(x, y, z) \leq 1$ (1.2; 1.8)

(−1 may be reached if x is, say, an existential statement and y its universal negation; +1 may be reached if x is, say, a universal statement and y is the same statement or one that is logically stronger, so that x follows from y.)

---

* See Popper (1959, [11]1983). It also is a special merit of the system referred to in the Appendix, that 1.7 is not assumed but can be deduced.

It may be asked why we need the relativised definitions 1.2 and 1.6. There are several answers. I shall mention here two, (a) and (b).

(a) We shall be interested in cases where x is some hypothesis, h, and y is some evidence e, supporting or countersupporting h. Now in some cases - the cases I shall call "generalising inductions" - we shall need only to consider $s(h, e)$. We start from the evidence e, for example:

e = All swans in Austria are found to be white in 1650.

and we proceed from this to the hypothesis

h = All swans in Austria and Bavaria are white in 1650 and also in the years from 1651 to 3000.

Then we ask for the measure of support given by e to h.

But there is also another type of argument which may be called "inductive testing"; and here we need a third kind of statement (corresponding to z) which sums up the relevant *background knowledge** and which I usually denote by b. It is needed, for it may be assumed to contain the initial conditions that allow us to deduce the test statement e from h. In this case, we shall have to ask for $s(h, e, b)$; that is, for the support given to h by e in the presence of b.

---

* The idea of "background knowledge" has been introduced in Popper (1963, [8]1983). (See the Index.) Carnap actually suggests that b ought to contain our "total knowledge", in order to make $p(x, b)$ operationally useful. Nothing of the kind is assumed by me.

(b) Another, in my opinion less serious reason to introduce 1.2 and 1.6 is this. Some famous theorists (John Maynard Keynes, Rudolf Carnap, and many others) do not allow absolute probabilities, as defined by 1.3, and used in 1.1. The reason for this rejection is usually that they adopt a psychological or subjective interpretation of probability: the probability $p(x, b)$ is interpreted as measuring the degree of a person's subjective belief (or reasonable belief) in x; and this measure is always relative to some given (personal) background of knowledge - to a given b; and as we *never* have only tautological background knowledge, these authors hold that absolute probability must be rejected.

But we can interpret the whole of probability theory objectively, interpreting absolute probability as a non-subjective logical measure of the logical *content* of a proposition; or more precisely, of the "degree of lack of content"; for the absolute probability of x *decreases* with the growing content of x; in fact, we can introduce a measure of content by making it rise with decreasing probability, and define the absolute content of x:

1.11 $ct(x) = 1 - p(x)$ (cp. Appendix, and also the paper of Popper and Miller (1983))

and the relative content of x given y

1.12 $ct(x, y) = 1 - p(x, y)$.

That these definitions are adequate can be seen from the fact that they lead to the following

1.13 $ct(x) \leq ct(xy) \geq ct(y)$

while we have (see Appendix, B)

1.13.1 $p(x) \geq p(xy) \leq p(y)$.

That is, the content grows with *additional* information. As to relative content, if y is "given", or regarded as present, then, in the presence of y, nothing will have content (additional information) that is entailed by y, (i.e., logically deducible from y). Writing "$y \vdash x$ " for "y entails x", we can say:

1.14 If $y \vdash x$, then $ct(x, y) = 0$.

This follows from 1.12 and

1.15 If $y \vdash x$, then $p(x, y) = 1$.

I shall end this section with an important

Theorem 1. For every x, y and z,

1.16.1 $s(x, y, z) = s(x \vee y, y, z) + s(x \leftarrow y, y, z)$

1.16.2 $s(x \leftarrow y, y, z) \leq s(x, y, z) \leq s(x \vee y, y, z)$

1.16.3 $s(x \leftarrow y, y, z) \leq 0 \leq s(x \vee y, y, z)$

1.16.4 $cs(x \leftarrow y, y, z) = ct(x, yz)ct(y, z) = Exc(x, y, z) \geq 0$*

1.16.5 $s(x \vee y, y, z) = ct(x \vee y, z) \geq 0$

1.16.6 All these formulae remain valid if we erase in each term the second comma (if any) and the variable z. That result can also be obtained by substituting $z \rightarrow z$ everywhere for the variable z. (See Appendix, D4.)

---

* $Exc(x, y)$ is defined on p. 307 of Popper (1966, [8]1984) and on p. 396 of Popper (1963, [8]1983); see there formula (22) and the 8 lines which follow it; see also here, below, 1.17 and 1.18.

The proof of this theorem is trivial with the possible exception of 1.16.4. In 1.16.4, $Exc(x, y, z)$ is the always positive *excess of the probability of the conditional over the conditional probability*; that is, *Exc* is defined*

1.17 $$Exc(x, y) = p(x \leftarrow y) - p(x, y)$$

and, more generally,

1.18 $$Exc(x, y, z) = p(x \leftarrow y, z) - p(x, yz).$$

That $Exc(x, y, z) = cs(x \leftarrow y, y, z)$ is easily seen. The lemma stating that $Exc(x, y, z) = ct(x, yz)ct(y, z)$ is not quite so easily seen; but it is proved in Popper and Miller (1983). The proof may be put, a little more briefly, as follows (a third variable, z, may be added everywhere; the references are to the Appendix).

Lemma. $Exc(x, y) = ct(x, y)ct(y)$

Proof: Since $p(x, x) = p(y, y) = 1$, (C; see also Popper (1959, [11]1983, pp. 349-350; and [8]1984, pp. 298-299.)

we have

$ct(x, y)ct(y) = ct(y) + p(xy) - p(x, y)$ (B, D1, D4)

$= p(x \leftarrow y) - p(x, y)$ (D3, D4)

$= Exc(x, y).$ (D6, D4)

* This is the definition given on page 396 of Popper (1963, [8]1983); see also D6 of the Appendix, below.

2. A PROOF OF THE IMPOSSIBILITY OF PROBABILISTIC INDUCTIVE SUPPORT

The following proof is a restatement of the proof in Popper and Miller (1983).

Let us start with *any* hypothesis h and *any* evidence e, whether supporting or countersupporting h, or independent of h.

We introduce an auxiliary hypothesis $g = h \leftarrow e$. This g is of course much weaker than h: we have $h \vdash g$, but in general not $g \vdash h$. However, *in the presence of* e, we find that h and g are always *logically interdeducible*. Of course, we also have

2.1 $p(h, e) = p(g, e)$,

since $p(g, e) = p(h \leftarrow e, e) = p((h \leftarrow e)e, e) = p(he, e) = p(h, e)$.

So in the presence of e, g contains everything that h contains: the relative contents (or relative deductive systems, in the sense of Tarski's Calculus of Systems*) of h and g, relative to e, or given e, or in the presence of e, are precisely equivalent, by propositional logic alone:

2.2.1 $ct(h, e) = ct(g, e)$.

We have, therefore,

Theorem 2. If $g = h \leftarrow e$, then $p(h, e) = p(g, e)$,

---

* Alfred Tarski (1956), Chapter XII. See especially the relativization (2), described in the last 8 lines of his book, p. 360 of his book.

nevertheless

2.2.2 $\quad s(g, e) \leq 0$

even if $s(h, e) \geq 0$.

So e always countersupports g. Thus if $s(h, e) \geq 0$, this is merely due to $s(h \vee e, e) \geq 0$, that is, to the fact that $s(h, e) = s(g, e) + s(h \vee e, e)$ (according to 1.6.1); but $s(h \vee e, e)$ is *wholly deductive support*. As shown by 1.6.1, the positivity (if any) of $s(h, e)$ cannot be due to any other but this deductive support. So there is no room here for anything like inductive support.

3. AN ALTERNATIVE PROOF

There are several other proofs. One is indirect.

Assume that there is an h and an e and a probabilistic support $s(h, e)$ whose positivity is *not* wholly due to the fact that $s(h \vee e, e)$ is positive. In other words, we assume that there is some kind of positive support, call it PS (> 0) which need not be itself probabilistic support. Since $s(h \vee e, e)$ is *always* part of $s(h, e)$ we would then have

$$s(h, e) = s(h \vee e, e) + PS,$$

so that the probabilistic support $s(h, e)$ would contain a positive term that is not a wholly deductive support (but may, perhaps, be some inductive support). But this is impossible: since $s(h \vee e, e)$ is an upper bound of every probabilistic support of any h by any e, the formula $s(h, e) = s(h \vee e, e) + PS$ (with $PS > 0$) proves that this $s(h, e)$ cannot be a probabilistic support, contrary to our assumption. There is no room for any positive term like *PS* in the calculus of probability and of probabilistic support. The calculus excludes the existence of a positive probabilistic support whose positivity is due to anything else but to a wholly deductive support.*

4. A VERY DIFFERENT PROOF**

The real idea of induction is this. We obtain (by observation, according to the usual belief) a number of statements such as "This swan is white" or "This raven is black". Having not found any counter-example within a finite spatio-temporal region, - say Austria in 1796 - we can sum up these statements by what can be called the evidence *e*, for example: "All swans in Austria in 1796 are white" (or perhaps "All observed swans in Austria in 1796 are white"). We then *generalize* the evidence *e*, *beyond the original spatio-temporal* region (of observation). The evidence statement *e* can be described as the conjunction of the statements *accepted as established* (by observation). The statement that generalizes (extends) our knowledge beyond the region of established statements is the generalization *g*. For example, *g* may be "All swans in Europe during the 18th century are white". Accordingly, the generalization *always entails the evidence*; and so, for any *g* that is a generalization of *e*, we have

---

* David Miller has drawn my attention to the fact that the statement printed in our (1983) in the two lines following formula (9) contains a mistake and should be deleted. Also delete the dash and the eight words following in the next (penultimate) paragraph. This mistake does not affect any other assertion of the paper.

** Compare this proof with the Appendices XVII and XIX of Popper ([8]1984).

$$g \vdash e$$

so that (provided $p(g) > 0$ and $0 < p(e) < 1$) we get

$$p(g, e) > p(g)$$

that is, positive probabilistic support:

$$s(g, e) > 0 ;$$

this is usually interpreted as inductive support.

However, this kind of interpretation is untenable.

We can show this by using the same e and a very different g_1 - one that satisfies the formal condition $g_1 \vdash e$ but which is otherwise as far away from being an inductive generalization of e as we like. For example, g_1 may be "All swans in the world are violet, except the Austrian swans in 1796 which are white". We can call such a g_1 an anti-inductive generalization. If probabilistic induction exists, g_1 should be of course less well supported by e than, say, the g described above.

We may give the absolute probability of g_1, that is, $p(g_1)$ any value we like. (Giving the absolute or *a priori* or prior probability a value which we "just find right" intuitively, and trusting that the mathematics of the calculus will nevertheless help to prove an "inductive effect" of the empirical evidence is part of the doctrine of the school that is called "Bayesian".)

In order to show that there is no probabilistic induction, we introduce the ratio of the prior (or *a priori*) probabilities

$$p(g_1)/p(g) = R_{prior} .$$

We now assert

$$p(g_1, e)/p(g, e) = R_{prior},$$

that is, the ratio of the *a posteriori* or empirical or inductive probabilities is the same as that of the *a priori* probabilities... .

Theorem 3: The evidence increases the probability of the "bad" anti-inductive anti-generalization g_1 in proportion to the increase of the "good" inductive generalization g.

Trivial as this theorem is, prominent Bayesians have admitted that it was new to them. (Some of them did not even admit its truth.) Others criticised my argument as "inadequate" because I "assumed" that both g and g_1 entailed e. But this alleged "assumption" is, of course, the formal condition for a statement being an inductive generalization: one would not call any g a generalization of e *in any sense* if it would not entail its inductive premise e. The classical inductive procedure is, of course: accept e and then *extend it inductively* and so obtain its support of the generalization. What I have shown is that you can extend it anti-inductively and obtain an identical support or increase of the probability if the *prior* (or *a priori*) probability was identical, and a proportional increase if the prior (*a priori*) probability was different (or *assumed* to be different, in the case of Bayesianism).

This proportional difference is the most that mathematics achieves; that is, the appeal to the calculus of probability is humbug.

However, just in order to show that the argument does not depend upon the inductive generalization of e, we can start from a completely arbitrary inductive hypothesis h and a completely arbitrary (anti-inductive) hypothesis h_1. We then take a completely arbitrary empirical evidence statement e, and consider the two ratios

$$R_{a\ priori} = p(h_1 e)/p(he)$$
$$R_{a\ posteriori} = p(h_1, e)/p(h, e).$$

What we can now show is that the ratio of these *relative probabilities* (which are probabilities in the light of some empirical evidence, or given some empirical evidence) is, trivially, the same as the ratio of the two *absolute probabilities* (without a comma!), $p(h_1 e)$ and $p(he)$. $R_{a\ priori}$ is an *a priori* ratio (not identical with our earlier R_{prior}).

$$R_{a\ posteriori} = p(h_1 e)/p(he) = R_{a\ priori}$$

even though, of course

$$p(h_1, e) > p(h_1 e) \ \&\ s(h_1, e) > 0$$
$$p(h, e) > p(he) \ \&\ s(h, e) > 0$$

which shows, clearly, that the increase, the support, must be regarded with far more critical eyes than it has been regarded in the past (for example, by Bayesians).

I should like to end with the remark that nobody doubts the significance of Bayes' theorem which is a trivial consequence of the product law $p(xy, z) = p(x, yz)p(y, z)$. (See Appendix, B.) All I assert is that such trivialities cannot be claimed to support inductive generalization, or predictions about the future.

There is an interpretation of the probability calculus, the propensity interpretation, which has a bearing on physics. But physics presupposes *physical laws* that are assumed to be time-invariant;

and it is *this* assumption which leads to predictions. This holds equally for probabilistic and non-probabilistic physical laws.

5. CONCLUSION

Because of my fight against induction I have sometimes been described as an irrationalist. But if it is true that there is no induction, then it is irrational to continue to have faith in induction.

What I advocate (as it were, in the place of induction) is the admission of the fact that our hypotheses, our conjectures, are our intuitive guesses, results of our creative imagination; results which, just because of their thrilling but dubious origin, ought to be submitted to the most gruelling tests. As opposed to this, the inductivist is bound to say (before experiencing in Norway, say, polar conditions) that the sun has been observed by him every day to rise, and will do so with high probability everywhere, in America, in the Azores, and therefore also in the polar regions.

Who is more rational? The believer in generalizing induction, or the critic who tries hard to anticipate, and to eliminate, the mistakes that may lurk in his conjectures - and who warns the scientist that his admirable and growing scientific knowledge remains uncertain conjectural knowledge? Is it irrational to teach the distinction between truth and certainty? To say that we ought to search for *truth*, which we *may* discover, though we may never be *certain* of it?

APPENDIX

For an axiomatic investigation of the calculus, see the new

Appendices *iii to *v in Popper (1959, [11]1983). A further simplified but equally powerful axiom system which assumes neither the propositional calculus nor Boolean algebra (but allows their derivation) is the following system of four axioms, A to D.

A $(Ex)(Ey)p(x, x) \neq p(y, x)$

B $p(xy, z) = p(x, yz)p(y, z) \leq p(x, z)$

C $p(x, x) \neq p(y, x) \rightarrow p(-z, x) = p(w, w) - p(z, x)$

(or: $p(-x, y) = p(z, z) - p(x, y) \leftrightarrow$

$\leftrightarrow (Ew)((p(y, y) \neq p(w, y)))$

D $x = y \leftrightarrow (z)p(x, z) = p(y, z)$

C and D are 'creative' definitions, and therefore axioms. The following definitions are non-creative (note that by C, $p(x, x) = = p(y, y)$, and by Popper (1959, [8]1984) $p(x, x) = 1$.)

D1 $ct(x, y) = p(x, x) - p(x, y)$ (see 1.11 above, and also Popper and Miller (1983))

D2 $p(x \rightarrow y, z) = ct(x, z) + p(xy, z)$

D3 $p(x \leftarrow y, z) = ct(y, z) + p(xy, z)$ $(= p(y \rightarrow x, z))$

D4 $((w)p(w, w) \leq p(z, w)) \rightarrow p(xy, z) = p(x, y)p(y)$

(Conditional Definition of absolute probability)

D5 $p(x \vee y, z) = p(x, z) + p(y, z) - p(xy, z)$.

D6 $Exc(x, y, z) = p(x \leftarrow y, z) - p(x, yz)$

Note: If we add to the Axioms A and B one or both of the following two:

AC $p(x, z) \leq p(y, y)$

BD $p(xy) = 0 \rightarrow p(z, yx) = p(z, xy)$

(or: $((x)p(x) \geq p(y) \geq p(z)) \rightarrow p(x, yz) = p(x, zy))$

then the axioms C and/or D respectively turn into non-creative definitions. This can also be achieved by adding (to A and B) the axiom

$$\text{AD} \quad ((x)p(x, y)) = p(x, z)) \leftrightarrow (x)p(x, x) \le p(y, z) \le p(z, y)$$

and weakening AC by substituting y for z.

REFERENCES

Popper, K. R., [1]1934, "Logik der Forschung," Springer, Vienna.

Popper, K. R., 1959, [11]1983, "The Logic of Scientific Discovery," Hutchinson, London.

Popper, K. R., 1963, [8]1983, "Conjectures and Refutations. The Growth of Scientific Knowledge," Routledge and Kegan Paul, London.

Popper, K. R., 1983, "Realism and the Aim of Science," Hutchinson, London (and Rowman & Littlefield, Totowa, NJ).

Popper, K. R., [2]1966, [8]1984, "Logik der Forschung," Mohr, Tübingen.

Popper, K. R. and Miller, D., 1983, A Proof of the Impossibility of Inductive Probability, Nature, 302:687-688.

Popper, K. R. and Miller, D., 1984, A Proof of the Impossibility of Inductive Probability (A Reply to some Critics), Nature, 310;433-434.

Tarski, A., 1956, "Logic, Semantics, Metamathematics," Clarendon Press, Oxford.

UNARY PROBABILISTIC SEMANTICS

Hugues Leblanc

Temple University
Philadelphia, PA 19122
USA

Writers in Popper's debt generally use *binary* probability functions when doing probabilistic semantics. I recount here results lately obtained when *unary* functions are used instead. I first describe the formal language (call it L) that I work with, provide a probabilistic semantics for it, and attend to such matters as strong soundness and strong completeness. This done I consider the relationship between unary probability functions and truth-value ones, and I demonstrate that and why unary probability theory is but a generalization of truth-value-theory. Lastly I study what Charles G. Morgan and I call *assumption sets*, here the assumption sets of unary probability functions. The unary probability functions in this text are in good standing: they are the probability functions in Chapter I of Kolmogorov (1933), with statements substituting for sets and provision made for the probabilities of quantifications.

I

L has as its *primitive signs* (i) anywhere from 1 to $aleph_0$

predicates, each identified as being of a certain degree *d*, (ii) $aleph_0$ (individual) terms, (iii) $aleph_0$ (individual) variables, (iv) the three operators '~', '&', and '∀', (v) the two parentheses '(' and ')', and (vi) the comma ','. L has as its *formulas* all finite (but non-empty) sequences of primitive signs of L. And L has as its *statements* (i) all formulas of L of the sort $Q(T_1, T_2, \ldots T_d)$, with Q here a predicate of L of degree *d* and T_1, T_1, ..., T_d (not necessarily distinct) terms of L, (ii) all formulas of L of the sort ~A where A is a statement of L, (iii) all formulas of L of the sort (A & B) where A and B are (not necessarily distinct) statements of L, and (iv) all formulas of the sort (∀X)A where for any term T of L you please A(T/X) - the result of putting T for the variable X in A - is a statement of L. Statements of the sort A(T/X) are known as *the substitution-instances in L of the quantification (∀X)A of L*. I refer to the set of them by means of 'SI((∀X)A)'.

In III it will help, given a non-empty set S of statements of L, to have something like a *register* of the members of S. To that effect, I understand by a *conjunction-associate of S* any statement of L of any of the sorts (i) A_1 where A_1 is a member of S, (ii) A_1 & A_2 where A_1 and A_2 are two distinct members of S, (iii) (A_1 & A_2) & A_3 where A_1, A_2, and A_3 are three distinct members of S, etc; and I refer to the set consisting of all these conjunction-associates by means of 'R(S)'. With (∀X)A a quantification of L and SI((∀X)A) the set of all its substitution-instances in L, the register R(SI((∀X)A)) will thus consist of all statements of L of any of the sorts (i) $A(T_1/X)$ where T_1 is a term of L, (ii) $A(T_1/X)$ & $A(T_2/X)$ where T_1 and T_2 are two distinct terms of L, (iii) ($A(T_1/X)$ & $A(T_2/X)$) & $A(T_3/X)$ where T_1, T_2, and T_3 are three distinct terms of L, etc.

L has as its *axioms* all statements of L of any of the following six sorts, where '⊃' is defined in the customary manner:

A1. $A \supset (A \,\&\, A)$

A2. $(A \,\&\, B) \supset A$

A3. $(A \supset B) \supset ({\sim}(B \,\&\, C) \supset {\sim}(C \,\&\, A))$

A4. $A \supset (\forall X)A$

A5. $(\forall X)A \supset A(T/X)$

A6. $(\forall X)(A \supset B) \supset ((\forall X)A \supset (\forall X)B)$,

plus all statements of L of the sort $(\forall X)(A(X/T))$, where A is an axiom of L; and L has as its one *rule of inference* Modus Ponens, the *ponential* of two statements A and $A \supset B$ of L being B.

Where A is a statement of L and S a set of statements of L, I understand by *a proof in L of A from S* any finite column of statements of L such that (i) each entry in the column is a member of S, an axiom of L, or the ponential of two earlier entries in the column, and (ii) the last entry in the column is A. I say that *A is provable in L from S* - $S \vdash A$, for short - if there exists a proof in L of A from S; and I say that *A is provable in L* - $\vdash A$, for short - if $\emptyset \vdash A$. And, with an eye to the Strong Completeness Proof in III and the material on assumption sets in V, I say that *S is consistent in L* if there is no statement A of L such that both $S \vdash A$ and $S \vdash {\sim}A$, *inconsistent in L* otherwise; *complete in L* if $S \vdash A$ or $S \vdash {\sim}A$ for each statement A of L; *deductively closed in L* if S has among its members each statement of L provable from S; and *maximally consistent in L* if S is consistent, complete, and deductively closed in L.

Considerable use will be made in the paper of the so-called *term-extensions* of L. These are all the languages exactly like L except for having anywhere from 1 to $aleph_0$ (individual) terms besides those of L. I refer to the term-extensions of L by means of 'L^+'. And, with L^+ an arbitrary term-extension of L, (i) I understand by a substitution-instance in L^+ of a quantification $(\forall X)A$

of L^+ any statement of L^+ of the sort $A(T/X)$, T here a term of L^+, (ii) I refer to the set consisting of all the substitution-instances of $(\forall X)A$ in L^+ by means of '$SI^+((\forall X)A)$', (iii) I write '$S \vdash^+ A$' for 'A is provable in L^+ from S', (iv) I say that a set S of statements of L^+ is consistent in L^+, complete in L^+, deductively closed in L^+, or maximally consistent in L^+ if the conditions in the previous paragraph, but with 'L^+' substituting for 'L' and '$\vdash^+$' for '$\vdash$', are met, (v) with an eye to a construction in V, I say that S^+ is *the deductive closure in* L^+ of a set S of statements of L if S^+ consists of all and only the statements of L^+ provable in L^+ from S, and (vi) with an eye again to the Strong Completeness Proof in III, I say that S is *omega-complete in* L^+ if, no matter the quantification $(\forall X)A$ of L^+, $S \vdash^+ (\forall X)A$ if $S \vdash^+ A(T/X)$ for each term T of L^+.

II

The sort of standard semantics for L that most are familiar with uses models, i.e. domains and interpretations relative to these domains of the predicates and the terms of L. Preference is given here to another, but equivalent, sort which uses truth-value functions for L and its term-extensions, and interprets the quantifications of the term-extensions of L *substitutionally*.

With L^+ an arbitrary term-extension of L, 0 the (truth-value) false, and 1 the (truth-value) true, I understand by *a truth-value function for* L^+ any function TV^+ from the statements of L^+ to {0, 1} that meets the following three constraints:

B1. $TV^+(\sim A) = 1$, if, and only if, $TV^+(A) \neq 1$

B2. $TV^+(A \& B) = 1$ if, and only if, $TV^+(A) = 1$ and $TV^+(B) = 1$

B3. $TV^+((\forall X)A) = 1$ if, and only if, $TV^+(B) = 1$ for each B in $SI^+((\forall X)A)$, or, equivalently,

C1. $TV^{+}(\sim A) = 1 - TV^{+}(A)$

C2. $TV^{+}(A \,\&\, B) = TV^{+}(A) \times TV^{+}(B)$

C3. $TV^{+}((\forall X)A) = glb\{TV^{+}(B)\colon B \in SI^{+}((\forall X)A)\}$,

where in *C3* the greatest lower bound $glb\{TV^{+}(B)\colon B \in SI^{+}((\forall X)A)\}$ of set $\{TV^{+}(B)\colon B \in SI^{+}((\forall X)A)\}$ is, in effect, the greater one of the two integers 0 and 1 which does not exceed $TV^{+}(B)$ for any B in $SI^{+}((\forall X)A)$. I call a function TV from the statements of L to {0, 1} *a truth-value-function for L* if for some term-extension L^{+} of L there exists a truth-value function for L^{+} of which TV is the restriction to L; and, with TV an arbitrary truth-value function for L and S an arbitrary set of statements of L, I take TV(S) to be 1 if S is empty, otherwise to be $glb\{TV(A)\colon A \in S\}$. I say of a statement A of L and a set S of statements of L that *A is logically entailed by S in the standard sense* if A evaluates to 1 on each truth-value function for L on which S evaluates to 1. And I say of a statement A of L that *A is logically true in the standard sense* if A is logically entailed by ∅ in that sense - i.e. if A evaluates to 1 on each truth-value function for L.

Proof of the following theorem can be retrieved from Leblanc (1983a):

Theorem 1. Let S be a set of statements of L, and A be a statement of L.

(a) *If S ⊢ A, then A is logically entailed by S in the standard sense; (= The Strong Soundness Theorem for L)*

(b) *If A is logically entailed by S in the standard sense, then S ⊢ A. (= The Strong Completeness Theorem for L)*

Hence, with S set at $\emptyset$:

Theorem 2. Let A be a statement of L.

(a) *If $\vdash$ A, then A is logically true in the standard sense; (= The Weak Soundness Theorem for L)*

(b) *If A is logically true in the standard sense, then $\vdash$ A. (= The Weak Completeness Theorem for L)*

Theorems 1 - 2 legitimize the accounts of logical entailment and logical truth submitted in the previous paragraph.

The reader will note that for each truth-value function TV for L (i) $TV(\sim A) = 1$ if, and only if, $TV(A) \neq 1$ and (ii) $TV(A \& B) = 1$ if, and only if, $TV(A) = 1$ and $TV(B) = 1$. However, $TV(A(T/X))$ may equal 1 for each term T of L and $TV((\forall X)A)$ nonetheless equal 0. The set

$$\{Q(T_1), Q(T_2), \ldots, Q(T_n), \ldots, \sim(\forall X)Q(X)\},$$

where $T_1, T_2, \ldots, T_n, \ldots,$ are *all* the terms of L, is consistent in L. So, by virtue of Theorem 1(b), there is sure to be a truth-value function for L on which $SI((\forall X)Q(X))$ evaluates to 1 but $(\forall X)Q(X)$ does not. The function will be the restriction to L of some truth-value function TV^+ (for some term-extension L^+ of L) on which Q(T) evaluates to 0 for some term T (of L^+) not among $T_1, T_2, \ldots, T_n, \ldots$. It is this interplay between the truth-value functions for the term-extensions of L (functions that treat quantifications substitutionally) and the truth-value functions for L itself (functions that don't) which permits proof of Theorem 1(b) and guarantees that the standard semantics of this text and the one using models do exactly the same work. (For a detailed study of the matter see Leblanc (1983a).)

III

It is time to trade truth-value functions for probability ones. Understand by *a unary probability function for a term-extension* L^+ *of L* any function P^+ from the statements of L^+ to the reals that meets the following constraints (the first six of which stem from Popper (1955) and the seventh from Gaifman (1964) and Bendall (1979)):

D1. $0 \leq P^+(A)$

D2. $P^+(\sim(A \,\&\, \sim A)) = 1$

D3. $P^+(A) = P^+(A \,\&\, B) + P^+(A \,\&\, \sim B)$

D4. $P^+(A) \leq P^+(A \,\&\, A)$

D5. $P^+(A \,\&\, B) \leq P^+(B \,\&\, A)$

D6. $P^+(A \,\&\, (B \,\&\, C)) \leq P^+((A \,\&\, B) \,\&\, C)$

D7. $P^+(A \,\&\, (\forall X)B) = glb\{P^+(A \,\&\, C): C \in R(SI^+((\forall X)B))\}$,

where in *D7* the greatest lower bound $glb\{P^+(A \,\&\, C): C \in R(SI^+((\forall X)B))\}$ of set $\{P^+(A \,\&\, C): C \in R(SI^+((\forall X)B))\}$ is the greatest real which does not exceed $P^+(A \,\&\, C)$ for any C in $R(SI^+((\forall X)B))$. Call a function P from the statements of L to the reals *a unary probability function for L* if for some term-extension L^+ of L there exists a unary probability function for L^+ of which P is the restriction to L; and, with P an arbitrary unary probability function for L and S an arbitrary set of statements of L, take P(S) to be 1 if S is empty, otherwise to be $glb\{P(A): A \in R(S)\}$.

The resulting probability functions, we shall see, are generalizations of the truth-value functions in II, and generalizations such that:

S $\vdash$ *A if, and only if, A evaluates to 1 on each unary probability function for L on which S evaluates to 1,* (1) and, hence,

> $\vdash$ *A if, and only if, A evaluates to 1 on each unary probability function for L.* (2)

So, one could say that *A is logically entailed by S in the probabilistic sense* if A evaluates to 1 on each unary probability function for L on which S does, and that *A is logically true in the probabilistic sense* if A is logically entailed by Ø in that sense. I did so in Leblanc (1983a) where I supplied proofs of (1) - (2), and in the abstract of this paper. Another and more intriguing account of these matters is possible, though. It stems from Field (1977).

Suppose S $\vdash$ A, S again a set of statements of L and A a statement of L; and let P be an arbitrary unary probability function for L. Then by the very definition of a proof in L there is sure to be a finite subset of S, say, $\{B_1, B_2, \ldots, B_n\}$ ($n \geq 0$), such that $\{B_1, B_2, \ldots, B_n\} \vdash$ A. So, $\vdash$ A when $n = 0$, and by the Deduction Theorem and Exportation $\vdash ((\ldots(B_1 \;\&\; B_2) \;\&\; \ldots) \;\&\; B_n) \supset A$ when $n > 0$. But, by virtue of (2) above, a statement of L, if provable in L, evaluates to 1 on each unary probability function for L. So, P(A) = 1 when $n = 0$, and $P(((\ldots(B_1 \;\&\; B_2) \;\&\; \ldots) \;\&\; B_n) \supset A) = 1$ when $n > 0$. But P(S) ≤ 1 by definition and the counterparts for P of constraints *D1* - *D5*. Hence, P(S) ≤ P(A) when $n = 0$. Suppose then that $n > 0$. It is easily ascertained that

If P(B ⊃ A) = 1, then P(B) ≤ P(A).

So, $P((\ldots(B_1 \;\&\; B_2) \;\&\; \ldots) \;\&\; B_n) \leq P(A)$. But $(\ldots(B_1 \;\&\; B_2) \;\&\; \ldots) \;\&\; B_n$ is a conjunction-associate of S, and by definition P(S) does not exceed P(B) for any B in R(S). Hence, P(S) ≤ P(A) when $n > 0$. Hence, in either case,

If S $\vdash$ *A, then* P(S) $\leq$ P(A) *for each unary probability function P for L,*

a welcome but surely anticipated result.

Suppose, on the other hand, that S $\nvdash$ A, and let L^{∞} be an arbitrary term-extension of L that has $aleph_0$ terms besides those of L. Then S $\cup$ {~A}, consistent in L, is sure to be consistent in L^{∞} as well and hence to extend (as shown by Henkin) to a set of statements of L^{∞} that is both maximally consistent and omega-complete in L^{∞}. Call that superset of S $\cup$ {~A}

H(S $\cup$ {~A}),

and for each statement B of L^{∞} define the function $P^{\infty}_{H(S \cup \{\sim A\})}$ thusly:

$$P_{H(S \cup \{\sim A\})}(B) = \begin{cases} 1 \text{ if } B \in H(S \cup \{\sim A\}) \\ 0 \text{ otherwise.} \end{cases}$$

It is easily verified that $P^{\infty}_{H(S \cup \{\sim A\})}$ meets each of constraints *D1* - *D7*, *D3* in particular because H(S $\cup$ {~A}) is maximally consistent in L^{∞} and *D7* because H(S $\cup$ {~A}) is omega-complete in L^{∞}. Hence, there is a term-extension L^{+} of L (= L^{∞}) and a unary probability function P^{+} for L^{+} (= $P^{\infty}_{H(S \cup \{\sim A\})}$) such that P^{+}(B) = 1 for each B in S and P^{+}(~A) = 1. Hence, there is a unary probability function P for L (= the restriction of $P^{\infty}_{H(S \cup \{\sim A\})}$ to L) such that P(S) = 1 and P(A) = 0, and hence such that P(S) > P(A). Hence, by Contraposition,

If P(S) $\leq$ P(A) *for each unary probability function P for L, then S* $\vdash$ *A,*

a welcome but possibly unanticipated result, except of course to readers of Field.

In light of the foregoing I propose that, with A a statement of L and S a set of statements of L, A be held *logically entailed by S in the probabilistic sense* if A evaluates to no less than S does on any unary probabilistic function for L, and A be held *logically true in the probabilistic sense* if A is logically entailed by ∅ in that sense - i.e. if A evaluates to 1 on each unary probability function for L. We shall then have:

Theorem 3. Let S be a set of statements of L, and A be a statement of L.

(a) *S ⊢ A if, and only if, A is logically entailed by S in the probabilistic sense;*

(b) *A is logically entailed by S in the standard sense if, and only if, logically entailed by S in the probabilistic sense.*

Hence, with S set at ∅:

Theorem 4. Let A be a statement of L.

(a) *⊢ A if, and only if, A is logically true in the probabilistic sense;*

(b) *A is logically true in the standard sense if, and only if, logically true in the probabilistic sense.*

IV

As indicated earlier, Kolmogorov dealt in his 1933 classic with sets, each of these a subset of a certain set E of "elementary events", and the probabilities he accorded them had to meet certain constraints. With the statements of L substituting for Kolmogorov's sets, '∼' for the complement sign, '&' for the intersection sign, and 'v' and '≡' defined in the customary manner, his constraints would read:

E1. $0 \leq P^{+}(A)$ (= *D1*)

E2. $P^{+}(\sim(A \,\&\, \sim A)) = 1$ (= *D2*)

E3. If $\vdash^{+} \sim(A \,\&\, B)$, then $P^{+}(A \vee B) = P^{+}(A) + P^{+}(B)$

E4. If $\vdash^{+} A \equiv B$, then $P^{+}(A) = P^{+}(B)$.

Provision for the quantifications of L could be made by enlisting as a fifth constraint the following special case of *D7*:

E5. $P^{+}((\forall X)A) = glb\{P^{+}(B) : B \in R(SI^{+}((\forall X)A))\}$.

It was Popper's insight in a 1938 paper that constraints *D3* - *D6* will do for *E3* - *E4*, hence, that one can characterize Kolmogorov's probability functions "autonomously" - i.e. withouth using such a deductive notion as that of provability or (equivalently) that of logical truth. Popper himself had constraints *D0´* - *D2´* below in place of *E1* - *E2* (see Popper (1955)), but in the presence of *D3* - *D5* these are equivalent to *D1* - *D2* (see Leblanc (1982)):

D0´. There are statements A and B of L^{+} such that $P^{+}(A) \neq P^{+}(B)$

D1´. $P^{+}(A \,\&\, B) \leq P^{+}(A)$

D2´. For each statement A of L^{+} there is a statement B of L^{+} such that $P^{+}(A) \leq P^{+}(B)$ and $P^{+}(A \,\&\, B) = P^{+}(A) \times P^{+}(B)$.

That in the presence of *D1* - *D2* (or, equivalently, *D0´* - *D2´*) the autonomous constraints *D3* - *D6* can supersede the non-autonomous ones *E3* - *E4* is a result of considerable significance: among other things, it made possible the accounts of logical entailment and logical truth in III, accounts in which unary probability functions supersede truth-value functions and, hence, models.

Proof that real-valued functions from the statements of L^{+} meet constraints *E3* - *E4* if they meet *D1* - *D6*, uses the following consequences of *D1* - *D6*:

$P^+(\sim A) = 1 - P^+(A)$ (4)

If $P^+(A \supset B) = 1$, then $P^+(A) \leq P^+(B)$. (5)

(The reader will find in Leblanc (1983a) proofs of (4) - (5) - and, hence, of (3), the counterpart for L of (5).)

(i) For proof of *E3*,

$$P^+(A \vee B) = 1 - P^+(\sim A \;\&\; \sim B)$$

by the definition of 'v' and (4). Hence,

$$P^+(A \vee B) = 1 - P^+(\sim A) + P^+(\sim A \;\&\; B)$$

by *D3*. Hence,

$$P^+(A \vee B) = P^+(A) + P^+(B \;\&\; \sim A)$$

by (4) and *D5*. Hence,

$$P^+(A \vee B) = P^+(A) + P^+(B) - P^+(B \;\&\; A)$$

by *D3*. But, if $\vdash^+ \sim(A \;\&\; B)$, then $\vdash^+ \sim(B \;\&\; A)$, hence $P^+(\sim(B \;\&\; A)) = 1$ by the counterpart for L^+ of (2) (cf. III above), and hence $P^+(B \;\&\; A) = 0$ by (4). Hence,

$$P^+(A \vee B) = P^+(A) + P^+(B).$$

(ii) For proof of *E4*, suppose $\vdash^+ A \equiv B$, hence $\vdash^+ A \supset B$ and $\vdash^+ B \supset A$, and hence $P^+(A \supset B) = 1$ and $P^+(B \supset A) = 1$ by the counterpart for L^+ of (2) (cf. III above). Then $P^+(A) \leq P^+(B)$ and $P^+(B) \leq P^+(A)$ by (5), and hence

$$P^+(A) = P^+(B).$$

Proof that real-valued functions from the statements of L^+ meet constraints *D3* - *D6* if they meet *E3* - *E4* is even simpler.

(i) For proof of *D3*, $\vdash^+ A \equiv ((A \& B) \vee (A \& \sim B))$. Hence,

$$P^+(A) = P^+((A \& B) \vee (A \& \sim B))$$

by *E4*. But $\vdash^+ \sim((A \& B) \& (A \& \sim B))$. Hence,

$$P^+((A \& B) \vee (A \& \sim B)) = P^+(A \& B) + P^+(A \& \sim B)$$

by *E3*. Hence

$$P^+(A) = P^+(A \& B) + P^+(A \& \sim B).$$

(ii) For proof of *D4* - *D6*, $\vdash^+ A \equiv (A \& A)$, $\vdash^+ (A \& B) \equiv (B \& A)$, and $\vdash^+ (A \& (B \& C)) \equiv ((A \& B) \& C)$. Hence,

$$P^+(A) = P^+(A \& A)$$
$$P^+(A \& B) = P^+(B \& A)$$

and

$$P^+(A \& (B \& C)) = P^+((A \& B) \& C)$$

by *E4*. Hence, *D4* - *D6*.

Incidentally, it is to *D3* (the one among constraints *D1* - *D6* to exhibit an arithmetical operator) and to *E3* (the one among constraints *E1* - *E4* to do so) that the functions picked out by *D1* - *D6* and by *E1* - *E4* owe their *probability* flavor. The remaining constraints merely guarantee that

(i) no statement of L^+ evaluates on P^+ to less than 0 (*D1* and *E1*),

(ii) no statement of L^+ evaluates on P^+ to more than 1, the real to which logical truths of L^+ of the sort $\sim(A \ \& \sim A)$ evaluate (*D2* and *E2*), and

(iii) any two statements of L^+ that are logically equivalent evaluate on P^+ to the same real (*D4* - *D6* and, less frugally, *E4*).

The truth-value functions in II and the unary probability functions in III are intimately related, as I discovered in 1981 and reported in Leblanc (1982).

Note first that:

Theorem 5. Let L^+ be an arbitrary term-extension of L, and TV^+ be an arbitrary 2-valued function from the statements of L^+ to the reals. Then:

(a) *If TV^+ meets constraints C1 - C2, then TV^+ has 0 and 1 as its values;*

(b) *If TV^+ meets constraints D1 - D4 (with 'TV^+' in place of 'P^+' there), then TV^+ again has 0 and 1 as its values.*

Proof: (a) Suppose TV^+ meets constraint *C2*, in which case

$$TV^+((\ldots(A_1 \ \& \ A_2) \ \& \ \ldots) \ \& \ A_n) = TV^+(A_1) \times TV^+(A_2) \times \ldots$$
$$\ldots \times TV^+(A_n)$$

and, hence, when $TV^+(A_1)$, $TV^+(A_2)$, ..., $TV^+(A_n)$ are all the same,

$$TV^+((\ldots(A_1 \ \& \ A_2) \ \& \ \ldots) \ \& \ A_n) = (TV^+(A_1))^n;$$

and suppose A_1 evaluated on TV^+ to some r other than -1, 0, and 1. Then TV^+ would have all of r, r^2, r^3, etc. as values and, hence, would not - as supposed - be 2-valued. Suppose next that TV^+ meets constraint *C1* as well. If TV^+ had -1 as a value, then TV^+ would have 0 and 1 as its values. (b) By *D2* $TV^+(\sim(A \,\&\, \sim A)) = 1$. But by *D3* $TV^+(A) - TV^+(A \,\&\, A) = TV^+(A \,\&\, \sim A)$, hence by *D4* $TV^+(A \,\&\, \sim A) \leq 0$, and hence by *D1* $TV^+(A \,\&\, \sim A) = 0$. Hence, (b). □

So:

Theorem 6: Let L^+ be as in Theorem 5, and TV^+ be an arbitrary function from the statements of L^+ to the reals. Then TV^+ constitutes a truth-value function for L^+ if, and only if, TV^+ is a 2-valued function that meets constraints C1 - C3.

Note next that:

Theorem 7: Let L^+ and TV^+ be as in Theorem 5. If TV^+ meets constraints C1 - C3, then TV^+ meets constraints D1 - D7 (with 'TV^+' in place of 'P^+').

Proof: Suppose TV^+ meets *C1* - *C3*, and hence by Theorem 5(a) has but 0 and 1 as values. (i) Proof that under these circumstances TV^+ meets constraints *D1* - *D2* and *D4* - *D6* is immediate. (ii) Proof that under these circumstances TV^+ meets *D3* is as follows:

$$\begin{aligned}
TV^+(A) &= (TV^+(A) \times TV^+(B)) + TV^+(A) - (TV^+(A) \times TB^+(B)) \\
&= TV^+(A \,\&\, B) + TV^+(A) - (TV^+(A) \times TV^+(B)) && (C2) \\
&= TV^+(A \,\&\, B) + TV^+(A)(1 - TV^+(B)) \\
&= TV^+(A \,\&\, B) + (TV^+(A) \times TV^+(\sim B)) && (C1) \\
&= TV^+(A \,\&\, B) + TV^+(A \,\&\, \sim B) && (C2).
\end{aligned}$$

(iii) Proof that under these circumstances TV^+ meets constraint *D7* is as follows. Suppose *first* that $TV^+(A \& (\forall X)B) = 1$. Then by *C2* $TV^+(A) \times TV^+((\forall X)B) = 1$; hence, $TV^+(A) = TV^+((\forall X)B) = 1$; hence, by *C3*, $TV^+(B(T/X)) = 1$ for each term T of L^+; hence, by *C2*, $TV^+(A \& C) = 1$ for each C in $R(SI^+((\forall X)B))$, and hence $glb\{TV^+(A \& C): C \in R(SI^+((\forall X)B))\} = 1$. Suppose *next* that $TV^+(A \& (\forall X)B) = 0$. Then by *C2* $TV^+(A) \times TV^+((\forall X)B) = 0$ and, hence, $TV^+(A) = 0$ or $TV^+((\forall X)B) = 0$. Now, if $TV^+(A) = 0$, then by *C2* $TV^+(A \& C) = 0$ for each C in $R(SI^+((\forall X)B))$, and hence $glb\{TV^+(A \& C): C \in R(SI^+((\forall X)B))\} = 0$. If, on the other hand, $TV^+((\forall X)B) = 0$, then by *C3* $TV^+(B(T/X)) = 0$ for at least one term T of L^+, hence by *C2* there is a C in $R(SI^+((\forall X)B))$ such that $TV^+(A \& C) = 0$, and hence again $glb\{TV^+(A \& C): C \in R(SI^+((\forall X)B))\} = 0$. Hence, $TV^+(A \& (\forall X)B) = glb\{TV^+(A \& C): C \in R(SI^+((\forall X)B))\}$, this whether $TV^+(A \& (\forall X)B)$ equals 1 or not, and in the latter case whether it is $TV^+(A)$ or $TV^+((\forall X)B)$ that equals 0. □

Proof of the converse of Theorem 7 calls for two lemmas. In the first of these TV^+ may have anywhere from two to $aleph_0$ values, but in the second it is understood to have just two.

Theorem 8: Let L^+ be as in Theorem 5, and TV^+ be an arbitrary function from the statements of L^+ that meets constraints D1 - D7 (with 'TV^+' in place of 'P^+'). Then:

(a) $TV^+(\sim A) = 1 - TV^+(A)$. (= *C1*)

(b) *If* $TV^+(A \& B) = 1$, *then* $TV^+(A) = TV^+(B) = 1$.

(c) *If* $TV^+(A \& B) = 1$, *then* $TV^+(A \& B) = TV^+(A) \times TV^+(B)$.

Proof: (a) is (4) (cf. IV above) in truth-value guise and is known to follow from *D1 - D6*. (b) $TV^+(A) = TV^+(A \& B) + TV^+(A \& \sim B)$ by *D3*. But $TV^+(A \& \sim B) \geq 0$ by *D1*. Hence $TV^+(A \& B) \leq TV^+(A)$. But by clause (a) of the present theorem and *D1* $TV^+(A) \leq 1$. Hence, if $TV^+(A \& B) = 1$, then $TV^+(A) = 1$, and hence by *D5* $TV^+(B) = 1$. (c) by (b).

Theorem 9. Let L^+ *be as in Theorem 5, and* TV^+ *be an arbitrary 2-valued function from the statements of* L^+ *to the reals that meets constraints D1 - D7 (again with '*TV^+*' in place of '*P^+*'). Then:*

(a) *If* $TV^+(A \& B) = 0$*, then* $TV^+(A) = 0$ *or* $TV^+(B) = 0$.

(b) *If* $TV^+(A \& B) \neq 1$*, then* $TV^+(A \& B) = TV^+(A) \times TV^+(B)$.

(c) $TV^+(A \& B) = TV^+(A) \times TV^+(B)$. (= *C2*)

(d) $TV((\forall X)A) = \text{glb}\{TV^+(B): B \in SI^+((\forall X)A)\}$. (= *C3*)

Proof: (a) Suppose $TV^+(A \& B) = 0$, and hence $TV^+(A) = TV^+(A \& \sim B)$ by *D3*. Suppose further that $TV^+(A) \neq 0$, and hence $TV^+(A) = 1$ by Theorem 5(b). Then $TV^+(A \& \sim B) = 1$; hence, $TV^+(\sim B) = 1$ by Theorem 8(b); and, hence, $TV^+(B) = 0$ by Theorem 8(a). Hence, $TV^+(A) = 0$ or $TV^+(B) = 0$. Hence, (a). (b) By Theorem 5(b) and clause (a) of the present theorem. (c) By clause (b) of the present theorem and Theorem 8(c). (d) Suppose *first* that $TV^+((\forall X)A) = 1$. Then by clause (c) of the present theorem and *D2* $TV^+(\sim(A(T/X) \& \sim A(T/X)) \& (\forall X)A) = 1$ (T here an arbitrary term of L^+); hence, by *D7*, $glb\{TV^+(\sim(A(T/X) \& \sim A(T/X)) \& C): C \in R(SI^+((\forall X)A))\} = 1$; hence, by clause (c) of the present theorem and *D2*, $glb\{TV^+(C): C \in R(SI^+((\forall X)A))\} = 1$; hence, by Theorem 5(b), $TV^+(C) = 1$ for each C in $R(SI^+((\forall X)A))$; hence, by Theorem 8(b), $TV^+(B) = 1$ for each B in $SI^+((\forall X)A)$; and, hence, $glb\{TV^+(B): B \in SI^+((\forall X)A)\} = 1$. Suppose *next* that $TV^+((\forall X)A) \neq 1$. Then by Theorem 5(b) $TV^+((\forall X)A) = 0$; hence, by the same reasoning as before, $glb\{TV^+(C): C \in R(SI^+((\forall X)A))\} = 0$; hence, by Theorem 5(b), $TV^+(C) = 0$ for at least one C in $R(SI^+((\forall X)A))$; hence, by clause (a) of the present theorem, $TV^+(B) = 0$ for at least one B in $SI^+((\forall X)A)$; and, hence, $glb\{TV^+(B): B \in SI^+((\forall X)A)\} = 0$. Hence, (d).

Hence:

Theorem 10. Let L^+ be as in Theorem 5, and TV^+ be an arbitrary 2-valued function from the statements of L^+ to the reals. If TV^+ meets D1 - D7 (with 'TV^+' in place of 'P^+'), then TV^+ meets constraints C1 - C3.

Hence:

Theorem 11. Let L^+ be as in Theorem 5, and TV^+ be an arbitrary function from the statements of L^+ to the reals. Then TV^+ constitutes a truth-value function for L^+ if, and only if, TV^+ is a 2-valued unary probability function for L^+.

And, hence:

Theorem 12. Let TV be an arbitrary function from the statements of L to the reals. Then TV constitutes a truth-value function for L if, and only if, TV is a 2-valued unary probability function for L.

So, as claimed in Popper (1959) but on quite different grounds, unary probability theory is a generalization of truth-value theory: allow truth-value functions (with those for L^+ meeting *D1 - D7* rather than *C1 - C3*) to have anywhere from 2 to $aleph_0$ values, and truth-value theory extends to unary probability theory. Or, to view it the other way round, allow unary probability functions to have but 2 values, and unary probability theory reduces to truth-value theory.

Note: Clause (d) in Theorem 9 holds only of 2-valued TV^+. Nor would we want '$SI^+((\forall X)B)$' for '$R(SI^+((\forall X)B))$' in *D7*. There are indeed unary probability functions P^+ for L^+ such that (i) $P^+(Q(T)) = 1/2$ for each term T of L^+ and yet (ii) $P^+((\ldots(Q(T_1) \& Q(T_2)) \& \ldots) \& \& Q(T_n)) = 1/2^n$ for any *n* distinct terms $T_1, T_2, \ldots, T_n$ of L^+. So, if $P^+((\forall X)Q(X))$ were understood as $glb\{P^+(A): A \in SI^+((\forall X)Q(X))\}$ rather than as $glb\{P^+(A): A \in R(SI^+((\forall X)Q(X)))\}$, $P^+((\forall X)Q(X))$ would equal 1/2 and hence for any *n* larger than 1 would exceed $P^+((\ldots(Q(T_1) \& Q(T_2)) \& \ldots) \& Q(T_n))$, which of course it should not.

V

As in some of the literature, probabilities are understood here as *degrees of rational credibility* - i.e. $A_1, A_2, A_3, \ldots$, being the various statements of L, $P(A_1), P(A_2), P(A_3), \ldots$, are understood, for each unary probability function P for L, as *degrees to which a rational agent might simultaneously believe* $A_1, A_2, A_3, \ldots$. (Under this construal, (i) a statement A of L is logically entailed by a set S of statements of L if, by whichever unary probability function for L rational credibility be measured, A is no less credible than S, and, hence, (ii) A is logically true if, by whichever unary probability function for L rational credibility be measured, there is no statement of L more credible than A.) That $P(A_1), P(A_2), P(A_3), \ldots$, qualify as degrees of rational credibility - in de Finetti's terminology, that P constitutes *a coherent odds function* - *only if* P meets constraints *D1* - *D7* can be shown by an extension of the so-called Dutch Book Argument. I save this for another occasion, though, and pass on to *assumption sets*.

Degrees of rational credibility are normally accorded to statements in light of other statements or, if you will, in light of certain assumptions. So, to sharpen the above characterization, $P(A_1)$, $P(A_2), P(A_3) \ldots$, are understood here as degrees to which *in light of certain statements of L as the assumptions of P* a rational agent might simultaneously believe $A_1, A_2, A_3, \ldots$.

I suggest in Leblanc (1983b) that, for each unary probability function P for L, the members of the set

{A: P(A) = 1}

serve as *the assumptions of P*, hence that {A: P(A) = 1} serve as *the assumption set of P*, and hence that the various sets of statements of L of the sort {A: P(A) = 1} serve as *the assumption sets of L*. My choice of {A: P(A) = 1} as the assumption set of P was dictated by the following considerations.

(1) Let P be an arbitrary unary probability function for L, and suppose a given statement A of L is one of the assumptions in light of which probabilities are accorded by P to the statements of L. Then the degree to which A is rationally credible in light of these assumptions - hence, in light of A and some other statements of L - is obviously 1. Hence, *if A belongs to the assumption set of P, then P(A) = 1.*

(2) As I put it in Leblanc (1983b), "The assumption sets of probability functions have got to be deductively closed. To be rational is to be alert to logical implications, those of what one knows, those of what one believes, and - in the present context - those of what one assumes. So, a rational agent ... would own as an assumption any statement of L logically implied by his assumptions, and hence accord probabilities in light of *none but* deductively closed sets of statements of L." So, *if S constitutes an assumption set of L, then S is deductively closed in L.*

(3) Incidentally, one of the sets of statements of L that are inconsistent in L is deductively closed in L: the set, call it S_L, that consists of all the statements of L. As indicated in Leblanc (1983b), I could see "according probabilities in light of 'contra-dictory' assumptions so long as *all* the probabilities accorded equal

1: all the statements of L are logically entailed by - and hence, should be equally and maximally probable under - such assumptions. However, the function P such that P(A) = 1 for each statement A of L violates the counterpart for P of *D3* and hence does not constitute a unary probability function for L. Rather than weakening *D3* ... I discount S_L as an assumption set of L." As a result, *if S constitutes an assumption set of L, then S is deductively closed and consistent in L.*

(4) But, as shown in Leblanc (1983b), there corresponds to each set S of statements of L that is both deductively closed and consistent in L one or more unary probability functions for L such that S consists of *all and only* the statements of L that evaluate to 1 on these functions.

So, let there be one or more unary probability functions for L of which a set S of statements of L is the assumption set. There will be by (3)-(4) one or more probability functions for L such that S consists of *all* - as well as *only* - the statements of L that evaluate to 1 on these functions. Hence my taking the assumption set of a unary probability function P for L to be {A: P(A) = 1}, a set that consists of *all* the statements of L evaluating to 1 on P. In keeping with (1), the set consists *only* of statements of L evaluating to 1 on P, and in keeping with (3) it is deductively closed and consistent in L.

The so-called *Fundamental Theorem for Assumption Sets*, to wit:

> *A set S of statements of L is deductively closed and consistent in L if, and only if, there is a unary probability function P for L such that* S = {A: P(A) = 1},

is proved in Leblanc (1983b) for a language L with just '~' and '&' as its logical operators. The argument there for the *if-part* of the theorem nonetheless holds with L as in this paper.

Suppose indeed P is a unary probability function for L such that S = {A: P(A) = 1}. (i) Let A be a statement of L such that S $\vdash$ A. Then {A: P(A) = 1} $\vdash$ A. But P(B) = 1 for each statement B of L in {A: P(A) = 1}. Hence, P(A) = 1 by (1) (cf. III); hence, A $\in$ S; and, hence, S is deductively closed in L. (ii) Suppose S were inconsistent in L. Then there would be a statement A of L such that S $\vdash$ A & ~A, hence by the hypothesis on P such that P(A & ~A) = 1, and hence by the analogue for P of (4) (cf. IV) such that P(~(A & ~A)) = 0, against the analogue for P of *D2*. Hence, S has got to be consistent in L. Hence:

Theorem 13. If there is a unary probability function P for L such that S = {A: P(A) = 1}, then S is deductively closed and consistent in L.

However, the argument in Leblanc (1983b) for the *only if-part* of the theorem must be adjusted to suit the present L. Needed now, given a set S of statements of L that is deductively closed and consistent in L, is a function - call it $P^{\infty}_{S^{\infty}}$ - from the statements of the term-extension L^{∞} of L to the reals which constitutes a unary probability function for L^{∞} and on which *all and only* the members of the deductive closure S^{∞} of S in L^{∞} evaluate to 1. The restriction of $P^{\infty}_{S^{\infty}}$ to L will then constitute a unary probability function for L on which all and only the members of S evaluate to 1.

Construction of $P^{\infty}_{S^{\infty}}$ is like that of P_S on pp. 385-386 of Leblanc (1983b), but with 'L^{∞}' substituting throughout for 'L' and '$\vdash^{\infty}$' for '$\vdash$', with the statement A in B understood to be *quantifier-free* (i.e. to contain no '$\forall$'), and with provision made as follows for an A of L^{∞} that is not quantifier-free:

C. A is in so-called *prenex normal form*, i.e. A is of the sort

$$(QX_1)(QX_2) \ldots (QX_n)B,$$

where for each i from 1 through n ($n \geq 1$) (QX_i) is either $(\forall X_i)$ or the customary abbreviation $(\exists X_i)$ of $\sim(\forall X_i)\sim$, and B is a quantifier-free formula of L^{∞}.

CASE 1. A is of the sort $(\forall X)C$. Then

$$P^{\infty}_{S^{\infty}}(A) = glb\{P^{\infty}(D): D \in R(SI^{\infty}((\forall X)C))\}.$$

CASE 2. A is of the sort $(\exists X)C$. Then

$$P^{\infty}_{S^{\infty}}(A) = 1 - glb\{P^{\infty}(D): D \in R(SI^{\infty}((\forall X)\sim C))\}.$$

D. A is not in prenex normal form. Then $P^{\infty}_{S^{\infty}}(A) = P^{\infty}_{S^{\infty}}(B)$, where B is any statement of L^{∞} that is in prenex normal form and such that $\vdash^{\infty} A \equiv B$.

With $P^{\infty}_{S^{\infty}}$ (and, hence, its restriction P to L) on hand, the argument on pp. 386-392 of Leblanc (1983b) can be generalized to show that:

Theorem 14. If S is deductively closed and consistent in L, then there is a unary probability function P for L (to wit: the restriction of $P^{\infty}_{S^{\infty}}$ to L) *such that* $S = \{A: P(A) = 1\}$.

That and how the statements in $\{A: P(A) = 1\}$, i.e. the assumptions in light of which P accords probabilities to the statements of L, affect these probabilities is illustrated in Leblanc (1983b), pp. 394-395.

The assumption sets of L can be arranged in the following three groups:

Group One, to consist of just one set: the set $\{A: \vdash A\}$ of all the statements of L provable in L and, hence, of all the logical truths of L,

Group Two, to consist of the remaining assumption sets of L that are not complete in L, and

Group Three, to consist of all the assumption sets of L that are complete in L, hence, of all the sets of statements of L that are maximally consistent in L.

Various results concerning the unary probability functions for L and their respective assumption sets will be found in Leblanc (1983b), among them: (i) the functions with $\{A: \vdash A\}$ as their assumption set are those Carnap acknowledged in Carnap (1950) as his *regular measure functions*, (ii) the functions with a set from Group Three as their assumption set are 2-valued, in point of fact they are *the* 2-valued unary probability functions for L, and hence in virtue of Theorem 12 they coincide with the truth-value functions for L in II, etc.

I close on a result which is quite elementary but neatly brings out the significance of assumption sets for probabilistic semantics. Let S be an arbitrary set of statements of L and A be an arbitrary statement of L, and suppose that, for each unary probability function P for L,

if $P(B) = 1$ for each B in S, then $P(A) = 1$.

Then, for each unary probability function P for L,

if $B \in \{C: P(C) = 1\}$ for each B in S, then $A \in \{C: P(C) = 1\}$;

hence, for each unary probability function P for L,

if $S \subset \{C: P(C) = 1\}$, then $A \in \{C: P(C) = 1\}$;

hence, for each set S′ of statements of L and each unary probability function P for L,

if $S' = \{C: P(C) = 1\}$, then $A \in S'$ if $S \subset S'$;

hence, for each set S′ of statements of L,

if $S' = \{C: P(C) = 1\}$ for some unary probability function P for L, then $A \in S'$ if $S \subset S'$;

and, hence,

if S′ is an assumption set of L, then $A \in S'$ if $S \subset S'$.

So, by virtue of (1) (cf. III),

$S \vdash A$ if, and only if, A belongs to each assumption set of L of which S is a subset.

So, given the Strong Soundness and Completeness results in II-III,

A is logically entailed by S if, and only if, A belongs to each assumption set of L of which S is a subset.

and, hence, with S set at $\emptyset$,

A is logically true if, and only if, A belongs to each assumption set of L.

For further results on unary probabilistic semantics, see Leblanc (1983a), (1983b), and (1984). While working on these matters I held a partial research leave and, in 1983, a Faculty Summer Research Grant from Temple University.

REFERENCES

Bendall, L. K., 1979, Belief-theoretic Formal Semantics for First-order Logic and Probability, J. Philosophical Logic, 8:375-394.

Carnap, R., 1950, "Logical Foundations of Probability," University of Chicago Press, Chicago.

Field, H. H., 1977, Logic, Meaning, and Conceptual Role, J. Philosophy, 74:379-409.

Gaifman, H., 1964, Concerning Measures on First-order Calculi, Isreal J. Math., 2:1-18.

Kolmogorov, A. N., 1933, Grundbegriffe der Wahrscheinlichkeitsrechnung, Ergebnisse der Math., 2:195-262.

Leblanc, H., 1982, Popper's 1955 Axiomatization of Absolute Probability, Pacific P. Quarterly, 63:133-145.

Leblanc, H., 1983a, Alternatives to Standard First-order Semantics, in: "Handbook of Philosophical Logic," D. M. Gabbay and F. Guenthner, eds., Reidel, Dordrecht.

Leblanc, H., 1983b, Probability Functions and their Assumption Sets - the Singulary Case, J. Philosophical Logic, 12:379-402

Leblanc, H., 1984, A New Semantics for First-order Logic, Multivalent and Mostly Intensional, to appear in Topoi.

Popper, K. R., 1938, A Set of Independent Axioms for Probability, Mind, 47:275-277.

Popper, K. R., 1955, Two Autonomous Axiom Systems for the Calculus of Probabilities, British J. for the P. of Science, 6:51-57, 176, 351.

Popper, K. R., 1959, "The Logic of Scientific Discovery," Basic Books, New York.

EPISTEMIC IMPORTANCE AND THE LOGIC OF THEORY CHANGE

Peter Gärdenfors

Lund University and
Stanford University

1. INTRODUCTION

In an ideal world science would be, if not definitive, then at least cumulative. New laws and facts would be added constantly to well established theories and their consequences would be determined. However, as modern philosophy of science has so painstakingly shown us, science is full of revisions and setbacks.

The logic of an expanding theory is well-known and fairly straightforward. If a theory has been given an axiomatic basis or at least is thought of as a deductive system, then expanding the theory by a new proposition (a new law or a new fact), consists simply in adding the proposition to the theory and then assuming that all logical consequences of the new proposition fused with the old theory are also in the new theory.

On the other hand, the logic of *theory revision* and *theory contraction* is much less understood. Some philosophers of science, notably Kuhn and Feyerabend, have claimed that there is no logic in large-scale theory changes, alias paradigm shifts, because they are intrinsically irrational processes. Here I will not be concerned with such large-scale theory changes but rather with revisions and contractions of theories within a paradigm or research program. The two most well-known accounts of the development within paradigms are Lakatos' 'research programmes' and Sneed's 'dynamics of theories'. Lakatos (1970) conceives of a 'research programme' as producing "a series of theories T_1, T_2, T_3, ... where each subset theory results from adding auxiliary clauses to ... the previous theory in order to accomodate some anomaly, ..." (p. 118). But accomodating an anomaly which conflicts with the older theory means that some part of the older theory has to be given up which entails that the series of theories do not represent an expanding science, but rather a series of revisions (and perhaps sometimes contractions). In general outline, Sneed's (1971) conception of 'the dynamics of theories' is similar, the main difference being that he has a more elaborate metatheory of the mathematical structure of the theories involved. It would take us too far to present Lakatos' and Sneed's metatheories in greater detail (for a lucid presentation of Sneed's theory, see Stegmüller (1976), and for a brief presentation, see Gärdenfors (1984a)). However, on this view of the dynamics of theories it is interesting to search for some rules that govern which parts of an old theory are retained when the conflicting principles of a new theory are added. Both Lakatos and Sneed separate out a 'core' of a theory which is not supposed to change during the series of revisions. Apart from this, they do not seem to say much about what determines which parts of the old theory to retain and which parts to retract. (For some schematic remarks on 'mistakes' in science, see Sneed (1971), p. 263 and pp. 285-286.)

The aim of this article is to outline a model of theory revision and theory contraction that will be a generalization of the process envisioned by Lakatos and Sneed. The key ideas are as follows:

1 It is possible to determine the relative *epistemic importance* of the elements of a theory.

2 When a theory is revised or contracted, the elements of the old theory that are given up are those with the lowest epistemic importance.

My goal is to show that these ideas, properly expanded, will make it possible to say something constructive about the logical properties of theory change.

As a model of a theory I will simply use a set of propositions closed under logical consequences. Admittedly, this is not a very realistic model of a scientific theory, but its simplicity will help us focus on some of the basic logical properties of theory contraction and theory revision. The notions of theory contraction and theory revision will be discussed in greater detail in section 3 and they will there be demarcated by a set of postulates. In section 4, I outline a representation theorem of Alchourrón, Gärdenfors and Makinson (1983) for these postulats. And in section 5 I show that in the finite case at least, this can be expressed in terms of a relation of epistemic importance over the theory itself. But before this can be done, the concept of epistemic importance must be highlighted.

2. EPISTEMIC IMPORTANCE

The central concept in this article is that of epistemic importance. The entities to which this concept is supposed to apply are the propositions accepted in a given theory. The notion of a theory will here be given a broad interpretation so that also an agent's state of belief can be said to be a theory of the world. (Here it should be noted that both Sneed (1971), ch. 8, and Stegmüller (1976), chs. 15 and 16, emphasize that 'holding a theory' essentially involves certain kinds of belief.) The propositions in the theory will be expressed by sentences from some appropriate language. A detailed account of the language need not concern us here; it will only be assumed that the language is closed under standard truth-functional connectives and that the language is governed by a logic L, which includes classical propositional logic.

The fundamental criterion for determining the epistemic importance of a proposition is how useful it is in inquiry and deliberation. Certain pieces of our knowledge and beliefs about the world are more important than others when conducting scientific investigations or planning future actions. For example, in present-day chemical theory, knowledge about the combining weights of different substances is much more important for the chemical experiments than knowledge about the color or taste of the substances. This difference of importance is reflected in that if the chemists for some reason changed their opinion concerning the combining weights of two substances, this would have much more radical effects on the chemical theory than if they changed their opinion concerning the tastes of the two substances.

This example also shows that the epistemic importance of different propositions need not be connected with their probabilities. If I have full belief in a proposition, i.e. if it is accepted in the theory, then I judge it to be maximally probable; but I do not regard all propositions which I accept as having equal epistemic importance. The following quotation from Levi (1983) emphasizes the same point:

> "In evaluating contraction strategies, we will be led to make discriminations between those items in the corpus to be contracted which are more vulnerable to removal from the corpus and those which are not. In this sense, we can talk of differences within the corpus with respect to grades of corrigibility.

It is tempting to correlate these grades of corrigibility with grades of certainty or probability. According to the view I advocate, that would be a mistake. All items in the initial corpus L which is to be contracted are, from X's initial point of view, certainly and infallibly true. They all bear probability 1." (p. 165)

Here Levi uses 'corpus' as I use 'theory' and 'grades of corrigibility' roughly as I use 'degrees of epistemic importance'. Rather than being connected with probability, the epistemic importance of a proposition is tied to its explanatory power and its overall informational value within the theory. For example, lawlike propositions generally have greater epistemic importance than accidental generalizations. This is not because the lawlike propositions are better supported by the available evidence (normally they are not), but since giving up lawlike sentences means that the theory looses more of its explanatory power than giving up accidental generalizations (cf. Gärdenfors (1984b), section 4, and Levi (1977), sections 2 and 3).

The epistemic importance of a proposition is dependent on the research program in which it occurs. This means that the epistemic importance of a proposition must be defined relative to a theory (or relative to a class of closely related theories, e.g. within a common 'research programme'). In the sequel, a theory will be modelled as a set of propositions, closed under logical consequences, and all theories will be assumed to be consistent. It will also be assumed that together with K comes an ordering of epistemic importance that is defined for propositions in K only. Different theories may thus be associated with different orderings of epistemic importance; even if the sets of propositions contained in the theories are overlapping, the orderings of epistemic importance need not agree on the common parts. In relation to the example above, it can be noted that within phlogiston theory qualitative facts, e.g. about the color and taste of substances, were more important than quantitative knowledge, e.g. about combining weights, while after Lavoisier and Dalton, the quantitative properties were put in the foreground and qualitative properties considered much less important (cf. Kuhn (1969)). On my own view of epistemic importance, a change of paradigm typically involves a radical change of the ordering of epistemic importance, and vice versa.

In this article, I will not assume that one can quantitatively measure degrees of epistemic importance, but instead I will formulate some postulates for the qualitative properties of epistemic importance. If A and B are propositions in a given theory K, the notation $A \leq B$ will be used as a shorthand for "B is at least as epistemically important as A". The strict relation $A < B$, representing "B is epistemically more important than A" is defined as $A \leq B$ and not $B \leq A$.

The first two postulates require $\leq$ to be a preordering:

(EI1) For any A, B, and C in K, if $A \leq B$ and $B \leq C$, then $A \leq C$. (Transitivity)

(EI2) For any A, B in K, either $A \leq B$ or $B \leq A$. (Connectivity)

Both of these postulates are idealizations of our intuitions about epistemic importance (transitivity less so). However, given the representation of theories used here, they are natural simplifications that will unify the sequel.

When a theory is revised or contracted some of the previously accepted propositions must be given up. The ordering of epistemic importance can be used to determine which propositions to retract, by requiring that the epistemically least important propositions be given up first so that the loss of information is minimal - this will be called the requirement of informational economy. (For similar ideas, cf. Gärdenfors (1984b), and Levi (1977, 1980).)

The third postulate requires that if a proposition is logically stronger than another, then it is epistemically less important:

(EI3) For any A, B in K, if A $\vdash$ B, then A $\leq$ B. (Dominance)

The justification of this postulate is that if A entails B, and either A or B must be retracted from the theory K, then it will be a smaller change to give up A and to retain B than to give up B, because then A must be retracted too, if we want to keep the revised theory closed under logical consequences.

At a first glance, this seems to go against the requirement of informational economy, since when A entails B, the informational value of A is greater than that of B. However, when giving up A, not all of the informational value of A will be lost in the revised theory - sometimes the content of B can be retained, while if B is given up, A must also be given up, so in this case more of the informational value of K is lost. This argument shows that the postulate (EI3) conforms with the requirement of informational economy. In fact, lacking a more precise definition of informational value, (EI3) seems to be all that can be postulated for a qualitative account of epistemic importance.

The fourth and final postulate perhaps looks innocent, but will turn out to be quite powerful:

(EI4) For all A, B in K, A$\vee$B $\leq$ A or A$\vee$B $\leq$ B. (Disjunctiveness)

The rationale for this postulate is as follows. If one wants to retract AvB from the theory K, this can only be achieved by giving up both A and B. On the other hand, the informational content of AvB cannot be greater than the maximal content of A and B taken separately. In other words, the epistemic importance of AvB is not greater than the maximum of the epistemic importance of A and the epistemic importance of B.

It will be clear from the sequel why (EI1) - (EI4) can be regarded as a complete set of postulates for the ordering of epistemic importance. Before turning to connections between the ordering of epistemic importance and other concepts, two simple consequences of the postulates will be presented.

<u>Lemma 2.1:</u>

Suppose the ordering ≤ satisfies (EI1) and (EI2). Then it satisfies (EI4) iff, for any A, B, and C in K, if A ≤ C and B ≤ C, then AvB ≤ C.

Proof: From left to right the proof is trivial. For the converse, suppose that the right-hand side holds. By (EI2) we know that either A ≤ B or B ≤ A. Suppose the former, the latter is similar. By (EI2) again, B ≤ B. So we have both A ≤ B and B ≤ B and thus, replacing C by B, AvB ≤ B. This completes the proof of the lemma.

<u>Lemma 2.2:</u>

Suppose the ordering ≤ satisfies (EI1) - (EI4). Then, for all A, B, and C in K, if A ≤ BvC, then A ≤ B or A ≤ C.

Proof: Assume that $A \leq B \vee C$. By (EI4) we know that $B \vee C \leq B$ or $B \vee C \leq C$. Hence by (EI1), $A \leq B$ or $A \leq C$ and the proof is complete.

It should be noted that the axiomatization of epistemic importance presented here is closely related to the axiomatization of 'comparative similarity' in Lewis (1973), p. 123 (cf. in particular the first footnote on p. 124). This connection is discussed in Gärdenfors (1984b), section 7.

3. THEORY CONTRACTION AND THEORY REVISION

The goal of this article is to show how, in the finite case at least, the ordering of epistemic importance can be used when constructing changes of a theory. In order to make this project more precise, I will now present different kinds of changes of theories (or belief states) and their properties.

For theories formulated as logically closed sets of propositions, there are three kinds of changes - expansion, contractions, and revisions. When *expanding* a theory K, a proposition A is added to K together with all the consequences of $K \cup \{A\}$, assuming that A is consistent with K, i.e. that $-A$ is not in K. The expansion of K with respect to A will be denoted K^+_A.

A *contraction* of a theory K consists in retracting, i.e. no longer accepting, some sentence that was accepted in K, but without accepting its negation. This kind of change may be made in order to open up for investigation some proposition that contradicts what was previously accepted in the theory. When contracting K with respect to some proposition A which is in K, it will be necessary to retract other propositions as well, in order to comply with the requirement that the resulting theory be closed under logical consequences. For example, suppose my present theory contains the beliefs that all philosophers are absentminded and that Wittgenstein is a philosopher, and consequently, that Wittgenstein is absentminded. If I now, for some reason, decide to give up my belief that Wittgenstein is absentminded, I must also give up either the belief that all philosophers are absentminded or the belief that Wittgenstein is a philosopher. According to the construction suggested in this article, I should give up one of these two beliefs which is less epistemically important. The contraction of K with respect to A will be denoted K_A^-.

When a theory K is *revised*, some proposition A is accepted, the negation of which was accepted in K. As with contractions, some propositions, earlier in K, must be given up in order to maintain consistency. A natural requirement is that the change of K not be greater than is necessary to accept A. The minimal change of K needed to accept A, which will be called the revision of K with respect to A, will be denoted K_A. The central problem here, which is similar to the corresponding problem for contractions, is to determine which sentences of K should be given up. The solution suggested here is the same as for contractions: When revising K with respect to A, keep the epistemically most important propositions that are consistent with A and give up less important propositions, if they in combination with more important ones contradict A.

We thus have two basic problems of determining which propositions to keep in contractions and revisions respectively. It has been argued (Gärdenfors (1981, 1982, 1984b), Harper (1977), Levi (1977)) that revisions can be defined in terms of contractions (and expansions) and that, conversely, contractions can be defined in terms of revisions (and expansions). If either of these definitions is accepted, the two problems will be reduced to one. Here I will adopt the definition of revisions in terms of contractions and expansions, which goes as follows (it has also been called the Levi identity):

(R) $K^*_A = (K^-_{-A})^+_A$

This means that when forming the revision of K with respect to A, one first contracts K with respect to -A and then expands the resulting theory K^-_{-A} with respect to A.

Elsewhere (Gärdenfors (1981, 1982, 1984b)) I have analysed contractions by suggesting postulates that a rational method of contraction ought to satisfy. These postulates can be formulated as follows (cf. Alchourrón, Gärdenfors, and Makinson (1983) or Makinson (1984)):

(-1) K^-_A is a theory whenever K is a theory

(-2) $K^-_A \subseteq K$

(-3) If $A \notin K$, then $K^-_A = K$

(-4) If A is not logically valid, then $A \notin K$

(-5) If A and B are logically equivalent, then $K^-_A = K^-_B$

(-6) $K = (K^-_A)^+_A$

(-7) $K^-_A \cap K^-_B \subseteq K^-_{A\&B}$

(-8) $K^-_{A\&B} \subseteq K^-_B$, whenever $A \notin K^-_{A\&B}$

The justifications for these postulates have been presented in the articles referred to above and will not be repeated here. Corresponding postulates for revisions can be derived from these postulates with the aid of definition (R). The main task is now to show how the ordering of epistemic importance can be used to construct a contraction procedure that will satisfy the postulates (-1) - (-8). If this goal can be achieved, we will thereby, via definition (R), also have a construction procedure for revisions of theories. In next section, an intermediate step in the construction procedure for contractions is presented.

4. PARTIAL MEET CONTRACTION FUNCTIONS

When forming the contraction K_A^- of a theory K with respect to a proposition A, a natural requirement is that K_A^- should contain 'as much as possible' from K. A first idea for constructing a contraction method would therefore be to choose K_A^- as a maximal subset of K that fails to imply A. However, as shown by Alchourrón and Makinson (1982), such *maxichoice* contractions will contain 'too much' in the sense that they have the following disconcerting property: If A is in K, then for any proposition B whatsoever, either $A \vee B$ or $A \vee -B$ is in K_A^-.

But the maximal subsets of K that fail to imply A can be used in other ways. Let us denote the class of these subsets by $K \bot A$. Since the result mentioned above shows that each of the elements in $K \bot A$ is 'too big' to represent the contraction K_A^-, a second idea would be to assume that K_A^- contains only the propositions that are common to all of the maximal subsets in $K \bot A$. More technically, this means that K_A^- is defined as the intersection of the elements of $K \bot A$. This contraction method will be called *full meet contraction*. Unfortunately, as is shown in observation 2.1 of Alchourrón and Makinson (1982), this leaves us with a contraction that is in general far too small - the only propositions left in K_A^- when A is in K are those propositions in K which are already consequences of -A considered alone. And thus, if revision is introduced via definition (R), the revision of K with respect to A will contain just the logical consequences of A considered alone; and this set is far too small to represent the result of an intuitive process of revision of K so as to bring in A.

A third idea for constructing a satisfactory contraction method, presented in Gärdenfors (1984b) and studied in detail in Alchourrón, Gärdenfors, and Makinson (1983), is to pick out a (non-empty) class of the 'most important' maximal subsets of K that fail to imply A, and then define K_A^- to be the intersection of the subset of K⊥A selected in this way. Thus a proposition B is in K_A^- iff it is an element of all the 'most important' maximal subsets of K. Contraction methods defined in this way are called *partial meet contraction methods*. These contraction methods do not in general have the 'inflation' property of the maxichoice methods and the 'drainage' property of the full meet contraction method.

The key problem when defining a specific partial meet contraction method is to determine which elements of K⊥A are the 'most important'. The most natural idea seems to be to assume that there is an ordering of all the maximal subsets of K, which can be used to pick out the top elements of K⊥A. Technically, we do this by introducing the notation M(K) for the union of the family of all the sets K⊥A, where A is any proposition in K that is not logically valid, and then assuming the existence of a relation ≦ over of M(K). An element M of K⊥A is then said to be among the 'most important' if M' ≦ M for all M' ∈ K⊥A. Note that the ordering ≦ of M(K) is not the relation of epistemic importance discussed earlier, since it is an ordering of the maximal subsets of K rather than of the elements of K. The connections between the two ordering relations will, of course, be the central topic in section 5.

One of the central results (observation 4.4 and corollary 4.5) in Alchourrón, Gärdenfors, and Makinson (1983) is that a contraction method satisfies postulates (-1) - (-8) iff there is some transitive ordering on M(K) such that it is a partial meet contraction method based on this ordering. In fact, it follows from a later result in that paper that, in the case when K is a finite theory, this result can be strengthened to the case when the ordering of M(K) is a preordering. When I say that a theory is *finite*, I mean that the relation of logical consequence partitions K into finitely many equivalence classes.

Theorem 4.1:

Let K be a finite theory. A contraction method satisfies postulates (-1) - (-8) iff there is some transitive and complete ordering ≦ of M(K) such that it is a partial meet contraction method based on this ordering.

This result shows if some contraction method satisfies postulates (-1) - (-8), then it is possible to find some ordering ≦ of M(K) that can be used to determine the contraction method. Since the postulates can be independently motivated, this strongly suggests that partial meet contraction functions based on transitive and complete orderings of M(K) can be used as ideal representations of the intuitive process of contraction. The key question, to be treated in next section, is how the ordering of M(K) can be connected with the ordering of epistemic importance of the elements of K.

5. CONNECTING THE TWO ORDERING RELATIONS

The orderings of K and M(K) respectively will be connected by investigating the consequences of two definitions, one defining the ordering of K in terms of the ordering of M(K), and the other defining the ordering of M(K) in terms of the ordering of K. The results of this investigation in combination with theorem 4.1 will show how a satisfactory contraction method can be constructed from an ordering of epistemic importance when K is a finite theory.

Before proceeding to the two definitions, let us recollect that the ordering ≤ of epistemic importance of K has been assumed to satisfy (EI1) - (EI4) and that the ordering ≦ of M(K) has been assumed to be transitive and connected (and hence reflexive).

The first definition gives us an ordering of the elements of K, assuming that we already have an ordering of M(K):

(I) Let A and B be in K. Then $A \leq B$ iff for all M' in M(K) such that $A \in M'$ there is an M in M(K) such that $B \in M$ and $M' \leqq M$.

The idea here is that A is epistemically less important than B if for any maximal subset of K containing A it is possible to find a maximal subset of K which contains B and which is at least as important (or in other words, the B-sets in M(K) 'dominate' the A-sets).

First of all, we want to check that this definition is appropriate in the sense that the defined ordering of K has the desired properties. This is asserted in the following lemma:

<u>Lemma 5.1:</u>

If $\leqq$ on M(K) is transitive and connected, then the ordering $\leq$ of K defined by (I) satisfies (EI1) - (EI4).

Proof: To check (EI1), assume that $A \leq B$ and $B \leq C$. Suppose $A \in M'$. By (I), there is an M" with $B \in M''$ such that $M' \leqq M''$. By (I) again, there is an M with $C \in M$ such that $M'' \leqq M$. Since $\leqq$ on M(K) is transitive, we conclude that $M' \leqq M$. Since M' was arbitrary, it follows that $A \leq C$ and hence (EI1) is fulfilled.

To prove (EI2), suppose that $A \nleq B$. By (I), there is then an M' with $A \in M'$ such that for all M with $B \in M$ it holds that $M' \nleqq M$. Since $\leqq$ on M(K) is assumed to be connected it follows that $M \leqq M'$.

By transposing the quantifiers of the earlier sentence, it follows that for all M with $B \in M$, there is an M' with $A \in M'$ such that $M \leqq M'$. Hence, by (I), $B \leq A$ and (EI2) is established.

For (EI3), suppose $A \vdash B$. For any M' in M(K), if $A \in M'$, then $B \in M'$. Since $M' \leqq M'$, it follows immediately from (I) that $A \leq B$.

Finally, we want to show that (EI4) is satisfied. First note that it follows from the definition of the maximal subset that if A and B are both in K, then for any M' in M(K) such that AvB is in M', either $A \in M'$ or $B \in M'$.

Suppose for contradiction that $A \vee B \not\leq A$ and $A \vee B \not\leq B$. It then follows from (I) that (a) there is an M' in M(K) with $A \vee B \in M'$ such that $M' \not\leqq M$ for all M in M(K) with $A \in M$; and (b) there is an M'' in M(K) with $A \vee B \in M''$ such that $M'' \not\leqq M^*$ for all M* in M(K) with $B \in M^*$. We can note that if $A \in M'$ then, by (a), $M' \not\leqq M'$ which gives us a contradiction. Hence we may assume that $B \in M'$. Similarly, if $B \in M''$ then it follows from (b) that $M'' \not\leqq M''$ which again gives us a contradiction. Hence we may assume that $A \in M''$. But $B \in M'$ entails, by (b), that $M'' \not\leqq M'$ and $A \in M''$ entails, by (a), that $M' \not\leqq M''$. However, this contradicts the assumption that $\leqq$ on M(K) is connected. This series of contradictions proves the lemma.

The second definition takes us from an ordering of K, assumed as given, to an ordering of M(K):

(II) Let M and M' be any elements in M(K). Then $M' \leqq M$ iff there is an $A \in M'$ such that for all $B \in M$ it holds that $A \leq B$.

Or in other words, M' is less important than M if some proposition in M' is epistemically less important than all the propositions in M.

Also for this definition, we want to check that the constructed ordering of M(K) has the desired properties. However, I have not been able to prove this in the most general case. I will show that if the theory K is assumed to be finite, the definition (II) works as desired. It is useful to note that if K is finite then the elements in M(K) can be identified with the aid of certain propositions in K, in the sense that for any M in M(K) there is some proposition A_M in M which logically entails all the other propositions in M. We say that A_M is a *determiner* for M.

Lemma 5.2:

Suppose that K is a finite theory and that the ordering $\leq$ of K satisfies (EI1) - (EI4). Then $\leqq$ on M(K) defined by (II) is transitive and connected.

Proof: For transitivity, suppose that $M'' \leqq M'$ and $M' \leqq M$. Then by (II), there is a $B \in M'$ such that for all $A \in M$, $B \leq A$. Furthermore there is a C in M'' such that $C \leq B$. By (EI1), there is a C in M'' such that for all A in M, $C \leq A$. Hence $M'' \leqq M$ as desired.

For connectivity, assume that $M' \nleqq M$. Then by (II), for all $A \in M'$, there is a $B \in M$ such that $A \nleq B$. By (EI2), it follows that $B \leq A$. Let C be determiner for M'. Then we know that there is a $B \in M$ such that $B \leq C$. By assumption $C \vdash A$ for all $A \in M'$ and hence, by (EI3), $C \leq A$, for all $A \in M'$. By (EI1), it then follows that there is a $B \in M$ such that for all $A \in M'$, $B \leq A$. Hence by (II), $M \leqq M'$ and the ordering of M(K) is connected. This completes the proof of the lemma. (Note that (EI4) is not used in the proof.)

Lemmas 5.1 and 5.2 show that the defined orderings have the necessary properties, at least in the finite case. But we also want the two definitions to be interchangeable in the sense that if we start with one kind of ordering and then use one definition to construct an ordering of the other kind and after that use the other definition to obtain an ordering of the first kind again, then we ought to have the original ordering back again. If this can be established, we will have shown that the two kinds of orderings are equivalent in a very precise sense.

For both of the two desired results we need the assumption that K is a finite theory. The first result concerns the case when we start out from a given ordering of M(K):

Theorem 5.3:

Suppose that K is a finite theory and that the ordering $\leqq$ of M(K) is transitive and connected. Let $\leq$ be an ordering of K defined by (I). Starting from this ordering, let $\leqq^*$ be an ordering of M(K) defined by (II). Then, for all M, M' in M(K), $M' \leqq M$ iff $M' \leqq^* M$.

Proof: Suppose first that $M' \leqq^* M$. By (II), there is then an $A \in M'$ such that for all $B \in M$, $A \leq B$. Let C be a determiner for M. It follows that $A \leq C$. By (I), for all M'' such that $A \in M''$ there is an M* with $C \in M^*$ such that $M'' \leqq M^*$. Since $A \in M'$, it follows that there is an M* with $C \in M^*$ such that $M' \leqq M^*$. Since C is a determiner for M we know that M* must be identical with M. Hence $M' \leqq M$.

For the converse, suppose that $M' \nleqq^* M$. Then by (II), for all $A \in M'$ there is a $B \in M$ such that $A \nleq B$. Let D be a determiner for M'. Then there is a $B \in M$ such that $D \nleq B$. By (I), there is an M'' with $D \in M''$ such that for all M* with $B \in M^*$, $M' = M'' \nleqq M^*$, and in particular $M' \nleqq M$. This completes the proof of the theorem.

The second result deals with the case when the original ordering is an ordering of K:

Theorem 5.4:

Suppose that K is a finite theory and that the ordering $\leq$ of K satisfies (EI1) - (EI4). Let $\leqq$ be an ordering of M(K) defined by (II). Starting from this ordering, let $\leq^*$ be an ordering of K defined by (I). Then, for all A, B in K, $A \leq B$ iff $A \leq^* B$.

Proof*): First suppose that $A \leq^* B$. Let $M_1, \ldots, M_n$ be all sets in M(K) that contain A, and let $A_1, \ldots, A_n$ be determiners for $M_1, \ldots, M_n$ respectively. It follows from a well known fact about finite boolean algebras that since K is finite, A is logically equivalent with the disjunction $A_1 \vee \ldots \vee A_n$. Now it follows from (I) that for all M_i with $A \in M_i$ there is an M with $B \in M$ such that $M_i \leqq M$. Then by (II), for all M_i, there is a $C_i \in M_i$ such that, for all $D \in M$, $C_i \leq D$, and in particular $C_i \leq B$. Since $A_i \vdash C_i$, for all i, $1 \leq i \leq n$, it follows from (EI3) that $A_i \leq C_i$ and hence, by (EI1), $A_i \leq B$. Since this holds for all (finitely many) A_i's, we can apply (EI4) and (EI2) via lemma 2.1 to conclude that $A_1 \vee \ldots \vee A_n \leq B$ and hence $A \leq B$ as desired.

For the converse, suppose that $A \nleq^* B$. This time, let $M_1, \ldots, M_k$ be all the elements in M(K) that contain B and let $B_1, \ldots, B_k$ be determiners for the M_i's. As before, B is logically equivalent with $B_1 \vee \ldots \vee B_k$. Since for each B_i, $B_i \vdash B$ and hence $B_i \leq^* B$ by lemma 5.1, it follows from the initial assumption and (EI1) that $A \nleq^* B_i$. Definition (I) then implies that, for each of the B_i's, there exists an M' with $A \in M'$ such that for all M with $B_i \in M$ it holds that $M' \nleqq M$. Since B_i is a determiner for M_i, this means that for each of the M_i's there is an M' with $A \in M'$ such that $M' \nleqq M_i$.

*) The idea behind this version of the proof is due to Carlos Alchourrón.

By (II) it now follows that for all $C \in M'$ there is a $D_i \in M_i$ such that $C \nleq D_i$. In particular $A \nleq D_i$. But since $B_i \vdash D_i$ and so by (EI3) $B_i \leq D_i$ it follows that $A \nleq B_i$. Since this holds for all the B_i's we can conclude from (EI4), via lemma 2.2, that $A \nleq B_1 \vee \ldots \vee B_k$ and hence $A \nleq B$. This completes the proof of the theorem.

We can reformulate the theorems in the following way: Definition (I) gives us a mapping from transitive and connected orderings of M(K) to orderings of K that satisfy (EI1) - (EI4); and definition (II) gives us a mapping from such orderings of K to transitive and connected orderings of M(K). Theorems 5.3 and 5.4 show that, in the finite case, these mappings are injective so that corresponding mappings will be the inverses of each other.

To sum up, the results in this section show that, at least in the case when K is a finite theory, one can start from either the ordering of epistemic importance of the elements of K or the ordering of maximal subsets of K, and then introduce the other ordering via one of the definitions (I) and (II) with equivalent results in the sense made precise in theorems 5.3 and 5.4. Thus either form of ordering can be taken as primitive when formulating an account of how contractions of theories are to be determined. Intuitively, it seems more natural to start from an ordering of K of epistemic importance since single propositions are conceptually easier to handle than maximal sets of propositions. (However, in the finite case, such maximal sets can be identified with single propositions - the determiners.)

6. CONCLUSION

The main reason for introducing the notion of epistemic importance is to show how it can be used in the process of constructing well-behaved contractions (and thereby also revisions) of theories. As described here, the contraction of a theory K with respect to a proposition A is construed from the ordering of epistemic importance in three steps: First, the ordering $\leq$ of K is used in definition (II) to obtain an ordering $\leqq$ of M(K). Second, the ordering of M(K) is used to select the set of most important maximal subsets of K that do not contain A. As the ordering over M(K) is connected, and M(K) is finite, we know that this set will always be non-empty. Finally, the intersection of these most important maximal subsets of K is defined to be the contraction K_A^-. And if we put together theorems 5.4 (or lemma 5.2) and 4.1 we know that this method of constructing contractions will, at least in the finite case, satisfy postulates (-1) - (-8), which shows that the construction procedure is satisfactory.

This procedure for constructing contractions assumes that there exists an ordering of epistemic importance that satisfies (EI1) - (EI4) (to be strict, only (EI1) - (EI3) are used in lemma 5.2). The results presented here can also be used to shed light on when this assumption is fulfilled: Let K be any finite theory. Take any contraction operation on K that satisfies (-1) - (-8). By theorem 4.1 we know that there is a transitive and connected ordering of M(K) that generates the contractions. And hence, by theorem 5.3 and lemma 5.1, there is an ordering of K that satisfies (EI1) - (EI4) and that also generates the contractions. Or in simpler words, for any well-behaved contraction method (or revision method, via the definitions mentioned in section 3) on a finite theory there exists an ordering of epistemic importance that generates the method. I believe that this result justifies the conclusion that the concept of epistemic importance is a useful tool when studying the dynamics of theories. --

Carlos Alcourrón and David Makinson have been extremely helpful by finding errors in earlier incorrect proofs and suggesting simplifications for the correct ones. Their criticism of my general program has made it less confused, I hope, even if it does not always agree with their opinions on the topic. I also wish to thank Isaac Levi for helpful comments.

REFERENCES

Alchourrón, C. E., Gärdenfors, P., and Makinson, D., 1983, On the Logic of Theory Change: Partial Meet Contraction and Revision Functions, to appear in *Journal of Symbolic Logic*.

Alchourrón, C. E., and Makinson, D., 1982, On the Logic of Theory Change: Contraction Functions and Their Associated Revision Functions, *Theoria*, 48:14-37.

Gärdenfors, P., 1979, Conditionals and Changes of Belief, *in*: "The Logic and Epistemology of Scientific Change" (*Acta Philosophica Fennica*, 30, issues 2-4), I. Niiniluoto and R. Tuomela, eds., North-Holland, Amsterdam.

Gärdenfors, P., 1981, An Epistemic Approach to Conditionals, *American Philosophical Quarterly*, 18:203-211.

Gärdenfors, P., 1982, Rules for Rational Changes of Belief, *in*: "<320311>: Philosophical Essays Dedicated to Lennart Åqvist on His Fiftieth Birthday," T. Pauli, ed., Philosophical Studies published by the Philosophical Society and the Department of Philosophy, University of Uppsala, No. 34, Uppsala.

Gärdenfors, P., 1984a, Sneed's Reconstruction of the Structure and Dynamics of Theories, to appear *in*: "After Kuhn: Method or Anarchy?," B. Hansson. ed., Doxa, Lund.

Gärdenfors, P., 1984b, Epistemic Importance and Minimal Changes of Belief, to appear in *Australasian Journal of Philosophy*.

Harper, W. L., 1977, Rational Conceptual Change, *PSA 1976*, Vol. 2, Philosophy of Science Association.

Kuhn, T. S., 1969, "The Structure of Scientific Revolutions," 2nd edition, University of Chicago Press, Chicago.

Lakatos, I., 1970, Falsification and the Methodology of Scientific Research Programmes, *in*: "Criticism and the Growth of Knowledge," I. Lakatos and A. Musgrave, eds., Cambridge University Press, Cambridge.

Levi, I., 1977, Subjunctives, Dispositions and Chances, *Synthese*, 34:423-455.

Levi, I., 1980, "The Enterprise of Knowledge," MIT Press, Cambridge, Mass.

Levi, I., 1983, Truth, Fallibility and the Growth of Knowledge, in: "Language, Logic, and Method," R. S. Cohen and M. W. Wartofsky, eds., Boston Studies in the Philosophy of Science, Vol. 31, Reidel, Dordrecht.

Lewis, D. K., 1973, "Counterfactuals," Blackwell, Oxford.

Makinson, D., 1984, How to Give It Up: A Survey of Some Formal Aspects of the Logic of Theory Change, to appear in Synthese.

Sneed, J. D., 1971, "The Logical Structure of Mathematical Physics," Reidel, Dordrecht.

Stegmüller, W., 1976, "The Structure and Dynamics of Theories," Springer-Verlag, New York.

LEŚNIEWSKI'S LOGIC AND ITS RELATION TO CLASSICAL AND FREE LOGICS

Peter M. Simons

Department of Philosophy
University of Salzburg
A-5020 Salzburg

1. INTRODUCTION

1.1 The Aim: Comparison

Understanding the relationship between the logical system of Stanisław Leśniewski and those of the Frege-Russell tradition is made difficult by a number of factors, some of them circumstantial, some substantial. The circumstantial ones include the fact that Leśniewski died in 1939, having published only a small fraction of his work, and his manuscripts were destroyed in the Nazi occupation of Poland. What survives is often compressed almost to the point of unintelligibility. His punctilious insistence on utmost rigour and his preference for an interesting but idiosyncratic notation isolated him from all but his students and a few contemporaries. While of those surviving some have, with their own pupils, reconstructed many of Leśniewski's achievements and pushed his work forward, they have tended not to spare much time for publicising Leśniewski's work to a wider audience. There exists to date no introductury logic textbook (outside Japan!) which devotes so much as a chapter to presenting even Leśniewski's basic ideas. On the substantial side, many of his opinions were then, and surprisingly many still are, uncompromisingly, even inconveniently radical.

Efforts to fruitfully compare his systems with those of the dominant logical tradition were spearheaded by the late Arthur Prior, a discerning though not infallible commentator. His successor at Manchester, Czesław Lejewski, pushed the work of comparison from the Leśniewskian side. I am attempting to carry on this Manchester tradition, and the present paper is part of the effort. While I by no means agree with all of Leśniewski's views, I still think we can learn much from him, so the process of bridge-building is well worthwhile.

It has frequently been noted that in some sense or other certain of Leśniewski's systems "contain" other familiar ones, e.g. that Ontology contains syllogistic, Boolean algebra, first-order predicate logic, that Mereology, Leśniewski's axiomatic theory of part and whole, contains the Leonard-Goodman Calculus of Individuals. While practitioners soon acquire the knack of "translating" from one system to another, it is less clear what this translatability precisely amounts to. That is what I here attempt to clarify. In particular I consider the relationship of Ontology to the following other logical systems: (1) classical first-order predicate logic with identity; (2) a first-order predicate logic with identity whose theorems are also valid on the empty domain (a universal logic); (3) a system of free logic with identity and descriptions developed by Lambert and Van Fraassen; (4) Lejewski's system of logic with non-reflexive identity; and finally (5) my own system of free logic with plural terms.

1.2 The Method: Extending and Embedding

The technique used in each case is the same. The language of Leśniewski's Ontology is enlarged by additional runs of nominal variables, for which special properties are axiomatically guaranteed, and the rules of Ontology are extended to cover the new expressions thus admitted. The axioms and rules of the compared systems are then found to have optically identical counterparts in the thus extended systems of Ontology, which are theorems and admissible rules respectively. Each such extension of Ontology however does not extend its expressive *power*, since every formula containing the newly-introduced signs is guaranteed to be logically equivalent to one containing only signs from the original, unextended Ontology. These equivalences, which will be outlined rather than proved in detail, then constitute translation metatheorems connecting each system with unextended Ontology, which turns out to be the system with the greatest expressive power of those considered. So when we speak of an *extension* of Ontology, this is to be understood in a literal linguistic and logical sense. Whether the extended systems of Ontology are *conservative* extensions of the original is something I conjecture but have not shown to be the case.

2. PROBLEMS OF COMPARISON

2.1 Nominalistic Conception of Logical Systems

There is one feature of Leśniewski's way of presenting and developing logical systems which, while it is of considerable philosophical interest, is a hindrance in effecting a comparison. This is Leśniewski's strictly nominalistic and finitistic conception of a logical system. For him, a system is a collection of concrete marks with a spatio-temporal location. Some such collections are in important respects alike. For instance those printed in what a Platonist would call different copies of the same book are typographically exactly alike. Others might be thus alike except for their two-dimensional layout on the page, or their three-dimensional distribution over several pages. Such discrepancies are logically insignificant provided all the versions yield the same sequential order of signs; all such systems may be considered equiform with one another - equiformity being an equivalence relation. Other systems may fall short of being equiform but are relevantly similar in other ways, e.g. being alphabetic variants of one another, or having different symbolic conventions regarding logical constants or formation rules. Such nitty-gritty details are not what a logician is interested in, though it is part of his craft to make sure they are not handled sloppily. More important logically are systems which have different initial segments but which converge, in that there comes a point in each system in which it has assembled the same (or rather equiform) class of theses (axioms, theorems, definitions) as another system, but in a different order. Such systems are then logically equivalent (assuming they have the same rules). One of the striking features of this way of looking at logical systems is that they are at any time finite in extent, but are capable of literally growing by the physical addition of new theses. Leśniewski understood this growth quite literally, and not as an abstract ordering of ideal formulae. He drew up detailed and unambiguous rules or *directives* stipulating how to add new theses to extant systems. Accompanying these directives are a large number of *terminological explanations* which describe the syntax of the language which is in the process of growing. The explanations and directives are formulated in a way which makes them self-adjusting: as new expressions are added to the system as theses, they and their parts fall under the descriptions given in the explanations and may be taken account of in further extending the system. The explanations and directives thus interweave the functions of listing primitive symbols, giving formation rules, rules of inference, and schemata for extensionality and admissible definitions. Their extreme complication has become somewhat notorious - Lejewski reports (Luschei, 1962, p.168) that their exposition normally took Leśniewski more than two semesters of advanced courses - but they are probably simpler by one or two orders of complication than the formation rules for well-formed programs in higher-level computing languages.

Now while (most) logicians do still get their hands dirty with physical marks on paper, most of them tend to look through or beyond these to formulae and logical systems conceived Platonistically. Whatever the philosophical credentials of this ideal intuition, the Platonistic way of viewing logical systems has its odd side too, for instance that of the denumerably infinitely many theorems most such systems are said to have, all but a small finite number remain forever unknown. Thus to compare Leśniewski directly with orthodoxy one must either Platonise Leśniewski or Leśniewski-ise Plato. The second option is in some ways the more interesting, but the first probably promises more ready intelligibility, so we follow it here (as in Simons, 1982).

2.2 Definitions

Before we can proceed however, another unusual feature of Leśniewski's systems must be accommodated, namely his handling of definitions. Leśniewski criticised previous logicians, above all Whitehead and Russell, for their sloppy account of definitions. In his view, the sign '$=_{Df}$' was an unacknowledged primitive of *Principia*, sanctioning the assertion of new material equivalences as theorems. So he treated definitions as object-language equivalences from the start rather than as metalinguistic abbreviations, expressions of the logician's will or anything else. That is why he developed the pure equivalential fragment of propositional calculus and made material equivalence the only primitive connective of his propositional logic (the other logical constant being the universal quantifier). Leśniewski gave conditions which material equivalences introducing a new sign must fulfil to be acceptable definitions.

One of the features of these definitions which has raised eyebrows is that they may be creative: sometimes it is possible to prove things not containing the defined sign via the definition which are unprovable without it. The definitions thus contribute to the logical power of a system. Most logicians think that this is a Bad Thing - a logical system should be fixed as to what can be proved in it from the beginning, and not successively souped up as we go along. In fact I think there is no real conflict here, just an equivocation on the word 'definition'. The sense in which a creative definition is Bad is that in which a sign is introduced as an abbreviation for a more complex group of signs. Mere shorthand should not enable one to prove more, although it should help one to prove the same things more quickly. But what Leśniewski calls a definition is not an abbreviation, although it may facilitate abbreviation. Rather it is tantamount to a special kind of axiom introducing a new term. Now of course extending an existing logical system with a new axiom is generally expected to enable us to prove new things - indeed it is a defect - non-independence - if it does not. If an axiom contains a term not present in the other axioms and yet with its help we can prove something new which does not contain this term, then we simply have a non-conservative extension. That, from the usual point of view, is all that creativity of Leśniewskian definitions really amounts to, and it is not the Bad Thing it was thought.

Since Leśniewski's stipulations govern only the form of admissible definitions relative to what has gone before, any number may be added to a system in conformity with the rules, so there is no fixed Platonic equivalent of a set of Leśniewskian directives, rather an unbounded multiplicity, according as we choose to extend the initial axioms and rules with definitions in Leśniewski's sense. Each such addition takes us to what would normally be considered a different system. If the extension thus obtained is however conservative, it is indifferent whether one chooses to see the definition as a metalinguistic abbreviation or as an introducing axiom. If the extension is not conservative, only the second option is available.

2.3 The Platonic Archetype of a Leśniewskian System

Take a given concrete Leśniewskian system, consisting of a finite sequence of theses, containing therefore finitely many constants and variables, some of the constants perhaps introduced by definition. We want to find a Platonic counterpart to this lump of logical earth, with all the usual Platonic properties like closure under substitution of equivalents, closure under deducibility and the like. How, in the face of the multiplicity just mentioned, to do this? Leśniewski's directives are very liberal as to what can be let in as a new sign, whether constant or variable. It is even possible to have a kind of contextually resolvable systematic ambiguity, as happens with the use of so-called higher epsilons. Let us suppose this variety tamed to the extent that we have, sitting in Plato's heaven, neat rows of symbols, all different, such that each constant present in the concrete fragment is there with the meaning intended, and each syntactic category has denumerably many variables such that those in the fragment are in the right category among them. Resolve any contextual ambiguity by the use of new signs, whether these be indices or whatever.

We now get a conventional system as follows. First list all the constants that actually occur in the fragment, with their category. Then list all the variables of all the categories which are used in the fragment. (If brackets are not counted among the *logical* constants they and other punctuation marks like commas must still be counted among the *syntactic* constants.) Take the axioms and definitions of the fragment as our axioms, and take the rules of substitution, inference and extensionality for the categories employed as our rules. *Leave out the rules of definition*. This is the basis; we then take its closure under the rules, given the listed infinite vocabulary, in the usual way. Assuming the directives (except for definitions) correspond to recursive stipulations of the usual kind, this gives us a unique Platonic Archetype, of which the clod of earth, the original fragment, is just a copy of a tiny but important corner. In some cases, namely when the fragment contains variable-binding term-forming functors like definite description operators, we need to add infinitely many axioms, corresponding to a schema (how this goes will become clear below). We fix the Leśniewskian definitions actually used as axioms, and do not allow them to be added to. We are then of course free to use metalinguistic abbreviations if we wish, borrowing suitable signs from other heavenly regions.

3. BASIC FEATURES OF LEŚNIEWSKIAN LOGIC

3.1 Protothetic

In his Protothetic Leśniewski gave the means for constructing what can grow indefinitely towards being a system of propositional types of the kind described by Church or Henkin, with quantifiers binding variables of each type, an axiom, rules of substitution, definition, quantifier distribution and extensionality for each type. The syntactic categories are all those which can be derived from the basic category S of sentence, where Leśniewski distinguishes e.g. the category S/(SS) of binary connectives from the functor-forming functor category (S/S)/S. I tend to find this rather over-fussy on Leśniewski's part. It enables him to keep rather simple rules of substitution, but the price for this is an abundance of definitions required to link analogous functors in what most categorial grammarians would regard as mere notational variants of the same constant. This fine discrimination among syntactic categories is continued in Ontology. The only undefined constants are material equivalence and the universal quantifier, which appears as a single constant without category rather than as a sheaf of constants as in Church. Though novel for its time, this system presents fewer interpretative difficulties for modern readers, though with its potentiality for adding (Leśniewskian) definitions as well as having variables in any category bound, it is probably the most powerful *extensional* propositional system it is possible to have.

3.2 Ontology

This is the most original and interesting of the systems Leśniewski developed. It combines features of the logic of Frege, whom Leśniewski admired tremendously, particularly for his exactness, and Schröder, whose work was the most widely read form of symbolic logic prior to *Principia*, and which Leśniewski may have encountered as a student of Twardowski in Lwów (see Dambska, 1978, p.123). Ontology adds the new basic syntactic category Name (N) to that of Sentence, and all the functor categories derivable from these two categories. All the syntactic categories thus obtainable fall into two disjoint groups: those whose index, in the normal quotient notation, begin with 'S' as the first letter, and those whose index begins with 'N'. Following a suggestion of Luschei (1962, p.169), we may call all categories whose index begins with 'S' (including sentences, connectives, predicates etc.) *propositive*, and all categories whose index begins with 'N' (including names, function names, subnectors etc.) *nominative*. An expression itself is propositive or nominative according as it belongs to a propositive or nominative category.

Ontology is built on Protothetic, in that it presupposes its axiom and rules, these merely being extended to cover the new expressions made available. In particular the rule for constructing definitions in Protothetic now applies to all propositive categories of expression, not just those whose index is built only from 'S', so it applies i.a. to predicates. This kind of definition is sometimes called 'Protothetical', but since it applies within Ontology as well it is better to follow Luschei and speak of propositive definitions. A second rule of definitions is added to cope with expressions of nominative category, and again we call these definitions nominative, though the more usual term is 'Ontological'.

Since the universal quantifier is already without category, its rules need merely be extended to allow it to bind variables of nominative category. While quantification in Protothetic is not without interest, it is certainly far less important in that extensional context than it is in an intensional propositional logic, and it really comes into its own first in Ontology, where it plays a role much more akin to that in predicate logic or type theory, and consequently appears more familiar (but see §3.4).

The possibility of reaching any finite type in a finite time in a concrete development of Ontology corresponds to a Platonistic system's already having all types available. But whereas for Frege and the early Russell the different types (of function) are a stratification of a vast universe of entities, for Leśniewski they amount to no more than tidy grammar: Leśniewski indeed used the term 'semantical category' rather than the later more usual 'syntactic category', but that does not mean that each expression is assigned an entity as its denotation. Leśniewski's categories were a development of Husserl's *Bedeutungskategorien*, and he chose the term 'semantic' to emphasise that the constant expressions in his languages had an intended meaning (as emphasised by Lejewski, 1958).

Nominal expressions in Leśniewski need not denote: he was the first to develop what is now known as a free logic. In addition, he also allows nominal expressions to denote more than one object at once. This fact is often misrepresented by saying that his names are in fact common nouns (see the arguments in Simons (1982) against this admittedly enticing interpretation).

Ontology adds a new axiom, usually based on the epsilon, 'ε', of singular inclusion. The original axiom of 1920 has been succeeded by shorter ones (see Sobociński (1967) for an account, though the work of providing a more compact basis is still continuing), and numerous other functors have been taken as primitive (see again Lejewski, 1958), but we shall stick in this paper to the original axiom for ε, which is still in many ways the most illuminating. In addition to the rules of detachment, substitution, quantification and definition, Leśniewski directed that a principle of extensionality can be formulated for every type. The system is extensional through and through. Sometimes definitions and extensionality have been used in finding shorter axiomatic bases equivalent to the original (see again Sobociński, 1967).

3.3 Ontological Neutrality of Logic

Ontology is a universal logic, in that its theorems remain true even for the empty universe, when none of its nominal expressions denote. That there are quantifiers binding variables of any cagegory does not lead to ontological commitments, since the quantifiers are taken to be free of ontological import (on what this means, see the next section). So although Ontology is a higher-order logic, it does not commit one to Platonism. While Leśniewski himself was a nominalist, and hence in a sense *needed* to decouple his logic from ontology, one need not be a nominalist to appreciate the freedom involved in being able to use a powerful system of logic without being plagued by ontological *Angst*. One is free to be as Platonistic as one wishes, but the decision to be so may be made independently of one's logic. Hence although Leśniewski called his system 'Ontology', it doesn't give one *an* ontology, but simply means for saying some of the things that can be said about what there (as it happens) is.

3.4 Interpretation of the Quantifiers

As we have pointed out, Leśniewski's quantifiers (or rather quantifier, for like Frege he only officially had the universal) are free of ontological import. There has been some controversy as to what this means and how it is possible. The two main options which have been canvassed are that his quantification is in some way substitutional or that it is neither substitutional nor referential, but rather ranges over extensional meanings. Quine has backed the former approach, Küng and Canty the latter (see the papers given in the references). Let us briefly consider these in turn.

If substitutional quantification is understood naively as involving quantification *over* expressions, then as is well known, problems arise over infinite domains, where there may not be enough expressions to go round. These problems are heightened in Ontology because of plural names: in a domain with c objects we need 2^c different names if all possibilities are to be covered. From Leśniewski's nominalist standpoint the problem is not even essentially connected with the possibility of an infinite domain. For the *actual* expressions in a system will at any time be finite in number, and fewer than the objects in the world, whether there are finitely or infinitely many of these - an empirical issue on which Leśniewski rightly would not pronounce. But even if we Platonise the language, we can always envisage a domain which is as large or larger than the number of expression-types. It is clearly against the spirit of ontological neutrality if we forego quantifying over objects only to end up saddled with a huge but still inadequate number of expressions. But quantification is in a way always *treated* substitutionally: introduction and elimination of quantified sentences in natural deduction always proceeds by substituting, whether in classical or Leśniewskian logic. There is also, as we shall see, an *implicitly* metalinguistic aspect to Leśniewskian quantification.

In its most straightforward form, the Küng-Canty interpretation of Leśniewskian quantification says that neither objects in the domain nor expressions are quantified over, but rather *extensions* of these expressions. Since to a domain of c objects we have 2^c extensions for names, 2^{2^c} for one-placed verbs, and so on, the arithmetic at least is right, and these extensions are ultimately built up out of objects of the domain. The names etc. do not *denote* these extensions, but rather *have* them.

But what are these extensions? The most obvious answer is that they are sets. So on this view, while Leśniewski does not *talk about* sets (or some equivalent), he still as it were covertly quantifies over them. This again looks like massive ontological commitment by the back door. Here we have the added difficulty that Leśniewski professed not to understand what a set is (Lejewski, 1967a, p.442). What is more, in order to provide extensions for all categories of expression, we should need to proceed through all finite levels in the set-theoretic hierarchy with the domain as our urelements. Leśniewski would have been deeply unhappy with this.

I said that this is the Küng-Canty account in its most straightforward form. Being as it were a back-door Platonism, no wonder Küng is forced to describe it as a 'nominalism *sui generis*' (Küng, 1977a, p.40)! But in later papers Küng has developed his idea of a prologue-functor, which allows us to be more discriminating. The idea of a prologue-functor reading for the quantifiers is that the quantifier and its associated variable(s) form a prologue, in which each such variable is *quoted*, to the rest (the body) of the sentence, in which the variables occur. This is not itself quoted, but *displayed* by being *run through* or *executed* in the normal fashion. So we can give a prologue reading to all kinds of quantification. For objectual nominal quantification "for all *a*: ϕa" may be read as

> "whatever '*a*' may be taken to denote, the following is asserted: ϕa",

a (Platonistic) substitutional reading as

> "whatever is substituted for '*a*' the following comes out true: ϕa"

(for a nominalistic reading see Küng, 1977, p.311), while the Küng-Canty reading is

> "whatever extension '*a*' may be taken to have, the following is true: ϕa".

There is textual evidence that Leśniewski might have found this acceptable: as Küng points out (Küng 1977, p.319; 1977a, p.39), in an early paper Leśniewski used the ordinary language reading "przy każdem znaczeniu wyrazu '*a*'","for every meaning of the expression '*a*'". Here 'meaning' is closer to Frege's *Bedeutung* than to his *Sinn*. Since, matters of *Sinn* aside, for Frege and Russell meaning *is bedeuten*, denoting, we can see how Leśniewski missed the difference between his quantification and Russell's (Küng, 1977, p. 319). But this textual evidence is insufficient to convict Leśniewski of countenancing sets. For it is not clear that for an expression to be meaningful, we must take there to be a set which it has as extension. Küng I think is beginning to move in this direction when he tries to insist that his reading is nominalistically acceptable because it does not *objectify* extensions (Küng, 1977a, p.38ff., p.52). This I take it means naming them by singular terms. Yet he still steers too close to the wind in taking the meanings to be extensions, and these to be sets (1977, p.318). If extensions are sets, they are already objectified, even if the singular terms naming them do not appear in the object language. A nominalist of Küng's stamp is a nominalist with double standards.

We ought to lay the ghost of the denotational theory of meaning which still haunts Küng's account. We could perhaps take a first step by offering a variant reading for Leśniewskian quantifiers as "whatever '*a*' is taken to mean" or "however '*a*' is interpreted". It is somehow less tempting to hypostatise "evers" or ways of meaning than it is if meaning consists in having something else, an extension. We can then say for various expressions what ways they can (extensionally) mean: sentences by being true or false, names by denoting no objects, one particular object, or several particular objects. We must of course *distinguish* different ways of meaning - being true is not the same as being false, etc. But if we look on ways of meaning more as alternative possibilities or routes to objects and truth, where for higher functors the routes become more tortuous, and take account of the lower level possibilities, then I think we are on the right lines. The semantics of functors then becomes in a sense *combinatorial* rather than referential, and it is more plausible to resist reification of ways and combinations than it is to resist (*per impossibile*) reification of sets. I think the germ of the idea of combinatorial semantics can be found in Wittgenstein's *Tractatus*. Wittgenstein criticised the (referential) Fregean account of propositional connectives as standing for truth-functions or sentences as standing for truth-values. Unfortunately most modern treatments follow Frege rather than Wittgenstein, who after all retained the referential account for names. In this respect one might claim that Leśniewski went still further.

We can now see why Leśniewski does not need substitutional quantification. He has all the expressions he needs right there in the prologue, namely the (token of the) quoted variable. We are then instructed to consider the various ways this may be meaningful in the mini-context which follows, the body of the sentence, and see whether we always, sometimes or never get truth. Yet the idea of substitution also gets its due: constant expressions, unlike variables, mean (perhaps relative to a domain) in only one way, but this way is one of the ways in which the variable ones may mean. So universal instantiation is explained because if the body of the quantified sentence is true no matter how the variable means, it is true when it means in the same way as the constant, so replacing the variable by the constant which means this way results in a true sentence. And dually for introducing the particular quantifier. The same sort of idea explains the validity of the distribution rule for universal quantification. Variations within variations always produce truth iff all variations carried out simultaneously do so.

4. BRIEF PRESENTATION OF ONTOLOGY

4.1 Nomenclature

All the formulae displayed are given compound tags consisting of a string of letters and perhaps a distinguishing numeral. The first letter signifies the system: 'O' for Ontology and 'O_1'-'O_4'

for its extensions. The next letter or letters give the status of the formula: 'A' for axioms, 'D' for Leśniewskian definitions, 'DS' for definitional schemata, 'ES' for extensionality schemata, and 'T' for theorems. Of these, the axioms, definitions and theorems are *theses*. Also any substitution instance of a definitional or extensionality schema is a thesis.

4.2 Notation

We use the following signs for sentential connectives: $\sim \wedge \vee \supset \equiv$, which are assumed to bind their arguments in the order given, with negation strongest and material equivalence weakest, unless overridden by parentheses or dots according to the system of Church, 1956, pp.75ff. The universal and particular quantifier are written respectively Π and Σ. Following Leśniewski we use special brackets, the upper corners $\ulcorner\ \urcorner$, to mark quantifier scope. Again these are omitted where no ambiguity results. This use of corners has nothing to do with Quinean quasi-quotation; it is simply that as a style of bracket corners leave the line nicely uncluttered. In Ontology there are no unbound variables in theses: every thesis is a sentence. But where a universal quantifier has the whole of a formula as its scope we conventionally omit the quantifier. No ambiguity results from doing so, and the convention is turned to good use later on.

The single primitive constant of Ontology is the binary predicate ε. A sentence '$a\ \varepsilon\ b$' is true iff 'a' designates exactly one object, 'b' designates one or more objects, and the object designated by 'a' is one of the one or more objects designated by 'b'. We may accordingly read '$a\ \varepsilon\ b$' as "a is one of b" (for a defence of this reading see Simons, 1982).

4.3 Definitions

Definitions in Leśniewski's sense are allowed to have one of the following two forms. Propositive definitions take the form

$$\text{ODS1} \quad \Pi\alpha_1 \ldots \ulcorner \phi(\alpha_1 \ldots) \equiv A \urcorner$$

where ϕ is the definiendum, a propositive expression (a sentence if there are no α_i), the α_i are variables of any category already introduced into the system, each of which occurs only once in $\phi(\alpha_1 \ldots)$, they are the only variables occurring free in the formula A, and this of course contains neither ϕ nor any other constant sign which has not previously been introduced. This form of definition is already present in Protothetic, where it may be used to define constant true and false sentences and all the sentential connectives apart from equivalence (how to define conjunction was the subject of Tarski's Ph.D. dissertation under Leśniewski). We use propositive definitions here mainly to define predicates.

Nominative definitions take the form

$$\text{ODS2} \quad \Pi a\alpha_1 \ldots \ulcorner a\ \varepsilon\ \Phi[\alpha_1 \ldots] \equiv a\ \varepsilon\ a \wedge A \urcorner$$

where the definiendum Φ is a nominative expression (a name if it has no arguments), the α_i are variables of previously introduced category, each occurring only once as argument of Φ and being, with a, the only free variables in the formula A. The clause $a\ \varepsilon\ a$ secures us against paradox-generating definitions. Were we to omit it, the following would be a well-formed definition: $\Pi a \ulcorner a\ \varepsilon\ R \equiv {\sim} a\ \varepsilon\ a \urcorner$. We could then obtain the analogue of Russell's Paradox by instantiating for R. Other forms are possible for nominative definitions which also block paradoxes, but this is the most straightforward.

If we were to define particular quantification dually to universal in the usual way as $\Sigma\alpha_1\ldots\alpha_n\ulcorner A\urcorner \equiv \sim\Pi\alpha_1\ldots\alpha_n\ulcorner\sim A\urcorner$ then we should notice that this scheme is neither propositive nor nominative, which is not surprising given that the quantifiers have no category. Leśniewski's own official language does not contain the particular quantifier, and this is perhaps the reason. When using Peano-Russell notation however Leśniewski did avail himself of the particular, which he seems to have regarded as an abbreviation, which is to say, the above is a definition not in his but in the more usual sense. We shall use further non-Leśniewskian definitions for other quantifiers below. One might square this discrepancy either by liberalising the rules of definition, or by bringing quantifiers within the ambit of propositive definitions by letting there be infinitely many universals, one for each category of variable, in the fashion of Church, 1940. Or one can regard the defined symbols as abbreviations. Nothing seems to turn on choosing between the first and third options for our purposes, so we leave the issue unsettled.

4.4 Axiom and Extensionality

The single ("long" - 1920) axiom of Ontology is

$$\text{OA}\quad a \,\varepsilon\, b \equiv \Sigma c\ulcorner c \,\varepsilon\, a\urcorner \wedge \Pi c\ulcorner c \,\varepsilon\, a \supset c \,\varepsilon\, b\urcorner \wedge$$
$$\wedge\ \Pi cd\ulcorner c \,\varepsilon\, a \wedge d \,\varepsilon\, a \supset c \,\varepsilon\, d\urcorner$$

Here the three clauses on the right hand side are analogous to those in a Russellian contextual definitions of a definite description. This axiom more than any of those which succeeded it makes the intended meaning of ε clear, and amounts to a kind of implicit definition of ε.

In addition to the rules of substitution, detachment and quantifier distribution, Ontology also embodies a principle of extensionality for each syntactic category, which conforms to the following schema for propositive categories

OES1 $\Pi\alpha_1 \ldots \ulcorner \phi(\alpha_1 \ldots) \equiv \psi(\alpha_1 \ldots) \urcorner \equiv \Pi f \ulcorner f(\phi) \equiv f(\psi) \urcorner$

Here if the propositive expressions ϕ and ψ are of category X, then the variable f has category S/X. For nominative expressions the extensionality schema is

OES2 $\Pi\alpha_1 \ldots \ulcorner \Pi a \ulcorner a \;\varepsilon\; \Phi[\alpha_1 \ldots] \equiv a \;\varepsilon\; \Psi[\alpha_1 \ldots] \urcorner \equiv \Pi F \ulcorner F(\Phi) \equiv F(\Psi) \urcorner \urcorner$

where again if the nominative variables Φ and Ψ have category Y, then F has category S/Y.

4.5 Some Definitions

The following are all propositive definitions. We define a predicate of existence (read: "there is an/at least one (of) *a*", "an *a* exists")

OD1 $\mathrm{E}a \equiv \Sigma c \ulcorner c \;\varepsilon\; a \urcorner$

uniqueness or non-plurality (read: "there is at most one of *a*")

OD2 $!a \equiv \Pi cd \ulcorner c \;\varepsilon\; a \wedge d \;\varepsilon\; a \supset c \;\varepsilon\; d \urcorner$

and unique existence or individuality ("there is exactly one of *a*", "*a* is an individual").

OD3 $\mathrm{E}!a \equiv \mathrm{E}a \wedge !a$

Readings are throughout approximate only: there is no perfect fit between Ontology and ordinary English, but the readings may help convey the intended meaning.

Next come predicates to do with identity: firstly neutral or unrestricted identity ("*a* is/are the same (individual(s)) as *b*")

OD4 $a \simeq b \equiv \Pi c \ulcorner c \; \varepsilon \; a \equiv c \; \varepsilon \; b \urcorner$

non-plural identity

OD5 $a \approx b \equiv \; !a \wedge a \simeq b$

and singular identity ("*a* is the same individual as *b*", "*a* is identical with *b*")

OD6 $a = b \equiv \mathrm{E}!a \wedge a \simeq b$

Only the first of these predicates deserves to be called identity in the logical sense, since it is the only one which conforms to the Leibnizian Law

OT1 $a \simeq b \equiv \Pi F \ulcorner F(a) \equiv F(b) \urcorner$

which follows directly from OD4 and the extensionality principle for names. The following nominative definition defines a standard empty term:

OD7 $a \; \varepsilon \; \Lambda \equiv a \; \varepsilon \; a \wedge \sim(a \; \varepsilon \; a)$

Restricted quantifiers may be defined as follows:

ODS8 $\forall aA \equiv \Pi a \ulcorner \mathrm{E}a \supset A \urcorner$

ODS9 $\exists aA \equiv \Sigma a \ulcorner \mathrm{E}a \wedge A \urcorner$

Unlike the unrestricted quantifiers, they do not satisfy the law of subalternation.

5. SYSTEM O_1: EMBEDDING CLASSICAL LOGIC

The nominal variables of Ontology may be empty or plural, and so do not share the limitations of the singular terms of classical logic. We can however extend the language of Ontology with a new run of singular variables x, y, ... which are non-plural, have values in all non-empty domains, are interchangeable with the neutral variables of Ontology where singulars are appropriate, and we add furthermore to Ontology the Leibniz-Heidegger axiom that there is something rather than nothing. These principles are formulated as

O_1A1 $\Pi xab \ulcorner a \varepsilon x \wedge b \varepsilon x \supset a \varepsilon b \urcorner$ (i.e. $\Pi x \ulcorner !x \urcorner$)
O_1A2 $\Pi x \ulcorner \Sigma a \mathrm{E}a \supset \mathrm{E}x \urcorner$
O_1A3 $\Pi x \Sigma a \ulcorner x \simeq a \urcorner$
O_1A4 $\Pi a \ulcorner \mathrm{E}!a \supset \Sigma x \ulcorner x \simeq a \urcorner \urcorner$
O_1A5 $\Sigma a \mathrm{E}a$

The first, second and fifth axioms ensure that every singular variable is non-empty. Therefore when only singular variables are bound, restricted and unrestricted quantification are equivalent. Since the classical quantificational principles apply to Π, Σ, they carry over to $\forall$, $\exists$, when these bind singulars. In particular we get subalternation, as in classical logic.

If we consider those theses of the thus extended Ontology O_1 in which only singular variables occur, bound only by restricted quantifiers, and the only constant predicate is '=', then it is clear that this includes all the principles of first-order predicate logic with identity, with one difference: where first-order predicate logic has free predicate variables, those in Ontology occurring in such sentences must be initially bound by Π. However in our convention we may omit such quantifiers, so the result is "optically" indistinguishable from a sentence in first-order logic. The effect of substituting predicates for predicate letters in first-order logic may be attained in this extension of Ontology by instantiation and definition. Systems of logic with free singular variables may also be given optically identical formulae of O_1 by binding these variables "invisibly" at the front with Π.

Since every singular term may be replaced by a neutral one, and the restricted quantifiers are eliminable, every formula in which singular variables and restricted quantification occur may be proved equivalent to one containing the expressions of unextended Ontology only. The axioms of first-order predicate logic with identity are therefore provably equivalent in O_1 to formulae which are theorems of the system O^+ of Ontology extended by the non-logical axiom O_1A5, and the inference rules are admissible.

One application of this embedding is that if we extend O^+ to a system M^+ of Mereology, it is possible to define mereological predicates which look like and have the same meaning as those in the Calculus of Individuals, while the Leonard-Goodman sum or fusion operator σ may be defined for non-complex predicates using the Mereological name-forming equivalent. I have dealt with this at slightly greater length elsewhere (Simons 198., Ch.2).

6. SYSTEM O_2: EMBEDDING UNIVERSAL LOGIC

Like classical logic, O_1 and O^+ commit us to the existence of at least one individual, which is, as Russell once admitted, a defect in logical purity. This was one reason for the dissatisfaction with classical logic which motivated the development of free logics in the Russellian mould. A logic where the theorems are valid even for the empty domain is called a universal logic, and we may obtain one with identity by simply dropping the incriminating axiom O_1A5, calling the resulting system O_2. In this system the subalternation principle for $\forall$ and $\exists$ fails even for singular variables: what we have left is the weaker scheme $\exists xB \supset. \forall xA \supset \exists xA$. The theorems of this system have equivalents in Ontology which are theorems of that system without requiring that something exists.

7. SYSTEM O_3: EMBEDDING FREE LOGICS

A second principle which classical logic accepts and which is rejected in free logic is that all individual parameters or free variables denote. Characteristic of free logic is dropping the assumption that parameters denote even on non-empty domains. This is usually reflected by distinguishing parameters from bound variables, as the quantifiers in free logic have the same meaning as they do in classical logic. To capture this kind of system we enlarge the language of O_1 and O_2 by adding a second run of non-plural variables s, t, ... subject to the following non-plurality and interchangeability conditions:

O_3A1 $\Pi s \ulcorner !s \urcorner$

O_3A2 $\Pi s \Sigma a \ulcorner s \simeq a \urcorner$

O_3A3 $\Pi a \ulcorner !a \supset \Sigma s \ulcorner s \simeq a \urcorner \urcorner$

These are, except for the last, similar to O_1A1-3, but O_1A4 commits the variables x, y, ... to denoting on all non-empty domains, whereas this does not apply to the new run. The system obtained by adding these variables and axioms to O_2 (N.B. not O_1) we call O_3. Chracteristic for O_3 is the lack of the usual principles of universal instantiation $\forall xA \supset A[s/x]$ and existential generalisation $A[s/x] \supset \exists xA$; we have only the weaker versions obtained from these by prefixing them with the condition E!*s*.

The identity predicate of Ontology which most resembles that usually employed in free logics is $\approx$, which is unrestrictedly reflexive on both runs of non-plural variables. In free logics with identity singular existence is defined: this definition is captured in O_3 by the theorem

O_3T1 $\Pi s \ulcorner E!s \equiv \exists x \ulcorner x \approx s \urcorner \urcorner$

Because O_3 is based on Ontology, we get the extensional result that "all non-existents are identical":

O_3T2 $\Pi st \ulcorner {\sim}E!s \wedge {\sim}E!t \supset s \approx t \urcorner$

Not all free logics have this as a theorem.

The theorems of a free logic with parameters, non-plural identity and existence and satisfying this extensionality condition may be represented as theorems of O_3 with the difference that the otherwise free variables, *s*, *t*, ... and the predicate variables, are initially bound by Π, which however we conventionally omit for optical effect. The advantage of making these quantifiers explicit as in Ontology is that they declare openly the claim to universality which theorems with free variables make tacitly. With Π at the front we are doing in this context what Frege with his Latin letters and Quine with '$\vdash$' do in the classical context.

The system O_3 may add definite descriptions. These may be readily captured in Leśniewskian systems by *explicit* nominative definitions. We here give a scheme for all such definitions, where it may be noted that the only use of non-neutral variables is in the operator itself:

$O_3DS1 \quad \Pi a \ulcorner a \, \varepsilon \, \iota xA \equiv a \, \varepsilon \, a \wedge A[a/x] \wedge \Pi b \ulcorner b \, \varepsilon \, b \wedge A[b/x] \supset b \, \varepsilon \, a \urcorner \urcorner$

This scheme allows us to derive the principles governing descriptions in Lambert and van Fraassen's system FD_2 of free logic with descriptions (see their 1967), namely

$O_3T3 \quad \forall y \ulcorner y \approx \iota xA \equiv \forall x \ulcorner A \supset x \approx y \wedge A[y/x] \urcorner \urcorner$

and an extensionality principle derivable immediately from O_3T1-2.

While we are here defining an expression for the individual such that A, it is worth noting in passing that we can also define a singular-or-plural (neutral) definite description, the individual or individuals such that A, according to the following scheme

$O_3DS2 \quad \Pi a \ulcorner a \, \varepsilon \, \hat{x}A \equiv a \, \varepsilon \, a \wedge A[a/x] \urcorner$

where we simply drop the uniqueness condition. Any resemblance to the axiom scheme of comprehension in naive set theory is purely intentional, but the clause $a \, \varepsilon \, a$ once more saves from paradox: we have simply

$O_3T4 \quad \hat{x} \ulcorner {\sim} x \, \varepsilon \, x \urcorner \approx \Lambda$

A different kind of free logic using non-plural variables has been developed from a Leśniewskian standpoint by Lejewski (1967). He uses as primitives the unrestricted quantifiers Π Σ and singular identity =, and adapts Leśniewskian principles of definition and extensionality to this context. We need only the variables s, t, ... to represent this system, and it can be readily checked that his axiom is a theorem:

$O_3T5 \quad \Pi ss't \ulcorner s = s' \equiv \Sigma t \ulcorner t = s \wedge t = s' \urcorner \urcorner$

and that his definition and extensionality schemata are also admissible:

O_3DS3 $\Pi s\alpha_1\ldots\ulcorner s = \Phi[\alpha_1\ldots] \equiv \phi(s) \wedge \Pi t\ulcorner\phi(t) \supset s = t\urcorner\urcorner$
O_3ES $\Pi\phi\psi\ulcorner\Pi s\alpha_1\ldots\ulcorner s = \Phi[\phi\alpha_1\ldots] \equiv s = \Phi[\psi\alpha_1\ldots]\urcorner \equiv \Pi F\ulcorner F(\phi) \equiv F(\psi)\urcorner\urcorner$

It was shown in Lambert and Scharle (1967) that there are principles of translation between this system and the system FD_2, and these translation rules hold also in O_3 provided we use the same run of variables, either x, y, ... or s, t, ..., in the formulation of both systems. In particular the quantifiers are connected by OD8 (adapted for the right variables) and

O_3T6 $\Pi sA \equiv \forall sA \wedge A[\Lambda/s]$

and dually for the particulars.

By virtue of the ubiquity of neutral variables and the definitions of unrestricted quantifiers, as well as the infinite sheaf of definitions covered by the definition schema for definite descriptions, every formula of O_3 may be shown to be equivalent to one in which only the vocabulary of unextended Ontology O occurs, so the extensions add only sentences which say something that can be already said (perhaps in a more roundabout way) in Ontology.

8. SYSTEM O_4: EMBEDDING A FREE LOGIC WITH PLURAL TERMS

The final system which can be embedded in an extension of Ontology is the one which is also closest to it in intent, namely my own system of empty, singular and plural terms (see Simons, 1982a). This differs from Ontology in using the restricted quantifiers $\forall\exists$ and in using separate runs for free and bound variables. It is thus a sort of cross between Ontology and free logic. Unlike Ontology it is based on the functor of strong inclusion $\Subset$ (also written '$\sqsubset$') defined thus

OD10 $a \Subset b \equiv \Sigma c\ulcorner c \; \varepsilon \; a\urcorner \wedge \Pi c\ulcorner c \; \varepsilon \; a \supset c \; \varepsilon \; b\urcorner$

The following theorem of Ontology shows it can be based on $\Subset$ alone (see Lejewski, 1958):

OT2 $a \; \varepsilon \; b \equiv a \Subset b \wedge \Pi c\ulcorner c \Subset a \supset a \Subset c\urcorner$

This difference is therefore inessential - the system could have been based on ε instead. In an effort to capture some of the features of plural terms in natural languages I had, besides the neutral terms of Ontology and the non-plural (singular-or-empty) ones we have met here, also non-singular (plural-or-empty) terms. Since there are two runs for each sort, there are no fewer than six runs of variable in my system, so we need to add three more to those of O_3. Firstly there are "bound" neutrals u, v, ... which, like the "bound" singulars x, y, ... are empty only on the empty domain:

O_4A1 $\Pi u\ulcorner \Sigma a\mathrm{E}a \supset \mathrm{E}u\urcorner$
O_4A2 $\Pi u \Sigma a\ulcorner u \simeq a\urcorner$
O_4A3 $\Pi a\ulcorner \mathrm{E}a \supset \Sigma u\ulcorner u \simeq a\urcorner\urcorner$

then non-singular variables i, j, ... for which

O_4A4 $\Pi i\ulcorner \mathrm{E}i \equiv \Sigma ab\ulcorner a \; \varepsilon \; i \wedge b \; \varepsilon \; i \wedge a \neq b\urcorner\urcorner$
O_4A5 $\Pi i \Sigma a\ulcorner i \simeq a\urcorner$
O_4A6 $\Pi a\ulcorner \sim\mathrm{E}!a \supset \Sigma i\ulcorner i \simeq a\urcorner\urcorner$

and finally non-singular "bound" variables m, n, ... for which, in addition to axioms O_4A7-9 exactly analogous to O_4A4-6 we have

O_4A10 $\Pi m\ulcorner \Sigma ab\ulcorner a \; \varepsilon \; a \wedge b \; \varepsilon \; b \wedge a \neq b\urcorner \supset \mathrm{E}m\urcorner$

The following definite description operators for neutral and non-singular variables define the union or maximum of all classes or pluralities such that A. This corresponds to one use of 'the' in ordinary language (see Sharvy (1980), Simons (1983) for more on this).

$$O_4DS1 \quad a \; \varepsilon \; \imath uA \equiv a \; \varepsilon \; a \wedge \Sigma u \ulcorner a \; \varepsilon \; u \wedge A \urcorner$$

$$O_4DS2 \quad a \; \varepsilon \; \imath mA \equiv a \; \varepsilon \; a \wedge \Sigma m \ulcorner a \; \varepsilon \; m \wedge A \urcorner$$

Russellian uniqueness descriptions may also be added for other variables. Now all the axioms and rules of my system are derivable within O_4, modulo the usual employment of Π to invisibly bind otherwise free variables. One axiom alone appears not to be derivable; this is an analogue of Zermelo's Disjoint Choice Principle (see Simons, 1982a, p.235).

By virtue of the ubiquity of neutral variables and the eliminability of restricted quantifiers, this language too says nothing that cannot be said, perhaps in a more roundabout way, in Ontology. The complications arose not from a love of complication *per se*, but rather in an attempt to mimic certain features of the logical behaviour of terms in natural language which are explicitly marked for singular or plural number.

9. MORAL. OPEN QUESTIONS AND FURTHER POSSIBILITIES

If we are looking for an extensional logic which combines maximum power with elegance, it seems we need look no further than Ontology. But sometimes for convenience we can use more restricted variables, and be sure we are not adding new substance to the system.

Arising from our comparisons are a number of interesting open issues concerning the relation between Ontology and other systems. Is the following Disjoint Choice Principle independent of Ontology?

$$\text{DJP}\quad \Pi\phi\ulcorner\Sigma a\ulcorner \mathrm{E}a \wedge \phi a\urcorner \wedge \Pi ab\ulcorner\phi a \wedge \phi b \wedge {\sim}a \simeq b \supset \mathrm{E}a \wedge \mathrm{E}b$$
$$\wedge {\sim}\Sigma c\ulcorner c\ \varepsilon\ a \wedge c\ \varepsilon\ b\urcorner\urcorner \supset \Sigma a\ulcorner\Pi b\ulcorner\phi b \supset \Sigma c\ulcorner c\ \varepsilon\ a \wedge c\ \varepsilon\ b$$
$$\wedge\ \Pi d\ulcorner d\ \varepsilon\ a \wedge d\ \varepsilon\ b \supset c = d\urcorner\urcorner\urcorner\urcorner\urcorner$$

Does it imply the Generalised Choice Principle expressed thus (cf. Davis, 1975)?

$$\text{GCP}\quad \Sigma\Phi\ulcorner\Pi ab\ulcorner a\ \varepsilon\ b \supset \Phi[b]\ \varepsilon\ b\urcorner\urcorner$$

Given that in Leśniewski we have potentially all types available, how does the simple theory of types look if we extend a Platonised Ontology with singular variables and their equivalents at each type? Does this then enable us to simulate class theory à la Russell? (Lejewski has some unpublished work which suggests that set theory can be simulated quite nicely within higher categories.) Conversely, what do classical and free logics look like if we treat them à la Leśniewski as growing systems? (Lejewski (1967) gives us a fair idea how this would go.)

More radically, what would an *intensional* logic look like if formulated in Leśniewskian fashion? How about adding λ-abstraction to Ontology or to an intensional logic and simplifying the use of definitions? If we are persuaded of the virtues of Leśniewskian logic, then these and similar questions need to be dealt with if working logicians and mathematicians are ever to be brought to adopt it and rescue it from its present esoteric status.

REFERENCES

Church, A., 1940, A Formulation of the Simple Theory of Types, JSL, 5:56-68.

Church, A., 1956, "Introduction to Mathematical Logic," Princeton UP, Princeton.

Dąmbska, I., 1978, François Brentano et la pensée philosophique en Pologne: Casimir Twardowski et son école, Grazer Phil. Studien, 5:117-130.

Davis, C. C., 1975, An Investigation Concerning the Hilbert-Sierpiński Logical Form of the Axiom of Choice, NDJFL, 16:145-184.

Küng, G., 1977, The Meaning of the Quantifiers in the Logic of Leśniewski, Studia Logica, 26:309-322.

Küng, G., 1977a, Nominalistische Logik heute, Allg. Zeitschr. f. Phil., 2:29-52.

Küng, G. and Canty, J. T., 1970, Substitutional Quantification and Leśniewskian Quantifiers, Theoria, 36:165-182.

Lambert, K. and Scharle, T., 1967, A Translation Theorem for Two Systems of Free Logic, Logique et analyse, 10:328-341.

Lejewski, C., 1958, On Leśniewski's Ontology, Ratio, 1:150-176.

Lejewski, C., 1967, A Theory of Non-reflexive Identity and its Ontological Ramifications, in: "Grundfragen der Wissenschaften und ihre Wurzeln in der Metaphysik," P. Weingartner, ed., Pustet, Salzburg.

Lejewski, C., 1967a, Leśniewski, Stanisław, in: "Encyclopedia of Philosophy," P. Edwards, ed., Macmillan, New York, Vol.4:441-443.

Luschei, E. C., 1962, "The Logical Systems of Leśniewski," North-Holland, Amsterdam.

Quine, W. V. O., 1969, "Ontological Relativity and Other Essays," Columbia UP, New York.

Sharvy, R., 1980, A More General Theory of Definite Descriptions, Phil. Review, 89:607-624.

Simons, P. M., 1982, On Understanding Leśniewski, Hist. and Phil. of Logic, 3:165-191.

Simons, P. M., 1982a, Plural Reference and Set Theory, in: "Parts and Moments," B. Smith, ed., Philosophia, Munich.

Simons, P. M., 1983, Class, Mass and Mereology, Hist. and Phil. of Logic, 4:157-180.

Simons, P. M., 198., "Parts. A Study in Ontology," forthcoming.

Sobociński, B., 1967, Successive Simplifications of the Axiom-system of Leśniewski's Ontology, _in_: "Polish Logic 1920-1939," S. McCall, ed., Oxford UP, Oxford.

Van Fraassen, B. C. and Lambert, K., 1967, On Free Description Theory, _Zeitschr. f. math. Logik u. Grundlagen d. Mathematik_, 13:225-240.

FOUNDATIONS OF LINGUISTICS: LOGIC AND LANGUAGE

ALGEBRAIC MODELS OF CATEGORIAL GRAMMARS

Wojciech Buszkowski

Institute of Mathematics
Adam Mickiewicz University
Poznań, Poland

Categorial grammars (the term introduced by Bar Hillel et al. (1960)) are the formal grammars which comprise two basic constituents: (1) an initial type assignment, i.e., a function which assigns a finite set of syntactic types to each atomic expression (word) of a given language, (2) a system of type reduction laws which enables one to produce the terminal type assignment, i.e., a function which assigns a set of syntactic types to each expression of that language (cf. Marcus (1967)). The types are intended to denote syntactic categories of expressions (we identify the categories with sets of expressions), and the type reduction laws reflect certain universal (that means, independent of a particular language) relations between categories. The very idea of categorial grammar should be credited to Ajdukiewicz (1935), though, of course, some origins can be traced back to Frege, Leśniewski, Tarski and others.

The concept of syntactic category underlies the very fundamentals of logic, philosophy of language, and mathematical linguistics. Accordingly it received a large number of explications, often only loosely connected with each other, being influenced by the tasks it was applied to. The one especially popular in last years rests upon a presupposed correspondence between syntactic structures and relations inside a (usually type-theoretic) semantics of language; syntactic categories (also called semantical categories) are to be identified with classes of those expressions which correspond to objects occupying a common semantical level. The approach had been anticipated by Tarski (1933), Bocheński (1947), and found a thorough elaboration in Suszko (1958, 1960), Montague (1974), Cresswell (1973), to mention some of the more prominent expositions. Especially the latter book exposes the idea of categorial syntax subordinate to a type-theoretic semantics in a fully conscious and consequent manner.

It is a characteristic feature of the "semantical" approach that each expression may be inserted into at most one syntactic category, namely that determined by its denotation (meaning, sense). Accordingly there remains no place for examining the reduction of categories, or more exactly, transformation of some categories into others. So, the second constituent of categorial grammar, as it was introduced in the first paragraph, actually disappears, if one neglects the trivial procedure of cancelling $(x/y)y$ to x, which corresponds to the "semantical" rule: if $f: X \rightarrow Y$, and $x \in X$, then $f(x) \in Y$.

On the other side, a detailed investigation of natural language structures discloses numerous situations where an expression of one syntactic category should also be considered as a member of other categories in order to accomplish a successful syntactic analysis of a more complex expression; that by no way is caused by the only syntactic ambiguity of some expressions (cf. Geach (1972), Heidrich (1979), van Benthem (1983)). It seems to be difficult to explain these phenomena without crossing the border-lines of "semantical" approach.

Fortunately a lucky way out of the troubles has been indicated as early, as in Lambek (1958). Surprisingly enough, that excellent paper did not influence the domain as much as it deserved to do. Perhaps it was caused by a too laconic style of Lambek's exposition. At any rate the most essential innovation was overlooked: simply supplying type reduction with a clear and natural algebraic semantics. Lambek and his followers (e.g. Cohen (1967), Lehrberger (1974)) put more emphasis on some peculiarities of a type reduction system (which we call Lambek Syntactic Calculus (LSC)) which indeed appears to be the most strong among classical systems of that kind (cf. Zielonka (1981)) and incorporates practically all the reduction laws proposed by Geach (1972), Montague (1974) and others to improve the syntactic analysis. More importantly, however, LSC may pretend to be called the complete reduction system, which means complete with respect to Lambek's semantics, and consequently the one best justified from the theoretical point of view. As a matter of fact, Lambek (1958) only claims his system be sound, which means all its theorems are universally valid.

By following Lambek's approach the present author (see the items quoted in references) managed to reveal a number of relevant properties of type reduction systems and categorial grammars, such as, e.g., completeness of such systems with respect to different variants of algebraic semantics, consistency and completeness of language description by means of categorial grammars, evaluating criteria for different sorts of categorial grammars, complexity of complete reduction systems, and so on. Some essential contributions have also been made by Zielonka (1981), (1981a), van Benthem (1983) and Došen (1984). Our aim in this paper is to survey the most characteristic results and to indicate some interesting directions of further research. A rather detailed presentation of these matters will appear in a forthcoming book (cf. Buszkowski (I)).

The very nature of our subject suggests we should proceed according to patterns being elaborated inside mathematical logic on the one hand and Chomsky's mathematical linguistics on the other. Accordingly the theory of categorial grammars may be viewed as connecting the two disciplines. It would be wrong to claim that categorial grammars in the algebraic setting attempt to compete with transformational grammars as well as with the "semantical" approach, for any championship. The author believes they simply form a necessary complement of and a mathematical advance in those great logico-linguistic enterprises.

Let me express the hope that the formal considerations given here will help linguists in a more effective application of categorial grammars to natural language. As rightly remarked by Batóg (1967), "a theory which is not sufficiently clear and precise will not work in practice, and the linguist who employs such a theory will be inclined to adjust it, for instance, to those features which are peculiar to the language he is examining or to the judgments of previous investigators of that language".

§1. SYNTACTIC CATEGORIES AND CATEGORY REDUCTION

We do not insist on any particular definition of syntactic category (cf. Hiż (1960), Lehrberger (1974) for details on that matter) since the concept does not play any fundamental role in our theory. More precisely, we assume categories may be quite arbitrary sets of expressions, and what is important is just some operations and relations on the totality of categories.

There is however a concept which needs to get a strict meaning at the very outset, namely that of (syntactic) functor. A clear algebraic interpretation of functor is given in Lambek (1958), although in an implicit manner. Given a set V, and $A, B \subseteq V^+$ (V^+ denotes the set of expressions over V, i.e., non-empty finite sequences of members of V), an expression $c \in V^+$ is called a right (resp.

left)-directed functor from A to B, if ca ∈ B (resp. ac ∈ B), for every a ∈ A; evidently, by ab we denote the juxtaposition (concatenation) of expressions a and b.

Starting from a family of sets of expressions (basic syntactic categories) one builds up an infinite hierarchy of functor categories. To mark the categories one uses structural indices, called (syntactic) types. We fix a countable set Pr of primitive types. The set Tp of types is the smallest set satisfying: (i) $Pr \subseteq Tp$, (ii) if x, y ∈ Tp then also (x/y), (x:y) ∈ Tp. We reserve the variables x, y, z (resp. p, q, r) to range over (resp. primitive) types, and the variables X, Y, Z to range over finite sequences of types. Any sequent X → x (X non-empty) will be called a reduction formula (r-formula), and the variable R is to range over sets of r-formulas.

By a category hierarchy (c-hierarchy) we mean any triple $M = (V_M, P_M, Cat_M)$, where V_M is a non-empty finite set (the vocabulary of M), $P_M \subseteq Pr$, and Cat_M is a function from P_M into the power-set of V_M^+. The sets $Cat_M(p)$, $p \in P_M$, are to be called basic (syntactic) categories in M. Now, the function Cat_M can be univocally extended to be defined on all the types built up from the primitive types in P_M (we denote that set of types by $Tp(P_M)$) by means of the recursive clause: $Cat_M(x/y)$ (resp. $Cat_M(y:x)$) consists of all the right (resp. left)-directed functors from $Cat_M(y)$ to $Cat_M(x)$. The sets $Cat_M(x)$, $x \notin Pr$, are to be called functor categories in M.

By CH we symbolize the class of c-hierarchies. Given M ∈ CH, a formula $x_1 \ldots x_n \to x$, where $x_i, x \in Tp(P_M)$, is said to be valid in M (write: $M \models x_1 \ldots x_n \to x$) if $Cat_M(x_1) \ldots Cat_M(x_n) \subseteq Cat_M(x)$. We write $M \models R$ if each formula in R is valid in M. We say that R CH-entails X → x if, for any M ∈ CH, $M \models X \to x$ whenever $M \models R$. An r-formula is said to be CH-valid if it is valid in all c-hierarchies M with a sufficiently large P_M.

The class of c-hierarchies coincides exactly with Lambek's algebraic semantics for categorial grammars. Given $M \in CH$, one interprets V_M to be the vocabulary of a language, and the categories in M to determine some linguistically relevant classes of expressions. Accordingly CH-valid formulas amount to "syntactic tautologies", that means, reduction laws which hold in all possible languages.

The classical type reduction system of Ajdukiewicz and Bar-Hillel produces exactly the r-formulas derivable from the axioms:

(1) $x \to x$, $(x/y)y \to x$, $x(x{:}y) \to y$, for $x, y \in Tp$,

by means of the inference rule:

(Cut) from $XyZ \to z$ and $Y \to y$ infer $XYZ \to z$.

That system, hereafter denoted by SCC (Simple Categorial Calculus) underlies Bar-Hillel's Categorial Grammars (BCG's; Bar-Hillel et al. (1960)), and is the one most frequently considered in the literature. Notice that also Cresswell (1973) and other representatives of "semantical" approach actually use the right-directional or :-free fragment of SCC.

There are, however, a number (infinite indeed) of CH-valid formulas which fail to be derivable in SCC, for instance:

(2) $x/y \to (x/z)/(y/z)$, $x{:}y \to (z{:}x){:}(z{:}y)$ (Geach's laws),
(3) $x \to y/(x{:}y)$, $x \to (y/x){:}y$ (Montague's laws),
(4) $(x/y)(y/z) \to x/z$, $(x{:}y)(y{:}z) \to x{:}z$ (Karlgren's laws).

The names we have attributed to (2) - (4) indicate the persons who have been concerned with their usefulness in syntactic analysis. As a matter of fact, all these laws were explicitly stated in Lambek

(1958) who also proposed a formal system, precisely LSC, capable of producing (2) - (4) and still more CH-valid r-formulas. LSC differs from SCC in that the former involves a wider collection of types; namely, apart from the right division / and left division : one respects the products sign •, to be interpreted as the concatenation of categories, that means, $Cat_M(x \cdot y) = Cat_M(x)Cat_M(y)$. For many purposes it is expedient to separate the conservative fragment of LSC restricted to product-free types. This calculus, to be denoted by L, can be axiomatized by supplying SCC with the new inference rules:

(/1) from $Xy \rightarrow x$ infer $X \rightarrow x/y$, (:1) from $xX \rightarrow y$ infer $X \rightarrow x{:}y$,

provided that X be non-empty.

By L(R) we denote the system that arises from L after one has added to it all the r-formulas in R as new axioms. We often identify the systems with their sets of theses. We also write R: $X \rightarrow x$ for "$X \rightarrow x$ belongs to R". We now state a simple but fundamental result (see Buszkowski (1982), (1985?) for the proof).

Completeness Theorem: L(R): $X \rightarrow x$ iff R CH-entails $X \rightarrow x$ (provided that the primitive types in $X \rightarrow x$ also appear in R). In particular, L: $X \rightarrow x$ iff $X \rightarrow x$ is CH-valid.

Accordingly the CH-complete systems of type reduction do coincide with the axiomatic extensions of L, and L yields exactly the CH-valid r-formulas. As shown by Zielonka (1981), no axiomatic extension of SCC by means of finitely many L-derivable axiom-schemas (as (2) - (4)) is equivalent to L, even in the scope of formulas $X \rightarrow p$. Consequently neither SCC nor other categorial calculi considered by different authors appear to be complete with respect to the standard algebraic semantics.

Perhaps an adequate semantics for those weak calculi can be obtained in the following way. For A, $B \subseteq V^+$, denote by (A/B) (resp. (B:A)) the set of right (resp. left)-directed functors from B to A. By a restricted category hierarchy (rc-hierarchy) we mean any triple $M = (V_M, P_M, Cat_M)$ where V_M, P_M have their previous meaning, and Cat_M is a function from $Tp(P_M)$ into the power-set of V_M^+ such that, for all x, $y \in Tp(P_M)$, $Cat_M(x/y) \subseteq Cat_M(x)/Cat_M(y)$ and $Cat_M(x:y) \subseteq$ $\subseteq Cat_M(x):Cat_M(y)$. One easily proves SCC be complete with respect to rc-hierarchies. Given an operator $F: P(V_M^+) \rightarrow P(V_M^+)$, satisfying $F(A) \subseteq A$, for all A, one may consider the rc-hierarchies M for which, for all x, $y \in Tp(P_M)$, $Cat_M(x/y) = F(Cat_M(x)/Cat_M(y))$, and similarly for x:y. Now, if $F(A)F(B) \subseteq F(AB)$ for all A, $B \subseteq V_M^+$, then a corresponding rc-hierarchy makes, e.g., (4) but not necessarily (2), (3) valid. We abandon a further exploration of these matters since their practical significance is yet not clear enough. In what follows we concentrate on our basic semantics CH (and some closely related variants) as it may pretend to be regarded as the simplest and most natural one, just as the two-element Boolean algebra for the case of propositional calculi.

The largest natural semantics for LSC consists of residuated semi-groups (cf. Fuchs (1963), Buszkowski (1984)), i.e., structures of the form $(A, \leq, \cdot, /, :)$, where $(A, \leq, \cdot)$ is a partially ordered semigroup, and /, : are binary operations on A, satisfying the equivalences:

(5) for a, b, $c \in A$, $a \leq c/b$ iff $a \cdot b \leq c$ iff $b \leq a:c$.

In fact, LSC amounts precisely to the atomic fragment of the elementary theory of residuated semigroups (cf. Buszkowski (1985?)). Evidently CH forms a fragment of the biggest semantics, as any structure $(P(V^+), \subseteq, \cdot, /, :)$, where A/B and A:B are to be defined as in the preceding paragraph, is a residuated semigroup; the latter structure will be called the residuated semigroup spread over the free semigroup V^+.

Though even that quite general semantics may be useful to model some kinds of category analysis, as, e.g., structures of categories of discontinuous phrases (cf. Hiż (1967)) or the structures considered by Došen (1984), for the majority of applications it suffices to deal with its proper subclass that consists of residuated semigroups spread over arbitrary semigroups, i.e. the structures $(P(G), \subseteq, \cdot, /, :)$ such that $(G, \cdot)$ is a semigroup, and, for $A, B \subseteq G$, the sets $A\cdot B$, A/B, $A:B$ are to be defined in the analogous way as it has been done for CH with substituting the operation $\cdot$ for concatenation. We denote the semantics by CH*. As it happens, CH* appears to be more appropriate for LSC than CH, since the consequence relation in LSC though CH*-complete fails to be CH-complete (cf. Buszkowski (1985?)). The question of whether LSC is CH-complete, although it is highly probable that it has a positive answer, seems to be difficult to solve.

An interesting fragment of CH* is CH_1, i.e., the residuated semigroups spread over free monoids V^* (instead of free semigroups V^+, as in CH). The models in CH_1 correspond to category analysis regarding the empty expression as a possible member of syntactic categories. Notice that CH_1 is not equivalent to CH, as, e.g., the formula $x/(y/y) \rightarrow x$ is CH_1-valid but not CH-valid. The system L_1 that produces the CH_1-valid r-formulas can be axiomatized by simply allowing L to deal with formulas $\rightarrow x$ (that means, $X \rightarrow x$ with X empty) and dropping the limitation "X is non-empty" in (/1), (:1) (this elegant axiomatization of L_1 was introduced by Zielonka (1981a)). Of course, L_1 is a proper extension of L, and the full analogue of the completeness theorem for L holds for L_1, if one replaces CH by CH_1 (for $M \in CH_1$, one defines $M \models \rightarrow x$ to mean that the empty expression be in $Cat_M(x)$). Evidently a similar extension can be constructed for

LSC. The extended calculus LSC_1 is complete with respect to CH_1^*, i.e., the residuated semigroups spread over monoids, and again its CH_1-completeness remains a hypothesis.

In the rest of this section we shall be concerned with an attractive way to accomplish category analysis with partial functors inside Lambek's framework. For an example of partial functor let us remember Lambek's (1961) observation concerning the category of pronouns. In particular, Lambek finds that "him" fails to be of category (s/n):s, as may be expected from patterns like "John likes him", since, for instance, there are non-sentences of the form "John likes poor him" (of course, we now interprete s, n to denote the categories of English declarative sentences, and proper noun phrases, respectively). In our terminology "him" is just a partial functor from the category s/n to the category s (left-directed, of course). The example seems to be rather typical for the structure of natural language. After one has started from a small family of basic categories then many expressions may be qualified only as partial but not as total functors of a given type. A similar view of the role of partially effective syntactic operations may be found in Cresswell (1973).

To model the structure of partial functors (in one of the possible manners, and, presumably, the most fruitful one; cf. Buszkowski (1981)) we must slightly depart from the basic semantics CH. Given a set $U \subseteq V^*$, and $A, B \subseteq U$, an expression $c \in U$ will be called a right (resp. left)-directed functor over U from A to B, if, for every $a \in A$, either $ca \notin U$ (resp. $ac \notin U$) or $ca \in B$ (resp. $ac \in B$). By a modified category hierarchy (mc-hierarchy) we mean any quadruple $M = (V_M, U_M, P_M, Cat_M)$, where V_M, P_M have the previous meaning, $U_M \subseteq V_M^*$ satisfies the condition:

(6) for $a, b, c \in U_M$, if $abc \in U_M$ then, $ab \in U_M$ iff $bc \in U_M$,

and Cat_M maps $Tp(P_M)$ into the power-set of U_M according to the clause: for $x, y \in Tp(P_M)$, $Cat_M(x/y)$ (resp. $Cat_M(y:x)$) consists of the right (resp. left)-directed functors over U_M from $Cat_M(y)$ to $Cat_M(x)$. We define: $M \models x_1 \ldots x_n \to x$ ($x_i, x \in Tp(P_M)$) iff, for all $a_i \in Cat_M(x_i)$, the following holds: if $a_i a_{i+1} \ldots a_j \in U_M$, for all $1 \leq i < j \leq n$, then $a_1 \ldots a_n \in Cat_M(x)$. Notice that the condition (6) is needed to guarantee that each mc-hierarchy be isomorphic with a structure in CH*; after neglecting (6) the resulting structures do not satisfy the associative laws $(x \cdot y) \cdot z \to x \cdot (y \cdot z)$, $x \cdot (y \cdot z) \to (x \cdot y) \cdot z$ (when expanded by putting $Cat_M(x \cdot y) = Cat_M(x)Cat_M(y)) \cap U_M$), hence they satisfy the laws derivable in the non-associative LSC (cf. Lambek (1961)). At any rate, (6) appears to have a wide spectrum of interesting models, e.g., any set U closed under concatenation or under cutting non-empty subintervals (in the latter case we can simplify the definition of validity: $M \models x_1 \ldots x_n \to x$ iff $Cat_M(x_1) \ldots Cat_M(x_n) \cap U_M \subseteq Cat_M(x)$).

Let now $\overline{M}$ denote the mc-hierarchy determined by: $V_{\overline{M}}$ is the English vocabulary, $U_{\overline{M}}$ is the totality of connected parts of English declarative sentences, that means, of syntactically connected English expressions, $P_{\overline{M}}$ comprises s and n, and $Cat_{\overline{M}}(s)$, $Cat_{\overline{M}}(n)$ have the usual meaning. We conjecture that the categories $Cat_{\overline{M}}(x)$, for $x \in Tp(P_{\overline{M}})$, cover all the expressions in $U_{\overline{M}}$, that means, $\overline{M}$ represents a complete category analysis of English. Moreover the analogous statement should be true for any natural language. In particular, "him" falls into $Cat_{\overline{M}}((s/n):s)$, and this is not affected by the pattern "John likes poor him" since, although "John likes poor" is in $Cat_{\overline{M}}(s/n)$, the former pattern fails to be in $U_{\overline{M}}$. In order to improve the effectiveness of such an analysis one might replace $U_{\overline{M}}$ by its superset which would contain the expressions not breaking a finite number of prohibitions (cf. Cresswell (1973)).

Let us stress that the above-sketched approach to partial

functors (being the author's proposal despite some loose relations to certain general ideas of Cresswell (1973)) is by no way an *ad hoc* appendix to Lambek's theory but surely a natural expansion of it. The crucial point is to regard a wider collection of models for LSC which still remain directly connected with the natural language structure. For other improvements of that kind we refer the reader to Buszkowski (1984).

§2. CATEGORIAL GRAMMARS

In this section we discuss some relations between categorial grammars and the standard semantics CH. Each categorial grammar is to be regarded as a "formal theory" of one c-hierarchy determined by the grammar (the standard model of the grammar). We formulate some natural conditions of compatibility between the grammar and its standard model; they lead to relevant evaluating criteria for categorial grammars. According to these criteria, the grammars based on L (or L(R)'s) appear to form the most adequate sorts of categorial grammars with respect to the standard semantics. Accordingly the usage of complete type reduction systems rather than their weak subsystems is not only aesthetically preferable but results in concrete improvements of language description. That strongly shakes the tradition of preferring just the poor systems (finite or categorial calculi in Zielonka's (1981) terminology). We also show some advantages of employing the non-universal systems (L(R)'s) instead of the traditional universal ones (L and its subsystems). Perhaps all these matters are only provinces of the general theory, nevertheless they seem to reveal its spirit and power in an especially striking manner. A preliminary study in this area has been published in Buszkowski (1982) and (1982b); a detailed exposition will be contained in Buszkowski (I) and (II) (forthcoming).

Formally, a categorial grammar (c-grammar) G may be identified with a quintuple (V_G P_G, I_G, s_G, R_G), where: V_G is a non-empty finite set (the vocabulary of G); $P_G \subset Pr$ is non-empty finite; I_G is a function which to any v in V_G assigns a finite set of types in $Tp(P_G)$ (the initial type assignment of G); $s_G \in P_G$; R_G is a set of r-formulas (the reduction system of G). One defines a function T_G (the terminal type assignment of G) from $Tp(P_G)$ into the power set of V_G^+ by putting $v_1 \ldots v_n$ ($v_i \in V_G$) into $T_G(x)$ iff R_G: $x_1 \ldots x_n \to x$, for some $x_i \in I_G(v_i)$, $1 \leq i \leq n$. A c-grammar G will be called an R-grammar if $R_G = R$. The set $T_G(s_G)$ will be called the behaviour of G (we prefer this term rather than "language of G" since the latter better fits the c-hierarchy described by G).

In the classical literature on the subject we find the following intuition behind the concept of c-grammar. By means of a c-grammar G one intends to describe the syntactic categories of a given language Lan, particularly to determine the scopes of basic categories, e.g., the category of sentences. By some empirical tests one establishes certain categories of words, which amounts to defining some initial type assignment I_G. One also chooses a reduction system R_G, just determining the sort of G. Finally, the categories of Lan are to be identified (at least approximately) with the sets $T_G(x)$, for $x \in Tp(P_G)$, P_G standing for the set of types for basic categories. In particular, the behaviour of G is to be interpreted as the set of sentences in Lan.

Clearly, for the description given by G to be truly informative about the structure of Lan at least two things should be taken care of: (i) that I_G be compatible with the real categories of words in Lan, (ii) that R_G or at least a fragment of it comprise no formula not valid in Lan. Provided that both the requirements are fulfilled one attains a sufficiently correct description. More exactly, if (i) holds and Lan satisfies R_G in the scope of all r-formulas $X \to x$,

$X \in T^+$, $x \in T$, where T is a set of types containing all the types mentioned in I_G, then each expression in $T_G(x)$, for x in T, surely belongs to the category of type x in Lan. In order to guarantee (ii) the classical theory preferred to consider c-grammars based on universal reduction systems, i.e., those R-grammars in which R consisted of CH-valid formulas. At the same time it totally abandoned any formal analysis of (i) and simply left this matter to purely empirical judgments. In fact there was no other possibility, since the structure of Lan had been quite dark and vague for the examiner before it was explicated by the formalism of G (of course the picture reflects what happens when one tries to describe a natural language, not an artificial one being precisely codified by a ready grammar of whatever sort).

The key innovation of our approach consists in assuming that any c-grammar G determines exactly one c-hierarchy M(G), to be regarded as the language described by G. This assumption seems to agree with those respected in other branches of mathematical linguistics, for instance, the theory of production grammars. We define M(G) by the equalities: $V_{M(G)} = V_G$; $P_{M(G)} = P_G$; $Cat_{M(G)}(p) = T_G(p)$, for all p in P_G. The last equality may be justified by the primary task to be accomplished by c-grammars: to determine the scopes of syntactic categories, and especially basic categories. Now, all the functor categories of M(G) are univocally defined as in the paragraph introducing the concept of c-hierarchy. We write $Cat_G(x)$ instead of $Cat_{M(G)}(x)$, and call the set the category of type x in (the language described by) G. Sometimes we refer to M(G) as the standard model for G. Returning to the problem of natural language description, the relation between G and Lan can now be put more clearly. Again one constructs G, guided by certain empirical (and usually vague) data of the structure of Lan. If, however, one has decided to fix a particular G, then one has also established its model M(G). Accordingly the question of compatibility of G with Lan splits in two clearly separated parts: (a) compatibility of G with M(G), (b) compatibility of M(G) with Lan. Now, (a) admits a strictly formal treatment while (b) still remains the area of empirical investigation - just as in other domains of mathematical linguistics. In what follows we explore (a) to illuminate some advantages of CH-complete reduction systems in generating syntactic descriptions.

Of course, our results will be strongly influenced by our choice of CH as the underlying semantics. Analogous theorems may be proved for different variants of CH with respect to appropriate reduction systems and c-grammars (often without any essential alteration). Therefore one should look at the further contents as illustrating the method rather than agitating for a new "doctrine of grammar".

First we introduce three fundamental conditions to be satisfied by a c-grammar G compatible with M(G). For $T \subseteq Tp$, let Red(T) denote the set of all $X \rightarrow x$ such that $X \in T^+$, $x \in T$. A c-grammar G is said to be: (i) adequate, if $M(G) \models R_G \cap Red(Tp(P_G))$, (ii) correct (consistent), if $v \in Cat_G(x)$ whenever $x \in I_G(v)$, for all $v \in V_G$, $x \in Tp(P_G)$, (iii) T-complete ($T \subseteq Tp(P_G)$), if $T_G(x) = Cat_G(x)$, for all $x \in T$. Let Tp_G denote the union of all $I_G(v)$, for $v \in V_G$. G is said to be (resp. weakly) complete if it is $Tp(P_G)$ (resp. Tp_G)-complete.

In other words, a c-grammar is adequate if its standard model satisfies the reduction system in the scope of the types involved in the mode. Evidently, each universal c-grammar G, i.e., a grammar G with $R_G \subseteq L$, is adequate. G is correct if T_G does not contradict the structure of M(G); equivalently, G "tells us" the truth about M(G) but not necessarily the whole truth. Finally, G is T-complete (resp. weakly complete, resp. complete) if it exactly describes M(G) in the scope of categories whose types fall into T (resp. types are mentioned by I_G, resp. in the full extent). The following simple lemma shows the logical connections between these notions.

Lemma 1. (i) Each complete c-grammar is adequate and weakly complete. (ii) Each weakly complete c-grammar is correct. (iii) If G is adequate then the following conditions are equivalent: (a) G is correct, (b) $T_G(x) \subseteq Cat_G(x)$, for all $x \in Tp(P_G)$.

Clearly, correctness is a requirement which must be satisfied by a c-grammar G if one wishes to derive from I_G and T_G any sound judgments about syntactic structures of expressions in the language described by G. We shall need a preservation property of this notion.

Lemma 2. Let G be correct, $R_G \subseteq R$, and $M(G) \models R \cap Red(Tp(P_G))$. Then $G' = (V_G, P_G, I_G, s_G, R)$ is adequate and correct, and $M(G') =$ $= M(G)$.

Two c-grammars are said to be weakly equivalent if their behaviours are equal. It is usually non-trivial to establish weak equivalence between c-grammars of different sorts (cf. Bar-Hillel et al. (1960), Zielonka (1978), Buszkowski (1985)). On the other hand, lemma 2 yields a striking general result which we formulate for the case of universal grammars.

Proposition 1. If $R \subseteq L$ then, for any correct R-grammar G, there exists a correct L-grammar G' such that $M(G') = M(G)$, and consequently G' is weakly equivalent to G. Accordingly the behaviours as well as the standard models of correct universal grammars are precisely those of correct L-grammars.

A similar theorem holds for L(R)'s and non-universal c-grammars. Consequently, the c-grammars based on L and its axiomatic extensions are powerful enough to replace any other sort of c-grammars in correctly describing language structure.

Unfortunately there is no natural sort of c-grammars which are all correct (notice that, for R comprising all r-formulas, each R-grammar is correct and even complete). To avoid non-essential complications we again restrict ourselves to universal grammars.

Proposition 2. For any $R \subseteq L$, there exist non-correct R-grammars.

By lemma 2, it suffices to find a non-correct L-grammar. Let V_G consist of v and w ($v \neq w$), P_G of p and q ($p \neq q$), $s_G = p$, $R_G = L$, and let I_G assign p/(p/q) to v, and p/q to w. Then, $Cat_G(q) = T_G(q)$ is empty, hence $Cat_G(p/q) = V_G^+$. Accordingly, $v \in Cat_G(p/q)$ but $vv \notin T_G(p) = Cat_G(p)$. Therefore $v \notin Cat_G(p/(p/q))$ and G is non-correct. Of course we might abandon w in the example. We have regarded the second word as making the grammar G more natural with $Cat_G(p)$ non-empty.

To any type x one assigns a non-negative integer o(x), called the order of x, by the following recursion: $o(p) = 0$, for p in Pr; $o(x/y) = o(y{:}x) = \max(o(x), o(y) + 1)$ (this concept of order is essentially due to Tarski (1933)). The order of a c-grammar G (o(G)) is just the maximal order of types in Tp_G. Notice that the G constructed in the preceding paragraph is of order 2. In fact, any universal c-grammar of order less than 2 (provided that its reduction system extends SCC) is correct. We shall return to this fact in the next section.

We say that G is extendable to $\overline{G}$ if $V_G \subseteq V_{\overline{G}}$, $P_G = P_{\overline{G}}$, $I_{\overline{G}}$ coincides with I_G on V_G, and $R_{\overline{G}} = R_G$. Notice that, if G is extendable to $\overline{G}$, then $T_G(x) = T_{\overline{G}}(x) \cap V_G^+$, for all x in $Tp(R_G)$; accordingly $\overline{G}$ is somewhat like a conservative extension of G. We now state two more sophisticated theorems which explain some connections between completeness of reduction system on the one hand, and correctness (weak completeness) of c-grammar on the other (see Buszkowski (1982b), (I) for the proofs).

Characterization Theorem I. For any R, the following are equivalent: (i) R = L(R), (ii) each R-grammar is extendable to a weakly complete R-grammar.

Corollary 1. L-grammars are the only sort of universal c-grammar generally extendable to weakly complete c-grammars.

Proposition 3. If R is finite, then every L(R)-grammar is extendable to an adequate and weakly complete c-grammar.

We say that R_1 almost amounts to R_2 if, for all $X \in Tp^+$, and $p \in Pr$, $R_1: X \to p$ iff $R_2: X \to p$.

Characterization Theorem II. For any R, the following are equivalent: (i) R almost amounts to L(R), (ii) each R-grammar is extendable to a correct R-grammar.

Corollary 2. L-grammars are the only standard sort of universal c-grammar generally extendable to correct c-grammar.

By a standard sort we mean, above, any sort of R-grammar where R admits a standard axiomatization, i.e., R = L or R is a finite categorial calculus (the extension of SCC by a finite number of L-derivable schemes). Now, by Zielonka's (1981) result, no finite categorial calculus almost amounts to L, which yields corollary 2.

Proposition 4. If R is finite and almost amounts to L(R), then every R-grammar is extendable to an adequate and correct R-grammar.

The extendability claimed by the above theorems may be supplied with a linguistic sense. Namely, in order to construct a correct (weakly complete) extension of an L(R)-grammar G one adds to V_G something like "syntactically unambiguous copies" of certain syntactically ambiguous expressions (cf. Buszkowski (I), (II)).

An interesting direction of research seems to be to look for some effective criteria for correctness, weak completeness, etc. In particular, we do not know whether the class of correct (weakly complete) L-grammars (also SCC-grammars and so on) is recursive, though we conjecture it is not. The answer is relatively simple for a very special form of I_G. Namely, G is said to be perfect, if it satisfies the conditions: (i) for any x in Tp_G, every subtype of x is also in Tp_G, (ii) for any x in Tp_G, there is v in V_G such that $I_G(v)$ contains the only type x.

Proposition 5. If G is perfect and $R_G \subseteq L$, then G is weakly complete (resp. correct) iff R_G coincides with L on $Red(Tp_G)$ (resp. on the formulas $X \to p$, where $X \in Tp_G^+$, $p \in P_G$).

Consequently, all perfect L-grammars are weakly complete. On the contrary, no perfect SCC-grammar G such that $p/(q/q)$, $q/q \in Tp_G$ is even correct. For the formula $(p/(q/q))(q/q)(q/q) \to p$ is derivable in L but not in SCC.

Among several c-grammars determining the same standard model one will surely prefer just those attaining a greater degree of completeness. As we now show, full completeness cannot be reached with applying universal c-grammars. A c-grammar G is said to be n-complete $(n \geq 0)$ if it is T-complete, T standing for the set of all $x \in Tp(P_G)$ such that $o(x) \leq n$.

Incompleteness Theorem. No universal c-grammar G is $(o(G)+2)$-complete.

As each universal G with $o(G) = 0$ is 1-complete, our bound $o(G)+2$ appears to be the best possible (it can be justified also for $o(G) > 0$ by some involved construction). A proof of this theorem, employing a rank-criterion for L-derivability, is given in Buszkowski

(1982). In opposition to the theorem, every c-hierarchy equals M(G), for some complete L(R)-grammar G, and R can be taken as finite provided that basic categories in M(G) be finite-state languages (cf. Buszkowski (1982b)). So, we have disclosed a remarkable difference in power between universal and non-universal c-grammars; only the latter are capable of providing a complete description of c-hierarchies. In general, the problems of completeness of non-universal grammars (and related ones, e.g., n-completeness) surely require a more thorough analysis.

§3. COMPLEXITY

In this section we briefly survey a more traditional area of research in categorial grammar, i.e., complexity of reduction systems and behaviours of c-grammars; the latter topic includes weak equivalence of different sorts of grammars.

That SCC is decidable is a rather obvious fact. The deepest result on SCC-grammars is still Gaifman's theorem on weak equivalence of SCC-grammars and context-free grammars (cf. Bar-Hillel et al. (1960)). In particular, by Gaifman's construction, for any context-free grammar G there exists an SCC-grammar G_1 such that $o(G_1) = 1$, I_{G1} does not involve the left division sign :, and the behaviour of G_1 equals the language generated by G.

Lambek (1958) proved decidability of LSC, hence also L, by a variant of the cut-elimination technique. As early as Chomsky (1963), it was suggested that L-grammars (or even c-grammars based on LSC) are weakly equivalent to SCC-grammars, hence to context-free grammars. An attempt to prove the conjecture was undertaken by Cohen (1967); unfortunately this proof is defective (cf. Zielonka (1981a), Buszkowski (1985)). More precisely, Cohen correctly shows each context-free language to be the behaviour of an L-grammar G with $o(G) = 1$; in fact, that is a simple consequence of Gaifman's theorem (recall that an SCC-grammar G with $o(G) < 2$ must be correct, so it is weakly equivalent to the L-grammar $\overline{G} = (V_G, P_G, I_G, s_G, L)$). Cohen's argument for the converse statement (each L-grammar yields a context-free language) rests upon a wrong claim; to any L-grammar G Cohen assigns an SCC-grammar F(G), intended to be weakly equivalent to G. Let x equal the type $(((p/p)/p)/p)/(((p/p)/p)/p)$, and G be the L-grammar defined by: V_G consists of two words v and w, P_G contains just p, I_G assigns p/x to v and p/p to w, and $s_G = p$. Then $vw \in T_G(p)$ but the behaviour of F(G) is empty, which contradicts Cohen's claim (see Buszkowksi (1985) for details). The latter paper yields a correct proof of Chomsky's conjecture for the restricted case of right-directional L-grammars. It seems very likely that this proof can be adapted for the general case via some rather involved tricks.

The equivalence results of the above kind have often been interpreted as diminishing the significance of c-grammars (as they bring nothing new). In the author's opinion, they are quite interesting characterization theorems for Chomsky's hierarchy. Namely, the context-free languages appear to coincide with the languages representable (in a special sense) in a logical system (L or the elementary theory of residuated semigroups). One should expect other nice characterizations of that form and derive from them more about the fine structure of Chomsky's hierarchy.

While universal c-grammars generate just the context-free languages (cp. proposition 1), the behaviours of L(R)-grammars, for finite R's, exhaust all the recursively enumerable languages. Accordingly c-grammars based on finitely axiomatizable CH-complete reduction systems are powerful enough to describe any language being covered by other types of formal grammar. For more about these matters see Buszkowski (1982a), (1982b).

Among other complexity question topics such as the following should be noted: effectively determining the types characterizing a complex expression (cf. Buszkowski (1982a), van Benthem (1983) who deals with "the range of outcomes for a sequence of types" and "the range of readings for an outcome"), finite model property in connection with cut-elimination and decidability (cf. Buszkowski (1982a)). An attractive perspective appears to be the generalization of the whole theory to categories in languages supplied with a number of syntactic operations (the traditional theory regards concatenation as the only distinguished operation, cf. Buszkowski (1984)).

My participation in the Congress was sponsored by The Organizing Committee and Professor V. Krumm. I wish to express my gratitude to all persons involved.

REFERENCES

Ajdukiewicz, K., 1935, Die syntaktische Konnexität, Studia Philosophica, 1:1-27.

Bar-Hillel, Y., Gaifman, C., and Shamir, E., 1960, On Categorial and Phrase-Structure Grammars, Bull. Res. Council Israel, F, 9:1-16.

Batóg, T., 1967, "The Axiomatic Method in Phonology," Routledge and Kegan Paul LTD, London.

van Benthem, J., 1983, The Semantics of Variety in Categorial Grammar, in: "Categorial Grammar," W. Buszkowski, ed., J. Benjamins B. V., Amsterdam (to appear).

Bocheński, I. M., 1949, On the Syntactical Categories, New Scholasticism, 23:257-280.

Buszkowski, W., 1978, Undecidability of Some Logical Extensions of Ajdukiewicz - Lambek Calculus, Studia Logica, 37, 1:59-64.

Buszkowski, W., 1981, Categories of Partial Functors, Lingua Posnaniensis, 24:63-70.

Buszkowski, W., 1982, Compatibility of a Categorial Grammar with an Associated Category System, ZML, 28:229-238.

Buszkowski, W., 1982a, Some Decision Problems in the Theory of Syntactic Categories, ZML, 28:539-548.

Buszkowski, W., 1982b, "Lambek's Categorial Grammars," Adam Mickiewicz University, Poznań.

Buszkowski, W., 1984, Fregean Grammar and Residuated Semigroup, in: "Proceedings of 2nd Frege Conference," G. Asser, ed., (to appear).

Buszkowski, W., 1985, The Equivalence of Unidirectional Lambek Categorial Grammars and Context-free Grammars, ZML, 31 (to appear).

Buszkowski, W., 1985?, Completeness Results for Lambek Syntactic Calculus, ZML, (to appear).

Buszkowski, W., I, "Logical Foundations of Ajdukiewicz - Lambek Categorial Grammars, Logic and Applications of Logic," PWN, Warszawa (to appear in Polish).

Buszkowski, W., II, Syntactic Functors in Grammar, forthcoming.

Chomsky, N., 1963, Formal Properties of Grammars, in: "Handbook of Mathematical Psychology," R. Duncan Luce, R. R. Bush, and E. Galanter, eds., John Wiley and Sons, New York and London.

Cohen, J. M., 1967, The Equivalence of Two Concepts of Categorial Grammar, Information and Control, 10:475-484.

Cresswell, M. J., 1973, "Logics and Languages," Methuen, London.

Došen, K., 1984, A Completeness Theorem for the Lambek Calculus of Syntactic Categories, ZML, 30 (to appear).

Fuchs, L., 1963, "Partially Ordered Algebraic Systems," Pergamon Press, Oxford.

Geach, P., 1972, A Program for Syntax, in: "Semantics of Natural Language," D. Davidson and G. Harman, eds., Reidel, Dordrecht.

Heidrich, H., 1979, Formal Capacity of Montague Grammars, in: "Logic, Methodology and Philosophy of Science VI," L. J. Cohen, J. Łoś, H. Pfeiffer, and K. P. Podewski, eds., PWN, Warsaw (1982).

Hiż, H., 1960, The Intuition of Grammatical Categories, Methodos, 48, 12:1-9.

Hiż, H., 1967, Grammar Logicism, The Monist, 51, 1:110-127.

Karlgren, H., 1974, Categorial Grammar Calculus, SMIL, 1-126.

Lambek, J., 1958, The Mathematics of Sentence Structure, American Math. Monthly, 65:154-170.

Lambek, J., 1961, On the Calculus of Syntactic Types, in: "Structure of Language and Its Mathematical Aspects,", R. Jakobson, ed., AMS, Providence.

Lehrberger, J., 1974, "Functor Analysis of Natural Language," Janua Linguarum, S. Minor, 197, Mouton, The Hague and Paris.

Marcus, S., 1967, "Algebraic Linguistics: Analytical Models," Academic Press, New York and London.

Montague, R., 1974, "Formal Philosophy," R. Thomason, ed., Yale University Press, New Haven.

Suszko, R., 1958, Syntactic Structure and Semantical Reference I, Studia Logica, 8:213-248.

Suszko, R., 1960, Syntactic Structure and Semantical Reference II, Studia Logica, 9:63-94.

Tarski, A., 1933, "Pojęcie prawdy w językach nauk dedukcyjnych," Warszawa.

Zielonka, W., 1978, A Direct Proof of the Equivalence of Free Categorial Grammars and Simple Phrase Structure Grammars, Studia Logica, 37, 1:41-58.

Zielonka, W., 1981, Axiomatizability of Ajdukiewicz - Lambek Calculus by means of Cancellation Schemes, ZML, 27:215-224.

Zielonka, W., 1981a, Equivalence Problems in the Theory of Syntactic Type Calculi, in Polish, unpublished Dissertation, Adam Mickiewicz University, Poznań.

ON THE INTERPRETED SENSE CALCULUS SC_{α}^{ν}

Aldo Bressan

Istituto di Analisi e Meccanica
Università di Padova
I-35131 Padova

N1 INTRODUCTION*

A. Bressan's communication at the congress, to which the present paper is related, concerned a memoir, written by Bonotto and Bressan (1984), and Bressan's forthcoming work "A transfinite sense theory for iterated belief sentences," [TST], which, in various respects, is strongly based on that memoir and generalizes it. The principal aim of the present paper is to give a brief but complete account of the basic semantics of [TST], with short explanations and without proofs. Thus a part of said memoir is embodied as a special case. The remaining part of the memoir and the present paper are briefly described in subsections (A) and (B) respectively of this introduction. Its subsection (C) is devoted to motivations for these works.

(A) The memoir refers to the interpreted modal calculus MC^{ν}, which substantially embodies the generalizations of the modal calculus

---

* The present work was performed within the activity sphere of CNR (Consiglio Nazionale delle Ricerche) in group no 3, during the academic year 1982-83.

MC^{ν} introduced in Bressan (1972a), that are presented in Bressan (1981a) and Bressan and Zanardo (1981). It is based on a type system τ_{ν}, with all finite levels, including the relation and function types constructed starting from (ν sorts of) individual types - as in Bressan (1972a) and in Bressan and Zanardo (1981) - and also from the sentence type - as is done in Bressan (1981a). Furthermore, MC^{ν} contains operator forms with non-logical operators, which expressions (disregarded in Bressan (1972a) and (1981a)) are treated in Bressan and Zanardo (1981). Then $\sim$, $\supset$, $\Box$, $=$, $\forall$ (all signs) and ι (for forming descriptions) are identified with suitable constants which occur in suitable axioms and have suitable interpretations. (A similar treatment is that of identity in Mendelson, 1964.) Below the formation rules for the language ML^{ν} on which MC^{ν} is based, various symbols including Church's λ are defined metalinguistically. In said memoir an interpreted theory $(\overline{T}, I) = (T, D, I)$ is considered, where the interpretation I is *admissible*, i.e., is a model for the definition system D. For it, first the particular synonymy notions $\asymp_o$ to $\asymp_2$ ($\asymp_o \subset \asymp_1 \subset \asymp_2$) are introduced.* They are regarded as binary relations among well formed expressions - briefly wfes - on $\overline{T}$. Let us stress that they are characterized only by means of conditions on the forms of the wfes among which they hold. The use of $\asymp_o$ in the memoir avoids complicated procedures also in the treatment of, e.g., $\asymp_1$ and $\asymp_2$. A certain requirement considered by Carnap (1947) pushes us to broaden $\asymp_2$ to $\asymp_3$. At this point it is natural to write a general rigorous definition of a synonymy notion $\asymp$ (with $\asymp_o \subseteq \asymp$).

---

* Synonymy is studied as a special subject in Bonotto and Bressan (1983/84) belonging to extensional logic, and in its extension (Bonotto, 1981/82) to modal logic. The thesis that several synonymy notions have to be considered is emphasized there in connection with an interpreted theory (T, D, I) endowed with a definition system D.

A main aim of the memoir is to introduce suitable quasi senses, briefly QSs, to represent the senses connected with any choice of $\asymp$, and to assign them to the wfes of $(\bar{T}, I)$. These QSs, to be denoted by ${}^{\asymp}$QSs or by ^{r}QSs for $\asymp = \asymp_r$ ($r = 0, \ldots, 3$), are constructed as suitable equivalence classes of ^{0}QSs. The ${}^{\asymp}$QSs (and the corresponding senses) are [fail to be] preserved by the principles of λ-conversion when the defining conditions of $\asymp_2$ hold [$\asymp$ is $\asymp_0$ or $\asymp_1$].

The ${}^{\asymp}$QSs have to fulfill certain natural requirements such as

(α) *the* ${}^{\asymp}$QSs *assigned to any two closed wfes* Δ_1 *and* Δ_2 *of* $(\bar{T}, I)$ *coincide iff* $\Delta_1 \asymp \Delta_2$.

Since open wfes are used in, e.g., belief sentences, they too must have senses. Therefore a criterium is considered in the memoir, which involves a certain extension $\underline{\asymp}$ of $\asymp$ to v-*valuated wfes*, i.e., couples $\langle \Delta, \mathcal{V} \rangle$ where Δ is a wfe and $\mathcal{V}$ is a v-*valuation* (an assignment of quasi-intensions to variables). The relations $\asymp$ and $\underline{\asymp}$ are extended to couples of theories such as $(\bar{T}, I)$; and the analogues for these extensions of the requirements hinted at above are proved to hold. Several auxiliary notions are introduced and several properties of them are proved in order to reach the afore-mentioned results, and in particular the designation rules for ${}^{\asymp}$QSs and (the proofs of) the adequacy requirements.

(B) By the space limits of this paper, it provides a brief presentation of only the basic semantics for a certain natural extension of the interpreted modal calculus MC^{ν} or MC^{ν} - see Bressan (1972a), Bressan (1981a) and the memoir - into the interpreted sense calculus SC^{ν}_{α}, capable to deal with belief sentences whose iteration orders may be transfinite. The logical symbols of the language SL^{ν}_{α} on which SC^{ν}_{α} is based, include $\sim$, $\supset$, $\Box$, $\forall$, $=$, ι, and primitive Church's lambda, λ^{p}; the other symbols are the variables v^{β}_{tn} and constants

$c^{\beta}_{t\mu}$, where the (*sense*) *order* β can take any value $< \alpha$, a possibly uncountable ordinal ($t \in \tau_{\nu}$ and the *index* μ may be transfinite unlike n). The wfes of SL^{ν}_{α} in which v^{β}_{tn}, c^{β}_{tn}, and $c^{\beta}_{t\mu}$ with $\beta > 0$ and μ transfinite fail to occur, are substantially those of ML^{ν}.

Any semantics to be considered for SL^{ν}_{α} on the basis of the memoir must involve senses and, hence, is to be based on a synonymy relation $\asymp$. The corresponding interpreted language [calculus] can be denoted by ${}^{\asymp}SL^{\nu}_{\alpha}$ [${}^{\asymp}SC^{\nu}_{\alpha}$] or by ${}^{r}SL^{\nu}_{\alpha}$ [${}^{r}SC^{\nu}_{\alpha}$] in case $\asymp$ is a natural extension of $\asymp_{r}$ to SL^{ν}_{α}, to be denoted by $\asymp_{r}$ again ($r = 0, \ldots, 3$). In NN2-7 only ${}^{0}SL^{\nu}_{\alpha}$ is treated. Therefore the index 0 is generally dropped there.

After presenting the formation rules for SL^{ν}_{α} [N2] and some useful definitions and conventions [N3], the main lines of the semantics for SL^{ν}_{α} are briefly described intuitively [N4]. Every wfe of ML^{ν} has a QI (quasi-intension) which represents its intension, and in every Γ-case (or possible world) γ it has a QE (quasi-extension) which represents its extension. Likewise every wfe$^{\beta}$ Δ - i.e., wfe Δ of order β - belonging to SL^{ν}_{α} has a HQI - i.e., a *hyper*-QI or an *order-endowed* QI - which represents its hyperintension. Furthermore, in every Γ-case γ, Δ has a HQE (a *hyper*-QE *or an order-endowed* QE) which represents its hyperextension.

More precisely Δ has [has in γ] a QI$^{\beta}$ [QE$^{\beta}$], i.e., a QI (or HQI) [a QE or HQE $\tilde{\Delta}_{\gamma}$] of order $\leq \beta$. In addition Δ has a QS$^{\beta}$, i.e., a (hyper-)QS $\breve{\Delta}$ of order $\leq \beta$, which represents its (hyper-)sense. There are rules which assign Δ uniquely both a HQI, $\tilde{\Delta} = \text{des}_{IV}(\Delta)$, and a QSs $\breve{\Delta} = \text{sens}_{IV}(\Delta)$ (at every c-valuation I and v-valuation V). Incidentally, by the presence of orders, it turned out convenient to choose the QI^{0}s [QE^{0}s] slightly different from the QIs [QEs] used for ML^{ν}.

The HQIs, HQEs, and QSs for SL_α^ν - to be also called more explicitly ^{o}HQIs, ^{o}HQEs, and ^{o}QSs (or ^{o}HQSs) respectively - are constructed in N5 by means of a complex transfinite recursive definition, which simultaneously defines also the restrictions of the functions $\text{des}_{IV}(\ldots)$ and $\text{sens}_{IV}(\ldots)$ to constant-free wfes for certain special choices of I and V. In N6 some properties of the above objects are listed and the functions above are defined for all wfes of an (arbitrary) theory T based on SL_α^ν (and possibly coinciding with SL_α^ν), and also for all wfes of a (weak) theory $T^w = (T, D)_w$ obtained from T by addition of a definition system D.

The description operators ($\imath$x) introduced for SL_α^ν directly in NN5-6, are (extensional and) *notional*. The corresponding *objective* description operators ($\imath^*$x) are defined, as well as a (more efficient) combination ($\imath_*$x) of ($\imath$x) and ($\imath^*$x) [N7]. Furthermore the usefulness of those operators is shown by treating technically six examples of (intuitive) descriptions [N7].

Admissible equivalence relations among ^{o}QSs can be defined, and corresponding designation rules can be stated. The relations $\asymp_o$ to $\asymp_3$, introduced in the memoir for ML^ν, can be extended to SL_α^ν; and rules of of sense and intension designations can be quickly written for any weak [strong] theory belonging to SL_α^ν and endowed with the semantics related to $\asymp_o$ or $\asymp_1$ [$\asymp_2$ or $\asymp_3$]. In connection with $\asymp_o$ these rules are equivalent to those stated in N6.

Let us add that, for α uncountable, SL_α^ν has uncountably many symbols; however, among other things, SL_α^ν can be used as a first step towards the construction of theories *belonging* to SL_α^ν, hinted at in N4; these theories can always be chosen with countably many wfes and, if preferred, with all wfes having a same order β ($< \alpha$). This constitutes a step towards a typeless and orderless (interpreted) sense calculus SC^∞ that generalizes the typeless modal calculus CM^∞ - see Bressan (1973/74).

(C) Many papers are devoted to sense logic, starting with Church (1951) and Carnap (1947) and (1955). The ways in which later works approach the problem of constructing a rather general and systematic theory of belief sentences are various. Those based on Church's view use extensional languages - see Kaplan (1975), Parsons (1981), and Parsons (1982). Others use Q-categorial languages or quotational ones. Among them let us mention Lewis (1970), Cresswell (1973) and (1975), Bigelow (1978b), and Cresswell (1980), where the literature and the situation with regard to the solution of the problem is described. In Lewis (1970) and Bigelow (1978), among other things, some ideas of Carnap are naturally extended and certain QSs are introduced. Cresswell (1975) heavily points out several deficiencies and limitations of the existing approaches to the problem and in some cases he expresses a strong pessimism;* and from Cresswell (1980) it emerges that the problem situation seems not at all to have improved much.

Bealer's (1982) recent theory has several interesting features (in particular, it does not refer to possible worlds) and is capable to deal with belief sentences of all finite orders, relations, and universal (and existential) quantifiers.

---

* Cresswell (1975, p.37, ftn. 16) says that "part of the problems is that the applications of categorial languages to linguistic analysis [in Cresswell (1973)] relied heavily on the principles of λ-conversion. It is not at all clear to me, whether and how these principles should be regarded as meaning preserving [...]". Furthermore, he says (p.27), that "the biggest philosophical test of Q-categorial languages will come of course when we try to formulate the truth conditions of specific hyperintensional functors such as 'says that', 'knows that', 'believes that', 'deduces that' etc. [...] And the plain fact is that the matter seems to be that we are almost completely in the dark about the semantics of these notions."

The main ideas underlying the construction of the interpreted calculus SC_α^ν go back, at least in part, to Carnap (1947); of course, much is new from the technical point of view. These ideas, on the whole, differ from those connected with the other works mentioned above, and in particular with the recent ones in Parsons (1982) and Bealer (1982). Uniformity and generality criteria are much taken into account in the construction of SC_α^ν; and SL_α^ν is, so to say, *purely intensional* in that there is no need to use in it, as a primitive notion, possible worlds or the sense of any entity Δ.* This does not prevent the extensionality thesis to hold for SC_α^ν (it is expected to be provable in analogy with its validity for MC^ν - see Bressan, 1972a, Chapter 3). Furthermore, the construction of SC_α^ν was planned with the aim of rich applications. Thus SC_α^ν contains descriptions, λ-expressions, and general operator forms; and the synonymy relation is defined within SL_α^ν. This allows us to treat also belief sentences of transfinite and possibly uncountable orders. Reasonable examples of such sentences can be made; e.g., roughly speaking, *Charles believes that* p_n *occurs for all* $n \in \mathbb{N}$, where p_n is (synonymous with) 3 *is* $\lg_1 8$ for $n = 0$, and (with) *George the n-th believes that* p_{n-1} *occurs* for $n > 0$.

The author took interest in possible worlds, or Γ-cases, in order to treat the foundations of classical particle mechanics according to Mach and Painlevé rigorously - see Painlevé (1922), Bressan (1962). In Bressan (1962) this aim is reached by using an extensional language which is simple but unusual in that (substantially) the notion of Γ-cases is regarded as primitive, which fact affects many

---

* However, some substitutes for Γ-cases can certainly be defined within SC_α^ν, the way they are within MC^ν - see Bressan (1972a, Chapter 9). Also the extension, intension, and sense of any entity Δ are definable within SC_α^ν.

ordinary notions. E.g., *the position of the mass point* M *at the instant* Θ *is changed into the position of* M *at* Θ *in (the* Γ*-case)* γ. Thus certain counterfactual conditionals essential in Painlevé's theory are reduced to obviously formalizable assertions. Note that Painlevé himself explicitly regards such a language not to be surely admissible; and thus he implicitly puts in evidence the interest of a modal formalization of physical theories - see Hermes (1959) and especially Bressan (1962, N10), and fnts 52, 53, and 67 to 69 in Bressan (1972a, pp.110-113).

The author has always regarded the extensional possibility devices used in Bressan (1962) as a first step towards a general theory of modal logic such as that in Bressan (1972a), capable of affording a logical basis for the languages used by Painlevé and teachers of (mathematical) physics. Of course, the semantics for such a theory is much more complex than the one for Bressan (1962); but in practice only the simplicity of deductive manipulations is relevant. In particular, this simplicity is greater for a modal theory than for its extensional translations (if any). Therefore, the author agrees completely with Carnap on the usefulness of modal logic even when the extensionality thesis holds - see ftn. on previous page and Carnap (1947, p. 142).

(Incidentally, Bressan's axiomatizational work conforms with Carnap's program of *axiomatizing any (physical) theory within a formal language*, when this program is meant in this reasonable version, grasped by the author from Carnap (1958): *to show that any theory is formalizable* - i.e., that a (possibly non-explicit) formalization of it exists. (Thus, e.g., any question of rigor arising at any point can be solved without taking the bulk of the preceeding part of the theory into account.) This is in accord with the fact that in the scientific community, e.g., an extensional axiomatization on Newtonian Mechanics would be regarded as trivial in itself - i.e., unless some interesting special aims are reached. These views of the author disagree with Stegmüller's (1976) point of view, essentially linked to the interpretation of Carnap's program as aiming at an explicit complete formalization of physical theories.* Note that Painlevé's afore-mentioned perplexity - see Painlevé (1922, p. 65) - has a counterpart in his axioms. In fact, certain possibility axioms are lacking - see Bressan (1962, N10). Generally, scientists regard foundations of theories on reality more as a specific matter of axiomatization than as a question of formalization.)

The notion of physical possibility is discussed in Bressan (1981b); examples of its usefulness in connection with well known theories and questions of determinism and physical completeness can be found in Bressan (1972b), (1980) and (1984). Among other physical theories usefully based on a modal language such as MC^{ν} and having some possibility axioms, let us mention (i) the axiomatic foundations of general relativity with inclusion of materials with memory in Bressan (1978, Chapter 8), (ii) the formalized foundations of probability calculus in Bressan and Montanaro (1981/83), and, in particular, the analysis of two much used concepts of random variables in Part 3 there, (iii) Bressan's foundations of wave mechanics in Bressan (1978/79), (iv) Pitteri's foundations of classical thermodynamics - see Pitteri (1984) - where, after an attempt of Zemansky, temperature is defined in terms of purely mechanical notions, and (v) the foundations of classical and (special) relativistic kinematics

---

* This point of view appears from the assertions "It is not possible for human beings to achieve Carnap's program ...", "adherents to Carnap's view are forced to use fictitious examples of instances of real science", "... had Bourbaki followed Carnap's program, he would still be at work on his first volume".

in Bressan and Montanaro (1982), where the two theories have the same primitive notions and differ only by an axiom. This paper examplifies and supports the following view or thesis.

When a scientific revolution changes the basic notions of a science, generally the old and new theories can be reformulated by using the same primitive notions, which are of the new kind for both theories, and suitable axioms; these, in connection with the old theory, cause the used notions to collaps into notions of the old kind. *

In Bressan (1974, p.298), the author remarked that no natural (modally) absolute concept - see, e.g., Bressan (1972a, N18) or Bressan (1972b, sect. 5)- of even point was known in general relativity. The difficult problem of constructing such a notion was solved by Zampieri (1982) and (1982/83).

Among the logical works connected with MC^{ν} - see Bressan (1972a) - let us mention Park's and Zanardo's completeness theorems - see Parks (1976), Zanardo (1981) and (1984), Omodeo's and Zanardo's remarks and refinements in Omodeo (1977) and (1980) and in Zanardo (1983), and Gupta's (1980) book.

---

* This thesis contrasts with some assertions of P. K. Feyerabend in his anarchical epistemology where, in the case of scientific revolutions, he speaks of mutual incommensurability of old and new theories. The author agrees only with some consequences of those assertions: the comparison of those theories is not easy, or not widely known, and in some cases it is not yet performed explicitly or rigorously.

N2 THE SENSE LANGUAGE SL_α^ν OF ORDER α. FORMATION RULES. SOME CONVENTIONS.

Let α be any ordinal number, possibly uncountable. I want substantially to extend the modal language ML_α^ν, dealt with in said memoir, into a sense language SL_α^ν of (sense) order α. This is interesting especially when $\alpha = \cup\alpha$, i.e., α is a limit ordinal. (Following Monk (1969) the relation $\alpha = \cup\{\beta \mid \beta < \alpha\}$ is accepted for every ordinal α.)

SL_α^ν is based on the same type system τ_ν used for ML^ν , i.e., the smallest set τ_ν such that

(i) $\{0, 1, \ldots, \nu\} \subset \tau_\nu$ and

(ii) *If* $n \in \mathbb{N}_* \ (=_D \mathbb{N} - \{0\})$ *and* $t_0, \ldots, t_n \in \tau_\nu$, *then the* $n+1$-*tuple* $\langle t_1, \ldots, t_n, t_0\rangle \in \tau_\nu$.

I say that 0 is the *sentence type* (because of the use made of it), 1 to ν are *individual types*, and $\langle t_1, \ldots, t_n, t_0\rangle$ with $t_0, \ldots$ $\ldots, t_n \in \tau_\nu$ and $t_0 = 0$ $[t_0 \neq 0]$, is a *relation* [*function*] *type*. I also set, in the fashion of Carnap (1958)

$$(2.1)\quad \begin{aligned} &(t_1, \ldots, t_n) =_D \langle t_1, \ldots, t_n, 0\rangle, \\ &(t_1, \ldots, t_n : t_0) =_D \langle t_1, \ldots, t_n, t_0\rangle \textit{ if } \\ &\qquad t_0, \ldots, t_n \in \tau_\nu \textit{ and } t_0 \neq 0. \end{aligned}$$

For $t_0, \ldots, t_n, \vartheta, \varepsilon \in \tau_\nu$ and $n \in \mathbb{N}$, I define, substantially following Bressan and Zanardo (1981), the operator type

$$(2.2)\quad (t_1, \ldots, t_n; \vartheta, \varepsilon) =_D \langle\langle t_1, \ldots, t_n, \vartheta\rangle, \varepsilon\rangle.^*$$

---

* See the remark below (3.4) in said memoir which explains why definition (2.2) differs from its analogue in Bressan and Zarnardo (1981).

The symbols of SL^{ν}_{α} are the following logical symbols: comma, left and right parentheses, the connectives $\sim$ and $\supset$, $\forall$, $\Box$, $=$ (for contingent identity), ι (for descriptions), and λ^{p} (primitive Church's lambda); furthermore, the variables v^{β}_{tn} and constants $c^{\beta}_{t\mu}$, of *order* β, *type* t, and *index* n or μ ($\beta < \alpha$, $t \in \tau_{\nu}$, $n \in \mathbb{N}_{*}$, and $0 < \mu < \alpha + \omega_{o}$ where ω_{o} is the first infinite ordinal).

If A is an *expression* of SL^{ν}_{α}, i.e., a finite sequence of symbols of SL^{ν}_{α}, then the largest among the orders of the constants and variables occurring in A will be called its (*sense*) *order* and will be briefly denoted by A^{ord}.

The class E_{t} of the well formed expressions, briefly wfes, (of SL^{ν}_{α}) of type t ($\in \tau_{\nu}$) is defined recursively by conditions (φ_{1}) to (φ_{10}) below, regarded to hold for $n \in \mathbb{N}$ and t, t_{o}, ..., t_{n}, $\mathcal{D} \in \tau_{\nu}$.

(φ_{1}) $c^{\beta}_{t\mu}$, $v^{\beta}_{tn} \in E_{t}$ *for* $\beta < \alpha$ *and* $0 < \mu < \alpha + \omega_{o}$.

(φ_{2}) *If* $\Delta_{i} \in E_{t_i}$ (i = 1, ..., n) *and* $\Delta \in E_{<t_1,\ldots,t_n,t>}$, *then* $\Delta(\Delta_{1}, \ldots, \Delta_{n}) \in E_{t}$.

(φ_{3}) *If* $\Omega \in E_{t}$ *with* $t = (t_{1}, \ldots, t_{n}; \vartheta, \varepsilon)$, x_{1} *to* x_{n} *are* n *(distinct) variables*, $x_{i} \in E_{t_i}$ (i = 1, ..., n), *and* $\Delta \in E_{\vartheta}$, *then* $(\Omega x_{i}, \ldots, x_{n})\Delta \in E_{\varepsilon}$.

(φ_{4-8}) *If* p, q $\in E_{o}$, *then* $\sim p$, $p \supset q$, $\Box p$, $(\forall v^{\beta}_{tn})p \in E_{o}$ *and* $(\iota v^{\beta}_{tn})p \in E_{t}$.

(φ_{9}) *If* Δ_{1}, $\Delta_{2} \in E_{t}$, *then* $\Delta_{1} = \Delta_{2} \in E_{o}$.

(φ_{10}) *If* $\Delta \in E_{t_o}$ *and* x_{1} *to* x_{n} *are* n *variables with* $x_{i} \in E_{t_i}$ (i = 1, ..., n), *then* $(\lambda^{p}x_{1}, \ldots, x_{n})\Delta \in E_{<t_1,\ldots,t_n,t_o>}$.

If A^{β} is a class depending on the ordinal β, I set

$$(2.3) \quad A^{<\beta} =_{D} \bigcup_{\delta<\beta} A^{\delta}, \quad A^{\leq\beta} =_{D} \bigcup_{\delta\leq\beta} A^{\delta}, \quad A^{\beta *} =_{D} A^{\beta} - A^{<\beta} \quad (A^{<o} = \emptyset).$$

For $t \in \tau_\nu$ I also set

$$(2.4)\quad E_t^\beta =_D \{\Delta \in E_t \mid \Delta^{ord} \leq \beta\}; \quad wfe^\beta =_D \bigcup_{t \in \tau_\nu} E_t^{\beta\nleq},$$

so that the wfe$^\beta$s are the wfes of order β.

The symbols of the modal language ML^ν considered in the memoir (see N1 A of the present paper) are comma, left and right parentheses, the variables v_{tn} and the constants c_{tn}, to be identified with v^o_{tn} and c^o_{tn} respectively ($t \in \tau_\nu$, $n \in \mathbb{N}_*$). By that identification, the wfes of ML^ν turn out to be those of SL^ν_α in which only symbols of ML^ν occur.

Note that the type system τ_ν allows ML^ν to contain (in particular) suitable substituta, possibly depending on types, for (all) connectives, $\Box$, $=$, $\forall$, $\neg$, and λ^p. In connection with orders I prefer to use also these logical symbols because the treatment of λ^p would be rather complex otherwise.

One regards $\wedge$, $\vee$, $\equiv$, $(\exists x)$, and $\Diamond$ to be introduced in the usual (metalinguistic) ways.

N3 ADDITIONAL CONVENTIONS AND METALINGUISTIC DEFINITIONS

Convention 3.1 *By* x, y, z, x_1, ..., *by* p, q, r, p_1, ..., *and by* Δ, Δ_1, ... *arbitrary variables, wffs, and wfes (of* SL^ν_α*) will be denoted respectively. By* x^β, ..., Δ^β, Δ^β_1, ... *one will denote wfe*$^\beta$*s of the respective kinds above.*

Def. 3.1. I say that Δ_1 is an *equivalent* of Δ_2, if Δ_1 and Δ_2 are wfes of the same length 1, and either

(i) $l = 1$ *and* Δ_2 *is* Δ_1, or

(ii) $l > 1$ *and* Δ_r *has the s-th of the forms* $\Delta_{ro}(\Delta_{r1}, \ldots, \Delta_{rn})$, $\sim\Delta_{r1}$, $\Delta_{r1} \supset \Delta_{r2}$, $\Box\Delta_{r1}$, *and* $\Delta_{r1} = \Delta_{r2}$ $(r = 1, 2)$ *where* Δ_{1j} *is an equivalent of* Δ_{2j} $(j = 0, \ldots, m)$, m *being the s-th of the numbers* n, 1, 2, 1, *and* 2 $(s = 1, \ldots, 5)$, or else

(iii) $l > 1$ *and* Δ_r *has the s-th of the forms* $(\Omega_r x_{r1}, \ldots, x_{rn})\Delta'_r$, $(\forall v^{\delta}_{tn_r})\Delta'_r$, $(\urcorner v^{\delta}_{tn_r})\Delta'_r$, *and* $(\lambda^{p} x_{r1}, \ldots, x_{rn})\Delta'_r$, *where* x_{r1} *to* x_{rn} *are* n *variables* $(r = 1, 2)$, x_{1i} *has the same order (and type) as* x_{2i} $(i = 1, \ldots, n)$, Ω_1 *is an equivalent of* Ω_2 *and* Δ'_2 $[\Delta'_1]$ *can be obtained from* Δ'_1 $[\Delta'_2]$ *by replacing simultaneously* x_{11} *to* x_{1n} $[x_{21}$ *to* $x_{2n}]$, *at their free occurrences, with* x_{21} *to* x_{2n} $[x_{11}$ *to* $x_{1n}]$ *respectively* $(s = 1, \ldots, 4)$.*

The relation of being an equivalent is obviously symmetric.

<u>Convention 3.2</u> *Every expression of* SL^{ν}_{α} *used in the sequel is assumed to be well formed, except otherwise noted (which makes several explanations unnecessary).*

<u>Convention 3.3</u> *If* (i) Δ *is a wfe,* (ii) x_1 *to* x_b *are* b *variables and* x_i, $\Delta_i \in E_{t_i}$ *with* $t_i \in \tau_{\nu}$ $(i = 1, \ldots, b)$, *then* $\Delta(x_i / \Delta_i)_b$, *as well as* $\Delta[x_1, \ldots, x_b / \Delta_1, \ldots, \Delta_b]$, *will denote the result of substituting* Δ_1 *to* Δ_b *simultaneously for* x_1 *to* x_b *respectively (at the free occurrences) in a certain equivalent* Δ' *of* Δ, *such that* Δ_i *is free for* x_i *in* Δ' *for* $i = 1, \ldots, b$ *(the precise description of this equivalent would have no interest for the sequel).*

---

* Clause (iii) in Def.3.1 can be justified by the equivalence stated in one of the (unpublished) logical axioms: $(\Omega x_1, \ldots, x_n)\Delta = \Omega[(\lambda^{p} x_1, \ldots, x_n)\Delta]$.

Convention 3.4 *If* x_1 *to* x_b *are* b *variables and a wfe* Δ *is denoted by* $\Phi(x_1, \ldots, x_b)$, *then* $\Phi(\Delta_1, \ldots, \Delta_b)$ *denotes* $\Delta(x_i / \Delta_i)_b$.

The cohesive powers of $\sim$, $(\Omega x_1, \ldots, x_n)$ - and, e.g., $(\forall x)$ or $\Box$ -, $\wedge$, $\vee$, $\supset$, $\equiv$, and $\equiv_D$ (equivalent by definition) decrease in the written order. Hence we can write, e.g.,

$$(3.1)\quad (\Omega x, y)p \wedge q \vee r \equiv ([(\Omega x, y)p] \wedge q) \vee r.$$

Division dots are used in a customary way, so that, e.g.,

$$(3.2)\quad p \wedge .\ q \vee r \equiv p \wedge (q \vee r),\ (\Omega x, y).\ p \wedge .\ q \vee r \equiv$$
$$\equiv (\Omega x, y)[p \wedge (q \vee r)].$$

As in Bressan (1972a) and (1981a) notations such as $=^\wedge$ and $=^\vee$ are used according to abbreviating definitions such as

$$(3.3)\quad \begin{array}{l} \Delta =^\wedge \Delta' \equiv_D \Box\Delta = \Delta',\ p \supset^\wedge q \equiv_D \Box(p \supset q),\ F^\wedge(x) \equiv_D \Box F(x), \\ \Delta =^\vee \Delta' \equiv_D \Diamond\Delta = \Delta',\ p \wedge^\vee q \equiv_D \Diamond.p \wedge q,\ F^\vee(x) \equiv_D \Diamond F(x). \end{array}$$

Furthermore

$$(3.4)\quad \begin{array}{l} (x)p \equiv_D (\forall x)p,\ x \in F \equiv_D F(x), \\ (\forall x \in S)p \equiv_D (x).\ x \in S \supset p,\ (\exists x \in S)p \equiv_D (\exists x).\ x \in S \wedge p, \end{array}$$

and, if y is the first variable non-free in p, with the type and order of x,

$$(3.5)\quad (\exists_1 x)p \equiv_D (\exists x).\ p \wedge (y).\ p[x / y] \supset x = y.$$

The synonymy relation $\asymp$ and the nonexisting object of type t can be defined within SL^ν_α itself metalinguistically:

$$(3.6)\quad \Delta_1 \asymp \Delta_2 \equiv_D (F)F(\Delta_1) = F(\Delta_2) \textit{ with } F^{ord} = = 1 + \max\{\Delta_1^{ord}, \Delta_2^{ord}\},$$

where $\Delta_1, \Delta_2 \in E_t^\beta$ *and* F *is the first variable of type (t) that satisfies* $(3.6)_2$ *and is nonfree in* Δ_1 *and* Δ_2.

$$(3.7)\quad a^* =_D a^*_t =_D (\urcorner v^o_{t1})v^o_{t1} \neq v^o_{t1}.$$

By rule (φ_9) in N2, = can be applied also to wffs, as a substitute for equivalence - an unpublished axiom is $p = q \equiv. p \equiv q$ - (and a^*_o will turn out to be equivalent to $(x)x \neq x$). Hence definition (3.6) applies also to wffs; and the definitions of the relational and functional Church's (nonprimitive) λ-operators can be embodied in a unique extension of definitions (3.2-3) in said memoir, for ML^ν:

$$(3.8)\quad (\lambda x_1, \ldots, x_n)\Delta \equiv_D (\urcorner f).\ (\forall x_1, \ldots, x_n) f(x_1, \ldots, x_n) = = \Delta \wedge (\forall y_1, \ldots, y_n).\ \sim(\exists x_1, \ldots, x_n) \bigwedge_{i=1}^{n} x_i \asymp y_i \supset \supset f(y_1, \ldots, y_n) = a^*,$$

where (i) $\Delta \in E_t^\beta$, (ii) x_1 *to* x_n *are* n *variables of the respective types* t_1 *to* t_n *and arbitrary orders,* (iii) f *is the first variable of type* $<t_1, \ldots, t_n, t_o>$ *and nonfree in* Δ, *such that*

$$(3.9)\quad f^{ord} = \max\{\Delta^{ord}, x_1^{ord}, \ldots, x_n^{ord}\},$$

and (iv) y_1 *to* y_n *are the first* n *variables different from* x_1 *to* x_n, *of the same order as* f, *and of the respective types* t_1 *to* t_n.

N4 BRIEF INTUITIVE CONSIDERATIONS ON THE SEMANTICS OF SL^ν_α

The semantics for SL^ν_α is substantially a natural extension of the one for ML^ν and hence of those considered in, e.g., Bressan

(1972a) and (1981a). The main differences, which affect also wfes of order 0, are that

(A) *The truth value* F *(false) is used as the nonexisting object (for* SL^{ν}_{α}*) of any type* $t \in \tau_{\nu}$*, and*

(B) *the* HQEs *(and* QEs*) for functions and attributes are in some sense partial functions, whereas the* QEs *for* ML^{ν} *are total functions.*

Since F is used for SL^{ν}_{α} - see (A) -, properties such as being inexistent, as well as their characteristic functions, can be dealt with in SL^{ν}_{α}; and by (B) certain complications otherwise arising in connection with orders are avoided.

The domain [counterdomain] of any function f will be denoted by $\mathcal{D}_f$ [$\mathcal{CD}_f$]. In connection with (B) let us set

$$(4.1)\quad \left\{ \begin{matrix} A \rightarrowtail B \\ A \leftarrowtail\!\!\rightarrow B \end{matrix} \right. =_D \{f \mid f \text{ is a function}, \mathcal{D}_f \left\{ \begin{matrix} = A \\ \subseteq A \end{matrix} \right., \text{ and } \mathcal{CD}_f \subseteq B\}.$$

One can regard $\mathcal{D}_1$ to $\mathcal{D}_{\nu}$ [Γ] as *proper individual domains* [class of *elementary possible cases,* or Γ*-cases*] for SL^{ν}_{α}, if

$$(4.2)\quad F \notin \mathcal{D}_1 \cup \ldots \cup \mathcal{D}_{\nu} \cup \Gamma,\ \Gamma \neq \emptyset,\ \mathcal{D}_i \neq \emptyset\ (i = 1, \ldots, \nu).$$

In every Γ-case γ any wfe Δ has a HQE $\tilde{\Delta}_{\gamma}$ of the same type as Δ and of order $\leq \Delta^{\text{ord}}$, which represents Δ's hyper-extension. The function $\tilde{\Delta}$, i.e., $\gamma \vdash \tilde{\Delta}_{\gamma}$, is the HQI of Δ and represents Δ's hyper-intension.

For $t = 0, 1, \ldots, \nu$, $\tilde{\Delta} \in (\Gamma \rightarrowtail D_t)$ no matter which order Δ has, where

(4.3) $D_s = \mathcal{D}_s \cup \{F\}$ $(s = 0, \ldots, \nu)$;
$D_o = \{T\}$, T *being the truth value true.*

Now let $t = \langle t_1, \ldots, t_n\ t_o\rangle$. Then $\tilde{\Delta}_\gamma$ is F in case Δ is meaningless. Otherwise $\tilde{\Delta}_\gamma$ is a partial function f from some n-tuples $\langle\sigma_1, \ldots, \sigma_n\rangle$ of QSs of the respective types t_1 to t_n and of suitable kinds, to proper QEs of type t_o; here *proper* means $\neq$ F; and f is a partial function in that, in case $\Delta(\Delta_1, \ldots, \Delta_n)$ is meaningless when σ_i is the QS of Δ_i $(i = 1, \ldots, n)$, we have $\langle\sigma_1, \ldots, \sigma_n\rangle \notin D_f$ - and not $f(\sigma_1, \ldots, \sigma_n) = F$.

A theory T is said to be *based* on SL^ν_α if its symbols are those of SL^ν_α except some (perhaps all) constants. The constants of T are regarded as primitive and are denoted by $\underline{\underline{c}}_j$ $(j < \pi)$ where π is an ordinal. Now let us briefly consider a definition system $D = \{D_\varphi\}_{\varphi<\chi}$, where χ is an ordinal and D_φ is the definition (in SL^ν_α) of a constant c_φ different from $\underline{\underline{c}}_j$ $(j < \pi)$ and c_ψ $(\psi < \varphi)$ - see N7 of the memoir for more detail.* The weak and strong extensions of T:

(4.4) $T^W = (T, D)_W$, $T^S = (T, D)_S$ $(D = \{D_\varphi\}_{\varphi<\chi}$, $D_\varphi \equiv_D \Delta_\varphi = \Delta'_\varphi)$

have the symbols of T added (only) with the constants c_φ $(\varphi < \chi)$. The wfes of T $[T^S]$ are those of SL^ν_α formed with symbols of T $[T^S]$, while the wfes of T^W are obtained (roughly speaking) from those of T and the definienda Δ_φ $(\varphi < \chi)$ by substitution of some among these wfes, or some among already constructed wfes, for some variables free in a wfe of the same kind - see the definition of E^*_t by (f^*_{1-4}) in N20 of the memoir. To consider T^S $[T^W]$ is useful in connection with a semantics for which the senses of wfes are [are not] preserved by

---

* The r-th of the definitions for $\cap$: (1) $\cap =_D (\lambda A, B)(\lambda x).\ x \in A \wedge \wedge\ x \in B$, (2) $A \cap B =_D (\lambda x).x \in A \wedge x \in B$, and (3) $(A \cap B)(x) \equiv_D \equiv_D x \in A \wedge x \in B$ is of degree $r - 1$ $(r = 1, 2, 3)$.

the principles of λ-conversion. Note that theory T^W, unlike T^S, generally fails to be based on SL^ν_α but it is a proper part of such a theory. Such proper parts will be said to *belong* to SL^ν_α. They may lack all variables with orders outside a given subset $\Sigma \subset \alpha$, hence they are called *Σ-reduced*. They may even lack the symbol λ^p. Thus they may have only countably many wfes even in case α is uncountable.

Let Δ be a wfe of a theory T' based on or belonging to SL^ν_α. Roughly speaking, its sense depends on its form and the senses of the variables and primitive constants occurring in it. For $T' = T^S$ the sense of c_φ with $\varphi < \chi$ certainly exists, while for $T' = T^W$ the sense of any wfe of T' that contains c_φ, is determined by a certain procedure involving the sense of Δ'_φ.

The sense of a primitive constant $\underline{\underline{c}}_j$ of T ($j < \pi$) is determined by its intuitive characterization. I say that it is *ostensive* - see N10 of the memoir - if either this characterisation consists in pointing at the object to be named by $\underline{\underline{c}}_j$, or it practically consists in an (intuitive) definition $\mathcal{D}$ involving some terms τ_1 to τ_a outside T, but $\underline{\underline{c}}_j$ is regarded not to refer to this particular definition, its replacement with any other equivalent one being considered as irrelevant.

If $\underline{\underline{c}}_j$ is explained by $\mathcal{D}$ and is also regarded to refer to this characterization, then the sense of $\underline{\underline{c}}_j$ is considered to be nonostensive, as well as the one of any (nontrivially) defined constant c_φ ($\varphi < \chi$). However in the last case τ_1 to τ_a can be regarded as primitive constants of an auxiliary theory T_o. Hence all cases can be reduced to the one where all primitive constants have ostensive senses. Likewise it is not restrictive to assume these senses to be distinct - see N10 in the memoir for more detail. It is natural to identify ostensive senses of type t and orders ≤ β, with hyperintensions of the same type and orders. The use of ostensive senses renders it possible to define objective (extensional) descriptions in terms of notional descriptions [N7] (which are introduced directly in SL_α^ν).

The class QS^β of the QSs that can be possessed by wfes of orders $\leq \beta$, is used to evaluate the wfes of orders (strictly) $> \beta$. Furthermore, the following equalities and proper inclusions will turn out to hold.

$$\begin{array}{ll} & QE_t^\beta = QE_t^o, \quad QI_t^\beta = QI_t^o \quad (t = 0, \ldots, \nu;\ \beta < \alpha). \\ (4.5) & QE_t^\delta \subset QE_t^\beta, \quad QI_t^\delta \subset QI_t^\beta \quad (t \in \tau_\nu - \{0, \ldots, \nu\},\ \delta < \beta < \alpha), \\ & QS_t^\delta \subset QS_t^\beta, \quad (t \in \tau_\nu,\ \delta < \beta < \alpha). \end{array}$$

For F and the *improper* QI I_F one has

$$(4.6)\quad F \in QE_t^\beta, \quad I_F \in QI_t^\beta, \text{ where } I_F =_D \{<\gamma, F>|\ \gamma \in \Gamma\}.$$

N5 A RIGOROUS RECURSIVE DEFINITION OF QSs AND HQIs FOR SL_α^ν

Convention 5.1 *If* V, $V' \in (A \rightarrowtail B)$, x_1 *to* x_n *are* n *elements of* A, $<\xi_1, \ldots, \xi_n> \in B^n$, $V'(x_i) = \xi_i$ $(i = 1, \ldots, n)$, *and* $V'(y) = V(y)$ *for* $y \in A - \{x_1, \ldots, x_n\}$, *then it will be written*

$$(5.1)\quad V' = V\binom{x_1 \cdots x_n}{\xi_1 \cdots \xi_n}.$$

In order to determine a semantics for SL_α^ν, based on the sets $\mathcal{D}_1$ to $\mathcal{D}_\nu$ and Γ - see (4.2) -, and precisely the weakest one to be considered in [TST] - see N1 -, a recursion procedure is used, which substantially defines also the QSs and HQIs designated (singularly) by constant-free wfes at certain partial v-valuations. More in detail one wants to define, for $\beta < \alpha$,

(a) the class QE_t^β [QI_t^β] of the HQEs [HQIs] that can be designated by (constant-free) wfes in E_t^β ($t \in \tau_\nu$),

(b) the class QS_t^β of the QSs designable by the wfes of orders $\leq \beta$,

(c) the class V^β of β-v-valuations, formed with certain functions defined on the variables v_{tn}^δ with $\delta \leq \beta$ (they are partial v-valuations),

(d) the hyper-quasi-intension (HQI) σ^I of any QS^β σ, and

(e) [(f)] the HQI $\tilde{\Delta} = des_{IV}(\Delta)$ [the QS $\check{\Delta} = sens_{IV}(\Delta)$] *designated* by any constant-free wfe Δ of order $\delta \leq \beta$ at the β-v-valuation V, where the c-valuation I is irrelevant (in this section) and can be identified with the function I_* defined (only) on constants, for which

(5.2) $I_*(c_{t\mu}^\beta) = F \quad (\beta < \alpha,\ t \in \tau_\nu,\ 0 < \mu < \alpha + \omega_o)$.

For any fixed value of β ($< \alpha$) let us order the objects (a) to (f) as follows: (1) QE_t^β *and* QI_t^β ($t \in \tau_\nu$), (2) V^β, (3) $\tilde{\Delta} = des_{I,V}(\Delta)$ ($V \in V^\beta$) *for* Δ *in* E_t^β *(and constant-free),* (4) $\check{\Delta} = sens_{I,V}(\Delta)$, *where* $V \in V^\beta$ *and* Δ *is as before*, (5) QS_t^β ($t \in \tau_\nu$), and (6) σ^I *for* $\sigma \in QS_t^\beta$ ($t \in \tau_\nu$).

Let N_Δ be the number of occurrences of operator forms in the (arbitrary) wfe Δ. The objects (1) to (6) are defined simultaneously by transfinite induction on β ($< \alpha$). (See, e.g., Theor. 11 in Monk (1967, p.75).) For fixed β ($< \alpha$) one determines recursively (1) for $t \in \tau_\nu$, then (2) , and lastly (3) to (6) in connection with $\Delta \in E_t^{\beta*}$, by simultaneous induction on N_Δ ($< \omega_o$) and recursion on $t \in \tau_\nu$.

The afore-mentioned definition is carried out by means of rules (h_o) and (h_{2-10}) for hyper-intensional designation, rules (ε_{1-10}) for sense designation, and conditions (5.9-12) and (5.16-17) below. These rules and conditions are regarded to hold under definitions (5.5-8) and assumptions (i) to (vii) below.

The same conditions and rules imply that, for $t \in \tau_\nu$ and $\beta < \alpha$,

(α) *the* QE^β_t's *are functions of domain* Γ,
(β) $F \in QE^\beta_t$, *so that*

$$(5.3)\quad QE^\beta_t = \mathcal{QE}^\beta_t \cup \{F\} \text{ for } \mathcal{QE}^\beta_t =_D QE^\beta_t - \{F\}$$

and the $\mathcal{QE}^\beta$s *- i.e., the elements of the sets* $\mathcal{QE}^\beta_t$ $(t \in \tau_\nu)$ *- can be called proper* QEs *of orders* $\leq \beta$, and

(γ) *as the name of* σ^I *suggests - see* (d) *above -*,

$$(5.4)\quad \sigma \in QS^\beta_t \Rightarrow \sigma^I \in QI^\beta_t, \text{ hence } \sigma^I(\gamma) \in QE^\beta_t \quad (t \in \tau_\nu,\ \beta < \alpha).$$

Furthermore, in writing the afore-mentioned conditions and rules one uses the class A^β_t of *entities assignable to variables in* E^β_t, the *order* ξ^{ord} $[\sigma^{ord}]$ of any HQI ξ [QS σ], the *relevant feature* $\sigma^{R,\delta}$ of any QS σ (which is relevant for determining the value of any n-ary HQE of order $\leqslant \delta$, at any n-tuple of objects including σ), and the †-*operation*:

$$(5.5)\quad A^\beta_t =_D QI^\beta_t \cup QS^{<\beta}_t, \text{ hence } A^o_t = QI^o_t \subseteq A^\delta_t \subset A^\beta_t \quad (t \in \tau_\nu,\ \delta < \beta < \alpha).$$

$$(5.6)\quad \begin{Bmatrix} \xi^{ord} \\ \sigma^{ord} \end{Bmatrix} =_D \text{ the ordinal } \delta \text{ with } \begin{Bmatrix} \xi \in QI^{\delta\dagger}_t \\ \sigma \in QS^{\delta\dagger}_t \end{Bmatrix} \text{ for some } t \in \tau_\nu .$$

$$(5.7)\quad \sigma^{R,\delta} = \begin{Bmatrix} \sigma \\ \sigma^I \end{Bmatrix} \text{ if } \sigma^{ord} \begin{Bmatrix} <\delta \\ \geq\delta \end{Bmatrix} \text{ for some } t \in \tau_\nu .$$

Convention 5.2 *If* $\mathcal{D}_f = \Gamma$, $\gamma \in \Gamma$, *and* $f(\gamma)$ *is either* F *or an n-ary function of domain* $\underline{\underline{D}}_\gamma$, *then for* $\gamma \in \Gamma$

$$(5.8)\quad [f(\gamma)](\xi_1, \ldots, \xi_n)^\dagger =_D \begin{cases} [f(\gamma)](\xi_1, \ldots, \xi_n) \text{ if } f(\gamma) \neq F \\ \text{and } <\xi_1, \ldots, \xi_n> \in \underline{\underline{D}}_\gamma, \\ F \text{ otherwise.} \end{cases}$$

The HQEs are given (for $\beta < \alpha$) by

$$(5.9)\quad QE^\beta_t = D_t \quad (t = 0, \ldots, \nu)$$

and - see (5.5), $(5.3)_2$, and $(4.1)_2$ -

$$(5.10)\quad QE^\beta_{<t_1\ldots,t_n,t_o>} = (A^\beta_{t_1} \times \ldots \times A^\beta_{t_n} \leftrightarrow QE^\beta_{t_o}) \cup \{F\}$$
$$(t_o, \ldots t_n \in \tau_\nu),$$

while HQIs are related to HQEs by

$$(5.11)\quad \xi \in QI^\beta_t \Leftrightarrow \xi \in (\Gamma \rightarrowtail QE^\beta_t) \quad (t \in \tau_\nu, \beta < \alpha).$$

The class V^β of β-v-*valuations* is defined by the condition

$$(5.12)\quad V \in V^\beta \Leftrightarrow_D (V \text{ is a function, } \mathcal{D}_V = \{v^\delta_{tn} \mid \delta \leq \beta,\ t \in \tau_\nu,$$
$$n \in \mathbb{N}_*\}, \text{ and } V(v^\delta_{tn}) \in A^\delta_t \text{ for } v^\delta_{tn} \in \mathcal{D}_V).$$

For every $V \in V^\beta$, any constant-free wfe$^\delta$ Δ with $\delta < \beta$ ($< \alpha$) is assigned a HQI, $\tilde{\Delta} = des_{I_*V}(\Delta)$ - see (5.2) -, by the hyper-intensional designation rules (h_o) and (h_{2-10}) below. They are regarded to hold under assumptions (i) to (vii) below.

(i) Δ, Δ_o *to* Δ_n, Δ', *and* Ω *are constant-free wfes of the respective types* t, t_o *to* t_n, t', *and* ($t_1, \ldots, t_n$; t', ε) *and the respective orders* δ, δ_o *to* δ_n, δ', *and* δ_Ω.

(ii) x_1 *to* x_n *are* n *variables and* $x_i \in E_{t_i}^{\delta_i *}$ (i = 1, ..., n) - see $(2.3)_3$.

(iii) $V \in V^{\beta}$, *while* δ, δ_o *to* δ_n, δ', *and* δ_{Ω} *are* $\leq \beta$ *(hence* $\delta_g \leq \beta$ - see (5.14) below -); $n \in \mathbb{N}_*$.

(iv) *Remembering* (5.1) *and* $(4.6)_3$, *set*

$$(5.13)\left\{\begin{matrix} g \\ {}_g I_{(\gamma)} \end{matrix}\right. =_D \{<\xi_1, \ldots, \xi_n \ \xi'> | \xi' = \left\{\begin{matrix} \text{sens}_{IV'}(\Delta') \neq I_F \\ \text{des}_{IV'\gamma}(\Delta')(\gamma \in \Gamma) \end{matrix}\right. , \ \xi_i \in A_{t_i}^{\delta_i} \ (i = 1, \ldots, n)\},$$

where $I = I_*$ *and* $\text{des}_{IV\gamma}(\Delta)$ *stands for* $[\text{des}_{IV}(\Delta)](\gamma)$, *so that*

$$(5.13') \quad \left\{\begin{matrix} g \\ {}_g I \end{matrix}\right. \in (A_{t_1}^{\delta_1} \times \ldots \times A_{t_n}^{\delta_n} \mapsto \left\{\begin{matrix} QS_{t'}^{\delta_g}) \\ QI_{t'}^{\delta_g}) \end{matrix}\right.$$

with

$$(5.14) \ \delta_g =_D \sup\{g(\xi)^{\text{ord}} \mid \xi \in \mathcal{D}_g\} \ \textit{for} \ \xi = <\xi_1, \ldots, \xi_n>.$$

(v) $\tilde{\Delta}' = \text{des}_{IV}(\Delta')$, $\tilde{\Omega} = \text{des}_{IV}(\Omega)$, $\tilde{\Delta}_j = \text{des}_{IV}(\Delta_j)$ (j = 0, ..., n).

(vi) $\breve{\Delta}' = \text{sens}_{IV}(\Delta')$, $\breve{\Omega} = \text{sens}_{IV}(\Omega)$, $\breve{\Delta}_j = \text{sens}_{IV}(\Delta_j)$ (j = 0, ..., n).

(vii) $\hat{\Delta}_i$ *(will turn out to be* $(\breve{\Delta}_i)^{R,\delta_o}$ *for* $\delta_o = (\Delta_o)^{\text{ord}}$ *in that it) is defined by*

$$(5.15) \ \hat{\Delta}_i =_D \left\{\begin{matrix} \text{sens}_{IV}(\Delta_i) \ \textit{if} \ (\breve{\Delta}_i)^{\text{ord}} < (\Delta_o)^{\text{ord}}, \\ \text{des}_{IV}(\Delta_i) \ \textit{otherwise} \end{matrix}\right. \qquad (i = 1, \ldots, n).$$

Rule	*If* Δ *is*	*then* $\tilde{\Delta}(\gamma) = des_{IV\gamma}(\Delta) =_D [des_{IV}(\Delta)](\gamma)$ *is*
(h_o)	v^{δ}_{tn},	$\xi^I(\gamma)\ [\xi(\gamma)]$ *for* $\xi = V(v^{\delta}_{tn})$ *and* $\xi^{ord} < [=] \beta$ - *see* (5.17) *below.*
(h_2)	$\Delta_o(\Delta_1, \ldots, \Delta_n)$,	$[\tilde{\Delta}_o(\gamma)](\hat{\Delta}_1, \ldots, \hat{\Delta}_n)^{\dagger}$ - *see* (5.8) *and* (5.15).
(h_3)	$(\Omega x_1, \ldots, x_n)\Delta'$,	$\tilde{\Omega}_{\gamma}(<\lambda^p, g>)^{\dagger}$ *for* $\delta_g < \Omega^{ord}$ - *see* (5.8) *and* (5.13-14) -; *and* $\tilde{\Omega}_{\gamma}(g^I)^{\dagger}$ *for* $\delta_g \geq \Omega^{ord}$ - *see* (5.13-14).
(h_4)	$\sim\Delta_1\ (t_1 = 0)$,	F[T] *if* Δ_1 *is* T[F].
(h_5)	$\Delta_1 \supset \Delta_2\ (t_1=t_2=0)$,	T *if* $\tilde{\Delta}_1$ = F *or* $\tilde{\Delta}_2$ = T; *and* F *otherwise.*
(h_6)	$\Box\Delta_1\ (t_1=0)$,	T *if* $des_{IV\gamma'}(\Delta_1)$ = T *for all* $\gamma' \in \Gamma$; *and* F *otherwise.*
(h_7)	$(\forall v^{\delta}_{tn})\Delta'\ (t'=0)$,	T, *if* $des_{IV'\gamma}(\Delta')$ = T *when* $V' = V(^{v^{\delta}_{tn}}_{\xi})$ *for all* $\xi \in A^{\delta}_{t'}$; *and* F *otherwise.*
(h_8)	$(\iota v^{\delta}_{tn})\Delta'$,	η, *if* η *is the unique element of* QE^{δ}_t *such that for some* $\xi \in A^{\delta}_t$, $\eta = \xi(\gamma)[\xi^I(\gamma)]$ *for* ξ^{ord} = [<]δ - *see* (5.17) *below* - *and* $des_{IV'\gamma}(\Delta')$ = T *for* $V' = V(^{v^{\delta}_{tn}}_{\xi})$; *and* F *if no such (unique)* η *exists.*
(h_9)	$\Delta_1 = \Delta_2\ (t_1=t_2)$,	T *if* $\tilde{\Delta}_1(\gamma) = \tilde{\Delta}_2(\gamma)$; *and* F *otherwise.*
(h_{10})	$(\lambda^p, x_1, \ldots, x_n)\Delta'$,	$g^I(\gamma)$ - *see* (5.13).

Note that by rule (h_8) *the description operators* (ιv^{δ}_{tn}) *are notional.*

In connection with every $V \in V^{\beta}$, any constant-free wfe Δ $(\delta \leq \beta)$ is assigned a unique QS $\breve{\Delta} = sens_{IV}(\Delta)$ by rules (ε_{1-10}) below, under assumptions (i) to (iv) and (vi).

Rule	*If* Δ *is*	*then* $\breve{\Delta} = \mathrm{sens}_{IV}(\Delta)$ *is*
(ε_1)	v^δ_{tn} *or* $c^\delta_{t\mu}$,	$V(v^\delta_{tn})$ *or* $I(c^\delta_{t\mu})$ *respectively.*
(ε_2)	$\Delta_o(\Delta_1, \ldots, \Delta_n)$	$<\breve{\Delta}_o, \breve{\Delta}_1, \ldots, \breve{\Delta}_n>$.
(ε_3)	$(\Omega x_1, \ldots, x_n)\Delta'$,	$<\breve{\Omega}, g>$ - *see* (5.13).
(ε_{4-8})	$\sim\Delta_1$, $\Delta_1 \supset \Delta_2$, $\Box\Delta_1$, $(x_3)\Delta'$, *or* $(\iota x_3)\Delta'$, *for* $t_1=t_2=0=t'$,	$<\sim, \breve{\Delta}_1>$, $<\supset, \breve{\Delta}_1, \breve{\Delta}_2>$, $<\Box, \breve{\Delta}_1>$, $<\forall, g>$, *or* $<\iota, g>$ *respectively* - *see* (5.13) *for* $V' = V(^{x_3}_{\xi 3})$.
(ε_9)	$\Delta_1 = \Delta_2$ $(t_1=t_2)$,	$<=, \breve{\Delta}_1, \breve{\Delta}_2>$.
(ε_{10})	$(\lambda^p x_1, \ldots, x_n)\Delta'$,	$<\lambda^p, g>$ - *see* (5.13).

Now let us define the class QS^β_t for $t \in \tau_\nu$, by

(5.16) $QS^\beta_t =_D \{\mathrm{sens}_{I_* V}(\Delta) \mid V \in V^\beta, \Delta \in E^\beta_t,$ *and* Δ *constant-free*$\}$.

On the basis of Theorem 6.1 below, the HQI σ^I of any QS^β σ can be defined by

(5.17) $\sigma^I = \mathrm{des}_{IV}(\Delta)$, *where* $\sigma = \mathrm{sens}_{IV}(\Delta)$,

for some constant-free wfe^δ Δ *and some* $V \in V^\delta$ *with* $\delta \le \beta$ $(I = I_*)$.

N6 SOME THEOREMS ON HQEs, HQSs, AND QSs; v- AND c-VALUATIONS; RULES OF INTENSION AND SENSE DESIGNATIONS FOR WEAK THEORIES

One can prove the following theorem, which justifies definition (5.17) of σ^I.

Theorem 6.1 *Assume that* $\sigma \in QS^\beta_t$ *with* $t \in \tau_\nu$ *and* $\beta < \alpha$, *and that condition* $(5.17)_2$ *in* V *and* Δ *is satisfied by* $<V_r, \Delta_r>$, *where* $V_r \in V^{\delta r}$ *and* Δ_r *is a constant-free wfe in* $E^{\delta r}_t$ *with* $\delta_r \le \beta$ $(r = 1, 2)$. *Then*

(6.1) $\mathrm{des}_{I_* V_1}(\Delta_1) = \mathrm{des}_{I_* V_2}(\Delta_2)$.

The function V [I] defined (only) on the variables [constants] of SL^{ν}_{α} will be said to be a v-*valuation* [c-*valuation*] (relative to Γ and $\mathcal{D}_1$ to $\mathcal{D}_{\nu}$) if, for $n \in \mathbb{N}$, $0 < \mu < \alpha + \omega_o$, $t \in \tau_{\nu}$, and $\beta < \alpha$, it satisfies the first [second] of the relations

(6.2) $V(v^{\beta}_{tn}) \in A^{\beta}_{t}$, $I(c^{\beta}_{t\mu}) \in A^{\beta}_{t}$ - see (5.5) -.

Note that *condition* $(5.17)_2$ *implies* $(5.17)_1$, *for all wfe* Δ *without defined constants, v-valuation* V, *and* c-*valuation* I.

On the basis of the main multiple recursive definition given in N5, one can check assertions (a) to (b) below.

(a) *Relations* (4.5-6) *hold, as well as the analogues of* $(4.5)_{1,3}$ *for proper* HQEs *- see* $(5.3)_2$ -: $\mathcal{QE}^{\beta}_{r} = \mathcal{QE}^{o}_{r}$, $\mathcal{QE}^{\delta}_{t} \subset \mathcal{QE}^{\beta}_{t}$ $(r = 0, \ldots, \nu;\ t \in \tau_{\nu} - \{0, \ldots, \nu\},\ \delta < \beta < \alpha)$.

(b) *By* (4.6) *and* (5.3), *for* $t \neq t'$ *with* $t, t' \in \tau_{\nu}$, *and* $\delta \leq \beta < \alpha$

(6.3) $\mathrm{QE}^{\delta}_{t} \cap \mathrm{QE}^{\beta}_{t'} = \begin{cases}\{F\} \\ \{F, \emptyset\}\end{cases}$, $\mathcal{QE}^{\delta}_{t} \cap \mathcal{QE}^{\beta}_{t'} = \begin{cases}\emptyset \\ \{\emptyset\}\end{cases}$, *and*

$\mathrm{QI}^{\delta}_{t} \cap \mathrm{QI}^{\beta}_{t'} = \begin{cases} I_F & \textit{for t or t' in } \{0, \ldots, \nu\}; \\ \Gamma \rightarrowtail \{F, \emptyset\} & \textit{otherwise}. \end{cases}$

Under conditions (4.2) one says that the (n + 2)-tuple

(6.4) $\mathcal{I} = \langle \mathcal{D}_1, \ldots, \mathcal{D}_{\nu}, \Gamma, I \rangle$ *with* I c-*valuation relative to* Γ *and* $\mathcal{D}_1$ *to* $\mathcal{D}_{\nu}$

is an *interpretation* for SL^{ν}_{α}, and the v-valuations relative to Γ and $\mathcal{D}_1$ to $\mathcal{D}_{\nu}$ are $\mathcal{I}$-valuations.

In connection with any interpretation I of SL_{α}^{ν} - see (6.4) - and any I-valuation V, the HQI $\tilde{\Delta}$ = $\text{des}_{IV}(\Delta)$ = $\text{des}_{IV}(\Delta)$ of any wfe Δ of the theory T based on SL_{α}^{ν} - see N4 - and its QS $\breve{\Delta}$ = $\text{sens}_{IV}(\Delta)$ = = $\text{sens}_{IV}(\Delta)$ are defined by simultaneous recursion on the type t of Δ, by means of rules (ε_{1-10}) and (h_{2-10}) in N5 and rule (h_1) below.

(h_1) $\text{des}_{IV\gamma}(\Delta)$ *is* $[V(\Delta)^I](\gamma)$ *or* $[I(\Delta)^I](\gamma)$ *if* Δ *has the form* v_{tn}^{δ} *or* $c_{t\mu}^{\delta}$ *respectively;*

the above rules being regarded to hold for all values of the (metalinguistic) variables occurring in them, that are compatible with assumptions (ii) and (iv) to (vii) in N5, as well as the assumption

(viii) Δ, Δ', Δ_o *to* Δ_n, *and* Ω *are wfes of* T, *of the respective types* t, t', t_o *to* t_n, *and* t_{Ω}; *furthermore their orders are* $\leq \beta$.

Let Δ be any wfe of T^w - see $(4.4)_{1,3,4}$ -. The T-*correspondent* Δ^T of Δ can be defined recursively, roughly speaking, by means of conditions (α) to (ε) below - after sects. 12 and 20 in said memoir.

(α) *If* Δ *is a variable or a primitive constant* $\underline{\underline{c}}_j$, *then* $\Delta^T = \Delta$ $(j < \pi)$.

(β) *If* Δ *has the form* $\Delta_{\varphi}(x_i / \Delta_i)_n$, *then* Δ^T *is* $\Delta'^T_{\varphi}(x_i / \Delta_i^T)_n$ - see $(4.4)_4$ *and Convention* 3.3.

(γ) [(δ)] *If* Δ *is* $\Delta_o(\Delta_1, \ldots, \Delta_n)[(\Omega x_1, \ldots, x_n)\Delta']$ *according to rule* (φ_2) $[(\varphi_3)]$ *in* N2, *then* Δ^T *is* $\Delta_o^T(\Delta_1^T, \ldots, \Delta_n^T)[(\Omega^T x_1, \ldots$ $\ldots, x_n)\Delta'^T]$.

(ε) *If* Δ *arises by rule* (φ_{3+s}) *in* N2, *then* Δ^T *is the s-th among the wfes* $\sim p^T$, $p^T \supset q^T$, $(v^\beta_{tn})p^T$, $\Box p^T$, $(\neg v^\beta_{tn})p^T$, $\Delta_1^T = \Delta_2^T$, *and* $(\lambda^p x_1, \ldots, x_n)\Delta^T$.

Recursion can be used on the length l of Δ and, for fixed l, on the largest φ with c_φ occurring in Δ.

It can also be checked that (c) *for any wfe* $\Delta \in E_t^\beta$, v-*valuation* V, *and* c-*valuation* I,

$$(6.5)\quad des_{IV}(\Delta) \in QI_t^\beta,\ sens_{IV}(\Delta) \in QS_t^\beta\ (t \in \tau_\nu,\ \beta < \alpha).$$

Def. 6.1 *The* HQI $des^w_{IV}(\Delta)$ (= $des^w_{IV}(\Delta)$) *and the* QS $sens^w_{IV}(\Delta)$ *designated in* T^w *at the interpretation* I *of* SL^ν_α *and at the* I-*valuation* V, *by the arbitrary wfe* Δ *of* T^w - *see* $(4.4)_1$, (6.4) - *are defined by*

$$(6.6)\quad des^w_{IV}(\Delta) =_D des_{IV}(\Delta^T),\ sens^w_{IV}(\Delta) =_D sens_{IV}(\Delta^T).$$

Note that only the restriction of I to the primitive constants of T (and T^w) is relevant for des^w_{IV} and $sens^w_{IV}$. However, it is preferable to choose I (and I) *admissible* for T^w in the sense that

$$(6.7)\quad des^w_{IV}(\Delta_\varphi) = des_{IV}(\Delta'_\varphi)\ (\varphi < \chi),$$

which is compatible with the condition

(η) $I(c_\varphi)$ *is a* HQI, *if the degree* g_φ *of* D_φ *is* > 0, *and* $I(c_\varphi) = sens_{IV}(\Delta'_\varphi)$ *if* $g_\varphi = 0$ $(\varphi < \chi)$ - *see* the ftn. placed above (4.4).

No trouble arises by the facts that, for $g_\varphi > 0$

$$(6.8)\quad sens^w_{IV}(\Delta_\varphi) \neq sens_{IV}(\Delta_\varphi)\ (g_\varphi > 0)$$

and c_φ is assigned an ostensive sense according to (η); in fact c_φ is no wfe of T^W and no sense is required for it.

Def. 6.2 (a) If $\text{des}_{IV\gamma}(p) = T$, briefly $\Vdash_{\overline{IV\gamma}} p$ (or $\Vdash_{\overline{IV\gamma}} p$) - see (6.4) -, I say that p is *true in* $\gamma(\in \Gamma)$ at I (or I) and at (the I-valuation V.

(b) [(c)] If $\Vdash_{\overline{IV\gamma}} p$ for all $\gamma \in \Gamma$ [and all I-valuations V], briefly $\Vdash_{\overline{IV}} p$ [$\Vdash_{\overline{I}} p$], then I say that p *is true* at I and V [*true* in I].

(d) If $\Vdash_{\overline{I}} p$ for every I, briefly $\Vdash p$, then p is said to be (*logically*) *valid*.

(e) If A is a class of wfes of SL_α^ν, then p is said to *follow semantically* from A; briefly $A \Vdash p$, in case for all I-valuations V and Γ-cases γ, $\Vdash_{\overline{IV\gamma}} p$ whenever $\Vdash_{\overline{IV\gamma}} q$ for every $q \in A$.

As examples let us note that, by definitions $(3.3)_1$ and (3.6),

$$(6.9)\quad \Vdash \Delta_1 \asymp \Delta_2 \supset \Delta_1 =^\wedge \Delta_2,\ \Vdash \Delta_1 \asymp \Delta_2 \supset \Delta_1 \asymp^\wedge \Delta_2$$
$$(\ldots \asymp^\wedge \ldots \equiv_D \Box \ldots \asymp \ldots).$$

That Δ has an ostensive QS in $QS_t^{\beta*}$ [QS_t^δ $(\delta < \omega_o)$] can be expressed within SL_α^ν by means of the metalinguistic definition $(6.10)_1$ [$(6.10)_2$] below, where x and y are $v_{t_m}^\beta$ and $v_{t_{m+1}}^\beta$ respectively, m being the first positive integer for which those variables are not free in Δ:

$$(6.10)\quad \Delta \in OS_t^{\beta*} \equiv_D (\exists x).\ x \asymp \Delta \wedge (y).\ y =^\wedge x \supset x \asymp y,$$
$$\Delta \in OS_t^\delta \equiv_D \Delta \in OS_t^{o*} \vee \ldots \vee \Delta \in OS_t^{\delta*}\ (\delta < \omega_o).$$

The definition of OS^{δ}_{t} can be extended to all $\delta < \alpha$ by stating certain three proper axioms (to be published elsewhere), e.g., on the constant $c^{\beta}_{<(t),(t)>,3}$, by which this constant expresses (in every model of those axioms) the strict inclusion relation $A^{\delta}_{t} \subset A^{\varkappa}_{t}$ for $0 \leq \delta < \varkappa < \beta$.

N7 OBJECTIVE DESCRIPTION OPERATORS. EXAMPLES OF DESCRIPTIONS

Now, at least for $\alpha = \omega_o$, the *objective description operators* $(\iota^{*}x)$ can be defined, by which $(\iota^{*}x)p$ expresses *the object* (pointable at in a broad sense) such that p:

$$(7.1)\quad (\iota^{*}v^{\delta}_{tn})p =_{D} (\iota v^{\delta}_{tn}).\ v^{\delta}_{tn} \in OS^{\beta}_{t} \wedge p\ (\iota^{*} = \iota^{*}_{\beta};\ \delta \leq \beta < \alpha).$$

A description operator more efficient than both (ιx) and $(\iota^{*}x)$ is the following combination $(\iota_{*}x)$ of them.

$$(7.2)\quad (\iota_{*}x)p = (\iota x).\ x = (\iota x)p \neq a^{*} \vee x = (\iota^{*}x)p.$$

Note that (for $1 \leq \beta$)

$$(7.3)\quad \Vdash v^{o}_{tn} \in OS^{\beta}_{t},$$

$$\text{hence}\quad \begin{cases} \Vdash (\iota x^{o})p = (\iota^{*}x^{o})p = (\iota_{*}x^{o})p; \\ (\iota x^{o})p \neq a^{*} \Vdash (\iota x^{o})p = (\iota^{*}x^{1})p = (\iota_{*}x^{1})p. \end{cases}$$

In order to construct some examples of descriptions, let R_i be the larger root of the i-th among the equations

$$(7.4)\quad x^2 - 5x + 6 = 0,\ x^2 - 7x + 12 = 0,$$
$$x^2 - 2x - 3 = 0,\ x^2 - 3x - 4 = 0,$$

whose respective root couples are <2, 3>, <3, 4>, <-1, 3>, and

<-1, 4>; and consider conditions (a_1), (a_2), (b_i) $(i = 1, \ldots, 4)$, and (c) to (e) below.

(a_1) $[(a_2)]$ A (Adam) believes that R_1 is 3 [4].

(b_i) A believes that $R_1 = R_i$.

(c) For every conceivable entity z believed (at the first order) by A to coincide with R_1, $z = R_1$. (By a psychological postulate, A believes that $R_1 = R_1$.)

(d) A is unable, roughly speaking, to point at any object believed by him to coincide with R_1.

(e) For all objects x and y believed by A to coincide with R_1 (and pointable by him in a broad sense), $x = y$ - which could be regarded as a psychological postulate.

Example 1 [2]. Assume (b_2) to (b_4) [and (d)]. Then (since $R_1 = 3 = R_3$ and $R_2 = 4 = R_4$) (c) fails to hold. This implies the truth of the first among the sentences (of SL^ν_α).

$$(7.5)\quad (\imath z^1)B^1(A, z^1) = a^*,\ (\imath z^o)B^1(A, z^o) = a^* = \\ = (\imath^* z^h)B^1(A, z^h) = (\imath_* z^h)B^1(A, z^h)\ (h = 0, 1),$$

where $B^1(A, \ldots)$ is a translation into SL^ν_α of "A believes (at the first order) that ... $= R_1$". [Furthermore, by (d) also $(7.5)_2$ is true and hence, by (7.1-3), all sentences (7.5) are true].

Example 3 [4]. Assume (b_2) to (b_4), (e), and (a_1) $[(a_2)]$. Then $(7.5)_1$ and the first [second] of the assertions

$$(7.6)\quad (\imath z^o)B^1(A, z^o = R_1) = 3,\ (\imath z^o)B^1(A, z^o = R_1) = 4, \\ (\imath z^1)B^1(A, z^1 = R_1) = a^*$$

is true, i.e., the object believed by A to coincide with $\mathcal{R}_1$ exists and is the right [wrong] one; and by (b_{2-4}), $(7.6)_3$ also holds. Of course, by (7.3), in $(7.6)_{1-2}$ z^o and ι can be replaced by z^1 and either ι^* or ι_* respectively.

Example 5 [6]. Assume (b_3), (c), and (d) [and (a_1)]. Then

$$(7.7)\quad (\iota z^1)B^1(A, z^1 = \mathcal{R}_1) = 3, \ (\iota z^o)B^1(A, z^o = \mathcal{R}_1) = a^*$$

[$(7.7)_1$ and $(7.6)_1$] are true.

Summing up, for $p \equiv_D B^1(A, z = \mathcal{R}_1)$ the following situations are possible: (i) $(\iota z^1)p$, $(\iota^* z^1)p$, and $(\iota_* x)p)$ fail to exist (Example 2), (ii) [(iii)] only $(\iota^* z^1)p$ and $(\iota_* z^1)p$ exist and they have the right [wrong] value (Example 3 [4]), and (iv) [(v)] $(\iota z^1)p$ and $(\iota_* z^1)p$ exist unlike [as well as] $(\iota^* z^1)p$ (Example 5 [6]).

In Examples 1 to 4 [5 to 6] 3, 4 $\in \mathcal{C}_A$ [$\{3\} = \mathcal{C}_A$], where $\mathcal{C}_A$ is the class of (objective) numbers coinciding with the conceivable numbers (or entities) believed by A to be $\mathcal{R}_1$:

$$(7.8)\quad \mathcal{C}_A =_D (\lambda z^o)(\exists z^1).\ z^1 = z^o \wedge B^1(A, z^1 = \mathcal{R}_1).$$

REFERENCES

Anderson, C. A., 1980, Some New Axioms for the Logic of Sense and Denotation: Alternative (0), Noûs, 14:217-234.

Bacon, J., 1980, Substance and First Order Quantification over Individual Concepts, J.S.L., 45:193-203.

Bealer, G., 1982, "Quality and Concept," Clarendon Press, Oxford.

Bigelow, J. C., 1978a, Believing in Semantics, Linguistic and Philosophy, 2:101-144.

Bigelow, J. C., 1978b, Semantics of Thinking, Speaking and Translation, in: "Meaning and Translation: Philosophical and Linguistic Approaches, M. Guenthner-Reutter and M. Guenthner, eds., Duckworth, London.

Bonotto, C., 1981/82, Synonymy for Bressan's Modal Calculus MC^{ν}, Part 1: A Synonymy Relation for MC^{ν}, Part 2: A Sufficient Criterium for Nonsynonymy, Atti Ist. Veneto di Scienze, Lettere ed Arti, 140:11-24, 85-99.

Bonotto, C. and Bressan, A., 1983/84, On a Synonymy Relation for Extensional First Order Theories, Part 1: A Notion of Synonymy, Part 2: A Sufficient Criterion for Non-Synonymy. Applications, Part 3: A Necessary and Sufficient Condition for Synonymy, Rend. Sem. Mat. Univ. Padova, 69:63-76, 70:13-19, 71:1-13.

Bonotto, C. and Bressan, A., 1984, On Generalized Synonymy Notions and Corresponding Quasi Senses, memoir in Atti Accad. Naz. dei Lincei (VIII), 17, sect.1:163-208.

Bressan, A., 1962, Metodo di Assiomatizzazione in Senso Stretto della Meccanica Classica ..., Rend. Sem. Mat. Univ. Padova, 32:55-212.

Bressan, A., 1972a, "A General Interpreted Modal Calculus," Yale University Press, New Haven.

Bressan, A., 1972b, On the Usefulness of Modal Logic in Axiomatization of Physics, in: "Proceedings of the Biennal Meeting of the Phil. of Sci. Association, 1972," K. F. Schaffner and R. S. Cohen, eds., 1974, pp.285-303 (see also pp.315-321 and 331-334).

Bressan, A., 1973/74, The Interpreted Type Free Modal Calculus MC^{∞} Involving Individuals, Part 1: The Interpreted Language ML^{∞} on which MC^{∞} is based, Part 2: Foundations of MC^{∞}, Part 3: Ordinals and Cardinals in MC^{∞}, Rend. Sem. Mat. Univ. Padova, 49:157-194, 50:19-57, 51:1-25.

Bressan, A., 1978, "Relativistic Theories of Materials," Springer, Berlin.

Bressan, A., 1978/79, On Wave Functions in Quantum Mechanics, Part 1:

On a Fundamental Property of Wave Functions. Its Deduction from Postulates with a Good Operative Character and Experimental Support, Part 2: On Fundamental Observables and Quantistic States, Part 3: A Theory of Quantum Mechanics in Which Wave Functions are Defined by Surely Fundamental Observables, Rend. Sem. Mat. Univ. Padova, 60:77-98, 61:221-228, 62:365-392.

Bressan, A., 1980, On Equilibrium in Rational Mechanics, Determinism, and Physical Completeness, Scienza e Cultura, 2:32-41.

Bressan, A., 1981a, Extensions of the Modal Calculi MC^{ν} and MC^{∞}. Comparison of them with Similar Calculi Endowed with Different Semantics. Applications to Probability Theory, in: "Aspects of Philosophical Logic," U. Moennich, ed., Reidel, Dordrecht.

Bressan, A., 1981b, On Physical Possibility, in: "Italian Studies in the Philosophy of Science," M. L. Dalla Chiara, ed., Reidel, Dordrecht.

Bressan, A., 1984, Substantial Uses of Physical Possibility in Principles and Definitions belonging to Well Known Classical Theories of Continuous Media, memoir in Atti Accad. Naz. Lincei (VIII), 17:137-162.

Bressan, A. and Montanaro, A., 1980/83, Contributions to Foundations of Probability Calculus on the Basis of the Modal Logical Calculus MC^{ν} or MC_{*}^{ν}, Part 1: Basic Theorems of a Recent Modal Version of the Probability Calculus Based on MC^{ν} or MC_{*}^{ν}, Part 2: On a Known Existence Rule of the Probability Calculus, Part 3: An Analysis of the Notion of Random Variable, Rend. Sem. Mat. Univ. Padova, 64:163-182, 65:263-270, 70:1-11.

Bressan, A. and Montanaro, A., 1982, Axiomatic Foundations of the Kinematics Common to Classical Physics and Special Relativity, Rend. Sem. Mat. Univ. Padova, 68:7-26.

Bressan, A. and Zanardo, A., 1981, General Operators Binding Variables in the Interpreted Calculus MC^{ν}, Atti Accad. Naz. Lincei (VIII), 70:191-197.

Carnap, R., 1947, "Meaning and Necessity," Chicago University Press, Chicago.

Carnap, R., 1955, Meaning and Synonymy in Natural Languages, Phil. Studies, 6.

Carnap, R., 1958, "Introduction to Symbolic Logic and its Applications," Dover Publ., New York.

Church, A., 1951, A formulation of the logic of sense and denotation, (a) (Abstract) J.S.L., 12:21, (b) (full article) in: "Structure, Method, and Meaning. Essays in honor of H. Sheffer," Liberal Art Press, New York, (c) Outline of a revised formulation of ..., Noûs 7:24-33, 8:135-156.

Cresswell, M. J., 1973, "Logics and Languages," Methuen, London.

Cresswell, M. J., 1975, Hyperintensional Logic, Studia Logica, 34:25-38.

Cresswell, M. J., 1980, Quotational Theories of Propositional Attitudes, J. Phil. Logic, 9:17-40.

Hermes, H., 1959, Modal Operators in Axiomatization of Mechanics, in: "Proceedings of the Colloque International sur la Méthode Axiomatique Classique et Moderne," Paris.

Gupta, A., 1980, The Common Logic of Common Nouns, Yale Univ. Press, New Haven.

Kaplan, D., 1975, How to Russell a Frege-Church, The J. of Philosophy, 72:716-729.

Lewis, D. K., 1970, General Semantics, Synthese, 22:18-67.

Mendelson, E., 1964, "Introduction to Mathematical Logic," Van Nostrand-Reinhold Co., New York.

Monk, J. D., 1969, "Introduction to Set Theory," McGraw Hill, New York.

Omodeo, E., 1977, The Elimination of Descriptions from A. Bressan's Modal Language ML^{ν} on which the Logical Calculus MC^{ν} is Based, Rend. Sem. Mat. Univ. Padova, 56:269-292.

Omodeo, E., 1980, Three Existence Principles in a Modal Calculus Without Descriptions Contained in A. Bressan's MC^{ν}, Notre Dame J. of Formal Logic, 21:711-727.

Painlevé, P., 1922, "Les Axiomes de la Méchanique," Gauthier, Villars, eds., Paris.

Parks, Z., 1976, Investigations into Quantified Modal Logic I, Studia Logica, 35:109-125.

Parsons, T., 1982, Intensional Logic in Extensional Language, J.S.L., 47:289-328.

Parsons, T., 1981, Frege's Hierarchies of Indirect Senses and the Paradox of Analysis, in: "Midwest Studies in Philosophy VI: The Foundations of Analytic Philosophy," Univ. of Minnesota Press, Minneapolis.

Partee, B. H., 1973, The Semantics of Belief Sentences, in: "Approaches to Natural Languages," J. Hintikka, J. Moravcsik and P. Suppes, eds., Reidel, Dordrecht.

Pitteri, M., 1984, On the Axiomatic Foundations of Temperature, appendix in the revised edition of Truesdell's book "Rational Thermodynamics," Springer, Berlin.

Stegmüller, W., 1976, "The Structure and Dynamics of Theories," Springer, Berlin.

Zampieri, G., 1982, Diffeomorphisms Constructively Associated with Mutually Diverging Spacetimes, which Allow a Natural Identification of Event Points in General Relativity, Atti Acc. Naz. Lincei (VIII), 73:132-137, 221-225.

Zampieri, G., 1982/83, A Choice of Global 4-Velocity Field in General Relativity, Atti Ist. Veneto Sci. Lettere e Arti, 141:201-216.

Zanardo, A., 1981, A Completeness Theorem for the General Interpreted Modal Calculus MC^{ν} of A. Bressan, Rend. Sem. Mat. Univ. Padova, 64:39-57.

Zanardo, A., 1983, On the Equivalence Between the Calculi MC^{ν} and $EC^{\nu+1}$ of A. Bressan, Notre Dame J. of Formal Logic, 34:367-388.

Zanardo, A., 1984, Individual Concepts as Propositional Variables, being printed in Notre Dame J. of Formal Logic.

SEMANTICS OF VAGUE CONCEPTS

Ewa Orłowska

Institute of Computer Science
Polish Academy of Sciences
PL-00-901 Warsaw

1. INTRODUCTION

For many years vagueness understood as a deficiency of meaning has been the subject of investigations and many authors are engaged in this research. The present paper is an attempt to show that problems concerning semantics of vague concepts may find their proper foundation in the theory of rough sets originated by Pawlak (1982). We give a formal framework to what is considered to be different ways of making vague concepts precise and we describe semantics within this framework. Following the idea accepted by many logicians that reasoning in a language containing expressions representing vague concepts requires a special logic, we present a kind of modal logic suitable for deductions in the presence of vagueness.

A natural language differs from any formalized language in many respects. One of the important distinguishing features of expressions of a natural language is their vagueness. We confine ourselves to considering predicates, that is expressions representing properties of entities of a certain universe. We shall consider epistemological vagueness of predicates consisting in unavailability of total information about the universe. The lack of information results in a deficiency of meaning of predicates for certain entities. It follows that predications obtained from vague predicates might be indefinite.

Consider for example the expression "adult man". We could hardly point out a set of all adult people since there is no crisp boundary between not yet adult and already adult, nor could we decide for any particular man whether he is or isn't adult. Thus, the notion involves vagueness manifested by the existence of borderline cases which make it impossible to identify the meaning of the expression corresponding to the notion with its standard extension. In general, we meet this kind of vagueness whenever in considering a property of some objects we emphasise its intension rather than its extension. "Being a tree" or "being a book" are among other examples of such properties.

Lack of sharp boundaries is semantically a deep phenomenon. It is a consequence of the fact that we describe a continuous world in observational terms, and usually there are entities or properties which cannot be grasped by observation. It follows that expressions describing inexact concepts have to involve tolerance which enables us to avoid conflict with the continuity of the world.

According to the standard approach to semantics, we define a meaning of expressions of a language by assigning to them the respective set-theoretical constructs such as sets, functions, and relations. However, the usual set-theoretic framework happens to be unsuitable to provide a basis for semantics of natural language.

Following Przełęcki (1980), we can classify attempts at defining interpretation of vague notions into two categories:

- one in which we look for a new ontology for semantics, different from set theory,

- one in which we try to find out some concepts which could provide a meaning to vague notions but which do not go beyond the set-theoretic framework.

The representative example of the research on a new foundation of semantics is the theory of semisets (Vopenka and Hajek, 1972; Vopenka, 1979). The concept of semiset is closely connected with a special understanding of infinity, different from the infinity in Cantor's understanding. In Vopenka (1979), infinity is treated as a phenomenon occurring when we observe large sets. Our abilities for observation are limited and we can neither grasp the set in its totality nor distinguish all the objects belonging to it. Such sets are said to have semisets as their subclasses. Thus semisets can be considered as formal counterparts of vague properties, and hence the theory of semisets could be considered as the ontology for semantics of vague expressions.

Research on semantics of vague concepts related to the second trend comprises two main tendencies: to define extensions of vague predicates by using fuzzy sets (for example Goguen, 1969; Lakoff, 1973; Sanford, 1976; Zadeh, 1965) and by using supervaluation (for example Lewis, 1970; Mehlberg, 1956; Rolf, 1980; Sanford, 1976; Van Fraassen, 1968).

Fuzzy sets, originated by Zadeh (1965), provide a tool to define degrees of membership of an element in a set. In logics with fuzzy set semantics extensions of predicates are identified with fuzzy sets. It enables us to define a kind of degrees of truth of predications.

The supervaluation approach consists in identifying an extension of a predicate not with one subset of a domain but with a family of such subsets. This family is intended to represent an admissible classification of the borderline cases of this predicate into its positive and negative instances.

This paper attempts to contribute to these trends. We are going to present a semantics based on special set-theoretical constructs invented to represent approximate information. At first, we consider a first order language and then we point out how to extend the approach to higher order languages. We also present a logic for reasoning in the presence of vagueness phenomena.

2. INDISCERNIBILITY

The starting point for our considerations is the notion of an approximation space (Pawlak, 1981; Zakowski, 1983) which serves as a formal counterpart of perceptual ability or observation. Our perception of reality is limited in many respects.

We assume that in the process of perception we distinguish entities (objects) and their properties. Properties of objects are perceived through assignment of some characteristics (attributes) and their values to the objects. For example, human beings can be characterized by attribute "age" taking values from the set of integers, or by attribute "colour of eyes" with values blue, green, hazel.

In this way we establish a universe of discourse consisting of objects and elementary information items providing a characterization of these objects in terms of attributes and attribute values. In general we are not able to distinguish single objects with respect to the admitted attributes, namely we identify those objects which have the same values for all these attributes. As a consequence we "grasp" not single objects but some classes of them. In each class there are elements which cannot be distinguished one from the other by means of the given attributes. The classes provide a covering of the universe of discourse, that is, the union of all the classes coincides with the universe. The classes may be disjoint or not. If the classes are pairwise disjoint then they can be considered to be equivalence classes of a certain equivalence relation (reflexive, symmetric, and transitive) in the given universe. If not all the pairs of classes are disjoint then they determine a tolerance relation (reflexive and symmetric).

Any pair (U, R) consisting of a nonempty set U, called a universe of discourse, and a binary relation R on set U, called an indiscernibility relation is said to be an approximation space. We assume that relation R is either an equivalence relation or a tolerance relation. The classes of undistinguishable elements determined by relation R are called elementary sets.

Given an approximation space S = (U, R) and a subset X of U, we say that X is definable in S if it can be represented as a union of some of the elementary sets determined by R or if it is empty. Usually, it is the case that not all the subsets of U are definable in S. Given a non-definable subset X of U, our observation restricted by R causes X to be perceived as a vague object. In fact, we perceive not the single set X but a family of those sets which cannot be distinguished from X. In other words, we do not observe a sharp boundary between set X and its complement, we observe X with some tolerance. The limits of this tolerance are determined by a pair of definable sets, called upper and lower approximation of X, respectively. The formal definition of these sets is as follows:

- an upper approximation $\overline{R}X$ of set X is the least definable subset of U containing X,

- a lower approximation $\underline{R}X$ of set X is the greatest definable subset of U contained in X.

Obviously, if X is definable then both $\overline{R}X$ and $\underline{R}X$ coincide with X, and this means that in such a case our perceptual abilities connected with R enable us to establish a sharp boundary between X and its complement. But if X is not definable, then all the sets which include $\underline{R}X$ and are included in $\overline{R}X$ are identified with X.

The following properties of approximations follow immediately from the given definitions:

- $\overline{R}X$ is a union of those elementary sets of relation R which have an element in common with set X,

- $\underline{R}X$ is a union of those elementary sets of relation R which are included in set X.

It follows that operations $\overline{R}$ and $\underline{R}$ of approximations are topological operations of closure and interior, respectively, in the algebra of all the subsets of universe U. Many set-theoretic properties of approximations are presented in Pawlak (1982).

Let us consider the following example. Let U consists of men and R be the relation "to have the same number of hairs". In each elementary set of this relation there are men who cannot be distinguished by the attribute "number of hairs". Assume that X is a set of bald men from U. In general the attribute "number of hairs" is not sufficient to define X in our approximation space, that is, we are not able to cover set X by the elementary sets of R. We can define the lower and upper approximation of the set of bald men. The lower approximation of X consists of those men who are definitely bald with respect to the number of hairs, and the upper approximation of X consists of men who are possibly bald with respect to this attribute.

3. PRECISIFICATION OF VAGUE PREDICATES

A predicate is an expression representing a property of elements of a certain domain U. In the ordinary logic, an extension of a predicate P is a subset X_P of the domain. An element u of U is a positive instance of P if and only if u belongs to X_P, and u is a negative instance of P if and only if u belongs to the complement $U - X_P$ of set X_P.

However, if our perception of elements of U is limited to some of their attributes, we might not be able to classify them into positive and negative instances of P. To deal with such cases we assume that we are given an approximation space (U, R), where U is a set of elements for which a property expressed by a predicate P is meaningful, and R is the indiscernibility relation in U related to the admitted attributes. Let X_P denote the subset of all elements from U for which P holds. In general, we are not able to decide for each element of U whether it belongs to X_P or not, we can decide it up to relation R. The following notions enable us to express all the situations:

- an element u is a positive instance of P if and only if u belongs to $\underline{R}X_P$,

- an element u is a negative instance of P if and only if u belongs to $U - \overline{R}X_P$,

- an element u is a borderline instance of P if and only if u belongs to $\overline{R}X_P - \underline{R}X_P$.

All the three sets of instances of P are definable in the space (U, R), and hence we can consider them as providing a means of making P precise.

We can easily reconstruct the above definitions for n-place predicates, where $n \geq 2$. Let Q be a n-place predicate and let Y_Q denote the subset of all n-tuples $(x_1, \ldots, x_n)$ of elements of U for which Q holds. Then the upper approximation $\overline{R}Y_Q$ of Y_Q is the set of all n-tuples $(y_1, \ldots y_n)$ for which there are $y_1', \ldots, y_n'$ which cannot be distinguished from $y_1, \ldots, y_n$ by means of R, respectively, and the tuple $(y_1', \ldots, y_n')$ belongs to Y_Q. Similarly, the lower approximation $\underline{R}Y_Q$ of Y_Q is the set of all n-tuples $(y_1, \ldots, y_n)$ where for all $y_1', \ldots, y_n'$ which cannot be distinguished from $y_1, \ldots, y_n$ by means of R, respectively, the tuple $(y_1', \ldots, y'_n)$ belongs to Y_Q. We define the set of positive, negative, and borderline instances of Q as $\underline{R}Y_Q$, $U^n - \overline{R}Y_Q$, and $\overline{R}Y_Q - \underline{R}Y_Q$, respectively, where U^n denotes the set of all n-tuples of elements of U.

4. HIGHER ORDER VAGUENESS

An indiscernibility relation R defined in a universe U is considered to be a representation of our ability to perceive U. Information about U is given by means of properties of elements of U, expressed through attributes. Usually a perception is a dynamic process and hence we should consider not a single indiscernibility relation but rather a family of them. In particular, if we extend our ability of perception determined by R, then we obtain an indiscernibility relation R' which is included in R. Thus, according to R' our perception of U will be finer, or more accurate than according to R.

Consider, for example, the concept "leukemia". We can characterize it by means of values of hemoglobin, erythrocyte, and leukocyte in the blood, obtaining an indiscernibility relation R in a set of patients. But if we take into account not only the blood parameters but also the results of a myeloblast test, we obtain the new indiscernibility relation R' which will provide a better characterization of the patients. The set of positive instances of the concept "leukemia" with respect to relation R' will be greater than the set of its positive instances with respect to relation R. Similarly, the set of negative instances of this concept with respect to R' will be smaller than the set of its negative instances with respect to R. It follows that the borderline area with respect to R' is less than the borderline area with respect to R. As a consequence, approximations of a set of patients suffering from leukemia determined by relation R' are closer to this set (with respect to inclusion) than its approximations with respect to R.

Any system $S = (U, \{R_i\}_{i \in I})$, where U is a nonempty universe, I is a nonempty set of indices, and for each $i \in I$ R_i is an indiscernibility relation in U is said to be a generalized approximation space. A subset X of U is said to be definable in S if, for each $i \in I$, X is definable in the space (U, R_i). In general, a set definable in (U, R_i) is not necessarily definable in a space (U, R_j) for a certain j different from i. However, if R_j is included in R_i, then each set definable in (U, R_i) is definable in (U, R_j), and, moreover, for any subset X of U the upper approximation $\overline{R}_j X$ is included in $\overline{R}_i X$ and the lower approximation $\underline{R}_j X$ is included in $\underline{R}_j X$. This means that if our perception of U becomes more accurate then the approximations of any set will be closer to it, with respect to inclusion.

Given a property of elements of a universe U, expressed by means of a predicate P, we define positive, negative, and borderline instances of P with respect to space S as follows:

- an element u is a positive instance of P if and only if for all $i \in I$ u belongs to $\underline{R}_i X_P$,

- an element u is a negative instance of P if and only if for all $i \in I$ u belongs to $U - \overline{R}_i X_P$,

- an element u is a borderline instance of P if and only if there is an $i \in I$ such that u belongs to $U - \underline{R}_i X_P$ and there is an $j \in I$ such that u belongs to $\overline{R}_j X_P$.

This means that element u is a positive (negative) instance of P with respect to a generalized approximation space $(U, \{R_i\}_{i \in I})$ whenever it is a positive (negative) instance in each space (U, R_i), for $i \in I$.

According to the given definitions we obtain a precisification of a predicate which is vague with respect to a family of indiscernibility relations by precisifying this predicate with respect to each of the relations.

A vagueness with respect to a generalized approximation space can be considered to be a higher order vagueness. The sets of instances of a predicate P may be definable in a certain space (U, R_j) and at the same time they may not be definable in another space (U, R_j) for a certain j different from i. This means that the boundaries which are observed as being sharp from the point of view represented by R_i are inexact from the point of view related to R_j. Thus in the framework of the generalized approximation spaces we can deal with hierarchy of vagueness phenomena for each predicate.

Moreover, such an approach provides an explanation of paradoxes of "sorites" (a heap) and "falakros" (a bald man). Namely, a degree of change in a status of an element determined by passing from R_i to

R_j is insufficient to alter the justification for deciding whether this element falls under a certain property. In other words, a very delicate change in the perception ability should not drastically alter an image of the perceived object.

Given a generalized approximation space $(U, \{R_i\}_{i \in I})$, we can define what we might call degrees of inexactness. For instance, we can say that "it is almost impossible that P(u)" whenever for all $i \in I$ element u does not belong to $\underline{R}_i X_P$ and for a certain $j \in I$ element u belongs to $\overline{R}_j X_P$. Similarly, "it might be possible that P(u)" whenever u does not belong to $\underline{R}_i X_P$ for a certain $i \in I$ and for all $j \in I$ element u belongs to $\overline{R}_j X$. These degrees can also be treated as a generalization of degrees of membership defined in the theory of fuzzy sets.

5. HIGHER ORDER PREDICATES

The method of precisification of first order predicates presented in the previous sections can easily be extended to higher order predicates. Given an approximation space (U, R), the indiscernibility relation R induces an equivalence relation E_R in the family 2^U of all the subsets of U, defined as follows:

- sets X_1 and X_2 cannot be distinguised by means of E_R if and only if $\overline{R}X_1$ coincides with $\overline{R}X_2$ and $\underline{R}X_1$ coincides with $\underline{R}X_2$.

Let P be a second order predicate, that is an expression representing a property of sets. To define sets of positive, negative, and borderline instances of a second order predicate P, we have to consider the approximation space $(2^U, E_R)$, and to proceed in the way described in Section 3.

It is easy to see that the same construction can be repeated for any level of a powerset hierarchy, and hence we are able to define semantics for all kinds of vague predicates.

6. REASONING ABOUT VAGUE CONCEPTS

The considerations on semantics presented in the previous sections provide a basis for developing a logic of inexact concepts. The former approaches to the problem consist in defining many-valued logics with semantics based on the theory of fuzzy sets or the theory of super-truth. However, such logics have some counterintuitive consequences. Consider, for instance, the predicate "bald", and suppose that John and Tom are borderline instances of this predicate. If we admit a three-valued logic then the sentences "John is bald" and "Tom is bald" will have the truth value 0.5. It follows that both the conjunctions "John is bald and Tom is bald" and "John is bald and John is not bald" take the truth value 0.5.

We established that to define a semantical domain in which we evaluate concepts we need to specify objects and some attributes meaningful for these objects. Then a meaning of expressions which are names of concepts depends on indiscernibility relations determined by these attributes. Thus in a formalism for reasoning about vague concepts we should be able to express both sets of objects being semantical counterparts of concepts and indiscernibility relations. Moreover, we should be able to formulate facts concerning an influence of a choice of attributes on definability of concepts. A formalized language developed in the present section is an attempt to satisfy the above requirements.

Expressions of the language are formed from symbols taken from the following pairwise disjoint sets:

- CONREL a denumerable set of constants representing indiscernibility relations,

- {$\cup$, $\cap$} the set of symbols of set-theoretical operations of union and intersection, respectively,

- VAR a denumerable set of propositional variables,

- {$\neg$, $\vee$, $\wedge$, $\rightarrow$, $\leftrightarrow$} the set of classical propositional operations of negation, disjunction, conjunction, implication and equivalence, respectively,

- {pos, neg, bor} the set of unary propositional operations,

- {(,)} the set of brackets.

We define set EREL of auxiliary expressions, called relational expressions, as follows:

CONREL $\subseteq$ EREL,
R, S $\in$ EREL implies R $\cup$ S, R $\cap$ S $\in$ EREL.

Relational expressions are intended to represent indiscernibility relations. In a definition of semantics of the relational expressions we shall assume that indiscernibility relations are reflexive and symmetric. We admit in the language operations of union and intersection of relations. It enables us to express explicitly in the formalism changes of indiscernibility relations related to changes of attributes.

Set FOR of formulas of the language is the least set satisfying the following conditions:

$VAR \subseteq FOR$,

$A, B \in FOR$ implies $\neg A$, $A \vee B$, $A \wedge B$, $A \rightarrow B$, $A \leftrightarrow B \in FOR$,

$A \in FOR$, $R \in EREL$ imply pos(R)A, neg(R)A, bor(R)A $\in$ FOR.

Formulas of the language are intended to represent concepts. A formula of the form pos(R)A(neg(R)A, bor(R)A) will correspond to a positive (negative, borderline) region of A with respect to an indiscernibility relation denoted by R.

Semantics of the language is defined by means of notions of model and satisfiability of the formulas in a model. By a model we mean a system:

$$M = (U, \{r_R\}_{R \in CONREL}, m)$$

where U is a nonempty universe; for each relational constant R r_R is a tolerance relation in set U; m is a meaning function such that

$m(p) \subseteq U$ for any propositional variable p,

$m(R) = r_R$ for any relational constant R,

$m(R \cup S) = m(R) \cup m(S)$,

$m(R \cap S) = m(R) \cap m(S)$.

Given a model M, we say that an element $u \in U$ satisfies a formula A (M, u sat A) whenever the following conditions are fulfilled:

M, u sat p iff $u \in m(p)$ for $p \in VAR$

M, u sat $\neg A$ iff not M, u sat A

M, u sat $A \vee B$ iff M, u sat A or M, u sat B

M, u sat $A \wedge B$ iff M, u sat A and M, u sat B

M, u sat $A \rightarrow B$ iff not M, u sat A or M, u sat B

M, u sat $A \leftrightarrow B$ iff M, u sat $A \rightarrow B$ and M, u sat $B \rightarrow A$

M, u sat pos(R)A iff for all $w \in U$ if $(u, w) \in m(R)$
then M, w sat A

M, u sat neg(R)A iff for all $w \in U$ if $(u, w) \in m(R)$
then not M, w sat A

M, w sat bor(R)A iff not M, u sat pos(R)A and not M,
u sat neg(R)A.

As usual, a formula A is said to be true in a model M whenever it is satisfied by all the elements of the universe of M. Below are listed some formulas which are true in all models.

$pos(R)A \rightarrow A$

$A \rightarrow \neg neg(R)A$

$\neg(pos(R)A \wedge neg(R)A)$

$pos(R)A \vee neg(R)A \vee bor(R)A$

$neg(R)A \leftrightarrow pos(R)\neg A$

$bor(R)A \leftrightarrow \neg pos(R)A \wedge \neg neg(R)A$

$pos(R)A \vee pos(S)A \rightarrow pos(R \cap S)A$

$pos(R \cup S)A \leftrightarrow pos(R)A \wedge pos(S)A$

In the given language we can discuss how definability of concepts depends on indiscernibility relations. For example, if a scheme

$pos(R)A \rightarrow pos(S)A$

represents true formulas in a certain model then in this model the relation represented by S enables us to characterize concepts more adequately than the relation corresponding to R, namely, for all concepts the positive regions with respect to S are greater than the positive regions with respect to R. As a consequence the above formula expresses the fact that the indiscernibility represented by S is included in the indiscernibility represented by R. The scheme

$$A \rightarrow \mathrm{pos}(R)A$$

expresses the fact that relation corresponding to R provides an adequate characterization of concepts, namely for any concept its positive area with respect to R coincides with the concept itself.

In the given language we can express separability of concepts up to indiscernibility relations. Given a model, we can consider concepts corresponding to A and B to be weakly separable in the model if the formula

$$\neg(\mathrm{pos}(R)A \wedge \mathrm{pos}(R)B)$$

is true in the model. Similarly the concepts represented by formulas A and B are strongly separable if both the above formula and the formula

$$\neg(\mathrm{bor}(R)A \wedge \mathrm{bor}(R)B)$$

are true in the model. We can consider the other forms of separability, e.g., separability of negative areas of concepts. Concepts which are not separable can be considered to be similar. We can define similarity with respect to positive and negative areas. Due to relational expressions we can express in the language a kind of degrees of similarity. If a formula

$$\mathrm{pos}(R)A \wedge \mathrm{pos}(R)B \rightarrow \mathrm{pos}(S)A \wedge \mathrm{pos}(S)B$$

is true in a certain model, then similarity of the respective concepts up to the relation corresponding to S can be considered to be stronger than their similarity up to the indiscernibility represented by R.

7. SUMMARY

In the paper we developed a method of dealing with vague concepts both on the semantic and syntactic level. We defined semantics of vague concepts on the basis of the rough set theory which enables us to give set-theoretical counterparts of the sets of positive, negative, and borderline instances of vague predicates. On the syntactic level, we introduced formalized language with special propositional operators, providing a formal tool for reasoning about vague concepts. In the language we have syntactic counterparts of concepts and indiscernibility relations. It enables us to express relationships between "views" of concepts in terms of various indiscernibility relations and to discuss degrees of vagueness determined by these relations.

REFERENCES

Black, M., 1937, Vagueness, Philosophy of Science, 4:427-455.

Black, M., 1963, Reasoning with Loose Concepts, Dialogue, 2:1-12.

Fine, K., 1975, Vagueness, Truth and Logic, Synthese, 30:265-300.

Goguen, J. A., 1969, The Logic of Inexact Concepts, Synthese, 19:325-373.

Kubiński, T., 1958, Nazwy nieostre (Vague Terms), Studia Logica, 7:115-179, in Polish.

Lakoff, G., 1973, Hedges: A Study in Meaning Criteria and the Logic of Fuzzy Concepts, Journal of Philosophical Logic, 2:458-508.

Lewis, D., 1970, General Semantics, Synthese, 22:18-67.

Mehlberg, H., 1956, "The Reach of Science," Toronto University Press, Toronto.

Orłowska, E., 1983, "Representation of Vague Information," ICS PAS Reports 503, Warsaw.

Pawlak, Z., 1981, "Classification of Objects by Means of Attributes," ICS PAS Reports 429, Warsaw.

Pawlak, Z., 1982, Rough Sets, International Journal of Computer and Information Sciences, 11:341-350.

Peacocke, Ch., 1981, Are Vague Predicates Incoherent?, Synthese, 46:121-141.

Przełęcki, M., 1980, Set Theory as an Ontology for Semantics, in: "Proceedings of the 4th International Wittgenstein Symposium," R. Haller and W. Grassl, eds., Hölder-Pichler-Tempsky, Vienna.

Rolf, B., 1980, A Theory of Vagueness, Journal of Philosophical Logic, 9:315-325.

Russell, B., 1923, Vagueness, Australasian Journal of Philosophy, 1:84-92.

Sanford, D., 1976, Competing Semantics of Vagueness: Many Values Versus Super-Truth, Synthese, 33:195-210.

Van Fraassen, B. C., 1966, Singular Terms, Truth-Value Gaps, and Free Logic, Journal of Philosophy, 63:481-495.

Van Fraassen, B. C., 1968, Presupposition, Implication and Self-Reference, Journal of Philosophy, 65:136-152.

Vopenka, P., 1979, "Mathematics in the Alternative Set Theory," Taubner-Texte zur Mathematik, Leipzig.

Vopenka, P., and Hajek, P., 1972, "The Theory of Semisets," North-Holland, Amsterdam.

Wright, C., 1975, On the Coherence of Vague Predicates, Synthese, 30:325-365.

Zadeh, L. A., 1965, Fuzzy Sets, Information and Control, 8:338-353.

Zadeh, L. A., 1975, Fuzzy Logic and Approximate Reasoning, Synthese, 30:407-428.

Zakowski, W., 1983, Approximations in the Space (U, Π), Demonstratio Mathematicae, 16:761-769.

INFORMATION SEMANTICS AND ANTINOMIES

Henry Hiż

Department of Linguistics
University of Pennsylvania
Philadelphia, PA 19104/USA

Among logicians and linguists there are long standing widespread opinions about the foundations of semantics which, like any other scientific opinion, should be scrutinized in the light of recent advances. According to one of the opinions in question, to keep a sharp distinction between a language and its metalanguages is necessary under the penalty of contradictions. The second opinion is that there is a substantive difference between the semantical antinomies and the set theoretical antinomies. To exemplify, the liar's antinomy is considered semantical (it supposedly confuses a language with its metalanguage) but Russell's antinomy is viewed as set theoretical (as it allegedly deals with the concept of a set). The third opinion to be critically examined holds that there is a sharp cleavage between syntax and semantics of a language. According to this view, syntax should determine all well formed sentences independently of any semantics. Only after that does semantics assign values to the well formed sentences and to their parts. Finally, among logicians, there is a suspicion that a natural language is doomed to trouble, inconsistencies, unresolvable ambiguities. Montague and others have done a great deal to allay some such fears but further defence of natural language and its own logic is needed.

The antinomies result from the supposition that every property determines an object and that if an object is determined by two properties then these properties apply to the same objects. If the objects determined by the properties are sets, the antinomies are called set-theoretical; if they are words, the antinomies are called semantical. The suppositions were stated by Frege; if the relation between the determined object and property is symbolized by 'α', his principles say

A1. $\Lambda f V a[a \alpha f]$

A2. $\Lambda afgx[a\alpha f \wedge a\alpha g \wedge f(x). \supset g(x)]$.

If we now add, as Russell did, the definition

$$\Lambda a[R(a) \equiv. \, Vf[a\alpha f] \wedge \Lambda f[a\alpha f \supset \sim f(a)]],$$

we can deduce by means of A2 alone that

$$\Lambda a[\sim a\alpha R],$$

contrary to A1.

The amendmendts to A1, A2 and the definition of R preoccupied many logicians in the first half of our century. If I add one more amendment, it is mainly because it leads to a semantic theory of some virtue, both in clarity and in applicability. The clarity is connected with a more restrained philosophy; the applicability will be illustrated by sketching a semantics of the utterance in which its later fragments change the assertions previously made in the utterance. Such is usually the case in conversation. But the semantics of a text is not a simple sum of semantics of its sentences. Every sentence uses what has been said before it, often adding conditions, corrections, elaborations.

In A2 the function f can be taken, and often was taken, to be not only of one argument but of two, three or any finite number of arguments. So that

A2'. $\Lambda afgxy[a\alpha f \wedge a\alpha g \wedge f(x, y) .\supset g(x, y)]$.

Similarly, we can take f to be a function of zero arguments so that A2 becomes

OA2. $\Lambda afg[a\alpha f \wedge a\alpha g \wedge f .\supset g]$.

From the form of OA2 we see that the symbols 'f' and 'g' are of the grammatical category of a sentence. It is customary then to use the letters 'p', 'q', etc. in this role:

OA2. $\Lambda apq[a\alpha p \wedge a\alpha q \wedge p .\supset q]$.

The Russellian definition then takes the form

$\Lambda a[R(a) \equiv. \vee p[a\alpha p] \wedge \Lambda p[a\alpha p \supset \sim p]]$.

The antinomy is not reconstructible in this case. Instead of $\Lambda a[\sim a\alpha R]$ one concludes

$\Lambda a[\sim a\alpha R(a)]$,

which does not contradict

OA1 $\Lambda p \vee a[a\alpha p]$.

Though no a is α-connected to R(a), there may be a b, different from a, which is α-connected to R(a).

In search of possible interpretations of 'α' I will first read it as 'says that'. It is taken not in the sense as in 'Peter says that he is hungry' but in the sense as in 'The French sentence 'Aujourd'hui c'est samedi' says that today is Saturday'. Says-that is a typical semantic relation between an utterance and, roughly speaking, its content. The content of a sentence is sometimes referred to as a proposition, a situation, real, possible, or even impossible. But we do not have to reify contents of utterances. If Carol utters 'Today is Saturday', we may not agree, but we will not impute to her a belief in abstract propositions. Sometimes I will use the terminology of 'situations', but I will not plead guilty to using it *à la lettre*.

By a sentence I will understand not only a stretch of speech represented in conventional writing occurring between two full stops. Rather, I will take it to be any stretch of speech from which we can draw consequences, or better, which can be a consequence. (Better, because we can draw consequences from an (unordered) set of sentences.) Thus

I ran. I was trying to catch the train. Too late.

is a sentence in this sense, even though for a logician it is not a conjunction of sentences.

Let us, therefore, introduce to our semantics the relation read in English as '*says that*'. The first arguments of that relation are, typically, sentences, utterances, and, normally, not nouns, verbs, determiners, etc. Only those phrases can occur in front of 'says that' which convey information. And I am not speaking here of conveying information by, for instance, lowering my voice when I signal that I am telling you a secret. (One may extend the semantic theory to such ways of conveying information, but this is *cura posterior*.) At present, I am dealing with utterances and those of their properties with which logicians deal when they speak about consequences. Here, the information of a text will be a particular subset of the consequences of the text. Similarly for vocal utterances. An example may illustrate a further delimitation of the problem. Suppose we are reading in the newspaper: "From what the President said we conclude that the government will cut the services; from how he said it we conclude that he was afraid to tell it to the public." Only the first kind of conclusion is the subject of the present study. The distinction between what he said and how he said it is important for linguistic study. If I ask a listener to repeat what the President said, I do not ask him to imitate the fear, or the timbre of voice, or the personal mannerisms, even though we do draw conclusions from these other aspects of his speech. The distinction between repetition and imitation is important for grammatical theory. Grammar studies invariants under repetition. This is not to say that we should not study imitation as well, under another heading.*

I understand here the relation of saying-that as saying exactly that and not as saying among other things that. To approximate that sense one can state some principles concerning saying-that. If in OA2 we interpret 'α' as 'says that', we obtain

If a says that p and a says that q and p, then q.

It seems plausible in the intended sense of 'says that'. 'Says that p' will be treated in the symbolism used as a functor of 'a'. Instead

---

* The relative absence of discussion of the distinction between repetition and imitation seems connected with the popularity of the distinction between knowledge and performance. In the knowledge-performance theory there is little room for the repetition-imitation distinction.

of 'a says that p', '$S<p>(a)$' will be written. Several sentences may have the property $S<p>$. In that symbolism OA2 becomes

$$\bigwedge paq[S<p>(a) \wedge S<q>(a) \wedge p \ .\supset q].$$

Let us call this statement the *Principle of Equivalence*, as its immediate consequence is

$$\bigwedge paq[S<p>(a) \wedge S<q>(a) \ .\supset. \ p \equiv q].$$

It is to be (tacitly) understood that a is in a specific language. In this interpretation, OA1 is not true. It is not true that whatever may happen or whatever may not happen is sayable in a language. There are situations indescribable in a given language. As an expression of inadequacy of any language let us proclaim the negation of OA1

$$\sim\bigwedge p \bigvee a[S<p>(a)]$$

and let us call it the *Principle of Inadequacy*. In connection with this principle let us observe that the concept of a sentence is highly theoretical and has little empirical support.

Just as there are no sentences to say whatever, so there are syntactically well formed sentences which do not say anything. One of them is '$a\alpha R(a)$' or - in the interpretation now under study - '$S<R(a)>(a)$'. Another is 'Every prime number is removable by turpentine'. It is not true that every sentence says something partly because the concept of a sentence depends on a specific grammatical theory. We may change our theories of grammar in interesting ways; but nothing in reality will be changed by it.

The next principle, the *Principle of Compactness*, states that if a says that p then every other sentence which says that p is inferentially equivalent to a; if a is any sentence that says that p, then the consequences of a are the same as the consequences of the class of all the sentences each of which says that p. In formulating this principle it is advisable to note that often consequences are drawn not only from a sentence alone, but that we use various assumptions, usually enthymematic, often unnoticed. The assumptions are really always with us. It is hard to imagine a discourse in which there are no assumptions. Therefore, when we speak about the consequences of a sentence, we will speak about the consequences of that sentence and the assumptions. The assumptions are not constant. They may vary from group to group of people, and they may change with knowledge and circumstances, so, we will keep it as a variable.

$$\bigwedge paX[S\langle p\rangle(a) \supset Cn(\iota a \cup X) = Cn(S\langle p\rangle \cup X)\ .$$

Although this concept of consequence is that elaborated by Tarski, a linguist may worry that some people draw further consequences than other people and that some people draw slanted consequences. (Perhaps all people draw slanted consequences, but slanted in various directions.) Also, some people often, and all people sometimes, draw wrong consequences. As a compromise, I take the relation of consequence to apply when a reasoning is valid and performed and recognized as valid in the social group whose language is under study.

Using the concept of saying-that, one can restate - perhaps more properly - many known semantical theorems. For instance, the *Deduction Theorem* becomes the semantic principle:

$$\bigwedge qpXa[S\langle q\rangle \subset Cn(S\langle p\rangle \cup X) \wedge S\langle p \supset q\rangle(a)\ .\supset S\langle p \supset q\rangle \subset Cn(X)].$$

I will accept the Principles of Equivalence, of Inadequacy, of Compactness and of Deduction without claiming that they suffice for the semantic theory and without claiming that saying-that is a primitive term of the theory. The concept of a primitive term makes sense for a well formalized version of a theory, and the sketch presented here is far from it.

In the semantic theory to which the present considerations may be a contribution there is no room, or need, for reference, denotation, or naming. The information is conveyed by sentences, but not by names unless they are used as short for a sentence. Though the meaning of names and some other words can be derivatively characterized in this theory, what is scrupulously avoided is, for example, saying that the word 'Chianti' refers to a kind of wine (or to a chain of mountains in Tuscany), or that the phrase 'red wine' refers to, names, designates, or denotes any red wine. This is why the theory is labelled 'an informational semantics' in contradistinction to a referential semantics.

Using the concept of saying-that one can define the concept of truth:

$$\bigwedge a[Tr(a) \equiv \bigvee p[S\langle p\rangle(a) \wedge p]].$$

From this it follows (by the Principle of Equivalence) that

$$\bigwedge pa[S\langle p\rangle(a) \supset . \ Tr(a) \equiv p].$$

Similarly, we define the concept of falsehood:

$$\bigwedge a[Fl(a) \equiv \bigvee p[S\langle p\rangle(a) \wedge \sim p]].$$

It is worth noting that falsehood and R from Russell's definition are equal, that

$$\bigwedge a[R(a) \equiv Fl(a)],$$

which, partly, resolves the mystery of the antinomy.

Using the presented Principles and definition, one can prove (see Hiż, 1984)

Theorem 1. $\wedge Xpqa[X \subset Tr \wedge S\langle p \supset q\rangle(a) \wedge Cn(S\langle p\rangle \cup X) - Cn(X) = Cn(S\langle q\rangle \cup X) - Cn(X) \wedge p \mathrel{.\supset} q]$.

Theorem 1 shows that in OA2 for α one can take the relation between the set $Y = Cn(S\langle p\rangle \cup X) - Cn(X)$ and p. The set Y may be called the information of a sentence saying that p. The following definition of the information of a sentence a relative to assumptions X is suitable

$$\wedge aXY[Inf\langle a, X\rangle(Y) \equiv \vee p[S\langle p\rangle(a) \wedge Y = Cn(\iota a \cup X) - Cn(X)]].$$

(This definition is a derivative of Carnap's work.)

From the fact that the concept of truth is definable by the concept of saying-that one should not conclude that the concept of saying-that is more fundamental than the other. Note that the concept of saying-that is definable by using the concept of consequence. The concept of consequence, though it is definable by truth, is helpful here in determining to some extent the concept of saying-that.

One must distinguish between the truth of a sentence and the truth of a completed (fulfilled) statement or text. *He told her the news* is a sentence. It obeys several logical laws, e.g. *Either he told her the news or he did not tell her the news*. We can draw conclusions from it, e.g. *She was told the news*, *The news was told her*, *She received the news*, etc. In that way, *He told her the news* creates its own system, its own field of consequences. We can reason correctly - to a point - without knowing who he is, who she is and what the news was about. *Every natural number divisible by 9 is divisible by 3* is a complete statement. It is hard to imagine a context which would change its message. And if somebody thinks that 2187 is not natural - because it is too large - or that it is not divisible by 9 - because he does not know how to perform the division - then he does not speak the sublanguage of arithmetic, but a language of his own limited arithmetical competence. Perhaps it is not prudent to take English, French, Italian, or Chinese as a language, as L in which a sentence a is coined. Perhaps there is no English, but only arithmetical English, chemical English etc. An ethnic language is too crude, too amorphous a structure for a refined semantics.

No possible fact is asserted by *He told her the news* alone. This sentence must be put in a context which would resolve all the referentials before it can be semantically evaluated in its extension.

Information content of a sentence has to be distinguished from the information given by the sentence in a particular context. I will examine the effect of the left context only.

$$\bigwedge baXY[Inf(b, a, X) = Y \equiv \bigvee pq[S\langle p\rangle(a) \wedge S\langle q\rangle(a^\frown b) \wedge Y = Cn(\iota(a^\frown b) \cup X) - Cn(\iota a \cup X)]]$$

The information given by b in the (left) context a relative to the set X of assumptions is the set Y which is the set of consequences of the text $a^\frown b$ (i.e. a followed by b), with the assumptions, less the consequences of the left-hand context a and of X, provided that there are two possible situations p and q such that a says that p and $a^\frown b$ says that q.

To exemplify, let the text $(a^\frown b)$ be

Once Peter visited France. When Peter was in France, De Gaulle was president.

and let X be a normal human knowledge, including *If somebody visited a country then he was in that country* as well as *France is a country* and *Peter is somebody*.

Peter was in France ε Cn(a, X),
Peter was in France ε Cn(b, X).

Therefore

Peter was in France $\tilde{\varepsilon}$ Inf(b, a, X).

It happens that

Inf(a⁀b, X) = Inf(a⁀*At that time De Gaulle was president*).

Also, *at that time* can be zeroed, i.e., removed from the text without changing information. (About zeroings see Harris, 1982, Chapter 1.)

Inf(a⁀b, X) = Inf(a⁀*De Gaulle was president*).

The possibility of zeroing and reconstructing the time may be connected not only with the identity of the tenses in a and in *De Gaulle was president* but also with the term *president*, as the presidency is for a period. (Compare *Carolo regnante*.) Such zeroing of *at that time* seems strange in

(*?) *Peter visited France. De Gaulle was anti-British.*

perhaps because De Gaulle being anti-British does not determine a period of time. If we add to this text some indication of time linked to the time of Peter's visit, e.g.

Peter visited France. De Gaulle was anti-British. It did not matter, for De Galle was no longer president.

the text becomes acceptable.

The definition of information in context allows us to assign information to sentences with an unresolved anaphora. In

He enjoyed the visit.

put after

Peter visited France.

both, *he* and *the visit* are resolved. The text

Peter visited France. He enjoyed the visit.

has among its consequences

Peter enjoyed the visit.
Peter enjoyed his visit to France.

They are in the information of *He enjoyed the visit* in the context of *Peter visited France.*

Sometimes it is asserted that to know these facts about consequence one has to know the rules of cross-reference. I would prefer to say that the rules are needed only for a description of the facts; speakers use the facts themselves. Every English speaker knows that *Peter enjoyed his visit to France* follows from *Peter visited France. He enjoyed the visit.* No rules help him, though they may help the linguist to make his theory of speaker's behaviour. To say that a speaker obeys the rule is a *post theoriam* metaphor.

In the structure Inf(a, b, X), b may be not a sentence, but a part-sentence, an adverbial, a quantifier, a noun phrase etc.:

> *Felice won the tournament. Yes, she did. (Easily; Delightful!; Almost; Only morally; No, Frank did; Frank, not her; It was Frank; No, she did not; No, no, Frank; Not quite; Possibly so; Perhaps; But it is not certain; There are conflicting reports about it.)*

Those bits of sentences in that context do give information. Some of them add to the previous information (*Easily*), some subtract or change it (*Almost; No, Frank did*). We call the latter *correctives*. The definition of information in context covers both cases. In case of a corrective (*Felice won the tournament. Only morally.*) one consequence of the text is *Felice did not win the tournament*. From the set Cn(ι(*Felice won the tournament*). *Only morally* $\cup$ X) we subtract the consequences of (ι(*Felice won the tournament*) $\cup$ X), among them the very *Felice won the tournament*.

To describe how we draw conclusions from texts with correctives, we note that correctives normally occur after the text which they correct. We give preference to the later part. If the negation of a follows from b, the negation of a follows from $a^\frown b$.

Taking another example of the information of a phrase in a context, in *Men are mortal. No exception*, the phrase *No exception* is like a quantifier over the first sentence. In *Men are corruptible. With rare exceptions*, the phrase *With rare exceptions* is also a quantifier for its predecessor *Men are corruptible*. The sentence *Men are mortal* alone could be understood as saying that men are usually due to die, just as *Men are vocal* is understood as saying that men usually can speak. The quantifiers *Normally*, *No exceptions*, etc. change the information content of their contexts.

The definition of the information of a phrase in a (left-hand) context contains a condition that $a^\frown b$ must be saying something, i.e. that $\bigvee q[S\langle q\rangle(a^\frown b)]$. But there may not be a possible situation asserted by $a^\frown b$. For instance, if a and b are in different sublanguages, $a^\frown b$ may be completely unacceptable.

* *9 is an even number. It is removable by turpentine.*

No speaker of both sublanguages, that of arithmetic and that of home cleaning can accept this sentence, even hypothetically; he cannot reason with it.

To reflect the relationship between what is said at the beginning of the text and what is said after the modifier is added, a more general concept of information in a context is useful.

A sentence a may be a consequence of a class Y of sentences, or a negation of a may be a consequence of Y, or it may be that neither is the case. We define a useful auxiliary function $Cn_a(Y)$ which states how a is related to Y. It is the verdict of a by Y.

D. $\bigwedge aY[Cn_a(Y) = \iota a$, if $a \in Cn(Y)]$
$= \iota neg\ a$, if $neg\ a \in Cn(Y)]$
$= \emptyset$ otherwise]

A lemma follows:

L. $\bigwedge aY[Cn_a(Y) \subset Cn(Y)]$

Proof.

Case 1. $a \in Cn(Y)$, then $Cn_a(Y) = \iota a$ and $\iota a \subset Cn(Y)$, therefore $Cn_a(Y) \subset Cn(Y)$;

Case 2. $neg\ a\ \varepsilon\ Cn_a(Y)$, then $Cn_a(Y) = \iota neg\ a$ and $\iota neg\ a \subset Cn(Y)$;
Case 3. $a\ \tilde{\varepsilon}\ Cn(Y)$ and $neg\ a\ \tilde{\varepsilon}\ Cn(Y)$, then $Cn_a(Y) = \emptyset \subset Cn(Y)$.

D. $\Lambda eaX[Inf_e(a, X) = Cn(\iota a \cup X) - Cn(Cn_e(\iota a \cup X) \cup X)]$

In particular,

$$\Lambda abX[Inf_a(a^\frown b, X) = Cn(\iota(a^\frown b) \cup X) - Cn(Cn_a(\iota(a^\frown b) \cup X) \cup X)].$$

The information about a given in $a^\frown b$ and X is the consequences of $\iota(a \cup b)$ and X less the consequences of Cn_a. Now we form a relation between a set of sentences and a situation: if after a we say that p, then we are in a new information state. The relation between this information state and the situation p is the relation $inf\langle X, a\rangle$.

D. $\Lambda YXap[Y\ inf\langle X, a\rangle p \equiv Vb[S\langle p\rangle(a^\frown b) \wedge Y = Inf_a(a^\frown b, X)]]$

One now can interpret 'α' from Frege's principle A2 as '$inf\langle X, a\rangle$' and a theorem resembling A2 can be proven. In addition to the conditions of the Theorem 1, it is now required that Cn_a of $S\langle p\rangle \cup X$ and of $S\langle q\rangle \cup X$ be the same.

If either b or c, when added to a, change the impact of a in the same way (i.e. if each asserts a or leaves it as it was, or each changes a to its negation or each declares ignorance about a), they still may do it with different additional items of information. (Compare *Only morally* with *No, Frank did*. Or compare *Perhaps* with *There are conflicting reports about it.*) If these additional items of information are identical as well, then if it is as $a^\frown b$ says, then it is also as $a^\frown c$ says. In other words, if $S\langle p\rangle(a^\frown c)$ and $S\langle q\rangle(a^\frown c)$ and if $Cn_a(S\langle p\rangle \cup X) = Cn_a(S\langle q\rangle \cup X)$ (i.e. if saying that p and saying that q result in the same verdict for a) and if otherwise the information contents of $a^\frown b$ and $a^\frown c$ are the same, then if p, then q

- provided that there is a sentence which says that $p \supset q$ and provided that the assumptions are true. The Theorem will assert that

$$\Lambda pabqcX[S\langle p\rangle(a^\frown b) \wedge S\langle q\rangle(a^\frown c) \wedge Cn_a(S\langle p\rangle \cup X) = Cn_a(S\langle q\rangle \cup X) \wedge Cn(\iota(a^\frown b) \cup X) - Cn_a(S\langle p\rangle \cup X) = Cn(\iota(a^\frown c) \cup X) - Cn_a(S\langle q\rangle \cup X) \wedge S\langle p \supset q\rangle(d) \wedge X \subset Tr \wedge p \mathrel{.\supset} q]$$

In terms of the relation $inf\langle X, a\rangle$ the same is stated in Theorem 2.

Theorem 2. $\Lambda YXapqd[Y\ inf\langle X, a\rangle p \wedge Y\ inf\langle X, a\rangle q \wedge Cn_a(S\langle p\rangle \cup X) = Cn_a(S\langle q\rangle \cup X) \wedge X \subset Tr \wedge S\langle p \supset q\rangle(d) \wedge p \mathrel{.\supset} q]$

Proof: If

1. $Y\ inf\langle X, a\rangle p$
2. $Y\ inf\langle X, a\rangle q$
3. $Cn_a(S\langle p\rangle \cup X) = Cn_a(S\langle q\rangle \cup X)$
4. $X \subset Tr$
5. $S\langle p \supset q\rangle(d)$
6. p, then

$.Vb, c$

7. $S\langle p\rangle(a^\frown b)$
8. $Y = Inf_a(a^\frown b, X)$ (1)
9. $S\langle q\rangle(a^\frown c)$
10. $Y = Inf_a(a^\frown c, X)$. (2)

I will abbreviate '$Cn_a(\iota(a^\frown b) \cup X)$' as 'E' and '$Cn_a(\iota(a^\frown c) \cup X)$' as 'C'.

11. $Cn(\iota(a^\frown b) \cup X) - Cn(E \cup X) = Cn(\iota(a^\frown c) \cup X) - Cn(C \cup X)$ (8,10)
12. $E \subset Cn(\iota(a^\frown b) \cup X)$ and $C \subset Cn(\iota(a^\frown c) \cup X)$ (Lemma)

If $Y \subset Cn(Z)$, then $Cn(Z) = Cn(Z \cup Y)$. Thus

13. $Cn(\iota(a^\frown b) \cup E \cup X) - Cn(E \cup X) = Cn(\iota(a^\frown c) \cup C \cup X) - Cn(C \cup X)$ (11,12)

14. $E = C$ (3)

15. $Cn(\iota(a^\frown b) \cup E \cup X) - Cn(E \cup X) =$

$= Cn(\iota(a^\frown c) \cup E \cup X) - Cn(E \cup X)$ (13,14)

16. $Cn(S\langle p\rangle \cup E \cup X) - Cn(E \cup X) =$

$= Cn(S\langle q\rangle \cup E \cup X) - Cn(E \cup X)$ (15,7,9)

q (Theorem 1,4,5,16)

The semantic characterization of a phrase used after its left-hand context a consists - roughly - in a set of sentences, which are consequences of $a^\frown b$, but are not consequences of a. The contextual import of *He is a teacher* after *You met my cousin* contains *My cousin is a teacher*, *My cousin whom you met is a man*, *You met a teacher* etc. But what is the semantic role of *He is a teacher* independent of the context in which it appears? A natural answer is that *He is a teacher* is a function from a set of sentences to another set of sentences, from information states to information states. The function is not a set of sentences but a relation between sets of sentences. The arguments of this function are the various information states before *He is a teacher* occurs. The values of the function are the information states after *He is a teacher* occurs. Though the value of the function varies with the argument, the function stays the same, and one who understands the sentence *He is a teacher* grasps the function rather than any particular value of it. The function assigned to *He is a teacher* is referred to as the intension of *He is a teacher* whereas the values of the function for particular left-hand environments are the extensions of the sentence. The intension of *He is a teacher* is: adding *d is a teacher* and *d is a man*, where *d* is the resolution of the anaphora *he*.

For Montague the intension of a sentence was the function from indices to truth-values. For a linguist the indices consist in information at different points of the text and the intensions are functions leading to further information states.

$$\text{D. } \Lambda fbX[f = \mathrm{Int}\langle b, X\rangle \equiv \Lambda pa[S\langle p\rangle(a^\frown b) \supset f(\mathrm{Cn}(\iota a \cup X)) =$$
$$= \mathrm{Cn}(\iota(a^\frown F(b)) \cup X)]]$$

From this definition of intension

$$\Lambda pabX[S\langle p\rangle(a^\frown b) \supset \mathrm{Int}\langle b, X\rangle(\mathrm{Cn}(\iota a \cup X)) = \mathrm{Cn}(\iota(a^\frown F(b)) \cup X)]$$

In a particular context a the phrase b may have number, gender, tense or modality, largely determined by a (*They will be teachers*, etc.). But $\mathrm{Int}\langle b, X\rangle$ may be kept in the form of unresolved dependence. The intension of predicating *teacher* is a process, the same process in all such cases. Furthermore, the intension of *d is a teacher* is the same as that of *d teaches*; i.e., the instruction "add *d is a teacher* to the information" amounts to the same change of information as the instruction "add *d teaches* to the information". *To be a teacher* is the same as *to teach*. The function, the instruction Int *d is a teacher*, consists therefore of *d teaches* in whatever form is appropriate in a given context. The form in general will be marked F(*teach*). This is the reason for writing '$\iota(a^\frown F(b))$' in the definition of intension.

The concept of a type, x, of elementary sentence with a phrase y is useful: if in a sentence with an occurrence of y the replacement of all phrases except y by their respective pro-forms results in a sentence x, then x is a type of elementary sentence with y. (I take *is*, *do*, *have* and their inflected forms as pro-forms form verb-phrases.)

To teach may appear with complements: *He teaches algebra*, *He teaches girls, He teaches girls algebra, He teaches algebra to girls*, *He teaches girls how to solve equations*. Each of these phrases has its own intension. So do *d F(teach) y to z, d F(teach) how to w, d F(teach) how to w*. (Note that *d F(teach) y* is ambiguous as to accusative or dative y, which in English practice is determined by the choice of words for y.) These intensions are different. But they are related. Whoever teaches something to somebody, teaches. The instruction to add *d F(teach)* is included in the instruction to add *d F(teach)y to z.*

$$\mathrm{Int}\langle d\ F(teach), X\rangle \subset \mathrm{Int}\langle d\ F(teach)y\ to\ z, X\rangle$$
$$\mathrm{Int}\langle d\ F(teach), X\rangle \subset \mathrm{Int}\langle d\ F(teach)\ how\ to\ w, X\rangle \text{ etc.}$$

Also, whoever teaches, teaches something to somebody.

$$\mathrm{Int}\langle d\ F(teach)y\ to\ z, X\rangle \subset \mathrm{Int}\langle d\ F(teach), X\rangle \text{ etc.}$$

so that

$$\mathrm{Int}\langle d\ F(teach), X\rangle = \mathrm{Int}\langle d\ F(teach)y_{accusative}, X\rangle =$$
$$= \mathrm{Int}\langle d\ F(teach)z_{dative}, X\rangle = \mathrm{Int}\langle d\ F(teach)zy, X\rangle =$$
$$= \mathrm{Int}\langle d\ F(teach)z\ how\ to\ w, X\rangle = \mathrm{Int}\langle d\ F(teach)how\ to\ w, X\rangle.$$

If in a particular context any of d, x, y, z or w is not specified, not determined, if it remains an anphora unresolved by the context, then it may be replaced in b by a pro-form: d and y by *somebody*, z by *something*, w by *do something.**

This shows that there is only one type of elementary sentence with *teach*: *One teaches somebody how to do something*. Others are short for it.

---

* Normally w = *do* y (*how to do algebra*). Often the relation between w and y requires special words instead of *do*, *teach violin* - *how to play the violin*; *teach medicine* - *how to practice medicine*.

REFERENCES

Harris, Z., 1982, "A Grammar of English on Mathematical Principles," John Wiley and Sons, New York.

Hiż, H., 1984, Frege, Leśniewski and Information Semantics on the Resolution of Antinomies, Synthese, 59.

INTERPRETATIVE MODEL FOR LINGUISTIC QUANTIFIERS

Irena Bellert

Department of Linguistics
McGill University
Montréal, Quebec H3A 1G5, Canada

1. INTRODUCTION

This paper attempts to give a model-theoretical account for the semantics of elementary English sentences (the basic units of the semantic structure of the entire language), as a necessary first step towards a compositional interpretive semantics of all the sentences of the language (see Bellert, 1983, for some applications of this proposal to complex sentences).

The proposed interpretive rules apply directly to a surface structure description of sentences. Assuming the generative transformational grammar, they apply to elementary S-structures with no modals, each consisting of an n-ary predicate (verb) with n NP-arguments (the Noun-phrase subject and the obligatory Noun-phrase objects) which are not semantically linked (i.e. independent of each other). Every NP-argument is analysed as a quantified term consisting of a linguistic quantifier (or a sign of quantity) and a term (a set expression). A linguistic quantifier may be explicit (e.g. a determiner, specifier or numeral) or implicit (lack of determiner before a proper name, a pronoun or an indefinite NP in the plural). A term may be explicit (a noun or a noun-phrase without its quantifier) or implicit, as in the case of a pronoun, for which the term is construed from the preceding (or extra-linguistic) context. In this paper, we do not discuss semantically linked arguments, and thus we do not include pronouns which are coreferential with a referring expression occurring in the same sentence, nor those usually interpreted as bound variables. (For an application of this proposal to semantically linked arguments, see Bellert, 1983 and 1984.)

The main points of the paper can be summarized as follows:

(1) Every NP-argument is interpreted according to the same unifying principle according to which, independently of whether an argument is a proper name, a pronoun or a quantified phrase, it is analysed in terms of a *sign of quantity* and a *term*. Such an approach is in accord with Leibniz's variant of traditional logic (Leibniz, 1966), where it is claimed that singular propositions have the logical form of general propositions, the only difference being that singular propositions have 'wild' or indifferent quantity. (See Sommers, 1982, for an interesting discussion of this matter and a comparison of categorical sentences in traditional logic with atomic sentences in modern predicate logic.)

In the present approach an argument is a linguistic expression interpretable in a sentence S by both the denotation class of its term and the features of its sign of quantity; together they determine a subclass, called here *reference class*, i.e. the class (or set of classes) of entities which can be selected by any user of S, and to which a given relation or property expressed by the predicate applies. Not every NP is, therefore, an argument. An argument position is one which allows only a quantified phrase. The predicate position following a copulative verb (*to be*, *to remain*, *to be turned into*) is not an argument position. The NP in a predicative position, e.g. the phrase in italics in

$$\left\{\begin{array}{l}\text{This man}\\ \text{John}\\ \text{Everyone}\end{array}\right\}\text{ is } \textit{a teacher}$$

does not determine any reference class. The reference class is determined here by the only argument in the subject position. The predicate *is a teacher* applies, like any other predicate in this position, to the reference class determined by the argument in the subject. The determiner, which occurs in this phrase, has no semantic function of a quantifying sign; it is only part of the predicate expression.

(2) Interpretive rules for elementary sentences are based on a lexical characterization of all linguistic quantifiers (and the implicit signs of quantity in proper names or pronouns), by means of the values of two formal features: *absoluteness* and *distributiveness* (defined in section 2). The set of rules (specified in section 4) predict all theoretically possible configurations of feature values in any cooccurring arguments in an elementary S-structure. Each such configuration of feature values determines a possible semantic reading of the sentence corresponding to that structure.

(3) This proposal is intended to account for the semantic properties of sentences which so far have been described by the scope method in terms of Logical Forms with fronted quantifiers, derived from S-structures by a Quantifier Movement Rule (as in May, 1977). The feature method is designed to interpret sentences with quantifiers in their actual syntactic position in S-structures (along with Chomsky's null hypothesis (1981), and similarly as in Barwise and Cooper (1981) or van Bentham (1983)). There is no need to front quantifiers in order or obtain different Logical Forms for distinct sem-

antic readings, nor is it necessary to use any additional rules. The proposed method correctly predicts the number of distinct readings in all those cases in which the scope method can do it, as well as in those cases in which the scope method cannot do it (see section 8, examples 3, 5). It also accounts for those readings which have to be considered as marked in the scope method (as in May, 1977, where the corresponding Logical Forms are derived by idiosyncratic 'conversion' rules, rather than by the rules of core grammar (see Bellert, 1983)). The definitions of feature values correspond closely to the way competent speakers of a natural language (rather than competent logicians) interpret quantified arguments, and the proposed interpretations are consonant with speakers' intuitions about the truth of such sentences in their ordinary use. The truth conditions for all sentences which correspond to the types of S-structures discussed, follow directly from the definitions of feature values.

(4) The proposal is *not* designed to account for the full lexical meaning of quantifiers or for some additional semantic distinctions between quantifiers (as in the case of *all*, *each*, *every* and *any* or *many* and *several*). It does not account either for quantified phrases which contain non-countable nouns (e.g. *a little water*, *some air*, *a lot of butter*), in which case the reference cannot be conceived of as a class of entities, and the interpretive rules will be different. Nor does it account for the generic use of determiners. For instance in

$$\begin{Bmatrix} \textit{the} \\ \textit{a} \end{Bmatrix} \textit{ lion is a wild animal}$$

the denotation is a species rather than a class of entities. Finally, so-called statistical sentences (e.g. 'A Belgian has 1½ children') are excluded, for the interpretation of such sentences is quite specific.

Let us now discuss some examples. Consider the sentence

(1) Each McGill student respects one professor

which has two distinct readings. In classical logic, the two readings could be represented schematically as (1a) and (1b), respectively

(1a) $(\forall x)(\exists y)(M(x) \wedge P(y) \rightarrow R(x, y))$

(1b) $(\exists y)(\forall x)(M(x) \wedge P(y) \rightarrow R(x, y))$

where M stands for *McGill student*, P for *professor* and R for *respects*. The difference in the order of quantifiers in (1a) and (1b) accounts for the difference in the meaning and the truth conditions. The order of the arguments in sentence (1) is, however, not decisive. This sentence can be interpreted either according to (1a) or according to (1b), if we disregard the fact that the more usual interpretation of 'one professor' is 'exactly one' rather than 'at least one', but this point is irrelevant for the present discussion.

In the case discussed above, the scope method would adequatly account for the ambiguity involved, by means of two different Logical Forms with a different order of the quantifiers fronted by the Movement Rule. And the number of distinct Logical Forms is indeed two, that is, the factorial (n!) of quantified phrases, as predicted by May (1977, 33). However, as we will see later, in many other cases it is impossible to account for distinct readings by the scope method. For instance, the well known example 'Two examiners marked six scripts' (where the numerals could be replaced by several other quantifiers with the same number of resulting interpretations), with its four readings discussed at length in several papers (Kempson and Cormack, 1981, 1982; Bach, 1982), cannot be accounted for by May's scope method. For, in general, the number of readings depends on the number of *ambiguously featured* quantifiers and on some general rules for cooccurring quantifiers (which will be proposed in section 4), rather than on the number and the respective scope of quantifiers, as it is claimed in the scope method. It is only incidental that the number of distinct readings for (1) coincides with the factorial of the quantifiers (as it also does for many other, but clearly not all, sentences).

The ambiguity, or rather the two possible interpretations, of (1) - it is worth noting - rests on two possible interpretations of the quantifier in the argument 'one professor', since the other quantifier 'each' is interpreted in the same way in both readings. This difference in the interpretation of (1) will be accounted for by two possible values of the feature *absoluteness*. The value *+absolute* is construed by analogy to what Copi (1967) calls the 'absolute' sense of an existential quantifier which precedes a universal quantifier, as opposed to the 'relative' sense of an existential quantifier which is in the scope of a universal quantifier. This notion is, however, modified and extended in the definitions to apply to various other linguistic quantifiers. The positive value of the feature 'absolute' can intuitively be described as an indication that the given argument has exactly one reference class (i.e. exactly one class of individuals may be referred to by means of an argument whose quantifier is interpreted as *+absolute*, on any particular use of the sentence in which it occurs), whereas a *-absolute* value will indicate that the given argument may have more than one reference class. According to the rules in section 4, 'one' which is assigned in the lexicon two possible values of absoluteness, will be interpreted as *+absolute* or *-absolute*, depending on the feature values of the cooccurring quantifying signs in the same S-structure. For some configurations of quantifying signs, 'one' will always be interpreted as *+absolute* (e.g. John respects one woman). In sentence (1), however, the rules will permit either of the two values, and (1) will thus have two distinct readings. But for some choice of the lexical material, one or the other reading may be excluded, only because the corresponding state of affairs would contradict our knowledge of the world (e.g. *Each girl married a handsome man*, where 'a' will be interpreted as *-absolute* in a monogamic society, or *Each catholic priest believes in one God* where 'one' will be interpreted as *+absolute*). Such readings are not excluded, however, by the rules of language. (The same assumption is made in May, 1977.)

The feature *distributiveness* is construed by analogy to the property of a universal quantifier in classical logic. This notion is, however, extended and defined in such a way that it applies to several other linguistic quantifiers. The linguistic quantifiers 'every' and 'each' are always interpreted as *+distributive*, that is, the predicate applies to each entity in the reference class of the argument quantified by such quantifiers. All the linguistic quantifiers which cooccur with plural noun phrases may, however, be interpreted as + or *-distributive*, and the choice of one or the other value is subject to the rules. Finally, *zero-distributiveness* indicates that the predicate applies to just one entity which is the only entity contained in the reference class. For instance, an argument consisting of a proper name or an argument quantified by a definite singular quantifier 'the', 'this' or 'that' will be interpreted as *zero-distributive*.

In the majority of ordinary sentences of a natural language, the linguistic quantifier and the term expression (the remaining part of the argument) are imprecise, insufficient for identification of the reference class, and sometimes even misleading (as in well known examples provided by Geach, 1976, or Donnellan, 1976). In a language theory, however, we have to assume that in any given context (model) such linguistic expressions are precise enough and sufficient for the identification of the entities in the reference classes. And if they happen to be misleading (or for that matter, if they contribute to a successful lie), this is not a problem for anyone interested in the rules of language, although it may be an interesting problem for a theorist of successful communication. In a language theory, we have to assume that in any given context (model), such linguistic expressions are precise enough and sufficient for the identification of their respective reference classes. A context (model) has to be assumed for another reason. Rarely, if ever, will ordinary language speakers use sentences, such as (2) or (3) (or similar sentences provided in the literature as examples)

(2) All babies are healthy.

(3) Some children are sick.

in a sense which could adequately be represented by means of an unrestricted universal quantifier or an existential quantifier, respectively, with the assumed context of the entire world. Ordinary speakers will normally use the arguments *all babies* or *some children* in the above examples in a restricted context, for which the reference class of *all babies* will be the class of all the babies in that context only, and the reference class of *some children* will consist of some specific individuals in that context only.

In its ordinary use, (3) may be true or false depending on the context. However, if the interpretive rules are not restricted to a given context, this sentence represented by means of an existential quantifier would always be true, since there are certainly some individuals in the world who are both children and sick. Similarly, (2) represented by an unrestricted universal quantifier would always be false, since certainly there is at least one baby in the world who is not healthy. A context will therefore be assumed for the interpretive rules, in order to account for the sense in which such or other quantified phrases may be intended.--

It follows: (2) definitions of features values; (3) assignment of feature values in the lexicon; (4) rules, theorems, and consequences; (5) corollaries; (6) truth conditions; (7) claims; and (8) examples.

2. DEFINITIONS OF FEATURE VALUES

We will consider elementary sentences with a predicate-argument structure consisting of an n-ary predicate (verb) with its n NP-arguments: the NP-subject and the obligatory NP-objects, each consisting of some kind of quantifying sign and some term. The following notation will be used in the definitions:

QT will stand for any NP-argument, where

Q is a linguistic quantifier, or a sign of quantity assigned to a proper name or a pronoun,

T is a term expression (the NP without its quantifier; in the case of a pronoun, the term is construed from its antecedent according to the rules of language, or from the context)

$||T||$ is the denotation class of T (the class of entities named by T)*

$||QT||$ is a family of all those subclasses of $||T||$ whose relative size or number of elements is indicated by Q.

Note: Intuitively, $||QT||$ represents a family of classes, each of which could possibly be a reference class of QT. Reference classes are, however, picked up in particular contexts on which they depend. We need therefore another notion:

$R_C(QT) \subset ||QT||$ is a particular subclass of $||QT||$, consisting of the reference class (or reference classes) of QT in a context C.

---

* For simplicity, we assume that $||T|| \neq \emptyset$.

Definitions of the Values of Absoluteness

Def. 1: In any given context C, Q is interpreted as *+abs* in QT iff Q requires exactly one class to be selected as a reference class of QT (that is, iff Q requires that R_C(QT) consist of exactly one class).

Def. 2: In any given context C, Q is interpreted as *-abs* in QT iff Q requires at least one class to be selected as a reference class of QT (that is, iff Q requires that R_C(QT) consist of at least one class).

It follows from the above definitions that a *+absolute* quantifier is a specific case of a *-absolute* quantifier, and thus any elementary sentence with an argument QT, where Q is interpreted as *+abs* will entail a sentence with the same structure, where Q will be interpreted as *-abs*. (It is worth noting that, similarly, any sentence represented by an existential quantifier followed by a universal quantifier will entail a sentence with the opposite order of quantifiers so that (1b) in the Introduction will entail (1a)). We will also introduce a stronger notion of *-absoluteness*.

Def. 2A: In any given context C, Q is interpreted as *strictly -abs* in QT iff Q requires more than one class to be selected as a reference class of QT (that is, Q requires that R_C(QT) consist of more than one class).

Note: If a quantifier Q is interpreted as *+abs* (*-abs* or *strictly -abs*), then by the same token the argument QT will also be said to be *+abs* (*-abs* or *strictly -abs*, respectively).

Definitions of the Values of Distributiveness

The relation of distributiveness indicates in what way the predicate applies to the entities in the reference class of its argument (if there is only one argument), or in what way the predicate relates (or connects) the entities in the reference classes of its arguments. If there are more than two arguments in any elementary predicate-argument structure, the predicate relates the entities in each pair of arguments. A quantifier Q_1 in an argument Q_1T_1 may then be *+dis* with respect to an argument Q_2T_2 (we will write Q_1*+dis*(Q_2)), and in the same structure Q_1 may be *-dis* with respect to another argument Q_3T_3 (we will write then $Q_{1\,-dis(Q_3)}^{\,+dis(Q_2)}$). In order to cover all the cases of distributiveness for arguments which are *+abs* (and have just one reference class) and for those which are *-abs* (and may have more than one reference class), we need another notion, namely, the range of an argument QT:

$RANGE_C(QT)$ stands for the union of all the reference classes of QT in any given context C (i.e. $RANGE_C(QT) = \bigcup R_C(QT)$).

Note: If an argument QT is interpreted as *+abs*, it has exactly one reference class, and then $RANGE_C(QT) = R_C(QT)$ (in such a case this notion is redundant). But if an argument QT is interpreted as *-abs*, this notion is a useful abbreviation in the definitions. In either case $RANGE_C(QT)$ represents the union of the reference classes, since the union of a family consisting of one class equals that class.

Le S be an elementary predicate-argument structure, let Q_1T_1 and Q_2T_2 be any two NP-arguments in S, and let P be the predicate:

Def 3: In any given context C, Q_1 is interpreted as *+dis*(Q_2) in S iff P relates each entity in the $RANGE_C(Q_1T_1)$ with each entity in one of the reference class $\in R_C(Q_2T_2)$ in such a way that each reference class $\in R_C(Q_2T_2)$ is related by P with at least one entity in the $RANGE_C(Q_1T_1)$.

Note: Notice that if Q_2 is *+abs*, that is, if Q_2T_2 has only one reference class $\in R_C(Q_2T_2)$, then the predicate P relates each entity in the $RANGE_C(Q_1T_1)$ with each entity in just one reference class, and the condition in Def. 3 is trivially satisfied, even in the case when that class contains just one entity.

Note: In a sentence with just one argument QT, Q is *+dis* iff the predicate P applies to each entity in the reference class of QT.

Def. 4: In any given context C, Q_1 is interpreted as *-dis*(Q_2) in S iff P connects each entity in the $RANGE_C(Q_1T_1)$ with at least one entity in the $RANGE_C(Q_2T_2)$, and each entity in the $RANGE_C(Q_2T_2)$ with at least one entity in the $RANGE_C(Q_1T_1)$.

Def. 4A: In any given context C, Q_1 is interpreted as *strictly -dis*(Q_2) in S iff (a) Q_1 is *-dis*(Q_2), (b) Q_1 is not *+dis*(Q_2), and (c) the $RANGE_C(Q_1T_1)$ and the $RANGE_C(Q_2T_2)$ both contain at least two entities.

Notes: The term 'predicate' is conceived here as including everything in S except for the two arguments quantified by Q_1 and Q_2, respectively, that is, the verb with adverbial particles and with prepositions, if such elements occur in S, as in the example below, where the predicate is in italics:

(3) Each student { *received* two letters / *served on* two committees / *signed in for* two courses }

Strictly speaking, the predicate 'P' in the definitions of distributiveness should be understood as 'interpretation of P'.

The three diagrams below represent examples of some possible connections between the entities in the reference classes, which correspond to some permitted configurations of feature values.

(4) Each boy spoke to these girls

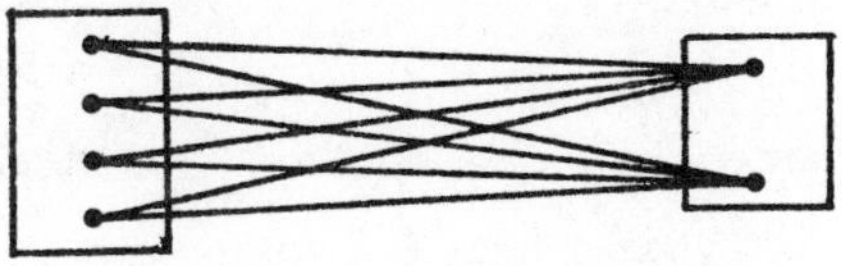

(in a context with four boys and two girls)

Q_1 *+abs* *+dis*(Q_2) Q_2 *+abs* *+dis*(Q_1)

(5) Each boy wrote two letters

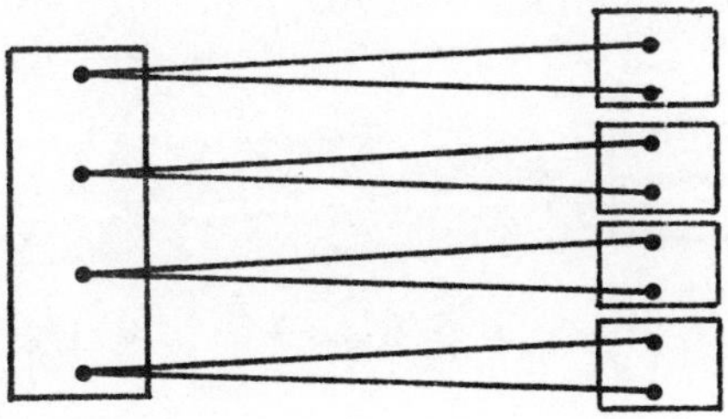

(in a context with four boys)

Q_1 *+abs* *+dis*(Q_2) Q_2 *−abs* *−dis*(Q_1)

(6) Seven pictures are located in two rooms

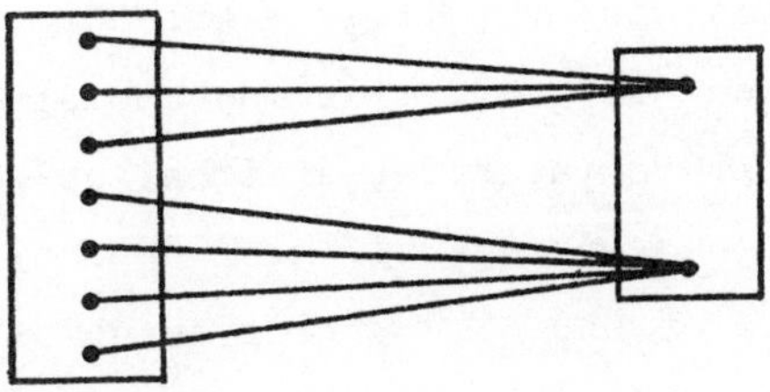

Q_1 *+abs* *−dis*(Q_2) Q_2 *+abs* *−dis*(Q_1)

Def. 5: In any given context C, Q_1 is interpreted as zero-distributive (*O dis*) with respect to any other cooccurring quantifier Q_2 iff Q_1 requires exactly one reference class which is a unit class to be selected as a reference class of Q_1T_1 (that is, Q requires that $R_C(Q_1T_1)$ be a one-element family consisting of one unit class).

Notes: A class containing more than one member may, however, be interpreted as a unit class but only in the case when all its members are construed as constituting one whole (one entity), and the predicate applies to the entire class conceived of as one whole. For instance, such is the case of the argument 'three brothers' in the example below.

(7) Three brothers inherited this house

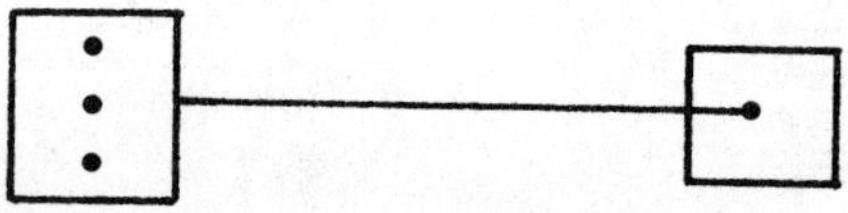

Q_1 *+abs* *O dis* Q_2 *+abs* *O dis*

We will write Q *O dis* without indicating to which quantifier Q is zero-distributive, since zero-distributiveness applies to any cooccurring quantifier. It is clear from Def. 5 that a definite singular quantifier (*the*, *this* or *that*) is always *O dis*, and so is any argument consisting of a proper name. An indefinite singular quantifier (*a*, *one*) is also *O dis* whenever it is *+abs*; but when it is *-abs*, the RANGE of the argument it quantifies may contain more than one entity, and then it will be interpreted either as *+dis* or as *-dis* with respect to the cooccurring quantifiers (depending on the corresponding feature values of the cooccurring quantifiers). See the example below, where the diagram represents a particular case in a context with six professors:

(8) Each professor wrote a letter to the Principal

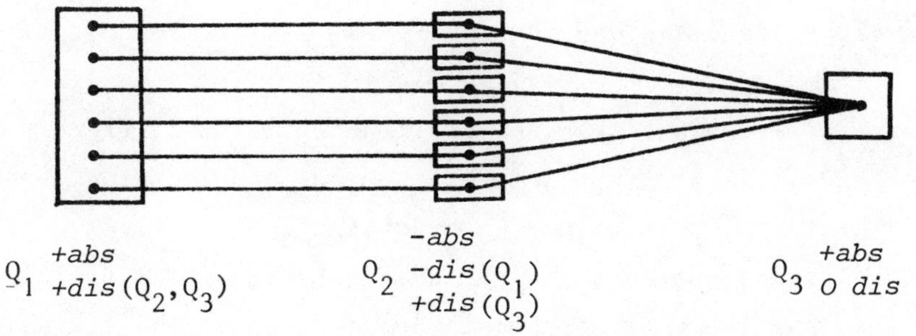

It is worth noting that a definite singular quantifier (e.g. *the*) and an indefinite singular quantifier (e.g. *a*, *one*) interpreted as *+absolute*, both require that there be exactly one reference class containing exactly one entity. However, an indefinite singular quantifier interpreted as *-absolute* requires only that there be at least one reference class with the number of entities indicated by the quantifier, so that *a* (or *one*) need not be interpreted as 'exactly one', but in some cases depending on the context, it may be interpreted as 'at least one'. Compare, for instance, (a) with (b): (a) 'A beaver came to the cabin', (b) 'Everyone has seen a beaver', where *a* in (a) can only be interpreted as *+absolute* (see the rules in section 4) but *a* in (b) can be interpreted in either way depending on the context.

There is also a pragmatic difference between a definite and an indefinite singular quantifier. Compare, for instance, (a) and (b):

(a) 'John hit the girl'

(b) 'John hit a girl' (where *a* will be interpreted as *+abs*).

A speaker will use (a) when he assumes that the hearer knows which individual is in question. Otherwise he will use (b) instead. This difference applies, mutatis mutandis, to other pairs consisting of a definite quantifier and the corresponding indefinite quantifier (e.g. *the three* vs. *three* interpreted as *+absolute*). The use of a definite quantifier gives an additional indication to the effect that the reference class can be identified from the context of use.

It is quite obvious that not all linguistic quantifiers function as 'pure' signs of quantity. Some of them have an additional lexical meaning. The feature method accounts for the quantitative and distributional relations expressed by the predicate-argument structures, and the remaining semantic or pragmatic features of the lexical items are left undefined (e.g. the distinction between *several, many* and *plenty of*).

3. ASSIGNMENT OF FEATURE VALUES IN THE LEXICON

Each linguistic quantifier in the lexicon may be characterized in terms of the potential feature values which it may assume. The five classes of quantifiers given below differ from each other with respect to the combination of feature values which they are assigned. Two of these classes are unambiguosly characterized, and the remaining three are ambigously characterized. The feature values are subject to the rules which determine all theoretically possible configurations of the cooccurring featured quantifiers.

Class 1: Q $\begin{smallmatrix}+abs\\+dis\end{smallmatrix}$ (includes: *each*, *every*, *any*, *no* (equivalent to *each* with negation))

Class 2: Q *+abs* (includes: *the*, *this*, *that*, zero with proper names, *this one*, *that particular one*, etc.)

Class 3: Q *+abs* or $\begin{smallmatrix}-abs\\+/-dis\end{smallmatrix}$ (includes: *a*, (at least) *one*, *some* with NP sg., *one of*, etc.)

Class 4: Q $\begin{smallmatrix}+abs\\+/-dis\end{smallmatrix}$ (includes: *these*, *those*, *the* with NP pl., a numeral preceded by *these*, *all* (*these*), etc.)

Class 5: Q $\begin{smallmatrix}+/-abs\\+/-dis\end{smallmatrix}$ (includes: *many*, *most*, any numeral greater than one, *some* with NP pl., *a group of*, etc.)

Zero-distributiveness is not indicated here. Quantifiers of class 1 can never be interpreted as *O dis*. Singular quantifiers of class 2 are assigned the value *O dis* in the lexicon, as they are always interpreted as *O dis* in elementary sentences. (Certain complex structures allow a reinterpretation of such quantifiers under well determined conditions, see Bellert, 1983.) Singular quantifiers of class 3 are *O dis* only when interpreted as *+abs*. All the quantifiers of the remaining classes, when interpreted as *+abs*, may be *O dis* under specific conditions stated in the note following Def. 5. In any case, whenever a quantifier is interpreted as *O dis*, it is subject to the rules as if it were a singular quantifier with one entity in its range (the reference class is interpreted as a unit class). It follows from the way these classes are specified, that no quantifier is *-absolute* by definition (in the lexicon). Some quantifiers may only be interpreted so in particular configurations of quantifiers according to the rules.

4. RULES, THEOREMS AND CONSEQUENCES

The set of basic rules specified below reduce the number of possible combinations of feature values (due to ambiguously featured quantifiers) to only those which are theoretically possible in any given configuration of featured arguments cooccurring in an elementary sentence structure. Thus certain configurations of feature values are excluded by the rules (these are ill formed and have no corresponding readings). Those which are permitted by the rules (i.e. those which are well formed and have the corresponding readings) describe the relations between the entities in the reference classes of the respective arguments according to the definitions of the particular feature values involved.

The Basic Rules and Laws

Note: In all the rules and laws specified in this section, the symbols '*-dis*' and '*-abs*' stand for '*strictly -dis*' and '*strictly -abs*', respectively.

For any quantifier Q_1, Q_2 in an elementary predicate-argument structure:

R.1. Q_1 *-abs* $\rightarrow \exists Q_3$ *+dis*(Q_1)
(A quantifier may be *-abs* only if there is a cooccurring quantifier which is *+dis* with respect to it.)

R.2. Q_1 *+dis*$(Q_2) \wedge Q_2$ *+abs* $\rightarrow Q_2$ *+dis*$(Q_1) \vee Q_2$ *O dis**

R.3. Q_1 *+dis*$(Q_2) \wedge Q_2$ *+dis*$(Q_1) \rightarrow [(Q_1$ *+abs* $\wedge Q_2$ *+abs*$) \vee$
$\vee (\exists Q_3$ *+dis*$(Q_1) \wedge Q_1$ *-dis*$(Q_3) \wedge Q_2$ *+abs*$)]$
(where Q_3 is a third cooccurring quantifier).

Laws of Transitivity: For any non-singular quantifiers Q_1, Q_2, Q_3 which cooccur in an elementary predicate-argument structure:

I. If $Q_1 \begin{matrix} \textit{+abs} \\ \textit{+dis}(Q_2) \end{matrix} \wedge Q_2$ *+dis*$(Q_3) \rightarrow Q_1$ *+dis*(Q_3)

II. If Q_1 *-dis*$(Q_2) \wedge Q_2$ *-dis*$(Q_3) \rightarrow Q_1$ *-dis*(Q_3)

Note: The restriction to non-singular quantifiers is necessary for Law I only (as no quantifier can be *-dis* with respect to a singular quantifier).

---

* The last clause, Q_2 *O dis*, may be omitted, as *O dis* is a specific case of *+dis*, but it is here for convenience (as a reminder).

Theorems or Consequences of the Basic Rules and Laws

R.4. $Q_1\ \mathit{-dis}(Q_2) \wedge Q_2\ \mathit{-dis}(Q_1) \rightarrow (Q_1\ \mathit{+abs} \wedge Q_2\ \mathit{+abs}) \vee$
$\vee\ (Q_1\ \mathit{-abs} \wedge Q_2\ \mathit{-abs})$

R.5. Q_1 is singular or *zero-distributive* $\rightarrow \sim Q_2\ \mathit{-dis}(Q_1)$
(No quantifier can be *-distributive* with respect to a unit class.)

R.6. If all the quantifiers are mutually *+distributive* or *zero-distributive*, then all are *+absolute*.

R.7. If all the quantifiers are mutually *-distributive* or *zero-distributive*, then all are *+absolute*.

R.8. At least one quantifier is *+absolute*.

R.9. $Q_1\ \mathit{-dis}(Q_2) \wedge Q_1\ \mathit{+abs} \rightarrow Q_2\ \mathit{-dis}(Q_1)$

R.10. $Q_1\ \mathit{+dis}(Q_2) \wedge Q_2\ \mathit{-dis}(Q_1) \rightarrow Q_2\ \mathit{-abs}$

Proofs: R.4. follows from R.1., R.2. and the two Laws of Transitivity. The proof is indirect. Assume that $Q_1 \begin{smallmatrix} \mathit{-abs} \\ \mathit{-dis}(Q_2) \end{smallmatrix}$ and $Q_2 \begin{smallmatrix} \mathit{+abs} \\ \mathit{-dis}(Q_1) \end{smallmatrix}$.* It follows then from R.1. that there is a third quantifier $Q_3\ \mathit{+dis}(Q_1)$. In such a case the following four possible configurations will be considered:

1. $Q_1 \begin{matrix} \mathit{-abs} \\ \mathit{-dis}(Q_2) \end{matrix} \quad Q_2 \begin{matrix} \mathit{+abs} \\ \mathit{-dis}(Q_1) \end{matrix} \quad Q_3 \begin{matrix} \mathit{+abs} \\ \mathit{+dis}(Q_1) \\ \mathit{+dis}(Q_2) \end{matrix}$

2. $Q_1 \begin{matrix} \mathit{-abs} \\ \mathit{-dis}(Q_2) \end{matrix} \quad Q_2 \begin{matrix} \mathit{+abs} \\ \mathit{-dis}(Q_1) \end{matrix} \quad Q_3 \begin{matrix} \mathit{+abs} \\ \mathit{+dis}(Q_1) \\ \mathit{-dis}(Q_2) \end{matrix}$

3. $Q_1 \begin{matrix} \mathit{-abs} \\ \mathit{-dis}(Q_2) \end{matrix} \quad Q_2 \begin{matrix} \mathit{+abs} \\ \mathit{-dis}(Q_2) \end{matrix} \quad Q_3 \begin{matrix} \mathit{-abs} \\ \mathit{+dis}(Q_1) \\ \mathit{+dis}(Q_2) \end{matrix}$

4. $Q_1 \begin{matrix} \mathit{-abs} \\ \mathit{-dis}(Q_2) \end{matrix} \quad Q_2 \begin{matrix} \mathit{+abs} \\ \mathit{-dis}(Q_1) \end{matrix} \quad Q_3 \begin{matrix} \mathit{-abs} \\ \mathit{+dis}(Q_1) \\ \mathit{-dis}(Q_2) \end{matrix}$

It will be shown that all these configurations are contradictory (excluded by the rules).

---

* The order of quantifiers is irrelevant here.

Ad 1. and ad 3.: We apply R.2. in the form: Q_3 *+dis*(Q_2) ∧ ∧ Q_2 *+abs* → Q_2 *+dis*(Q_3) ∨ Q_2 *O dis*. Since Q_2 is not *O dis* (since by assumption Q_2 *-dis*(Q_1)), then Q_2 *+dis*(Q_3).

However, Q_3 *+dis*(Q_1), and therefore by virtue of the First Law of Transitivity Q_2 *+dis*(Q_1). We have thus a contradiction: Q_2 is both *+dis*(Q_1) and *-dis*(Q_1).

Ad 2. and ad 4.: By virtue of the Second Law of Transitivity we immediately arrive at a contradiction: Q_3 *-dis*(Q_2) ∧ Q_2 *-dis*(Q_1) → → Q_3 *-dis*(Q_1). Hence Q_3 ist both *+dis*(Q_1) and *-dis*(Q_1). The proof is therefore completed.

Note: This proof is due to Vetulani (1983), who reformulated my original proof in (Bellert, 1983) and gave me some helpful suggestions for reorganizing the rules.

R.5. is a direct consequence of Definition 5.
R.6. is a direct consequence of R.3.
R.7. is a direct consequence of R.1.
R.8. is a consequence of R.1., R.3. and the Second Law of Transitivity. (A proof is given in Vetulani, 1983.)
R.9. is a consequence of R.2. (A proof is given in Bellert, 1983, and a different one in Vetulani, 1983.)
R.10. is a consequence of R.9. (A proof is given in Bellert, 1983.)

5. COROLLARIES

Among the definitions of section 2, there are two which have not been used so far. These are Definition 2 (*-absolute*, in the weak sense) and Definition 4 (*-distributive*, in the weak sense). There are two corollaries, for which we need these two definitions. The symbols *-abs* and *-dis* will thus be used in this section according to these two definitions, respectively.

Corollary 1. For any two elementary sentences S and S', which have the same S-structure and lexical items, except that a quantifier Q_1 in S is interpreted as *+absolute*, while the corresponding quantifier Q_1' in S' is interpreted as *-absolute*, S entails S', but S' does not entail S.

This Corollary is a welcome consequence of the definitions, for it is analogical to the rules of classical logic:

$$(\exists x)(\forall y)R(x, y) \vdash (\forall y)(\exists x)R(x, y) \text{ but}$$
$$(\forall x)(\exists y)R(x, y) \nvdash (\exists y)(\forall x)R(x, y)$$

Withouth moving quantifiers from their actual syntactic position in S-structures, and without necessarily deriving two distinct Logical Forms with a different order of quantifiers, we have an analogical rule, which may be used as an inference rule for deriving consequences. It holds good for sentences with linguistic quantifiers which differ only in that one is *+absolute*, while the other one is *-absolute*. For instance, it accounts for the relation of entailment between the sentences (a) and (b), respectively:

(a)		(b)
Most kids have seen the beaver.	$\vdash$	Most kids have seen a beaver.
John loves the girl.	$\vdash$	John loves a girl.
Each doctor examined the two men.	$\vdash$	Each doctor examined two men.
Each doctor showed these pictures to the director.	$\vdash$	Each doctor showed some pictures to the director.
Each doctor showed this picture to these five patients.	$\vdash$	Each doctor showed this picture to five patients.

Corollary 2: For any quantifier (or sign of quantity) Q:

$$Q\ \mathit{O\ dis} \text{ implies } Q \begin{smallmatrix}\mathit{+abs}\\ \mathit{+dis}\end{smallmatrix} \text{ implies } Q \begin{smallmatrix}\mathit{+abs}\\ \mathit{-dis}\end{smallmatrix}$$

This corollary is an abbreviation for the following statement. It follows from the definitions of feature values that any quantifier (or sign of quantity) interpreted as *O dis* is a specific case of (satisfies the condition for) that quantifier interpreted as $\begin{smallmatrix}\mathit{+abs}\\ \mathit{+dis}\end{smallmatrix}$, which in turn is a specific case of that quantifier interpreted as $\begin{smallmatrix}\mathit{+abs}\\ \mathit{-dis}\end{smallmatrix}$. Hence the *zero-distributive* interpretation is a specific case of both $\begin{smallmatrix}\mathit{+abs}\\ \mathit{+dis}\end{smallmatrix}$ and $\begin{smallmatrix}\mathit{+abs}\\ \mathit{-dis}\end{smallmatrix}$ interpretations with respect to any other cooccurring quantifier. This corollary corresponds thus to Leibniz's characterization of singular terms by wild (indifferent) quantity, for a singular term (proper name) is always interpreted as $\begin{smallmatrix}\mathit{+abs}\\ \mathit{O\ dis}\end{smallmatrix}$ (its sign of quantity is $\begin{smallmatrix}\mathit{+abs}\\ \mathit{O\ dis}\end{smallmatrix}$). The corollary is thus relevant for inference rules, as Leibniz has demonstrated (Leibniz, 1966). Let me quote Sommers:

> "This traditional doctrine treats singular sentences as if they were universal and it implicitly denies the Fregean thesis that singular sentences are syntactically more primitive than general sentences. Instead, the difference between 'Socrates is mortal' and 'every man is mortal' is semantically accounted for by the difference between 'Socrates' and 'man', i.e., by the difference between a term expressly designed to apply to no more than one thing, and one that is not restricted to unique application. Leibniz has an interesting variant of the traditional doctrine that singular terms are syntactically general. According to Leibniz, 'Socrates is mortal' is a particular proposition whose proper form is 'Some Socrates is mortal'. But 'Some Socrates is mortal' entails 'Every Socrates is mortal' so we are free to choose either way of representing the sentence. Leibniz thus views the singular proposition as equivalent to a particular

proposition that entails a universal one. In effect 'Socrates is mortal' has wild or indifferent quantity ('some-or-every Socrates is mortal') (...) it is understood that neither quantity is actually specified. However, in justifying inferences we must sometimes be explicit in assigning a given quantity to a singular proposition" (Sommers, 1982, 15-16).

6. TRUTH CONDITIONS

Truth conditions for sentences which are instances of elementary predicate-argument structures discussed in this paper, are given in a straightforward way in the definitions of feature values. This seems to be another advantage of the proposed feature method, for the reasons described by Quine in the following passage: "The grammar that we logicians tendentiously call standard is grammar designed with no other thought than to facilitate the tracing of truth conditions. And a very good thought it is" (Quine, 1970, p. 35, discussed in Sommers, 1982). The feature method can indeed be said to facilitate the 'tracing of truth conditions'. The conditions specified in each definition of a feature value apply to any sentence which is an instance of an elementary structure with arguments characterized by the corresponding feature values. Consider, as an example, the application of the conditions in Definitions 1 and 3, which are translated here into the language of the first-order predicate calculus:

Any sentence which is an instance of a two-argument S-structure of the type $P(Q_1{}^{+abs}_{+dis(Q_2)}T_1,\ Q_2{}^{+abs}_{+dis(Q_1)}T_2)$ (where P stands for the predicate) is true in any given context (model) C iff:

(a) $(\exists!X)(\exists!Y)(X \in R_C(Q_1T_1) \wedge Y \in R_C(Q_2T_2))$, and

(b) $(\forall x)(\forall y)(x \in RANGE_C(Q_1T_1) \wedge y \in RANGE_C(Q_2T_2) \rightarrow \langle x, y\rangle \in \|P\|_C)$

where $\|P\|_C$ stands for the interpretation of P in the context C). In other words, any sentence which is an instance of the predicate-argument structure described above is true in a given context just in case the conditions specified in the definitions of these particular feature values are satisfied.

Note: The existential quantifier is used in the definitions throughout this paper with no ontological commitment with respect to the entities in question, as the conditions are relativized to a given context (which can be the context of a novel). The interpretation of the predicate is also made relative to the context, in order to account for the differences in the meaning of some predicates (e.g. 'This ant is small' vs. 'This elephant is small').

When a predicate-argument structure contains more than two arguments, the corresponding truth conditions must be specified pairwise with respects to the arguments, so that they consist of a conjunction of truth conditions for each pair of arguments. For instance, in the case of a structure with three arguments:

$$Q_1 \begin{matrix} +abs \\ +dis(Q_2) \\ +dis(Q_3) \end{matrix} T_1,\ Q_2 \begin{matrix} -abs \\ -dis(Q_1) \\ +dis(Q_3) \end{matrix} T_2,\ Q_3 \begin{matrix} +abs \\ o\ dis \end{matrix} T_3,$$

we will have a conjunction of truth conditions for the following pairs of arguments:

$$(1)\ Q_1 \begin{matrix} +abs \\ +dis(Q_2) \end{matrix} T_1 \qquad Q_2 \begin{matrix} -abs \\ -dis(Q_1) \end{matrix} T_2$$

$$(2)\ Q_1 \begin{matrix} +abs \\ +dis(Q_3) \end{matrix} T_1 \qquad Q_3 \begin{matrix} +abs \\ o\ dis \end{matrix} T_3$$

$$(3)\ Q_2 \begin{matrix} -abs \\ +dis(Q_3) \end{matrix} T_2 \qquad Q_3 \begin{matrix} +abs \\ o\ dis \end{matrix} T_3$$

In each case the predicate expression is assumed to include everything in a given sentence except for the two arguments which it relates. A three-argument structure interpreted according to the above configuration of feature values could be exemplified by the following sentences:

Each professor wrote two letters to the Principal.
Everyone submitted two petitions to Pierre Trudeau.

When a predicate-argument structure contains just one argument, any corresponding sentence consists of a predicate P (an intransitive verb) and its NP-subject. The rules predict in such a case that the quantifier Q can only be interpreted as: (a) $\begin{smallmatrix}+abs\\+dis\end{smallmatrix}$, or (b) $\begin{smallmatrix}+abs\\0\ dis\end{smallmatrix}$ (which is a particular case of (a)). The truth conditions are thus:

(a) Any sentence which is an instance of a predicate-argument structure of the type $P(Q_{+dis}^{+abs}T)$ is true in any given context C iff $(\exists!X)(X \in R_C(QT) \wedge (\forall x)(x \in X \rightarrow x \in \|P\|_C))$.
(b) Any sentence which is an instance of a predicate-argument structure of the type $P(Q_{0\ dis}^{+abs}T)$ is true in a given context C iff $(\exists!X)(X \in R_C(QT) \wedge (\exists!x)(x \in X \rightarrow x \in \|P\|_C))$.

A general statement may thus be formulated, as a conclusion of this section,* with respect to truth conditions pertaining to the predicate-argument structures discussed in the paper.

* The idea that reference classes (and therefore the truth conditions) depend on the context is not at all new. Let me quote Dummett: "According to Frege, a word does not have a reference *on its own*, 'considered in isolation' (...) it does not by itself has a reference at all (...) only a particular occurrence of a word or expression in a sentence has a reference, and this reference is determined jointly by the sense of the word and the kind of context in which it occurs" (Dummett, 1973, p. 268).

Any sentence which is an instance of an elementary predicate-argument structure interpreted according to a configuration of feature values predicted by the rules, is true in a given context iff
all the conditions specified in the definitions of the corresponding feature values with respect to each pair of arguments are satisfied in that context.

Note: If there is only one argument, then obviously the conditions pertain to just one argument.

7. CLAIMS

The following claims are made in this paper:

(1) For every elementary sentence, the number of theoretically predictable configurations of feature values in the cooccurring quantifiers is the maximal number of the possible semantic readings of that sentence.

(2) Every sentence, for which the rules predict only one configuration of feature values in its quantifiers, has indeed only one reading consonant with the definitions of the feature values involved. However, for some selection of the lexical material, the reading may be hardly acceptable or even excluded, because of some specific properties of a lexical item and because of what speakers know about the world (that is, the corresponding state of affairs would be bizarre, improbable or contradicting the laws of nature, as e.g. 'Each woman gave birth to the child.').

(3) Every sentence for which the rules predict more than one configuration of feature values in its quantifiers will indeed have more than one reading, each corresponding to a predicted configuration

and consonant with the definitions of those values (with the same proviso for the lexical material, as in (2); for instance, in the sentence 'Each patient swallowed two pills', *two* will not be interpreted as *+abs*, and one of the predicted configurations will be excluded). For each reading it is possible to construct a paraphrase by the addition of expressions such as *each*, *the same*, *some or other*, *different*, *more than one*, which explicitly render the meaning of the given quantifier unambiguous and consonant with the corresponding definition of the feature value involved.

(4) No example can be found for configurations of feature values which are excluded by the rules (there are no corresponding readings).

8. EXAMPLES

We will now consider some examples and apply the rules, which reduce the number of configurations of featured quantifiers to only those which are predicted as possible. The number of predictable readings is the maximal number, and the number of actual readings may in some cases be smaller, because of some specific choice of the lexical material and extralinguistic factors mentioned in section 7. Moreover, if a given sentence has many possible readings because of its quantificational structure, speakers usually avoid using such a sentence, and instead disambiguate the interpretation of a quantifier by adding words such as 'each of', 'the same', 'different', etc. unless the context makes it clear which reading is intended. It is therefore helpful to conceive of a specific context for some of the predicted readings, in order to realize that such readings are available. A syntactic position may also be a factor in selecting one reading rather than another one. For instance, the preferred reading of a quantifier in the subject position (and the only one available without a specific context) is the one with a *+absolute* interpretation. However, the rules in the present proposal are designed to account for all theoretically possible readings, and the problem of preference of readings (interesting as it may be) is not discussed here (see Fodor, 1982, for a discussion of this problem).

Example 1: This student has read five books

+abs *+/-abs*
0 dis *+/-dis*

The rules predict only one configuration of feature values (i.e. one reading), although there are four possible combinations of values:

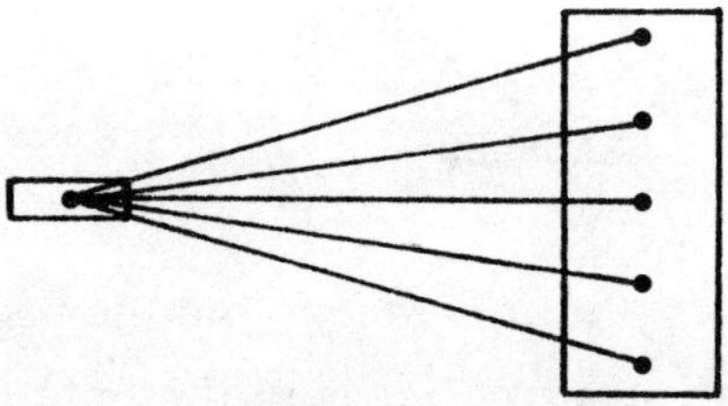

1. Q_1 *+abs* $Q_2 \begin{smallmatrix} +abs \\ +dis \end{smallmatrix}$

2. Q_1 *+abs* $Q_2 \begin{smallmatrix} +abs \\ -dis \end{smallmatrix}$ excluded by R.5.

3. Q_1 *+abs* $Q_2 \begin{smallmatrix} -abs \\ +dis \end{smallmatrix}$ excluded by R.1.

4. Q_1 *+abs* $Q_2 \begin{smallmatrix} -abs \\ -dis \end{smallmatrix}$ excluded by R.1.

Note: In this and in the remaining examples we use the symbols *-abs* and *-dis* in the sense of *strictly -abs* and *strictly -dis*, i.e. in the same sense as they are used in the rules.

In fact, this sentence has only one interpretation, although the quantifier 'five' may, in general, assume anyone of the four possible combinations of feature values. Notice that the same configuration of feature values is predicted for any other sentence containing two quantifiers which belong to the same two classes, respectively, Q_1 *+abs* and $Q_2 \begin{smallmatrix} +/-abs \\ +/-dis \end{smallmatrix}$, and since the order of featured quantifiers is irrelevant for the rules, for any one of the examples below only one configuration of feature values will be predicted by the rules, and in fact each sentence has only one reading:

The man visited several cities

John has written many books.

The Pope met the majority of cardinals.

Many students read this book.

Several people visited Ann.

A group of priests met the Pope.

Example 2: Four children have seen a beaver.

+/-abs *+/-dis*	*+abs/-abs* *+/-dis*

There are twelve possible combinations of values but only two configurations are predicted by the rules. Six cases in which *four* is *-dis* (with respect to a singular quantifier) can immediately be excluded by Rule 5. The remaining six cases are the following ones:

1.	Q_1	*+abs* *+dis*	Q_2	*+abs* *O dis*	
2.	Q_1	*-abs* *+dis*	Q_2	*+abs* *O dis*	excluded by R.1.
3.	Q_1	*+abs* *+dis*	Q_2	*-abs* *+dis*	excluded by R.3.
4.	Q_1	*-abs* *+dis*	Q_2	*-abs* *+dis*	excluded by R.3.
5.	Q_1	*+abs* *+dis*	Q_2	*-abs* *-dis*	
6.	Q_1	*-abs* *+dis*	Q_2	*-abs* *-dis*	excluded by R.1.

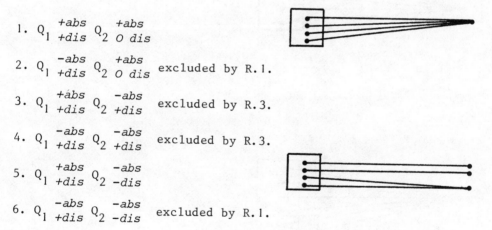

In fact, there are only two readings possible (*Four children have seen the same beaver*, and *Four children have seen some beaver or other*). The same configurations will be predicted for any other examples with two quantifiers of the same type, independently of their order.

Example 3: Two professors marked six scripts.

+/-abs *+/-abs*
+/-dis *+/-dis*

There are sixteen possible combinations of feature values, but only four are permitted by the rules. This example is borrowed from Kempson and Cormack (1982), who also analyse this sentence with its four interpretations. The feature method is compatible with their interesting analysis, but it gives an alternative account of the facts.

1. Q_1 *+abs* *+dis* Q_2 *+abs* *+dis*

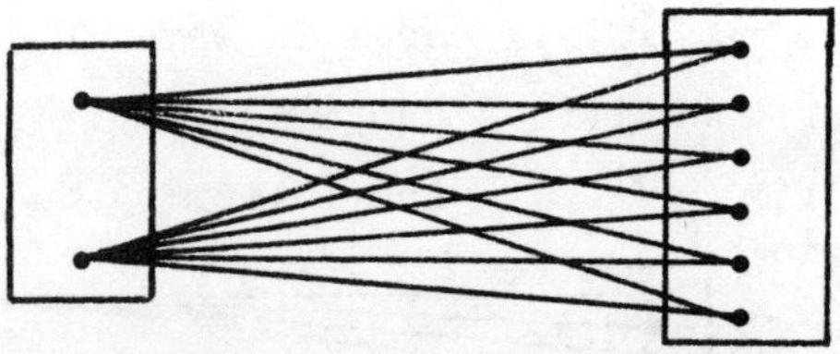

2. Q_1 *+abs* *+dis* Q_2 *-abs* *-dis* excluded by R.2.

3. Q_1 *+abs* *+dis* Q_2 *-abs* *+dis* excluded by R.3.

4. Q_1 *+abs* *+dis* Q_2 *-abs* *-dis*

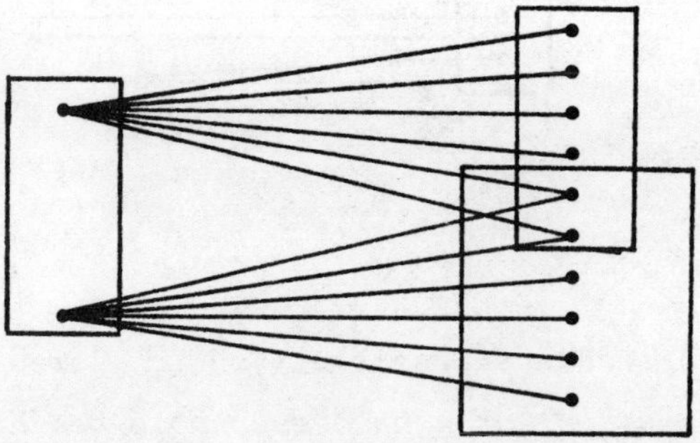

5. Q_1 *+abs* *-dis* Q_2 *+abs* *+dis* excluded by R.2.

6. $Q_1 \begin{matrix} +abs \\ -dis \end{matrix}$ $Q_2 \begin{matrix} +abs \\ -dis \end{matrix}$

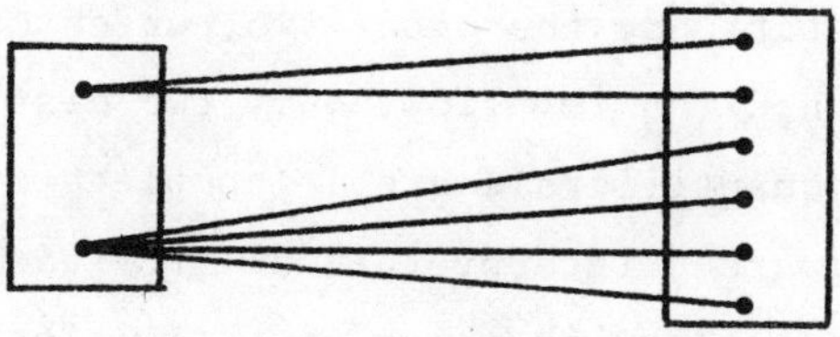

7. $Q_1 \begin{matrix} +abs \\ -dis \end{matrix}$ $Q_2 \begin{matrix} -abs \\ +dis \end{matrix}$ excluded by R.2.

8. $Q_1 \begin{matrix} +abs \\ -dis \end{matrix}$ $Q_2 \begin{matrix} -abs \\ -dis \end{matrix}$ excluded by R.4.

9. $Q_1 \begin{matrix} -abs \\ +dis \end{matrix}$ $Q_2 \begin{matrix} +abs \\ +dis \end{matrix}$ excluded by R.3.

10. $Q_1 \begin{matrix} -abs \\ +dis \end{matrix}$ $Q_2 \begin{matrix} +abs \\ -dis \end{matrix}$ excluded by R.2.

11. $Q_1 \begin{matrix} -abs \\ +dis \end{matrix}$ $Q_2 \begin{matrix} -abs \\ +dis \end{matrix}$ excluded by R.1.

12. $Q_1 \begin{matrix} -abs \\ +dis \end{matrix}$ $Q_2 \begin{matrix} -abs \\ -dis \end{matrix}$ excluded by R.1.

13. $Q_1 \begin{matrix} -abs \\ -dis \end{matrix}$ $Q_2 \begin{matrix} +abs \\ +dis \end{matrix}$

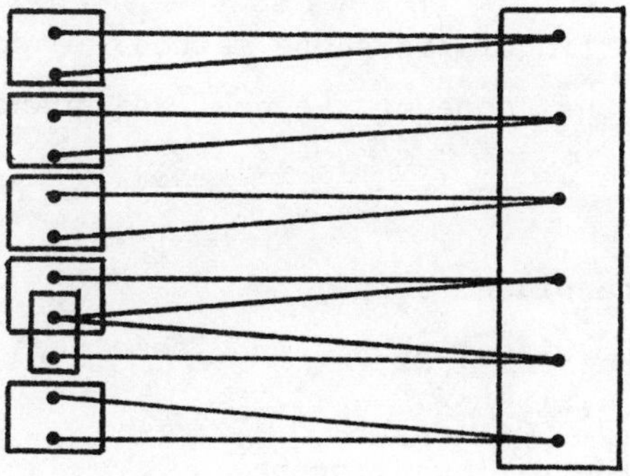

14. $Q_1 \begin{matrix} -abs \\ -dis \end{matrix}$ $Q_2 \begin{matrix} +abs \\ -dis \end{matrix}$ excluded by R.4.

15. $Q_1 \begin{matrix} -abs \\ -dis \end{matrix}$ $Q_2 \begin{matrix} -abs \\ +dis \end{matrix}$ excluded by R.1.

16. $Q_1 \begin{matrix} -abs \\ -dis \end{matrix}$ $Q_2 \begin{matrix} -abs \\ -dis \end{matrix}$ excluded by R.1.

The four configurations predicted by the rules correspond to the four readings distinguished in Kempson and Cormack (1982): 4 and 13 are scope differentiated interpretations, the other two, which cannot be accounted for by the scope method (as it allows only two distinct readings for a sentence with two quantifiers), are 1 (complete group interpretation) and 6 (incomplete group interpretation). For each reading, it is possible to find a context in which it will clearly be the intended reading (see Bellert, 1983). Each diagram which corresponds to a configuration with a quantifier *-dis*, represents an example of a possible state of things which satisfies the definitions, while the diagram in 1 obviously represents the only possible state of things.

Example 4: Everyone discussed $\left\{\begin{matrix}\text{a}\\ \text{some}\\ \text{one}\end{matrix}\right\}$ problem with each minister.

In a restricted domain (e.g. with four people and two ministers), 'every' and 'each' could be represented by a universal quantifier, and 'some' by an existential quantifier. This sentence would then have four possible readings accounted for by four logical forms in quantificational logic (or in the linguistic scope method), each corresponding to a difference in the scope of the prefixed quantifiers.

(1) $\exists x \forall y \forall z$ (where 'some' has the widest scope)

(2) $\forall z \exists x \forall y$ (where 'each' has the widest scope, and 'some' has a wider scope than 'every')

(3) $\forall y \forall z \exists x$ (where 'every' has the narrowest scope)

(4) $\forall y \exists x \forall z$ (where 'every' has the widest scope and 'some' has a wider scope than 'each')

(Two other possibilities are excluded as they are equivalent to (1) and (3), respectively.)

For this example, the feature method also gives four possible readings, accounted for by four predicted configurations of feature values due to the quantifier *some* (the remaining two quantifiers are always interpreted as *+absolute* and *+distributive* with respect to any cooccurring quantifiers). In the first case *some* is interpreted as *+absolute*.

(1) *some +abs*

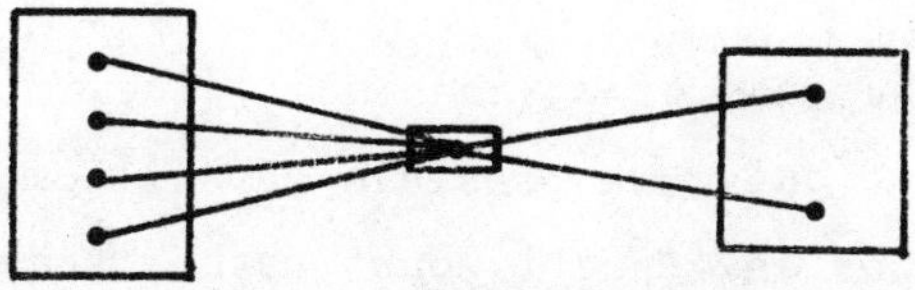

In the remaining three cases, when 'some' is interpreted as *-absolute*, it may be interpreted as + or *-distributive* with respect to the cooccurring quantifiers:

(2) *some* *-abs*
-dis(every)
+dis(each)

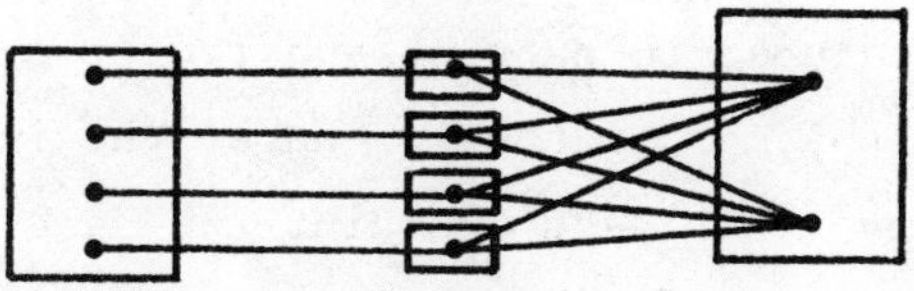

(3) *some* *-abs*
-dis(every)
-dis(each)

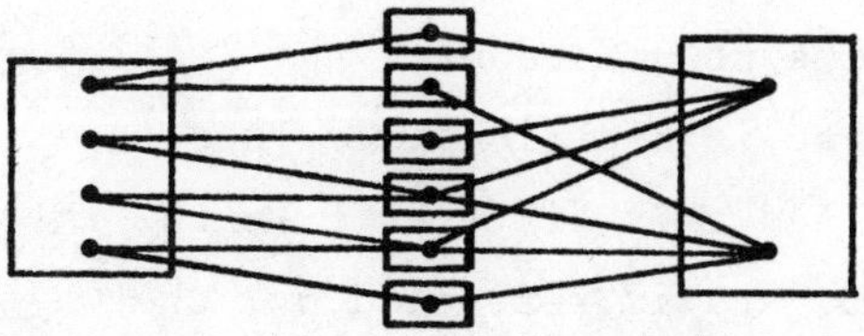

(4) *some* *-abs* *+dis(every)* *-dis(each)*

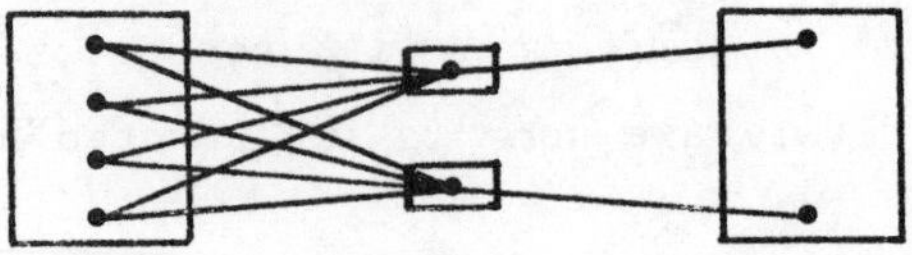

The last case, when *some* is *-abs* *+dis(every)* *+dis*, is excluded by Rule 3.

It is worth noting that in the case of a *-absolute* value, a corresponding diagram can represent only one possible case. 'Some' is interpreted in the above diagrams as 'exactly one' rather than 'at least one', which might also be the case for a *-absolute* singular quantifier. But the difference is irrelevant for the discussion.

In this case, the number of readings accounted for is the same as it would be in the scope method. The difference lies, however, in the fact that in the present proposal the different interpretations follow from the way the quantifier 'some' is interpreted, the only quantifier which is differently featured in each of the four configurations. And in fact, for any speaker of the language, the interpretation of the quantifiers 'every' and 'each' remains the same in the above four readings. What changes from one reading to another is the way the speaker will interpret the quantifier 'some': whether it requires just one unit class as a reference class or it requires more than one reference class, and the way the speaker interprets how the reference class (classes) of the argument quantified by 'some' is (are) to be related by the predicate with the remaining reference classes (how the predicate is distributed). This is exactly what the feature method captures. And this difference in the interpretation of 'some' corresponds to, and is reflected by, the ways in which speakers paraphrase these readings:

(1) Everyone discussed the same problem with each minister.
(2) Everyone discussed some problem or other, the same one with each minister.
(3) Everyone discussed some problem or other, a different one with each minister.

The fourth reading is hardly available without a very specific context (it can best be rendered by the converse sentence: 'Each minister discussed some problem or other with everyone'). However, for a different choice of the lexical material, this reading is available:

(4) Everyone signed a protest letter to each minister.
(4a) Everyone contributed to a present for each minister.
(4b) Everyone participated in a meeting with each minister.

Example 5: Everyone discussed some problem with two ministers.

This example differs from the preceding one only in that the quantifier 'two' occurs here instead of 'each'. Thus in addition to the four configurations of feature values corresponding to those in Example 4, we will have some additional ones due to the additional possible feature values of 'two', which in general may be + or -*absolute* and + or -*distrubutive*. In this particular configuration of quantifiers, 'two' can only be +*distributive* with respect to 'some' (by Rule 5), and if it is +*absolute*, it can only be +*distributive* with respect to 'every' (by Rule 3). The only additional configurations permitted by the rules will then be the following three:

(5)	*+abs* *every +dis(some),* *+dis(two)*	*some +abs,*	*-abs* *two +dis(some)* *-dis(every)*

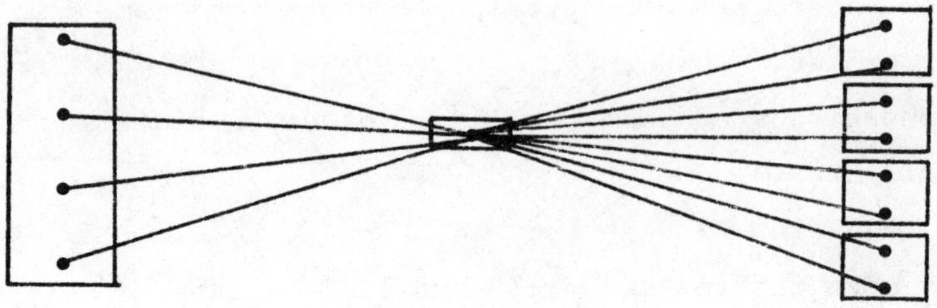

(6)	*+abs* *every +dis(some),* *+dis(two)*	*-abs* *some +dis(two),* *-dis(every)*	*-abs* *two +dis(some)* *-dis(every)*

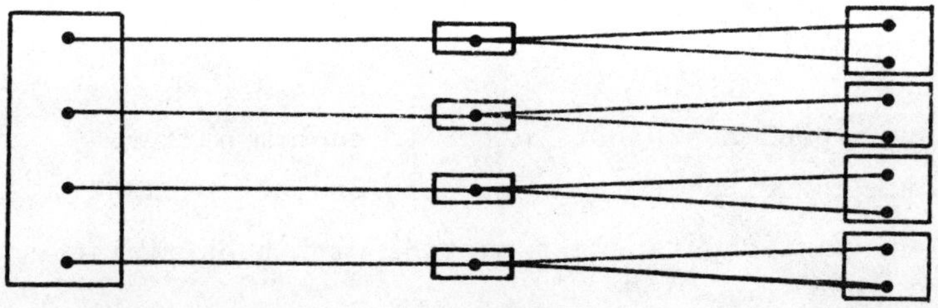

(7)	*+abs* *every +dis(some),* *+dis(two)*	*-abs* *some -dis(two),* *-dis(every)*	*-abs* *two +dis(some)* *-dis(every)*

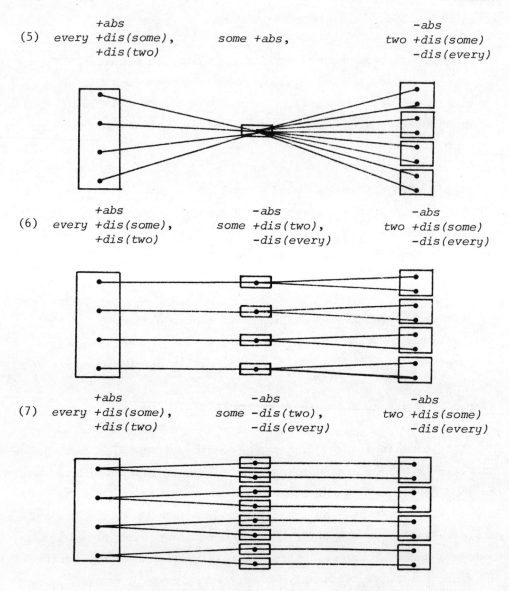

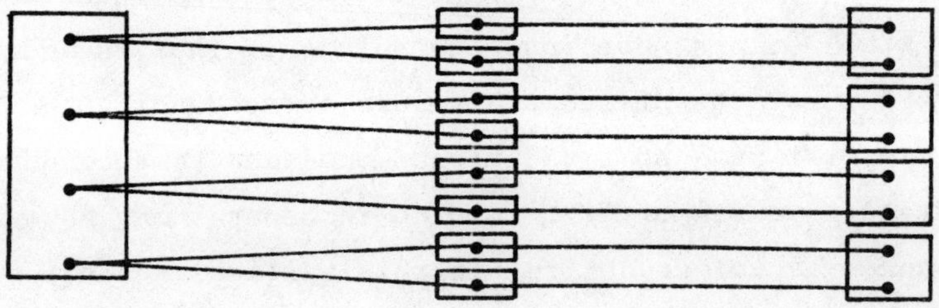

The three additional readings will be, respectively, the following:

(5') Everyone discussed the same problem with two ministers or other.

(6') Everyone discussed some problem or other, (the same one) with some two ministers or other.

(7') Everyone discussed some problem or other, a different one with each of some two ministers or other.

For this example, the scope method would allow only two additional forms due to the reordering of the three quantifiers, as the maximal number of Logical Forms is only six in this case (the factorial of the number of three different quantifiers). Moreover, just a different order and scope of these three quantifiers would not suffice to account for the differences in the readings discussed above, which are captured by the feature method. (See, however, an alternative proposal in Kempson and Cormack (1981), which would account for all these readings.) --

I am indebted to Dr. Zbigniew Stachniak and Dr. Zygmunt Vetulani for many critical and helpful suggestions and for corrections of my errors. The remaining inadequacies in the form of presentation, which as a linguist (not a logician) I am evidently liable to, are obviously my own. I am thankful to Paul Weingartner for several helpful discussions. I also wish to express my indebtedness to Robert May's work (1977), which was used as guidelines for my paper (1983). My proposal, whatever its value may prove to be, would have been hardly possible without the knowledge and inspiration I got from May's work. I also learnt a lot from Higginbotham's papers. I have demonstrated some advantages of the feature method over the scope method on the level of elementary sentences only. Though both authors accept the framework of the scope method with variables for interpreting linguistic quantifiers, their insights and findings in the domain of quantification in natural language go well beyond elementary sentences. And thus no comparison of the two methods can be made at this point with respect to the interpretation of complex sentences. This remains an open project, yet to be explored. However, it seems to me that the general approach to the interpretation of linguistic quantifiers, as initiated by Richard Montague, as assumed similarly by Fred Sommers (1982), and as proposed independently and somehow differently by Barwise and Cooper (1981) or by van Benthem (1983), is more promising for a theory of natural language. Although I wrote my paper for Salzburg Congress independently of these papers, I see it as a further contribution to this approach. Finally, I am thank thankful to Evelyn Styan for editorial comments.

REFERENCES

Bach, K., 1982, Quantification and Pragmatics, Linguistics and Philosophy, 4:607-618.

Barwise, J. and Cooper, R., 1981, Generalized Quantifiers and Natural Language, Linguistics and Philosophy, 4:159-219.

Bellert, I., 1983, Interpretive Model for Quantification Structure: I. Elementary Structures, II. Further Applications, typescript (80 pages).

Bellert, I., 1984, Interpretive Rules for Pronouns (in preparation).

van Benthem, J., 1983, A Linguistic Turn: New Directions in Logic, paper presented at the 7th International Congress of Logic, Methodology and Philosophy of Science, Salzburg, 1983.

Chomsky, N., 1981, Lectures on Government and Binding, MIT press, Cambridge, Mass.

Copi, I. M., 1967, "Symbolic Logic," MacMillan, London and New York.

Donnellan, K. S., 1978, Speaker Reference, Descriptions and Anaphora, in: "Syntax and Semantics," P. Cole, ed., Academic Press, New York.

Dummett, M., 1973, "Frege, Philosophy of Language," Duckworth, London.

Fodor, J. D., 1982, The Mental Representation of Quantifiers, in: "Processes, Beliefs, and Questions," S. Peters and E. Saarinen, eds., Reidel, Dordrecht.

Geach, P. T., 1976, Back Reference, in: "Language and Focus," A. Kasher, ed., Reidel, Dordrecht.

Kempson, R. M. and Cormack, A., 1981, Ambiguity and Quantification, Linguistics and Philosophy, 4:259-309.

Leibniz, G. W., 1966, Logical Papers, G. H. R. Parkinson, ed., Clarendon Press, Oxford.

May, R., 1977, "The Grammar of Quantification," unpublished doctoral dissertation, MIT, Cambridge, Mass. (Distributed by Indiana University Linguistics Club, 1980).

Quine, W. V. O., 1970, "Philosophy of Logic," Prentice Hall, Englewood Cliffs.

Sommers, F., 1982, "The Logic of Natural Language," Clarendon Press, New York.

Vetulani, Z., 1983, Proof of some Theorems in Bellert's Interpretive Model for Quantificational Structure, (typescript in Polish), Institute of Mathematics, UAM, Poznan, Poland.

HOMOGENEOUS AND INDIVIDUATED QUANTIFIERS IN NATURAL LANGUAGE

Alice G. B. ter Meulen

Taakgroep Formele Linguistiek
Rijksuniversiteit Groningen
NL-9718 CA Groningen

1. INTRODUCTION

In mathematical model-theory it is commonly assumed that the domain has a fixed and absolute structure, independent and prior to the interpretation of a language on that domain in a model.

In this paper it is argued that the semantics for natural language should not blindly inherit this assumption. The structure of the world to which we make reference with expressions of natural languages largely underdetermines what we say. In making reference to a part of the world we determine largely how we are to refer back to it with anaphora and under what change its identity is preserved. Thus we construct a representation of the world consisting of semantic entities that vary in stability, i.e. the more stable the more information can be incorporated about changes in its parts while preserving its identity. Three modes of reference are to be distinguished from a semantical point of view: divisible reference, reference that is indivisible with respect to some descriptive expression of the language, and maximally indivisible reference. Natural languages allow considerable leeway in using a given expression in any of these three modes of reference. For this reason the semantic interpretation of an expression cannot be determined solely by the semantic type corresponding to its lexical category, in the way familiar to us from Montague-grammar. Instead, the three classes of semantic entities arising from the three distinguished modes of reference are all constructed employing a set of processes in a process-structure on which models are defined. No conceptual or ontological priority is hence claimed for individuals, but all semantic entities to which natural language expressions refer, no matter what their internal structure is like, are obtained with closure-conditions on subsets of the set of processes.

The organization of this paper is as follows. First, two preliminary methodological remarks are made concerning the advantages of the strategy of direct model-theoretic interpretation in semantics as opposed to translational theories of semantics, and, secondly, we review the well-known problems of logical atomism, which appears to enjoy a recent revival in some Russellian-flavoured semantic theories. The third and fourth section present the body of the paper: the issues of homogeneous and individuated quantification and the formalization in process-structures. The final section reviews these results and concludes with a more philosophical deliberation on the nature of the representation of the world in a linguistically motivated modeltheory.

2. METHODOLOGICAL PRELIMINARIES

Before expounding the issues of homogeneous and individuated quantification, two topics deserve to be commented upon while clarifying the overall strategy I pursue in semantics for natural languages. It also provides some more philosophical background to the main argument of this paper, the thesis that all semantic entities to which reference is made with natural language expressions are constructions from primitive processes.

2.1 Direct Interpretation

From Richard Montague we have inherited two quite distinct methods for doing semantics of natural language. First, the PTQ-strategy, as I shall call it, formalizes semantic interpretation indirectly by translating the generated expressions of a fragment of a natural language to an appropriately enriched formal language of intensional logic. This language receives its interpretation in a possible world semantics formulated in set-theory. The main burden in developing an interpretation for a fragment consists in defining a Fregean compositional translation to some suitable formal language. In actual practice - we have about a decade of hindsight by now - this strategy of indirect interpretation has proven to be a most appealing and productive paradigm for Montague-grammar and formal semantics. However, by diverting attention from the third component, the model-theory, the explanation of semantic phenomena was sought primarily in the recursive definition of the translation. Scope-ambiguities, for instance, were explained by defining translations for the sentence that varied the order of quantifiers, which necessitated two distinct syntactic trees for reasons of compositionality.

The second semantic strategy, which Montague pursued in his 'English as a Formal Language' (cf. Montague (1974)), obviated the intermediate component of a formal language by interpreting expressions of the fragment directly in the set-theoretic language of the model-theory. As the models employed for this purpose were extremely rich and defined with only total functions, the direct interpretation of a given sentence was often a tremendously complicated set-theoretic expression with complex functionals. The overly rich and universal possible world models that Montague deemed necessary concealed the important methodological advantages of direct interpretation for the semantics of natural language. Semantic relations of informational dependencies or independencies, synonymy or equivalence or entailment are defined as set-theoretic notions on the model-theoretic objects. Furthermore properties useful for explanatory purposes can be defined or derived from more fundamental ones in the set-theoretic language. In dropping the unnecessarily strong requirement that all functions be total, an important flexibility is gained that allows finer-grained models and stronger semantic relations on their objects.* Contexts are themselves set-theoretic objects, constructions out of individuals, properties and relations, so that various forms of context-dependent interpretation and indexical reference can be treated as relations between set-theoretic objects. In this paper the strategy of direct interpretation allows the definition of three classes of semantic entities as sets of processes closed under certain conditions. Properties of these respective sets serve to explain the linguistic data on scope, anaphora and ellipsis. Obviously, for every direct interpretation of a fragment we may have a wide choice of non-equivalent translations into any number of formal languages between the natural language syntax and the set-theoretic language of the modeltheory. But the explanations offered by such indirect interpretation can only appeal to the form of the translations or the relations between them as syntactic counterparts to the semantic relations between the set-theoretic objects that constitute their interpretation. For this reason, it is at least misleading to claim that direct and indirect interpretations are merely notational variants, as was often thought in the early studies in Montague-grammar. The two strategies offer fundamentally different explanations of the same issues and it cannot be just a matter of taste to prefer the clear and simple world of set-theoretic objects over the largely arbitrary choice of a formal language for translation in an indirect interpretation, which only provides insight if we understand all its

---

* See Barwise (1981a), (1981b) and Barwise and Perry (1983), but Kamp (1983) for a piercing study of 'strong consequence' in situation-semantics.

expressions in their own set-theoretic interpretation. Much more remains to be said about this issue of direct and indirect interpretation, but the following sections of this paper are intended to provide an immediate illustration of the advantages of direct interpretation.

2.2 Logical Atomism Revisited

Logical atomism is the metaphysical view, ascribed primarily to Bertrand Russell (cf. Russell (1971)), that the world consists of single atomic facts, all independent of one another, described by atomic propositions consisting of a name and a predicate or an *n*-place relation with *n* names in its argument places. This is not the place to review the massive arguments, both metaphysical and epistemological, that were advanced against logical atomism in philosophy earlier this century. But one central problem can be isolated that deserves some discussion in the present context.

Names refer rigidly to individuals, i.e. their referents are the same no matter what context the name occurs in. But individuals consist of parts, some of which may be individuals too, since we name parts of referents of names. A simple example is a state which is part of a union or larger named whole: California is part of the United States or Groningen is part of Holland. It may be less customary to name parts of persons with independent names, but I see no principled objection against doing so. Perhaps not all parts of the entire world are equally on a par to refer to using proper names, but there cannot be genuinely semantic grounds for denying a part of the world its qualification for bearing a name. Referents of proper names, individuals, change parts constantly, but in naming we agree to ignore such changes and consider the individual as remaining the same throughout such change. Spatio-temporal continuity of an individual, which philosophers often consider a *conditio sine qua non* for qualifying as an individual, holds only at a level relative to other parts of the world that are considered individuals. Indeed, all individuals scatter their parts constantly, even at a common sense level. John remains John even though he sheds his hair, gains weight, loses his arm in an accident and gets artifact replacements for his vital organs. Obviously, individuals can be part of other individuals and, consequently, atomic facts cannot describe indecomposable states of affairs, as any part of the world contains other parts and the world lends itself in principle to infinite divisibility. The semantic problem here is to account on the one hand for the rigidity, or the relative stability as I would like to put it, of an individual, while, on the other hand, acknowledging that parts of it change. Another way of putting the problem is the following example, which shifts the terminology slightly. In a situation in which John's arm is moving, John himself is moving as well, as John's arm is part of John and if part of a larger whole moves, it moves as well. A syntactically atomic description of the situation is <<*move*, j> = 1>, but the situation itself is constituted of many parts, amongst which is John's moving arm. Atomic descriptions may hence describe situations always have other situations as parts even if they are just constituted of one individual and one property. Information can be coarse or finer-grained in that it conveys less or more precisely how part of the world is individuated from its surrounding physical context. If a model-theory starts out with a given set of individuals as constituents of situations, the part-of relation between them is to be analyzed as descriptive relation like all transitive verbs. Similarly, the constitutive relation is an overt relation between an individual and a set of individuals, its parts. Perhaps it can be done, but such an analysis loses its contact with the syntactic form of the interpreted expression, since such relations of part-of and constitution do not have to appear in the sentences themselves. Furthermore, it is puzzling to explain how an individual at a location may scatter its parts over various disconnected locations while it also remains intact as identity at the same location.

Summarizing then, the world does not come in neatly packaged atomic parcels, but our linguistic descriptions of complex and continously changing parts of the world can be atomic. Names in such atomic descriptions preserve the identity of their referent while disregarding the internal changes that take place. The model-theory presented in this paper constructs individuals as maximally fine descriptions of parts of the world that are stable under addition of information concerning their internal parts. The following two sections give this as yet metaphysical idea a precise content.

3. HOMOGENEOUS QUANTIFICATION AND DIVISIBLE REFERENCE

Quantifiers may be conceived as functors D assigning to a domain E some binary relation between its subsets A and B : D_E AB (cf. van Benthem (1983) for a systematic study of the relational theory of generalized quantifiers). The domain is usually considered to be a set of individuals, structured prior to and independently of the language interpreted in that domain. Consequently little attention has been directed to quantification in a multi-sorted domain with various kinds of entities beside individuals. Noun-phrases as *some water*, *no gold*, *little money*, or with comparative determiners like *more tea than coffee* are interpreted on a domain of quantities rather than individuals. Quantities are entities that have entities of the same kind as parts. Reference to a quantity, like the sentence *Here is some water*, is divisible in the sense that parts of the quantity of water referred to are quantities of water too. Individuals, on the contrary, cannot have parts of the same kind, and, consequently, reference to them is indivisible. Individuals, as was argued above, do have other individuals as part, but they must be of a different kind, described by a different predicate (cf. ter Meulen (1984)). Not only for homogeneous quantification in NPs is a domain of divisible quantities required, but also for the interpretation of the activity-VPs like *be writing*, *run around*, *push a cart*, *damage a car*. Such VPs are to be interpreted as events, with an as yet indeterminate agent, that are divisible in having parts that are the same kind of event. They are usually contrasted to the accomplishment and achievement VPs which have an indivisible internal structure, discussed in section 4.

How do we formalize the domain of divisible entities that may serve to interpret homogeneous quantification on a par with the relational analysis of generalized quantifiers? We start with a primitive set P of spatio-temporally extended processes, which we may understand as recognized similarities or uniformities across parts of the world. No natural language expressions correspond directly to processes, but every descriptive atomic expression is interpreted as a subset of P. Only two primitive relations are needed between processes, providing sufficient structure for all required relations between entities. Recognized uniformities can be ordered in time, that is, a process may (strictly) precede another one. And, secondly, processes may or may not overlap in space.

Note that there is no requirement that any process that does not precede another one, must overlap with it.

Precedence is an irreflexive and transitive relation, whereas overlap is symmetric and reflexive. This provides the fundamental structure of our model-theory which is called process-structure: $\mathcal{P} = \langle P, <, o \rangle$, in which P is a non-empty set of processes, $<$ denotes the strict precedence-relation on P x P, and o denotes the spatial overlap on P x P. A process-model is a process structure $\mathcal{P}$ together with an assignment function ⟦ ⟧ which assigns every descriptive (i.e. non-logical) expression of *L*, the natural language to be interpreted, a subset of P or a subset of (P x P x ... x P) *n*-times for *n*-ary expressions. To construct semantic entities as sets of processes closed under certain conditions, three definitions are required, for x, y, z, u ε P;

Def. 1. x *is a temporal part* of y = df. for all z if z < y then z < x and y < z then x < z.

Def. 2. x *is a material portion* of y = df. for all z if z o x then z o y.

Def. 3. x *is decomposable into* y and z = df. y and z are material portions of x and for all u if u o x then u o y or u o z.

Note that in the last definition y and z may be overlapping processes. Furthermore, we assume that if x is a material portion of y then x is a temporal part of y. With these tools divisible entities are constructed as subsets of P that satisfy the following condition:

Continuity: for all x, y ε X, there is a z ε X, z is a material portion of x and z is a material portion of y.

The condition of Continuity requires that relative to X ⊆ P no gaps occur between any two elements x, y ε X. Sentences with homogeneous quantification or divisibly referring expressions are interpreted on a domain E consisting of divisible entities X ⊆ P closed under Continuity. Homogeneously quantified expressions are dependent on individuated quantifiers which is customarily in translational theories called their lack of wide-scope reading. Witness the following sentence

(1) Every blacksmith melted some iron.

which cannot describe a situation in which there is one and the same quantity of iron that every blacksmith melted. In opaque contexts homogeneous quantifiers similarly depend on the individuated quantifiers, as in

(2) Every blacksmith believed some iron was melting on the fire.

Although every blacksmith may believe *de re* of a piece of iron that it is melting on his fire, there is a definitely preferred interpretation that it depends on the blacksmith what piece of iron the belief is about, unless some very restricting context forces a unique piece of iron to be the interpretation of *some iron*. Elliptical VPs demonstrate the same point,

(3) Mary melted *some iron* and John too,

which, without any further restricting context, describes the situation in which each was melting a different piece of iron.

Anaphora depending on homogeneous quantifiers are more restricted than anaphora depending on individuated quantifiers. Although this claim deserves a more thorough study and linguistic underpinning than the brief review in this paper, the following examples may illustrate the point.

(4) Every blacksmith melted *some iron*.

$\left\{\begin{array}{l}\text{*}\textit{It}\text{ was}\\ \text{*}\textit{They}\text{ were}\end{array}\right\}$ in the fire

but acceptable is

(5) Every blacksmith who melted *some iron*, put *it* in the fire.

Backwards anaphora are excluded, like the case of indefinite individuated quantifiers:

(6) *Every blacksmith melted *it* by putting *some iron* in the fire.

Homogeneous quantifiers are dependent on individuated quantifiers in general, and have also more restricted possibilities for coreferential anaphora.

4. INDIVIDUATED QUANTIFIERS AND INDIVISIBLE REFERENCE

Individuated quantifiers are interpreted on a domain E of individuals, which are subsets of P satisfying additional closure-conditions, besides Continuity. Conceptually individuals are indivisible with respect to a descriptive expression R, that is, no part of a situation <<R, a> = 1> is itself a situation <<R, b> = 1> where b is a part of a. Noun-phrases as *some glasses*, *three tables*, *several books* or the comparative *more tables than chairs* are interpreted as relations between sets of individuals of an individuated domain E.

Just like homogeneous quantification, individuated quantifiers occur both in NPs and VPs. The Vendler-classes of accomplishments and achievements are interpreted by events that have an indivisible internal structure, like individuals in a temporal domain. Examples of such tenseless VPs are: *write a letter*, *cross the street*, *demolish a car* and *knock*, *die* or *score*. No part of the action of writing a letter is itself writing a letter, nor is part of a crossing of the street itself a street-crossing, although in nominalizations we easily construct divisibly referring expressions like *street-crossing* or *streets-crossings*.

Obviously, individuals constructed as subsets of the set of processes P, have to satisfy Continuity, prohibiting gaps within one individual. The indivisibility with respect to R is obtained with the decomposition of processes within ⟦R⟧ ⊆ P to the point at which a smallest x ε ⟦R⟧ is reached, if such is ever the case. The following closure-condition defines this requirement:

Splitting: for all x ε X if x is decomposable into y and z then either y ε X or z ε X but not both (x, y, z ε ⟦R⟧)

To render this more intuitive, imagine an R-continuum, and divide it into any number of smallest R-stretches that all overlap with the R-continuum. The domain of individuals is identified with a set of subsets of P that are closed under Continuity and Splitting. As the two closure-conditions provide a finer-grained structure to individuals than to quantities individuated quantifiers show more varieties of dependencies than homogeneous quantifiers.

(7) Every blacksmith melted some horseshoe.

which may describe two distinct situations: one in which each blacksmith was melting his horseshoe, and, second, a situation in which, just one horseshoe was being melted by all blacksmiths, either over and over again in single, temporally distinct melting-actions or in a collective action by all blacksmiths together.

Belief *de re* can be expressed about a single individual in

(8) Every blacksmith believed some horseshoe was melting in the fire.

which may either describe a collective belief about one horseshoe, or, alternatively, also the *de re* beliefs of each blacksmith separately about various distinct horseshoes.

Elliptical VPs show a similar ambiguity.

(9) Mary melted some horseshoe and John too.

which may be interpreted, contrary to (3), by a situation in which Mary and John both, either together or at different times, melted one and the same horseshoe. The anaphora depending on individuated quantifiers have a wider range of occurrences than those depending on homogeneous quantifiers, witness

(10) Every blacksmith melted *some horseshoe*.
{*It* was / *They* were} in the fire.

The sentences in (10) demonstrate how anaphoric reference may disambiguate a preceding sentence. *It* is used if the first sentence is intended to be about just one horseshoe melted in collective action, whereas *they* is used if the horseshoes melted each by a single blacksmith were all in one common fire. Both anaphora are equally acceptable, as opposed to the two unacceptable anaphora in (4) that could not depend on a homogeneously quantified expression across a sentence-boundary. Finally, (11), (12) and (13) demonstrate that, analogous to (5), coreferential anaphora are possible with individuated quantifiers in a relative clause, and, if definite, with backwards anaphoric dependencies in which the dependency-relation is the reverse from the actual order of the expressions in the sentence, and, finally, if indefinite, with donkey-like pronouns.

(11) Every blacksmith who melted *some horseshoe*, put *it* in the fire.
(12) Every blacksmith melted it by putting
{*his* / *the*} *horseshoe* in the fire.

(13) If every blacksmith melted *a horseshoe*, he put *it* in the fire.

Proper names and all definite individual NPs, together with the achievement VPs, form a special class of quantifiers, interpreted on a domain in E of individuals that are constructed as maximally indivisible entities, subsets of P that contain processes decomposed into their parts. Such $X \subseteq P$ satisfy a third closure-condition in addition to Continuity and Splitting, namely

Atomicity: for some $x \varepsilon X$, for all $y \varepsilon P$ if y is a material part of x then $y \varepsilon X$.

An alternative, and perhaps more transparent formulation of this closure-condition would be to generalize Splitting to all descriptive expressions in L. Atomicity implies such a generalized Splitting condition in an infinite P, but if P is finite, and I see no semantic reason to assume that it is not, Atomicity and Generalized Splitting are equivalent.

The three requirements on $X \subseteq P$, Continuity, Splitting and Atomicity, define increasingly stronger closure-conditions, which give rise to three classes of entities with different internal structure. E_1 is the domain of divisible entities, E_2 the domain of entities indivisible relative to some $R \varepsilon L$, and E_3 is the domain of atomic entities, indivisible relative to any $R \varepsilon L$. Obviously, since the three conditions form a cumulative hierarchy, $E_1 \supseteq E_2 \supseteq E_3$.

In accounting for dependency-relations, both the traditional scope-relations, the *de dicto/de re* issues as well as anaphoric dependencies, the three closure-conditions provide the semantic characterization of three classes of entities:

(i) the class of divisible entities, $\{X \subseteq P : X$ closed under Continuity$\}$, are the semantically weakest entities, they depend strongly on other entities, and have restricted coreference conditions.

(ii) the class of entities indivisible with respect to some descriptive expression R, $\{X \subseteq P : X$ closed under Continuity and Splitting$\}$, are semantically stronger, and have freer dependency-relations and coreference conditions.

(iii) the class of maximally indivisible entities, $\{X \subseteq P : X$ closed under Continuity, Splitting and Atomicity$\}$, are semantically strongest in that they have greatest independency of other entities and the most liberal coreference conditions.

Again it may be helpful to think in terms of a two-dimensional space, with one spatial coordinate and one temporal coordinate, in which a divisible entity is a bounded continuum, an R-indivisible entity an R-atom that does not contain any R-parts, and a maximally indivisible entity an absolute atom, i.e. a point. The latter have strongest 'fixing powers', a metaphor for determining the location of the referent in the two-dimensional space and tracing it along the temporal axis. R-atoms are then clusters of absolute atoms that have no R-atoms as part. The bounded continua have least 'fixing powers' and get fixed only via the R-atoms or atoms. This is only a suggestive image, processes in fact have four-dimensional extension in the process-structures, and there are no point-like processes since they are all extended.

Process-models may be ordered into possibly infinite chains $P_0 \subseteq P_1 \subseteq \ldots \subseteq P_n \subseteq P_{n+1} \ldots$, where the order is determined by the inclusion relation on the domain $P_o \subseteq P_1 \subseteq \ldots \subseteq P_n$, and the interpretation assignment-function $[\![\ ]\!]$ is preserved throughout. Two kinds of new information may provide expansions of the set of processes: either refinements of given processes, or new processes that allow formation of new $X \subseteq P$, new semantic entities, closed under some of the three conditions, disjoint from the entities defined in the preceding process-model. In the first case, when refinements are possible of already defined entities, the construction of indivisible entities with Splitting and Atomicity, which are $\forall\ \forall$ and $\exists\ \forall$ conditions, 'for *all* x and for *all* y and z' and 'for some $x \in X$ and for *all* $y \in P$', require that, in any extension P_{n+1} of a given process model P_n in which some $X \subseteq P_n$ satisfying Splitting and/or Atomicity is defined, such $X \subseteq P_n$ are updated by incorporating the additional processes in $P_{n+1} - P_n$, in satisfying the same conditions again for $X \subseteq P_{n+1}$.

Indivisible entities behave consequently relatively stable by this procedure of updating the $X \subseteq P$ that constitute them, preservation of identity is explained as stability by updating and incorporation of new processes. The entire updating-idea needs to be developed and more rigorously formalized. Divisible entities are in this respect less stable since the condition of Continuity, being formulated only with $\forall\ \exists$ does not require updating as any $X \subseteq P_n$ that satisfies Continuity in P_n will satisfy Continuity in any P_{n+m} automatically. Updating is not required, even when new processes are added to P_n that refine a process in an $X \subseteq P_n$ that satisfies only Continuity. Divisible entities preserve their identity as set-theoretic identity of the sets of which they consist. Identity of indivisible entities is not set-theoretic identity, but stability under extensions.

This provides the outline of a more comprehensive program for semantic explanation of dependency-relations in a model-theoretic framework. One important area that was not touched upon in this paper are the VP-anaphora, but Partee (1983) provides an interesting exposition of these issues in the framework of Discourse Representation Structures.

5. CONCLUSION

5.1 Semantic Atomism

The process-structures and models based upon them have been strongly inspired by the Russell/Wiener/Whitehead method of abstraction, which derived moments as maximally pairwise overlapping sets of events or experiences. Kamp (1979) revived this method in the context of temporal reference and English and French tenses, but had no concern with homogeneous quantification and divisible reference. A thorough study of the model-theoretic issues and the relations between period-structures, based on bounded continuous periods, and point-structures can be found in van Benthem (1982). It was argued in this paper that from a linguistic point of view it is more natural, since it fits with the empirical evidence, to derive the interpretation of all nonlogical expressions of a natural language from a set of primitive processes, and to construct divisible entities and indivisible ones on a par by closure-conditions on subsets of these. This captures the important parallel between NPs and VPs and generalizes the method of abstraction to spatio-temporal structures.

It has been emphasized that divisibility of reference cannot be fixed at a lexical level, since almost any expression can be used divisibly or indivisibly. Proper names, our common paradigm of indivisibly referring expression, are used predicatively in a sentence like

(14) Another Reagan for president will destroy the world.

and divisibly in

(15) We have not seen much of Reagan lately.

The interpretation of any expression as referring to divisible or indivisible entities is dependent upon its context, inside but also outside sentence-boundaries. The thesis constitutes what I would like to call *semantic atomism*, which acknowledges that atoms are language-dependent representations of the world, but dissents to the idea that the world consists of independent atomic facts, as fundamental building-blocks of a complex external world. In a translational semantics, as in ter Meulen (1981), homogeneous quantification was analyzed on a par with individuated quantification, and divisibility was imposed by an additional meaning-postulate for mass terms. It seems to allow for a more satisfactory semantic explanation to reconstruct relations between semantic entities with purely set-theoretic means, rather than impose requirements on a wide and principally unrestricted set of models. The methodological shift from indirect interpretation to direct interpretation squares nicely with the typically linguistic concern to employ tools, whether in syntax or in semantics, that have the right generative capacity, i.e. they do not overgenerate, which necessitates later filtering, nor undergenerate, which fails to capture the correct empirical generalizations. Universal grammar, as Richard Montague endorsed, was motivated primarily from a mathematical point of view, in which elegance and abstraction were going hand in hand. A linguistically motivated universal grammar, which is not just restricted to syntax, would seek the appropriate model-theoretic tools to explain inferences, anaphora restrictions and other dependency-relations between interpreted expressions by defining model-theoretic relations and concepts which can be used in proving properties of relations between expressions. I have been more explicit than usual on methodological matters in semantics, not only to do justice to the nature of this meeting, but also because I believe there still remains a certain amount of obscurity concerning the options of semantic methods and the nature of explanations we may be expecting from model-theoretic semantics.

5.2 Model-theoretic Representation

In interpreting a natural language we define models for it that formalize to a certain extent how the language describes the external world. The world and the models are, however, entities of an entirely different realm. Model-theoretic interpretations construct representations of the external world that indicate how our language ascribes structure to the continuously changing chaos, stability is obtained by ignoring irrelevant changes, order is imposed by recognizing similarities. The world lends itself to a multitude of structured representations, all equally 'true' of it and in the same sense about it. A physical theory may tell us that the world consists of atoms, but a semantic theory may reconstruct atoms as indivisible entities that preserve their identity under changes of their parts. The two notions are wide apart, and we may even deny that they have anything in common. But it is important to realize that human beings are capable of entertaining a variety of mutually incompatible representations of their environment at the same time, which provides the essential flexibility to efficiently manipulate and change it.

REFERENCES

Barwise, J., 1981a, Scenes and Other Situations, Journal of Philosophy, 78.

Barwise, J., 1981b, Some Computational Aspects of Situation Semantics, in: "Proceedings of the 19th Annual Meeting of the Association for Computational Linguistics," C. R. Perrault, ed., SRI, Menlo Park, California.

Barwise, J., and Perry, J., 1983, "Situations and Attitudes," Bradford Books, MIT Press, Cambridge, Mass.

van Benthem, J., 1982, "The Logic of Time," Reidel Publ. Co., Dordrecht.

van Benthem, J., 1983, Determiners and Logic, Linguistics and Philosophy, 6.

Kamp, H., 1979, Events, Instants and Temporal Reference, in: "Semantics from Different Points of View," R. Bäuerle, A. v. Stechow, and U. Egli, eds., Springer Verlag, Berlin.

Kamp, H., 1983, A Scenic Tour Through the Land of Naked Infinitives, ms. University of Texas, Austin.

Link, G., 1983, The Logical Analysis of Plurals and Mass Terms: A Lattice-theoretical Approach, in: "Meaning, Use and Interpretation of Language," R. Bäuerle, C. Schwarze, and A. v. Stechow, eds., de Gruyter, Berlin.

ter Meulen, A., 1981, An Intensional Logic for Mass Terms, Philosophical Studies, 40.

ter Meulen, A., 1984, Events, Quantities and Individuals, in: "Varieties of Formal Semantics," F. Landman and F. Veltman, eds., GRASS 3, Foris Publ., Dordrecht.

Montague, R., 1974, "Formal Philosophy," R. Thomason, ed., Yale University Press, New Haven.

Partee, B., 1983, Temporal and Nominal Anaphora, ms. University of Massachusetts, Amherst.

Russell, B., 1971, The Philosophy of Logical Atomism, in: "Logic and Knowledge," R. C. Marsh, ed., Capricorn, N.Y.

A SIMPLE RELEVANCE-CRITERION FOR NATURAL LANGUAGE AND ITS SEMANTICS

Paul Weingartner

Department of Philosophy
University of Salzburg
A-5020 Salzburg/Austria

0. INTRODUCTION

The purpose of this paper is to propose a simple relevance-criterion - called A-relevance - which is claimed to be adequate for inferences in Natural Language and to give its semantics by way of truth tables (finite matrices).

In addition the following by-product (BP) is obtained:

(BP) If it is correct (as claimed in the paper) that A-relevance is representable by the finite truth tables offered then intuitionistic propositional calculus is decidable. On the other hand if it is false that A-relevance is representable by the finite truth tables offered then Chomsky's theory of grammar is correct.

Before I give a precise definition of A-relevance I want to throw some attention to the "by-product" BP: BP is true, because implication "if ... then" is used as in standard two-valued propositional calculus; i.e., any implication is true if its consequent is established by a proof of logic to be true and also if its antecedent is logically false (since if it is false that A-relevance is representable by finite matrices this is again a matter of a proof of logic). Thus, though BP is true it is in fact not a result of this paper, but trivially true. And in fact the decidability of intuitionistic propositional calculus and the correctness of Chomsky's theory of grammar have nothing to do with the result reported in this paper, namely that a certain kind of relevance is representable by finite truth tables. In other words this result is *irrelevant* for both intuitionistic propositional calculus and Chomsky's theory of grammar. Nevertheless, one can "connect" these "irrelevant" states of affairs with an implication of standard logic.* Needless to say that such "theorems" as BP are not derivable with inferences used in Natural Language. More generally I think that the inferences in Natural Language have the property that one cannot infer (derive, conclude) something from premisses which is new in the sense that it is completely unrelated to the premisses. Therefore, the Aristotelean Relevance Criterion mentioned below seems to mirror adequatly at least one of the essential features of inferences in Natural Language even if probably not all of them.

Such and similar kinds of paradoxes as BP were the reason to propose the socalled relevant logics. From its very beginning proponents of relevant logics considered the two properties of implication of standard logic mentioned above as paradoxical or as irrelevant; i.e., relevant implication has to exclude the ex falso quodlibet (an arbitrary contradiction logically implies any arbitrary proposition) and the verum ex quodlibet principle (any arbitrary logically valid proposition follows from any arbitrary proposition). There is a general condition proposed by Anderson and Belnap for *A* to entail *B*

---

* The stimulation for BP the author got from Anderson and Belnap (1975), p. 17.

(or for "*A* relevantly implies *B*"): *A* and *B* must have some propositional variables in common.* But as was criticized by several people** this condition is too weak. And in fact it allows $(p \wedge \neg p) \rightarrow \rightarrow (p \wedge q)$ as a relevant implication since antecedent and consequent share at least one variable. And by the same reason (sharing at least one variable) it allows also $p \rightarrow [p \vee (q \rightarrow q)]$ as a relevant implication. Thus the paradoxical cases discussed above in connection with BP enter again in a more complicated form.

1. THE ARISTOTELEAN RELEVANCE-CRITERION

In Aristotle's syllogistics the following relevance-criterion is incorporated: No predicates occur in the conclusion which did not occur already in the premisses. More accurately: The conclusion of any syllogistic mode contains subject-term and predicate-term only whereas the premises contain in addition the middle-term which is eliminated by the inference. Although not mentioned explicitly by Aristotle this criterion is an essential feature of syllogistic inference. If this idea is applied to propositional logic one gets the following criteria, formulated for implicational formulas and inferences.

1.1 A-relevant Implicational Formulas

Writing α, β, γ ... for formulas and p, q, r ... for propositional variables of the standard 2-valued Propositional Calculus

---

* This condition was also called "variable sharing condition". Cf. Anderson and Belnap (1975).

** Cf. Meyer (1984).

and presupposing the usual recursive definition for well-formed formulas and one of the well known axiomatizations for the valid formulas A-relevance can be defined thus:

Def 1: A valid implicational formula $\alpha \to \beta$ of Propositional Calculus is A-relevant iff there is no atomic formula which occurs in β but not in α.

1.2 A-relevant Inferences

Def 2: A valid inference $\alpha \vdash \beta$ of Propositional Calculus is A-relevant iff its respective valid implicational formula $\alpha \to \beta$ is A-relevant.

1.3 Examples

It is easy to see that the valid formulas (or their respective inferences) $p \to p$, $p \to \neg\neg p$, $\neg\neg p \to p$, and the laws of commutation, association, distribution, DeMorgan, modus ponens, modus tollens, hypothetical syllogism in the form $[(p \to q) \wedge (q \to r)] \to (p \to r)$, disjunctive syllogism, simplification, i.e., $(p \wedge q) \to p$, $(p \to \neg p) \to p$, $(p \to q) \to (\neg q \to \neg p)$ ... etc. are all A-relevant.

However, the following valid formulas (or their respective inferences) are not A-relevant: $(p \wedge \neg p) \to q$, $\neg p \to (p \to q)$, $q \to (p \to q)$, $p \to (p \vee q)$, $p \to (q \to q)$, $(p \wedge \neg p) \to (q \wedge \neg q)$, $[p \to (q \wedge \neg q) \leftrightarrow \neg p$, $(p \to q) \to [(p \wedge r) \to (q \wedge r)]$.

1.4 Properties of A-relevance

In another paper it is proved that A-relevant implication (or inference) is (1) transitive, (2) not A-relevance preserving, (3) not closed under modus ponens, (4) closed under substitution.*

1.5 A-relevance Helps to Solve Paradoxes

Here I may mention other reasons (in addition to those discussed in the introduction) in support of the A-relevance criterion.

1.5.1 When introducing value-judgments or norms into scientific discourse (of which it is assumed that standard propositional logic is applicable to it) one has the paradoxes of deontic logic and analoguous ones of value theory as immediate consequences. For instance, since $p \rightarrow (p \vee q)$ is valid in propositional logic one gets - by the usual additional assumptions: what is logically true ought to be and by distribution concerning → (which is available in every deontic logic) - the Ross paradox: $Op \rightarrow O(p \vee q)$. An analoguous paradox follows if 'O' is replaced by a value-operator "it is valuable that".

The application of A-relevance, however, rules out almost all of the paradoxes of deontic logic and value theory.

1.5.2 In addition, A-relevance is a great help in solving the Paradoxes of Explanation and Confirmation. In this case a part of them are ruled out by A-relevance and almost all of them are ruled out by a strengthening of A-relevance.**

---

* Cf. Wronski and Weingartner (198.).

** Cf. Weingartner and Schurz (198.). There we do not restrict relevance to valid formulas since paradoxical sentences are not always valid.

2. FINITE TRUTH-TABLES FOR A-RELEVANCE

2.1 The Main Point of A-relevance

In order to construct finite truth-tables (matrices) for A-relevance one has to observe the main point of the criterion: no new atomic formula in the conclusion (or in the conclusion-part or consequent of a valid implication). But to find out whether the formula is new it has to be distinguishable from the others. This is done in the formal language by using different letters like 'p', 'q', 'r' ... etc. The well formed formulas (wffs) are the same as in two-valued standard propositional calculus. But in a truth table in which no atomic formulas enter (take a conjunction $p \wedge q$ or a disjunction $p \vee q$) the truth values of p are distinguished from the truth-values of q by the special arrangement of these values. For instance, if 1 and 0 are the truth-values true and false, $p \wedge q$ has the following matrix,

$p \wedge q$	1	0
1	1	0
0	0	0

where the values of p and that of q are arranged in different directions. In order to have a more general method of distinguishing these values I propose to introduce indices: for p index 1, for q index 2, for r index 3 ... etc. such that p has then the truth-values 1^1 and 0^1, q has 1^2 and 0^2, r has 1^3 and 0^3. Further observe that the truth-values of a compound proposition are functions of the truth-values of the elementary ones such that they have to carry the indices of all the elementary ones which enter. This means that the new truth-tables for the conjunction and disjunction with all the indices are these:

$p \wedge q$	1^2	0^2
1^1	1^{12}	0^{12}
0^1	0^{12}	0^{12}

$p \vee q$	1^2	0^2
1^1	1^{12}	1^{12}
0^1	1^{12}	0^{12}

2.2 Meaning of A-relevance Expressed by Truth-tables

Remember the truth-table properties of standard material implication (the only case when it has the truth value 0 is for $1 \rightarrow 0$). Then one can explain already the meaning of A-relvance in respect to the two formulas $(p \wedge q) \rightarrow q$ and $p \rightarrow (p \vee q)$ of which the first is A-relevant, the second is not. It amounts to this: A valid implicational formula is A-relevant iff it satisfies the following two conditions:

2.2.1 Its truth table (constructed according to the rules of the standard truth table for material implication) contains only truth-values 1.

2.2.2 The set of indices of the consequent-part (conclusion-part) is a subset of the set of indices of the antecedens-part (premiss-part).

In fact the condition 2.2.1 is superfluous because we speak only of *valid* formulas (or *valid* inferences) as relevant or not relevant.

Applying condition 2.2.2 to the formulas $(p \wedge q) \rightarrow q$ and $p \rightarrow (p \vee q)$ with the help of the above matrices gives perceptual evidence that condition 2.2.2 lets through as relevant the first but rules out the second: i.e., going from values 1^{12} and 0^{12} to 1^2 and 0^2 is o.k., but going from 1^1 and 0^1 to 1^{12} and 0^{12} is not o.k. according to 2.2.2.

Thus all what one has to do in constructing a truth-table for A-relevant implication is to observe that condition 2.2.2 is satisfied (in addition to the standard requirements for the truth-values for a true implication).

This gives the following matrix for A-relevant implication ($\overset{A}{\rightarrow}$) with two variables *p* and *q*. Observe that *p* and *q* as atomic formulas can have only the values 1^1, 0^1 and 1^2, 0^2. But if one takes instead of *p* for example the formula $(p \wedge \neg p) \wedge q$ then this formula has the values 0^{12}, such that for $[(p \wedge \neg p) \wedge q] \overset{A}{\rightarrow} q$ the matrix has to tell the result of $0^{12} \overset{A}{\rightarrow} 1^2$ and $0^{12} \overset{A}{\rightarrow} 0^2$. That means that one needs all the possible values when formulas with two propositions are involved.

$\alpha \overset{A}{\rightarrow} \beta$	1^1	1^2	1^{12}	0^{12}	0^2	0^1
1^1	1^1	0^{12}	0^{12}	0^{12}	0^{12}	0^1
1^2	0^{12}	1^2	0^{12}	0^{12}	0^2	0^{12}
1^{12}	1^{12}	1^{12}	1^{12}	0^{12}	0^{12}	0^{12}
0^{12}	1^{12}	1^{12}	1^{12}	1^{12}	1^{12}	1^{12}
0^2	0^{12}	1^2	0^{12}	0^{12}	1^2	0^{12}
0^1	1^1	0^{12}	0^{12}	0^{12}	0^{12}	1^1

2.3 Completing All Possible Values for Formulas with Two Propositions

Though the truth values of *p* and *q* are completely given by 1^1, 0^1 and 1^2, 0^2 compound formulas may have different values such that the connectives have to be defined also for further combinations of values like $1^2 \wedge 1^2$, $1^1 \wedge 1^{12}$ or $0^2 \wedge 1^{12}$ ... etc. In other words, one has to define the connectives and negation for all possible values, i.e., for 1^1, 0^1; 1^2, 0^2; 1^{12}, 0^{12} and all their combinations. If more than two variables are involved the definitions are analoguous (i.e., like truth-tables of standard propositional calculus with more than two variables (see 2.5)).

These definitions are constructed through a simple advice: (1) the truth-values are determined as in standard propositional calculus, (2) the result of a combination of sets of indices is always the union-set of the sets of indices. Thus the matrices for negation, conjunction, disjunction and implication are these:

α	$\neg\alpha$
1^{1}	0^{1}
1^{2}	0^{2}
1^{12}	0^{12}
0^{12}	1^{12}
0^{2}	1^{2}
0^{1}	1^{1}

$\alpha \wedge \beta$	1^{1}	1^{2}	1^{12}	0^{12}	0^{2}	0^{1}
1^{1}	1^{1}	1^{12}	1^{12}	0^{12}	0^{12}	0^{1}
1^{2}	1^{12}	1^{2}	1^{12}	0^{12}	0^{2}	0^{12}
1^{12}	1^{12}	1^{12}	1^{12}	0^{12}	0^{12}	0^{12}
0^{12}	0^{12}	0^{12}	0^{12}	0^{12}	0^{12}	0^{12}
0^{2}	0^{12}	0^{2}	0^{12}	0^{12}	0^{2}	0^{12}
0^{1}	0^{1}	0^{12}	0^{12}	0^{12}	0^{12}	0^{1}

$\alpha \vee \beta$	1^{1}	1^{2}	1^{12}	0^{12}	0^{2}	0^{1}
1^{1}	1^{1}	1^{12}	1^{12}	1^{12}	1^{12}	1^{1}
1^{2}	1^{12}	1^{2}	1^{12}	1^{12}	1^{2}	1^{12}
1^{12}	1^{12}	1^{12}	1^{12}	1^{12}	1^{12}	1^{12}
0^{12}	1^{12}	1^{12}	1^{12}	0^{12}	0^{12}	0^{12}
0^{2}	1^{12}	1^{2}	1^{12}	0^{12}	0^{2}	0^{12}
0^{1}	1^{1}	1^{12}	1^{12}	0^{12}	0^{12}	0^{1}

$\alpha \rightarrow \beta$	1^{1}	1^{2}	1^{12}	0^{12}	0^{2}	0^{1}
1^{1}	1^{1}	1^{12}	1^{12}	0^{12}	0^{12}	0^{1}
1^{2}	1^{12}	1^{2}	1^{12}	0^{12}	0^{2}	0^{12}
1^{12}	1^{12}	1^{12}	1^{12}	0^{12}	0^{12}	0^{12}
0^{12}	1^{12}	1^{12}	1^{12}	1^{12}	1^{12}	1^{12}
0^{2}	1^{12}	1^{2}	1^{12}	1^{12}	1^{2}	1^{12}
0^{1}	1^{1}	1^{12}	1^{12}	1^{12}	1^{12}	1^{1}

As one can see from the matrices the connectives (except relevant implication) are interdefinable such that two connectives suffice to determine the others. Thus the pairs $\{p \wedge q, \neg(p \rightarrow \neg q)\}$, $\{p \vee q, \neg p \rightarrow q\}$, $\{p \wedge q, \neg(\neg p \vee \neg q\}$, $\{p \rightarrow q, \neg p \vee q\}$, $\{p \vee q, \neg(\neg p \wedge \neg q)\}$, $\{p \rightarrow q, \neg(p \wedge \neg q)\}$ have the same matrices and are therefore relevantly interchangeable, i.e., the arrow in both directions is a relevant implication.

Equivalence is defined in the usual way: $(p \leftrightarrow q)$ =df $[(p \rightarrow q) \wedge \wedge (q \rightarrow p)]$ (where '=df' means that the respective matrices are identical).

2.4 Substitution

As one can see easily from the matrix for relevant implication $\alpha \overset{A}{\rightarrow} \beta$ two formulas are A-relevantly substitutable iff they have the same matrices, i.e., their matrices have (1) the same truth-values at the same place and (2) the same indices at the same place (see the diagonal from left top to right bottom).

2.5 Definition of A-relevant Propositional Calculus

In order to give a general definition one has to observe first 2.5.1, 2.5.2 and 2.5.3.

2.5.1 The truth values have as indices sets of natural numbers. If for instance four propositions are involved the sequence is continued thus: $1^1 1^2 1^{12} 1^3 1^{13}$ ... $1^4 1^{14}$ ... $1^{1234} 0^{1234}$ ... $0^{14} 0^4$ ... ... $0^{13} 0^3 0^{12} 0^2 0^1$ (where the parenthesis to indicate sets are omitted).

2.5.2 If any formula α (atomic or compound) is combined by a connective ($\wedge$, $\vee$, $\rightarrow$, $\leftrightarrow$, $\overset{A}{\rightarrow}$) with any other formula α (atomic or compound) then the indices of the resulting truth-values are the union-sets of the sets of indices of the respective truth-values of α combined with the sets of indices of the respective truth-values of β.

If for instance the pairs $\{1^{1}, 1^{12}\}$, $\{1^{23}, 1^{12}\}$, $\{1^{34}, 1^{12}\}$ are combined by one of the connectives $\wedge$, $\vee$, $\rightarrow$, $\leftrightarrow$ then the resulting truth-values have the respective union-sets of the sets of indices: 1^{12}, 1^{123}, 1^{1234}.

2.5.3 In general the truth-values with arbitrary indices can be defined as T (true) = $\{1^{x} : x \subset \mathbb{N}, x \neq \emptyset, x \text{ is finite}\}$ and F (false) = $\{0^{x} : x \subset \mathbb{N}, x \neq \emptyset, x \text{ is finite}\}$.

If an arbitrary truth value with index x, i.e., v^{x} is combined by a connective with an arbitrary truth-value with index y, i.e., w^{y} then the resulting truth-value has the union-set of the sets of indices of v and w, i.e., the result is either $v^{x \cup y}$ or $w^{x \cup y}$ (if $v \neq w$).

2.5.4 According to 2.5.3 one can define the connectives in a general way thus:

p	$\neg p$
1^{x}	0^{x}
0^{x}	1^{x}

$p \wedge q$	1^{y}	0^{y}
1^{x}	$1^{x \cup y}$	$0^{x \cup y}$
0^{x}	$0^{x \cup y}$	$0^{x \cup y}$

$p \vee q$	1^{y}	0^{y}
1^{x}	$1^{x \cup y}$	$1^{x \cup y}$
0^{x}	$1^{x \cup y}$	$0^{x \cup y}$

$p \rightarrow q$	1^{y}	0^{y}
1^{x}	$1^{x \cup y}$	$0^{x \cup y}$
0^{x}	$1^{x \cup y}$	$1^{x \cup y}$

$p \leftrightarrow q$	1^{y}	0^{y}
1^{x}	$1^{x \cup y}$	$0^{x \cup y}$
0^{x}	$0^{x \cup y}$	$1^{x \cup y}$

2.5.5 Following 2.5.3 and 2.5.4 the definition of A-relevant implication $\overset{A}{\rightarrow}$ is this:

$p \overset{A}{\to} q$	1^y	0^x
1^x	$v^{x \cup y}$	$0^{x \cup y}$
0^x	$v^{x \cup y}$	$v^{x \cup y}$

$$\text{where } v^{x \cup y} = \begin{cases} 1^{x \cup y} & \text{if } y \subseteq x \\ 0^{x \cup y} & \text{otherwise} \end{cases}$$

2.5.6 Definition. The system of A-relevant propositional calculus can be defined as the set of all wffs which are satisfied by the matrix Mat = $\langle T, F, \neg, \to, \overset{A}{\to} \rangle$ where T, F and the operations $\neg$, $\to$ and $\overset{A}{\to}$ are defined as in 2.5.3, 2.5.4 and 2.5.5.

An unpleasant feature of the matrix of 2.5.6 is its infinite universe containing the usual truth-values 0 and 1 indexed by arbitrary finite and non-empty sets of natural numbers. But if one wants a single matrix to work for all possible formulas and at the same time for any n-variable formula one needs each of the truth values with $2^n - 1$ indices then the trouble seems to be hard to avoid. However, a nice way out may be found by observing that it is not necessary to attach different indices to different propositional variables because the desired result may be achieved if only we assure that an extra-variable in the conclusion (if it exists) is given a different index then all the rest. Thus we can use as our indices all subsets of an arbitrary singleton - say s - and replace 2.5.3 with the following:

2.5.7 Truth values of our matrix are elements of the following two sets: T (true) = $\{1^{\emptyset}, 1^{s}\}$, F (false) = $\{0^{\emptyset}, 0^{s}\}$.

Then leaving all the remaining definitions unchanged we arrive at a four-element matrix capable of doing the same job as one of 2.5.6. Indeed, any implication having an extra-variable p solely in the conclusion is refuted in our new matrix when p takes the value 1^s and all other variables the value $1^{\emptyset}$. [This improvement was suggested by A. Wronski.]

3. STRENGTHENING OF A-RELEVANCE

The following strengthening of A-relevance (A^+-relevance) seems worthy of further investigation.

Def 3: A valid implicational formula is A^+-relevant iff it satisfies conditions (1) and (2):

(1) as in Def 1.

(2) If the atomic subformula s_a of β occurs also in α it does not occur there only as a subformula of a valid wff (which is a subformula of α) except s_a occurs also in β as a subformula of a valid wff (which is a subformula of β).

Thus for instance $[(p \wedge \neg p) \wedge (q \rightarrow q)] \rightarrow q$ is A-relevant but not A^+-relevant whereas $[p \wedge (q \rightarrow q)] \rightarrow (q \vee \neg q)$ is also A^+-relevant.

REFERENCES

Anderson, A. R. and Belnap, N. D., 1975, "Entailment. The Logic of Relevance and Necessity," Vol. I, Princeton University Press, Princeton.

Bellert, I. and Weingartner, P., 1982, On Different Characteristics of Scientific Texts as Compared with Every-Day Language Texts, in: "Sublanguage. Studies of Language in Restricted Semantic Domains," R. Kittredge and J. Lehrberger, eds., deGruyter, Berlin and New York.

Meyer, R. K., 1984, A Farewell to Entailment, in: this Volume.

Weingartner, P. and Schurz, G., 198., Paradoxes Solved by Simple Relevance Criteria, (forthcoming).

Weingartner, P. and Wronski, A., 198., Relevance Criteria Based on Classical Logic, (forthcoming).

A FAREWELL TO ENTAILMENT

Robert K. Meyer

The Research School of Social Sciences
Australian National University
Canberra ACT 2600, Australia

"DON'T FENCE ME IN"

I am not a Relevantist. But, were I one, I might speak something like this. "In their epochal work *Entailment* (vol. I, Anderson and Belnap, 1975, with others), Relevant Logicians have led us out of the Material dominions of the great Boole. They wave the Archetypal Form of Inference $A \rightarrow A$, and the Truth-functional Sea parts, that the Children of Relevance might reach the far side in safety, there to practice Natural Deduction according to the systems of their choice in peace, tranquility, and mathematical exactitude. But the Sea returns to claim the pursuing Official Logicians, who are weighed down by false theorems. Just is the fate of these Officials. For they have bowed down before Irrelevant Entailments in which antecedents and consequents share no variable. And they have allowed the Accidental Premiss to beget the Necessitive Conclusion. Drowned are they in their own Paradoxes and Contradictions; and in the Flood of Nonsense that follows therefrom."

"The Way to the One True Logic leads first through the deserts of Strict Implication, tempting the Followers of Our Intuitions into errors and idolatries not far from those of the great Boole himself. But they are fed by systems from Pittsburgh - among them, E, R, EM, RM, and T - whose axioms and rules are just right. Of commandments, there is only one. Thou shalt not use the disjunctive syllogism. Or else one will be like the heathen."

"The result is a 'new branch of mathematical logic'. It is 'the logic of relevance and necessity'. Of these the Chosen Logicians were deprived when they were forced to make the Brick of Valid Argument without the Straw of Traditional Wisdom. But, while there are many Relevant logics, there is only one Promised Logic. EM and RM fall by the wayside, plagued by fallacies of relevance. Even the beloved system R also sins, enticed into fallacies of modality. Applying the process of elimination (and hoping, perhaps against hope, that this does not violate the One Commandment), this leaves only E. Inspect the Tablets of Rationality, and see what is written on them. Is it not the axioms and rules of E? (Together, perhaps, with the One Commandment - since that's the tradition in these matters, and E is big on Tradition.) For E, and only E, is presented as the *system of entailment*."

Even were my Poetic License revoked, I am not sure that anybody would stick up for E in just this manner. But, on the central points, it does seem a not unfair reading of the work of Anderson and Belnap, set out in its presumptively definitive form in the treatise cited above. For that matter, it is (save for the emphasis on E as the best Relevant logic) not an unfair reading of many things that I have said myself. (But, to oneself, all is forgiven.) But I see things these days in more sombre hues. Among Relevant logics, E is not even a particularly good one. It is certainly not *the* system of entailment. On wide motivational points, the "archetypal" $A \rightarrow A$ is a question-begging fallacy. The "natural deduction" systems for E are baroque, *ad hoc*, and not very natural. There is no "logic of relevance"; were there one, it would scarcely be E. The whole "fallacies of modality" story is circular; it motivates very little. Most significantly, the One Commandment is dead wrong. The claim that Relevant logics reject the disjunctive syllogism has been a millstone around the neck of these logics for a full quarter century. It has dominated philosophical discussion, almost to the exclusion of the more interesting technical and philosophical questions that Relevant logics raise. I show here that the claim itself is *false*, whence its false presupposition dismisses much of the discussion. (Briefly, the Relevant attitude toward the disjunctive syllogism is subtle. But it is not malicious.)

On all these counts, Relevant logics stand now at a point of motivational crisis. There are *old* motivating lines, which the world has found unpersuasive. By and large, the world is right. But these failed lines never exhausted the project, which antedated them and which will survive them. Making these points is the purpose of this paper. In doing so, we bid farewell to the system E of entailment; and to much balderdash that has accompanied it.

Thus went, more or less, the introduction to what I assumed would be the final form of this paper. If it is sharply polemical (as much that follows will be), it is warranted by the motivational situation. For a long time, the *picture* presented of the world of Relevant logics has been seriously misleading. Given the weight of Relevant authority that has been attached to that picture, efforts to change it have not only been unavailing, but mainly unnoticed. Perhaps the most important *desideratum* is that of securing some rapprochement between Relevant and Material insights. The technical foundation exists on which to do it. The $\supset$E issues that I examine below are part of that foundation; perhaps even more important is the direction taken by Relevant semantical analysis, especially when provided with the "Boolean" negation that I introduced with Routley in our 1973 paper, and have studied subsequently. (Urquhart, 1972, makes similar suggestions.)

However, since I prepared these remarks, a copy of Belnap (1984) has crossed my desk. It is, as President Nixon used to say, "at variance" with some of the previously published opinions of its author. While I do not propose to discuss this paper (since it is marked "not for publication"), I trust that it will violate no confidences to say that it is a fine piece of work, which takes a sane and balanced view of the accomplishments and prospects for a Relevant understanding of logic. Some of what I say below would, no doubt, have been said differently had I had that paper in hand when preparing this one. While this may be *too* revealing, the fact that Belnap notes that, in his own practice, he also uses the disjunctive syllogism is too significant to omit; there must be something wrong with the view that it will drive you mad. (There are also some odd resonances between Belnap's paper and this one, evidently mutually unintended; compare what I say below about "asserting the consequent" with Belnap's observation that it is everybody's favourite formal fallacy. Save for the assurance that I have not been cribbing, I leave the informed reader to ferret out variations on other themes.) To say more about Belnap (1984) would not be fair, save that I hope that it becomes generally available, if only as evidence for the Defence. Meanwhile, here is the case for the Prosecution.

I FAREWELL TO THE ONE COMMANDMENT

In their 1981 paper, Belnap and Dunn reject the disjunctive syllogism as incompatible with a Relevantist philosophy. While this has been an old focus of debate between Relevant logicians and their critics, the Relevantist line, if allowed to stand, goes a long way toward reducing the Relevant side of the case to absurdity. For one thing, if there is anything *else* to a Relevantist philosophy *except* the rejection of the disjunctive syllogism, Belnap and Dunn do not dwell on it. (This has the effect of making what purports to be *the* philosophy appropriate to Relevant logics look like a pet peeve.) Moreover, the Relevantist view removes some of the sugar-coating to be found in previous discussions of the topic - for example, in Anderson and Belnap (1975) - which suggest that the real disjunctive syllogism depends on an *intensional* reading of the 'or' of its major premiss, whence the relevantly invalid form of the principle may be viewed simply as an extensional counterfeit of a traditionally, and relevantly, valid inference. For Belnap and Dunn mince no words in suggesting that it is the Traditional disjunctive syllogism - the Fifth Indemonstrable - that Relevantists should deny. (They add the quip that it is better to deny an indemonstrable than a demonstrable. But, since much of the rest of their 1981 paper is an attempt to weasel out of the fact that the prohibited inference has been *proved* admissible for E and many other Relevant logics and theories, they seem stuck after all in the quagmire of denying demonstrables. I shall return to this subject.)

Before dissecting it, I remark in passing that this hardening of the Relevantist position has had numerous side effects, all bad. One is simply the bickering that it has produced among Relevant logicians themselves - though, insofar as genuine differences of opinion are involved, perhaps that could not be helped. Next, in its narrow focus on and utter rejection of the disjunctive syllogism, long viewed by philosophical opponents as the Achilles heel of the Relevant logics, the Relevantist view has given aid and comfort to these opponents - which, as might be expected, they have not been slow to seize. While perhaps that, too, could not be helped, there is something disheartening about seeing a *reductio ad absurdum* of one's own position presented as its purest form. A quarter of a century spent debating when and whether we use the disjunctive syllogism in everyday good argument is long enough; the case seems overwhelming that we do. This leaves it as the duty of Relevant philosophers of logic either to *account* for the fact, from the viewpoint of their own systems, or to show that what counts as everyday good argument rests here on mistakes, fallacies, and philosophical presuppositions that will not stand the test of time. To a degree, both approaches have been tried. But the Belnap-Dunn paper seems to me simply to abnegate responsibility on the point, exposing the Relevantist view to the obvious counterexamples, while offering no defence save the coherence with Relevant logics as previously formulated and motivated. While Belnap and Dunn castigate some objections to the Relevantist program as involving "leaps of faith", the whole program seems a leap of faith, and one likely to be well-nigh universally rejected.

While this is bad enough, the inconsistency with Anderson and Belnap (1975) is worse. If anything in its motivating style remains persistently appealing, resisting subsumption under special pleading for particular systems, it lies in a concern for Traditional ingredients of good argument, which currently fashionable Boolean reconstruction has lost sight of. Logic is responsible to its data. To be sure, Logic has also a prescriptive element; it indicates not merely how we do argue, when we are arguing well, but how we should argue, if we would argue well. We pursue theory, in the last analysis, to get clear about how we should act. Otherwise it is sterile, and a mere codification of behaviour. So theoretical reconstruction can change our views about what constitute good arguments (and Boolean reconstruction has certainly done so). But the interplay between theory and practice remains delicate. The paradoxes of material and strict implication remain offensive because, at the practical level, they correspond to inaccurate predictions about how we will argue, if we are arguing well. It is as much a refutation of Boolean reconstruction of logic that people do not infer what they please from contradictions as it is a refutation of Newtonian physics that the planet Mercury does not appear on photographic plates where that theory says it should be. Special pleading that we should overlook the brute facts of our rational behaviour - and even that we should regiment that behaviour until it accords with prevailing theory - is as unacceptable as the plea that the photographs should be doctored until Mercury is relocated to fit the theory.

So much one can read in (or at least read into) Anderson and Belnap (1975). And one has heard enough of the widespread assumption that one cannot bring an objective rationality to bear on the claims of competing logics, presumptively because logic itself is involved in judging those claims; or because, if you deny certain theses, you must *mean* something different by the *informal* logical particles. Such pessimism is on a par with a view that, because we are components of physical systems, we cannot make rational judgments between competing physical theories. For we do not need logical theory to make us rational, any more than we need physical theory to make us physical objects. Logic is a product of our rationality, not its cause. While we may hope also that it will cause an improvement in the product (and flatter ourselves that it has done so), the circles that philosophers spin rarely enmesh us as completely as claimed. We can still stand outside them, equipped with our everyday reason - fallible, error-prone, imprecise, self-interested, and even biased though it may be - and determine that some word-smith is making the worse appear the better cause. Because it does not accord with the facts of the case.

So it is, I think, with Relevantist rejection of the disjunctive syllogism. Relevant logics do have new views on the topic. Leaving aside the slings and arrows of outrageous philosophy, no subject has been more thoroughly examined *technically* by Relevant logicians. And how odd it is that, if Relevant logics are held simplistically to *reject* this principle, so much effort has gone into *verifying* it.

There must, in that event, have been something wrong with the propaganda. Or else the effort has been misdirected. I shall quarrel here with the propaganda - or, at least, with some elements of it. For Friends and Foes of Relevant Logics have been besotted by the fact that the following is not a Relevant theorem scheme:

(1) $(A \supset B) \,\&\, A \rightarrow B$

Few of the Foes and too few of the Friends have been equally attentive to the status of the following as a *rule of inference* in Relevant logics and theories.

$\supset$E) $A \supset B$ and $A \Rightarrow B$

And it has gone almost without comment, as unworthy of association with the question, that the following *is* a Relevant theorem scheme:

(2) $(A \supset B) \,\&\, A \supset B$

To facilitate comparison, here are another theorem scheme and rule of E and its kin:

(3) $(A \rightarrow B) \,\&\, A \rightarrow B$

$\rightarrow$E) $A \rightarrow B$ and $A \Rightarrow B$

While $\supset$E has been contentious, no one has ever doubted that $\rightarrow$E is in the spirit of E, if only because it shows up as a primitive rule whenever the system is specified. But you and I will shortly doubt it. And, I hope, restore some Parity.

I pause for notational points. $A \supset B$ is defined as usual by $-A \vee B$, where $-$ is the DeMorgan negation with which Relevant logics have traditionally been equipped. I shall not dwell here on the issues raised by Boolean negation, save to note that I think that Belnap and Dunn (1981) are unduly nervous in associating its discovery with that of nuclear fission. And mouthwash. (I am planning a paper, "Boole bites back", to deal with those issues.) & and $\vee$ are as usual. $\rightarrow$ is relevant implication (or entailment). $\Rightarrow$ is metalogical 'if' (or, if one prefers, the record of a license to infer); for the moment, I do not analyse further. To read formulas, let binary particles be ranked &, $\vee$, $\supset$, $\rightarrow$, in order of increasing scope; mixed use of formal and English particles (as in $\supset$E, $\rightarrow$E above) is, I trust, self-explanatory. Otherwise, associate to the left, and use dots as parentheses as usual.

Surviving Stoics, perplexed by all those $\supset$'s, are now excused. For the Relevant "disjunctive syllogism" debate is about $\supset$E, and we henceforth drop the conceit that it is about anything else. (If anybody cares, we note that the Fourth Indemonstrable of the Stoics went like this: "A or B; but A; so not B." So anybody who thinks that the 'or' of the Fifth one was $\vee$ seems at least to have got the wrong truth-function, with an even more severe anachronism being a distinct possibility.) This calls for a candour that past participants have not always exercised (except privately). The *contentious* question, in Relevant logics, is whether, and to what degree, $\supset$ is a *bona fide* implication (in Quinese, read 'conditional'). The core of that question is *modus ponens* for $\supset$. Relevant logicians, with a taste for the Anderson-Belnap *bon mot* that material implication is no more a kind of implication than a blunderbuss is a kind of buss, have preferred a "disjunctive syllogism" question to a "material implication" question. (Well, some blunder. Some buss.) Their foes, I fear, have joined the conspiracy to obfuscate the question; in holding to the "disjunctive syllogism", they seem for once to have Tradition on their side, which is not so clear if they are simply sticking up for a naked material $\supset$. This brings up another level of aversion to calling a spade a spade. $\supset$E is the rule (γ) of Ackermann

(1956); and we Relevant logicians have stuck also to that name - so technical, so impressive, so Greek. But this is, surely, getting the precedence wrong; ⊃E, fair enough, is the very first primitive proposition of *Principia Mathematica*, whence a real regard for Logical Tradition should at least enjoin us to call it 1.1.

Many authors have, over the years, joined the ⊃E debate. A few of them are Read, Mortensen, Burgess, Kielkopf, Woods, Bennett, Curley, Plumwood, Routley, Anderson, Belnap, and Dunn. Even Kripke, according to Belnap and Dunn, has had his say. It has even been discovered that some Scholastics had it in for ⊃E (in, I suppose, its 14th century form). That's as these things go; old-timers grow wiser as modern theory develops. The semi-published Meyer (1979), which by backwards causation is a response to Belnap and Dunn (1981), develops some of my own views; these led to an immediate increase in my hate mail, including withdrawal of an invitation that I had accepted 5 years earlier to collaborate as an author of volume II of *Entailment*. (So, in a sense, entailment has already said farewell to me.) Those who missed them the first time round will find the gist of these views below, somewhat updated.

In calling this a ⊃E debate, I mean simply that, when some informal appeals to the disjunctive syllogism are analysed relevantly, they are most naturally parsed as involving ⊃E. I do not mean that they *do* involve ⊃E, which is a principle (or property) of formal theories, and which can at best apply by analogy to our informal reasoning. Nor am I moved by the fact that, parsed classically, these arguments would almost certainly involve ⊃E. For classical logic is sufficiently impoverished that, quibbles aside, it has no choice. Nor can one sensibly beg the question by examining it from the viewpoint of just one theory, outside of which there is no salvation. Says who?

Next, I do not wish to rule out alternative Relevant parsings of 'or', on which a given informal appeal to the disjunctive syllogism might rest on $\rightarrow$E rather than $\supset$E. Many, perhaps most, classical invocations of $\supset$E are so transformed in the context of Relevant theory. The problem is with the residue. Since trading examples and counterexamples is not to my taste, I see little value in discussing these things outside of a theoretical context. But there are theoretical examples. In the system of relevant arithmetic introduced in Meyer (1975), one finds the theorem $x \neq 0 \supset 0 < x$. The system becomes incoherent if one strengthens this to $x \neq 0 \rightarrow 0 < x$. So we are stuck, at best, with a material $\supset$. But $7 \neq 0$. It seems to me a reasonable conclusion that $0 < 7$ (which is, thank goodness, a theorem). And the task is to find some systematic Relevant way of drawing such reasonable conclusions.

But, since Meyer and Dunn (1969), we have known the way. I hold, accordingly, that the Relevant *problem* of $\supset$E has been solved; and that it has been solved, moreover, in the affirmative. Since, infuriatingly, most of the discussion has ignored the solution, there is no need to dwell on a pre-scientific approach to these things. Even more infuriatingly, Belnap and Dunn, who do attend to the solution, do so primarily to undermine it, at least from the Relevantist standpoint. On this I must dwell.

Here is the Meyer and Dunn alternative - in which, whatever Dunn may now think, I still have confidence. There are many theories that, for good reason, do not and ought not to admit $\supset$E as a *global* principle. Inconsistent theories are the familiar example. The well-known Lewis path goes A, $-$A, $-$A $\vee$ B, A $\supset$ B, B. Trivial truth-functional maneuvers, combined with a final $\supset$E step, yield a (theoretical) psychotic break. I have never doubted that, in this case, it is the

$\supset$E step that is wrong. But, because we impose a Relevant quarantine on diseased theories, is it reasonable to impose the same quarantine on healthy theories? Should we not look rather for criteria that separate the healthy theories form the diseased ones? If we find such criteria, may we not have our cake and eat it too, objecting to $\supset$E where it is objectionable, without depriving ourselves of a useful principle where it is *not* objectionable?

The question then is whether there is a Relevant *warrant* for our everyday appeal to $\supset$E. Again there is little sense to be made of this question outside of a theoretical context. The best warrant is *proof*. One shows, for the theories for which $\supset$E is wanted, that they do admit the principle. The most conspicuous such theory is Logic itself. It would be shocking were both $A \supset B$ and A to be theorems of (say) E, but for B to be a non-theorem. This would make Logic itself a diseased theory. Demonstrably it is not, as Meyer and Dunn (1969) show for E and its close kin. Moreover, the *method* of proof has permitted almost indefinite refinement and modification, in its application to richer Relevant logics and to more concrete Relevant theories. One can almost say that, if we have good grounds for thinking that a given Relevant theory formalizes stable and coherent insights, sooner or later somebody will prove that $\supset$E holds for this theory. (I confess, though, a vested interest. As often as not, that somebody has been me.)

So the Prosecution has an indictment to return. There is probable cause that the Relevantist has committed a Crime against Reason, even as Reason is enshrined in Relevant logics. (This raises the question whether motivational suicide is an indictable offence.) Relevant logics and theories do make room for $\supset$E. Whether they attach to it the honorific "universally valid" is more or less beside the point. (Why must logicians always project their intuitions *that far* upon the galaxy?) But, to show that the Relevantist is guilty as charged, we must establish this Crime beyond reasonable doubt.

The rejection of ⊃E as a Relevant principle has generally rested on rejection of (1), $(A \supset B) \& A \rightarrow B$. But why would anybody *want* (1) in the first place? Primarily, I suppose, to guarantee that ⊃E is an *applicable* rule, not only in logic but in concrete theories. So it well may be, in many circumstances of interest, but the theoremhood of (1) is a *perverse* way of making that point. For suppose, in some regular theory T of which (1) is a theorem, that $A \supset B$ and A are both theorems. Conjoining, and invoking →E with (1) as *major* premis, we get B. So, in ordinary circumstances, one may take ⊃E to be justified by (1). But note that it is →E, not ⊃E, that is the inferential principle that was *used*. What (1) conveys, in short, is that if you believe →E, you will believe ⊃E.

In the context of Relevant logics, this is absurd. For not all circumstances are "ordinary". And → is wanted as a strong, durable connective, good not merely for driving one's arguments down the freeway of humdrum inference, but equally serviceable on dusty back roads where mishaps threaten, and able to make some headway even in those swamps of paradox where ⊃ just gets bogged. And it is as *incoherent* to apply to → to guarantee ⊃ as to think that, in cleaning out underbrush, the family sedan will do just as well as a bulldozer. Huge advertising campaigns have been mounted for the classical sedan. They are replete with assurances that (a) all the bugs are now out, (b) if you hear a rattle, it's probably just your imagination, and (c) research projects now under way will fix the remaining difficulties in, maybe, 20 years. In fact, there are some inferential tests that ⊃E *always* fails. I hate to drone away on the old saw, but giving a credible account of how Rationality remains possible in the presence of contradiction is still one of them. Whence it is about time to sack the Advertising department and to pester Engineering for a better product. Still, if one wants to zip down to the coast with the kids for a picnic on a clear day, the full power of the family bulldozer may not be required. Granted, a fallen tree *might* be blocking the way. But the sane course is to make reasonable allowance for reasonable risk. We can choose a middle way between the carefree dismissal of real risks ("This little beauty of a set theory will take you anywhere, and is safe at any speed") and neurotic preoccupation with unreal ones ("Keep your foot on the brake when you test-drive truth-tables, in case they are inconsistent.")

A word is now in order about the relation among theorems of logic, inferential principles, and metalogical assertions. We are often enjoined to keep such things straight. Up to a point, the advice is sound. But only up to a point. For levels of logic interact *fruitfully*. Specifically, it is sometimes suggested that there is an enormous difference between *inference* (which connotes activity, motion, and the general urge to be doing things) and mere indicative *assertion* (similarly connoting passivity, static truth, and in general just lying around). There is less to this suggestion than meets the eye. For Logic, after all, is *about* Inference. And there is not much for its arrows, hooks, horseshoes, and other pieces of onward-pointing notation to do *except* to serve as a Rational guide to the inferences that we may perform when we are up and dressed. Conversely, if we have a license to infer, we know something about the *theories* in which that license is exercised - namely, that they are closed under the relations that correspond to the licensed inferences. In a word, we make no mistake in correlating relational *truths* involving logical particles with licensed inferential *actions*. For, otherwise, investigating the theses that contain these particles is an empty exercise.

Accordingly, many Relevant logicians have been guided by a Principle of Parity in relating the *theorems* of a logic to its *rules*. This is evident in how Belnap (1959) formulates E. From one viewpoint, E is just the Ackermann (1956) system Π' of *strenge Implikation*. Not only do E and Π' have (as it turns out) exactly the same theorems, but Anderson and Belnap present E as the result of tinkering with Ackermann's axioms and rules. The crucial element in the tinkering is dropping ⊃E as a primitive rule. The *reason* given by Belnap (1959) is an application of the Parity Principle. Since (1) is not a theorem, Ackermann's ⊃E rule is *unsupported* by a corresponding theorem. Contrast →E, which remains a primitive rule. It is supported by an E-theorem; for example, (3) above.

The Parity Principle, thus applied, seems strange. Granted, it is natural to tie provable *implications* to *rules*. But this natural tie exists between the theorems of *Logic* and the rules appropriate to concrete *Theories*. In a nutshell, a theorem of Logic provides a rule on which we can rely, when we are *applying* Logic. What Belnap seems to insist is that the *rules of proof* generating the theorems of logic should conform to this natural tie. But is this after all so strange? Logic is itself a theory; and if it is its job to tell us what, in general, are good ways of passing from premisses to conclusions, ought we not to respect its dictates when the theory being formulated is Logic itself? Granted, the Principle of Parity is in this case circular. But Logic is full of this sort of circularity – as when we say that A ∨ B is true just if A is true or B is true, in setting up a completeness proof. Unless you know that *or* is supposed to mean what ∨ is supposed to mean, you won't get far.

But, even if we concede the Parity Principle, has it really disposed of ⊃E, as a *rule* appropriate to E? Has it even established that E and Π' are *distinct* systems? No, it has not. What if ⊃E is not backed up by (1)? It is still backed up by (2). Is this formal undergirding? Well, does (3) justify →E? Suppose that one can prove A → B and A in E. Conjoining, and applying →E with (3) as major premiss, we get B. So, if you believe (3), and believe *moreover* that the → of E supports *modus ponens*, then you will believe that (3) justifies →E. (The reader who catches a hint of Lewis Carroll in all of this will not have missed the point.) If you believe all this, and if you also believe that the primitive rules of E should be thus justified by E itself, then you will think that →E is a good primitive rule for E. (Belnap, 1959, prefers A → B →. A → B as the justifying thesis; but the same points are to be made.) The story does stick together. But it is *no more* than coherent. To be sure, it accords with the motivating intention, of those who devised E, that → be a particle that supports *modus ponens*. But this is, at best, a psychological fact about them.

Now cannot ⊃E stand guard for itself in the same way? Why should it look to Big Brother to fight its battles, invoking some principle like (1)? Does (2), (A ⊃ B) & A ⊃ B, undergird ⊃E? If one can prove A ⊃ B and A in E, conjoin them and apply ⊃E with (2) as major premiss, getting B. After this, the story is as above. Its last twist is that the Parity Principle may be invoked on Ackermann's behalf. Why not retain ⊃E as a primitive rule of E? Again, the story is *no more* than coherent. But why should it be?

But now let us look for *direct* Relevant justification of ⊃E (aside from Mackenzie's observation that denying it can get one into a lot of trouble in bars). There is such justification, though it will come as a shock. The *entailment* that grounds ⊃E is just B → A ⊃ B. For, as a truth-functional compound statement, the *truth* of A ⊃ B is putatively conferred upon it either by the falsity of A or by the truth of B. A *true* A is not up to this job. What is up to the job is a true B. Frenzied readers will wonder where we were when elementary logic was being taught. Is not getting B in this situation from A ⊃ B a blatant assertion of the consequent? If that's what we were doing, of course. But, actually, A ⊃ B came from B. We pause to note that logicians who have equated 'If A then B' and 'A only if B' have mashed both the direction of dependence conveyed by English 'if' and the meaning 'only'. (Thistlewaite notes that "I'll cut the grass only if you wash the dishes" is, if uttered, a legal ground for divorce whenever the dishes are washed and the grass is uncut. Oh, truth-functional logicians will tell us, 'if and only if' was meant. Tell it to the judge!) To be sure, English 'if' is not always that clear on which way relations of dependence go, and these tend to be but partial anyway; we don't want that much to hang on usage. But we can all distinguish 'X causes Y' from 'X is the *only* cause of Y', to pick a kindred notion. In either case, the direction of dependence is from X to Y. But in the latter case, the presence of Y is a sure sign of the presence of X, even though the relation of dependence goes the other way.

This will not cut much ice with the Relevantist that Belnap and Dunn (1981) hold up for our admiration, as a sort of Platonic ideal of what Relevant philosophers should (more accurately, should *not*) be up to. For Relevantist philosophy has cut loose from the awe that previous articles expressed for our ordinary logical intuitions. (In itself, this may be just as well.) For the Relevantist eschews $\supset$E even where it is demonstrable. One can think of only two grounds. First, the demonstration might not be acceptable. Second, what has been demonstrated might not justify the *use* of $\supset$E. We have a go, as Belnap and Dunn did, on both of these points.

On what grounds might our demonstration that $\supset$E holds for E be unacceptable? Let no weight be placed on its acceptance by a prominent logic journal. They have made mistakes before. Nor that it was reprinted in *Entailment*. They have made mistakes since. What Belnap and Dunn (1981) suggest is that, although the proof may be O. K. on other criteria, it may offend Relevantist ones. This violates what I claimed (1979) as "Meyer's thesis": to embrace a logic L is *already* to hold that L accounts for everyday good argument. Granted, one can *study* logics without embracing them. But a Relevantist has not merely embraced E (or some subsystem thereof) but married it. The Relevantist holds that E *is* Logic. This may be a "prescriptive" view. But the prescription does not make much sense unless the job of E is recognizably to formalize good argument (and not, say, Molecular Biology). Of course I am not holding that E is logic; even if I thought so, I would not appeal to the above thesis to show that the ⊃E argument is Relevantly Valid (whatever that may mean); that's as may be. But I am trying to show that the *burden of proof* is here on the Relevantist. If there is some specific Relevantist objection to extant ⊃E arguments - some step that most of us would accept that, parsed naturally, is objectionable in E - then this must be taken seriously. But the only attempt to do so, in a draft version of Belnap and Dunn (1981), involved a serious misreading of the extant ⊃E proof. This was duly excoriated in my 1979 paper (and perhaps unduly so, since the error was eventually corrected). What is left to the Relevantist here is only the *argumentum ad ignorantiam; perhaps* some hole can be poked in the ⊃E proof. (Well, *Entailment* did say that it intended to spend more time with the fallacies at the front of the logic book; but we didn't realize that the intention was to commit them.)

That point, in short, is a red herring. But it merges with one that is not. At issue are not merely the *steps* in the proof (which I expect can be formulated relevantly, if anybody cares to do so), but *what has been proved*. It is now time to disambiguate our metalogical ⇒. Belnap and Dunn may be taken to have suggested that, if we also formalized the metalogic in a Relevant way, we would discover that what we have proved for E is the follow:

(4) $(\vdash A \supset B)$ & $(\vdash A) \supset (\vdash B)$.

That is, the *if* of ⊃E, taken as the claim '*if* A ⊃ B and A are both theorems of E, *then* so also is B', is at best a *material if*.

A standard objection now seems to me in order, against all claims that, if one finds an 'if' in a piece of technical argument, conducted according to our usual informal canons, it is to be taken as a material 'if'. For the presupposition behind such claims seems to be that, if we are reasoning as we ordinarily do, we are reasoning "classically". For this is to confuse our informal reason with one particular recipe for its formal reconstruction. Moreover, it tends to confuse also the reasonably secure and traditional parts of "classical" logic with claims that are both more modern and more dubious. Even the identification of this logic as "two-valued" tends to beg questions. In the clearest sense, 'true' and 'false' are not *values* of sentences, but *predicates* of sentences. One can very well hold that exactly one of these predicates applies to every meaningful sentence, without holding that English particles are to be interpreted *truth-functionally*. In particular, English 'if' means whatever it means; it does not *especially* mean $\supset$.

But the standard objection, which I had hoped would contain the Relevantist threat, cannot be urged here with much force. For what, fairly, Dunn and I showed was that contradiction issues from the assumption that $A \supset B$ and A are theorems of E but that B is not. On Relevant reconstruction of that argument, this justifies the main $\supset$ in (4), but it would not justify an $\rightarrow$ in its place. Moreover, it seems highly plausible that Dunn and Belnap have the right technical intuition for the case. For one thing, there is the Parity Principle. If $\supset$E goes with (2), and not with (1), then one would *expect* to find a $\supset$ in (4), and not an $\rightarrow$. There might even be a plan, I think, to make this rigourous; one can envision a "wipe-out" argument, in an appropriately constructed Relevant theory, on which any metalogical argument with an $\rightarrow$ form of (4) as its last line could be transformed into a proof that, after all, (1) itself is a theorem scheme of E. To be sure, the point is delicate; for we are here in the realm of intuitions, not proofs; before we have a Relevantly formulated metalogic, we have some hard problems to solve, that are part of a Relevant program for reconstructing mathematical reasoning generally. For all one knows, perhaps the paradoxes of implication will turn out as *non-logical* theses of such a metalogic, which should make the → form of (4) easy.

Still, to live outside the Classical law, one must be honest (with apologies to Bob Dylan). So I shall take up the Belnap-Dunn challenge; (4) looks right to me, and I shall assume that it is right. But does this justify the Belnap-Dunn conclusion - namely, that the Relevantist is a "hero", especially faithful to the philosophical spirit of Relevant logics, in rejecting ⊃E in all its forms? The Relevantist allows, on the main hypothesis of the Belnap-Dunn discussion, that there is a Relevantly valid proof of (4). That is, there are *no counterexamples* to ⊃E. What is to be made of this? Belnap and Dunn bite the bullet. The Relevantist, even if presented with proofs in E of A ⊃ B and A, responds with a shrug of the shoulders if you ask whether B is a theorem. For only an appeal to ⊃E itself, with (4) as major premiss, could justify that conclusion. For this there is no license.

I shall bite another bullet - which, for a Relevant logician, may be even less tasty. First, the ⊃E proof has settled something. In the ten years or so that the problem was open, opinions were divided as to whether ⊃E held for E or not. In the usual manner in which one tackles open problems, one spent part of the time trying to show that ⊃E holds; and another part of it in the search for counterexamples. Nobody - not even Relevantists and their friends - pursues the latter search any more. Why not? Because, demonstrably, there are no counterexamples. This leaves the Relevantist in a situation at least ticklish, and probably untenable.

For the balance of this discussion, fix A ⊃ B and A as theorems of E, whose proofs are in hand. For this is the case on which Belnap and Dunn (1981) dwells. Moreover, Relevantists have *proof* that it can't happen also that B is a non-theorem. What is the open option? That B is a theorem, of course. They *confuse* the fact that this is not *entailed* by theoremhood of A ⊃ B and of A with absence of a license to infer it. After all, if Relevantists want to be *convinced* that B is a theorem of E, all that must be done is to enumerate the theorems of E, quitting when one hits B. The ⊃E argument assures us that B will always be on this list. When the Relevantist *finds it* on the list, as a Relevant consequence of Relevantly valid axioms and rules, then (finally) it must be admitted that there are conclusive grounds to be committed to B. All of this seems unnecessary labour, for an arcane point of philosophical principle. For is it not disturbing indeed to think oneself without a license to infer what one can never have a license to deny? Intuitionists, perhaps, can and do think like that. But it is false to the nature and character of Relevant logics that their adherents should thus turn themselves into *ersatz* Intuitionists, out-Brouwering Brouwer by making ⊃E their "excluded middle". For the *coherent* view, surely, is not that Relevant logics *deny* this principle, but that they *accept* it.

Thus far, in some respects, these remarks sound like those of Routley (1983) and Mortensen (1983). (This is not surprising, since, in these respects, these authors sound like me.) I think that ⊃E is good for some theories, and not good for others. One could engage in a more precise specification, as Routley and Mortensen do. For, to follow the argument and terminology of my original paper with Dunn, ⊃E holds for E because E is the intersection of its *normal* extensions. More generally, it will hold of any E-theory which is the intersection of its *prime*, *consistent* extensions. But, in the end, what such specification comes to is that ⊃E is good for a theory that admits ⊃E. While this is a reasonable thing to hold, it is easy to exaggerate the *independence* with which one holds it. (Nor are other suggested grounds particularly convincing as a justification for ⊃E - e.g., simple negation consistency, which has sometimes been urged as *sufficient* for the principle. For ⊃E may be as undesirable in a *false* theory as in one actually inconsistent.) At any rate, these considerations do *not* avoid the Belnap-Dunn problem; for, fairly parsed, the *statement* that a prime, consistent theory admits ⊃E remains a *material* one. That is, it is *contradictory* to hold that each of A, -A ∨ B belong to such a theory but that B does not. For, by primeness, either *both* of A, -A belong, or else B belongs. That is, either the theory is inconsistent, or B belongs to it. But it is consistent. So either it is both consistent and inconsistent, or else B belongs to it. We still require a metalogical ⊃E to guarantee the membership of B in the theory, which was the Belnap-Dunn point. So Routley's apparent confidence that one can remain a (sort of) Relevantist while still holding ⊃E for prime, consistent theories seems to miss the point. We *still* require a metalogical ⊃E, to be able to *use* our ⊃E at the object level for these theories, and even Routley's softened Relevantism does not seem to provide one, except by fiat.

But let us speak less formally. A theory that admits ⊃E is one in which, at least to that extent, our truth-functional intuitions are operating *normally*. I see it as no part of Relevant philosophy to *preclude* this possibility. To the contrary, it is the *preferable* one. What is wrong with the Classical philosophy is that it thinks it the *only* one, becoming faithless to reason *in use* on that account.

However, I am convinced by champions of Relevantist views of something of which, perhaps, they did not wish to convince us. It is that its theory of Material ⊃ is an *integral* part of Relevant understanding, without which we will scarcely understand Relevant logics themselves. Relevant motivation, after all, has reserved a consistent sneer for the *mere* material. Almost unnoticed is the fact that Relevant *logics* have failed to make good on this sneer. While Boolean ¬ and not DeMorgan - is perhaps the "real" truth-functional negation appropriate to Relevant logics, the amazing thing about these logics is not how much of the Material has been expunged, but how much of it has survived. One might almost think, reading Relevant logicians, that they were motivating some other systems from those for which they were laying down axioms and rules.

This is crucial. For the Relevantist refuses to use ⊃E logically, even in theories demonstrably closed under this principle, lest ⊃E be used metalogically in so doing. As noted, this can be avoided. The theorems can be proved, one by one. But *why* should it be avoided? Material ⊃ is a perfectly good particle of E. There are perfectly good theorems in it - all the material tautologies, to begin with. Whether we choose - in one particular inferential situation or another - to follow the properly Relevant recommendations of E, or the merely Material ones, is our business. E gives *both* sorts of recommendations; it does not *just* give Relevant ones. And one thing that a formal system *cannot* do is to specify the conditions of its application.

So, instead of a ceaseless "paradigm clash" between Relevant and Material insights, one has the opportunity to reconcile these insights. If Material logic is not so much wrong as crude, we can avail ourselves of its crudities, without being bound by them when they lead to Trouble. There is a Relevant *attack* on ⊃E. I have not abandoned that attack. But let us confine it to its proper place - where the crudities of truth-functional analysis groan under the assault of paradox. But there is also a Relevant *defence* of ⊃E, grounded in objective demonstration and available to secure this principle where it is ordinarily wanted. For let none suppose that it is not ordinarily wanted - the valid core of Irrelevantist objection to much Relevant propaganda.

This defence, the Relevantist charges, is circular. But this is a refined philosophical circularity, which fails to distinguish the theory for which ⊃E fails (or remains unproved), in which there might be an actual counterexample, from a theory for which a ⊃E proof is in hand. Which indeed is the more coherent and "philosophical" view? That only provable → statements license inference? That may have been the initial idea. But it doesn't seem eventually to work, even in getting clear on what the Relevant logics themselves involve. Or is the more coherent view that, when we have proved something, what we have proved is also true?

The Belnap-Dunn paper, with what seems to me more superficial cleverness than substantive fairness, slants the case the Relevantist's way. To accept the conclusion of ⊃E when one has accepted its premisses may be to hold that "I'm all right, Jack." Or it may be to take a "leap of faith". (Routley, 1983, criticizes me for the concession that we all take leaps of faith. He doesn't, he says. Accordingly, I withdraw the concession, which at any rate was not intended to preclude *rational* discussion of any purported logical or philosophical position. One looks for the best reasons that one can in defence of whatever position one holds, and presumptively will change that view if better reasons show up on the other side. As for the source of this abuse, a Meinongian in whose ontology there is room for more impossible objects than one can shake a round square at, I have a certain sense of having been condemned as the kettle. Nor do I find very convincing the Routley, 1983, thought that Real Relevantists will end up with a *preferred* Relevant formal system. Now there's an article of faith for you, devoid of confirming evidence. It risks exactly the criticism that Relevant philosophers have made of their Classical opponents: namely, that the System has been the thing, which has been invoked to explain away recalcitrant elements of our logical behaviour. We can, let us hope, construct better systems. But the will-o'-the-wisp of the One True Logic has not previously given good service in yielding an all-purpose formal model of what passes for informal Rationality; a more modest but more enduring contribution of Relevant logics to thought, one hopes, is the idea that, in developing formal logics, we are *modelling* informal Rationality, not *capturing* it. If so, there is room for many such models, both Relevant and Irrelevant. There is no room for the dogmatic arrogance on which, if you don't like one formal system, you must be irrational. Routley takes mine as the Opportunist view, which he charges me with holding. If so, the Opportunist view is that Formal Systems are made for Man (not excluding Woman), not Man for Formal Systems. Relevantist views, of all persuasions, seem to me to take Relevant formal systems too seriously - as the ground for new "philosophies", which tend to turn out somewhat queer; the real job of logic is to account for good argument, and, while this job is not devoid of (or uncorrupted by) philosophy, the job becomes perverted to unwholesome ends when it is linked to that of *devising* philosophies.)

But while Relevantists of Routley's persuasion may be somewhat less than consistent, in supposing that they can invoke ⊃E where they want it in a way that does not itself presuppose this principle, this is a minor vice. The consistency of (what Routley calls) the Bone-headed Relevantist commended to us by Belnap and Dunn (1981) is the greater evil. For let us look in detail at what these authors identify as the heroic course. Let C be the formula $(A \supset B) \& A$. On the hypothesis of the main case, either C is unprovable or B is provable; moreover, C is provable. On an E-valid move, we conclude that either C is *both* provable *and* unprovable, *or* else B is provable. Is there any way that we can hold this *without* holding that B is provable? The 4-valued "American plan" semantical analysis of Belnap and Dunn (1981) does allow this possibility in general. One blocks (1) by allowing that A might be true and false while B is just false, whence (1) is rejected as an entailment because its antecedent is true (among other things), while its consequent is not true at all.

But applying the 4-valued plan in this situation is, to say the least, disturbing. We avoid the apparent conclusion that B is provable by holding open the possibility that it is both true and false of C that it is provable. What can this mean? Not, evidently, what we ordinarily think that we mean by 'true' and 'false' in this situation, which is uncustomarily crisp. It is true of C that it is provable in E just in case C follows from axioms and rules in a precisely specified manner. Moreover, this has been granted, on the hypothesis of the case. So how can it also be false of C that it is a theorem? If one is to take this seriously, the best try would seem to be that C meets some criterion of formal *refutability* as well. Perhaps it does. In that case, the natural thing to say is that our criterion for refutability is in error. But, just maybe, this is an error that we don't know how to remove. Maybe it is an error that all thinking people have made since Pythagoras was a toddler. Maybe it is an error necessary for any sort of mathematical thought whatsoever - in which case one would hardly call it an error, but one of those profound mystical truths - like the doctrine of the Trinity - which both confound and ground our pale human thought.

Well, maybe. In other circumstances, I am not averse to thinking this sort of thing, welcoming rather the protection that Relevant logics give against the spread of this sort of profundity, to encompass, and confound, all of thought. Here, however, it seems more like insincerity. The notion of what it is to be a theorem of E is too clear to entertain the further thought that it can be truly said of such a theorem that it is *unprovable*. A theory that says so is just wrong, not profound. Now it could be, of course, that the informal metalogical theory in which $\supset$E was proved was in fact just wrong; and that formalizing the theory relevantly shows up the error. But, while our theories may be wrong (every program has bugs), we can scarcely *entertain* them as wrong. We are back to "asserting the consequent" (if, as I doubt, it is here a fallacy). C is unprovable or B is provable. Having demonstrated it, do we not believe it true? And do we not then believe that a disjunct is true? But, on the hypothesis of the case, we have an E-proof of C in hand. Can it be that the truth of the disjunction was conferred upon it by the *denial* of that fact? Some second-grade epistemic falsity may (as Belnap and Dunn suggest) perhaps be conferred upon a truth by a botched theory. But the truth, in that case, is hardly *truly* denied. The disjunction is true, in short, *because* B is provable, in virtue of the valid entailment that takes us from 'B is provable' to 'B is provable, or C isn't provable'. And, if it is true that B is provable, it is provable.

Still, I am not contesting the circularity alleged by Belnap and Dunn. What I am contesting is its viciousness. There are many similar examples in logic. For example, are we to make nothing of the Ackermann and Gentzen proofs that arithmetic is consistent, given the Gödel theorem that these proofs must use methods not formalizable in the system proved consistent? We should, I think, make a good deal more of these proofs than that. One could, after all, have shown that arithmetic is *inconsistent*. In one sense, Gentzen and Ackermann did not provide *extrinsic* verification of the picture. But they did show that the picture *hangs together*. In formal logic, that is often (and perhaps always) the best we have. Or let me cite an example from my own work in (Relevant) arithmetic. The system R# partially escapes Gödel's theorem, since there is an elementary proof that (for example) 2 + 2 = 5 is a non-theorem of the system. Suppose that we could prove this relevantly; still, according to Belnap and Dunn, DeMorgan - is not an *exclusion* negation. So what, in that case, would our elementary proof be worth? For the intention, surely, was to *exclude* 2 + 2 = 5, not merely to *deny* it. Unless DeMorgan - can also bear its *normal* sense, as well as the abnormal ones that have been devised for abnormal theories, this intention cannot be realized; and we should go on seeking to prove that 2 + 2 = 5, undeterred by the assurance that this will never happen.

In short, what I think, against Relevantists of every ilk, is that the *normal* interpretation of DeMorgan - is the underlying one. It is, indeed, the point of ⊃E proofs to provide evidence for just this fact. Granted, Relevant semantical interpretations, both on the American plan and on the contrasting Australian plan of Routley and Routley (1972), have also provided *abnormal* interpretations of this particle. Inspection of these plans (which I do in considerably more detail with Martin in our 1984 paper) makes it clear that they interpret - *by analogy* with its usual interpretation, under circumstances where our normal truth-functional intuitions have (at least partially) broken down. While we have been charged by some critics with forsaking what all good persons and true mean by 'not', I think that the exact opposite is the case; we have done our best to *retain* what 'not' means, under circumstances (e.g., inconsistent ones) of which a naive truth-functional account can give no reconstruction whatsoever. But a Relevantist seems to be somebody who takes the *analogy* as the *intended* account, overlooking in the process the very large concessions to a *normal* view of truth-functionality that are ubiquitous in E and other Relevant logics. Against this, one can only say that although one wants one's logic to be able to *cope* with theories and inferential situations in which the truth-functional particles *will not bear* their normal interpretations, and although it is a grave defect of the received wisdom that it places such situations beyond the pale of logical analysis, one does *not* wish extraordinary understanding to cancel ordinary understanding. In the technical development of Relevant logics (and, I think, in the conceptual order of things), it has worked the other way round. We have built extraordinary formal intuitions on ordinary ones, where otherwise we would have no intuitions at all (except grounding ones, like 'contradictions do not entail what you will'). Note that this is still not a blanket defence of ⊃E. For I have set out *reasons why*, in the Belnap-Dunn case, to deny that it applies seems insincere, if not downright frivolous. Can this be extended to all circumstances?

Of course not; the circumstances in which 'I am lying' is true do not exclude its falsity; viewed straightforwardly, they enforce it. That the truth-functional writ does not run everywhere is not the same as the assertion that it does not run somewhere. Where it runs, it may be invoked.

But even Relevantism must be conceded its point. That point, as I read it, is that fallibility runs through all human enterprises, even the demonstration of truths about logic. But here too there is a burden of proof, which cannot sensibly be reversed. If we *will not* act on what we have demonstrated, we need reasons; we do not need *further* reasons to act. The Relevantist hedge - that we should go around saying, "Either B, or I am in error", when anybody else would say B - is too facile. Since we are usually in error about something, the hedge too easily becomes true by truth of the wrong disjunct. It is time, too, to end the discussion on which →E is a rule of E, while ⊃E may or may not be. The idea is that → is more vertebrate. We might reflect this distinction by designating some rules of E, like →E, as Inner Rules; by contrast, ⊃E would be an Outer Rule. Logic is closed under both sorts of rules. It is *other theories* for which a decent → is wanted; for some of them will be closed only under the Inner Rules. For sometimes (again, the inconsistent case), ⊃E is just silly.

For, while logic can lead us to *modus ponens*, it can't make us drink it. The same, in the end, can be said of →E as well. We have seen that, so far as *systematic* justification is concerned, →E and ⊃E are on a par; they are both *self-justifying*, and no more. But some paradoxes - specifically, the Curry and Feys (1958) version of Russell's paradox - seem to depend most on the assumptions surrounding *modus ponens* as such, and are not especially linked to deficiencies of ⊃, -, or other truth-functional connectives. (That is, affirming *modus ponens* can get one in trouble, in bars and other places.)

Without dwelling on particular anomalies, let us return to the thought that Relevant logics try to limit the damage done by unwholesome premisses. If the premisses get unwholesome enough, applying *modus ponens* - any *modus ponens* - is just going to make things worse. (In fact, it is not part of the characterization of an L-theory, where L is a Relevant logic, that it is closed under →E; E-theories are so closed, but this is a special fact, depending on (3).) For damage *control* is not damage *avoidance*. And this completes the circle. If it is vicious to think ⊃E justified, because it is in the end self-justified, the same holds of →E. Whatever motivational gleam may have been in the parental eye at the moment of conception of a particular system is irrelevant to this point. Similarly, if there are reasons - in terms of unwelcome consequences - to avoid ⊃E sometimes, the same will ultimately hold of →E as well. The advantages of → over ⊃ are relative, not absolute. To attempt to hold the contrary is to make Relevant logics susceptible to the very same arguments that they have used against their Truth-functional foes. A relative advantage is still an advantage; it can be a very great one. But the Relevant Crusade against the disjunctive syllogism has gone on too long, for any good that it may have done. To the One Commandment, farewell!

II FAREWELL TO RELEVANCE

I have dwelt on the need for a proper Relevant attitude toward the disjunctive syllogism. While this is justified by the topicality of the subject, and by the serious harm done to the general motivational case for Relevant logics by making the rejection of ⊃E the keynote of the case, it requires us to abbreviate our treatment of other topics. This is unfortunate, for the *real* case lies in these other topics. So what is said here is more or less a summary of views that I (together with colleagues like Plumwood and Routley) have formed, and to some degree expressed in other places. And no question occupies a higher place on the motivational agenda than that of relevance itself.

Relevant logics capture relevance. Or so one would hope, since, otherwise, what would they be good for? It is clear, at least, what Anderson and Belnap (1975) *thought* they had accomplished. They say, speaking of Ackermann, "We argue below that one of the principal merits of his system of *strenge Implikation* is that it, and its neighbors, give us for the first time a mathematically satisfactory way of grasping the elusive notion of *relevance* of antecedent to consequent in "if ... then ---" propositions; such is the topic of this book." (p. xxi)

I argue rather that capturing relevance does not have much to do with the nature or purposes of Relevant logics. This has spawned an amusing terminological dispute, which (as often happens) has now grown into a substantive one. The plot begins with Bacon (1966), who affixed the name "relevance implication" to the system R. In this he was followed exactly by nobody at all, while being followed approximately by everybody. R was called 'relevant implication' in Belnap (1967), and that has stuck. So I, and most other authors, began to speak of 'relevant logics' in our papers. The idea was simply that the *specific* name of the system R would do also for the *genus*. If that connoted that logics in the *genus* had *something to do* with relevance, we were content to let that connotation stand. But Anderson and Belnap - wishing, presumptively, to make *not merely* the point that Relevant logics are akin to R *but also* to claim that they are logics *of relevance* - undertook to switch the then prevailing usage to 'relevance logics'. (As, perhaps, a sort of consolation prize to Bacon, following his usage on *another* point after rejecting it in its original habitat.) While other authors have twisted and turned amenable, I have not - preferring to remain consistent with my own usage, which at any rate antedated the switch by many years. Here are my reasons.

First, there is simple English grammar. Adjectives belong in adjectival position. Logicians, though they often have not had much of an ear for natural language, have usually had enough to send an adjective, not a noun, to do an adjective's job. Thus they speak of classical logic, modal logic, many-valued logic, paraconsistent logic, and so forth. (And nobody, I hope, supposes that classical logic is the logic of classics.) The usage is not invariant, nor does it necessarily apply to languages besides English. It is *natural* in German to string nouns together, forming new nouns. It is *possible* in English ('ice cream', for example - or, more to the point, 'significance logic'). But, if English is not to sound like Newspeak, we should think twice about departing from the natural grammar of the language. To use 'relevance logics' to insinuate that these are *logics of relevance* is not a good reason.

Second, technical phrases, once coined, assume a life of their own. The more unnatural these phrases are, the more one's discussions tend toward pleonastic jargon. Accompanying Relevant logics, one can expect a Relevant philosophy. To those who object that this is a technical and not an ordinary sense, I must again reply that a Classical philosophy of logic is not one grounded in Homer, Thucydides, and the works of the Roman republic. More jargon is the ugly alternative. Now we have a Relevantist philosophy. (A little more of this, and we shall have a Relevantistical one, as G. Monro has suggested.) As the jargon deepens, it becomes in application more perverse. The Relevantist sticks up not for Relevant logics in general, nor even for E in particular, but for one peculiar slant on Relevant Philosophy.

But is E, or anything like it, a logic of relevance? For that matter, is relevance worth capturing? A generally satisfactory analysis is not to be found anywhere; the "elusive notion" has proved elusive indeed. The word 'relevance' does not, in itself, mean much.

It is a weasel word. In the '60's, and even later, it was appropriated by almost everybody to stand vaguely for what there should be more of. Since opinions differ about what there should be more of - to achieve individual, social, and even logical goals - the *cover* of a weasel word has some appeal. Choose a word, and of course it will be difficult to say precisely what it means. Perhaps, at root, all that we can make out of 'A is relevant to B' is 'A and B are interestingly associated'. Already we are begging questions. How much association is required? Of what sort? How interesting does it have to be? To whom, and for what purpose?

In these times, 'relevance' has an anachronistic ring. It has been worn out by too much use, which never dispelled its underlying vapidity. This is as true in logic and philosophy as anywhere else. To be sure, we all wish to avoid being *irrelevant*. If this means anything in logic, it means that we want what the premisses of a valid argument state to be *related* to what its conclusion states; and we at least wish to avoid arguments whose purported conclusions follow from *totally unrelated* premisses. A decent implication is *essentially relational*. And I must observe again that modern logic, so fertile in insisting that Logic *take account* of genuine relations, not reducible to simple monadic predication, has abandoned this insistence when it comes to the fundamental logical relation of entailment. Here an *accidental conjunction* of truths will do (if one thinks of *materially sound* arguments); if one wants one's arguments to be *formally sound* (in a sense attributable to Russell, which, despite claims that he was "confused", has dominated the subject since), all that one requires moreover is that the accident be *universal*. (As in the phrase, "*Whenever* the premisses are true, the conlusion is also true.")

Vertebrate implication is relational. But here we strike another circle. For what is the relation linking premiss to conclusion, in virtue of which we have a valid argument? It is scarcely anything but the relation of logical entailment itself. The relevance *requisite* for inference is precisely that *supplied* when one proposition stands to another in the entailment *relation*. (Relevant logicians don't even pretend to analyse *any other sort* of relevance save that which enters into an account of implication. Far from supplying a general "logic of relevance", they aren't even trying.) If A does entail B, then A *must have been* relevant to B, in the wanted logical sense. Defenders of strict implication (Prior, for example) have made just this point. Since, according to them, A & -A entails every B, they conclude that A & -A is (logically) relevant to absolutely everything. If this sticks in one's craw, it is not because we have pre-theoretic notions of *relevance* which stick it there. (Who knows about A & -A, which is not ordinarily the sort of proposition that we enjoy entertaining?) Rather we have pre-theoretic notions of what constitutes a good *argument*, that the inference in question offends. Relevance is not an *ingredient* of a theory of logical entailment. Insofar as logical sense can be assigned to the notion, it is a *consequence* of holding such a theory. Logical Tradition, to which Anderson and Belnap so often appeal, is quite clear on this point. Premisses are *irrelevant to* their conclusions if one cannot find a valid syllogism to link them. And it is an unequivocal Middle Term that links the premisses of a valid argument, the harbinger of Relevance.

But *Entailment* argues otherwise, claiming a "mathematically satisfactory" way of isolating relevance as a component of good argument. It has two main strings to its bow (whose arrows fly, again for specificity, on behalf of E). One rests on the fact that, if A → B is a theorem of E, there is some variable p that occurs in both A and B. This variable-sharing property is a nice one for a decent theory of entailment to have. If one likes, it rules out what Belnap has called *raw irrelevance*. But, as a criterion of relevance, its sting is not in what it says but in what it omits. Sharing a single variable is not, after all, a very impressive guarantee that two propositions are deeply entwined logically; there may yet be 20 million unshared variables, which may (or may not) make a candidate a fallacy of relevance nonetheless. It is protested, to be sure, that the criterion is merely necessary, not sufficient. Since it is a criterion that most familiar logics flunk, it retains some merit in separating the logical sheep from the irrelevant goats. (Here in Australia, any criterion that favours sheep will carry a lot of weight with us. But we don't like being fleeced by criteria that insinuate much more than they actually convey.)

We proceed to the sting. Variable-sharing, as an idea, has been demonstrated in more satisfactory ways for logics *outside* the Relevant family than *inside* it. (Inside, Brady's *depth relevance* is also more comprehensive; but it doesn't apply to E.) One example is Parry's analytic implication. This system requires that *every variable* in the consequent of a valid entailment occur also in its antecedent. Even more painful is the fact that Craig's Interpolation Theorem, which is known to hold classically but which is not known to hold for E (though McRobbie, 1979, has nice results on fragments of R), furnishes truth-functional logic with a more satisfactory account of variable-sharing relevance than Relevant logics (save weak ones, or fragments) are known to have. Moreover, this theorem better reflects traditional relevance also, with its emphasis on the Middle Term. For, according to Craig, if $\vdash A \supset C$, then there exists a B in *exactly* the variables common to A and C, such that $\vdash A \supset B$ and $\vdash B \supset C$. More significantly, the appropriate generalization holds for Classical Predicate Logic also. (There are the usual exceptions, which different authors handle on different plans, where A is contradictory or C tautologous.) It is to be hoped that Relevant logics will offer improved versions of this theorem, dropping the exceptional cases. McRobbie's results do offer promise. But, even if they do, the most that will be supplied is another necessary condition, not something that can plausibly be taken to capture relevance as such.

But the main burden of the "mathematically satisfactory" account of relevance that Anderson and Belnap (1975) purport to give does not lie with variable-sharing, which is conceded to be a minimal criterion, but in its analysis of deduction. The basic idea, which is borrowed from Church (1951), is reasonably clear. If A follows from a bunch of premisses S, in a relevant sense, then there must exist a deduction in which all members of S are used. In its most immediate application, the idea looks good. Given the bunch of premisses, A, B, it does *not* in general follow relevantly that A, for there may be no plausible way of using B in a deduction of A from itself. In a word - irrelevant premisses can *spoil* a deduction, if one intends "follows from" in a relevant sense. What follows relevantly from *less* does not necessarily follow relevantly from *more*. Granted, mere inelegance does not necessarily spoil a deduction; the criterion is not that all the premisses *must* be used, but that they *may* be used. But a premiss that can *never* be used, in any valid deduction, is another matter. One fails one's IQ test if, given the list '*1 3 5 blue 13*', and challenged to find the one that doesn't fit, one detects no anomaly in the presence of *blue* on the list. One similarly fails one's logical IQ test if, given 'snow is white' and 'R is wonderful', one supposes that the second of these true premisses is part of a relevantly valid deduction that snow is white. Given the appropriate version of the deductive theorem, this rules out the paradox $A \rightarrow . B \rightarrow A$ as unmotivated; other paradoxical inferences are ruled out on similar intuitions. Since Anderson and Belnap view the technical development of this "use criterion" as both *necessary* and *sufficient* for the isolation of relevance as a component of valid inference, they may, after all, rest their case to have captured the elusive notion in the logical sense.

So far, so good. At one time, I found this case quite persuasive. What it *claimed* to do, in the first instance, was to motivate the system R of relevant implication. One then motivated E ("the logic of relevance *and* necessity") by adding properly modal considerations, of the sort to be examined in the next section. But, despite its immediate appeal, the case breaks down in practice. It breaks down especially if the sense in which relevance has been captured has been taken as *univocal*. In the first place, the treatise *Entailment*, like the rest of us, thinks that A is entailed by A & B. Does this not rest on a deduction of A from A, B in which B is not necessarily used? Well, yes. And, if one reads the fine print, one discovers that *Entailment* is mixing (at least) *two* senses of deduction, one a properly "Relevant" one for which the "use criterion" does count, and the other not far from the "Official" notion that, officially, *Entailment* is engaged in lacerating. As a result, and as we stressed in the last section, the Relevant *systems* are not so resistant even to Material thinking as some of the propaganda would suggest. Forget $-$, $\vee$, $\supset$, and other truth-functional particles likely to be viewed as problematic. While &, the most straightforward of the Material connectives, retains its Material properties, it will always be possible to undercut the "use criterion", in E and associated systems, by assuming that the premisses of an argument have been bunched in a Materially conjunctive way, instead of viewing them as "fused" in a way that activates the properly Relevant machinery. (Systematically, C follows from the "fusion" of A, B if $A \rightarrow. B \rightarrow C$ is a theorem; from their conjunction, of course, if $A \& B \rightarrow C$ is. It is useful to consider these *not* to be relevantly equivalent, denying exportation in E and R, and importation also in some other systems.) This undermines the use criterion in practice, save when one is making very fine distinctions. We note in passing that Church (1951), the source of these ideas, avoids truth-functional &, though, (interestingly) it does have an explicit fusion particle. So the use criterion is pure in Church, uncontaminated by later Material admixtures.

There is no attempt to *conceal* these facts in *Entailment*. There is simply a certain *tension* between earlier and later motivating remarks. Nor is it a defect, in my view, of Relevant logics that they offer *alternative* ways of understanding fundamental logical particles and relations. It is rather an advantage. But this advantage is best seen as *deepening* our previous understanding of deductive methodology; the propaganda that suggests instead that we are *cancelling* it, while it may have served some good in awakening interest in Relevant logics, is now best scrapped. For it is useful to have a sense of deducibility in which premisses must *collaborate* to produce their conclusions, to be distinguished from the more familiar sense in which they need not do so. Here too, Relevant logics have room for old Material ideas as well as for newfangled Relevant ones. Sometimes, informally, we do wish to dwell on the collaborative sense of deducibility, and it is nice to have formal systems that enable us to do so. But note yet again that any sense that we have explicated relevance is here too a by-product of our theory of deducibility, not an ingredient. Certainly nobody would think it intuitively irrelevant that we should derive A & B from A, B by conjoining them; the E-thesis A & B → A & B testifies to this fact. But we should have the paradoxes back, lickety-split, were A →. B → A & B to be a theorem of E. We cannot use A and B, *in this sense*, to derive A & B. Technically the latter counts, according to *Entailment*, as a fallacy of relevance. But this is merely to say that it presents a theory of entailment that *makes it such*. Inasmuch as the theory would hardly be coherent with A →. B → A & B, this is fair enough. But, at the level of ideas, there is a basic equivocation about use. There is Relevant use, that, by Church, blocks the paradoxes. There is Material use, that doesn't. (Further halfway houses are possible; the Relevantist who likes &I, but who foreswears ⊃E, occupies one of them, having sanctioned enough Material use to get *into* Trouble, but not enough to get *out*.) Again, it would be unfair to charge Anderson and Belnap with obscuring these points; while their technical contributions often antedate (necessarily) the working out of some of the details, they do note and seek to give an account of the complexities involved, tying their use criterion to application of the →E rule and recognizing that &I works on other principles. Once again it is not the technique, but the accompanying motivational propaganda, that tends to invite confusion. (Before throwing too many stones, I should observe that this is no doubt the fate of motivational propaganda generally, including the present exercise.) But it is not fair to say that, as the use criterion works in Relevant logics, it has captured what philosophers from Aristotle to Nelson Goodman have sought to mean by 'relevance'.

This becomes all the more evident when one attends to the formal mechanisms, via systems of "natural deduction", that *Entailment* develops to account for relevance. These systems are replete with taggings and flaggings designed to keep track of what depends on what, as one threads one's way through a deduction. (Though, on Dudman's observation that it is not very natural to instantiate to the first free variable not free on a preceding line of a derivation, perhaps the "naturalness" of natural deduction systems has been in general overadvertised. Again, such systems *model* Reason in Use. It is a Bold Falsehood that they *capture* it.) These technical flaggings, whether or not we find pre-theoretic intuitions in which to ground them securely, do have their point; we keep track of assumptions, in an E-valid deduction, in a way that causes these assumptions relevantly to entail their conclusions as the logic E determines that they shall. They have *another* point only if we can find some independent ground for the specific maneuvers. In the large, this is easy enough to come by; one of the maneuvers, for example, is →E, and I shall not gripe here that B may appear as a new line in a deduction when A → B and A are already in hand.

But these lines in deduction do come with *tags*, and we can gripe about the principles of tag manipulation. Indeed, we can gripe in several different ways. First, the tags are *sets* of things. Why sets? This already assumes a principle of tag organization - and, eventually, it makes assumptions about how premisses are structured - that is open to challenge. Second, when one applies an applicable rule, given certain tagged formulas, the tag to be attached to the conclusion is also determined. This also is open to challenge, both with respect to *when* the rule may be applied, and to *what* tag shall be affixed to its conclusion. If we combine this with our first point, allowing different principles of organization, obviously a great many possibilities arise. Nor should it be overlooked that some of the Anderson-Belnap "natural deduction" rules are evidently cooked to motivate the corresponding E-theses. Some of these theses have been controversial. If we subtract these rules, or replace them with related ones, we get a different collection of theses.

These points are not just theoretical. For example, McRobbie and I (1982) preferred a *multiset* organization of tags, in formulating a natural deduction system for R. The reason is that, when one bunches R-premisses relevantly (that is, fuses them), the order of these premisses doesn't matter, but the number of times that a particular premiss is repeated may matter. The mathematical notion of a multiset, which abstracts from order but not from number of repetitions, is exactly what is wanted; by contrast, set collection counts each member of a set only once; accordingly, one must just somehow or other *simulate* multisets as sets if one insists on organizing one's tags into sets, when giving a natural deduction formulation of R. This is, as I now view it, what the Anderson-Belnap natural deduction system for R in fact accomplished. But it is hard to convince some people (who, while they have not heard of many sorts of mathematical entities, have heard of sets) that this is what the process amounts to, and that what R systems of natural deduction in fact capture are R theories of deducibility, and not anything more magic and wonderful. I don't say that disparagingly; I *like* the R theory of deducibility, for several dozen reasons on which it is not the purpose of this paper to dwell (though others have so dwelt). (The contrary views expressed in Routley *et. al.*, 1984, are not mine.) But the thought that this theory is in some way univocally motivated, because it is the meal that one gets if one follows one particular recipe for natural deduction, is going too far.

For it is possible to vary the Anderson-Belnap plan, or to choose quite a different plan, so that one gets a *very* different collection of theses. This is important when one considers some theorems, such as the "contraction" axiom (A →. A → B) →. A → B, which has become controversial. For it appears absolutely ineluctable on the "natural deduction" plan of *Entailment*. Vary the plan while preserving its main thrust, and the ineluctability is revealed as an illusion, and not necessarily even a very good illusion. Blatantly *ad hoc*, though, is the *Entailment* distribution rule that takes us from A & (B v C) to A & B v C. Distribution of & over v is wanted in E for *semantic* reasons; it is accordingly just *assumed* deductively. While I think that the semantic reasons are good ones, it is of course interesting to drop the *ad hoc* rule and to study the resultant system LR. (Otherwise known as OR, or as R-distribution. The 'L' is for *lattice*, since LR formalizes general Relevant lattice logic, in contrast to R, which specializes to distributive lattice logic. LR, as McRobbie and Thistlewaite saw, is well adapted to automatic theorem proving. Thistlewaite, 1984, develops an elegant proof theory for the system, and demonstrates that it is artificially intelligent, adapting Kripke, 1959, to that end.)

But I have said enough, I trust, to make my main point. The pre-theoretical questions that one has about relevance - what sort of association is required for A to be relevant to B? - are also systematic questions. Answer them differently, and one will have different notions of what is relevant to what. While it is a great merit of Anderson and Belnap to have raised the question, the elusive notion will remain elusive so long as the human mind is capable of entertaining alternative views as to what entails what. *Entailment*, far from diminishing this capability, has in fact enhanced it; we now have new alternatives to consider, many of them hardly touched upon, if at all, in this work. Relevance, as a component in Relevant motivation, has, over the years, been producing steadily diminishing philosophical and technical returns. While an occasional appeal thereto may still be useful in fixing the logical intuitions, nothing hangs on it, any more. To relevance, farewell!

III FAREWELL TO NECESSITY

I have made it clear that, in bidding farewell to relevance above, I am not bidding farewell to R. R remains a stable and interesting Relevant logic from many viewpoints - semantic, algebraic, and in concrete application. In company with RM (which is even simpler than R, though less plausible), R remains the best laboratory for the presentation of relevant ideas, if only because it does not depart quite so drastically from its Irrelevant progenitors as do certain other Relevant logics. Research thus far suggests that we can live quite happily without the principles that R chops out (to the degree that it chops them out at all, which we have already taken issue with). For these principles do not seem to have been doing as much for theoretical inference as had been alleged, though the issue is hardly settled at this stage of the game. This is far less clear for Relevant logics that depart even more dramatically from received principles; one reason, to be sure, is simply that less research has been done on these systems. But the most to be said *against* R, at this stage, is that it is one theory of relevant implication among many. There are alternatives, and, in the long run, others may seem more suited to the development of relevant insights. But, instead of appealing any further to general preconceptions, or on prejudices favourable or unfavourable, I suggest that R is now sufficiently well-developed, as a logic, that its main challenges henceforth will lie in application. Can one use R to do the things that one expects a logic to do? Does it suggest a plan for the reconstruction of mathematics? Will the work cited above help the Japanese (or anybody else) in their search for machines that think faster and more efficiently than we do? Does R leave room for philosophical subtleties that truth-functional logic has erased? For example, will it ground a genuine theory of relations, not reducible to truth-functional accidents? These are areas of active research, even though they are presently being investigated by a mere handful of widely scattered researchers. (Oh for a mere handful of megabucks, to instill some concentration into these efforts! Tokyo, please come in. Megayen are also acceptable. But it is depressing when one thinks of how much work could be done in logic, with, as Douglas once noted, the price of two kilometers of any modern freeway, anywhere in the world. One modern missile, and we could have Goldbach's conjecture settled by yesterday. Meanwhile, let us tighten our belts, darn up the old socks, and get back to work.)

But there are some things that R is clearly not good for. It does not, for example, *limit* the damage done by Russell's paradox in the way that Brady (1982) shows that weaker Relevant logics protect naive set theory against the worst. And it still validates $A \to A$, the archetypal question-begging fallacy, against the sane insistence of the system S (for syllogism) that such fallacies form no part of Logic. (The profound technical investigations of Martin, 1978, establish that S has this property.) For, if such recent fallacies as $A \to. B \to A$ must succumb on grounds of Relevance, and because we are agreed that they cannot reasonably be used, should not the ancient fallacy $A \to A$ share their fate? Most assuredly, nobody ever justifiably uses that one. And nobody ever should. $A \to A$ is not, as Anderson and Belnap assert, a trivial truth on which all Reason rests. It is a trivial falsehood that contradicts all Reason.

(Interestingly, on the semantical analysis that Martin and I developed, all Reason may rest on A → A nonetheless, in the sense that every logical truth is *entailed by* some A → A. But it is a *bad* instance of asserting the consequent to hold on that account that A → A is itself *true*; logical truths may be *grounded* in identities; it does not follow that these identities are themselves logical truths.) But can we proceed further and more profitably in weaker Relevant logics? There are some more nice results, provided by investigators like Routley, Priest, and Slaney - for example, Slaney (1982), which frees the irrationality of the square root of 2 from its apparent dependence on the "contraction" principle. But it is perhaps a little too easy to engage in more or less idle speculation on these topics. Here also what is called for is some hard work, and we shall defer judgment until we see how it turns out.

Towards E, however, I cannot be so charitable. There is little likelihood that any purported deficiencies of R, as a vehicle for the development of Relevant insight in concrete ways, will not be shared by E as well. Moreover, E rests on a mistake. The mistake is to think that one needs some *modal* intuitions to formalize entailment. Anderson and Belnap may have made that mistake, but C. I. Lewis provoked them to it. (Even as Lewis, according to Quine, was himself provoked by Russell's mistakes; as, one has to add, was Quine.) But *requiring* such modal intuitions is overkill. If one has a decent →, the *theoremhood*, as a matter of Logic, of A → B is what is needed that A should entail B. Lewis introduced (in effect) the □ of modern modal logics because he did *not* have a decent →; he only had ⊃. So he tried to cook up a decent → (again, in effect) by *defining* A → B as □(A ⊃ B). But, if one *already* has a decent →, it is at best redundant to *characterize* A → B as □(A → B). It may be *worse* than redundant; why should a decent → have a □ built into it in this way? Moreover, we may not have the theory of □ that we thought we had. And what we think is our theory may simply tempt us into fresh confusions.

I seek below to give some substance to all these "may's". Meanwhile, a preliminary look at E is in order. From the viewpoint of formal naturalness, E has some obvious deficiencies. While R has a certain smoothness, either on the algebraic analysis of Dunn (1966) or on my 1973 semantical analysis, with Routley, a look at the corresponding postulates for E in Routley (*et. al.*) (1984) (or in the similar treatments by Fine and Maximova) is somewhat disappointing. Nor did Dunn fare better, in his 1966 efforts to provide E with an algebraic analysis like that which he furnished R. For a look at the semantical postulates for E leaves one in little doubt that they have been chosen precisely because they verified the axioms of E, and for no other plausible reason. One ought not to complain too much about this. A great deal of purported objective verification in logic is self-verification, when one examines it closely; as we noted above, *any* semantic completeness proofs tend to rank high on the self-verifying list. Still, one does seek *some* conceptual independence - a sense that, if one looked at Logic *another way*, one would have a fighting chance to get a system stipulated by some fixed collection of axioms and rules. Simplicity and formal elegance do count in giving one this sense; those who proclaim their passion for truth-tables rely on little else (and, since it is also desirable to be Rational, the virtues of being *that* simple are a little dim).

But no way of looking at E, that I know of, gives one such a fighting chance. The nearest approximation is the equivalence of E and Ackermann's Π'; being based on the admissibility of ⊃E for E, it is at least non-trivial. But, since E was presented as a recasting of Ackermann's system, one does not have much sense of conceptual independence. Otherwise, the results have been disappointing. What at one time seemed the best hope to ground E in other insights did not work out. The idea (which I'm afraid was mine) was to define

'A *entails* B', in the sense of E, as '*Necessarily* A *relevantly implies* B'; where, near enough, S4 supplies the □, and R the relevant →. This would have made E the confluence of the modal ideas of S4 and the relevant ideas of R, in conformity with the motivating ideas as one understood them. The idea did work out for some fragments of E. But Maximova (1973) presented a devastating counterexample (which Minc, apparently, had suggested). I have discussed "natural deduction" systems already. While, when they were discovered for E by Anderson in the early days of Relevant logics, such systems constituted a theoretical advance of great import, they too seem to have come to a dead end. At least they don't seem to furnish the desired conceptual independence. Granted, the natural deduction systems do confer a certain stability on E (especially its pure → part), which has its genuinely natural features as well as the *ad hoc* ones touched on above. But, when these systems are used as a basis for semantic analysis, as they were by Urquhart (1972), they seem to lead in other directions from those that produce E and R. Nor is it clear how, save on the application of logical brute force, Urquhart's work could be modified to produce E exactly.

So developments that have conferred stability and interest on other Relevant logics - from B+ and S to R and RM - have had a way of passing E by. Granted, there have been some results that the defence attorneys for E should cite. Most notable among them are those that E contains other logics, such as S4, on philosophically motivated translations. But, in general, such results have not singled out E as a specially interesting system. Typical here, perhaps, is the ⊃E result, or the semantical ones, which apply to E as one among a great number of logics satisfying certain conditions. That such results have been announced as results about E in particular has more to do with the sociological fact that E had been advertised as the Relevant logic *par excellence* than with any facts about E tending to justify the advertisement.

Since E lacks those signs of *formal* stability that commend other Relevant logics to us (save mainly for sharing *pervasive* properties of this class of logics), we must look rather to the special motivation that has been urged for this system. This lies in the claim that E, unlike its kin, has a viable theory of necessity, and that necessity no less than relevance has been an important element in logical tradition that prevailing logics overlook. Even the last claim is open to some doubt; while modal logics long did lie under a cloud (chiefly, I think, on account of the criticisms of Quine), they have been an extremely active area of logical and philosophical research during the past quarter century. So, no less than in the "relevance" case, the motivating remarks in *Entailment* have a somewhat anachronistic ring. Still, while it was Ackermann who furnished E with its theory of modality, it has been Anderson and Belnap that have dwelt upon it. And they do have some new things to say.

At first, the formal basis of modality in E looks somewhat strange. E differs from the nearby systems R and T most notably on the so-called Law of Assertion $A \rightarrow . A \rightarrow B \rightarrow B$. R asserts this principle. T may be taken as denying it. E tries to take a middle position. It affirms the principle when A is of the special form $C \rightarrow D$, but it does not affirm it generally. While *Entailment* gives reasons for this course, they had better be good reasons. For it is easier to live with, or without, a principle than to live with part of one. And the indecisiveness of E on this point afflicts all that is peculiar to it, rendering it cumbersome where its neighbours are smooth.

And what of the theory of necessity that we have bought at this price? First, one might ask again, is there any particular reason why Relevant logics should *have* a theory of modality? Their job is to formalize implication, or perhaps entailment. Now there is, of course, a long tradition that valid entailments are necessary truths.

But, on what seems to be the solid part of Quine's critique of modal logics, this is no reason why we have to build necessity into the → that we are formalizing. (The gaseous part, that we had better not call that → 'implies', is a piece of linguistic superstition (not to say, a mere taboo) that we have all dwelt on enough elsewhere to ignore here; see especially the appendix to *Entailment*.)

We all know the truth-functional recipe; B follows from A just in case A ⊃ B is a tautology; nothing modal enters into ⊃. If, tired of truth-functional lassitude, we want a more vertebrate theory of logical consequence, we can get ourselves a straighter →, aimed toward its consequent and not just bending in its general direction. But nothing modal has to enter into this → either, for the same reason. Once we are free from the taboo, it is easy to see that we have need for a notion of *true implication* that falls short of *logically true implication*. What Kennedy said to Khrushchev implied that there would be trouble in the Caribbean. The implication was more than truth-functional; it did rest on a connection. But it was less than logical. Granted, attempts have been made to *reduce* all implication to logical implication, aided and abetted by the thought that that was the only real kind. They tend to be *enthymematic*, suggesting that to say with the masses that A implies B meant really that A and t logically imply B, where t is some contextually suppressed truth. While the attempts tend to founder on the project of characterizing the suppressed t, we may appeal to Logic for a reasonably sensible recommendation on the point. What suppressed truth is wanted? The truth that, after all, A and B are connected, not necessarily as a Matter of Logic, but at least in a Vertebrate Way. That is, the truth that commends itself to us, as the one that has been suppressed, is exactly A → B, where → expresses a true implication that is not necessarily logically true. For think through the story in a Classical way. If A and t logically imply B, then t logically implies A ⊃ B. Since t is a suppressed truth, so is A ⊃ B. So A ⊃ B will do, on the story, as the suppressed t, whence it is both necessary and sufficient, in the proposed enthymematic sense, for A to imply B that $A \supset B$ should be true; that is, the purported reduction only produces Material implication, confounding the claim that, on sanitized classical stories, it is only a *facon de parler* to call this 'implies'. For Russell, not Quine, was right on this point. Garden-variety 'implies', on Classical reconstruction, can scarcely be anything but '$\supset$'. All the efforts to say that it is something else (because 'logically implies' is indeed something else) have come to nought.

So, while there are some valid insights in the attempt to ground non-logical true implications in the logical ones, in eventual application they are all wet. (Perhaps they too have had trouble in the Caribbean.) But what one can say is that, *if* $A \to B$ *is asserted on logical grounds*, it signals logical consequence of the appropriate sort. In a word, we do not have to build any theory of necessity (or of logicality) into $\to$ itself to develop a Relevant theory of the entailment *relation*. For the defects of modal logics, as theories of entailment, do not lie in their analysis of $\Box$. They lie in the underlying analysis of $\supset$, as one may take Quine to have pointed out. So, if we wish to fix up our account of 'entails', as a logical notion, what most needs fixing is the logic of 'implies', in the broad and not the narrow sense.

These considerations have been used sometimes to argue for R, and against E. The response, from defenders of E, has been that we might want not merely an entailment relation, *indicated* by provable $\to$ statements, but an entailment *connective*, which $\to$ expresses directly. And this connective, the brief continues, *would* be modal. Again, however, if this is what is wanted, there are well-known ways of getting it. The NR way, adding $\Box$ to R, is one of them. For if one insists on having a $\Box$ in one's Relevant logics, it can be added explicitly, together with those principles that one takes to govern it. Since, even in the case where modalities are added to truth-functional logic, there has been great disagreement about what these modal principles should be, this course offers Relevant logics similar latitude (as Bacon has suggested). Given a Relevant logic L, we can extend L in an S3 way, an S4 way, an S5 way, and so forth, to encompass a modal theory. For there is no *a priori* reason to suppose that we shall get the right modal theory on the cheap, by using → to define □, ◇, etc.

This runs into the claim that E has a modal theory already, which, more or less, is that of S4. Viewed straightforwardly, the claim is surprising, since on taking the → of E as strict implication E is a subsystem not only of S4 but also of S3. Accordingly, Routley has argued that, conceptually, thinking E an S4-like system has been a mistake, and that its insights go much more naturally with S3. There is something here that is perhaps more than historical accident. Lewis, though he later changed his mind, initially favoured S3 as the system of strict implication. His purpose was to find the intuitive principles governing entailment. Ackermann, many years later, devised an S3-like system to serve the same purpose, which *Entailment* transmuted to make the claim that E is the system of entailment. One can allow, perhaps, that S3-principles are those that *first* commend themselves to people trying to capture entailment. But it is a different question whether these are the ones that should *ultimately* commend themselves. S3, these days, is mainly a topic of historical interest. The same, I think, will be true of E. At any rate, if we take its suggested E-definition as a *serious* definition of □, which allegedly gives E an S4-theory of modality, we find a cute twist. For the same moves can be made in S3. This suggests that S3 also has an S4-theory of modality. And that does sound strange.

Nor should we be impressed that □A is defined in E as (A → A) → A, a point also criticized by Routley and Routley (1969). One may take this, to be sure, as a systematic accident. Ackermann's definition, in essence, made □A into t → A, where t is an appropriate standard logical truth. Being entailed by the standard truth does have something to commend it as an inferential definition of necessity. As Anderson and Belnap showed, this happens in E to be equivalent to A → A → A. So, when sentential constants are chopped in the interest of conceptual economy, the latter definition survives. But, if so, so much the worse for E. We suppose that the definition commends itself in *Entailment* because of the identification of A → A as the "archetypal form of inference, the trivial foundation of all reasoning." Anything that follows from the archetype is, one supposes, necessary. Martin's and my view that A → A is false does undermine that line, but I won't press that view further here. For the converse of what passes as a reasonable intuition still seems *ad hoc*. Why, to be necessary, must a proposition follow from its entailing *itself*? (Routley and Routley, 1969, make this point also.) If any B → B entails A, surely it suffices, on this intuition, that A should be necessary. If, in E, A → A itself will always do, the reason surely lies in systematic peculiarities of the system E, not anything general.

Such complaints have been made before. But I turn now to the heart of the Anderson-Belnap case that, unlike other systems, E is free of modal fallacies. We can illustrate by commenting on the non-theoremhood of p →. p → p. This would not *seem* a fallacy of relevance (though it is a non-theorem of R also, which is advertised as careful about such things). But it may be a fallacy of modality. As Anderson and Belnap (1962) put it, does one convince someone that 'snow is white' entails itself by displaying some snow? Trying to be sympathetic, the root idea seems to be that there is no path from the non-logical to the logical - from the contingent to the necessary, if one wants to put it that way. For the logical truths are those that are true in virtue of their form, and we ought not to be holding them merely on the basis of what is true as a matter of fact.

Thus put, the root idea is probably particularly appealing to philosophers, who have enjoyed dividing the world into its conceptual and its factual parts. (Similarly, in ethics, there has been a philosophical pull to divide the world into its natural and its normative parts, producing an "is-ought" gap.) That philosophers should have something to do, it is nice to have fences around their special areas, marked "No admittance" to people wearing lab coats and others whose concern is merely with this world. The tendency is to be disapproved in principle; the ultimate concern of all philosophy is with this world, not with ones that we know not of. If one thinks about it, to hold that there are areas so fenced in - shielding one from outside inferences as thick lead walls supposedly shield one from nasty particles - is simply to uncover another sort of *fallacy of relevance*. Purported "modal fallacies", I think, are just that - fallacies of relevance in another guise. Their ultimate import is, "You can't get there from here". We now wish to inquire whether *Entailment* has presented this message in ways that are non-vacuously true.

First, what we took a paragraph ago as the "root idea" doesn't work. (Routley and Routley, 1969, pointed this out, and Anderson and Belnap, 1975, concedes it.) After all, while $p \to . \ p \to p$ is a non-theorem of E, $p \to p \vee -p$ is a theorem. One is allowed to convince somebody that snow is white, or not, by displaying some snow, though what is shown is a logical truth. This, perhaps, has already been conceded; the main claim was that entailments did not follow from contingent propositions. But that was still wrong; where p is 'snow is white', $p \& (p \to p)$ is presumptively no less contingent than is p itself. But, in E, $p \to p$ follows from $p \& (p \to p)$, in virtue of $A \& B \to B$. Whence, it would seem, one can break into the safe of logical entailment with a contingent crowbar.

So a repair of the earlier fallacies-of-modality line was required. *Entailment* claims to have found one, credited to Coffa, whose work appears therein. First, the assertion that the *necessary* propositions occupy an isolated world of their own has now been abandoned (to the extent that it was ever made). What the case rests on now is not that the logical truths are true according to their form, but (in essence) on the fact that → statements are → statements according to their form. While true, it is hardly the old intuition. By varying the playing field, we shall show that it has nothing to do with modality, or even with Relevant logics, at all. For the *ideas behind* Coffa's repair can be put as follows.

Let everything of the form A → B be classed as a *necessitive*. Let us now form the *ideal* (in, near enough, the lattice-theoretic sense) determined by these formulas; we call this ideal I. Specifically, all formulas A → B ∈ I. We lay it down also that, if C → D is a theorem of E, then if D ∈ I then C ∈ I as well. That is, I is closed *down* under provable entailment (on the "Hasse diagram" picture on which 'entails' points *up*). Consider now the class L - I of all formulas in the language L of E which do *not* belong to I. It is trivial that, since I is closed *down*, its set-theoretic complement is closed *up*; that is, L - I is closed under 'provably entails, according to E'.

There are some facts in Coffa's account of real technical significance for E, and perhaps of continuing philosophical interest as well. But, viewed starkly, it merely brings the modally fallacious chickens home to roost. One cannot, to be sure, get *into* I from *outside* I. But the root reason is a simple set-theoretic one. If you close *any class* I under the converse of *any relation* R, then the *complement* of I will be closed under R. So, if you start off in the complement, and take an R-trip, you won't get into I from there. To see this, take any class of sentences at all - the ones that you uttered last month about Belisarius, for example. Form I by closing those Belisarius-sentences under the converse of entailment. It is now a *Belisarius-fallacy* if any sentence not in I entails a Belisarius sentence. The reader will be relieved to know that *all logics* are free of Belisarius-fallacies. It is, in this case, hardly a particular merit of E to be free of them. The same goes of fallacies of modality. To sum up: if you *can't* get there from here, you *won't*. If the E case retains *some* interest nonetheless, it lies not in general considerations but in *particular* classes of entailments known to be blocked. E.g., neither wholly truth-functional expressions nor negations of entailments will entail in E any entailments, or any conjunctions or disjunctions of entailments. I leave it open whether this is a good thing; save to note that, if it is, all subsystems of E will have these properties also, when again they hardly motivate E in particular. But, on the whole, it has been a bad idea to prefer E because of its purported theory of necessity. It is to be questioned whether Relevant logics even require such a theory. The one supplied for E is cumbersome and unpersuasive, if not actually vacuous. If its theory of □ recommends E, E is not to be recommended. To necessity, farewell!

IV FAREWELL TO E

While it has been necessary to be polemical about some things, we close on a note of sadness. While antedated to some degree by R, the system E of entailment was the first Relevant logic to be taken very seriously, either on the technical or the philosophical level. Conceived essentially by Ackermann, it provided the impetus for almost all the early work in Relevant logics, culminating in *Entailment* (and its promised sequel). While E has never been my favourite Relevant logic - indeed, save in a few well-known quarters, it seems almost universally agreed among Relevant logicians that E is not a very good system - E and its problems served as an important stimulus for my work, and that of many colleagues. Amidst the follies of youth, I have had some good things to say about it. Moreover, ideas developed to make E plausible, if they have not particularly succeeded in that task, have had wide application to logics that remain appealing. I do reserve, naturally, the right to change my mind again. The fallacies-of-modality idea, for example, showed up in altered form in R# (which was not supposed to be modal); if it is interesting there, the possibility remains open that the story would be more coherent if we based arithmetic on E instead (which, I expect, would be straightforward on the R# plan).

But, as the land appears to lie, the time has come for the old war horse to be put out to pasture. The cries under which she charged - Relevance, Modality, and Woe to the Disjunctive Syllogism - no longer rally the troops. The battles that have been won have conferred some degree of philosophical and technical respectability upon the Relevant logics. Those that have been lost are best abandoned. If there is, as I hope and trust that there is, a wider appreciation these days of what non-Classical points of view can do for Logic generally, the considerations that have been urged in behalf of E, and the results that have been proved about it, are not the least of the causes. If some of the old shibboleths that rendered Material logic more secure than it had any right to be have now collapsed, encouraging broader and less partisan views in the philosophy of logic generally, the old war horse played her part in keeping the classical hordes at bay. But Relevant logics will not survive, as a subject of serious interest, if they and their philosophy are thought to cluster around ideas and systems that have, at best, only partially worked out. Of the systems that have not worked out, the most conspicuous is E itself. And so, with all due thanks for services once rendered, we bid farewell to E. --

My thanks are due to a great many people with whom I have discussed the topics of this paper, over the years. They are preeminently due to Richard Routley and to Val Plumwood, who have long shared my discontent with E, and who in some respects have shaped it. Accordingly, the abstracted version of this paper was joint with these authors, as I had intended this final version to be. Two developments have changed that plan. First, Routley (*et. al.*) (1984) has now appeared. I am both annoyed and relieved with this development. I am annoyed because the book has been published as merely "with" Plumwood, Brady, and me. This ill accords with the use that has been made of my own work, published and unpublished (and presumptively of the work of these other authors as well). So I shall affirm here, to set the record straight, that the early published "Routley-Meyer" semantical papers on which the book builds have in *every* sentence, and in every *line* of every *proof*, the following well-known property: I am solely responsible for the errors therein. But, for present purposes, I am relieved. For Routley's version of the ideas relevant to this paper is now in print. On essential points, I take this to be Plumwood's also, since what is said extends and develops the views set out in the earlier Routley-Plumwood papers cited here. So the interested reader has the direct opportunity to find out what Routley and Plumwood think about E (basically, they don't think much of it), without refraction through the perspectives of this paper. Second, and more immediately important, the more revisions this paper went through, the more that it came to dwell on the disjunctive syllogism. For, while I have regretted the fact, this does seem to be the hot issue in philosophical discussion of Relevant logics. People who know nothing else about them know that these logics "reject" the disjunctive syllogism. (On the line taken here, what they know is false.) But it does not seem fair, either to their views or to mine, to try to associate Routley and Plumwood with the plea here for some rapprochement between Classical and Relevantist views on the topic. Routley (1983) is in many ways a direct attack on my 1979 version of that plea, which he judges deficient in Relevantist ardour. And Plumwood, when I described the words that I intended to put in her mouth, protested that, while general and not exact agreement would do for a joint paper, it seemed to her that, where the disjunctive syllogism was concerned, I was asserting p on her behalf where she is committed to not-p. So, regretfully, it seems best to change the plan, and to assert p on my own behalf, and not on behalf of anybody else. Among other debts, those to Anderson, Belnap, and Dunn also deserve mention, since their thinking continues to loom large in what I now make of Relevant logics, despite the immediate evidence presented above to the contrary. Disagreeing with Dunn about the Relevant significance of ⊃E has been especially painful, since our intuitions on the subject grew up together. When I wrote my 1979 paper, I had hoped that some of my disagreements with these authors might turn out more apparent than real, especially since Belnap and Dunn (1981) did not actually endorse what they described as the Relevantist option, however favourably they were (in my view, mistakenly) seeking to portray it. For the ground of my side of some of these issues lies no less in the work of these and other authors than it does in my own. For example, it was the truth-functionally normal semantics for first-degree formulas of Relevant logics presented in Belnap (1967) which first suggested to me that Relevant logics could be developed in the Boolean direction that Belnap and Dunn (1981) disparage. (For that matter, it was Belnap, whose enthusiasm for their problems proved contagious, who awakened my own interest in Relevant logics.) But the sequel leaves little doubt, I fear, that the differences are not only real, but mortally so. At issue, eventually, is whether Relevant logics shall outgrow the chrysalis from which they sprang, or whether they shall be entombed within it. Also at issue is whether a permanent chip on the shoulder toward all that is truth-functional is part of the Relevant program; or whether, having made their motivational points, these logics should now grow up, accepting the truth-functional (in normal and not abnormal perspective) as part of what shapes their own insights, and becoming less strident in their polemic and more objective in their outlook. Finally, and as ever, thanks are due especially to the members of the Logic Group of the Australian National University, past and present, and to visitors who have been from time to time among us. These have included, I think it fair to say, most logicians who would count Relevant logics as a major research interest, though by no means all. Thanks do not imply agreement, as some among these colleagues would be the first to insist, especially with a paper advocating as many sharp turns in previous Relevant Tradition as this one is. But, if I have made the point that one doesn't have to be insane, or irrational, to like Relevant logics, that will be a start. For, like all logics, it is sanity and rationality that they exist to serve.

REFERENCES

Ackermann, W., 1956, Begründung einer strengen Implikation, Journal of Symbolic Logic, 21:113-128.

Anderson, A. R. and Belnap, N. D. Jr., 1962, The Pure Calculus of Entailment, Journal of Symbolic Logic, 27:19-52.

Anderson, A. R. and Belnap, N. D. Jr., 1975, "Entailment, the Logic of Relevance and Necessity," vol. 1, Princeton University Press, Princeton.

Bacon, J., 1966, "Being and Existence: Two Ways of Formal Ontology," Ph.D. thesis, Yale University, New Haven.

Belnap, N. D. Jr., 1959, "The Formalization of Entailment," Ph.D. thesis, Yale University, New Haven.

Belnap, N. D. Jr., 1967, Intensional Models for First Degree Formulas, Journal of Symbolic Logic, 32:1-22.

Belnap, N. D. Jr., 1984, Return to Relevance, typescript, Pittsburgh.

Belnap, N. D. Jr. and Dunn, J. M., 1981, Entailment and the Disjunctive Syllogism, in: "Contemporary Philosophy: A New Survey," G. Floistad and G. H. von Wright, eds., Martinus Nijhoff, The Hague.

Brady, R. T., 1982, Non-Triviality of Dialectical Set Theory, in: "Paraconsistent Logic," R. Routley, G. Priest and J. Norman, eds., Philosophia Verlag, Munich (forthcoming).

Church, A., 1951, The Weak Theory of Implication, in: "Kontrolliertes Denken, Untersuchungen zum Logikkalkül und der Logik der Einzelwissenschaften," A. Menne, A. Wilhelmy, and H. Angstl, eds., Alber, Munich.

Coffa, J. A., 1975, Fallacies of Modality, in: "Entailment, the Logic of Relevance and Necessity," A. R. Anderson and N. D. Belnap Jr., eds., Princeton University Press, Princeton.

Curry, H. B. and Feys, R., 1958, "Combinatory Logic," vol. 1, North-Holland, Amsterdam.

Dunn, J. M., 1966, "The Algebra of Intensional Logics," Ph.D. thesis, University of Pittsburgh, Ann Arbor.

Kripke, S. A., The Problem of Entailment, Journal of Symbolic Logic, 24:324.

Maximova, L., 1973, Semantics for the Calculus E of Entailment, Bulletin of the Section of Logic, Polish Academy of Sciences, 2:18-21.

Martin, E. P., 1978, "The P-W Problem," Ph.D. thesis, Australian National University, Canberra.

McRobbie, M. A., 1979, "A Proof Theoretic Investigation of Relevant and Modal Logics," Ph.D. thesis, Australian National University, Canberra.

Meyer, R. K., 1975, Arithmetic Formulated Relevantly, typescript, Australian National University, Canberra.

Meyer, R. K., 1979, Why I am Not a Relevantist, Research Paper No. 1, Logic Group, Australian National University, Canberra.

Meyer, R. K. and Dunn, J. M., 1969, E, R and γ, Journal of Symbolic Logic, 34:460-474.

Meyer, R. K. and Martin, E. P., 1984, Logic on the Australian Plan, typescript, Australian National University, Canberra.

Meyer, R. K. and McRobbie, M. A., 1982, Multisets and Relevant Implication I and II, Australasian Journal of Philosophy, 60:107-139, 265-281.

Meyer, R. K. and Routley, R., 1973, Classical Relevant Logics I, Studia Logica, 32:51-66.

Mortensen, C., 1983, The Validity of Disjunctive Syllogism is Not So Easily Proved, Notre Dame Journal of Formal Logic, 24:35-40.

Routley, R., 1983, Relevantism and the Problem as to When Material Detachment and the Disjunctive Syllogism Argument Can be Correctly Used, Research Paper No. 12, Logic Group, Australian National University, Canberra.

Routley, R., and Meyer, R. K., 1973, The Semantics of Entailment I, in: "Truth, Syntax and Modality," H. Leblanc, ed., North-Holland, Amsterdam.

Routley, R. and Routley, V., 1969, A Fallacy of Modality, Nous, 3:129-153.

Routley, R. and Routley, V., 1972, Semantics of First Degree Entailment, Nous, 6:335-359.

Routley, R. with Meyer, R. K., Plumwood, V. and Brady, R. T., 1984, "Relevant Logics and Their Rivals, Part 1: the Basic Philosophical and Semantical Theory," Ridgeview, Atascadero, California.

Slaney, J. K., 1982, The Irrationality of the Square Root of 2, typescript, University of Queensland, Brisbane.

Thistlewaite, P. B., 1984, "Automated Theorem-Proving in Non-Classical Logics," Ph.D. thesis, Australian National University, Canberra.

Urquhart, A., 1972, "The Semantics of Entailment," Ph.D. thesis, University of Pittsburgh, Ann Arbor.

FOUNDATIONS OF LINGUISTICS: PHILOSOPHY OF LANGUAGE

DUMMETT'S CONCEPTION AS THEORY OF MEANING FOR HINTIKKA'S TYPE OF GAME-THEORETICAL SEMANTICS (I) ('USE' AND 'LANGUAGE-GAME' IN WITTGENSTEIN AND DUMMETT)

Heda Festini

Filozofski fakultet
Zadar, Yugoslavia

0. INTRODUCTION

It is well known that three types of semantics have been developed in relation to transformational grammar (TG). From the standpoint of the philosophy of linguistics it seems that the main achievement in the field of semantics for TG are Montague grammar and Lakoff's (1972) type of fuzzy-set theory. When Hintikka formed his game-theoretic conception, TG had already passed through many phases: in early Chomsky, semantics was independent of syntax; for Katz-Postal the deep structure was semantics; for late Chomsky semantics was dependent on both surface and deep structure; for McCawley and Lakoff the beginning generation of syntax already included semantical representations. Montague pleaded for the parallelism of semantical and syntactical rules. Hintikka's semantics (1975) represented (according to his own words) a confrontation with Fregean semantics, as was the case with the proposals of Montague and Davidson. Gabbay (1973) described Montague's grammar as a form of Suppes probabilistic semantics, and it seems very plausible that fuzzy-set theory can also be described as a probabilistic semantics.

Hintikka's conception would then be an external approach to TG and an alternative to both versions of probabilistic semantics. We believe this theory deserves some attention concerning its consequences for some fragments of languages other than English (Italian, French, Russian, Croatian), as well as inclusion in a general theory of meaning. The issue to be explored here is the possibility of using Dummett's falsificationist conception as the theory of meaning for this purpose. The question can be put more precisely in this way: is Dummett's conception a philosophical theory of meaning, and if it is, can it incorporate the semantics of Hintikka's game theory as its own part or not? That is, are these theories parallel, analoguous or neither? Hintikka imlicitly allowed for such a development with his verificationist/falsificationist/language-use interpretation of language-games (for formal logic in 1968), and Dummett (1976) explicitly pointed out the "obvious affinities" of his own theory with "the language-game type of semantics developed by Hintikka and others". In Saarinen's (1979) words "it remains to be seen whether both theories can be tied together with more systematic links". The present paper is a suggestion for an analysis of such an attempt. This kind of investigation should include these questions: 1) Wittenstein's influence on both authors, 2) their attitude toward Frege, 3) the forming of the theory of meaning involving verification/falsification. In this paper we will consider only the first question: the growth of Dummett's conception out of Wittgenstein's claims about use and language games.

Although Dummett and Hintikka criticise Wittgenstein's view of language, they both develop his theses about language-games and the importance of the use of language. Dummett doesn't think that Wittgenstein's conception can be a systematic theory of meaning, because it impugns the "legitimacy of any distinctions corresponding to that of Frege between sense and force"; and if it must be "a wholly new kind" of the theory of meaning, "there is not sufficient indication" even for "the general outlines of such a new type of theory" (1978). He accuses Wittgenstein of "linguistic holism" (1975) and finds a similar defect in the picture-theory (1981). On the other hand, Hintikka thinks that Wittgenstein's device "is not unequivocal" (1968) and that the notion of a game is vague (1971). However, according to Dummett (1963), merely identifying meaning with use doesn't "by itself accomplish very much: but to reject the identification is to abandon all hope of an explanation of meaning".

Hintikka claims that Wittgenstein's picture theory already suggests a theory of language use (1969), and that the idea of language games doesn't refute his earlier picture theory (1971). So Hintikka wants to relate Wittgenstein's device closely to the notion of language-game, a notion which he believes "sits especially happily" with his own conception of "language-games of seeking and finding" (1968), providing for Wittgenstein's notion "the precise sense of the mathematical theory of games" (1971). As Hintikka (1976) himself says, he by and large accepts Wittgenstein's notion of "language-games as the mediators between language and reality".

It is obvious that Dummett and Hintikka differ with regard to Wittgenstein. The question is: won't such a difference be so great as to compromise the possibility of Dummett's conception being a theory of meaning for Hintikka's GTS? Or can such a difference be explained as a difference only at a level, as Dummett seems to suggest by his conception of a philosophical theory of meaning that would also provide a semantics for a fragment of natural language? An investigation of the origin of such a difference in these attitudes toward Wittgenstein's thoughts may facilitate an answer to this question.

Dummett's "Truth" (1959) already was an announcement of his plan to accommodate Wittgenstein's concept of use to Frege's theory.

Frege's term 'sense' he no longer identifies with the truth-conditions of a sentence, but with its use, i.e., with what is accomplished by making several kinds of statements, in this case, conditionals. He invokes the "Tractatus" distinction between saying and showing as it "might have been useful to Frege" in distinguishing between meaning and sense. Dummett emphasizes the "force" which in Frege's "Begriffsschrift" had the role of determining "the connection between the truth-condition of an arbitrary sentence and what we effect by uttering the sentence".

But in "Frege, Philosophy of Language" (1973) Dummett remarks that the late Wittgenstein didn't understand the term 'sense' very well, because he captured only one aspect of sense by 'use'. Frege's theory, according to Dummett, didn't neglect to employ both approaches, atomic and molecular, toward the relation between words and sentences. Wittgenstein overvalued one approach: for him the sentence is the smallest unit of meaning. In this connection Dummett draws the "crude analogy" between a simple code and the understanding of a sentence as derived from the understanding of its constituent words, and our understanding of the words through grasping the way in which they may figure in a sentence in general. (Wittgenstein also employed the term 'code' in his *PG*, but Dummett doesn't mention it.)

Dummett points out that Frege's conception of meaning accounted for three important notions: sense, tone, and force. The notion of sense presupposed the distinction between sense and reference. In his examination of Frege's notion of reference, Dummett mentions Wittgenstein's discussion about 'Moses', incorporating it into Frege's account of the problem of reference. But in examining Frege's term 'denotation', he doesn't say anything about Wittgenstein's term in *PG*. He points to Wittgenstein's later writings as an attack upon Frege's distinction between sense and force. Dummett repeatedly emphasizes the importance of force in our understanding of a sentence (1967, 1975a, 1975b, 1976).

In "Frege's Distinction Between Sense and Reference" (1975) Dummett, interpreting Frege, writes, "Sense is an ingredient in meaning." The sense of the words contributes to the determination of the condition under which the sentence is true. This claim is explained as in previous texts, but now the stress is on Frege's thesis that the "sentences play a primary role in the theory of meaning" because the smallest linguistic complex with which one can say anything is a sentence. In order to support such a claim, Frege employed the distinction of which, as we know, Dummett approves. Dummett claims that the main attack on the sense/reference distinction today comes from holism and the causal theory of reference. This claim is important not only with regard to his objection to Wittgenstein, but also in regard to the emphasis he places on the notion of force. Dummett thinks that for Frege sense determines reference, and the force is an aspect of meaning without which it is impossible to consider the different categories of sentences.

At the end of his paper "Was Frege a Philosopher of Language?" (1979a), Dummett affirms that it is possible to connect Frege's conception of the sense of a sentence with the idea of its use, but that "no statements of this thesis is to be found in Frege." Later, in "Comments on Professor Prawitz's Paper" (1980), Dummett includes the notion of use as the central notion in the theory of meaning, i.e., in its part (I). In his book "The Interpretation of Frege's Philosophy" (1981), he is concerned with indications that Frege didn't succeed in his attempt to explain the notion of sense independently of psychology, because the understanding of a sense was a mental process. Eventually, according to Dummett, Wittgenstein found the solution: understanding is not a mental process.

At the outset we can find reason to suspect Dummett's accommodation of Wittgenstein to Frege's framework. We already have some indication of a negative answer to the putative question: can Dummett accommodate Wittgenstein's thesis in Frege's framework? If this accommodation is not possible, it seems that we would have a reason for precisely the reverse strategy. Our question should then be: can Dummett accommodate Frege in a Wittgensteinian framework?

1. 'SENSE' AND 'FORCE' VS. 'USE' AND 'LANGUAGE GAME'

1.1 We can find some indications of this reverse strategy in Dummett's treatment of language-games in his early article "Truth" (1959). Dummett employs the characteristic terms from board games, 'winning' and 'losing', which he says coincide with formal descriptions of what happens in natural language. He makes a comparison between winning and losing and the determination of the sense of a statement by knowing in what circumstances it is true or false. The notion of sense becomes separated from a truth-conditional treatment. At the end of this paper, he credits Wittgenstein with being the author of the doctrine of meaning explained in terms of use, which involves dethroning truth and falsity from their central role in the theory of meaning. Dummett adds that the point of Wittgenstein's doctrine has not been generally understood. Dummett connects this doctrine with Frege's notion of contextual definition in the "Grundlagen". He explains, in "Frege's Philosophy" (1968), that Frege seems to be aiming at what Wittgenstein was after with his notion of "making a move in the language game". According to Wittgenstein, says Dummett, the linguistic act of uttering a sentence - the smallest linguistic unit - is making a move in the language game.

In "Postscript" (1972) to "Truth", he reiterates the claim that "the comparison between the notion of truth and that of winning a game still seems" to him good; but he doesn't mention Wittgenstein here.

In his book "Frege, Philosophy of Language" Dummett mentions playing cards, and connects it with the problem of sense. He points out in the same connection Wittgenstein's dictum 'make a move in the language'.

Our first insight, then, is that, when the Wittgensteinian notions of use and language-game were introduced as candidates for the central notions of Dummett's theory of meaning, this is done only implicitly. If we bear in mind that Dummett claims to supplement Wittgenstein's thesis, then it seems that our candidates don't have much of a chance. But we can try to find another possibility.

1.2 In "Frege's Distinction between Sense and Reference" Dummett asserts that a Fregean theory of meaning must be capable of accounting for the actual use of language. This direction can be taken as an indication of another way of emphasizing the relation between Wittgenstein and Frege, one that would combine Wittgenstein's thesis and Frege's 'force'. In "Can Analytical Philosophy be Systematic, and Ought it to Be?" (1975) Dummett allows that the notion of language-game that Wittgenstein employed was connected to various activities, e.g., linguistic acts. But he points out that the category of the sentence is still one aspect to the meaning based on different acts, which Wittgenstein didn't respect because he proposed rejecting the linguistic act of assertion in *PI*.

This objection deserves much attention. For instance, C. Wright (1980) doesn't share it. It is strange that Dummett didn't connect the problem of force with Wittgenstein's notion of language-game, although in his text he mentions it and considers it together with Frege. He claims (1975a) that Wittgenstein employed the notion in the "Brown Book" and elsewhere, regarding a language-game as a "fragment of the language which is displayed as actually spoken" and which is constituted by "the complex of activities with which the utterance of sentences of the language are interwoven". Dummett points out that Wittgenstein's example of a coin in *PI* is the best illustration of what he meant with the term "use", i.e., he meant the institutionalized character of the linguistic activities. To both Wittgenstein and Frege, Dummett attributes the insight into the ineradicably social character of language. However, he must admit that Frege took the institution of language as autonomous, whereas for Wittgenstein, language is interwoven with our non-linguistic activities. Dummett doesn't restrain his criticism of Frege's disregard of the social character of language, but he does glide rather quickly over such difficulties of Wittgenstein's as "the remoteness of the connection between linguistic activities and non-linguistic ones" (1975a). However, we can admit it is visible in the trace of his supplementation of so-called Fregean force with Wittgenstein's notion of social games. The Russian philosopher Grjaznov in 1982 considers Dummett's assimilation of Wittgenstein's theory of language-game as a form of life as a supplementation to Frege's theory, which so neglected the social character of language.

In "What is a Theory of Meaning? (II)" (1976) Dummett once again claims that the theory of force must be viewed as a supplementation to Wittgenstein's thesis identifying meaning with use, since the distinction between sense and force, disregarded by Wittgenstein, is important especially for the linguistic act of assertion. Thus, Dummett insists on his radical interpretation of Wittgenstein, but he doesn't supply any reason for preferring the Fregean notion of force. Dummett here favors a theory of meaning in which it is possible to obtain a formulation of "the general principles in accordance with which the language games of assertion, question, command, request, etc. are played". So far, we don't know whether such a claim is in accordance with Wittgenstein or not. The problem requires further analysis, especially if we bear in mind Wright's disagreement with Dummett's opinion about Wittgenstein's denial of the sense/force distinction.

In his lecture at Stockholm University, entitled "What Do I Know When I Know a Language?" (1978), Dummett, developing Wittgenstein's tenets, thinks that it is also necessary to take into account the three well-known ingredients of meaning. Here we have more evidence that the supplementation of Wittgenstein with Frege is the accommodation of Frege to Wittgenstein's conception of meaning as use in a language-game.

He repeats in "What does the Appeal to Use Do for the Theory of Meaning?" (1979) the importance of the theory of force, which he connects with the use the sentence has in actual linguistic practice. But at the same time he repeats his claim that Wittgenstein repudiated Frege's distinction between senses and force, particularly assertoric force in general, a repudiation that one finds in *PI* and not in *PG*. So we now have one more element for discussing the assertoric problem in Wittgenstein.

In the beginning of his "Comments on Professor Prawitz's Paper" (1980) Dummett repeats that there is no clear idea of 'use' of a sentence without an explanation of what a speaker does by uttering it. He emphasizes that "it will have to envoke some general principle". But in the discussion with Prawitz he agrees that it is possible to take 'use' as the central notion of the theory of meaning. But he also pointed out to Prawitz that it remains necessary to take force into account. Dummett's answer to the problem of force seems so far to be only a half an answer.

Wright (1981) has shown that it isn't very certain that Wittgenstein did deny the sense/force distinction, and has explained why Wittgenstein didn't consider the entire theory of force necessary. We can add that Wittgenstein did seem to make this distinction in many texts (for instance in *PI*, *OC*, *RFM*), and that the various linguistic activities provide a natural basis for it, i.e., they constitute the general principle of the distinction. It seems that to Dummett it is not so strange an idea. We can raise the question - why has it remained only implicit? Let us try to make it more explicit.

1.3 In his book "Frege, Philosophy of Language" we find the exposition of Frege's thesis about thought which has as its vehicle the sentence. According to Dummett, Wittgenstein is indebted to Frege for such an idea, and for denying that thoughts are mental entities.

In other papers Dummett is occupied with this topic also. In the book "Truth and other Enigmas" (1978) he stresses the public character of Frege's thesis, and he adds that Wittgenstein was very forceful in rejecting the private interpretation. The direct contribution of Frege and Wittgenstein to the fundamental outlines for the insight of how language functions is in their thesis that thoughts are communicable by means of language. An analysis of employment of language must, therefore, according to Dummett, make explicit the principles regulating our use of language, of which we already have an implicit grasp. He reiterates that they both treated language as a vehicle for thought and a means for communication. Nevertheless, Dummett thinks, "although these are ideas with which any future attempt to construct a theory of meaning must come to terms, Wittgenstein's work did not provide a foundation for such an attempt" (p. 453). A systematic theory of meaning must enclose a vast complex of interconnections in an account of the mastery of language which doesn't consist "in a number of principle isolable practical abilities" (p. 454). According to Dummett, the further development comes after Frege, since, as a result of his work, we know enough of "underlying syntactical structure of our language and about what is demanded of a theory of meaning" (p. 454).

In his Stockholm lecture he repeats both Frege's and Wittgenstein's theses regarding language as the vehicle of thought, characterizing it not as a means for thoughts, which becomes important for further interpretation.

In his "The Interpretation of Frege's Philosophy" (1981) Dummett is concerned with defending Frege's conception of thought. Frege didn't believe in incommunicability of thoughts in the sense in which Wittgenstein denied them to be possible. Wittgenstein was clearer, Dummett admits, denying the thoughts as mental processes. Dummett can't deny that Frege took into account an individual speaker's mastery of language and connected it with his idiolect. The whole point of Wittgenstein's attack, admits Dummett, had its origin in his treatment of language as a public language, which essentially involves reference to the linguistic community. This reference was obscure in Frege's conception, and, according to Dummett, equally far from Putnam's idea of the division of linguistic labour. This public character of a language Dummett points out also in his paper "Realism" (1982).

The previous analysis shows that Dummett vacillates between a partial and a complete denial of Frege's so called public interpretation of language. It is remarkable that he displays such vacillation not merely in the articles from different periods of his writing, but often in a single article. His relation to Wittgenstein is interesting in this regard: he admits Wittgenstein's advantage over Frege, but persists in the thesis that the further development comes from Frege and not from Wittgenstein. In most of his papers his objections to Wittgenstein are sharper than they are to Frege, but in his last book (1981) he admits the full advantage of Wittgenstein over Frege. We can conclude that these elements of Dummett's own theory became more explicit when we consider their origin.

In his last book he is more explicit, but even there insufficiently, because Putnam's idea about the division of linguistic labour, to which he only alludes, is possible only if it is based upon Wittgenstein's notion of public linguistic activities.

2. CONVENTIONAL AND SOCIAL LINGUISTIC ACTIVITIES

2.1 Closely related to the notion of public linguistic activities is the problem of the interpretation of a code. In his book "Frege, Philosophy of Language" Dummett points out that a code is not a good comparison with a word or with a sentence. In his Stockholm lecture Dummett emphasizes his and Fege's repudiation of the conception of a language as a code. He claims that in such a conception it would be required "that we may ascribe concepts and thoughts to people independently of their knowledge of language". He cites Frege's and Wittgenstein's counterexamples. For more light it is useful to turn back to 1963 article "The Philosophical Significance of Gödel's Theorem". In his examination of meaning and use, he says that recent philosophers have tended to reverse Aristotle's approach. His useful analogy with a code drops out. According to Aristotle, we use sentences to communicate thoughts that we can't transmit directly, therefore we code them by means of audible or visible signs. The sentence is in that case the code-symbol for the thought. Dummett says, that Wittgenstein's analogy with chess-pieces and their posers is better. The code-symbol for that power isn't considered as something which could in principle exist on its own, but only in the practice of moving it in accordance with certain rules. It seems that he is in agreement with Wittgenstein's treatment that we don't code our thoughts. But, consequently, since Dummett considers only these particular thoughts of Wittgenstein and not the others, we can conclude, that Dummett hasn't provided a complete account. So Frege received the better treatment. Dummett is too severe with Wittgenstein and too mild with Frege. We can't forget here that, according to Dummett, Frege couldn't give up his unpublic conception of language and the mental character of thought. If this is so, how can we admit that Frege reversed Aristotle's approach? Wittgenstein's attitude toward thought was uncompromisingly unmentalistic. Dummett was forced to admit this, at least in his second book on Frege, more explicitly. We have seen that this problem has to do with implicit knowledge and with problems about rules. We shall now pursue these topics.

2.2 In his Stockholm lecture Dummett stresses the question: do we really know the theory of meaning when we know a language? Following first Wittgenstein and further Frege he asserts that "the conception of mastery of a language" consists "in implicit knowledge of a theory of meaning", i.e., "what makes the utterances of a speaker to be expressions of thought is a piece of internal equipment". In his attempt to make this implicit knowledge manifest in the speaker's use of the language, it becomes evident that invoking the knowledge isn't necessary at all, because we must take into account "the social practice in which that mastery enables" the speaker to participate.

In his last book about Frege Dummett says that we can't dispense with the notion of a purely implicit understanding, and points to Frege's analysis of the expression of generality of which we have implicit knowledge. He points also to Wittgenstein's 'tacit conventions' "governing the working of our language" (p. 236). So, it appears, that we must take into account such terms as 'implicit', 'tacit', and so forth. Implicit knowledge of which Dummett earlier wished to dispense, in reality is the problem of implicit knowledge of the rule.

2.3 In his book "Frege, Philosophy of Language" Dummett speaks about rules of inference and of proof. Paraphrasing Wittgenstein's "move can be made in the language" (p. 194), he explains what for Frege was the problem of the relation between words and sentences, and then he employs the term 'rule'. He also makes a comparison with playing cards. The rule for a word functions together with the rules which govern other words, which in turn constitute the words of a sentence. In "Frege's Distinction Between Sense and Reference" Dummett (1975b) says that, according to Frege, "in our everyday speech we are not playing a game whose rules we have not fully formulated, but one for which no consistent set of rules could be drawn up". In "Can Analytical Philosophy Be Systematic, and Ought It To Be?" we find Dummett emphasizing the proximity of Frege's and Wittgenstein's descriptions of the conventional principles which govern the practice of speaking the language and of the concept of following a rule. In "What is a Theory of Meaning? II", speaking of an anti-deterministic theory of meaning, Dummett stresses as the main claim, the studying of the rules and strategies of a game which even in principle couldn't be predicted by any one speaker. In the Stockholm lecture he makes the comparison with a board player. If we wish to explain what the mastery of a rule for a player consists in, we describe the practice of playing the game, i.e., we simply "state the rules". So, the individual player's practice is based on implicit knowledge of the rules, but in the question of language we must take into account "the social practice". As we have already seen, for such a purpose we don't need to "invoke the knowledge at all". We already encounter in Dummett's last book his stress on Wittgenstein's "Tractatus" appeal to 'tacit convention'.

In our second fragment, we see that Dummett hesitates. He applies Wittgensteinian language-game terminology to Frege and asserts that Frege didn't think that it is possible to formulate a consistent set of rules for natural language. Who doubts the existence of a systematic theory, Wittgenstein or Frege?

After this, Dummett thinks that both Frege and Wittgenstein are interested in the description of conventional principles which govern linguistic practice. It is clear that, according to Dummett, Frege didn't believe in the possibility of such a description. Finally, Dummett claims that the rules are constituted by conventional and social linguistic practice, a view which, Dummett claims in his last book, Frege couldn't hold. Hence, Dummett must change his negative opinion about Wittgenstein in an explicit way, or we can conclude that he was merely using Wittgenstein as a supplementation to Frege. In the second fragment we saw that the problem of interpretation and understanding the rule includes the question about the relation between words and sentences, i.e., it is included in the main problem of meaning, to which we now turn.

3. COMPONENTIAL AND CONTEXT PRINCIPLES

3.1 In his book "Frege, Philosophy of Language" Dummet discusses Quine's holism, which can't allow the notion of language "as something decomposable into significant parts", with different levels. In "Frege's Distinction Between Sense and Reference", he reiterates this objection to Quine and especially to Davidson's holism as well. Though the holist theory has difficulties, he admits that for some kinds of sentences - ones with proper names - it seems to be true. But nevertheless he pursues the objection in "What Is a Theory of Meaning? (I)". The holistic theory precludes the possibility of providing a systematic theory of meaning for natural language, because it has the wrong basis - a specific class of sentences - and because the notion of language is reduced "to that of an idiolect". Throughout his writings Dummett is opposed to the social character of language. In this sense he ascribes to holists the omission of the phenomenon called by Putnam "the linguistic division of labor". He criticizes the holist for applying the case of Wittgenstein's

'Moses' to all the words in the language. In "The Justification of Deduction" Dummett makes the distinction between the radical Wittgensteinian holistic position and a possible modification of it. Wittgenstein's holism renders the characterisation of the meaning of an individual sentence without "giving an account of the entire language of which it forms a part". According to Dummett, in modified holism the molecular view is lacking, too, because we can find no way of ascribing an individual content to each sentence of the language without a knowledge of the entire language. Either holism cannot "consider the sentence as a smallest unit of the language". Therefore, according to Dummett, we must reject holism if we wish to retain both the claim that each sentence has a content depending only upon its internal structure, and the claim that the sentence can't have "a meaning independent of *all* the rest of the language". Dummett contends in "Can Analytic Philosophy be Systematic, and Ought it to Be?" that Wittgenstein's language-games "give an account of some very small fragments of language" which "do not appear a promising model for a systematic account of an entire language". Confronting Dummett's own text, one gets the impression that his objection to Wittgenstein involves contradictions, which we ought now to try to resolve.

3.2 In his article "Nominalism" (1956), Dummett for the first time points out that probably the most important of Frege's philosophical statements, quoted by Wittgenstein in both the "Tractatus" and the "Investigations", was his "doctrine that only in the context of a sentence does a name stand for anything". Dummett wrote very often after that about Frege's treatment of proper names, of complex names, i.e., of the reference of words and expressions. The term 'reference' Dummett (1973a) explicitly applies to the relation between words and things. He tried to explain Frege's own view as the name/bearer relation, which, as the prototype of reference, forced him to the distinction between intensional and extensional contexts. Dummett

(1973a) reveals difficulties that made Frege's conception much too weak. Of course, for Frege the most important question always concerns the truth or falsity of a sentence: a sentence without a bearer has no truth value. And, as we know, a truth-conditional approach is the standpoint neither of Wittgenstein nor of Dummett. However, Dummett tries to explain in his last book some misunderstandings about the terms 'referent' and 'reference' connected with Frege's interpretation of predicates. He must finally admit in "Realism" (1982) that, by Frege's principle, "we do not need to invoke the notion of reference" in applying to terms, but "we continue to ascribe reference to terms for directions" (p. 68). The previous stress on the distinction between sense and reference became superfluous, and Dummett's criticism of the causal theory of names becomes unconvincing. The first insight renders the criticism of Wittgenstein's holism and holism in general unconvincing. Dummett claims that Wittgenstein's example of 'Moses' indicates the correct schematic use of the form which a specification of the use of the name must take (1975c). But, he thinks that the typical holistic requirement of the entire language for the understanding of any part isn't avoided (1976). In his last article (1982), he employs the same interpretation of Wittgenstein's treatment of words and expressions of inner sensations. But at the same time he approves of Wittgenstein's view of the ascription of inner sensations as involving a radical divergence from the principle of bivalence (1982). How can we combine this with the previous criticism? Dummett's theory of reference isn't so firm anymore. Why?

In "What is a Theory of Meaning? (II)", Dummett presents his own ideas of the correct theory of meaning as composed of two, rather than of three parts, the central part providing the theory of sense and reference, and the second part being supplementary. In the first part, Dummett lays out the features any sentence must have, and in the second part provides a uniform means of deriving such features for every aspect of a sentence's use. But on the very next pages, we see that he advocates a theory in which "the theories of reference and of sense merge", a theory in which the candidate notion is verification or falsification. This new theory "has obvious affinities, not only with Popper's account of science, but also with the language-game type of semantics developed by Hintikka and others". It is very important to see here how much closer Dummett's interpretation of Frege is to Wittgenstein's account of the relation between words and sentences.

3.3 In the beginning, Dummett ascribes to both Frege and Wittgenstein a theory that is both atomistic and molecular at the same time (1956). The sentence is primary only "on the ground that we can learn the meaning of a word only by learning the meaning of a sentence in which it occurs". There are the sentences "which we understand only by already knowing the meanings of the constituent words". For Dummett it is quite wrong to ascribe to Frege "the doctrine that the unit of significance is not the word but the sentence" (1973, 1956). In both cases Dummett appeals to Wittgenstein supporting Frege's doctrine with Wittgenstein's idea of making a move in a game (1973). The word is another kind of linguistic unit: it is the smallest bit of language to which one can attribute sense. The first is named the "context principle" (1968), and the second may be called the compositional principle, i.e., the componential principle (1975b). Dummett makes a "crude analogy" with a code-word to illustrate such a double relation. A code-word may consist of a numeral followed by a string of letters. The analogy with our understanding of a word independently of any particular sentence containing it is established in the following way: the determination of the encoded word proceeds only by applying the general rule of a code word. The analogy with our understanding such a word consists in grasping the way in which it may figure in a sentence in general. It follows that the significance of the code of any numeral or letter is not explainable without the reference to the general notion of the representation of a normal word by means of a code word (1973). But in the same book he mentions Wittgenstein's comparison of the word with a chess piece, which for Dummett is a better comparison than with a code: "the word has a sense, and is not, as on the first view, a code for it, just as the rook has certain powers of movement and is not a code for them" (p. 156). It remains for us to choose which example is better or to accept Wittgenstein's treatment of codes in *PG*, as we already suggested. Wittgenstein employed the terms 'code', 'denotation', 'designation', in *PG*. He spoke about "the grammar of denotation" and made an example with designation. The rules of the language-games, according to Wittgenstein, codify different characteristics of words. The code with the key for deciphering we can explain as a connotative code for the sentences encoded (1982). Since, according to Wittgenstein, the "meaning is the role of the word in the calculus" and "the proposition has its content as part of a calculus", this gives to denotation a character of identification of one part of sentence content, as we explained before (1982). So, the denotative code denotes the primary content and the connotative code is the 'undercode' (1982). The 'multifariousness' of language in *PG* must be understood as the cultural systems of codes. Wittgenstein wasn't satisfied with some general theory. He allowed for a generality (*PG*) which can't concern the language alone, but involves the cultural and social systems with which the language is interwoven. The terms 'denotation' and 'designation' in *PI*, in *OC*, and 'designation' and 'reference' in *RC* have the same role. In this manner, Wittgenstein tried to save the individual content of a sentence through the compositional principle, and to guarantee the sentence as a unit of language through the context principle.

Let us consider the distinction between syntax and semantics which, according to Dummett, was the source for Frege of his double principle. Dummett explains that Frege didn't directly provide "any syntactic analysis of natural language". The sentences comprising his formalized language, however, have a precise syntactic structure, manifested in their surface appearance, which can provide the basis for a semantics for a large fragment of natural language, even though Frege didn't believe in the possibility of such semantics (1975b). Frege's syntax has two stages: first we construct the simplest form of sentences, then out of them the complex sentences by means of iterable devices of sentence-composition.

In "What Is a Theory of Meaning? (I)", Dummett says that holism has a tendency to disregard the atomistic standpoint only at first sight. Given the continuous needs of the relation "to the language as a whole", this tendency becomes apparent and unsuccessful.

In "The Justification of Deduction", Dummet speaks about a modified Wittgensteinian doctrine which would throw out also the "molecular conception of language under which each sentence possesses an individual content which may be grasped without a knowledge of the entire language". Therefore, he concludes, we must reject holism if we wish to suppose that each sentence has a content which depends "only upon its internal structure". But, "of course, even on a molecular view of this kind, no sentence can have a meaning which is independent of *all* the rest of the language". He admits this double principle, and at first it is hard to see the difference between a point of view which is molecular and one which is atomistic. But in "What Is a Theory of Meaning? (II)", Dummett proceeds with explaining the difference between a molecular and a holistic view: for a "molecular view, there is, for each sentence, a determinate fragment of the language a knowledge of which will suffice for a complete understanding of that sentence", and for a holistic view, "it is impossible fully to understand any sentence without knowing the entire language". In "Was Frege a Philosopher of Language?"

(1979), Dummett attempts to explain further the same claim in connection with Frege's problem of thought: "the structure of the sentence reflects the structure of the thought and the senses of the constituent parts of the sentence are parts of the thought, which is the sense of the sentence". Such a view Dummett sees, as before, as close to a possible interpretation of natural language. He says, "the surface form of the sentence does not reveal its true structure", which is not an unfamiliar idea to Chomsky and other linguists. Such a conception aims at what Dummett calls 'essential structure', even though it wasn't "intended [by Frege] as a contribution to a syntactical theory; it was concerned to explain Frege's account of what is involved in grasping the thought expressed by a complex sentence". Dummett claims that such a treatment, which Frege pointed out, "Wittgenstein, Chomsky and others are never tired of pointing out".

In his book of 1981, Dummett defends himself against Sluga's attack that he has not given enough weight to the context principle. But, even now, he gives more weight to the other compositional principle. Here Dummett writes about Frege's unsuccessful attempt to reveal how the thought is constructed out of its constituents. He examines Wittgenstein's proposal in *RFM*, pp. 41-43, that the meaning of a complex sentence consists in what we can do with it, or in what is involved in accepting it (as an assertion). Dummett remarks, that this is essentially explained by the rule governing the deduction of simpler sentences from it. What Dummett needs is a stronger principle. Frege didn't find the solution. Wittgenstein came closer with his anti-mentalistic approach, but exaggerated, according to Dummett, the context principle. However, Dummett emphasizes Wittgenstein's approach in his last article (1982). In his last book (1981) he rejects the Wittgensteinian picture theory as a possible solution of the role of the thought in such problems.

In our third section, an analysis is provided of the problem of proper names, words, and expressions. Dummett settles this, yielding, as was promised, to holism (to Wittgensteinian holism à la Quine), and to some kind of causal theory as well. Wittgenstein's conception of a name is nearer to some aspects of the theory of direct reference, as we can conclude from Salmon's interpretation of possible refinements of an orthodox Fregean theory (1982). Dummett insists so much upon a distinction between sense and reference, but already from 1973 on, he began to "incorporate" the reference into sense. Finally they "merge" and give way to another notion, that of verification and falsification. We can conclude that until "What Is a Theory of Meaning? (I)" Dummett didn't find in Wittgenstein any exaggeration of the context principle. He starts then to accuse him of holism, but at the same time asserts that his model of language is not promising, because it can be only for a small fragment. Frege's conception is promising for a large fragment of language, but Dummett once accepted that the molecular view required the treatment of linguistic fragments! After all, what are language-games, and what is Hintikka's type of GT semantics to which Dummett appeals? Is it for a small or a large fragment of language? Wittgenstein's language-games are in language; they are the fragments, some of the examples explored by Hintikka. On the other hand, Hintikka (1971) shows that his idea of GTS is connected with the picture theory explicitly. We have tried to show that Wittgenstein's explanation of word-meaning and sentence-meaning is better than Frege's (if the code principle is convincing!). Our conclusion is that the fragment of conception of language must be better also. And so the question isn't whether Frege or Wittgenstein are working in the same direction as TG, but rather, which of them is closer to an anticipation of Hintikka's GTS. In the last section we provided the most explicit answer that Dummett implicitly accommodated Frege to Wittgenstein. This is the reason for his errors.

Comparing and confronting Dummett's texts, we conclude: Dummett, by his own words, began as a follower of Wittgenstein (1978). Then he attacked Wittgenstein, using Frege. But, step by step he was forced to concede. If he intended to accommodate Wittgenstein's notions in a Fregean framework he should have made it in conjunction with Frege's truth-conditional theory. Dummett didn't want to do this, and can't, as we saw generally, leaving the details for another essay. Considering further the converse possibility, the difficulties in accommodating Wittgenstein's notions into the central and second part of Dummett's theory of meaning, we come to Wright's interpretation of 'force', developed more explicitly than Dummett's own concession to Wittgenstein's unmentalistic, conventional, and social rule-governed treatment of linguistic activities. Such a conception leads Dummett to abandon the previous approval of the strict distinction between sense and reference, and to acknowledge some interpretations of certain representatives of the theory of direct reference and holism. The candidates he proposes for a central part of his theory are verification and falsification, which he finds later in Hintikka's semantical notions. It remains for another essay to explain the question of Wittgenstein's views upon this topic.

The investigation which we have undertaken shows that Dummett must be closer to Wittgenstein, especially in the tolerance of a language fragment as a theoretically acceptable topic, if he wants to include Hintikka's context-dependent semantics as a counterexample to TG and his own conception as an attempt at a general philosophical theory of meaning.

REFERENCES

Dummett, M., 1956, Nominalism, in: "Truth and Other Enigmas," 1978, Duckworth, London.

Dummett, M., 1959, Truth, in: ibid.

Dummett, M., 1963, The Philosophical Significance of Gödel's Theorem, in: ibid.

Dummett, M., 1967, Frege's Philosophy, in: ibid.

Dummett, M., 1972, Postscript, in: ibid.

Dummett, M., 1973a, "Frege, Philosophy of Language," Duckworth, London.

Dummett, M., 1973b, The Justification of Deduction, in: "Truth and Other Enigmas," op.cit.

Dummett, M., 1975a, Can Analytical Philosophy be Systematic, and Ought it to Be?, in: ibid.

Dummett, M., 1975b, Frege's Distinction between Sense and Reference, in: ibid.

Dummett, M., 1975c, What is a Theory of Meaning? (I), in: "Mind and Language," S. Guttenplan, ed., Clarendon Press, Oxford.

Dummett, M., 1976, What is a Theory of Meaning? (II), in: "Truth and Meaning," G. Evans and J. McDowell, eds., Clarendon Press, Oxford.

Dummett, M., 1978, What Do I Know When I Know a Language?, Lecture at the Centenary Celebrations of the Stockholm University, printed as summary.

Dummett, M., 1979a, Was Frege a Philosopher of Language?. Revue Internat. de Philosophie, 130:786.

Dummett, M., 1979b, What does the Appeal to Use Do for the Theory of Meaning?, in: "Meaning and Use," A. Margalit, ed., Reidel, Dordrecht.

Dummett, M., 1980, Comments on Professor Prawitz's Paper, in: "Logic and Philosophy," G. H. von Wright, ed., Martinus Nijhoff, The Hague.

Dummett, M., 1981, "The Interpretation of Frege's Philosophy," Duckworth, London.

Dummett, M., 1982, Realism, Synth., 52:55.

Festini, H., 1982, Is Wittgenstein's Concept of Proposition in *Philosophical Grammar* Intensional, Extensional, or Something Else?, in: "Language and Ontology. Proceedings of the 6th International Wittgenstein Symposium," W. Leinfellner, E. Kraemer, and J. Schank, eds., Hölder-Pichler-Tempsky, Vienna.

Gabbay, D. M., 1973, Representation of the Montague Semantics as a Form of the Suppes Semantics, in: "Approaches to Natural Language," K. J. J. Hintikka, J. M. E. Moravcsik, and P. Suppes, eds., Reidel, Dordrecht.

Grjaznov, A. F., 1982, Teorija značenija Majkla Dammita, Voprosy filosofii, 4:114.

Hintikka, K. J. J., 1968, Language-Games for Quantifiers, reprinted in: "Logic, Language-Games and Information," 1973, Oxford University Press, Oxford.

Hintikka, K. J. J., 1969, Quantification and the Picture Theory of Language, reprinted in: ibid.

Hintikka, K. J. J., 1971, Quantifiers, Language-Games, and Transcendental Arguments, reprinted in: ibid.

Hintikka, K. J. J., 1975, On the Limitation of Generative Grammar, in: "Filosofiska Studier. Proceedings of the Scandinavian Seminar on Philosophy of Language," Uppsala Universitet, Uppsala.

Hintikka, K. J. J., 1976, Language-Games, in: "Game-Theoretical Semantics," E. Saarinen, ed., Reidel, Dordrecht.

Lakoff, G., 1972, Hedges: A Study in Meaning Criteria and the Logic of Fuzzy Concepts, in: "Papers from the Eighth Regional Meeting of the Chicago Linguistic Society," P. M. Peranteau, J. N. Levy, G. C. Phares, eds., University of Michigan, Chicago.

Salmon, N. U., 1982, "Reference and Essence," Blackwell, London.

Saarinen, E., 1979, Introduction, in: "Game-Theoretical Semantics," E. Saarinen, ed., Reidel, Dordrecht.

Wittgenstein, L., 1953, "Philosophical Investigations," (Abb. *PI*), Blackwell, Oxford.

Wittgenstein, L., 1956, "Remarks on the Foundations of Mathematics," (Abb. *RFM*), Blackwell, Oxford.

Wittgenstein, L., 1969, "On Certainty," (Abb. *OC*), Blackwell, Oxford.

Wittgenstein, L., 1977, "Remarks on Colour," (Abb. *RC*), Blackwell, Oxford.

Wright, C., 1980, "Wittgenstein on the Foundation of Mathematics," Duckworth, London.

INDETERMINACY OF MEANING

Bengt-Olof Qvarnström

Department of Philosophy
University of Turku
Finland

1. INTRODUCTION

In this paper we shall critically examine the two main arguments that W. V. Quine has presented in various forms to support his thesis of the indeterminacy of translation. If somebody objects that we have, from the very beginning, misrepresented the thesis by calling it "indeterminacy of meaning" whereas Quine names it "indeterminacy of translation", here is our answer. Since translation as normally understood is a way of explaining meaning and there is considerable evidence that Quine intends that the word "translation" should be understood in its normal sense, his thesis could also be interpreted as a thesis of the indeterminacy of meaning. Here we shall discuss the thesis only in this sense.

In 1973 Føllesdal argued very convincingly that Quine has in fact presented two quite different arguments in support of his thesis: one based on holism and the verification theory of meaning, the other on certain crucial differences between a theory of nature and a theory of translation [meaning] (Føllesdal (1973) especially p. 290, see also Føllesdal (1975) pp.28-33). As far as we can see, however, Quine does not only present two different arguments but tries to establish with each a different thesis: in one case "the indeterminacy of empirical meaning" and in the other case "the indeterminacy of normal meaning" as we shall call these theses. In the second case meaning should be understood in its ordinary everyday sense, according to which meanings are roughly ideas in the mind.

In Section 3 we treat Quine's main argument for the indeterminacy of normal meaning. First we present some relatively precise formulations of this thesis and examine them. Then we give various interpretations of "meaning is indeterminate". We end the section by discussing the truth of the thesis of indeterminacy of normal meaning. Our conclusion is that it can hardly be true.

In Section 4 we scrutinize Quine's argument for the indeterminacy of empirical meaning. The concept of empirical meaning is of course very important because it is used in the formulation of the thesis. Therefore its introduction must be firmly justified as it differs considerably from the normal concept of meaning, with which it should not be confused. Since Quine's justification for introducing empirical meaning is not perfectly clear our first goal in Section 4 is to clarify and improve it. To the extent that we succeed in this, we also strengthen Quine's argument for the indeterminacy of empirical meaning. The latter part of Section 4 is devoted to Quine's main argument for the indeterminacy of empirical meaning where he crucially uses the concept of empirical meaning. Our conclusion is that the thesis of empirical meaning is probably true.

Section 2 is of a preparatory character. Here concepts, ideas and claims in Quine's philosophy of science are explained because we believe that without such explanations his arguments concerning indeterminacy cannot be easily understood.

2. FUNDAMENTAL CONCEPTS AND IDEAS IN QUINE'S PHILOSOPHY OF SCIENCE

First, we let Quine in his own words describe the content of his concepts 'observation sentence' and 'standing sentence'. It should be observed that the concept 'occasion sentence' is used to explain "observation sentence":

> It [the occasion sentence] is a sentence like 'This is red' or 'It is raining', which is true on one occasion and false on another; unlike 'Sugar is sweet', whose truth value endures regardless of occasion of utterance. Quine (1975a) p. 72.

> Assent to an occasion sentence has to be prompted anew, whenever the sentence is queried, by what is currently observable. The sentence simply has no truth value apart from the occasion. A standing sentence, once assented to, remains as a standing commitment for a while at least. Quine (1974) p. 63.

> Such, then, is an observation sentence: it is an occasion sentence whose occasion is not only intersubjectively observable but is generally adequate, moreover, to elicit assent to the sentence from any present witness conversant with the language. Quine (1975a) p. 73.

(These concepts are described in detail, for example, in Chapter II, Quine (1960) and further clarified on pp. 85-89 in Quine (1969b).)

A 'theory' is a set of (theoretical) standing sentences and a subset of these constitutes its axioms. Theories are different if and only if they are not logically equivalent (Quine (1975c) p. 318). Quine is obviously an empiricist who accepts the hypothetico-deductive method as the only method of science (see, for example, Quine (1975a) pp. 71-72; Quine (1975c) pp. 316-319): a theory is, in the last instance, tested by deriving from it observation sentences which, if true, confirm the theory and, if false, disconfirm it. The above account is, however, not quite correct, because "The observation sentences cannot, as occasion sentences, be implied by theory; we must first change them into standing sentences by incorporating specifications of place-times" (Quine (1975c) p. 316). The standing sentences obtained by such specifications in the observation sentences Quine calls "pegged observation sentences". For example, the transformation of "It is raining" into "Rain at Heathrow 1600 G.M.T. 23 February 1974" results in a pegged observation sentence (Quine (1975a) p. 75). Thus in fact a theory is tested by logically deducing from it pegged observation sentences of which most are of conditional form in the context of theory testing, i.e., they are if-then sentences (Quine (1975c) pp. 317-318). From now on we use the term "standing sentence" to refer only to standing sentences that are not pegged observation sentences.

Since the concept of observation sentence plays an important role in the hypothetico-deductive method we shall remind the reader of some of its features which ought to be kept in mind. An observation sentence is true (false) in a situation, if all (or nearly all) speakers would assent to (dissent from) it when asked in that situation. Thus the observation sentence is an intersubjective unit. Furthermore, Quine defines the observation sentence as an amorphous unstructured whole. For example, "The cat is on the mat" is only an unstructured sound sequence which all speakers would assent to (dissent from) in situation *s* if at least one speaker assented to (dissented from) it in *s*. Nor does the sentence contain such units as 'the', 'cat', 'is' etc. in which it is normally analyzed (Quine-Ullian (1978) pp. 25-26).

We now introduce some additional concepts which are also needed below. We say that two theories are *empirically equivalent* if and only if they are compatible with exactly the same pegged observation sentences, and that they are *scientifically equivalent* if and only if they are empirically equivalent, and equally well satisfy those criteria (simplicity etc.) which are normally used or should be used when one tries to choose the best between empirically equivalent theories. Quine probably accepts as such criteria the five properties presented as the virtues of a hypothesis in Quine-Ullian (1978), Chapter VI. We say, furthermore, that a theory T_1 is *empirically underdetermined by its observation sentences O*, if there is at least one different or incompatible theory T_2 that is empirically equivalent to T_1 in respect to *O* and only the members in *O* are used for testing T_1 and T_2. By substituting the concept of scientific equivalence between theories for empirical equivalence in the preceding definition we obtain a definition which says when a theory is *scientifically underdetermined by its set of observation sentences*.

In the year 1975 Quine considerably changed the concept of theory described above. The beginnings of these changes are to be found in Quine (1975a, p. 80) and are more fully elaborated in Quine (1975c, pp. 318-322). The axioms of a theory in the old sense are now by definition a theory formulation. An equivalence relation 'expresses the same theory as' is defined for theory formulations. The definition uses, among other things, the concept 'empirical equivalence'. Theories are then trivially defined as the equivalence classes generated by the relation 'expresses the same theory as'. The main reason why Quine introduces the new concept of theory is that he wants to take better account of the normal intuitive use of the term "theory" which, according to him, allows that theories might be identical although their formulations are incompatible. The old concept of theory does not allow this, because incompatible formulations cannot be logically equivalent. It should be observed that theories in the old sense also are equivalence classes generated by 'expresses the same theory as'. In this case this relation is of course defined as 'logical equivalence'.

Here we shall only treat Quine's arguments to the extent they are based on the old theory concept. This seems fair to us, because as far as we can see, the main results of our discussion are the same *mutatis mutandis*, independently of on what theory concept it is founded. However, if this is not true, there is another perfectly satisfactory justification for basing our discussion only on the old concept: all Quine's explicit formulations of indeterminacy are from earlier than 1975, the year he first introduces, as far as we know, the new theory concept. Considering how important the idea of underdetermination is in Quine's philosophy of science, the new concept has perhaps a less desirable feature: it seems to be of such a character that even in principle it is very hard to find out whether there are any empirically underdetermined theories in *actual* science. Quine is also aware of this (see Quine (1975c) pp. 326-328).

With the concepts above available, certain statements which Quine has regarded as important truths in his philosophy of science can be concisely formulated:

> All (most?, many?) theories are empirically (scientifically?) underdetermined by their observation sentences.

On the basis of various relevant passages it is very difficult to find out which of our formulations comes closest to Quine's intentions because the passages are unclear. For example, although the following passage eliminates those interpretations that are formulated in terms of scientific underdetermination, it does not suffice to show which of the remaining three is the correct one:

> Science is *empirically* [our emphasis] underdetermined: there is slack. Quine (1966) p. 241.

It is of course very difficult to confirm the truth of any of our renderings of Quine's statements concerning underdetermination, especially the more general renderings or those in which scientific equivalence is involved. At least the passages in Quine's writings that can be adduced in their support are not convincing. Therefore we are inclined to believe that the statements obtained by putting the phrase "It is possible that" in front of the formulations above better capture Quine's message, the message being simply that he wants to make clear that the belief that there is a unique true theory for every (or most) field(s) of enquiry is not the only possibility, although common among scientists, because in practice they normally work with only one successful theory. Such an interpretation is strongly supported by the following passage:

> [...] we have no reason to suppose that man's surface irritations [codified in observation sentences] even unto eternity admit of any systematization [=theory] that is *scientifically better or simpler* [our emphasis] than *all possible others* [our emphasis]. It seems likelier, if only on account of symmetries or dualities, that countless alternative theories would be tied for first place. Scientific method is the way to truth, but it affords even in principle no unique definition of truth. Quine (1960) p. 23.

which could be succinctly rendered as

> It is possible that any theory of the whole world or universe is scientifically underdetermined by all observation sentences.

This interpretation also obtains support from more recent formulations in Quine (1975c, pp. 327-328). The passage quoted clearly indicates that Quine is not a scientific realist in the normal naive sense, according to which there is only one true description of reality. The following passage, also from Quine (1960), together with the quotation above shows that he is a "sophisticated" realist:

> Everything to which we concede existence is a posit from the standpoint of a description of the theory-building process, and simultaneously real from the standpoint of the theory that is being built. Nor let us look down on the standpoint of the theory as make-believe; for we can never do better than occupy the standpoint of some theory or other, the best we can muster at the time. Quine (1960) p. 22.

Thus Quine seems to claim that the different entities talked about in different scientifically equivalent theories are not only real but even equally real.

3 INDETERMINACY OF NORMAL MEANING

First we make some introductory remarks. If the thesis concerning normal meaning were true, some of its consequences would be revolutionary. For example, one could not construct a semantic theory, i.e., a theory of meaning for the individual sentences in a natural language, which implies that translation in any scientific sense is not possible. This conflicts with the traditional view, according to which it is possible to create such theories of meaning or of translation, although satisfactory theories have not yet been constructed.

We now present some rather precise formulations of the indeterminacy thesis.

Version I

(1) Any theory of meaning for all standing sentences of any language *L* is scientifically underdetermined by the set of all observation sentences *O* in *L* (or the set of all observation sentences independently of in what language they are formulated).

(2) For any two theories of meaning for *L* thus underdetermined by *O* there is at least one standing sentence in *L* such that one theory assigns to this sentence a meaning which is incompatible with, or different from, the meaning assigned to it by the other theory.

Version II

(1) above

(2') For almost any standing sentence in *L* there are, among the theories of meaning underdetermined by *O*, at least two such that one theory assigns to this sentence a meaning which is incompatible with, or different from, the meaning assigned to it by the other theory.

Version III

(1) above

(2") The theories of meaning for the standing sentence of *L* underdetermined by *O* are such that each of them attributes to any standing sentence of *L* a meaning which is incompatible with, or different from, the meaning attributed to it by all the other meaning theories.

II, perhaps better than I, corresponds to Quine's thesis as it is formulated in Quine (1960) for there we find passages on page 27 which indicate that he wants to say that an infinite number of sentences of a language are indeterminate with respect to meaning.

It is very important to note that, since a language *L'* is needed in which a meaning theory for *L* is expressed, I, II and III, because they concern all languages, also hold true for *L'*. In the case of III this is particularly important because, in this case, as many different or incompatible meanings as there are theories of meaning for *L'* are assigned to any standing sentence in *L'* assigning a meaning to a standing sentence in *L*. III makes sense of Quine's statement, made on various occasions, that one cannot find out what an expression means by asking questions, because the language in which the questions and answers are formulated is itself subject to indeterminacy (see, for example, Quine (1960) pp. 52-53 and particularly Quine (1970) p. 180, the end of the longest paragraph). It should be noted that according to I and II a standing sentence in *L'* assigning a meaning to a standing sentence in *L* is not necessarily itself subject to indeterminacy.

The weakest version of the indeterminacy thesis is presented in Quine (1969b, p. 29) and in Quine (1970, pp. 180-181) for here Quine states something which can more precisely be interpreted as conditional statements such as the following:

> *If* (1) a theory of meaning for all standing sentences of some language *L* *were* scientifically underdetermined by the set of all observation sentences *O* in *L* and (2) for any two such theories underdetermined by *O* there *were* at least one standing sentence in *L* such that one theory assigned to this sentence a meaning which is incompatible with, or different from, the meaning assigned to it by the other theory, *then* it *would* make no sense to ask whether the first or the second meaning is the real meaning of the standing sentence in question.

By substituting *mutatis mutandis* (2') and (2") for (2) above we obtain other conditional statements which are also reasonable interpretations of the thesis as is stated on pages 180-181 in Quine

(1970). In view of these conditional formulations Quine's thesis, which was originally a very strong factual claim, seems in 1969-1970 to have been reduced to a highly speculative hypothetical claim which is rather uninteresting, because everybody subscribes to it. Therefore we shall not discuss the thesis further in this form.

Our formulations of the indeterminacy thesis could be criticized on the grounds that they are formulated in terms of incompatible or different meanings, which implies that meanings exist although Quine denies this. However, it is by no means clear that Quine denies that they exist although many passages suggest such an interpretation (see, e.g., Quine (1975a) below on p. 80), because other passages can be found, e.g., in Quine (1969b) below on page 28, where he describes the standard theory of meaning (calling it "the museum myth theory of meaning") as attributing *determinate* meaning to expressions. In view of this, passages indicating that he does not attribute existence to meanings should perhaps be interpreted as only stating that he only denies that expressions and in particular standing sentences have a *determinate* meaning, although they have also meaning according to him.

One might also criticize Quine on the grounds that he must assume that (determinate) meanings exist when, in the formulations of his thesis, he talks about incompatible translations. We think, however, that this criticism is inadequate. It assumes that the relation of incompatibility only makes sense when holding between meanings, while as far as we can see Quine holds the view that incompatibility makes sense only when holding between *sentences* but not between meanings. These critics take for granted that the traditional view is correct, according to which incompatibility prevails between meanings, while Quine with his thesis tries to show that meanings or determinate meanings do not exist. The critics confuse the intuitions of incompatibility with a theory which tries to explain them by means of meaning, a theory which, since childhood, they have been conditioned to accept without critical reflection. Does then incompatibility between standing sentences make sense? Surely it makes sense indirectly for two standing sentences each of which is a conjunction of the standing sentences in different theories if one theory logically implies an observation sentence that is incompatible with an observation sentence derivable from the other theory, for clearly, according to Quine, observation sentences can be incompatible without assuming that they have normal meaning. Whether incompatibility also makes direct sense for standing sentences constituting theories in the manner described without invoking meaning is, however, a more difficult question. It should be noted that Quine, for the sake of consistency, must answer this question in the affirmative if he claims that it is possible for two empirically equivalent theories to lack normal meaning although they are incompatible. In this case the incompatibility is of course not reflected in any incompatibility of observation sentences. Note, furthermore, that both theories have of course the same empirical meaning, i.e., the set of observation sentences that would confirm or disconfirm each theory is the same. In Quine (1975b) we find very sceptical remarks concerning the understanding of any standing sentence which is not a theory, for example, the following:

> Perhaps the very notion of understanding, as applied to single standing sentences, simply cannot be explicated in terms of behavioural dispositions. Perhaps therefore it is simply an untenable notion, notwithstanding our intuitive predilections. Quine (1975b) p. 89.

Before we study whether the arguments based on underdetermination which Quine has presented in support of his thesis are valid, we shall investigate in what sense meaning is indeterminate assuming the truth of I, II and III. We study first those readings, which do not contain "is different from". Under these readings all three versions imply in each language a standing sentence *S* and two theories of meaning, one of which assigns to *S* a meaning that is incompatible with the meaning assigned to *S* by the other theory. Adherents of the standard theory of meaning, according to which the meaning of any linguistic expression is determinate (fixed) quite independently of any theory of meaning, must admit that the phrase "meaning of a standing sentence" is used in the same sense in both theories. This, however, leads to inconsistency, for if the phrase "meaning of a standing sentence" is used in the same sense in both theories, then *S* has both those meanings which are incompatible. Thus the general concept of meaning of a standing sentence has incompatible instantiations and is empty. Under the readings under discussion indeterminacy of meaning is simply emptiness of the general concept of meaning.

We shall now show that a concept 'the (physical) structure of a concrete object' in a hypothetical physical theory could be shown to be empty by an argument of the same form as that presented above. We do this in order to further elucidate the reasoning above and because we believe that it is a universal belief that a physical concept cannot be shown to be empty in this manner.

Let us assume that we want to construct a physical theory of the structure of all concrete physical objects and that the statements (1_{ph}) and (2_{ph}) below corresponding to (1) and (2) in I are true:

Version I_{ph}

(1_{ph}) Any theory of the physical structure of all concrete objects is scientifically underdetermined by the set of all observation sentences *O*.

(2_{ph}) For any two theories of the physical structure of all concrete objects thus underdetermined by *O*, there is at least one concrete object such that one theory assigns to it a physical structure which is incompatible with, or different from, the physical structure attributed to it by the other theory.

II_{ph} and III_{ph} are of course obtained by analogy from II and III respectively.

It is easily realized that an argument of the same form as that presented above establishes that we do not have a general concept of the structure of a concrete object which is independent of theory. How would Quine react to this similarity between meaning and physical structure? Perhaps he would say that one of the main points of his indeterminacy thesis is the truth of the statement that a general concept of meaning that is independent of theory is as empty as the corresponding concept of the structure of a concrete object would be in our hypothetical physical case. Perhaps he would continue by pointing out that physicists would immediately reject such a concept as empty, because for centuries it has been at least implicitly common knowledge among physicists that theoretical concepts are not independent of the theories in which they occur, whereas meaning theorists, unaware of this elementary fact in the philosophy of science, do not reject the general concept of meaning, although they should.

We have so far clarified in what sense meaning is indeterminate under all other readings of I-III except those in which only the phrase "is different from" is taken account of, but not the phrase "is incompatible with". Is it possible to make sense of "meaning is indeterminate" also in these cases? We think so. In order to show this we first observe that an infinite regress can be generated by starting from a language *L* and constructing a meaning theory in language *L*' for *L* (more precisely for the standing sentences in *L*) and by continuing in a similar manner (by constructing a meaning theory in language *L*'' for *L*' etc.). We also observe that another infinite regress can quite analogously be generated which begins with a physical theory of the structure of concrete objects. At the second stage in this process a theory is obtained that could roughly be described as a theory of the structure of the structure of the original concrete objects. The theory of the third stage is of course about the structure of the structure of the structure. All other members of the regress are obtained similarly. In the physical regress it would be rather obvious that the description of the structure, to which an earlier structure in the sequence is reduced, refers to quite different entities than the description of the reduced structure (at least this seems to be true in actual cases of reduction in natural science). However, in the semantic regress a later theory that does not refer to similar kinds of entities, for example, meanings, words or sentences, etc. as a preceding theory, would probably not be called a meaning theory by meaning theorists. Possibly the statement that meaning is indeterminate is, in this case, short for: meaning theories of the above kind are in fact empty, because the explanatory theories refer to the same kind of entities as the explananda and are thus possibly circular or semicircular, although this is seldom realized. Evidence for this interpretation is found in Quine (1975b) pp. 86-87.

For the readings of I-III just discussed there is also a second way of making sense of "meaning is indeterminant". We showed earlier that, according to Quine, the different entities talked about in different, scientifically equivalent theories are not only real, but even equally real. In view of this one naturally asks why Quine cannot accept that scientifically equivalent semantic theories referring to meanings also talk about them as real entities? Many passages in his writings suggest that the reason is that he is a "sophisticated" physicalist (= a person who only attributes existence to entities referred to in physical theories including numbers and sets but no intensional entities) who believes that meanings can never in principle be reduced to physics and therefore do not exist. However, Quine's physicalism seems to be unjustified. This has been demonstrated by many writers who convincingly show that Quine has not presented good arguments in its favour (see, e.g., Gardner (1973) pp. 388-390, Hockney (1975), Friedman (1975)). Føllesdal (1973, 1975) shows how one can make good sense of indeterminacy if one accepts sophisticated physicalism, but he does not attack Quine's physicalism, probably because its dogmatic character is so obvious. On the basis of the above it clearly follows that in cases where the readings of I-III containing "is incompatible with" are left out of consideration, the phrase "meaning is indeterminate" can also be taken to mean 'meaning is irreducible to physics'.

There is still a third possibility of making sense of the readings under discussion. In this case "meaning is indeterminate" says that the meaning of some or all standing sentences in any language varies with the theory chosen, which contradicts the almost universally held belief that the meaning of any sentence in any language is determinate (fixed). However, this interpretation is not so good because it would make the concept of the structure of a concrete object indeterminate in the same sense under the corresponding readings of I_{ph}-III_{ph}, although Quine would probably deny that a physical concept could be indeterminate in this manner. Nevertheless, there is evidence for indeterminacy of meaning in this sense. Quine's reply to Chomsky's criticism (Quine (1969a) pp. 303-304) constitutes the best evidence for this, although it is also strongly supported by Quine's statement that in such a situation it does not make sense to ask of a sentence indeterminate in meaning whether one really believes it with the meaning attributed to it by one theory or with the meaning attributed to it by another (Quine (1970) pp. 180-181).

All our interpretations of "meaning is indeterminate" also make sense of Quine's statement that indeterminacy of meaning is additional to the empirically underdetermined character of physics (Quine (1970) p. 180). In our first case the additional feature is emptiness of the general everyday concept of meaning. In the second, it is circularity or semicircularity. In the third, irreducibility to physics and in the last case it is the variable character of meaning.

We conclude this section by investigating to what extent Quine's arguments for the indeterminacy of normal meaning establish its truth or the truth of I-III. We first observe that the content of the statements to be established is of such a character that it is very difficult to present general arguments which confirm them to an acceptable degree. We shall consider a general argument in Chapter II, Quine (1960) which, although it does not have the required force, is interesting as correct criticism. It is an indirect argument because Quine argues for the truth of his thesis by showing that there is no support for the almost universally held belief that linguistic expressions have determinate meanings. Quine admits that the rules in practice used by linguists and others for specifying the meaning of an expression are such that they assign to it a determinate meaning. His main point, however, seems to be that, although these rules are practically justified, they lack completely a theoretical motivation and are therefore arbitrary and that, furthermore, the rules clearly do not have the status of a scientific theory which has been accepted on the basis of the usual criteria of theory choice. As examples of such scientifically unjustified rules we can mention: one should not assign to a sentence a meaning which makes it false when all or most speakers consider it true (Quine (1960) p. 59); one should assign to an expression a meaning that is expressed by an expression which is of approximately the same length as the original expression (Quine (1960) p. 74). We think that this criticism is essentially correct since many rules relied on in practice, when meanings are specified, in fact seem to be of the sort described. However, it is easy to see that this criticism, although correct, by no means suffices to make the thesis minimally plausible.

In order to minimally confirm the thesis, one could also take a different approach which does not involve general arguments applying to all languages at the same time. One could try to make the thesis minimally plausible by showing that it holds true for some particular languages (or at least a sufficiently large fragment of some language).

In Quine (1969b, particularly pp. 35-38) this approach is also adopted. Here Quine tries to establish the truth of his thesis for Japanese. Quine claims (if we reformulate him more precisely) that there is a sound sequence occurring in Japanese standing sentences and two theories of meaning for *all* the Japanese standing sentences such that one theory assigns the meaning 'five oxen' to the sequence and the other approximately the meaning 'five head of cattle' to it where 'cattle' is understood as a mass term covering only 'bovines'. However, in order that this should be a genuine case of indeterminacy of normal meaning both theories should as wholes, i.e. as theories for all standing sentences, be scientifically equivalent. For some reason Quine takes this for granted without argument although it might very well be the case that the theory assigning, for example, the meaning 'five oxen' to the sound sequence in question, might assign meanings to other standing sentences in a way that makes it necessarily more complicated than the other theory attributing the other meaning to the sound sequence (or vice versa). Nor does Quine show that there cannot, in principle, be a third empirically equivalent theory which, however, better satisfies the rules of theory choice (simplicity, etc.) than the other two. It is of course necessary to establish this in order for the semantic indeterminacy of Japanese to follow. The criticism above applies to Quine's attempts to establish indeterminacy for other natural languages. Perhaps it should be said that the argument concerning Japanese should be taken quite seriously and not as a simplified artificial heuristic example only presented in order to make understanding of the indeterminacy thesis easier, for Quine comments on the example as follows:

> [...] here is a question that remains undecided by the totality of human dispositions to verbal behavior. It is indeterminate in principle; there is no fact of the matter. Quine (1969b) p. 38.

4. INDETERMINACY OF EMPIRICAL MEANING

We first explain the concept of empirical meaning: the empirical (verificational) meaning of a sentence is defined as the observational evidence (according to Quine codified in observation sentences) "that would support or refute it" (Quine (1974) p. 38). It should be noted that this concept of meaning is the logical positivists' concept of meaning in their verification theory of meaning. According to Quine it is also C. S. Peirce's concept of meaning (see, e.g., Quine (1969b) p. 80).

A paragraph on page 81 in Quine (1969b), the approximate content of which also occurs in other writings by Quine (see, e.g., Quine (1974) p. 38), contains what seems to be Quine's clearest argument for the importance of empirical meaning. We only quote the most revealing sentences of this paragraph.

> The sort of meaning that is basic to translation, and to the learning of one's own language, is *necessarily* [our emphasis] empirical meaning and nothing more. A child learns his first

words and sentences by hearing and using them in the presence of appropriate stimuli. These must be external stimuli, for they must act both on the child and on the speaker from whom he is learning.

The paragraph in question and in particular the sentences quoted suggest that one of the reasons why Quine considers empirical meaning important is that a successful theory of language acquisition not using the concept of empirical meaning cannot be constructed, i.e., this concept is necessary for a theory of language acquisition. It appears to us that Quine's argument for empirical meaning is similar to the familiar argument which is normally taken as establishing the importance of the concept of the atom and other theoretical concepts: the concept of atom is important because a successful physical theory uses this concept. However, in all places where Quine states that empirical meaning is involved in language acquisition he only presents a very speculative theory of language acquisition which uses empirical meaning. Because of this we shall here describe the form of such a theory which is also based on actual research in linguistics.

According to this theory the child, on the basis of the verbal or non-verbal behaviour (codified in observation sentences) of members of his language community, constructs successive theories for what sound sequences are accepted as sentences and how they are understood and used by the community. It then tests these theories by deriving predictions concerning the verbal and non-verbal behaviour (again codified in observation sentences) of members of this language community. The theories are successive because the child revises its theory when predictions derived from it are proved false. Since the child, when starting his learning, has very few data (codified in observation sentences) at his disposal, his first theory is very soon falsified. When the child has completely learned his language, very few or no false predictions can be derived from the theory adopted at this final stage (if indeed there is a final stage). According to the above picture of language learning, the child behaves, albeit unconsciously and instinctively due to its innate abilities, like a scientist. The child rather speculatively, on the basis of scarce data, constructs a theory, puts the theory to a test by deriving predictions from it and revises it when it makes false predictions. This kind of hypothetico-deductive theory of language learning, which was originally proposed by Chomsky, uses the concept of empirical meaning in the same manner as all other hypothetico-deductive theories since the observation sentences by means of which, in the last instance, such a theory is tested constitute by definition its empirical meaning. Chomsky also points to evidence which supports this kind of theory. He has found features in sentences of natural languages the acquisition of which can hardly be explained, if one does not postulate that language learning proceeds according to the hypothetico-deductive method or at least according to a method that closely resembles it. Chomsky and his associates very convincingly argue that, in order to account for language learning, one must postulate a much stronger innate mechanism than that assumed by current, mostly behaviouristic, theories of language learning. In a context where one tries to make more precise sense of Quine's statement that empirical meaning is necessary to language learning, the idea that this mechanism might be the hypothetico-deductive method or something similar sounds quite reasonable.

In the name of objectivity it must also be mentioned that Chomsky's conception of an innate mechanism has been heavily criticized as too speculative. However, in particular in recent years he has been able to strengthen certain arguments for strong innateness, for he has found results by others that support his concept of innateness (see, e.g., Chomsky (1976) pp. 8-9). These results show that not even learning by "simple" sense experience in animals and humans can be accounted for without assuming rather complex innate structures. Most illuminating in this respect is the following statement about animals quoted in Chomsky (1976) page 9:

> survival would be improbable if learning in nature required the lengthy repetition characteristic of most conditioning procedures

Thus perhaps not only language acquisition but all learning in humans and animals presupposes a strong innate mechanism, which might be the hypothetico-deductive method or a method very close to it.

After establishing that the concept of empirical meaning is justified, we shall treat Quine's argument for the indeterminacy of empirical meaning. This, as noted before, is formulated by means of the concept of empirical meaning. However, we first quote a passage from Quine (1969b, pp. 80-81) which shows that Quine considers the thesis a consequence of combining Peirce's concept of empirical meaning with Duhem's scientific holism, which says that a scientific theory is tested only as whole:

> If we recognize with Peirce that the meaning of a sentence turns purely on what would count as evidence for its truth, and if we recognize with Duhem that theoretical sentences have their evidence not as single sentences but only as larger blocks of theory, then the indeterminacy of translation [meaning] of theoretical sentences is the natural conclusion.

We now give a more precise reformulation of Quine's original argument which is contained in various passages in Quine (1969b) pages 78-82. We reformulate the argument as an intuitively valid inference:

No single sentence in a theory implies alone any observation sentence.

The empirical meaning of a sentence is the set of all observation sentences that would support or refute it.

Conclusion: No single sentence in a theory has empirical meaning.

This argument if of course intuitively valid. Is it also factually valid? In other words, are its premises also factually true? The second premise is of course true, because it is a definition (Peirce's definition of empirical meaning). The first premise, which expresses Duhem's holism, is also true if, with Quine, we accept the standard conception of how a theory is tested. According to it one or more sentences in a theory *only together with statements of initial (or antecedent) conditions and rules of correspondence* entail observation sentences. From this it follows that only in a case where the theory consists of only one sentence, and initial (or antecedent) conditions and rules of correspondence are of such a character that they could be correctly expressed by observation sentences, would the single theoretical sentence indirectly have separate empirical meaning. This presupposes, of course, that one agrees with Quine that the empirical meaning of an observation sentence is its stimulus meaning (defined, e.g., in Quine (1960)), which remains the same independent of in what context of other sentences it occurs. However, there hardly exist any one-sentence theories with initial (or antecedent) conditions and rules of correspondence as described above. Of course, we do not here count the conjunction of sentences in a theory as a one-sentence theory for if such a conjunction were a one-sentence theory, then every theory would be a one-sentence theory.

According to our reformulation of Quine's argument the empirical meaning of any single sentence in a theory is indeterminate in the sense that the sentence lacks empirical meaning. This interpretation seems to be the only reasonable possibility in view of the following passage in Quine (1969b) page 79:

> The component statements [of a theory] simply do not have empirical meanings, by Peirce's standard; but a sufficiently inclusive portion of theory does.

We find Quine's argument for the indeterminacy of empirical meaning much more plausible than his argument for the indeterminacy of normal meaning because the latter relies on assumptions that are much more problematic than those used in the argument under scrutiny. The argument reconstructed above employs hardly any other problematic assumption than that which says that the correct theory of language learning is a hypothetico-deductive theory. Although this assumption is problematic because nobody has so far been able to present such a theory explicitly, it is nevertheless plausible in view of the findings of Chomsky and other transformational grammarians.

If the thesis about empirical meaning is true, it has very far-reaching consequences because all concepts and activities that presuppose that each single sentence in a theory has empirical meaning are made impossible. For example, if translation presupposes this, translation of single sentences in a theory is impossible. The same also applies to the theory of sentence understanding according to which understanding a sentence means grasping its empirical meaning.

REFERENCES

Chomsky, N., 1976, "Reflections on Language," Temple Smith, London.

Friedman, M., 1975, Physicalism and the Indeterminacy of Translation, Noûs, 9:353-374.

Føllesdal, D., 1973, Indeterminacy of Translation and Under-Determination of the Theory of Nature, Dialectica, 27:289-301.

Føllesdal, D., 1975, Meaning and Experience, in: "Mind and Language," S. Guttenplan, ed., Clarendon Press, Oxford.

Gardner, M. R., 1973, Apparent Conflicts between Quine's Indeterminacy Thesis and his Philosophy of Science, BJPS, 24:381-393.

Hockney, D., 1975, The Bifurcation of Scientific Theories and Indeterminacy of Translation, PS, 42:411-427.

Quine, W. V., 1960, "Word and Object," MIT Press, Cambridge.

Quine, W. V., 1966, "The Ways of Paradox," Random House, New York.

Quine, W. V., 1969a, Reply to Chomsky, in: "Words and Objections," D. Davidson and J. Hintikka, eds., Reidel, Dordrecht.

Quine, W. V., 1969b, "Ontological Relativity and Other Essays," Columbia University Press, New York and London.

Quine, W. V., 1970, On the Reasons for Indeterminacy of Translation, JP, 67:178-183.

Quine, W. V., 1974, "The Roots of Reference," Open Court, La Salle.

Quine, W. V., 1975a, The Nature of Natural Knowledge, in: "Mind and Language," S. Guttenplan, ed., Clarendon Press, Oxford.

Quine, W. V., 1975b, Mind and Verbal Dispositions, in: "Mind and Language," S. Guttenplan, ed., Clarendon Press, Oxford.

Quine, W. V., 1975c, On Empirically Equivalent Systems of the World, Erkenntnis, 9:313-328.

Quine, W. V., and Ullian, J. S., 1978, "The Web of Belief," Random House, New York.

COLORS AND LANGUAGES

Wolfgang Wenning

Joachim-Friedrichstraße 54
D-1000 Berlin 31

Colors are unsettled entities suspicious to exist in the mind as well as in the world outside. It is hard to say what they "really" are. If they are in the mind, how do they find their place in the world and if they are in the world how do they enter into the mind? If colors "really" are physical states of the brain (or Platonic ideas), how are these related to mental states of color experiences? Much progress has been achieved in understanding color vision as a neural information processing system obeying psychophysical laws. No comparable progress occured - since Plato - in the philosophy of mind. There is much truth in Sokrates' mythological allusion - in the dialogue Theaitetos - that the goddess of the rainbow, Iris, is in fact known to be the daughter of Thaumas, that is, of somebody who is puzzled. Meanwhile the rainbow is not a puzzle anymore for the physicist, yet it became a puzzle for the linguist. If the stripes of the rainbow - the veils of Iris so to speak - are counted using color terms in different languages, one gets different numbers. For instance in Tzeltal there is only one term for both blue and green. That is why linguists came to believe, that speakers of different languages perceive the rainbow in different ways. If, what is a continuum in physics, is - initially - also a continuum in perception, structure appears to become a matter of linguistic convention. Indeed, according to the view of linguistic relativity, the perceptual space of color is partitioned, like a cake, into named pieces (categories) of arbitrary size and number to fulfil the needs and demands of particular language communities. If this view is generalized, a whole continuum of language based - or language biased - "worldviews" (in the sense of W. v. Humboldt) comes into appearance. In fact, the domain of color became one of the principle paradigms for the view that language structures perception. The opposite view that perception structures language seemed to be difficult to defend in the domain of color, until Berlin and Kay (1969) revealed certain semantic universals in the alleged paradigm of linguistic relativity. These semantic universals correspond to universal psychophysical as well as neurobiological features of human color vision. In 1. these universal features of color vision are outlined in the frame of a historical perspective. In 2. the universal semantic schema of Berlin and Kay (based on a comparison of color vocabularies of 98 languages) is summarized together with slight modifications urged by later more rigorous studies. In 3. the connection between the perceptual and the semantic universals is demonstrated.

1. UNIVERSALS OF COLOR VISION

Thomas Young conjectured in 1806 that three different light sensitive "particles" or "resonators" in the human retina would account for the outcome of Newton's additive color mixture experiments which establish that colors can be matched by use of three spectral lights. Helmholtz adopted and further developed this idea by proposing (hypothetical) absorption curves for three kinds of retinal photoreceptors. These give rise to a three-dimensional color space, of which each point is a representative for an (infinite) equivalence class of physically different spectral energy distributions of the *same* color. Based empirically on the Grassmann laws of color matching (additivity, scalar multiplication, trichromacy) the Young-Helmholtz theory found wide acceptance long before Wild and Brown (1965) photochemically vindicated Young's original hypothesis by identifying three types of photopigments in retinal cones (and a fourth one in the rods - for scotopic vision). It is obvious that Young applied some principle of psychophysical correspondence in his conclusion from the phenomenology of additive color mixture to the physiology at the retinal surface. Deeper levels of neural processing correspond to other color phenomena:

Leonardo da Vinci had insisted (abstracting from the pecularities of subtractive color mixture on his palette) that (phenomenologically) there are four basic hues: Red, Green, Yellow, and Blue. Similarly Goethe (abstracting from the peculiarities of additive color mixture) insisted that (phenomenologically) white is not a mixture of any hues, and to come to know this (introspectively) Goethe did not have to bother about Newton's experiments. Drawing on these phenomenological insights Mach (1865) postulated - on the basis of his principle of psychophysical parallelism - that in contrast to the Young-Helmholtz theory there should be more than three light-sensitive elements in the human retina. Hering (1878) concluded from certain phenomenological inadequacies of Mach's theory (with respect to Black and White) that Mach's physiological assumptions were insufficient (later Mach adopted Hering's view). Hering assumed that there exist three systems of antagonistic physiological processes: the Black/White-, the Red/Green-, and the Yellow/Blue-system. In each system - Hering supposed - the antagonistic mechanism consists of two kinds of activity ("assimilation" and "dissimilation") which cancel each other out at an equilibrium point, whilst moving away from this point the one or the other activity prevails. Hering's three opponent color systems are comparable to three "scales" the equilibrium of which corresponds to grey. Incompatible colors like a "reddish Green" or a "yellowish Blue" are thereby naturally excluded, since the "pointer" in each of the two chromatic opponent color systems can not simultaneously point into two directions. (According to Mach's "Die Analyse der Empfindungen" (1911) the two chromatic opponent color systems are "homodrom" whilst the achromatic Black/White-system is "heterodrom", since the sensation of grey partially includes the sensations of black and white.) Physiologists (e.g., S. Hecht in the thirties) predominantly rejected Hering's views until around 1950 Kuffler's electrophysiological techniques of single-cell recordings led to the discovery of opponent color systems in the retina of the carp (Svaetichin (1953)), the monkey (De Valoise, et al. (1966), Wiesel and Hubel (1966)), and humans (see Mollon (1982)).

The retina of the eye is a neural network which transmits signals of the photoreceptors via the bipolar to the ganglion cells whose axons form the optic nerve. Laterally to this flow of information the retinal network is synaptically connected by interneurons (horizontal cells and amacrine cells) which integrate and modulate the activity of the bipolar and ganglion cells in local circuits. After crosswise branching in the optic chiasm the optic nerves on both sides reach the lateral geniculate nucleus and from there neurons project to the primary visual cortex. In general, a single neuron of the visual pathway receives input from a receptive field, which contains a large number of photoreceptors spread over some area of the retina. Single cell recordings of such neurons for varying stimuli of light reveal a variety of functional characteristics including neural coding of color. Retinal ganglion cells encode Bright versus Dark, Red versus Green, and Yellow versus Blue antagonistically by increasing/decreasing firing rates depending on excitatory/inhibitory influences of two concentric so-called ON/OFF receptive field areas. The center and surround of these areas contain the same types of photoreceptors (cones) in the Bright/Dark-system and different types of cones in the spectrally opponent Red/Green- and Yellow/Blue-system. (Red-ON, Green-OFF) / (Green-ON, Red-OFF)-cells are excited by Red/Green and inhibited by Green/Red light. (Yellow-ON, Blue-OFF) / (Blue-ON, Yellow-OFF)-cells are excited by Yellow/Blue and inhibited by Blue/Yellow light. Excitation and inhibition cancel each other out, if the two receptive field areas are both stimulated at the same time. Hering's opponent color theory had been motivated also by phenomena of simultaneous contrast (a grey spot on red/green background appears slightly greenish/reddish). In the primary visual cortex color contrast neurons get maximally stimulated, if one opponent color hits the center and the other opponent color hits the surround of their dual-opponent color receptive fields (Michael (1978a, b)), which consists, e.g., of a number of (Green-ON, Red-OFF)-receptive fields in the center and a number of (Red-ON, Green-OFF)-receptive fields in the surround. Along the visual pathway neurons widen their scope by surveying neural activity at earlier levels. Simple, complex and hypercomplex neurons of the primary visual cortex integrate and modulate incoming signals in columnar circuits to build up opponent color tuned feature detectors for dots, oriented lines, edges, rectangles and - abstracting from retinal position - movement of these shapes. The importance of contour detection for higher visual functions suggests that simultaneous contrast of opponent colors is also exploited at higher levels of visual processing.

A psychophysical demonstration of the correctness of Hering's opponent color theory had to wait until Jameson and Hurvich (1955) developed their method of chromatic cancellation. By this method a spectral orange, for instance, is measured by cancelling its redness with a green light and its yellowness with a blue light. Similarly a spectral bluegreen is measured by a portion (intensity) of yellow and a portion of red light. The resulting chromatic cancellation functions are linear functions of the trichromatic color matching functions. That means that the color space based on Hering's opponent color theory is a linear transform of the color space based on the trichromatic Young-Helmholtz theory (Krantz (1975)). This shows that the method of chromatic cancellation (which tests at which point - under achromatic adaption and surround conditions - a light stimulus appears to be of neutral hue (grey)) is not less objective than the method of trichromatic color matching (which tests only if two light-stimuli can be visually distinguished or not). On the basis of trichromatic color matching the existence of the four psychologically "unique" (or phenomenologically "pure") colors Red, Green, Yellow, and Blue (defined to be those hues, which subjectively contain no infusion of neighbouring hues), could not be objectively verified in psychophysics. Jameson's and Hurvich's method, however, allow to elicit the four unique hues objectively without referring to them. In fact, the chromatic cancellation functions have four zerocrossings which coincide with unique Green, Yellow, and Blue, and approximately Red (spectral red appears slightly yellowish; unique (pure) Red contains some light from the blue side of the spectrum).

The perceptual reality of three opponent color pairs and the existence of four unique hues (Red, Green, Yellow, and Blue) is universally established on neurobiological as well as on psychophysical grounds. The physical continuum of the equal energy spectrum has a universal perceptual structure in human vision. How do those perceptual universals constrain human color naming?

2. UNIVERSALS OF COLOR NAMING

Although color vocabularies have been studied for more than a century (see the bibliography in Bornstein (1975)), the dominant doctrine of linguistic relativity has not been seriously challenged before Berlin and Kay (1969) - comparing color vocabularies of 98 languages - revealed that there are semantic universals in the domain of color naming. Berlin and Kay applied a new strategy in doing two things: First, they restricted color vocabularies to what they call *basic color terms*. Second, they asked not only for the "boundaries" (that is the extension of basic color terms in color space) but also for the "foci" (that is the most typical referents of basic color terms).

For each language *basic color terms* are defined to be: (1) monolexemic, ruling out, e.g., terms like 'bluegreen', (2) not hyponymous to other color terms of the same language, ruling out, e.g., 'crimson' which designates a shade of red, (3) not restricted in application to a narrow class of objects, ruling out, e.g., 'blond', (4) representative or salient with respect to frequency of use, constancy of reference, and independance of idiolect, ruling out, e.g., 'mauve' or 'puce'. Additional criteria for borderline cases were (5) morphematic complexity, borrowing from other languages and derivation from natural kind terms like 'gold'. Applying these criteria Berlin and Kay determined the basic color terms of 98 languages. No language contains less than 2 or more than 11 basic color terms.

Berlin and Kay compared basic color terms of different languages with respect to a representative part of color space by using an array of maximally saturated, equally spaced chips in 40 steps of hue and 8 degrees of brightness together with a few chips of neutral hue (white, black, and intermediate greys). Although the boundaries of basic color categories vary considerably in color space from one language to the next, the foci of basic color categories turned out to be as stable across languages as for the same language for different speakers. Thus basic color categories can be identified across languages by using the English basic color terms as a label for their foci. Berlin and Kay found that there are seven synchronic ("distributional") *types* as well as diachronic ("evolutionary") *stages* (i) - (vii) of languages such that there is a fixed partial order in which basic color categories are encoded into language:

(i) "black", "white", (ii) in addition: "red", (iii) in addition: either "green" or "yellow", (iv) in addition: "yellow" respectively "green", (v) in addition: "blue", (vi) in addition: "brown", (vii) in addition: "pink" and/or "orange" and/or "purple" and/or "grey".

Despite much criticism in a number of reviews and further investigations the main results obtained by Berlin and Kay were given additional support even in the most critical studies with few corrections: (1) In type (i) languages the two basic color categories are not achromatic ("black", "white") but panchromatic: The Dugum Dani in New Guinea - according to Heider (1972) - use 'mola' for bright or "warm" colors in the area of white, red and yellow, and 'mili' for dark or "cold" colors in the area of black, blue, and green. - Since 'mola' is focussed by 69 % of the speakers also in red the Dugum Dani seem to be prepared to develop a type (ii) language. - (2) Few languages of type (iii) and (iv) encode a basic color category with focus in blue: In Aguaruna 'winka' is focussed in blue by 97 % of the speakers; in Futunese 'wiwi' is focussed predominantly in blue rather than green; in Eskimo 'tungu' is focussed equally in blue and green; in Tzeltal 'yas' is sometimes focussed in blue rather than green; 'ao' in Old Japanese is a further example. For these reasons Kay (1975) proposed to substitute "green" by "grue" (green and blue) in the above scheme. (3) The basic color category "grey" is encoded also in some type (vi) languages.

3. COLOR VISION AND LANGUAGE

What is the connection between the perceptual universals of color vision and the semantic universals of color naming? Hering's opponent color theory fits the linguistic data of Berlin and Kay in several respects: The first six colors encoded stepwise from stage (i) - (v) are the six opponent colors of Hering's theory. As observed by McDaniel (1972) and Zollinger (1972, 1973) the four chromatic foci at these stages agree with the unique hues Red, Green, Yellow, and Blue of Jameson and Hurvich. That means that there is indeed a strong connection between the psychophysics and neurobiology of color vision on the one side and the ethnosemantics of color-naming on the other.

Why are Hering's six opponent colors encoded into language in the fixed order layed down in the universal semantic schema of Berlin and Kay? Under the dimensions of color sensation (brightness, hue and saturation) brightness is the only one present also in scotopic vision at night. Visual perception depends predominantly on brightness contrast. Indeed the detection of brightness contrast is biologically the most deeply rooted visual information processing task. The opposition of bright and dark is the only universal visual function. It seems not surprising that the semantic opposition of bright and dark is universally - stage (i) - the first one encoded into language. What can be said with respect to the four chromatic opponent colors? Microspectral measurements of cone sensitivities establish that long wavelength (red) cones are much more sensitive than short wavelength (blue) cones. In addition, "red" cones but not "blue" cones contribute to both chromatic opponent color systems (Ratliff (1976)). The most central part of the retina (Fovea centralis) is most sensitive for red and insensitive for blue. If viewed indirectly 40° apart from the fovea in the periphery, red does not loose saturation in contrast to green, yellow and blue (see Ratliff (1976)). These observations - not to mention evidence on the psychological level - suggest that red is the "strongest" and blue the "weakest" opponent color. Indeed red is universally the first chromatic opponent color encoded into language - stage (ii) and blue the last one - stage (v) -. At the intermediate stages (iii) and (iv) either yellow is encoded before green or green before yellow. Only five languages (see above) encode "grue" rather than "green" at these two stages; it is remarkable, that no language joins a pair of opponent colors into the same semantic category (e.g., "bluellow"). It may be argued that 'green' makes a better binary opposition (in the semantic sense) to 'red' encoded at the previous stage; yet on the other hand there is the extreme luminosity of yellow. However, since language allows both orders of encoding, why scramble up evidence on the side of perception.

At the two remaining stages (vi) and (vii) brown is universally encoded earlier than pink, orange and purple. Each of these colors (remarkably) contains red (the most salient and first encoded chromatic color). In addition, brown contains black and yellow while the others contain white, yellow and blue, respectively. If these components are decreasingly "wieghed" downwards from stage (i) to (v) the sum of these weighed components gets maximal for brown. Thus the arguments given already with respect to the stages (i) to (v) may be exploited also with respect to the order of encoding at the stages (vi) to (vii). Finally there is the "wild cart" (Kay (1975)) grey which is not bound to a fixed stage. Since grey corresponds to the equilibrium of the opponent color system from where color vision starts, it is indeed exceptional.

Kay and McDaniel (1978) propose a model of color category formation within "fuzzy set" theory (Zadeh (1965)). At the foci "fuzzy membership" is 1 and at the boundaries it reaches 0 in color space. *Primary* basic color categories correspond to Hering's opponent colors and are psychophysically defined by Jameson's and Hurvich's opponent color cancellation functions with respect to the "degree" of fuzzy membership between 0 and 1. *Composite* basic color categories (at the stages (i) - (iv)) are formed from the primary ones by "fuzzy union". For instance, mili and mola (the stage (i) color categories of the Dugum Dani in New Guinea) are represented by the fuzzy union of the primary basic color categories white, red, yellow, and black, green, blue, respectively. Similarly the composite color category "grue" of stage (iii) and (iv) languages (s.a.) is represented by the fuzzy union of the primary basic color categories green and blue. At stage (v) the primary basic color categories are encoded into language. *Derived* basic color categories (brown, purple, pink, orange) are added at stage (vi) and (vii) and are formed from the primary ones by "fuzzy intersection" and further operations ("multiplication", "the absolute value of", "the complement of"). Kay and McDaniel (1978) propose that these fuzzy set operations "correspond in some way to actual neural and/or cognitive events" (p. 634) such that two mathematically equivalent descriptions involving different operations are supposed to "make different claims about the cognitive processes available for derived basic color category formation" (p. 634) as for instance in the case of the two equivalent descriptions "orange (x) = 2 times the fuzzy union of red(x) and yellow(x)" and "orange (x) = 1 minus the absolute value of the difference of red(x) and yellow(x)" (see p. 633). The authors speculate that "one might be able to examine experimentally the hypothesis that different individuals - or a given individual under varying conditions - would process the semantic category orange in ways that sometimes suggest 3 [the one] and sometimes 4 [the other formalisation]" (p. 634). These projections of the fuzzy set operations into the brain are problematic since there are certainly more and presumably different types of neurological processes involved than the two or three operations appearing in the above formalisations. The simplicity measure proposed by the authors (counting the number of operations) does not reduce the number of "alternative claims" since it is doubtful that this measure corresponds to "neural and/or cognitive" simplicity. Why should the fuzzy set formalism give us a better access to neural processes than any other extensionally equivalent formal approach as long as our knowledge about these processes is rather limited? Kay and McDaniel start with the precise fuzziness of the primary basic color categories (based on psychophysical data) and end with a kind of fuzzy preciseness for the derived ones.

Returning to the question of "linguistic relativity" in the domain of color naming it is evident so far that universal neurobiological and psychophysical features of color vision constrain the encoding of color categories into language: The formation of linguistic color categories starts with the opposition of bright and dark and "crystallizes" around the unique (focal) hues Red, Green, Yellow, and Blue before further color categories are formed from these components. The internal structure of color space limits the degree of linguistic relativity to a large extent.

On the side of language, however, there is still some freedom to shape linguistic color categories even in the domain of basic color categories. Let me summarize some results from Iijima, Wenning, Zollinger (1982) in this connection (see this paper for technical details): Color naming tests with Japanese children in Yonezawa (Yamagata Prefecture), Tokyo and at the Japanese school in the German town Düsseldorf revealed characteristic differences in the application of color terms. From Yonezawa via Tokyo to Düsseldorf, the basic color category *midori* (green) shifts stepwise towards the longwavelength side of the hue scale while the basic color category *ao* (blue) shifts towards the shortwavelength side (the maxima growing in steps of 20 %) such that the data become similar to the data - based on the same test - for English and German speakers. This hue shift in different directions is remarkable also with respect to the diachronic development of Japanese color naming: In Old Japanese 'ao' was used for both blue and green. Berlin and Kay (1969) therefore regarded 'ao' as an exception to their universal schema; when the other exceptions (s.a.) became known, "grue" was introduced into the schema (Kay (1975)). In modern Japanese 'ao' is confined to blue although in poetry 'ao' rather than 'midori' (green) is sometimes applied, e.g., to green leaves. The observation that in Yonezawa the basic color categories *ao* and *midori* are less separated in color space than in Tokyo seems to show that the language variety in the Yamagata Prefecture is - in this respect - closer to Old Japanese than in the capital city. Although this may be due partly to the internal diachronic development of Japanese, external influences are also relevant: A color vocabulary test showed that in Yonezawa the terms 'daidai' (orange) and 'momo-iro' (pink) are still in use, while in Tokyo they are nearly eliminated by the English substitutes 'orange' and 'pink'. Similarly the salience rank of 'cha-iro' (brown, literally "colored like tea") increases from Yonezawa (18 %) via Tokyo (45 %) to Düsseldorf (62 %) where it reaches the salience rank of 'brown' (62 %) for English and of 'braun' (57%) for German speakers. A specific trait of Japanese, however, is preserved with respect to the salience rank of 'kuro' (black) and 'shiro' (white) which is quite exactly the same at the three test locations and significantly higher than for German and English speakers. This may be due to the fact that black and white are not regarded to be less genuine "colors" by Japanese speakers or may be interpreted to be a specific Japanese cultural trait present also in painting.

It has been shown that although color vocabularies are primordially structured by perception, there is still some freedom on the side of language to shape even basic color categories.

According to Krantz (1972) the color space may be regarded to be a "microcosm of psychology". If this is correct, similar results are to be expected in other realms of structured inner/outer experiences. The organisation of cultural "boundaries" around universal "foci" may be understood then - more generally - to mean that human nature contains enough "universal foci" to rely on globally, and enough "relative boundaries" to keep life interesting locally.

REFERENCES

Berlin, B. and Kay, P., 1969, "Basic Color Terms: Their Universality and Evolution," University of California Press, Berkeley and Los Angeles.

Bornstein, M. H., 1975, The Influence of Visual Perception on Culture, American Anthropologist, 77:771-798.

Carterette, E. C. and Friedman, M. R., 1975, "Handbook of Perception, Vol. V," Academic Press, New York.

Collier, G. A., 1973, Review of Berlin and Kay, Language, 49:245-248.

DeValoise, R. L., Abramov, I. and Jacobs, G. H., 1966, Analysis of Response Patterns of LGN Cells, Journ. Opt. Soc. America, 56:966-977.

Gipper, H., 1972, "Gibt es ein sprachliches Relativitätsprinzip?," Fischer, Frankfurt a. M.

Heider, E. R., 1972, Probabilities, Sampling, and Ethnographic Method: The Case of Dani Color Names, Man, 7:448-466.

Heider, E. R., 1972, Universals in Color Naming and Memory, Journal of Experimental Psychology, 93:10-20.

Hering, E., 1878, "Zur Lehre vom Lichtsinne. Sechs Mitteilungen an die Kaiserl. Akad. der Wissenschaften, Carl Gerold's Sohn, Vienna.

Hurvich, L. M., Jameson, D. and Cohen, J. D., 1968, The Experimental Determination of Unique Green in the Spectrum, Perception and Psychophysics, 4(2):65-68.

Iijima, T., Wenning, W. and Zollinger, H., 1982, Cultural Factors of Color Naming in Japanese: Naming Tests with Japanese Children in Japan and Europe, Anthropological Linguistics, 24:245-262.

Jameson, D. and Hurvich, L. M., 1955, Some Quantitative Aspects of an Opponent-Colors Theory. I. Chromatic Responses and Spectral Saturation, Journal of the Optical Society of America, 45:546-552 45:546-542.

Kay, P. 1975, Synchronic Variability and Diachronic Change in the Basic Color Terms, Language in Society, 4:257-270.

Kay, P. and McDaniel, C. K., 1978, The Linguistic Significance of the Meanings of Basic Color Terms, Language, 54:610-646.

Krantz, D. H., 1972, Measurement Structures and Psychological Laws, Science, 175:1427-1435.

Krantz, D. H., 1975, Color Measurement and Color Theory: I. Representation Theorem for Grassmann Structures, II. Opponent-Colors Theory, Journ. of Mathematical Psychology, 12:283-327.

Mach, E., 1865, Über die Wirkung der räumlichen Verteilung des Lichtreizes auf die Netzhaut, in: Sitzungsbericht d. k. Akad. d. Wiss., 52.

Mach, E., 1911, "Die Analyse der Empfindungen," 6. edition, Fischer, Jena.

Marr, D., 1982, "Vision: A Computational Investigation into the Human Representation and Processing of Visual Information," W. H. Freeman and Company, San Francisco.

McDaniel, C. K., 1972, "Hue Perception and Hue Naming," A.B. honors thesis, Harvard College.

Michael, C. R., 1978a, Color Vision Mechanism in Monkey Striate Cortex: Dual-Opponent Cells with Concentric Receptive Fields, Journ. Neurophysiol., 41:572-588.

Michael, C. R., 1978b, Color Sensitive Complex Cells in Monkey Striate Cortex, Journ. Neurophysiol., 41:1250-1266.

Mollon, J. D., 1982, Color Vision, Ann. Rev. Psychol., 33:41-85.

Platon, 1958, Theaitetos, in: "Platon IV," Rowohlt, Hamburg.

Ratliff, F., 1973, The Logic of the Retina, in: "From Theoretical Physics to Biology," M. Marois, ed., S. Karger, Basel and New York.

Ratliff, F., 1976, On the Psychophysiological Bases of Universal Color Terms, Proc. of the American Philosoph. Soc., 120:311-330.

Svaetichin, G., 1953, The Cone Action Potential, Acta Physiologica Scandinavica, 29 (Suppl. 106):565-600.

Wald, G. and Brown, P. K., 1965, Human Color Vision and Color Blindness, Cold Spring Harbor Symp. on Quant. Biol., 30:345-359.

Wenning, W., 1982, Wittgensteins 'Logik der Farbbegriffe' und die Geometrie des Farbraums, in: "Language and Ontology. Proceedings of the 6th International Wittgenstein Symposium," W. Leinfellner, E. Kraemer and J. Schank, eds., Hölder-Pichler-Tempsky, Vienna.

Wenning, W., 1983, Parallelen zwischen Sehtheorie und Wittgensteins Sprachphilosophie, in: "Epistemology and Philosophy of Science. Proceedings of the 7th International Wittgenstein Symposium," P. Weingartner and H. Czermak, eds., Hölder-Pichler-Tempsky, Vienna.

Wenning, W., 1984, Farbwörter und Sehen, in: "Festschrift für H. Schnelle," T. Ballmer and R. Posner, eds., deGruyter, Berlin.

Wiesel, T. N. and Hubel, D. H., 1966, Spatial and Chromatic Interactions in the Lateral Geniculate Body of the Rhesus Monkey, Journal of Neurophysiology, 29:1115-1156.

Zadeh, L. A., 1965, Fuzzy Sets, Information and Control, 8:338-353.

Zollinger, H., 1972, Human Color Vision as an Interdisciplinary Research Problem, Palette, 40:25-31.

Zollinger, H., 1973, Zusammenhänge zwischen Farbbenennung und Biologie des Farbensehens beim Menschen, Vierteljahresschrift Naturf. Ges. Zürich, 118:227-255.

CONTRIBUTORS

Professor Irena Bellert, Department of Linguistics, McGill University, 1001 Sherbrooke Street West, Montreal, Quebec, Canada H3A 1G5

Prof. DDDr. Josef M. Bocheński, Pl. G. Python 1, CH-1700 Fribourg

Professor Aldo Bressan, Università di Padova, Istituto di Analisi e Meccanica, Via Belzoni, 7, I-35131 Padova

Dr. Norbert Brunner, Institut für Mathematik und angewandte Statistik Universität für Bodenkultur, Gregor Mendel-Strasse 33, A-1180 Wien

Dr. Wojciech Buszkowski, Institute of Mathematics, Adam Mickiewicz University, Matejki 48/49, PL-60-769 Poznań

Professor Heda Festini, Filozofski fakultet, Obala M. Tita 2, YU-57000 Zadar

Professor Peter Gärdenfors, Department of Philosophy, Lund University, Kungshuset, Lundagård, S-223 50 Lund

Professor Yuri Gurevich, Department of Computer and Communication Sciences, The University of Michigan, 435 South State, 221 Angel Hall, Ann Arbor, MI 48109, USA

Professor Henry Hiż, Department of Linguistics, University of Pennsylvania, Room 619 Williams Hall CU, Philadelphia, PA 19104, USA

Professor Hugues Leblanc, Department of Philosophy, College of Liberal Arts, Temple University, Philadelphia, PA 19122, USA

Professor Alice G. B. ter Meulen, Taakgroep Formele Linguistich, Centrale Interfakulteit, Rijksuniversiteit Groningen, Westersingel 19, NL-9718 CA Groningen

Professor Robert K. Meyer, The Research School of Social Sciences, The Australian National University, P. O. Box 4, Canberra ACT 2601, Australia

Professor Ewa Orłowska, Institute of Computer Science, Polish Academy of Sciences, P. O. Box 22, PL-00-901 Warsaw PKiN

Dr. Peter Päppinghaus, Universität Hannover, Institut für Mathematik, Welfengarten 1, D-3000 Hannover 1

Professor Regimantas Pliuškevičius, Academy of Sciences of the Lithuanian SSR, Institute of Mathematics and Cybernetics, 54, K. Poželos st., SU-232600 Vilnius

Professor Sir Karl R. Popper, Fallowfield, Manor Close, Manor Road, Penn, Buckinghamshire HP10 8HZ, England

Doz. Dr. habil. Tadeusz Prucnal, Instytut Matematyki WSP, ul. Konopnickiej 21, PL-25-406 Kielce

Professor Bengt-Olof Qvarnström, Department of Philosophy, University of Turku, SF-20500 Turku 50

Professor Wolfgang Rautenberg, Institut für Mathematik II (WE2), Freie Universität Berlin, Arnimallee 3, D-1000 Berlin 33

Dr. Peter Schroeder-Heister, Philosophische Fakultät, Fachgruppe Philosophie, Universität Konstanz, Postfach 5560, D-7750 Konstanz 1

Professor Saharon Shelah, Mathematics Department, Hebrew University, Jerusalem 91904, Israel

Professor Wilfried Sieg, Department of Philosophy, Columbia University in the City of New York, New York, N.Y. 10027, USA

Dr. Peter M. Simons, Institut für Philosophie, Universität Salzburg, Franziskanergasse 1, A-5020 Salzburg

Professor V. Stepanov, Department of Mathematical Logic, Faculty of Mathematics and Mechanics, Moscow State University, SU-113808 Moscow

Professor H. C. M. de Swart, Katholieke Hogeschool Tilburg, Centrale Interfaculteit, Postbus 90153, NL-5000 LE Tilburg

Professor Jari Talja, Department of Philosophy, University of Turku, SF-20500 Turku 50

Professor Paul Weingartner, Institut für Philosophie, Universität Salzburg, Franziskanergasse 1, A-5020 Salzburg

Dr. Wolfgang Wenning, Joachim-Friedrich-Strasse. 54, D-1 Berlin 31

Professor Andrzej Wroński, Department of Logic, Jagiellonian University, ul. Grodzka 52, PL-31-044 Kraków

INDEX